Waking the Dictator

Latin American and Caribbean Series

Waking the Dictator
Veracruz, the Struggle for Federalism, and the Mexican Revolution, 1870-1927

Karl B. Koth

The Spirit of Hidalgo
The Mexican Revolution in Coahuila

Suzanne B. Pasztor
Co-published by Michigan State University Press

Clerical Ideology in a Revolutionary Age
The Guadalajara Church and the Idea of the Mexican Nation 1788-1853

Brian F. Connaughton, translated by Mark Allan Healey
Co-published by Michigan State University Press

WAKING
THE
DICTATOR

Veracruz, the Struggle for Federalism, and the
Mexican Revolution, 1870-1927

Karl B. Koth

UNIVERSITY OF
CALGARY
PRESS

University of Calgary Press
2500 University Drive NW
Calgary, Alberta
Canada T2N 1N4
www.uofcpress.com

National Library of Canada Cataloguing in Publication Data
 Koth, Karl B.
 Waking the dictator
 (Latin American and Caribbean series, ISSN 1498-2366)

 Includes bibliographical references and index.
 ISBN 1-55238-031-9

 1. Veracruz (Mexico : State) — History
 2. Mexico — History — Revolution, 1824–1870. I. Title. II. Series.
 F1371.K67 2002   971'.62   C2002-910100-X

We acknowledge the financial support of the Government of Canada
through the Book Publishing Industry Development Program (BPIDP)
for our publishing activities.

The Canada Council for the Arts
Le Conseil des Arts du Canada

Printed and bound in Canada by AGMV Marquis.
∞ This book is printed on acid-free paper.

Page, cover design, and typesetting by Kristina Schuring.

To
Charles, Christopher, Natalya, and Eric

Series Editor's Preface

It is a very great pleasure to introduce the first volume of the Latin American and Caribbean Series published by the University of Calgary Press. Not only will this series embrace a variety of historical, literary, and postcolonial themes; it is the only one of its kind in Canada. Our intention is to publish cutting-edge and revisionist studies that reinterpret our understanding of historical and current issues in Latin America and the Caribbean.

Karl Koth's book on the Mexican State of Veracruz before and during the Mexican Revolution is a fine example of fresh archival research, new thinking, and reinterpretation that poses questions about the nature of the Mexican Revolution. First a strategically situated province of New Spain and later a Mexican state, Veracruz had a long history of opposition to outside forces and access to the world through the ports cities of Veracruz and Tampico. From the sixteenth century forward, the port of Veracruz was the export entrepôt for Mexican silver and mineral wealth and the entry point that led inland to Mexico City and the interior of Spain's greatest and most powerful American possession. Even before the outbreak of the War of Independence in 1810, the people of Veracruz province had a reputation for truculence, riots, and uprisings against outside influences that sometimes taxed the available military forces. During the Independence epoch (1810–21), many Veracruzanos embraced the insurgent cause and developed effective guerrilla warfare based in the rugged mountains, deep barrancas, and almost impenetrable forests. Resistant to malaria, yellow fever, and other diseases that decimated outside invaders, they played a significant role in defeating the royalist Spanish armies. Having developed an entrenched tradition of regionalism, the population resisted any surrender of local authority to distant bureaucrats and politicians. Through different constitutions and the rule of some colourful caudillos such as Antonio López de Santa Anna, a local son, the Veracruzanos defended themselves with tenacity and dedication.

Koth's study, based upon research in many archives of Veracruz state and other Mexican collections, develops these themes and presents a quite different view of the late nineteenth-century and early twentieth-century Mexican Revolution. This is an important book that illustrates the importance of Mexican regional history and sheds new light upon many aspects of the Revolution.

Christon I. Archer
Series Editor

Contents

Preface   viii

Acknowledgments   x

1   The Path Taken:
    The Modernization of Veracruz, 1870–1905   1
2   Revolution in Veracruz:
    The PLM Phase   41
3   Revolution in Veracruz:
    The Maderista Phase   79
4   The Revised Revolution   115
5   Revolution and Counter-Revolution:
    From Orozco to Díaz   145
6   The Neo-Porfirian Experiment   173
7   Constitutionalists, Conventionists, and Félix Díaz   195
8   Experiment with Socialism   223
9   Conclusion:
    Tomorrow Never Comes   253

Notes   259
Glossary   317
Abbreviations   319
Bibliography   321
Index   339

Preface

This work focuses on a crucial region of Mexico, the state of Veracruz, during a critical time in its history, the Mexican Revolution. It first problematizes that radically modernizing period known as the Porfiriato. I trace the failure of that regime to provide a legitimization of power that could have survived into the twentieth century and I elucidate the bitter and virulent battle for a new socioeconomic order in Veracruz: the local struggles and contributions of the peasants, Indians, industrial workers, and other marginalized Veracruzans as well as the role of the local elite. More specifically, I illuminate not only the confusing and contradictory alliances that obtained between the lower classes and the elite, but also the struggles of both against an encroaching central government. In short, I examine the centralizing processes that resulted in the construction of the modern, Mexican national state, consummated, I argue, in Veracruz in 1927. This book is, therefore, a work of military and social and political history as these elements are inextricably intertwined in the period under consideration.

I argue, albeit from the perspective of Veracruz, that in social and political terms 1910 was not the beginning nor 1920 the end of the Mexican Revolution. The continuities of peasant rebellion and working-class resistance to exploitation in the years preceding 1910 are too stark to be consigned to the status of mere "precursor" uprisings.[1] Nor can one argue that the final product, the construction of the Mexican state, under which Mexico would be ruled to the present, was completed in 1920. One is yet forced to reconsider the meaning of the violence and social protest that erupted after the turn of this century. For the promises of the Revolution that await implementation are still capable of triggering violent outbursts of protest.[2]

My search for information took me into a variety of private and public archives in Mexico City as well as to others in Veracruz, especially the Archivo General del Estado de Veracruz. A significant amount of my evidence comes from primary sources. Where possible, I have utilized personal archives such as those of Teodoro A. Dehesa (now in Xalapa) and the Carranza and Félix Díaz archives at CONDUMEX in Mexico City. I also conducted research within official government agencies such as the Archivo General de la Nación and the Archivo Histórico de la Secretaría de la Defensa Nacional. Documents of the U.S. Department of State as well as certain of those of the British Foreign Office were particularly interesting for their first-hand consular accounts (albeit somewhat biased) of contemporary events. Newspapers, too, despite their own proclivities, were an indispensable source of information.

Like others before me who arrived at similar conclusions, I find the implications of this study extremely disturbing.[3] Neither the democratic nor the social goals of the Revolution have been realized in Veracruz nor elsewhere in Mexico. Certainly, in some areas of Mexico, land distribution has satisfied some of the legitimate demands of *some* peasants, Indians, and rural and urban workers. But as recent events have attested, these measures have been embarrassingly insufficient. Most notably, a large number of rural workers and Indians have been effectively denied participation in government; hence the struggle for democracy and human rights, first manifested during the independence movement and continuing throughout the nineteenth century and the Mexican Revolution, cannot but continue.

Acknowledgments

In the course of preparing this work I have incurred many debts. The late Herman Konrad first suggested I consider Veracruz as the focus of a possible dissertation topic. His subsequent encouragement and interest in my work are deeply appreciated. I am also deeply indebted to Timothy Anna, who saw me through doctoral studies and remains both mentor and friend.

I conducted the majority of my research in Mexico and owe archives and personnel there a heartfelt thank you for graciously tolerating my constant demands. Special thanks are due to Señora Alicia González Martínez, in charge of the Madero archive at INAH; the personnel of the AGN; the director and personnel of the CONDUMEX centre; Maestra Olivia Domínguez Pérez, director of the Archivo General of Veracruz; personnel of the Archivo Municipal in Veracruz port; and others at the Hemeroteca Nacional at UNAM. Dr. Xavier Garciadiego kindly arranged for permission to work in the stacks at El Colegio de México.

To Bill French and David LaFrance, who read the draft and made encouraging suggestions, I remain especially indebted.

Thanks are also due to Hernán Lama, Paty Lutrillo, Milagro Rosales, Julia Mawhinney and Tara King, student assistants at various times, and to the Work Study program of the Ministry of Education, British Columbia, for funding their time. Sophie

Lawrence rendered invaluable and dedicated service as my research assistant. Señorita Josefina Sentmanat helped in ways too numerous to mention during my stays in Mexico as did Dr. Pedro Castro Martínez of UAM, Xochimilco, and Maestra Soledad García Morales of the Instituto de Antropología e Historia, Xalapa,Veracruz. To Rosalvo Quintero and her sons Rodrigo and Adrián I extend my appreciation for opening their house to me over a number of years.

Beverly, Charles, Christopher, and Natalya put up with moods and frustration while I was writing the doctoral thesis on which the first part of this book is based. The children generally thought the whole enterprise was a curious one, but were patient and supportive.

At the institutional level there are also debts to be acknowledged. The Social Sciences and Humanities Research Council of Canada afforded me a fellowship to pursue doctoral research and a further fellowship to undertake the research on the Revolution. Okanagan University College has also been generous with grants-in-aid, as well as release time to research and write this book. This book has been published with the help of a grant from the Humanities and Social Science Federation of Canada, using the funds provided by the Social Sciences and Humanities Research Council of Canada. To Faith Peyton and Rose Cresswell in the Inter-library loan Department, Gwen Zilm, Garth Homer and Anne Cossentine, I owe special thanks for their friendly and efficacious handling of all my requests. *The Canadian Journal of Latin American and Caribbean Studies, Mexican Studies/Estudios Mexicanos,* and *Historia Mexicana* kindly granted me permission to use sections of my previous publications.

My gratitude goes also to Walter Hildebrandt, director of University of Calgary Press, to John King, production editor, as well as to the staff at the press, especially Sharon Boyle, Kristina Schuring, and Terry Teskey. Thanks also to the readers of the University of Calgary Press and those of the Aid to Small Publications branch of SSHRC, for their helpful comments.

Finally, I am deeply indebted to my friend and colleague Sukeshi Kamra for her patience, encouragement, enlivening "interdisciplinary" discussions, and her keen eye. Needless to say, I alone am responsible for any errors, omissions, or defects of the text.

xii

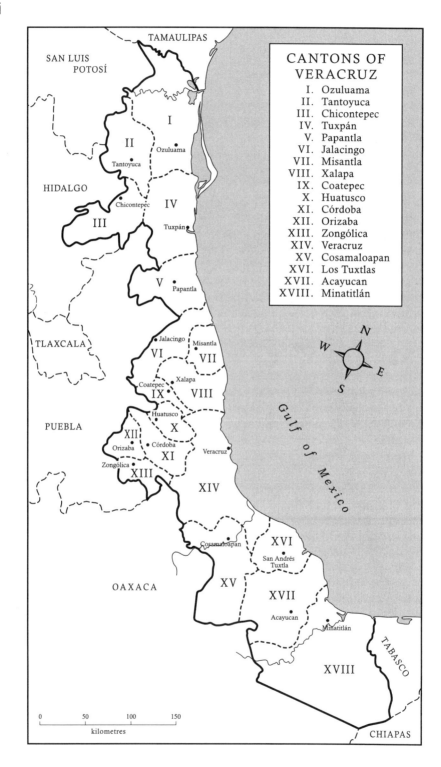

TAMAULIPAS

SAN LUIS
POTOSÍ

I

II
Ozuluama

Tantoyuca

HIDALGO

Chicontepec   IV

III   Tuxpán

V
Papantla

TLAXCALA

Jalacingo   Misantla
VI   VII

Coatepec   Xalapa
IX   VIII

PUEBLA   Huatusco

XII   X
Orizaba   Córdoba
XI
Veracruz
Zongólica

XIII
XIV

OAXACA

Cosamaloapan   XVI
San Andrés
Tuxtla
XV
XVII
Acayucan
Minatitlán

TABASCO

XVIII

CHIAPAS

Gulf of Mexico

N
W   E
S

CANTONS OF
VERACRUZ
I. Ozuluama
II. Tantoyuca
III. Chicontepec
IV. Tuxpán
V. Papantla
VI. Jalacingo
VII. Misantla
VIII. Xalapa
IX. Coatepec
X. Huatusco
XI. Córdoba
XII. Orizaba
XIII. Zongólica
XIV. Veracruz
XV. Cosamaloapan
XVI. Los Tuxtlas
XVII. Acayucan
XVIII. Minatitlán

0   50   100   150
kilometres

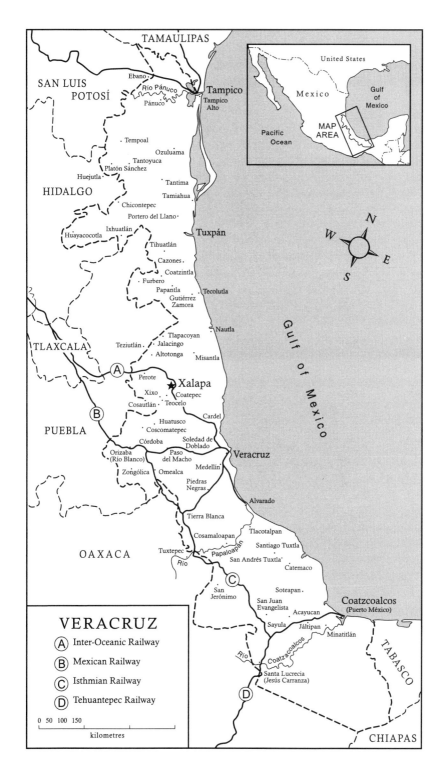

1

The Path Taken

The Modernization of Veracruz, 1870–1905

In late March, 1876, Mexico stood on the brink of one of the most influential periods of its history. General Porfirio Díaz was poised with a few hundred men on the U.S.-Mexican border, ready to initiate the revolution that would propel him into the presidency. From the time of that revolution, called the Revolution of Tuxtepec, Porfirio Díaz was the master of Mexico – with the brief exception of the years between 1880–84 when the country was guided by Manuel González (with Díaz in the background watching carefully) – until he was ousted in 1911. In 1876 he inherited a country that had lived through fifty-five years of turmoil and that could hardly be described as a unified nation. One of the forces besetting unity was the strong regional tendencies that had matured since the country gained its independence and that would have to be controlled if Mexico was to establish the stability necessary for modernization. Among these powerful regions was the state of Veracruz, gateway to Mexico in the nineteenth century and, due to its geography and physical attributes, destined to become one of the richest states of the Mexican union.

Veracruz: An Economic and Political Geography

At the onset of Díaz's career, however, that destiny was yet only a potential, a derivative of the physical geography that blessed this Gulf Coast state. Veracruz occupies almost all of the land between the vast mountain range known as the Sierra Madre Oriental and the Gulf of Mexico. It is bounded on the north by the Pánuco and Tamesí rivers and on the south by the Tonalá, and covers approximately 72,000 square kilometres of territory. The coastline is 700 kilometres long, and from the coast to the mainly eastern and southern borders its width varies between 32 and 222 kilometres.[1] Veracruz borders on the state of Tamaulipas to the north; San Luis Potosí, Puebla and Hidalgo to the west; Oaxaca and Chiapas to the south; and Tabasco to the southeast.[2] Its position on the east coast was the key to Veracruz's importance. It was the gateway to Mexico in the historic as well as the geographic sense: not only was the coast the arrival point for the Spanish *conquistadores*, it was also the natural destination for invaders from other parts of Europe as well as the United States. Perhaps for this reason, and certainly because of its commercial orientation, the port of Veracruz acquired a cosmopolitan character and considerable influence on the rest of the state.

The abundant natural resources of the state derive from the variety of its topography and climate. The coastland is low and studded with many bays and inlets (utilized by both smugglers and rebels), except for the southern extremity of the state, where the mountains thrust out towards the sea. In a few places the low ground extends inland for quite a distance, as in the southern cantons of Los Tuxtlas, Acayucan, and Minatitlán. Generally, however, the land rises fairly quickly from the coast, giving way to lush mountains with a wide variety of fauna and flora, including vast pine forests. The highest points of the Sierra Madre Oriental are found in the state, as are the famous extinct volcanoes, the Pico Orizaba (5,700 metres) and the Cofre de Perote (4,000 metres).

Numerous streams and rivers form in the Sierra watershed, making Veracruz one of the best-watered states of the Mexican union. On the way to the coast these form a variety of waterfalls, cascades, and rapids that give Veracruz an advantage in the production of hydropower, the basis for the late-nineteenth-century development of its textile industry.[3] Naturally, its coastal location confers on it a fishing industry, as well as relative ease of communication with the northern and southern extremities of the state.

Its rivers also provided an important means of communication. In the north, the Pánuco River is navigable for its course through Veracruz. Before the building of an extensive highway system, regular river steamers provided a commercial connection between Alvarado on the coast with San Juan Evangelista via the San Juan Michapán River, and with Tuxtepec, just across the border in Oaxaca, via the Papaloapán River. Important

international ports were and are to be found in the natural har-
bours of Tuxpán and Coatzacoalcos (later Puerto México) and the
historic port city of Veracruz, whose artificial harbour and dike
systems were built during the governorship of Teodoro Dehesa.[4]
Veracruz's riparian structure also permitted the use of coastal
vessels in transporting troops inland, for example, during the
Acayucan uprising, affording rebels ingenuous means of mounting attacks, for example, via the Papaloapán River (see Chapter 8).

The climate of Veracruz is as varied as its topography, ranging
from the torrid heat of the coastal area to the freezing tempera-
tures on the ice-bound peaks of the highest mountains. Rainfall
and wind conditions are difficult to predict and generalize. There
are areas with very little rainfall, such as the Central Plain; by
contrast, mountain convection brings considerable precipitation
to the upland regions.[5] The sea breezes blow inland during the
day, having a slight cooling effect on the hot areas as well as
carrying the moisture that produces the precipitation in the
upland areas. The rainy season is between May and October. In
the winter the dreaded *nortes* (north winds) appear on the coast,
turning the harbour at Veracruz into a broiling cauldron to be
avoided by sailing vessels.[6]

In general, the climate is able to favour agriculture, as is
the fertile soil. The extensive forests contain various species of
wood, allowing for a modest lumber industry. Of greater economic import is the vigorous agricultural sector developed in the
nineteenth century, in which maize, beans, sugar cane, bananas,
citrus, coffee, sarsaparilla, vanilla, tobacco, cacao, potatoes, wheat,
maguey, and sisal were cultivated.[7] Sugar cane and coffee early on
established themselves as the most important cash crops and continue to occupy first place in the state's agricultural production.
In addition to these, cattle and dairy ranching are made possible
by the state's extensive plains with good pastureland, especially
in the Huasteca to the north and in the southern areas. The soil
is blessed with a number of valuable ores and minerals, among
them gold, silver, copper, iron, lead, manganese, cinnabar, and sul-
phur, as well as marble and various hard stones useful in construction. The most significant mineral resource discovered around
the turn of the century and today occupying the most important
position in the Mexican economy, is oil. In 1901 upwards of ten
thousand barrels were produced in the northern region, with production reaching twelve million barrels by 1912.[8] The strategic
importance of this vital commodity was the central factor in the
annihilation of the federalist system, as we shall see in Chapter 8.

The tremendous agricultural and industrial potential of Veracruz was not, however, exploited in the colonial era; there simply wasn't sufficient population to do so. In the first decade of the nineteenth century, Veracruz had only 185,935 residents, of which almost 138,000 were Indians, just over 9,000 were Spanish, and 28,000 plus were of mixed blood.[9] Most of the whites lived in the upland area, avoiding the coast and the ever-present danger of tropical diseases. The corridor connecting Xalapa, Orizaba, and Córdoba, which was connected to Mexico City, was their favoured area. In it most of the wealth of Veracruz, from tobacco farms and *haciendas* as well as sugar plantations, was produced. The other regions were almost devoid of economic activity again due to the lack of a workforce. For their part, the Indians who remained after the devastating if unintentional "biological warfare" of the sixteenth and seventeenth centuries had withdrawn inland to their traditional areas. They kept to themselves, subsisting on their traditional lands and displaying no inclination to participate in the vice-regal – (Spanish colonial) – economy. However, the mixed-blood groups, or *castas*, were spread across the state. Some farmed small *ranchos*, others fished for a living. Since many of these *castas* had developed immunity to tropical diseases, they worked in the port city, the only vital locus of economic activity in the state. It was the only port through which flowed the goods from Spain necessary for New Spain.

Nevertheless, growth at the end of the colonial period was unspectacular. The first decades of the nineteenth century actually saw a decline in economic output due, for the most part, to the debilitating independence movement. That struggle interrupted industrial and agricultural growth for at least the first half of the century. Over the first two decades the money supply fell from sixteen million pesos to just over three million, a tremendous drop. By the middle of the century, it has been estimated, the money supply still had not returned to the level it had reached at the end of the colonial period.[10] This contraction had a number of effects. First, it made it very difficult to obtain capital for the resumption of activities, let alone expansion. It also led to a very slow recovery in the mining sector, which had a negative effect on the terms of trade. Governments had little money to cover expenses, which in itself had a disastrous effect on foreign affairs. But apart from the army, which was forever underpaid, government simply had no money to repair or improve the infrastructure. Repairing roads and building railways, which might have stimulated the economy, was not possible.[11] This fiscal problem may be the key to explaining the political chaos of the first half of the century: there was no money to do anything. Veracruz state, however, was better off than most. Whatever government revenue there was had to flow through its gates. And the politician who was the most influential in Mexican politics during this near half-century, General López de Santa Anna, was a Veracruzan.

Veracruz's economic potential had already been established before the independence wars. With independence, it seemed as if the state was not only going to continue in this importance, but would be the linchpin in the early plans for Mexican development. These were based on agricultural possibilities and centred on the *tierra caliente*, the coastal and lowland area of Veracruz with potential for growing sugar, cotton, and coffee in addition to tobacco. The latter, already grown on the temperate slopes of Orizaba and Córdoba, had been one of the mainstays of the vice-regal economy, aided by the monopoly it enjoyed. With the establishment of the constitution in 1824, and in the climate of euphoria over the idea of free trade, that monopoly was restructured, with the national government sharing the marketing with the states.[12]

In addition, the industrial potential of Veracruz was recognized from the first days of the young Mexican republic. Lucas Alamán set up the Banco de Avío to fund a Mexican textile industry in the Orizaban highlands of Veracruz. Seeing the potential of the state's hydraulic resources, between 1835 and 1840 the bank financed the establishment of the first textile factories in Xalapa and Orizaba. This development quickly converted Veracruz into one of the prime manufacturing centres in Mexico. By 1845 it possessed just over seventeen per cent of the textile spindles in the country.[13] The state, therefore, offered a tremendous power base to a governor who was shrewd enough to use these resources to his advantage. It also offered temptations to the central government, for reasons we shall examine, to exert increasing control over this lucrative state for the benefit of the nation. Veracruz's geography became an integral factor determining the eventual outcome of that struggle.

The Porfiriato

That dictatorships are very rarely completely dictatorial is a truism. That the dictatorship of Porfirio Díaz, who ruled Mexico from 1876 to 1911, was hardly authoritarian at the local and regional levels, that the entire system rested instead on a complex network of negotiated outcomes, has been accepted by scholars of the period.[14] Veracruz was no exception. Unlike Yucatan, however, where *camarilla*[15] politics was the order of the day, in Veracruz the Porfirian system rested, from 1892 onwards, on an accommodation between the president and a powerful governor, who was genuinely popular in the state because of his developmentalist policies. That accommodation was significant because it emphasized a traditional element in Veracruz politics, one that had been a bone of contention in the Juárez settlement after 1867: the issue of federalism. Veracruzans had expressed their adherence to a federalist interpretation of the Constitution of 1857 and had thrown their support behind Díaz and against Lerdo de Tejada in 1876 because of it.[16] Even before he became governor, Teodoro Dehesa identified with this position, one that he maintained steadfastly throughout his life.

Dehesa was born in Veracruz port on October 1, 1848, of an Aragonese father who settled in Veracruz and a Xalapa mother from a distinguished family. At an early age the little boy came face to face with social reality in Mexico, for his parents continuously discussed the plight of the poor. Dehesa's sympathy for the impoverished class dates from this time. The story is told that he once raided a small cash box of his father's, distributing the contents to some poor children who were attending the municipal school that faced his house. Another factor in Dehesa's formation was the fervent religious education imparted by his mother, a devout Roman Catholic. He attended private schools and then entered the Lyceum in Xalapa, whose headmaster at the time was the well-known and influential educator Teodoro Kerlegand. Dehesa was an excellent student at the top of his class. He took over his father's bakery upon the latter's death, but was also apprenticed to a local businessman who owned a drygoods store. He soon became a trusted employee, eventually becoming the owner's private secretary.

In the 1860s, the young Dehesa followed the events surrounding the French invasion of Mexico with considerable trepidation over the imposition of a foreign monarch on the nation. It was during this time that he became aware of Porfirio Díaz and began to admire the victor of the battle of Puebla. This initial sympathy grew with time, especially when Díaz began to demonstrate opposition to the re-election of President Benito Juárez some years later. This adhesion to the *caudillo* (strong man) would last throughout the Porfiriato.[17] Dehesa then joined the

Porfirian movement in 1870 and was elected to the executive of the "Republican Club" of Veracruz. In the election of 1871, the club championed Porfirio Díaz, who lost. Dehesa then argued that since electoral means had failed to bring Díaz to power, the only remaining option was rebellion.[18] On October 12, 1871, in fact, the day after Juárez was declared elected by the Mexican Congress, a revolt was launched. This came to be known as the Revolt of La Noria, named after the *hacienda* Díaz owned in Oaxaca.[19] Several months later, Díaz's brother was brutally killed in the field and the defeated Porfirians were seeking a way out of the country.[20] Porfirio Díaz's flight through Veracruz and the valuable help given him by the young Dehesa are described in the latter's memoirs:

> The revolt having failed, in order to escape abroad Don Porfirio found it necessary to seek refuge in Veracruz where he knew he had friends and followers. Together with General Galván he went through the *sierra* of Zongólica towards Coscomatepec. There they encountered Colonel Honrato Domínguez, who knew the country and who directed them towards the coast, putting them up in the house of Don Juan Viveros. Without doubt Domínguez told Don Porfirio that one of his loyal followers lived in Veracruz, and from there I suppose that General Díaz wrote me the letter asking for my help in securing passage on a ship out of the country, either to Havana or to the United States. In my youthfulness I was eager to serve General Díaz and Providence complied.[21]

With the help of friends, Dehesa managed to secure passage for Díaz and General Pedro A. Galván aboard the English vessel *Corsica*, which left Veracruz on February 1, 1872, for New York.[22] This was the beginning of a long and lasting friendship between the two men that was to result in close co-operation throughout the Porfiriato, especially after Dehesa assumed the governorship of Veracruz in 1892.

After Díaz's flight, Dehesa became even more involved with the Porfirian movement, deciding to enter active politics himself. In the meantime, President Juárez had died of a heart attack and the president of the Supreme Court, Sebastian Lerdo de Tejada, another Veracruzan, had been sworn in as president. Lerdo de Tejada cleverly issued an amnesty to which Díaz decided to submit on October 13, 1872.[23] However, the Porfirian party was not dead. Cosío Villegas remarks that, in fact, Díaz began thinking about the next revolt right after arriving in the capital where Lerdo received him. For the moment, however, he retired "completely" from politics and returned to agriculture. But the sugar business at La Noria being rather poor, he decided to take over a small sugar ranch near the Veracruzan town of Tlacotalpan called La Candelaria, which was awarded to him by the Veracruz legislature.[24]

Happily for the Porfirian followers in Veracruz, President Lerdo removed the Juarista governor, substituting the well-liked and distinguished Veracruzan Francisco Landero y Cos, who sympathized with the Porfirians. In the October 1872 elections for the state legislature, Dehesa, only twenty-four years of age, won a seat to represent Xalapa, the state capital.[25] Dehesa's victory rested on the acclaim he received from many Veracruzans over his stand against re-election. Dehesa and his followers then tried to encourage Díaz to re-enter Mexican political life through the open door of Veracruzan politics. General Luis Mier y Terán, another close and fervently loyal supporter of Díaz, proposed that he seek the governorship of Veracruz. Since Landero y Cos was about to resign, and since it was possible to name an interim governor, Dehesa proposed this manoeuvre to Díaz. Díaz politely refused. However, he did accept an offer from the state government, Mier y Terán and Dehesa, to run for a vacant seat for the Mexican Congress in a Veracruz district. Díaz believed that if he were not able to win a seat, the opportunity for higher office would be lost forever. Dehesa then compiled a list of candidates he felt would best represent Porfirian interests in the forthcoming state election of 1875, featuring Díaz as congressional deputy. The majority of these were subsequently elected, including Díaz, with the result that he again appeared officially as a political figure, awakening hopes in the hearts of many of those who were becoming disillusioned with Lerdo's presidency.[26]

With the election of a governor as well as a slate of representatives from within the ranks of the Porfirians, Díaz' political fortunes again began to wax. His political movement in Veracruz, lead by Dehesa, gathered momentum. Together with General Mier y Terán, Dehesa founded political clubs throughout the state to campaign for Díaz as president. Certainly, in Veracruz, as elsewhere, Díaz was popular, especially with the commercial sector, which wanted above all the peace and order that would permit them to do business.[27]

The pro-Díaz movement in Veracruz, which had spread to other parts of the country, was not the only source of opposition to Lerdo. In the capital, too, leading newspapermen were spearheading a movement severely critical of the president.

Vincente Riva Palacio in *El Ahuizote* (Papantla) and Ireneo Paz in *El Padre Cobos* (Mexico City) were constant in their criticism, and towards the end of 1875 published a book in which they attempted to raise their criticisms "before the tribunal of history."[28] The support he enjoyed and Lerdo's declared intention to seek re-election, probably motivated Díaz to think about initiating plans for a revolt since it was unlikely that Lerdo would be able to win an election without massive corruption.[29]

In June 1875, there were unfounded rumours that Díaz had left La Candelaria for Oaxaca, his home state, where he would be raising an army. Actually, Díaz had had his passport extended by the military commandant of Veracruz, and on December 3, together with Manuel González, had left the port by ship for Brownsville, Texas. From there he proceeded to solicit funds, buy arms, and raise an army. In March he issued the Plan of Tuxtepec, charging Lerdo *inter alia* with violating the sovereignty of the states. On March 20, 1876, he crossed the northern frontier with about four hundred men.[30]

In Veracruz his followers indicated their support quite openly. In Xalapa there was a bold attempt to score an early Porfirian victory. An attempted *coup d'état* by a Porfirian supporter, Manuel García, was easily defeated by a captain of the Rurales, the federal mounted police, who also arrested the ineffectual governor, María Mena. Shortly after, General Marcos Carillo was named commandant and military governor of the Lerdista government in Veracruz and restored order of a kind. Of these events Dehesa writes:

A movement was initiated in the capital, Xalapa. The governor, Don José María Mena, was an illustrious Cordoban. However, he was completely indolent, and, because of this a chief of the Rurales, Captain Merino, took him prisoner. So the situation changed there. The legislative and judicial powers were removed to Veracruz and I went along. The events in Veracruz had such repercussions on the rest of the country, that the Federation declared a state of siege there, naming General Marcos Carillo as Governor and Commander-in-Chief. Since I continued to express my opinions with absolute freedom, Gen. Carillo called me to him one day and said, "I don't want to have to give Veracruz a day of mourning, and you therefore can consider yourself under arrest."[31]

Dehesa was then removed from Veracruz to Orizaba, where he was detained for a few days until he could be moved to Mexico

City. He was well treated in Orizaba and in Mexico City, where he was kept under house arrest in the Hotel Iturbide. He was removed to a prison on March 24, 1876 and remained there until December of that year, keeping in touch with political events through daily visits from the editor of the influential newspaper *El Monitor Repúblicano* (Mexico City), Vincente García Torres. He was also in correspondence with Díaz, writing under the assumed name of Estanislao Mendoza and giving accounts of the political climate in the capital.[32]

In the meantime, the Revolution of Tuxtepec gathered momentum in Veracruz and the rest of Mexico. Revolts had broken out in Acayucan and Coscomatepec, and thereafter extended into the Huatusco, Jalacingo, Misantla, Papantla, and Córdoba. The Battle of Tecoac in Tlaxcala, which took place on November 16, 1876, decided Lerdo's fate. Five days later, on November 21, Díaz entered Mexico City; Lerdo embarked for the United States from Acapulco. After Lerdo's flight from the capital, Dehesa made his way back to Veracruz with General Mier y Terán, eventually meeting up with Díaz in the home of a Spaniard. Dehesa returned to the port, where he was named Inspector of Maritime Customs, an important post. Here his task was to inspect the operations of the customs, and in particular to uncover corruption and smuggling, which were a constant drain on this source of government revenue. Dehesa remained at this post through Díaz's first presidential term. He also served Díaz's successor, President Manuel González, until the end of González's mandate in 1884, doing an excellent job of suppressing corruption within the customs service.

Dehesa used this time well by cementing his political contacts and promoting the Porfirian cause. This was important work, as neither the state nor the country were completely pacified with Díaz's victory. There were significant Lerdista uprisings in Veracruz as well as the rest of the country. It is therefore understandable, although not excusable, that General Mier y Terán, stung by the nervous president Díaz's constant accusations of a conspiracy in Veracruz, which he equally constantly denied, resorted to some extreme and brutal measures. When the crew of the warship *Libertad* mutinied in the harbour at Tlacotalpan and Mier y Terán was informed that there was, indeed, a plot underfoot in the port city, he acted on Díaz's orders conveyed in the famous telegram "*Matalos en caliente*" (kill them cold-bloodedly). On the night of November 24, nine leading citizens were hauled from their beds and executed brutally and without trial. The public outcry was so great that the governor was forced to resign.

In the next elections in 1880, Apolinar Castillo was elected governor.[33] Dehesa, who was not involved in any way with the executions, was thus in an excellent position to continue his own political march. He had already been thrice elected as a member of the legislature, and enjoyed a reputation as both an honest and an effective administrator. In 1884 he was also elected as a deputy to the Mexican Congress. By this time both his loyalty and his administrative ability had been proven. On Díaz's return to the presidency in 1884, Dehesa was given the top position of Administrator of the Customs House with an enormous salary.[34] From here he would be able to hone other administrative skills and further enhance his political reputation.

Veracruz in 1884 was in the hands of an extremely able and popular governor, Juan de la Luz Enríquez, known for his heroism against the French. He was also a liberal politician with avowedly democratic leanings. Under his governorship the state continued to flourish materially and culturally. In 1890 the Inter-Oceanic Railway from Veracruz port through Xalapa to Mexico City was finally completed. The state *alcabalas* (internal commercial duties) were rescinded, and special attention was given to education. A normal school was established to train teachers, directed by the eminent Swiss educator Enrique Rebsamen, and primary schools were established in cantonal capitals.[35] In addition, Enríquez initiated a beautification campaign for the major towns.

These measures, however, served the middle classes, rather than the poor and Indians. The latter had already signalled their antipathy to the liberal ideas of "progress," especially the *Ley Lerdo* and its attempt to privatize land. However, the state government had no intention of altering the trajectory that had been implicitly agreed on since the 1840s. This relentless implementation of the liberal program forced Indians in two distinct areas to rebel in the 1880s and 1890s. From 1881 to 1884 Popolucas in the Soteapan, objecting to the theft of their lands by the *hacienda*, Corral Nuevo, had taken to arms, only to be repressed. The family who owned the *hacienda*, the Cházaro Solers, was too powerful, and in any event it is clear, with hindsight, that Mexican development in this era – as before – was accomplished by actively marginalizing Indian peoples who were considered not to be sufficiently "progressive." In Papantla as well, the Totonacs, finding no redress in the courts, rose up against the invasion of their lands by would-be vanilla growers, also to no avail.[36]

De la Luz Enríquez, although genuinely popular among certain groups, and despite his successes as governor, engendered opposition among not only Indians but also his political peers. His decision to run for a third term aroused much hostility in Veracruz. This paradox of principle and praxis is quite interesting, and it is typical of the Porfiriato. The people of Veracruz state had been among the most fervent supporters of the principles of Tuxtepec, which called for no re-election. The eight-year period since Díaz's revolt had not been sufficient to dim these memories, and there were many Veracruzans who wanted these principles respected. *El Reproductor*, the influential paper printed in the former Veracruzan capital, Orizaba, tried to calm the political storm by pointing out the advantages of continuity, which it suggested should take precedence over principles that had been rooted in a different political context. Its efforts were not successful, however, and speculation about other possible candidates increased as the election of 1892 drew close.[37]

Teodoro Dehesa, seeing his chance to obtain the governorship under the Anti-re-electionist banner, unleashed a furious campaign against Enríquez. The newspaper *El Nacional* (Mexico City) supported him. It revealed a unique approach to the logic of "principle," which had become the guiding political concept of the Porfiriato. According to this concept, principles such as "no re-election" might be sacred, but could and should be subsumed under another principle, that of "national necessity." In other words, re-electing Díaz was all right, but Enríquez had to go.

As early as February 1891, Dehesa's friends were at work in various parts of the state setting up political clubs. Dehesa's political platform was based on the Plan of Tuxtepec with its demand for no re-election. Naturally, although Dehesa was campaigning vigorously under the slogan of "no re-election" in Veracruz, he had no doubt that the best thing for the country would be Díaz's own re-election, a view that was shared by many people and justified by the principle of national necessity enunciated above.[38] At the same time he appealed to the president that such reasoning did not apply to Veracruz: the electorate wanted and the state needed a change of administration. So he left no stone unturned in consistently petitioning Díaz on his own behalf, reminding the president of his, Dehesa's, consistent loyalty and friendship.[39] Dehesa's difficulties were considerable. Enríquez had been a good governor and, moreover, enjoyed Díaz's confidence. The decision must have been painful for Díaz. On March 17, Dehesa sent him copies of newspaper articles from the port city in support of various candidates. He specifically recommended that the president read one particular article, by Dehesa's friend, Salvador Díaz Mirón, supporting his own candidacy.[40]

In fact, Enríquez's popularity was waning, especially among the press. In Veracruz the press had always enjoyed considerable freedom but was now under attack from the governor because of its support for the principle of no re-election. On March 9, Pedro Castillo, editor of *El Ciudadano Libre* and *El Imparcial* in the port city, wrote to the president giving a personal example of the governor's application of "justice." Castillo had written an article censuring the administration, accusing it of immorality and of disregarding the very laws that it was supposed to uphold, because it had incarcerated a justice of the jeace and notary public for drunkenness. And since Enríquez did not permit anyone to criticize his administration, he had ordered the *jefe político* to accuse Castillo of defamation of character and had him sent to prison for two months until his release on bail.[41]

Happily for Dehesa and the opposition, and, indeed, Díaz, Enríquez died suddenly on March 17 of a heart attack. Manuel Leví, secretary of *Gobierno* (government: a position second only to the governor) in Veracruz, was named interim governor. Enríquez was buried on March 20 with full honours and attended by a huge cortège.[42] Dehesa's campaign could now proceed without much fear of opposition, although there were still obstacles to overcome: the late governor's supporters still occupied all important government posts, and their support was essential if Dehesa was to prevail. Then Díaz stepped in. On the same day of Enríquez's funeral, he wrote to the interim governor, Manuel Leví, reminding him that new employees were to be followers of Dehesa, but he also warned Dehesa not to be vindictive against the Enriquistas.[43] Dehesa, however, was not a vindictive person. Besides, Díaz's advice was politically wise. Dehesa therefore wrote to assure Díaz that he had communicated with "our friends" in diverse places, asking them to cease publication of articles critical of the previous administration, in view of not only the president's wishes but also his own.[44]

The close co-operation between Díaz and Dehesa was obvious well before Enríquez died. Díaz realized the importance of having a genuinely popular governor in office, one who could be counted on for support and who was, moreover, a civilian. Despite the presence of an interim governor, the business of state was already being carried on between Díaz and Dehesa.[45] The two exchanged reams of letters after March discussing such government business as the choice of *jefes políticos* and how to ensure that the new interim governor, Leandro Alcolea, did their bidding. Nor did Díaz hesitate to exert his influence in the local matter of selecting representatives to the state legislature.[46] Here already, Dehesa demonstrated that he was not to be treated as a mere yes-man to the president and that he was determined to keep as free a hand as possible in the affairs of the state. For example, to Díaz's request that he appoint Guillermo A. Esteva to the state legislature, he answered:

> With Esteva the enriquistas will have four out of the eleven representatives. As this will mean a representation of more than one third, I would agree that Esteva come with a little false restraint, that is, as a substitute representative for someone with whom he would not agree. This will fulfill his desires and we will have prevented any capriciousness in the future, because I know him since college and he is a little mischievous.[47]

Díaz answered with thanks for Dehesa's consideration, adding that, given the reasons cited, he approved of the way the matter would be handled.[48]

In the elections for governor, held in July, Dehesa received a majority of ballots and was duly confirmed and sworn in by the state legislature, despite objections that there had been some rigging.[49] This election began Dehesa's governorship, which was to last until 1911, contrary to his own stated principle of no reelection but, in the minds of most contemporary observers and later historians, to the decided benefit of Veracruz. More importantly, by choosing Dehesa, Díaz put an end to *camarilla* politics in the state. He did not allow any other group to command his attention. No "political carousel" was utilized in controlling this state, one of the few that Díaz did not need to worry about unduly.[50] This is not to say, however, that the president did not use other checks and balances.

The Porfirian System in Veracruz

Dehesa's success in developing Veracruz was such in part due to his abilities as an administrator and in part to his friendship with the president. This connection, forged during the La Noria and Tuxtepec revolts, was an essential part of the system known as the Porfiriato. To accomplish the modernization of Mexico, Díaz had cleverly utilized the sentiment of federalism to gain power, allowing the states considerable freedom to manoeuvre as long as they acquiesced in the general trajectory of economic growth under a capitalist system.[51] On the other hand, the consolidation and retention of power in the hands of the president was accomplished through the skillful employment of a number of manipulative political techniques.

First, Díaz almost always had his military cronies elected as governors and *jefes políticos* to oversee the running of the various states.[52] Trained in carrying out orders, these men would be more likely to enforce the president's will than would civilians. Second, power was concentrated at the federal level, specifically in the person of the president, who oversaw all government activity, but especially correspondence with the governors and *jefes políticos.* Third, Díaz surrounded himself with close members of his own family, wherever possible, and with intimate friends to ensure that he would be obeyed and that plots or incipient revolts would be uncovered before they could be brought to fruition. A fourth tactic was the skillful use of the concept *divide et impera*, in which rival groups were played off against one another, so that no group ever seemed to have finally and irrevocably enjoyed the president's favour. Wells and Joseph have provided a compelling portrait of the use of intrastate elite rivalry and *camarilla* politics in Yucatan, although this tactic was not utilized within every state.[53]

In other states, such as Veracruz, the regime was built around the unconditional support that Díaz gave to his governors, and which they in turn gave to him.[54] Even in cases where Díaz had to countermand a governor's position, it was done without the removal of the governor, as in the case of the unpopular Carlos Díez Gutiérrez of San Luis Potosí. For their part, the governors did the same in respect to their state institutions and offices, nominating the members for the legislature, the judiciary, and the municipal offices. At the same time, they were made responsible for any "violations" of constitutional and federal laws that occurred in their states.[55] In practical terms, this measure gave them the opportunity to centralize all state power in their own hands. Thus, Díaz allowed the creation of a series of state political machines, which were completely dependent on him and were allowed to maintain themselves as long as they kept order. In other words, the federalism that had hitherto been defined and incorporated into the Constitution of 1857 existed not just in name, but frequently in practice, to a certain degree.

Governors did not often implement any kind of independent policy under the Díaz regime. It was, however, possible for strong personalities, such as governors Bernardo Reyes in Monterrey and Dehesa in Veracruz, who were genuinely popular in their states, to imprint their own style and ideas on their particular bailiwicks. And the country was quick to respond with approbation for governors who actually took their mandates seriously and with integrity, as was the case with Dehesa. Applauding a good governor, after all, was one way of getting around the strict and implacable censorship of the press. Some papers like *La Patria* (Mexico City) and *El Diario del Hogar* (Mexico City), did level criticism, but paid the price.[56]

The other important bulwark of the regime was the *jefe político* as head of each canton.[57] The origin of this office has been traced to the early years of the nineteenth century when Liberals, anxious to strengthen local government against the encroachments of central power, had local representatives appointed by the governor. Since 1887, the governor usually appointed this individual after consultation with the president. Díaz, however, completely changed the role of these appointees: from standing on guard against the heavy hand of the central government, they became its local representatives, with roles akin to that of the Intendant in France, Spain, and New Spain. They were responsible to the governors, although it was expected that they would report directly to the president, and they often did. They were given executive power in their cantons and judicial power in certain cases. They were also in control of the Rurales, as well as state gendarmery. The *jefe político* was definitely the "man on the spot" during the Porfiriato, for he ensured that the government's chosen candidates won local elections and that the president's and governor's wishes were carried out.[58]

Because of their far-reaching powers, *jefes políticos* had to be closely watched by both president and governor. Numerous were the occasions in which private citizens, for one reason or another, complained to the president about one of these officials, prompting an investigation by the governor. Dehesa, however, knew his men. He also took the trouble to inquire about those the president asked him to appoint, and often sharply rejected the president's accusations against some who were the target of vicious slurs levelled by Díaz's friends and acquaintances. For example, in 1908 various citizens from the canton of Jalacingo, Veracruz, complained to the president of the cruelty of their *jefe político*, his rigidity and arbitrariness, and his levying of heavy fines and jailing of citizens. Dehesa's reply was that the charges were "completely untrue" and that the real reason for the complaint was that the individual in question was protecting Indians from exploitation by unscrupulous lawyers (*tinterillos*).[59]

Sometimes, too, the accusations were couched in abjectly

general terms. Residents in the canton of Minatitlán petitioned the president in February 1902, complaining about the conduct of a *jefe político* who was sowing "ill-feeling" with his behaviour. Specific charges were not made, yet the president wrote Dehesa that the individual was not worthy of the confidence that the governor had placed in him. Dehesa's reply was that the *jefe político* was a person of good background, that the complaint was probably from a man who felt he ought to be in charge, and that the president should consult with the minister of finance, who knew the *jefe político* personally. Similarly, during the investigation of a murder in the canton of Cosamaloapan in 1898, Díaz asked Dehesa to order the *jefe político* to cease bothering an old friend. Dehesa's investigation revealed that the police had entered the old man's house looking for his son who was wanted for questioning and had not molested him. When a few years later the same *jefe político* was accused of protecting the secretary of the municipality, who had been accused of corruption, Dehesa promised that if it were true the situation would be "radically corrected."[60]

In the case of a *jefe político* of San Andrés Tuxtla, repeated charges appearing in the press and citizens' complaints that he was in league with cattle thieves caused Dehesa to undertake a special journey to that canton, which resulted in the official's removal. However, his replacement was unable to gain the confidence of the citizenry and was in turn replaced by a man who had been born in the canton and was, in addition, an old friend of the president's. Unfortunately, this Colonel Ortiz was not liked by one of the Porfirian factions, called the "rich," who disliked him particularly because he was said to be always surrounded by the other faction, called the "poor."[61] Because of the continued rivalry but also because of Ortiz's apparent favouritism, Dehesa had him replaced with his own appointee, who did not work out either – this canton was obviously difficult to please! Other *jefes políticos* were replaced because they were a focus of opposition to the governor, as in the case of Ignacio Betancourt in Misantla, or because their families tried to take personal advantage of their connections. Sometimes, too, they were replaced because of personal problems such as alcoholism, as was the case with Demetrio Santaella in Zongólica.[62]

The press was also quite active in reporting on local conditions and alleged abuses, contributing to the removal of some *jefes políticos*. In February 1901, *El Paladín* (Mexico City), a newspaper representing Spanish interests in Mexico and a virulent opponent of Dehesa, printed a strongly worded article complaining of abuses committed against the Indian population in San Juan Evangelista in the canton of Acayucan. The *jefe político* was said to have imposed heavy fines on the Indians of Sayula because their cattle had caused damage to the lands of a *hacendado* and he was also accused of drunkenness. He was transferred to another canton. In that same year, the *jefe político* of Papantla was accused of molesting the poor. His sarcastic rejoinder was that he had given them "all manner of guarantees that they were free and could continue their travels to the *Valle Nacional* [a work camp in Oaxaca in which conditions akin to slavery existed] and receive the necessary military instructions so as to be able to defend the integrity of the country against the threatened Yankee invasion."[63] The following month, Dehesa had him replaced.

The position of *jefe político* was so sensitive that it is no wonder frequent replacements were necessary. Factional strife was always present, as were people who tried to use their friendship or acquaintance with the president to obtain preferential treatment in some business matter. And while the president's appointments were made with an eye to keeping order, he was sensitive to abuses and tried to correct them. With the guidance of a governor like Dehesa, who demanded scrupulous honesty and justice from his *jefe políticos*, there were many cases where this local authority performed well and was praised by citizens and even the opposition press. Ignacio Canseco, the *jefe político* of Huatusco, appointed in 1892, was truly popular; some considered him to be the best *jefe político* the canton had ever had.[64] The *jefe político* who replaced Santaella in Zongólica was also considered to be doing a good job, especially in the area of public morality, which meant that he was trying to contain gambling and drunkenness.

Even *El Paladín*, whose criticisms of Dehesa could be strident, had to admit that his choices for *jefes políticos* were sometimes excellent. Other newspapers went further, listing the actual achievements of the local authority. A prisoner in the jail at Jalacingo wrote to *El Nacional* praising conditions in the jail, which had been improved by the new *jefe político*. The prisoners had been treated to a succulent Christmas dinner, and a gallery had been constructed in the prison where prisoners could make arts and crafts for sale in order to help support their families. The *jefe político* of Cosamaloapan, Lorenzo Gómez, who had been there for eight years, built a boys' school, a public market, a parade square, a theatre, and a women's jail. His financial administration was also sound, the tax intake was properly monitored, and the entire administration was considered one of the best in the state. *La Patria* commented that his success "reinforced our thesis that a government as progressive as that of Veracruz needs secondary officials who are as competent as those to whom they are subordinate."[65] In Orizaba, too, the administration of Angel Prieto instituted similar reforms.[66]

Dehesa was not always able to have his own men appointed, however, and was careful not to take his opposition to the president too far. Nor did Díaz always consult the governor over appointments, although he sometimes later questioned the behaviour and loyalty of those he had imposed on the state. This was the case with the appointment of Demetrio Santibáñez to Minatitlán in 1905. This man had been imposed on Dehesa after he had made another choice. Such had been the arbitrariness of the appointment that Dehesa had to request Santibáñez's address from the president in order to send him the official notice of appointment. But when Díaz accused Santibáñez of disloyalty a few years later for giving aid to the Madero revolutionaries, Dehesa had to point out that, although Santibáñez had his faults, disloyalty was not one of them.[67]

There seems to have been no consistency in the way the president handled appointments or complaints. At times, he could be arbitrary; at other times, an implacable sense of justice would prevail. This, of course, made it extremely difficult to deal with him, and lesser men than Dehesa might have succumbed to the temptation of merely carrying out orders. But Dehesa always pressed his point as far as he could, not hesitating to give the real facts in any situation. During the sensitive period prior to the Revolution, army commanders were quick to abuse their authority and sometimes committed grave offences against innocent people. The army commander for Acayucan, Colonel Jasso arrested a man in December 1910 – the colonel and some of his subalterns had been drinking heavily in a bar, and when asked to leave, had arrested the proprietor – without informing the *jefe político*, José María Camacho, under whose jurisdiction such an action fell. The latter complained to Dehesa, who told him to remind Colonel Jasso tactfully of the harmony that had always existed between the two offices. Jasso still refused to release the man. When Dehesa informed the president, a direct order was sent to have the man released. Later, the colonel was severely reprimanded.[68] This system of local authority with direct access to the president was extremely efficient in maintaining control. That it could also be arbitrary or oppressive is without doubt.

Another method Díaz used to maintain political control was

to undermine the authority of ministers in the cabinet. Between 1892 and 1900, the cabinet served as an administrative body, with the ministers taking orders directly from the president. But when any group seemed to be gaining ascendancy another group swiftly arose to oppose them. This was the case until 1900, when Díaz tried to oppose the Científico[69] group, headed by his father-in-law, Manuel Romero Rubio, by constantly playing them off against Joaquín Baranda, whose close friend was Teodoro Dehesa. Whenever he wished to make the Científicos uneasy, he would confer exclusively with Baranda and Dehesa. In similar fashion, governors who were too popular, or too ambitious could be counteracted by playing them off against military commanders, as was the case with Dehesa and Rosalino Martínez, a rivalry which reached its peak at Río Blanco (see Chapter 2).[70]

The reduction of both the Chamber of Deputies (Lower House) and the Senate to the status of rubber stamps completed the system of controls. At no time were elections to Congress the result of the popular vote and, after 1892, the president personally selected the members of those bodies. Lists of candidates were submitted to him, from which he would indicate individuals to be accepted or rejected. Suggestions by governors were naturally possible. Francisco Dehesa, the governor's brother, and Teodoro Dehesa's eldest son Raúl were both representatives in the Chamber of Deputies for Veracruz. The same system was true for the state legislatures, where Díaz would send lists to the governors. Dehesa, however, frequently kept his own council, and would indicate that he had already made a choice, which he did not wish to compromise. At other times, he simply refused to abide by Díaz's wishes to select the president's friends.[71]

Control of the press was another element in this system, albeit not always a successful one. Throughout the Porfiriato there was always an opposition press. Some publishers and writers were willing to risk imprisonment for criticizing the government. Others praised governors or officials who had acted honestly and justly, a more subtle form of criticism. Newspapers were supported for carrying the government line, but even when there was general support for the regime, some papers attacked particular states or governors with singular ferocity. *La Patria*, whose publisher, Ireneo Paz, was an old friend of Díaz, did level heavy criticism at some of the badly governed states and their governors while reserving unstinting praise for others, such as Veracruz under Dehesa, who was "doing an excellent job."[72]

Dehesa himself had his own idiosyncratic methods of dealing

with the press. Indeed, he protected *El Dictámen* of Veracruz, which was considered an opposition paper, and which seemed to take the side of the workers' movement, although it consistently supported Dehesa. And when Díaz accused him of disloyalty because of his protection of the paper, Dehesa answered icily:

> I have always told you the truth, and intend to continue doing so even when you have the patience to listen to many stories about me which are intended to raise doubts about my loyalty to you.[73]

Instead of taking arbitrary action, Dehesa tried to confront the writers of inflammatory articles against him, forcing them to substantiate their charges or publicly withdraw their accusation. Dehesa's primary enemy was the newspaper *El Paladín*. This paper consistently hurled charges that his administration was ineffective and that he was doing nothing for the state. Every conceivable petty incident was used as the basis for an article repeating these charges, as if their veracity had already been established. Not all Spaniards supported the paper (which supposedly represented their interests), let alone its accusations. In response to the continuing vilification, one Spanish citizen living in Veracruz, Ramón Alvarez Soto, wrote to the publisher of *El Paladín* asking him to cease the campaign against Dehesa. "The Spanish colony of this state," he wrote, "is rich and numerous and is completely satisfied with the present administration."[74]

Some Spaniards even began countering with a broadsheet distancing themselves from the paper. However, the *El Paladín* articles made Díaz nervous, and he asked Dehesa to deal with them.[75] Dehesa's tactic was to invite the authors of articles that accused him of misconduct to Veracruz, where, in front of the *jefe político* of the canton in which abuses were alleged to have taken place, they were asked to repeat and substantiate the charges. This they were always unable to do.

Díaz was extremely sensitive to the press, especially when he found himself unable to influence or control it. Such was the case in Yucatan in 1905 when some periodicals printed articles attacking the federal government. The problem here was that the governor, who was also helping these publications financially, protected them. Díaz then asked Dehesa, who was a friend of the governor, to "call attention to his (the governor's) anti-patriotic conduct." Dehesa discreetly dropped some hints, although the records do not indicate whether the matter was solved to the president's satisfaction. The president also kept a close watch on what the foreign press was saying about him.[76]

The president, surrounded by factions and groups all of whom wanted a share of the power, and sometimes more than a share, never knew exactly whom to trust. Even close and loyal friends such as Dehesa were spied on if Díaz had the slightest doubt that matters were not being handled entirely his way. Dehesa must have been aware of this, yet his support of the president never wavered, as far as can be ascertained. On the other hand, he never shirked from reporting his objections to the president whenever he found "dirty hands" at work in the government, obliging Díaz to take energetic measures to investigate and punish offenders.[77]

There is no doubt that the political system in the Porfiriato was highly centralized and authoritarian. Yet this did not mean there was no room for flexibility. A governor like Dehesa, who was not afraid to speak his mind, could resist the pressure of his enemies and demand that certain actions be taken. In this limited sense only, however, can one speak of a continuation of the federal system. Furthermore, there were forces at work, ironically promoted by Dehesa himself – the capitalist growth of the state and the nation – that would severely test that system. The root ideological motive, fuelled by those developing forces, was the resistance to the increasingly centralized nature of the Porfirian state.

Veracruz's Economic Development

In 1876, at the beginning of the Porfiriato, Veracruz was still relatively underdeveloped and sparsely populated, but efforts to exploit its potential brought about rapid change. This was aided by the overall recovery of the Mexican economy in the 1860s and 1870s, led by the increased output of the mining industry and the stimulus from railway construction. This recovery reverberated throughout the economy and affected the cotton textile industry as well. In 1892, the basis was already being laid for the expansion of the textile industry that was to become so important for Veracruz and Mexico, not only economically but politically as well.[78] In 1892, President Díaz inaugurated the modern textile factory of Río Blanco at Orizaba. With spindles, a thousand looms, and six large presses, it allowed Veracruz and indeed, the country to compete with the best of British cotton imports.[79] Total capital investment in the textile industry in Veracruz was between 2.5 and 3 million pesos in 1892, rising to 6.5 million in 1896 and 15 million in 1908. The capital increase was due to the completion of the large hydroelectric plant at Rincón Grande in 1897. By 1895, Río Blanco was producing a dividend to shareholders of twenty-five per cent on investment, which averaged twenty per cent in the years 1894–99. In 1896 a rival conglomerate, La Compañía Industrial Veracruzana, with French and German capital, was established in the town of Necoxtla near Orizaba, and constructed the Santa Rosa factory for stamping cloth and producing yarn. Nearly one thousand workers were involved in the construction, and a road was built to join the two towns. Total capital investment there was 3.5 million pesos, and the factory continuously paid dividends of approximately thirteen per cent.[80] With these investments, Veracruz accumulated forty-four per cent of the spindles in the country and became one of the most important manufacturing centres.[81]

In addition, by 1895, there were more than 465 other manufacturing establishments representing total capital of 4.3 million pesos, the most important of which produced cigars and cigarettes, lumber, and fish products. Commerce was also of relative importance.[82] In other areas of the economy, the growth rate was also quite spectacular. By 1911, Veracruz accounted for half of the entire coffee output of Mexico, and between 1876 and 1910 there was a 350 per cent increase in the output of sugar and oil.[83] In 1901, a new mineral law was passed to allow for exploration of the subsoil without taxes for ten years: this benefited companies like Sir Weetman Pearson's Compañía Mexicana de Petroleo, which was to become the largest Mexican oil company in the ensuing years.[84] In 1897, Prescotte and Co. of New York acquired large tracts of land for growing rubber trees as well as setting up the processing machinery. In 1905, agriculturists in the canton of Zongólica, formed a company investing over 400,000 pesos to grow rubber trees whose product had a ready market in New York.[85] A hydro-electric plant was constructed in that year too, in Córdoba, utilizing one of its waterfalls, to supply power to a huge new sugar factory as well as to the city's tramways. In Tuxpán in the north, between Lake Tamiahua and the Gulf, another company was established to market daffodils.[86] In 1905, in the south, in Minatitlán, a sugar factory utilizing the most modern refining process was built with capital amounting to over one million pesos. One year later a U.S. company sent agents to both Zongólica and Papantla to acquire lands for the commercial growing of vanilla.[87]

Such was the promise and reputation of Veracruz that outside investors were eager to take advantage of its potential. Letters requesting information on Veracruz were continuous and showed a vigorous interest in establishing industries in that state.[88] In 1905, the minister of the interior, Ramón Corral, requested Governor Dehesa's help for a businessman who had established an office in Mexico City in order to transmit economic information on the various Mexican states. However, the state government had already established an information office run by a U.S. citizen, Alex M. Gaw. Dehesa's answer to Corral was curt, indicating not only the emphasis that Dehesa placed on economic development but also his intention to maintain control of that development without interference from the central government. In a sense, Dehesa's reply reflects the bitter fight for control of the state economy he was forever waging with the central government, and in particular against his enemies the Científicos. (See Chapter 3.)[89]

The Demographic Results of Modernization

Certainly the rapid growth of the state caused problems for the government, especially from agriculturists who resented the concessions granted the new industries. Dehesa tried to facilitate the industrial sector, which was obviously expanding at the behest of the central government, but he was careful to maintain harmony between the two sectors and was not about to give the new industries an absolutely free hand by removing all taxes.[90] Nevertheless, by the turn of the century, industry was of far greater importance than agriculture. This development modified the social structure of the state and would have important consequences in the future.[91] One of these consequences was a rapid increase in the population of Veracruz. At the beginning of the Porfiriato, Veracruz was home to merely 542,918 persons. By 1885, this number had reached only 621,476. But over the next ten years there was a massive influx of people; the population increased by over thirty per cent, reaching 866,355, due to industrial as well as agricultural expansion. That growth continued unabated until 1910, when the state population reached 1.1 million people. Only the state of Jalisco counted more people. Of that one million plus, however, the vast majority – 887 thousand – were engaged in agricultural pursuits. And of that number, twenty-four per cent worked as peons, mainly on tobacco, sugar cane, and coffee plantations. The rest of the agricultural population worked as free laborers, sometimes farming small parcels of land as well as hiring themselves out by the day. In contrast, only 12.9 per cent of the labour force, or 56,421 people, were hired as factory workers, and of these, 31,199 worked in the textile industry.[92] The central region of Veracruz, containing four of the largest cities Veracruz, Xalapa, Córdoba, and Orizaba, was the most populous. It was, via trade, a region connected inextricably with the outside world.

By virtue of its agricultural and industrial production, therefore, Veracruz was of great importance within the Mexican economy. With only 8.32 per cent of the national population in 1910, and covering 3.65 per cent of the national territory, it furnished 11.23 per cent of industrial, and 10.42 per cent of agricultural output.[93] With economic ascendancy came a corresponding shift in Veracruz's political position vis-à-vis the national government. In view of its role as the international gateway of Mexico as well as its manufacturing establishments, not to speak of its agricultural output and mineral potential, Veracruz had by the year 1910 come to be regarded by the federal government as one of the most important Mexican states.

Much of its development was due to the opening of new lands and the capitalist exploitation of agro-industries, but also to rapid industrialization, especially in the Orizaba area, which had brought thousands of immigrant workers from other parts of Mexico. In the north and south, the Huasteca and Minatitlán, the discovery of oil also transformed the state. As expected, wherever oil was discovered, land patterns and agricultural practices had to change drastically. Unsurprisingly, hostile reactions to Porfirian development strategies would occur in those areas most affected by foreign penetration, either in zones of commercial agriculture or in the vast lands needed for oil exploration. And these reactions did not wait for the call to revolution announced in 1910 by Francisco Madero: they came much earlier.

The Land Question in Veracruz

To understand the seriousness of the rural rebellions during the Porfiriato, one must bear in mind the history of these recurring rebellions since the early nineteenth century. The first uprisings were the rural and indigenous revolts in Veracruz beginning with the Olarte rebellion in 1836. These saw as their main enemy the domination of Mexican politics by the centre in Mexico City, although only the early revolts document this stance.[94] The motivation for later revolts was the destruction of communal property in the nineteenth and early twentieth centuries by the Reform Laws. In August 1865, in Misantla, there was a revolt of Totonac Indians against the Mexicans derisively called the *gente de razón* (men of reason) in respons to the plunder of traditional lands as well as the forcible conversion of these lands from communal to private property. The government had then ordered the armed forces "not to leave one seed of the Totonac Indians in Misantla." Indians who fled were pursued into the mountains and ruthlessly slaughtered. The military was assiduous in its pursuit of this end, seriously reducing the Indian element in this region of Veracruz.[95] Equally significant uprisings occurred some years later, in 1891 and 1896, when another Totonac group protested against the loss of land in Papantla. The source of both these uprisings had been the implementation of the Reform Laws passed during the presidencies of Juárez and Lerdo de Tejada. But, as Emilio Kourí argues, the land issue was a complex one, especially in the region of Papanatla, and there needs to be a more distinctive reading of the causes behind these land revolts. Not a purely ethnic divide but a socio-economic one was the background to the later Papantla revolts.[96] As the economic viability of producing vanilla became apparent, fortunes were made both among the *gente de razón* as well as within Indian communities, producing social tensions that were reflected in the growing demand for the privatization of land.[97]

Nevertheless, both uprisings are evidence of the problem, at the turn of the century, of attempts to modernize Mexico. These two land disputes were symptomatic of general land problems during the Porfiriato. They reveal the complexity of the task of reconciling modern ideas of development in the late nineteenth century with the older Indian traditions of Mexico. They also mirror one of the central truths about the Porfiriato that has never been stressed: that behind the president was a nation of Mexicans determined to enrich themselves at the expense of the Indian element, a determination that the autocratic regime could not contain. And they point to the need for analytical sophistication: it was not the *reparto* (division and allotment of communal lands) alone, but "the interplay of growing commercial, demographic, fiscal, and political pressures during this period," that resulted in serious violence.[98]

The handling of these land problems was another matter. It displayed clearly the sharp differences between the methods and policies of Governor Dehesa, and at times President Díaz himself, as against those of the group known as the Científicos. Here were reflected, again, the problems of not only political control but the way in which development was perceived. The issue was not one of ends but means. Whereas Dehesa believed that modern Mexico needed private property and small farmers as a basis for its prosperity and tried patiently to explain this to the Indians, the Científicos wanted to proceed as rapidly as possible. The latter had two reasons: they wanted to expedite the process of modernization, and they were not squeamish about seeing Indians defrauded of their land. In their minds, the Indians were a backward element anyway. Dehesa was aware of this and therefore tried to proceed slowly, in an attempt to explain to the Indians the benefits of private property and also to ensure that proper titles were issued so that they would not lose their individual plots. His attempt to proceed in this manner is attested to by the fact that the state laws calling for the conversion of communal into private property were postponed every year up to the Revolution.

The entire land question during the Porfiriato was the subject of endless debate, and the issue is not yet settled. There is general agreement that the Reform Laws, and in particular the Lerdo Law of June 1856, had the consequence of transferring of Indian communal lands throughout Mexico to private individuals. Some of the recipients were Indians themselves. However, there has been no agreement as to how much land was retained by the Indian groups. Neither has the role of the president been clarified. He has been variously described as the chief agent behind the despoliation of lands and also as a protector of Indian property. The truth is probably closer to Steven's assertion that Díaz, who was a respecter of property rights, did not wish to deprive the Indians of their land, but was limited in his power to prevent his more avaricious countrymen from doing so.[90] He was especially limited by expectations and a *modus operandi* (which had become common during the presidency of Juárez and which was contrary to the spirit of the Reform Laws) of defrauding the Indians of their land wherever possible. The laws in question, the Lerdo Law of 1856 and its subsequent inclusion into the Constitution of 1857, prohibited religious communities from holding land that was not used for religious worship. These laws were then extended to include Indian *ejido* (communal land) property. The *ejidos* were ordered subdivided and then allotted to individuals on the basis of one plot for each head of family. Although the express aim of these Laws of Disamortization, as they have been called, was the creation of a solid middle class, the policy did not work out as planned, and the Indians were left to the mercy of their more numerous *mestizo* (people of Indian and Spanish origin) countrymen. Communal *ejidos* did not provide sufficient income to enable individuals to purchase their plots or pay for the surveying fees, let alone hire lawyers to contest the well-funded, large-estate claimants who saw here an opportunity to enrich themselves at the expense of poor Indian peasants.[100]

The land problem was further exacerbated in 1875 with the passage of the Colonization Law, which allowed the president to approve of foreign immigration. To facilitate immigration through land grants, survey companies were allowed to survey unused lands (*baldíos*), keeping one third of all land surveyed as payment for their efforts. This law was modified in 1884 by limiting to 2,500 hectares the amount of land any one company could obtain. On the other hand, any individual was allowed to "denounce" communal or public lands that he thought were not legally owned. The occupiers would then have to come up with titles proving ownership, or lose the land to the individual or company who had denounced it. The object of this law was again to attempt to create medium-sized farms and to avoid monopolization of land by a few people. There was apparently sincerity behind the government's intentions. In 1889, President Díaz had issued a circular to officials warning them to be just and to ensure that "the disinherited classes of the people were given land."[101] Governor Dehesa was also a fervent believer in this policy. As he pointed out to the president a few years later, in discussing the subdivision of lands in Chicontepec, there were many advantages to be obtained from land division accompanied by the issuance of individual titles. For one, it would prevent the encroachment of large landowners on Indian lands, once these were clearly marked off and in the possession of individuals; furthermore, there would be growth in agricultural production and, as a consequence, a greater tax intake for the state. Dehesa also believed that owning their own land would give peasants a chance to develop personally, which could only be of benefit to themselves and the state.[102]

However, from the outset, this general land policy was faced with insurmountable difficulties. The laws were ineffective because the elites who had a stake in land, and who had access to the necessary legal means, continually frustrated government efforts. And because this was also the group, or class, of people who supported the regime, it was almost impossible to take action against them. In 1893, the Survey Law was replaced by a new law lifting the limit on the amount of land a company could obtain. This law was reconfirmed a year later, but with an important addition. No longer were the survey companies required to populate the lands or even have them properly marked off. This amendment was the real cause of the despoliation of Indian and peasant lands, which were already encircled by huge *haciendas* often too powerful to be resisted.[103] Influential families such as the Armentas in Misantla or the Cházaro Solers in Acayucan did as they pleased. So powerful were they that, despite the policies of the Mexican Revolution, including the return of *ejido* lands, these families today still retain the vast amounts of land they accrued before and during the Porfiriato. Indeed, it was not until 1931 that the *ejido* of Juchique de Ferrer, for example, was able to secure a return of some of its land, owing no doubt to their possession of clear titles received under Dehesa's governorship. The Armenta family was forced to return 335 hectares, a tiny percentage of their entire property.

In addition, social factors were responsible for Indian loss of land. Indian groups who could not speak Spanish were obviously at a disadvantage. To see the scope of the problem, consider that in 1885 in Veracruz, about one third of the population, or 228,966 people, were classified as Indians. As late as 1946, over ten per cent of the state's population could not speak the national language.[104]

In 1889, the government reaffirmed the law outlawing communal landholding, giving the *ejidal* communities just over two years in which to convert their lands into individual holdings. In 1893, it rescinded communal rights altogether. Although Dehesa postponed the effects of this law in Veracruz by consistently extending its implementation every year until the Revolution, the individualization of land ownership created serious problems during the Porfiriato, problems that were never resolved. While it can be argued that the porfirian regime did not create the problems associated with land-holding, it sanctioned passively the redistribution of land into the hands of large landowners and private companies. The result of this was the loss of small plots and farms hundreds of thousands of peasants and Indians.[105] The myriad entanglements and conflicts resulting from disputes over boundaries and titles or, for that matter, the lack of titles, resulted in decisions usually favourable to the large landowner. The president himself saw the danger in these. In 1894, he directed a letter to the governor of San Luis Potosí, Carlos Díez Gutiérrez, pointing out that some states had adjudicated land to their peoples without cost. Others, like Veracruz, Chiapas, and San Luis Potosí, had given lands to outsiders because of lack of demand, and this was causing bad feeling. The practice, he counselled, ought to be avoided. If President Díaz really believed that the regeneration of Mexico lay in the destruction of Indian communal organization and the assimilation of the Indians into the rest of the population, his actions give the lie to his convictions. It was not uncommon during the Porfiriato for Indian delegations to journey to the capital in search of titles under the protection of governors like Dehesa, as well as the president himself.[106] Yet there was no surety that every Indian group would be treated alike. Indeed, the inconsistent handling of the land question was the main cause of rural uprisings, which began in the 1830s and appear to continue to this day.[107] In the last days of the Porfiriato, it was even acknowledged that the monopolization of land had been the result of sheer neglect on the part of the government. Furthermore, only a thorough break-up *(fraccionamiento)* of large properties would ensure the creation of a middle class on which the economic and political equilibrium of the country could be based.[108]

In 1901, Article 27 of the Mexican Constitution was amended to allow the existence of communal property. This was probably too late to be of much good. In Veracruz, much of the damage to rural, Indian communities had occurred by 1892. The division of communal lands had almost been completed in the central and southern portions of the state. Under the previous governor, Enríquez, most of the land distribution had been completed. Dehesa conscientiously dealt with what was left. Shortly after Dehesa gained office in 1892, President Díaz sent an agent to Veracruz on a secret mission, concerning the disposition of Indian lands. The interim governor, Herrera, disclosed the agent's mission, and the latter was forced to seek Dehesa's help in conveying his report to the president. He had been spied on at every turn, he said, and prevented from carrying out his investigations regarding the outright theft of land from the Indians by various citizens of Huamantla. The land question there was fraught with such difficulties, and with opposition from so many quarters, that the governor had to maintain the utmost vigilance. Dehesa tried to have the work of surveying and land division done by people who were diplomatic, honest, and completely trustworthy. When one of his most trusted engineers was transferred to the Military College in Mexico City, Dehesa put up hefty resistance until Captain Luis Ulloa was returned to the state. The study that Ulloa had made of the various titles, Dehesa explained, was so complex that this knowledge could not easily be transmitted to another individual. Ulloa was therefore allowed to remain in Veracruz.[109]

In 1892, Dehesa asked the president for a suspension of the

work of a survey company in the canton of Chicontepec that was surveying so-called unused land, even though it was clear there was no public land left in that canton. Furthermore, Dehesa explained, he had examined all the existing titles and had found them in order. Díaz complied suspending the surveying work.[110]

The riots in Chicontepec, in March 1892, are a good example of the complexity of the Mexican land question, not only in its legal dimension, but also in regard to the difficulty of reconciling problems when friends or supporters of the president were involved. The riots were the continuation of a small, armed uprising by Otomís of both Hidalgo and Veracruz states, which had begun the previous September. Their leader, Antonio Granada, had convinced them that they had lost land under a recent division and succeeded in leading them in an invasion of two Veracruzan villages bordering on the state of Hidalgo. Granada had been apprehended and then released, and was again trying to stir up the Indians. In June 1892, Dehesa wrote to the president asking him to use his influence with the governor of Hidalgo in maintaining the borders of that state with Veracruz and helping in the arrest of Granada. In addition, Dehesa believed that if the Hidalgan governor enforced the state borders, this would end a certain dispute between a *hacienda* owner and the Indians who were claiming his land. The *hacienda* in question bordered on the village of San Pedrito, which was in the state of Hidalgo; the property line between the hacienda and the village coincided with the Hidalgo–Veracruz border. It was owned by Julian Herrera, a friend of both Dehesa and Díaz.[111]

On another occasion, when it became obvious that a survey company was proceeding with work that was contrary to the wishes of the people of the village of Citlaltepec in the canton of Ozuluama, Dehesa requested that the president forbid the company to continue its work. The request was granted. In 1894, a delegation of Indians from Cosamaloapan complained to the president about a circular ordering the division and distribution of their lands. Díaz asked Dehesa to look into the matter, adding that in his opinion the land ought to be divided among the heads of families, which was the governor's intention and practice anyway. Two years later, President Díaz asked the governor what the result had been, because a citizen had informed him that the people of Cosamaloapan had had their lands expropriated. Dehesa then paid the man's way to Veracruz, asking him to find the titles and present them. These were found and duly examined, and the man had to apologize, admitting he had been wrong in his assertions.[112]

The 1891 and 1896 Papantla Revolts

No better example of the immense complexity of the land question and the emotions it generated is to be found than in the
causes of the Papantla uprisings of 1891 and 1896. The canton
of Papantla, situated between Tuxpán to the north and Jalacingo
to the south, contains one of the ancient peoples of Mexico, the
Totonac-Huastecas (descendants of the builders of the city of El
Tajín). It was in this area that numerous uprisings against the
central government, from the days of Moctezuma to the nineteenth century, had taken place. The Totonacs, with a population
of some 85,000 in 1876, lived in forty-five villages in Veracruz.
They cultivated maize and produced sugar and alcohol as well as
arts and crafts. They were an extremely proud and independent
people who had been struggling since 1813 against attempts
to divide their communal lands for distribution to individual
owners. By 1876, much of the land had been divided into large
lotes (lots). Some of this land had been declared *baldío*, or public
land, and had been sold to other people.[113] Many inhabitants
of Papantla, Indian and non-Indian alike, were awarded shares
of the land as *condueños*, or shareholders. Nevertheless, in a fair
number of the municipalities Indians were excluded from this
reparto.[114] Kourí argues that it was this devolution into *condueñazgos* (owners of a *condueño*) that provides the basis for understanding the revolts of 1891 and 1896. Their cause, he says, was
not simply an attempt to preserve a traditional way of life, as has
been argued by other historians, but the alteration of the historic forces around the region. And the main protagonist in this
alteration was the production of vanilla, and the industry that
had grown up around it.[115]

The 1880s to middle 1890s were the boom years of vanilla production. Thereafter, a combination of drought and frost affected
production, seriously eroding the livelihood of the many people
engaged in production. But in general, in this climate it was
obvious that there would be pressure from the large commercial
houses to obtain more land as freehold, or to at least control
vanilla production as much as possible. Another serious problem
in the region was that over the years the *condueñazgos* had become
"cauldrons of social strife," leading many of the shareholders to
wish for privatization and, with it, their own piece of land.[116]

In the winter of 1890, surveyors appeared in the Papantla
valley, which contained 20,000 Totonacs. They were ordered to
leave by local Indian authorities. The surveyors then called in

Rurales and federal troops. An armed clash resulted in which about six thousand Indians were reported killed. One year later, Governor Enríquez declared that "public tranquility has been completely restored in Papantla and the Indians are now disposed to the subdivision of their lots." However, the resistance had been only temporarily crushed; the Totonac–Huastecas continued to make plans for an uprising, collecting arms and gunpowder for the purpose.[117]

In July 1892, General Huerta was put in charge of a military survey party and sent out to Papantla to complete the *deslinde* (surveying and subdividing the communal lands) once and for all. He soon complained that he was not receiving the co-operation of the *jefe político*, Lucido Cambas. President Díaz consequently asked Dehesa to undertake a comprehensive investigation, especially in regard to the advisability of proceeding with the subdivision of the Papantla lands. He pointed out that the local businessmen who were in control of the silver mine had succeeded in tricking and seducing the local authority into impeding the engineers' work, which gambit was, in his opinion, contrary to the interests of the Indians. In using the word, "interests" Díaz was obviously referring to his own conception of what that entailed, not that of the Totonacs. Since Díaz's letter ended on a note of sarcasm, Dehesa was quick to point out that he, as well as the *jefe político*, shared the view of the president that the breakup of communal land was essential for the prosperity of the nation. In addition, he continued, he had given the requisite instructions to Cambas, which Huerta was very well aware of. The president was still not satisfied. He remained extremely agitated and was anxious for the subdivision to be settled peacefully.[118] There was good reason for the president to worry. In 1892 and 1893, the nation's finances were at a low ebb, and Díaz did not want to have to waste money on government surveyors nor have to engage in a costly military campaign to pacify an angry Indian group.

In 1894, Veracruz authorities continued the subdivision of the remaining large lots and their distribution to heads of families. Governor Dehesa expected that this would produce a marked increase in agricultural production, as the lands had remained unworked for a long time. Instead, the renewed attempts at subdivision roused the dormant hostility of the Totonacs, of which Dehesa and the president were only too well aware. In September 1894, Díaz warned Dehesa that something was happening in Papantla, which he should investigate because it "would produce lamentable effects."[119] What the president was

referring to was a potent mixture of old problems and new prov-
ocations, unrelated to the hostility to the subdivision. The combination of these elements makes it very difficult for the observer
to arrive at a clear picture. Nevertheless, it seems that the new mix
of problems involved eight different groups of people, all with
differing interests and points of view: the federal government,
the state government, the *jefe político* in Papantla, the surveyors
of the Federal Geographic Commission, local businessmen, the
Ayuntamiento (town council), some Indian leaders, and some of
the Totonac-Huastecas. Complicating matters, was the division of
the Totonac "community" into two groups: *leales*, supporters of
the government and owners of individual parcels of land, and
the *insurrectos*.[120] The latter, it seems, were upset by news of the
surveying of the remaining communal lands. The businessmen
were interested in maintaining a dominant presence because of
a small silver mine and the valuable vanilla crop produced in
Papantla. The local authority and the surveyors, led by General
Victoriano Huerta, wanted to hang onto their petty authority.
The state government was interested in promoting agriculture
but within the existing market system, so as to increase its tax
intake, and the federal government wanted to ensure the further
development of the country, for which, it thought, the elabora-
tion of private property was essential. Needless to say, a climate
of intrigue and flurries of complaints accompanied the work of
subdivision, making it impossible for the governor to decide who
was telling the truth.[121]

Dehesa therefore commissioned the *jefe político* to investigate
and submit a report. Cambas's report was, to say the least, confusing. If, however, one accepts Dehesa's suggestion that one of the
sources of the discontent was business interests, then the report
makes sense. The businessmen probably had been motivated to
support the break-up of the communal lands in the hope that
they would be able to "denounce" some of them as *baldíos* and
thus obtain a portion for themselves. But having rediscovered the
silver lodes, and realizing the potential profit to be made by having
the Totonacs produce a vanilla crop, which was increasingly in
demand, they would have seen it in their interest to halt the subdivision and keep the Indian lands intact. The president, unfortunately, was nervous and unwilling to listen to complicated rational
explanations. He preferred to listen to unfounded rumours, and
accepted a report that one of the surveyors was at the root of
the problems. He suggested that Dehesa have the man arrested.
This Dehesa refused to do and invited the municipality to write a

letter to the president clearing the man of all charges, including the claim that the local authorities had bribed him.[122]

For the next few months the work of subdivision went well, and there were no incidents. Some of the large lots had been distributed, although more remained to be subdivided. Governor Dehesa tried to foster better relations with the Indians by asking the president to order the release of those who had been consigned to the army punishment battalions for their part in the uprising of 1891. Díaz agreed to do so. The governor also commissioned a special

Teodoro A. Dehesa

agent, an engineer, to oversee the survey work in the canton. This man reported in May that some Indians, who had previously been in the rebel camp, had changed their minds and peacefully accepted their parcels of land.[123] However, the president was still nervous. In a letter to the governor he suggested that, since the subdivision had met with such resistance, it might be better to stop it altogether and accept the fact that the Indians would live "in slavery under the businessmen and Spaniards." He believed that the difficulties were due to the *jefe político* and that that official ought to be removed temporarily. He remarked:

> I do not personally care whether the settlements are made one way or the other but I do not believe the Indians understand and appreciate the benefits of private ownership and, if they will not appreciate the favours granted why not allow them to live as they always have.[124]

The president, who seemed to favour quick solutions and always showed a short fuse when complicated matters were at hand, apparently preferred that things take their "natural" course. This would have meant the exploitation of the Indians by businessmen. Dehesa wanted to avoid this, for he realized how much more dangerous it could be. He believed the Indians would be

better off if they held clear titles to their land, but he wanted
to do things his way. So he avoided concluding the subdivisions
until every step had been taken to explain carefully to the Indians
what their rights and benefits would be, utilizing Cambas for this
purpose.[125]

The situation by September 1894 was further complicated by a
number of individuals who saw their opportunity to take advantage of the law on common lands by denouncing tracts of land
that ran through the Indian holdings in Papantla. The denunciations came to the attention of the president, who again asked
Dehesa to investigate. The *jefe político's* investigation revealed
that the lands in question had already been subdivided. On the
request of the governor, the president agreed that no lands in
the village of Papantla should be adjudicated to strangers (i.e.,
those who had not been previously resident in the village), but
only to the Indians. Still, there was an air of intrigue surrounding
the land question in the village, and Governor Dehesa decided to
investigate further. His enquiries revealed that one of the trouble-
makers had been the person in charge of land distribution under
the previous governor. Papantlans disliked this man, Juan Vidal,
because he had taken land from some neighbours without payment. In addition, he had framed his own nephew as a "vanilla
thief," was an enemy of his own brother, and was hated by
the Indians for having originally divided their communal lands
into large lots. The distribution had been so badly conducted
that much reparation was needed.[126] He had also exploited the
Indians by paying them for vanilla at a reduced rate or not at all.

Indeed, an independent report Dehesa commissioned told in
lurid detail of centuries of wrongdoing against the Indians who
had originally been given their land by the colonial government.
Outsiders had moved onto the land, exploiting its resources to
the fullest and maltreating the Indians, without even bothering
to pay taxes on their operations. With the passage of the Reform
Laws, the lands had been divided into large lots, but without
designating clearly who or what entity was the owner. This had
been the first mistake. It was followed by a sequence of others, the
importance of which was the allotment of some land to Mexicans,
Spaniards, Italians, Frenchmen, Americans, Englishmen, which
was, of course, plain theft. Then the state had demanded taxes
from the new owners. In most cases, the Indians had paid theirs,
but the newcomers refused to do so. The Indians were further
required to pay steep taxes to the state government for commis-
sions, interpreters, and scribes. They claimed someone had told
them that they should not have to pay taxes on land that was

ancestrally theirs if they could produce their titles. But since they could no longer afford to continue the search for titles and pay taxes at the same time, they soon began to withhold their contributions altogether. Their land was declared *baldío* and soon sold to various *gente de razón*. As well, unscrupulous bureaucrats in Mexico City told the Indians that they should disregard the local authorities, which led to the first rebellion at the time when Vidal was *jefe político*. The Indians had thus come to resist any further subdivision of their land because throughout they had consistently been the victims. The report went on to suggest that subdivision was indeed the answer to the present situation. In addition, it recommended that the Indians be given clear titles and maps of their properties, not at their expense, and that federal troops ought to be stationed in Papantla to ensure public order.[127]

To validate the report, Dehesa asked his friend, engineer Ignacio Muñoz, the president's nephew, to go to Papantla and investigate. He further tried to make quite clear to the president the reason for the Indians' resistance to subdivision:

> If the Indians resist the subdivision they are acting for the most part on instinct. Unfortunately mercenary speculation has been the usual means of subdividing lands.... The Indian living communally knows that he has something. With subdivision he knows he will lose what he has had and will be worse off. His ignorance is exploited and through unscrupulous means he ends up with nothing. This he does not perceive but he senses it, and therefore, remains opposed to any subdivision, the operations of which have been a gold mine for others.[128]

President Díaz accepted the report, recommending that its terms be implemented, although he suggested that it might be prudent to wait on Muñoz, "whose impartiality is irrefutable." By December 1894 Muñoz's report was ready. As was to be expected, it did not differ from the conclusions already drawn. Díaz was satisfied and did not see the necessity of sending a battalion to Papantla. By this time, too, most of the land in the canton had been subdivided, including the municipality of Papantla, although there was still resistance in one or two places.[129] Unfortunately, on December 17, a horrible incident took place in the canton. A teacher had gone out to his ranch to pay some Indians for a crop of vanilla, and because he apparently did not pay them what they were owed, he was ambushed on the way back, his head cut off, and his heart removed and eaten.[130] Still the authorities did not appear to be unduly alarmed, since it was an isolated incident.

In May 1895, the *jefe político* journeyed to Mexico City to
bring the president up to date on the continuing subdivisions.[131]
Progress towards completion was slow because of the sensitivity
that had to be brought to dealings with the Indians on the matter
of land policy. In spite of the legislature's exhortation to complete
the subdivisions as quickly as possible, Dehesa had extended
the deadline for completion each year, by one year, until 1911.
He had also replaced Huerta with Muñoz, whom Dehesa felt
he could trust. Nevertheless, the unrest in the canton was the
result of more than just the land question. The people there
had been neglected in other ways. *El Monitor Republicano* (Mexico
City), admittedly no friend of the Díaz regime, reported that in
Papantla there were no police, no lights, no hospital, only a gathering place for the sick, no proper prisons but only pig-sties,
and no cantonal school except a dilapidated building. Yet under
Muñoz the subdivision seemed to be going ahead according to
schedule and would probably be finished in a year.[132]

The newspaper report was, however, not without substance.
In March 1896, a group of Indians had a petition drawn up
by the local authorities in which they expressed similar complaints. Reminding the president of the supplement to the Plan
of Tuxtepec, the Plan of Palo Blanco, which had promised the
Indians retention of their lands, they also pointed to "the ambition of a great part of the capitalists of the village who are trying
to appropriate our property." They added that the majority of
villages in the municipality were without any schools, in order,
they felt, "to keep us in idiocy and therefore make it easier to
exploit us." The petitioners made six requests of the president: to
suspend the subdivision, to indicate to them which crops would
produce the best revenue for the state so that they could plant
them, to return to them their share certificates to the land that
the rich in the village had taken through deception, to draw up
and enter property titles in the national registry, to give them
possession of the large lots, and pay them for their work as well
as paying for stamp duties and other state fees.[133]

Dehesa asked Muñoz to report quickly on the state of affairs
and sent him to Mexico City to speak with the president. Muñoz
had been proceeding rapidly with the subdivision. Five large lots
had been divided and eight hundred property titles had been
distributed. He complained, however, that there were constant
meetings in the home of a man connected with Galicia – an engineer whom Dehesa charged with the responsibility for stirring
up the Indians – and that Indians appeared to be leaving the
meetings in an agitated state. Despite various reports, Dehesa

probably never realized that the situation was extremely serious and that it would have been prudent to leave the subdivision for a later date. Certainly neither he nor Muñoz expected what was about to happen.

On June 23, 1896, in Papantla and on June 24 in the smaller towns of Polutla and Arroyo Grande, 900 Totonacs rose up in arms and attacked the state authorities as well as other objects of their anger. In Papantla, they attacked the telegraph office and the *jefatura* (headquarters of the *jefe político*), assassinated some citizens, and kept the town under siege for hours. Other towns also came under attack before federal forces could be brought up to relieve the few state police, who were being assisted by local citizens, including Totonac *leales*. General Rosalino Martínez was dispatched from Mexico City with the Twenty-Third Battalion. By the middle of July, the rebellion had been crushed, and things began returning to normal. Ringleaders, including the heads of some villages, were rounded up and executed.

The objects of the attacks allow one to penetrate a bit deeper into the causes of the rebellion. One such object was definitely the *jefe político*, who was apparently disliked because at some point he had promised the Indians that their lands would not be divided, and then went back on his word. Other targets of the revolt were the small farmers who were the middlemen in the vanilla trade. One rich merchant in particular, Manuel Patino, was the object of anger, but his life was saved because he happened to be away in Tampico on business.[134]

There have been a number of theories on the cause of the revolt. *El Diario del Hogar* of Mexico City saw the main cause as the "lamentable and legendary question of land" and the many enemies that the *jefe político* had made. Historians, too, have generally considered that the break-up of communal property and the many successful attempts at robbing the Indians of their land were the causes of this and other revolts by the Indian peoples. Dehesa himself had another, if completely inadequate, explanation. He saw the bad harvests in the north in 1895 and 1896 as well as the slow pace of subdivision, which had kept the Indians in a state of expectation, as the main causes. He also admitted that the state had not paid sufficient attention to the poorer classes in the preceding years. These may well have been contributing factors in this particular revolt; the truth is complicated, and deeper and more complex causes were at the root of so many Indian rebellions, in and beyond the borders of Veracruz.[135] In a very general sense, modernization had done its job: "the old communal lands of the Totonac *pueblo* had been fractionalized, but only after the land-holding community had itself been fractured."[136]

In Veracruz, there were six Totonac and four Popoluca rebellions in the nineteenth century. These Indians were rebelling both against an alien system of landholding that would destroy their traditional culture, and against the practice of defrauding them of their inheritance.[137] Nevertheless, the policy of land division was accelerated after Díaz came to power, especially in Veracruz. And its consequences were as spectacular as the rate of progress. In Veracruz, by 1910, there were sixty-five people with estates of more than 10,000 hectares, and 116,000 rural families without any land at all. The census of 1910 listed 135 *hacendados* (estate owners with more than 1,000 hectares) and 1,801 *rancheros* (less than 1,000 hectares.) Some estates had grown to an enormous size. In the canton of Minatitlán, the Hearst family had an estate of 116,000 hectares, Felipe Martell had 87,775, and the Mexican Tropical Planter Company had 50,000. In all, by 1910, six of the largest landowners controlled more than twenty per cent of the land.[138]

Dehesa's claim that the Indians did not have a political motive was a rationalization of the highest order. The rebelling Totonacs had no political motive in the sense of a clearly recognizable political ideology of the Western kind, understandable to the Mexican hierarchy. But they certainly were equipped with a very clear idea of the social and economic system they did or did not wish to live under, and it was not individualistic capitalism. They knew that their property had been stolen and that their traditional way of life was a thing of the past. In contrast, the Popolucas of the Soteapan valley in the canton of Acayucan not only expressed that fact, but also had a very clear political ideology as they attempted to put paid to the Díaz regime by fomenting a revolution in 1906.

2

Revolution in Veracruz

The PLM Phase

I f the uprising of the Totonacs of Papantla was a response to local conditions consequent on national and state policy, the violence at Acayucan and subsequently at Río Blanco were direct responses to national policy formulated by the Científicos. Unlike the Papantla uprising, however, the two later occurrences increased the mounting tension between the Veracruz state government and the national government over the issue of state sovereignty. The labour dispute at Río Blanco strained to the limit relations between the central government and Veracruz. It opened a fissure in the regime that could not be bridged. The rift between the policies of the president and the Veracruz governor that had developed by 1907 was a determining factor in Francisco Madero's successful attempt to topple the dictator.

Political Opposition

Between 1900 and 1910, the government of Porfirio Díaz, buffeted by mounting social unrest, continued to be confronted with open challenges to the regime. In 1901, the First Liberal Congress was organized by Camilo Arriaga. It recalled the anti-clerical and federalist themes of mid-nineteenth-century Mexican liberalism – seriously attenuated during the Porfiriato – as well as the much-violated Constitution of 1857. Over the next decade, Arriaga's efforts to mount a constitutional, that is, democratic challenge to the regime gave way to two ideologically distinct movements: the first of these demanded adherence to the democratic tenets of the Constitution of 1857, while the second called for fundamental change to the accepted political ideology of liberal capitalism. The outspoken Ricardo Flores Magón advocated this latter position at that congress. Four years later, the Flores Magón brothers organized the first radical national opposition to the Díaz regime, the anarcho-syndicalist Partido Liberal Mexicana (Mexican Liberal Party or PLM), and called for a violent revolution to overthrow the dictator.[1]

These combined efforts of radicals and democrats finally resulted in the Mexican Revolution, a phenomenon that was extremely violent as well as enduring. One of the world's first extreme responses to modernization, it has produced a long and distinguished line of historical accounts as well as interpretations, including a recent revision that has seen one major interpretation – that this was a genuine popular revolution, a mass movement – again become dominant.[2] Such an interpretation, of course, throws out the additional question of what prompted the rural population to revolt.[3] In addition, we also need to consider the periodization of the Revolution. It has usually been assumed that it was Francisco Madero's mainly political revolution (the first of the two currents mentioned above) of November 20, 1910, that began the upheaval that toppled Porfirio Díaz. And not only is the date of the "beginning" of the Revolution in question, but the very notion of a "beginning" itself.[4] For attempts to resist the economic and social coercion of the Porfiriato are to be found throughout the period, not least of all in Veracruz. Furthermore, it is there that one finds some of the most prescient examples of attempts to overthrow the system. Interestingly, violent opposition to the system occurred in the countryside as well as the town, on land as in the factory, by Indians and peasants as well as workers, and by members of the middle class. In Veracruz, however, it was peasants and Indians who were the first to rise up.

The Acayucan Uprising

The 1906 uprising in southern Veracruz, in the vicinity of the town of Acayucan, was the second most serious one in the state's modern history, but far surpasses the 1896 revolt of the Totonacs in its intent, ferocity, and ideological underpinnings. The Acayucan revolt, which some historians have described only as a minor rebellion, if a rebellion at all, was the result of an alliance between the Popoluca Indians and middle – and working – class revolutionaries of the PLM, the anarcho-socialist party led by Ricardo Flores Magón.[5] In a number of senses, it was the first distinct shot in a mélange of peasant unrest and violent revolutionary activity, which initiated the chain of events that was to culminate in the fall of President Díaz and his government in 1911.[6] The unrest was not a spontaneous protest against local grievances, as was the case in 1896 with the Papantla uprising. Acayucan was neither protest nor rebellion: it was revolution.[7] And the ground had been carefully prepared by the PLM Liberal clubs, which had sprung up all over Mexico since the founding of that political party in 1905.

What were the factors that contributed to the formation of a relatively homogeneous revolutionary army comprised mainly of indigenous Popolucas? This group lived on ancestral lands in the southern cantons of Veracruz, the Tuxtlas, Acayucan and Minatitlán. The area covered 19,418 square kilometres, one quarter of the state, with a total population of 102,945 persons. The population density was 5.3 persons per square kilometre, less than half that of the entire state.[8] It is an area of vast plains traversed by a variety of rivers and streams some of which, like the Papaloapán and Coatzacoalcos, are navigable for considerable distances (a factor that was of inestimable value in putting down the revolt). Of the population, 10,884 were listed as Popolucas in the census of 1900. They have been described as "honorable, industrious and hospitable," and as having never enjoyed the protection of the government. The majority of these lived in the municipality of Soteapan, canton of Acayucan, where sixty-five per cent of the population spoke the Popoluca language. The rest of the population there consisted of *mestizo* peasants, most of whom worked in the tobacco industry, where physical maltreatment, the climate, and the infamous *enganche* (draft) system of recruiting labour contributed to a miserable existence and often an early death.[9] With its forests of valuable woods, and plains that were well-suited for grazing cattle or planting tobacco, the area had considerable economic value, a fact recognized as far back as the Spanish Conquest.[10] In addition, because of its proximity to the Isthmus of Tehuantepec, the region possessed a strategic value that was not lost on the Mexican government as well as the United States. In 1871, a United States expedition had been sent to reconnoiter the territory as the possible site of a canal connecting the two oceans.[11] The Mexican government, however, had no intention of letting this valuable territory fall under U.S. control – an important factor in the development of events that led to the revolt.

More germane to the question of causes of the rebellion was

that, in all three areas under discussion, land had been gradually stolen from the Indians and had passed into the control of
three families. In 1892, the *hacienda* Corral Nuevo passed into the
hands of the Cházaro Soler family, rich landowners and friends
of the president. The *hacienda* comprised an area of 78,759 hectares, including eight cattle ranches that had been consistently
claimed by twenty-seven Indian communities, among them the
municipality of Acayucan; these had long asked for a survey
and eventual allotment of these ranches. Some years earlier, the
Cházaro Solers had given one ranch as a gift to an *ejido* after
allegedly locking the municipal aldermen in a church and forcing them, as "ransom," to accept the ranch as compensation.[12]
After 1902, these Indians found common cause with those from
other municipalities, especially with claimants against the estate
of Díaz's father-in-law, Romero Rubio. Together they proceeded
to present a common front to the state government, which struck
a commission to investigate. In 1903, however, Dehesa personally gave orders to the *jefe político* to disregard the findings of
the commission, because it had ruled in favour of the Indians.[13]
In 1904, the Cházaro Soler *hacienda* had its boundaries clearly
marked, but because of the continued claims of the Popolucas,
the state government turned the matter over to the president for
arbitration. In 1906, the well-known jurist Emilio Rabasa gave his
decision, which ruled against the Indian land claims. The reason,
he stated, was that the Indians gave no proof of ownership. This
was probably true, as not all the Indian peoples in Mexico had
formed communities or had had their land confirmed during the
colonial period. It was, therefore, perfectly legal, although unfair,
to declare these lands as *baldíos*. Failing to secure their livelihood
by legal means, the Indians saw rebellion as their last hope.[14]

  Much the same could be said of the municipality of Soteapan,
canton of Acayucan, where the despoliation of land had been
underway for decades, and where almost the entire municipality
had been gathered together in one huge estate owned by
President Díaz's father-in-law. The conversion of these lands into
private property had begun in 1826. The major beneficiaries of
the subdivision had not been the Indians, however, but the aldermen of the municipality and their associates. The reasons for
this were manifold: the Indians had no clear understanding of
Spanish land law; they were shy, kept to themselves, and constantly displayed an attitude of hostility to strangers; the territory had been vastly underpopulated and no one, including the
Indians, knew exactly where their lands began or ended. In 1890,

these lands had been declared *baldíos* and all 149,404 hectares were adjudicated to Romero Rubio.[15] Rubio died in 1895 and left the lands to his daughter Carmen Díaz, the president's wife. However, Rubio's death and the probation of the will had again opened up the question of land ownership, and the Indians had pressed their claims. Now, the president, on behalf of his wife, was pressing for a prompt settlement of the will. In 1897, he complained that the appointment of a certain Ceballo to handle the probation was unfortunate as "he is the most terrible enemy of the terms of the will and regarding land negotiations." The man was promptly removed.[16]

Indeed, there had been much hostility to a settlement of the will in the way the Díaz family expected. Notwithstanding the family's presentation of the bills of sale for the properties dated 1889, Dehesa felt it necessary and advisable to call a conference of all the parties concerned in the state capital in 1902. The resulting resolution, signed by the lawyers of the Rubio estate, the representative of the municipality, and the *jefe político* of Acayucan, recognized that eleven *sitios* (sites, equivalent to approximately 1,700 hectares of land) out of a total of 19,476 hectares were in fact the property of the municipality. However, when the subdivision that had been initiated in 1896 and 1900 was terminated, the lands were not subsequently made available to the municipality, and the Indians were left with absolutely nothing for their trouble.[17]

The main reason for this failure to implement the agreement soon became apparent. The crux of the matter was *raison d'état*. At stake was what the president believed to be an attempt by the United States to get hold of land in the isthmus, and so ultimately to wrest political control of the area from Mexico. Díaz reasoned that Sir Weetman Pearson, the British engineer and entrepreneur who had already done significant work in Mexico, would be an invaluable help in the attempt to forestall the suspected U.S. intentions, simply because Pearson was a British subject. Díaz, therefore, went out of his way to help Pearson, but at the same time made it appear that he was being totally neutral in any confrontation between Pearson and U.S. companies.[18]

Pearson had discovered oil seepage at San Cristóbal in the southern states while working on the Tehuantepec railroad and had decided to secure an option for the oil business. Taxation rights were ceded to the company, although in January, 1903, a lawyer for the company complained that his employees were not enjoying the protection of the authorities in Minatitlán, or, to put it differently, they were being treated in a hostile manner.[19] The matter was more serious than this. Díaz had reason to believe that neither Dehesa nor the local *jefe político* were expediting the transfer of the Rubio property to the Pearson company. In very sharp terms, Díaz wrote Dehesa:

> Mr. Varela with whom I spoke on the business of Acayucan has mentioned his belief that the authorities are not very scrupulous in their duty of defending property. In bringing this to your attention please tell me if *it is the authorities who do not obey you or is it you who believe that the rights of the estate of Romero Rubio are not well defined* since I myself have no doubt about it.[20] [emphasis added]

In replying to these accusations, Dehesa questioned the veracity of Díaz's source of information. He also told the president clearly where he thought legality took precedence over friendship, remarking caustically:

> The political authority no doubt renders me obedience because if it didn't, the world would turn in reverse. With respect to the Rubio will, I have never examined it and thus my opinion would be rash, either in favour of or against it.
>
> In the other matter I limited myself, with all the loyalty that distinguishes me, to support your recommendations with all *efficacy and nothing more*.[21] [emphasis added]

In fact, the matter had become so sensitive that the judge of the higher court of Acayucan decided to resign and had to be replaced. The matter was indeed delicate since it involved huge tracts of land that were to be turned over to the Pearson company, in addition to which the company would receive state and federal concessions concerning subsoil rights.[22]

At the same time, Díaz was neither unaware of nor unconcerned about the general state of the growing political opposition. He saw that the political danger was mounting with the increasing alienation of lands from Indians and Mexican peasants. In 1906, he secretly commissioned a supporter, Rafael de Zayas Enríquez, to draw up a report on the general political involvement of labour and the extent of socialist agitation in the country. The report was submitted to him two weeks before the Acayucan uprising and revealed conditions that were truly alarming for the government. The author cited unrest in every state, led by the middle classes against the Científico clique; it indicted the conditions under which peons and labourers were forced to live; and it pointed to growing socialist agitation, especially in Veracruz.[23] This ideological development was attributable to the movement that the Flores Magón brothers had spawned. In 1901, at the Liberal Congress held in San Luis Potosí on the initiative of Camilo Arriaga, the Magón brothers had played a leading role.[24] A second meeting was held in February, 1902, but shortly after, the regime realizing the potent extent of their criticism, most of these Liberals were arrested and jailed, Arriaga among them. In 1903, the leaders of the Liberal movement, including the Magón brothers and Arriaga, migrated to the United States where they published a radical newspaper, *Regeneración*, which was distributed in Mexico.[25] Arriaga broke with the Magón brothers after they began to drift towards the anarchist camp, and in 1905 the PLM was officially born. In 1905 and 1906, a number of "Liberal" clubs associated with the PLM began to appear in Mexico. One important and active state was Veracruz, where local initiative was very strong. One of the first Veracruz clubs was founded by Hilario Salas and Cipriano Medina in Coatzacoalcos (later called Puerto México) and was given the name Valentín Gómez Farías Club. Another important Liberal centre was the Vicente Guerrero Club of Chinameca, also in the south, whose president was Margarito Nava and whose vice-president was Enrique Novoa. The membership of these clubs consisted of artisans, railroad mechanics, and employees as well as small businessmen. Their aims were all similar: foment uprisings throughout the state and hasten the fall of the Díaz government. While the clubs worked assiduously to enlarge their membership and to denounce the regime, a newspaper, *La Voz de Lerdo*, was founded and public meetings were organized. By mid-1906, the two leading clubs together had more than a thousand members. In a public demonstration on March 21, 1906, Medina denounced the regime and was promptly arrested and imprisoned.[26]

Besides his work in the towns, Hilario Salas was especially active in 1905 in the Soteapan among the Popolucas, to whom he brought the message of the PLM and the impending revolution. In every village of the Soteapan, it is said, there were PLM leaders organizing the overthrow of Díaz.[27] Salas himself went to Missouri, where he worked on the draft of the PLM program that was published and clandestinely distributed throughout Mexico on July 1, 1906. It called for revolution and the overthrow of the Díaz regime. With the publication of this PLM manifesto, the

Veracruz government began a systematic crackdown on the clubs and imprisoned scores of their members.[28] In response, the PLM leadership accelerated the plans for a revolution.

By August 1906, there were approximately forty clubs in Mexico allegedly ready for an uprising, the plans for which were already known to the government. Early in June, President Díaz sent Dehesa a copy of a newspaper the headline of which he considered an open call to rebellion and urged the governor to proceed with "all energy and activity against such a dangerous and transcendental business."[29] Consequently in July Dehesa ordered the *jefe político* of Minatitlán, Demetrio Santibáñez, to close all the Liberal clubs. At the same time the government kept abreast of PLM plans by intercepting their letters. In one of these, Novoa revealed that there were plans to start the rebellion on September 29. Ricardo Flores Magón then ordered the club in Coatzacoalcos to cease holding meetings so as not to attract the attention of the authorities. On September 3, he repeated the advice, reminding members that they must remain free in order to be able to take part in the uprising. Furthermore, they were asked not to waste precious money, which could be used to buy arms. A week later, he wrote to a friend in a Veracruz prison that it was only a matter of days before the uprising would begin.[30]

The junta in St. Louis must not have been anticipating much resistance, or perhaps they felt the regime would just wither away after the first shot, because their lack of planning and careful preparation is obvious from reading the documents, as is their naïveté. No attempt was made to evade the country's clandestine police apparatus. Letters were smuggled in and out of Mexico but passed through many hands. Obviously, there was the possibility of infiltration by police spies. Yet many letters were written without code and in an absolutely open manner. One would-be revolutionary wrote Magón that his club did not have sufficient arms and asked if there were any other rebels in his district who could be contacted. He also requested Magón to send some heavy guns so that they would be able to take Veracruz by land and sea.[31]

Under Praxedis Guerrero the forty-four guerrilla groups were alerted for a coordinated uprising. These were to take their cues from the attacks that would break out in three areas: from Texas across the border, led by Villareal and Juan Sarabía; in Chihuahua, led by P. Silva; and in Acayucan, Veracruz, led by Hilario Salas and Cándido Donato Padua. However, the initial surprise was lost when the government got wind of the exact time of the attack on the northern town of Jiménez. Immediately, the junta contacted Salas in Veracruz, advising him to do what he could in the situation. Salas with his thousand men in Acayucan consisting mainly of *mestizos* and Popolucas, decided to attack immediately. Before he could launch his attack, however, a force of about fifty men attacked the border town of Jiménez, continuing their harassment of the defenders for the next few days. Salas then decided to attack, dividing his group into three units: Enrique Novoa was to attack the plaza at Minatitlán; Román Marín and Juan Alfonso, Puerto México; and the third force, commanded by Salas, was to attack the town of Acayucan.[32]

Municipal Building, Acayucan

Salas was the first to reach his objective. The attack on Acayucan began at 11 p.m. Sunday, September 30. During the fight Salas was shot in the stomach, and his troops, demoralized, retreated. Novoa meanwhile advanced towards Chinameca, but with such delay that federal troops were able to reach the town first. Novoa's men then decided to rampage through the countryside instead, and attacked various *haciendas* and villages. The third group was delayed even longer because of differences between the leaders, and so Puerto México was also fortified with federal troops that arrived by sea. The rebels then took to the hills, and on October 4 Salas encountered the 25th Battalion, which badly mauled his troop. He himself was able to escape, but hundreds of his men, as well as many club members, were arrested and jailed.[33] The expected general uprising failed to materialize, and the government was able to contain and suppress the rebellion in a few days. Some rebels, including Salas and Padua, managed to elude federal forces and escape to the hills. Although the press remained fairly muted about the events, no doubt because the government would not reveal what had occurred, and although President Díaz tried to explain away rumours of the attacks as being the result of mere local discontent, the government's actions reveal how seriously shaken it was.[34] On October 8, an additional 150 soldiers from the 17th Battalion were rushed to the area by train from Veracruz. At the same time, two gunboats, the *Bravo* and the *Yucatan*, were put on the alert for possible immediate departure. A number of people were apprehended, and three judges interrogated them in an attempt to pinpoint the origins of the insurrection. A special judge, Bullé Goyri, was also seconded to take charge of interrogations and to expedite convictions as well as to release the many innocent people who had been apprehended. On October 16, Goyri returned from Acayucan to Veracruz, bringing some of the captured weapons, including a cannon and gun carriage, and set about continuing his investigations among the prisoners who were being held in the infamous San Juan de Ulúa fortress. From San Andrés Tuxtla, in the neighbouring canton to the north, came a report from the *jefe político* that a group of people with "Magonist" ideas, discontented with the mayor of Catemoco and emboldened by the rebellion at Acayucan, were under surveillance; the *jefe político* feared they might try to attack the jail. Dehesa prudently advised him not to take any hasty action.[35] That same day the *jefe político* of Acayucan, Sentíes, sent his own report to the president. The region was quiet, he reported: there were sufficient horses, harnesses, provisions, and telegraph connections in case of another attack, and he was in constant contact with the army commanders. He claimed that there was no political plan and no program of action beyond the affair itself, and he assured the president that all the citizens who claimed to belong to the middle class were condemnatory of the affair. There was only one bit of bad news, he wrote: as troops left the village of Soteapan, they had had to leave behind eleven wounded in the house of a woman who was attending their wounds. Sometime later, a group of "savages" locked the house and set it on fire, and all that could be recovered were the charred remains of their comrades. According to Sentíes, outsiders as well as a few locals

had been inciting the "illiterate masses," reading them periodicals from the United States in order to find proselytes for their
cause. The centre of the movement, it seemed, although Sentíes
was not certain, had been the port city of Coatzacoalcos. He also
thanked the president for removing the prisoners to San Juan
de Ulúa because he feared that there might be an epidemic of
unrest if they remained in Acayucan.[36]

Although the army tried to capture the few remaining and
dangerous participants, the immediate danger of recurring violence seemed to be over, and the government now concentrated
on trying to ascertain the causes. Despite the efforts of the various secret services and the detective agency to obtain access to
documents and letters, it appears that the president was either
reluctant to admit that this had been a planned overthrow of
his government, or he had difficulty interpreting the documents.
Díaz actually thought that the cause might have been the cruelty
of the *jefe político* of Acayucan.[37] But Judge J.M. Camacho, head
of a special commission appointed by Dehesa to investigate the
rebellion, thought he had found the reason:

> In respect of the causes of the movement, I have discovered no
> others except the ambition and turbulence of a few perverse
> people without name or prestige, and the stupid credulity of the
> Indians, who were easily seduced with promises of a return of
> some land.[38]

He included a letter from Enrique Novoa, alias Dantón, to
Ricardo Flores Magón dated September 26, 1906, giving the
names of the main members of the junta organizing the rebellion and specifying September 29 as the date on which it would
take place. This letter was what the authorities had been seeking
because it gave unquestionable proof of the connection between
the PLM and the events at Acayucan.[39]

It is difficult in view of the evidence to say why the president
did not take the revolt more seriously. As he would do in regard
to worker unrest at Río Blanco, he appeared to view the revolt
as an isolated incident in which the majority of the participants
were really innocent seductees of some unscrupulous person
rather than participants in a movement to ovethrow his government. Yet the opposite was clearly the truth. On November 22,
the district judge in Veracruz sent Dehesa the code used by the
PLM in their correspondence with Novoa, and Dehesa was able
to intensify his search for the remaining rebels. Three days later,

the special judge in Acayucan wrote that he now had thirty-two prisoners who, for the most part, had confessed and been convicted. He also requested further orders. On the 27th, Díaz ordered the arrest of three more citizens on suspicion, and the next day Dehesa was able to report the capture of the two most wanted men, Enrique Novoa and Cristóbal Vásquez. By mid-December, Dehesa considered that order had been restored and ordered the auxiliary police paid and released from service. He also told Camacho to return to Veracruz.[40]

Dehesa, convinced that the *jefe político* of Acayucan was partly to blame for the events, secured his resignation and put one of his own men, Ignacio Canseco, in place, with instructions to submit a detailed report. Canseco's report was shocking and confirmed Dehesa's worst fears. The report itself merits detailed consideration here as it reveals the corruption that could and did exist with the collusion of a corrupt *jefe político*. Moreover, it reveals the sociopolitical situation that existed in the Porfiriato, where the absence of the rule of law was legend and many petty tyrants were armed with extensive powers. Canseco found that the people of the canton were, in general, docile, hard working, and respectful of those in authority. However, he described the local officials as a band of thieves and robbers. In the central office of the *jefe político*, there was one Antonio Mateo Rodríguez, the municipal mayor, who was also the leader of a gang of cattle thieves. The most intrepid member of his gang was the official treasurer in the municipal government, Francisco Ortíz. Two or three days after taking office, Canseco caught two of this man's brothers *in flagrante delicto* and with a herd of stolen cattle. Two other brothers, one of whom was the alderman in the town assembly and the other head of the town police, had a nasty habit of cutting the wire fences of various properties at night, introducing strange cattle into the fields, arresting the unsuspecting and innocent farmer, and fining him at least one hundred pesos before releasing him.

Another example was the secretary to the *jefe político*, Eduardo González, who, while enjoying the complete protection of his chief, jailed people arbitrarily. The municipal mayor of the town of Soconusco, too, was the leader of the cattle thieves in his area. In Soteapan, the secretary to the mayor, Genaro Ambielle, ran a protection racket, exploiting the unfortunate Indians mercilessly, assuring them that for one or two hundred pesos they would not be molested. In addition to this, he helped himself to their corn, sometimes using the police force for greater effect. In San Juan

Evangelista, there was another well-organized gang protected by the local mayor. In Texistepec, the leader of the local gang of thieves was the mayor, Alvaro Díaz, who with his three sons devastated the local farms, keeping the cattle in his own fields where he sold them to the highest bidder. The information, Canseco concluded, was given to him by a majority of the people of these villages.[41]

Unfortunately, and for reasons that could not be ascertained, Canseco was not allowed to remain in his post for long. On September 29, 1907, José Beltrán wrote to Dehesa from Chapultepec Castle informing the governor that, since there was to be a change of *jefe político* in the canton, he had been recommended for the job by Ignacio Muñoz as well as the president.[42] The heavy hand of the president had obviously fallen on a subordinate who had taken his job too seriously. Dehesa was left to answer Muñoz, not without a subtle hint of anger and frustration, that he could not send Beltrán any papers since he did not know his address.[43] What the president's reasons were for removing Canseco, without extending the courtesy of asking for Dehesa's nominal approval, is a matter for conjecture. He certainly did not share Dehesa's views on the seriousness of the uprising. Neither did he agree that a scrupulous and diplomatic representative would be able to do very much to keep things quiet in the area. To the contrary, Díaz did not intend to take a more benevolent view of Indian land claims, especially since *raison d'état* as well as his own family's interests were involved.

Díaz's replacement of the *jefe político* was clearly interference in the state's affairs. The governor viewed the appointment as impolitic since the replacement was quite corrupt. Beltrán's first measure was to get rid of all state employees, replacing them with his own men. Unfortunately, this housecleaning threw out good men as well as bad ones. Furthermore, at an extraordinary, and illegal, session of the town council, Beltrán had the mayor removed and his own brother, Marcelino, elected in his stead. The nepotism was blatant. Dehesa immediately dispatched Pedro Gómez, the ousted mayor, to Mexico City and informed Ignacio Muñoz, asking him to see that the ex-mayor was able to see the president.[44] Explained Dehesa:

> Only the governor has the right to suspend or remove members of the town council....We must believe that Beltrán did this out of ignorance. Substituting his brother is also irregular as the mayor is chosen by popular election which is prescribed by law.... Gómez

believes that the person behind his ouster is Isidro Montera who has some disputes with the people over land. I am sending you the president's telegram, as well as letters from my brother. Gómez is no relation to Martin Gómez the cattle thief, and the letters I have included should prove this to the president. You know that I am no friend of villains who do not enjoy my benevolence whatsoever.[45]

Dehesa was furious at the intervention of the *jefe político* and the support given him by the president, who did not know what was going on but accepted scandalous rumours rather than his governor's reports: unscrupulous persons had written to the president saying that the Dehesas were protecting a man named Gómez who was a cattle thief. Dehesa replied that he had no intention of releasing Martin Gómez, the cattle thief; and that *Pedro* Gómez was indeed a friend of Francisco Dehesa, his brother, but his brother did not exert any influence on the governor of Veracruz nor was he stirring up any trouble.[46] In this correspondence, relations between the president and Governor Dehesa reached their lowest point. Díaz obviously did not accept Dehesa's explanations, for he refused to see Gómez. The governor, however, continued to receive complaints and reports from various citizens about the arbitrariness of Beltrán's actions. Arbitrary his actions might have been, but there were some powerful forces supporting him. Apparently, Pedro Gómez had done everything in his power to save the municipal lands from being taken over by two powerful families, the Franyuttis and Cházaro Solers of the *hacienda* Corral Nuevo.[47] Dehesa's hands, it seems, were also tied, and there was not much he could do except extend his protection to the ex-mayor. Eventually, however, he was able to convince the president that Beltrán was not the man for this important and delicate canton, literally begging Díaz to find him some other employment.[48]

From the president's actions subsequent to the Acayucan rebellion, the trend in the later Porfiriato becomes clear. Due to the influence of the Científicos, cynical exploitation involving total disregard of fundamental justice was common.[49] Consequently, the government's solution to opposition, or even any attempt to address grievances, was to call in the army and suppress the people who had brought the matter out into the open. This was the way Díaz dealt with Acayucan and its aftermath, and this was the way he would deal with the labour problems in the textile industry.

But there is a second important aspect to the Acayucan debacle: it was the cause of Dehesa's first disagreement with the president and would not be the last. It is perhaps here that Dehesa first encountered the president's lack of intellectual acumen, which must have brought home to him the unfortunate fact that modern Mexico was a complexity led by a man who was not given to thinking in complex terms. More importantly, Dehesa was upset that the president was ignoring the opinions of the man who was most likely to be well informed of events taking place: the governor.

Most galling to the governor was the fact that he was correct in his assessment of the situation. The uprising at Acayucan was not the simple affair that the president would have liked to believe. Mere rebellion can be described as "overt opposition directed at particular laws, practices or individuals," as was the case in Papantla in 1896.[50] It demands only specific changes. No doubt most of the Indians involved in the Acayucan events were fighting for limited aims; but their leaders were of a different cut. In this sense, the outbreak at Acayucan cannot be considered a rebellion: it was an armed struggle that was informed by a coherent political ideology. The political movement that adhered to this ideology was not concerned with a mere redress of grievances. The PLM and many of the Populucas wanted the overthrow of the Díaz regime and its replacement with a government that would change the existing social order in Mexico. Furthermore, the men who led the attack at Acayucan fully expected that they were initiating a general uprising throughout the country. They were also ready to replace government and bureaucracy with their own people. In general as well as historical terminology, what occurred at Acayucan in 1906 was an uprising of revolutionary intent.

By October 1906, then, this first cadre of revolutionaries in Veracruz had undergone their initial test of fire. The second cadre was just about to undergo theirs, but with one major difference. The first element, the Indians from Acayucan, had reacted to "developmentalist" policies, (i.e., the *Ley Lerdo*) that had been thought through in the early years of the republic and incorporated into the Constitution of 1857. The second cadre would consist of those opposed to another aspect of the same policies, the capitalist development of Mexican industry: the working class. Not coincidentally, this second element developed in the oldest area of industrial development, Orizaba, Veracruz, whose geography had invited the establishment of the first textile mills in Mexico.

The Río Blanco Labour Dispute

The second event, that widened the breach between the president and Dehesa over the issue of political control of the state was the unrest in the Mexican textile industry. It began at the end of 1906 and culminated in the brutal massacre of workers on January 7, 1907, at Río Blanco.[51]

The role of the PLM is central in understanding this labour dispute. But it has created a historiographical divide; on one side are those who deny any ideological motivation on the part of the workers, on the other are those who see at least some workers as being motivated by ideology. There are also differing claims about the amount of influence, if any, of the PLM. Moreover, the debate has been obscured by differences in perspective as well as methodological weaknesses. Contemporary newspaper accounts saw the workers as being motivated by bread-and-butter issues. In general, Alan Knight concurs. Rodney Dean Anderson has argued that workers at Río Blanco were motivated by the ideals of *La Reforma*, the period of Liberal government after 1855 that included promulgation of a new constitution in 1857 guaranteeing freedom of speech, press, and assembly, rather than "more radical doctrines." In his later monograph, Anderson also rejected James D. Cockroft's claim that the "PLM was the main political force behind the strike." Cockroft had viewed the PLM as the main influence behind the spread of radical ideas among the workers via their paper *Regeneración*. John Mason Hart agrees with Cockroft that PLM presence at Río Blanco was not visible but recognizes that its influence was. Among his evidence is that on January 6, 1907, in Orizaba, a "large and loud minority" using "PLM-like rhetoric" shouted "Death to Porfirio Díaz."

There are a number of problems with these interpretations. First, while the attempt to generalize about the attitude of Mexican workers is a legitimate endeavour, it obscures the truth. Second, with the exception of Cockcroft and Anderson's monographs, there is frequent use of the same secondary works and insufficient archival verification in the literature. Anderson's methodological caveat in his 1974 paper that we need to listen to what workers said about themselves is sound. But we should not fall into the opposite trap of accepting at face value everything workers say about themselves. Anderson's attempt to prove that workers were not revolutionary because they expressed themselves in the non-revolutionary terms of "justice, liberty, law, equality and fraternity" taken from the Constitution of 1857 is questionable. The demand for "equality and fraternity" was in itself revolutionary given the social conditions of the Porfiriato. Furthermore, neither the expression of revolutionary nor of older "liberal" ideas precluded bona fide membership in the PLM – at this stage, the PLM included many political shades united by a common opposition to the regime. Moreover, the argument, cogently rebutted by Salvador Hernández, that worker association with the PLM disappeared after 1907 and therefore could not have been very strong to begin with fails to take into account the impact of brutal army repression. Neither PLM presence nor influence should be underestimated. However, a full explanation of the Orizaba labour dispute goes beyond the actions and influence of the PLM. The popular union leaders were members of the PLM, but at the same time, many workers, either influenced by the ideas of the newspaper *Revolución Social* or generating these ideas from their immediate work environment, called for a victory over the capitalists and an end to the Porfirian regime.[52] These workers were neither weak nor passive in their reaction to the exigencies of capital, a considerble amount of which had been invested in the little village of Río Blanco.

Río Blanco is near the major city of Orizaba, located on the Río Blanco River and about halfway between the port of Veracruz and Mexico City. Río Blanco was also the name given to one of the largest and most modern Mexican textile factories, the Compañía Industrial de Orizaba (CIDOSA), situated on the outskirts of Orizaba and owned by a group of Frenchmen. The Río Blanco factory accounted for fifteen per cent of the total spindles and looms in Mexico and was opened on October 9, 1892.[53]

When Dehesa became governor in 1892, the Veracruz textile industry had been in existence for over sixty years. Already by 1845, Veracruz occupied third place in Mexico both in terms of the number of textile factories it owned and the number of spindles it operated. The factories, which initiated the Mexican industrial revolution, were installed at Xalapa and Orizaba primarily because of the availability of water power from the rapidly descending rivers in those areas. The principal entrepreneurs in this development were the Mexican state, through the Banco de Avío, and the small but vigourous French business community in Mexico. Their impact on the hitherto insignificant city of Orizaba, indeed on the entire state, was considerable. In 1838, the largest spinning mill in Mexico, the Cocatapán factory, was established in Orizaba, stimulating further industrial and urban expansion. Whereas in 1831 there were only twenty-nine persons making a living by weaving cotton, a year after the factory began operating, that number had risen to 160. The population of Orizaba likewise grew rapidly from 17,000 to 24,000 in the same period, while there was a significant increase in the numbers of skilled workers engaged in secondary and tertiary services.[54] During the 1880s, industrial expansion continued, and between 1887 and 1906, the population of the entire canton of Orizaba almost doubled. By 1906, the textile industry had expanded into the smaller towns around Orizaba itself, which contained important factories. The Río Blanco factory was considered modern by world standards. The other large textile factory in the area, Santasa in Necoxtla, was owned by the Compañía Industrial Veracruzana (CIV). The Veracruz textile industry accounted for one quarter of total sales in Mexico and almost one fifth (6,000) of the textile workforce. French capital, connected with the name of Antonio Reynaud, who was both director and secretary of CIDOSA and president and treasurer of CIV, controlled both companies.[55] In fact, much of the impetus for industrial development had come from foreign capital. Indeed, it was the express policy of the government to allow such leadership in manufacturing and other industrial areas in order to modernize the Mexican economy.[56]

But while industrialization had the initial effect of raising the standard of living of industrial workers between 1877 and 1898 by some fifteen per cent (due in part to the great demand for workers), after 1900, wages tended to fall back to the level of 1877, producing misery and discontent. The conditions of work were also debilitating, if not thoroughly cruel. Workers were accustomed to a fourteen- or fifteen-hour day beginning, in the summer, at 5:30 a.m. One and one-half hours per day were allowed for breakfast and lunch. Working hours did not differ significantly from those in other countries, but the atrocious working conditions particularly incensed the Mexican worker.[57] Moreover, wages were unacceptably low, barely sufficient to cover the cost of food for a day, and could be further reduced by the supervisors' arbitrary imposition of fines, against which workers had little recourse. Other grievances included child labour, which was against the law; the lack of sufficient schools for workers' children; and the degrading demand that workers refrain from entertaining friends in their company homes. Particularly odious was the sexual harassment and coercion of all kinds to which female workers were subjected.[58]

Workers did not meekly accept these conditions. During the

entire Porfiriato, there were some 250 strikes in the textile, tobacco, railway, mining, and baking industries. The largest number of strikes occurred in the textile industry after the turn of the century. There were good reasons for this militancy. The first was price inflation caused by the decline in the price of silver. In addition, the introduction of machinery caused a reduction in the workforce. As if these were not sufficient, the 1907 Wall Street crisis lowered the prices of henequen, cotton, and minerals and led to violent strikes in the last five years of the Porfiriato. But these were not the first such strikes. As early as 1891, in Nogales, another small town close to Orizaba, there was a strike of textile workers.[59] In March 1896, the El Destino tobacco factory in San Andrés Tuxtla installed blankets in all the windows to keep out dust during a severe drought. The intense heat led to bitter complaints by workers. When the management refused to take down the blankets, a strike was called that eventually bankrupted the company. In the same year, workers at the Río Blanco factory successfully resisted an attempt by management to increase the night shift to twelve hours.[60]

The militancy and determination of workers was not lost on their national leaders, who on visiting Nogales factory in 1898 remarked on the "unpatriotic atmosphere" in the town, where there were no flags flying for the May 5 celebration.[61] In 1903, workers at the Río Blanco factory tried to resist the employment of a supervisor who had a bad reputation. Incensed that a strike had begun not over wages or increased hours of work, which he might have accepted, but over the company's decision to hire a particular foreman, President Díaz ordered the *jefe político* of Orizaba to evict all the strikers from their homes if they refused to return to work. Dehesa and his *jefe político*, Carlos Herrera, were intent on settling matters more amicably, but their task was not made easier by the president's order or by the intransigence of the company. On June 15, Herrera cabled Dehesa that he could have settled the matter of the supervisor if the owner of the company store had not wanted to punish workers by changing price lists (raising some prices while lowering others), thus forcing some workers to seek employment elsewhere. However, two days later, the strike fizzled out, due, it seems, more to lack of organization than anything else.[62] In 1905, there were two further strikes in Veracruz, the first at El Valle Nacional, the tobacco factory in Xalapa, and the second at the San Gertrudis jute factory in Orizaba. In both cases, the strike was settled in favour of the workers after Dehesa or Herrera intervened pesonally.[63]

Despite these successes, conditions in general continued to worsen. Newspaper editorials expressed alarm and mortification at the treatment that the unprotected workers were forced to endure and began to inform the public. In March 1906, *El Paladín* of Orizaba reported that in one department of the Río Blanco factory a foreman had been hired who was behaving "like a Sultan," firing females who refused his sexual advances. In May, Carlos Herrera forced the factory management to reprimand a supervisor for having intentionally injured a worker. In addition, he obtained CIDOSA's agreement to abolish the system of arbitrary fines in all their mills in the area.[64] But in June workers at the San Lorenzo factory, protesting again against the arbitrary fines imposed by some supervisors, opened the sluice gates of the hydraulic system and brought the factory machinery to a halt. They then sought out the factory manager, Hartington, who listened courteously to their complaints and arranged a meeting between the workers and the foremen, at which Carlos Herrera was present. On this occasion, too, the work stoppage was diplomatically handled, and after being given some concessions, the workers returned to work that afternoon. As the *jefe político* and the head of the union, José Neyra, explained in a letter to *El Paladín*, they had convinced Hartington to remove the fines. Yet the company continued to find new ways of exploiting the workers, such as increasing the length of finished cloth for which they were paid by three metres yet paying them the same.[65]

In June, the textile industry had also begun to experience the worst effects of the depression and to accumulate a surplus of merchandise. Díaz and Dehesa discussed this worsening economic situation, but their suggestions to the factory owners were ignored.[66] None of the factories would comply with their proposal to utilize an hourly wage since they preferred to operate according to the cheaper piece-rate system. Hartington opposed these suggestions as well. But he also warned the owners that they had better undertake a radical reform of production facilities and working conditions if they were to achieve the necessary efficiency to remain competitive; he firmly believed that, if factories in Mexico operated a sixty-hour week, the workers would be able to produce more.[67] Hartington's efforts at rationalizing production and reducing costs may have been reasonable given the effects of international factors, but they were opposed by a labour movement incensed by working conditions and becoming conscious of its own power. Rafael de Zayas Enríquez, in his July report to the government, confirmed that conditions in the industry were deplorable. He called for sweeping labour reforms throughout Mexico. Dehesa also informed Díaz of the impending labour troubles. The labour movement as such was not new either to Mexico in general or to Veracruz. It had distinct Mexican roots with a definite anarchist tinge, which has been traced to the 1860s. It was initially controlled by cooptation of its leaders, but the worsening economic situation produced new leaders who saw in the radical anarchist ideas of the newly formed PLM an ideological justification for their demands. In Veracruz, the first step towards a worker's organization was the formation of a Mutual Savings Society.[68] Sometime after the turn of the century, however, a small group began to hold clandestine meetings in Orizaba with the purpose of proselytizing among the workers. The group consisted of two textile workers, Manuel Avíla and José Neyra, who had been influenced by the anarchist ideas of the PLM, and José Rumbía, a Methodist minister and teacher. They initiated the labour movement that began among Veracruz workers in 1903 and that gradually spread to other workers in Mexico. In the spring of 1906, the group formed a union called the Gran Círculo de Obreros Libres (Great Circle of Free Workers or GCOL) and named Avíla and Neyra president and vice-president, respectively. Their manifesto called for the overthrow of capitalism and the Díaz dictatorship. A secret charter also called for relations with the militant PLM.[69]

Faced with this almost open call to rebellion, which was circulated in the workers' newspaper, *Revolución Social*, the president countered with repression. On June 14, 1906, eleven days after the appearance of the newspaper in Orizaba, the *jefe político* appeared with a group of Rurales to arrest the GCOL leaders during a secret meeting. He caught some of them, but others were able to get away. With the dispersal of the original leaders, the workers chose a moderate foreman from Río Blanco, José Morales, to be their next president. Morales immediately resigned from his job so as to devote all his time to the union and petitioned the state government for official recognition of the union. He acknowledged the past mistakes of the GCOL and promised both to obey the law and to support the government in the future. Because Dehesa insisted, Díaz acquiesced in this new development, although he "grumpily" informed Dehesa that the governor would be responsible for any illegalities committed by the union. Dehesa's recognition was formally accorded the union in September, an act that one noted historian has called a

The GCOL was founded in this house, home of Andrés Mota, a worker at Río Blanco.

feat because it gave the GCOL a status no other labour organization in Mexico had hitherto enjoyed.[70]

Meanwhile, Dehesa commissioned Ramón Rocha, judge of the
first district court in Orizaba, to investigate not only seditious
acts but also the underlying causes of the workers' unrest. This
was a clever move on Dehesa's part. He knew that the PLM had
infiltrated the workers' movement. But he felt that if he could
identify and deal calmly with concrete and specific issues, he
would be able to undercut PLM influence. So he had to try to
convince the president that, not ideology, but workplace grievances were the real reasons behind the unrest. Rocha submitted
a tentative report in July. He wrote:

> Permit me, governor, to indicate to you the motives, which the
> workers allege are the causes of their discontent. These are the
> fines, which are imposed without any reason as well as the bad
> treatment received at the hands of the foremen. The present lead-
> ers of the GCOL who were said to be originators of the anarchist
> paper, are poor and ignorant men, who are well-intentioned and
> who, it appears, are only following philanthropic ends. They all
> believe themselves to be the victims of injustice.[71]

Rocha presented the detailed report in October. In it he denied the rumours that had been circulating about an armed uprising by workers. There had been no increase in gun sales in the area nor was there any increase in payments to pawn shops that would have pointed to some unusual activity. Second, he turned his attention to problems in the jute factory, specifically the reduction in wages because of a reduction in the price of certain products. He and Herrera had forced the company to come to an agreement with the workers over wages. However, the agreement had not been implemented and this had led to a strike, which lasted one month. Rocha also explained that he met regularly with Morales, the GCOL leader, and with Herrera, and that Morales understood that respect for the constituted authority was imperative. Nevertheless, Rocha warned that the workers would not stand for any violence from foremen and that such violence would completely "transform this serene and tranquil" group. He reported, too, that he had cultivated Morales's confidence and that the latter was coming to him regularly for advice. Rocha closed his report by assuring Dehesa that there was not the least cause for alarm in the canton and that things were improving daily.[72]

Díaz was obviously pleased with Rocha's efforts to get one of Dehesa's own followers into the GCOL in a confidential position.[73] Nevertheless, this attempt by the state government to co-opt the GCOL or at least to know its intentions was not entirely successful. Within the GCOL, there were factions. In November 1906, one of these succeeded in removing Morales from the presidency and substituting a more militant worker, Samuel A. Ramírez, a member of the PLM. Ramírez's attitude was expressed clearly in an aggressive letter directed to Hartington, demanding an end to various abuses. In a bid to regain the leadership of the union, Morales visited other GCOL leaders in Puebla. He obtained sufficient support, and, at a meeting in the Gorostiza Theatre in Orizaba, he was re-elected.

This, however, did not end dissension in the union. The *jefe político* in Orizaba told the workers that they were free to elect whomever they pleased, but not Ramírez. The latter continued to find support, especially among the workers of the Santa Rosa factory, and the president and vice-president of their local, Rafael Moreno and Manuel Juárez.[74] This group was to be among those accused of responsibility for the forthcoming massacre. Hartington wrote to Reynaud in November, pointing out the growing strength of the union and recommending a reduction in the hours of work, which he believed would have the additional benefit of increasing productivity. In addition, he recommended the adoption of the European system of workers' committees in each factory, which would present their grievances and hopefully result in an end to the many strikes.[75] He was ignored. The industrialists, grouped together under the umbrella organization Centro Industrial Méxicana (Mexican Industrial Centre or CIM), instead decided to break the power of the union.

If the attitudes of both capitalists and workers were clear, what about the positions of the federal and state governments? The historiography, while generally acknowledging Dehesa's attempts at a solution to the benefit of the workers, has been more critical of the president and the federal government. Certainly there is much ground for criticism, but the view of Díaz simply adopting an anti-labour stance is not accurate. On the contrary, Díaz was working secretly to improve the lot of the workers in the textile industry.[76] Nor was he necessarily bound to the implacably anti-labour policy of the Científicos. On the other hand, he was concerned about alienating French capitalists, whom he needed to offset the weight of U.S. investments. This dilemma explains the fact that orders from the minister of the interior, Ramón Corral, also a leading Científico, to arrest all persons "dangerous" to the government and to make copies of all messages relating to any workers' movement, while they were obeyed by some governors, were ignored by Dehesa. And he continued to enjoy the confidence of the president. Díaz, not always inclined to Científico solutions, gave sufficient reign to the popular Veracruz governor whose diplomacy he felt might solve the labour disputes.[77] (See Chapter 3.)

Indeed, Dehesa, long an advocate of conciliatory labour policies, was convinced that an intransigent attitude on the part of the government would only exacerbate the labour situation. Since 1896, he had studied the labour problem. He had commissioned his secretary, the well-known legal consultant Silvestre Moreno Cora, to draw up a labour code that was promptly approved by the state legislature and then forwarded to Mexico City, where it was not even allowed to reach the floor of the Chamber of Deputies for debate.[78] Dehesa's sympathies were well known. He had clashed more than once with the factory owners in Orizaba, suggesting that it was the owners' greed that was the source of all the trouble. Dehesa viewed the role of the state as neutral in the struggle between workers and owners, but he also tried to have the state play the role of mediator, which often led to peaceful settlement of disputes. His fears for the future led him to take the side of the workers. During Christmas 1906, when the workers of Orizaba and Puebla were locked out, he had the *jefe político* distribute beans, corn, and money among them. Some workers expressed thanks for the support from their state government in letters to newspapers.[79]

Such actions made Díaz suspicious. He complained that Herrera was too "complacent" towards the workers and that they were "animated" by the thought that they could always count on help from the state government. However, in June 1906, the president wrote Dehesa affirming the right of workers to withhold their labour, a right that he publicized in his speech to the Mexican Congress in September 1906. And a request from the workers themselves directed to the president asking for help with their problems resulted in Dehesa being invited to Mexico City, where together they worked out a new set of factory rules, eliminating some abuses. Companies were required to post regular hours of work. Another measure was the inclusion of grievance procedures and the arbitration by the *jefe político* of any fine over one peso. Dehesa would have liked more comprehensive rules, but he was unable to convince the president. He continued discreetly to investigate the situation of workers who had been transported to the army punishment battalion in Quintana Roo for having circulated "socialist" ideas. And he also carried on his fight for better working conditions with one of the richest and most powerful capitalists, Enrique Tron.[80]

As a direct result of the government's entry into the labour arena, the factory owners decided to form the CIM. Early in November, matters began to come to a head. Textile workers in Puebla presented a series of demands to the companies. These were discussed in Orizaba also, and workers there began presenting their own demands to the factory management. On November 6, Hartington warned Herrera that the workers' demands were so extensive the companies intended to close all their factories in order to force the workers to accept their conditions. Díaz, preoccupied with the possibility of an uprising by the PLM (the attempt in Acayucan at coordinated revolution mentioned above), now gave in completely to the industrialists abandoning his efforts to regulate working conditions. He wrote resignedly to Dehesa that there was probably no other way to "obtain the compliance of the workers." On December 2, the CIM countered the workers' demands by issuing their own set of revised factory regulations, clearly an attempt to break the union and lower wages.[81] The new rules fixed working hours between 6 a.m. and 8 p.m.;

workers had to work the entire week without a break to receive their week's wages; they were forbidden visitors in their homes; and there were to be no objections to the fines levied for defective work. The new rules were onerous, to say the least, and completely unacceptable, since fatigue induced by long working hours would make it impossible to avoid mistakes on the job.[82]

Finally, on December 4, 1906, the GCOL with 6,000 workers declared itself on strike against the thirty factories situated in the states of Puebla and Tlaxcala. Even *El Imparcial*, not usually friendly to labour, called their demands entirely reasonable. These consisted of two rest periods of forty-five minutes each for breakfast and lunch; conclusion of the Saturday working day at 5:30 p.m.; no loss of pay for workers who were unable to work because their helpers were not available; suppression of the infamous *tiendas de raya* (company stores); half pay for accident victims; a twenty-five per cent premium for the night shift; the establishment of a factory commission to rule on defective work; and no employment of children under the age of fourteen.[83] *El Diario*, another major Mexico City daily, also commented that the demands were reasonable, and that some "respectable" factory owners wanted to concede them, but that this was difficult owing to the competition from cheaper cloth imports from the United States.

A delegation of workers from Puebla now travelled to Orizaba on December 6, convincing the non-striking members of the GCOL to help their comrades by contributing an additional sum of ten centavos per week to the strike fund.[84] Despite the increase, however, the fund was insufficient, and in a short while it became obvious that, with no end in sight, something else would have to be done. Consequently, in mid-December, Morales cabled the president asking for his intervention to settle the Puebla and Tlaxcala strikes. Díaz agreed, but the CIM refused the president's good offices. Apparently, management had already come to the decision, which had earlier been communicated to Carlos Herrera, to impose a lockout throughout the entire industry.[85]

The strategy was clear: deprive all the textile workers of their incomes and they would not be able to contribute to the strike fund, which was supporting their striking comrades. According to labour historian Luis Araiza, a meeting had been held between representatives of CIM and the minister of finance, José Yves Limantour (a shareholder in the Moctezuma beer factory in Orizaba), in the national palace at the end of December. There, Limantour reputedly told them that the best way to end the strike was through a lockout, which had been successful in other countries. Consequently, when workers in Orizaba, Puebla, and Tlaxcala arrived for work on Christmas Eve, they found the factory doors shut.[86] Throughout the country, 30,000 workers were suddenly without an income for the Christmas of 1906. The term "Río Blanco Strike," therefore, which occurs in much of the literature, is absolutely misleading.

On Christmas Day, Herrera cabled Dehesa, telling him that union president Morales was asking the president to intervene to end the lockout. In the meantime, citizens of Orizaba offered their help to the destitute workers. One *hacienda* owner offered work on his estate, some businessmen collected bread, meat, and seeds for planting, and a doctor offered his services free. The press, even the official pro-government organs, came down squarely on the side of the workers. *El Reproductor*, an Orizaban newspaper, warned that the lockout would have no effect because the workers were firm in their demands. The writer also castigated the owners for the lockout, hoped that the workers would give up their socialistic ideas, but demanded, in the name of progress, that the owners show more regard for their employees. *El Diario* commented that the workers' living conditions were bad, and that only the president's intervention, which the workers but not the owners had requested, would settle things. *La Patria* called the situation "A Question of Stomach." The paper declared that this was the worst strike the country had ever experienced, even though it was peaceful. But, it went on, the workers were firm in their demands because they were organized, and in this way wanted to become, men. Some periodicals claimed that the strike was politically motivated by socialism. This was not so, argued *La Patria*:

> All demands for justice are called socialism; the cry against hunger is called sedition; those that ask for clemency for the poor or reproof of the avarice of the rich are called revolutionary, anti-government and anti-social. Why do we have to improve the lot of the rich who feed on the misery of the poor? Why do we not censure the moneylenders who demand twenty and thirty percent interest? We do not see the specter of socialism but only tangible realities.[87]

The reference to moneylenders was aimed, of course, at one of the most iniquitous practices in the Porfiriato, the *tienda de raya*, which was itself responsible for much of the poverty of worker and peon alike. Since workers were paid with company scrip, not actual money, they were forced to purchase their necessities in the company store. But with the retail price of goods at inflated prices set by the company, the workers were thus continuously in debt. The company store was the parallel to the debt-peonage practised on *haciendas* and was one of the prime sources of worker anger. And this anger was about to find violent expression.

The attitude of the press must have had some effect on the factory owners for on December 31 the CIM asked the president if he would intervene. Subsequently, the GCOL workers also voted to take the advice of their leaders and accept the president's arbitration unconditionally. His *laudo* (arbitration award) was announced on January 4, 1907, to a joint assembly of GCOL and CIM representatives.[88] It has, of course, been viewed in a number of different ways. Some historians have overlooked it or treated it as meaningless. For others, it was an important milestone in Mexican labour history, since in effect it "negated the liberal principle" according to which economic matters were supposed to be self-regulating. Others saw it as a significant victory for the workers, since there were some concessions to earlier demands, and these were to be binding on the industrialists.[89] Reports that the two GCOL leaders, Morales and Mendoza, greeted it with shouts of thanks to the president could not be corroborated. The very opposite, in fact, was the case.

In Puebla, the GCOL membership, packed into the Guerrero Theatre, instantly reacted against the award, which did not contain one article conceding to the workers any amelioration of conditions. Only by reminding them that they had agreed to abide by the president's arbitration, and invoking their religious faith as well as threatening to resign, did Mendoza succeed in calming them and getting them to agree to return to work the following morning.[90] In Orizaba, the situation was quite different. There, Morales was jeered by the entire body of workers when he finished reading the *laudo*. Other speakers, among them Manuel Juárez, were cheered when they denounced both Morales and the document, remarking that "they were expected to accept conditions, which were worse than they had been before." Shouts of "death to Porfirio Díaz" and "down with the dictatorship" are supposed to have filled the room. Morales felt obliged to leave the hall quickly in order to avoid the wrath of the workers.[91]

In retrospect, one must recognize that the *laudo*, far from being a "substantial victory" for the workers, was a substantial defeat. For example, the only article (2.IV), which allowed the workers to receive more pay through a bonus, was limited by the right of the administration to decide the amount arbitrarily. In addition, Article 3 introduced a new measure, a passbook, in which the workers' conduct and work history would be noted. The hated system of fines remained, as did the long working hours; and the main reason for the workers' impoverishment, the *tienda de raya*, was not even mentioned. And it is this institution, which is the key to understanding the subsequent disturbances at Río Blanco.

Despite their by now almost destitute position, the workers vehemently rejected the *laudo*. This was a desperate move for one must also remember that additional payments from the Orizaba workers and the strike fund had supported the Puebla workers, and so the strike fund was thus exhausted by the time the Río Blanco lockout occurred. The Orizaban workers were totally without means of support except for the grain that was distributed by Herrera. Dependent on credit from the company store to keep them alive between pay periods, they were in dire straits during the lockout for now credit was refused. Still, many of them were reluctant to resume work the next morning.[92]

During Sunday night, groups of workers milled about Orizaba, discussing the events, and it seems that a majority of them had decided not to return to work. On Monday morning at 5:30 a.m., the factory whistles summoned the workers as usual. At Río Blanco, some workers entered the factory to begin work, but others remained in discussion outside the gate and some were prevented from entering. Accounts of what happened next differ. What is certain is that there was discussion about the local company store, operated by Victor Garcín, who had reputedly told his clerks not to give the workers anything, not even water. After a three-hour discussion, a group of workers started towards the store where a frightened employee is said to have fired a shot.[93] Whatever the pretext, the store was raided and set on fire. It contained a large tank of alcohol, which exploded and the entire building was consumed in a short time. By this time, the *jefe político* had arrived on the scene with the local gendarmerie, but despite provocation and being wounded by a thrown stone, Herrera calmly ordered his gendarmes not to shoot.[94] By about 9:00 a.m., everything was quiet. When members of the 13th Infantry Battalion arrived, Herrera had them posted around the mill. Some of the workers then decided to go to Santa Rosa and Nogales to set fire to Garcín's stores there. People from the villages joined the procession, which finally reached Nogales, where another of Garcín's stores was burnt. On the way back to Río Blanco, the group of workers and villagers were surprised by

a section of the 13th Battalion under the command of Colonel
José María Villareal. The soldiers fired on the crowd of march-
ers, killing some of them. The soldiers then marched to Santa
Rosa, where there was another encounter in which workers were
shot and some soldiers injured. By about 4:00 p.m., calm had
been restored. The district judge arrived and was busy making
out death certificates. Many workers fled the town for the hills,
afraid of reprisals.

   Then the disturbance broke out again. A small group of workers went looking for Morales to vent their anger on him. Not
finding him, they set his house ablaze, causing the entire block
of workers' dwellings to burn. Afterwards, there were a few isolated incidents, but in general, with the departure of the workers for the hills, things were quiet in Orizaba and neighbouring
towns that night. At 1:30 a.m., more troops arrived. By 7:00 a.m.,
Colonel Francisco Ruíz with the 24th Artillery Battalion, accompanied by General Rosalino Martínez, Under-Secretary for War,
was in Orizaba. Immediately, Carlos Herrera was replaced by
Colonel Ruíz as *jefe político* and was ordered to return to Xalapa.
A number of workers were rounded up and summarily executed, most of them in front of the burnt-out company store.[95]
How many people were killed in total is unknown. Although
the number has been estimated at between fifty and seventy,
Mexicans believed at the time that hundreds of deaths occurred.
The reputation of the president and his government was seriously damaged, and the events remained in people's minds for a
long time. Dehesa was incensed by the infringement of state sovereignty and the brutal repression that followed. He also resisted
the replacement of Herrera by Ruíz for as long as he dared.[96]

   Within the next few days, however, he undertook certain measures to ensure that both the president and the public were
aware of the real course of events. Dehesa would not believe that
Díaz was behind the massacre. On Friday, January 11, Herrera
wrote him an official report of the events of the previous Monday,
which Dehesa had printed in the official state newspaper, *Diario
Oficial*, and also in *El Dictámen* (Veracruz City) as well as *El
Reproductor*. The next day, he wrote the president asking him to
receive Carlos Herrera, "who desires to inform you of the dis-
graceful events at Río Blanco." Dehesa also sent Díaz a copy of
a letter from Rocha giving his account of the incident and the
reasons for the riot. According to Rocha, the lockout was the
principal cause of the disturbances, coinciding with a state of
excitement among the workers caused by the squabbles over the

union presidency. There was not only a clash of personalities but also disagreement over the moderate line taken by Morales and the radical socialist one taken by Ramírez and the group behind the paper *Revolución Social.*[97] For Dehesa, however, the root cause of all the disturbances was not socialist agitation but the greed of the factory owners, an opinion that he circulated. They, in turn, supported by the Científicos, were equally determined to minimize Dehesa's influence.[98] Besides the greed of the industrialists, Dehesa laid the blame squarely on the shoulders of the government, without, however, specifying whom he thought responsible. A few days later, Dehesa went to the capital to see the president and told Díaz "with all clarity that the government had committed a grave error." In fact, he listed a number of serious mistakes committed by the federal government. These were: the removal of Herrera from his post; the ordering of federal troops to the area, which the situation did not demand; sending a general with a bad reputation; trying to solve the problems by force of arms when more prudent measures were called for; and violating the territorial sovereignty of the state of Veracruz. The president conceded that he had judged the situation precipitately and agreed to withdraw federal troops. But when Díaz chided him with the comment that Dehesa was taking matters too seriously, that the events at Acayucan the previous September and at Río Blanco were only mutinies, Dehesa replied:

> No general, it is necessary that you accept reality and do not allow yourself to be deceived by the Científicos. *It is not a question of a mutiny; it is a question of a revolution.*[99] [emphasis added]

The Political Fallout

Privy to the ideological and social causes of the uprising at Acayucan, as well as the reasons behind the bloody events at Río Blanco, Dehesa knew that dissatisfaction in Mexico was widespread. From his subsequent actions between 1908 and 1911, especially his meetings with Madero, one can infer that Dehesa was also thinking in terms of a thorough political change. It was not that he desired to remove Díaz, but rather, the Científico clique, whom he held responsible for much more than the events and massacre at Río Blanco. The misreading and mishandling of the situation had so angered Dehesa that, years later, he was still preoccupied with it.[100]

Strong rumours circulated that Dehesa had been so disgusted with the federal government's actions that he was considering resignation. The main reason cited was that he had not been consulted. In fact, Dehesa's anger was also directed at the government over the summary executions carried out on the orders of Colonel Ruíz or General Martínez. Dehesa had Herrera continue to gather evidence, which showed the complicity of the company. Some employees and managers had indicated which workers should be punished as ring-leaders. Many of these had then been shot in front of their colleagues.[101]

Dehesa then consulted with Moreno Cora on the events of December-January in Orizaba. Moreno Cora's opinion that Herrera's actions had been correct under the circumstances was subsequently sent to Díaz, resulting in some measures to alleviate working conditions. Colonel Ruíz ordered an end to the use of company store scrip and lowered the rent on workers' homes. Díaz then replaced Ruíz with Miguel Gómez (another hard-liner, but a civilian, and again without consulting Dehesa) at the end of the month. The minister of the interior, Ramón Corral, ordered that particular care be taken in seeing that articles 4 and 7 of the *laudo* regarding hygiene, the employment of young children, and the establishment of schools were carried out under the supervision of the state government. He himself, he stated, was enforcing the stipulation that young children not be put to work. As a precaution, however, Dehesa asked the president to keep the 13th Battalion in Orizaba.[102]

The massacre and repression of workers and the implementation of the president's *laudo* were not sufficient to prevent further strikes. It is amazing that the workers, after a massacre in which 1,571 of their comrades had either fled or been wounded or killed, continued to use the strike tactic. In April, 1907, there were strikes in Xalapa, Nogales, and Río Blanco as well as the jute factory in Orizaba. Grievances and requests were presented to the governor, including the prohibition of child labour under fifteen years of age; the establishment of a night school and time off in order to attend, with the time to be made up by work on religious holidays; the establishment of a commission of workers to handle grievances; and a strenuous effort on the part of the company to end bad treatment at the hands of foremen and supervisors. But the regulations were ignored, and the workers walked off the job again.[103]

Since the president (nervous because of the continuing strikes across the country, not to speak of revolutionary preparations) was behind Dehesa, CIDOSA unwillingly accepted the governor's recommendations. They were: an increase of the minimum age for child labour to ten, three years above the minimum stated in the *laudo*; a reduction in maximum working hours for all employees to twelve hours per day; time off on Sundays, national holidays, and the five religious holidays, without pay; and establishment of an arbitration committee at a worker's request, with the worker's right to agree on the arbitrator. In addition, the time limit for vacating homes was raised to ten days; complaints had to be answered in eight, not fifteen, days; foremen were prohibited from taking money from workers; workers were to be treated with "moderation"; factories with over one hundred workers would employ a physician; and there would be eight day's notice for a change in wage scale. There was, however, no mention of the hated passbooks.[104] The new regulations removed some abuses and calmed the workers for a while but, needless to say, the labour situation was not "solved." Grievances remained and strikes continued, and, although there were minor successes for the workers, threats by management and the fear of being transported to Quintana Roo or going to jail kept these at minimum.[105]

After Cananea[106] and Río Blanco, the Mexican government decided not to attempt to deal with the labour problem in any positive way. Nor did it pay any attention to the festering social problems and the mounting political opposition. The Científicos, it seems, had finally gained the upper hand. Moreover, the energy that Díaz had been able to show even in 1907 appeared to be running out by 1908. The president was considering retiring, the Creelman interview (Chapter 3) had set off an unprecedented wave of intrigue and speculation, and the country was stirring after more than thirty years of the dictatorship. After 1906, Dehesa was occupied with his bitter fight to remove the Científicos from their positions of power, including making a bid for the vice-presidency. He realized that with this group in control he would have little or no influence on any policy and less and less control in his own state. It was for precisely this reason that he had consistently espoused the cause of federalism.

The massacre at Río Blanco had discredited Díaz in the eyes of Mexicans, not only because of the brutal way things had been handled and because of the government's unwillingness to devise a labour policy, but because of the serious breach of state sovereignty. Dehesa, as a clever and introspective individual, realized after he spoke to the president in January 1907 that the heavy-handedness of the central government was leading to

revolution. Yet because of his personal loyalty to Díaz, and perhaps too because of his conceit, he did not react at Río Blanco
with integrity, for his course of action could and should have
been resignation. Instead, he felt that he might have sufficient
influence with the president to counteract the Científicos and
rescue the situation. This was a serious error of judgment on
his part. Nevertheless, Dehesa's attitude influenced not only the
workers but also the gathering opposition. Nor was such opposition from a respected political figure who was also a close friend
of the president lost on those who followed political events
closely. In any event, the brutalities committed at Río Blanco, following so closely on the heels of Acayucan and Cananea, were
signs that the regime had run its course.

The Revolutionary Pact of Mata de Canela

The men who had fled Río Blanco now joined those who had
started the uprising at Acayucan. In July, 1908, Hilario Salas
received a letter from Samuel A. Ramírez, the former president
of the GCOL at Río Blanco, who was in hiding in Puerto
México, requesting a meeting. The two and Padua met at a place
called Mata de Canela, near Catemoco, in the house of Pedro A.
Carbajal, and agreed to fuse the two groups, the revolutionary
workers from Río Blanco and the remnants of the Acayucan
uprising. They also agreed not to end their struggle until the Díaz
regime was overthrown.[107] In addition, they united with some of
the Indians from Lomo Larga and other parts of the Soteapan
who had fought with Salas in 1906.[108] It is important to understand that this revolutionary group operated under the banner of
the PLM. In February of the following year, Salas named Padua
chief of operations in the south of Veracruz, with headquarters
in the Soteapan, near Padua's home at Chinameca. Ramírez
returned secretly to Río Blanco to inform other revolutionary
workers in the factories there. Salas himself undertook a propaganda trip through Tlaxcala, Puebla, and Mexico states, and by
mid-1910, the organization of the PLM for the next phase of the
revolution was in full swing.[109]

In July 1910, the rebel forces gained an important ally in the
person of Santana Rodríguez. Rodríguez, or Santanón as he was
popularly known, was a bandit whose main area of operations
was to the southeast of the port of Verazcruz. He was "regarded
by many in the region as a sort of Robin Hood and more than
a little respected throughout the nation for his bold defiance

of Porfirian authority."[110] Together with his lieutenants Eduardo Díaz, Fermín Cortés, Odón Camacho, Nicanor Pérez, and two women, one of whom was named Angela, he met on July 19 with Padua at Jalapilla, where they formed an alliance. Santanón would not discuss politics, indicating that the only reason he was joining the rebels was that government forces had been pursuing him for reasons he did not want to go into.[111] Padua was very happy to have such an important and experienced military ally, whatever his motives, for even though Santanón claimed to be uninterested in politics, his type of banditry meshed very well with the ideological purposes of the Vercacruz rebels. At the end of May, Santanon had attacked large *haciendas* like Corral Nuevo and San Anastasio and to the north in the municipality of Tlacotalpan.[112] Three days later, on May 31, he appeared at the *hacienda* Bella Vista in the state of Oaxaca where he murdered the German manager, Robert Voigt.[113] Important supplies arms and money were thus provided for the cause. And Santanón was not squeamish about whom or how he robbed as long as there was sufficient booty to be had. On the night of July 15, the gang surprised Julio Mendoza and his wife María Ravelo, merchants who traded up and down the San Juan Michapám River close to its confluence with the Papaloapán. They shot Mendoza but let his wife go, stealing all their money, some four thousand pesos.[114]

Convinced of his adherence to the cause, Padua dispatched Santanón and his two lieutenants, Díaz and Cortés, together with six of his own men under Espiridion Pérez to reconnoiter a place where he wanted to store arms. The immediate goal was to open a path across the range to the San Martín Mountains in order to be able to get closer to the city of San Andrés Tuxtla.[115] But the Díaz government was out to get this audacious bandit who thumbed his nose at the authorities. Detachments of the 6th Rurales were first assigned to the task of finding Santanón. In August, two of his men, Isauro Ponce and Felipe Cruz, were captured; in October, two others. In addition, an expeditionary force of the 24th Battalion under Colonel Manuel Jasso was dispatched to the area from Acayucan to aid in the search for the rebels.[116]

In the meantime, Padua was trying to recruit more people for the revolutionary struggle. On October 6, 1910, he attacked the sugar plantation of San Carlos, where there were some fifty Yaqui forced labourers who wanted to join the movement. With only four men, Padua assaulted the works, capturing the watchman. He found twenty-five labourers, fourteen women, and many children. The Yaquis begged Padua to take the women with them, "as they could be useful in the preparation of tortillas."[117] On October 14, on their way to the town of Amamaloya, about one-half kilometre from Huazuntlán in the municipality of Mecayapán, canton of Acayucan, they encountered a troop of state Rurales under Francisco Cárdenas, who were put to flight.[118] With Cárdenas' Rurales under pressure, the minister of the interior ordered the Rurales' inspector general to dispatch another twenty-five men of the 12th Rurales under Corporal José Espinosa to Nopalapám to join Cárdenas. They were also advised to coordinate actions with the commander of the gunboat *El Morelos*. A 2,000-peso reward was posted for Santanón's capture.[119]

Padua had sent word to Santanón to expect the wounded from his encounter with the Rurales on the 14th. Instead of waiting, however, on October 17, Santanón with fifty-nine men went out to meet them. Taking a different route, he was unable to locate them, arriving instead at the place where the previous battle had been fought. At about the same time, Corporal Ignacio Gutiérrez with Rurales of the 1st Corps was ordered to the ranch Apa, and then to Guasutlán, the scene of the earlier battle. Gutiérrez was ordered to advance with five men to within three hundred metres of the campsite. The rebels suddenly opened fire and the federal forces were caught by surprise because the people of the surrounding area had given no indication that Santanón was near. After an exchange of fire that lasted about forty-five minutes, seventy to eighty of the rebels took off for the hills, leaving their leader and a few others. These kept up the fight until they were all killed; Santanón, Eduardo Díaz, and seven others lost their lives.[120] Among the interesting documents found on the dead were letters signed by Santanón as General-in-Chief of the Eastern Revolutionary Army and a dispatch from Los Angeles, California, addressed to the Chief of the 1st Revolutionary Military Zone, together with a list of the names of fifty-six of his men and codes using Japanese symbols.[121] Santanón's body was taken to the nearby town of Acayucan, where he was identified by the district judge and various other people. His picture was also published in the *Periódico Oficial* in Xalapa on October 29, to make sure that the death of the legendary figure was an object lesson to all those who might want to emulate him.[122] His men scattered in various small groups in the southern cantons, where they were subjected to an intense hunt by the authorities, who succeeded in capturing only some of them.[123] The elimination of Santanón was not, however, the end of the PLM struggle in Veracruz.

In Acayucan, people who had taken part in the uprising in Lomo Larga and the Soteapan in general, but who had been too afraid or unable for various reasons to continue their activity under Padua, began to drift back to the PLM revolutionary cause after Madero's November 20 call for revolution. Indeed, the government was seriously concerned about the military situation in the southern cantons. Additional state police were sent to Chinameca and Acayucan. The military commander, Colonel Jasso, began reconnaissance around Minatitlán by cutting a road into the mountains, with two hundred men recruited for the task. Jasso's hunches were correct: a well-established and -fortified camp built of stones and lumber, together with numerous buildings was discovered. The rebels had abandoned it after burning the houses but were apparently still in that remote area.[124]

Early in 1910, the signs of a complex and exasperating military situation were beginning to appear. Although one cannot claim that the PLM group in the south of Veracruz posed a serious military threat by itself, still its presence was embarrassing, more so because the government was unable to put paid to the band, estimated at about two hundred. At the same time, conditions in the central area of the state necessitated a fairly large stationary garrison around Córdoba and Orizaba, placed there to intimidate the textile workers. This area was obviously strategic, as it was not only the main communications link between the port of Veracruz and Mexico City, but was the heart of the textile industry. More than seven thousand workers laboured in the textile mills of CIDOSA located there, many of them militant, constantly striking over working conditions. Because of fears of revolt, made more urgent by an inability to gauge the full extent of bitterness surrounding the memory of the massacre in 1907, the government felt it wise to keep the 15th Battalion permanently stationed in Río Blanco.

For the moment, the Porfirian regime could breathe easy. The challenges of Acayucan and Río Blanco had not been able to spark a general uprising, nor bring the regime to a halt. Other offensives and alliances would be necessary, although very few people envisaged what was about to happen, for a double challenge now developed from within as well as without the regime. From within, Dehesa's public condemnation of the government over the Río Blanco massacre, but especially his opposition to the Científico's centralist politics, opened a breach in the legitimacy of the regime. Certainly, it gave moral strength to the growing opposition without and became an additional factor in the events that would hasten the demise of the Díaz regime. Dehesa's condemnation was to have broad implications as the presidential election of 1910 approached.

3

Revolution
in Veracruz

The Maderista Phase

The strength of Mexican Liberalism had always resided in the provinces, where it attracted a motley following made up of "middle and lower socioethnic groups."[1] The Acayucan uprising and the labour problems at Río Blanco both reflected an alliance between the lower-middle class and the lower classes. Town and country, lower-middle class citizens and landless Indians, peasants, and exploited workers, all collaborated in these first attempts to dislodge the porfirian regime. In fact, many of the revolutionaries who appear after 1910 – Hilario Salas, Heriberto Jara, and Gabriel Gavira – received their "ideological," if not military, preparation from these two events.

The uprising at Acayucan and the massacre at Río Blanco stengthened the fault line between the state and central governments. And the fissure in both instances was precisely the issue of political control. Problems, such as these were not handled and mediated at the municipal or state level. Had they been, the outcomes might have been different. Instead, solutions were imposed from the centre in Mexico City. But this was antithetical to the spirit of Mexican Liberalism, whose central tenet was the concept of the autonomous municipality.[2]

Although the Plan of Tuxtepec, which brought Díaz to power, did explicitly call for the autonomous municipality, implying regional sovereignty, the praxis of the Porfiriato in this regard was quite different from the intent of the wording in the Plan as well as the Constitution of 1857. In fact, it has been acknowledged that, while the Porfirians "openly exploited the radical Liberals' federalist stance" to obtain power, that power was ironically used to undercut federalism and state sovereignty.[3]

The paradox of the Porfiriato after 1907, then, was precisely that some of those same people who had brought the regime into existence and supported it now saw fit to turn against it, all the while operating with a semblance of legality. For now, the provincial elite of Veracruz, headed by the governor, blamed the Científicos rather than Díaz for the political and social unrest in the state. And the Científicos were vulnerable because they were blameworthy. The debacle bought about by the interference of this group in Río Blanco definitely crystallized the anti-centralist opposition. Many Mexicans felt that the proper authority to handle the affair was the state governor. Dehesa himself was adamant on this point. Díaz's decision to call in the troops, therefore, was not only ill-advised; it was politically disastrous. Mexicans felt that the intellectual source of this decision must have been the Científicos. The mounting political opposition, therefore, tended to first coalesce around calls for the removal of Vice-President Corral, a leading Científico. And the man, who spearheaded this demand was none other than governor of Veracruz.

The argument presented in this chapter is that Dehesa's vehement opposition to this ruling clique and their centralist policies was instrumental in opening the breach into which Francisco Madero and the Anti-Re-electionists could slip, thus affecting the political climate in a crucial manner. And the initial vehicle for this opposition (one can hardly call it a movement yet) was the behind-the-scenes manoeuvreing around the choice of vice-president in the election of 1910.

The Anti-Científico Political Revolt

We have seen that in and of themselves the PLM efforts were not strong enough to overthrow the regime. Indeed, it has been acknowledged elsewhere that peasant and workers' movements alone are usually incapable of overthrowing a dominant bourgeois regime, even with the participation of the lower-middle class. An alliance with the rest of the middle class is needed to accomplish that end and is more often than not perceived as the deciding factor in leading a revolutionary possibility to a victorious conclusion.[4] That alliance usually becomes possible only when there is a breakdown in the political-administrative partnership within a state during a political crisis. In Mexico, by early 1910, then, the necessary conditions for such an alliance had appeared. And stirrings within the middle class had been building but had yet received no catalyst through which to forge that alliance.

After 1908, middle class citizens who could now be counted among the opposition, but who were opposed to the radical tenets of the PLM, were attracted to Francisco Madero's Partido Antireelectionista (Anti-Re-electionist Party or PA). Others directed their increasing dislike of the system into support of the various opposition *foci* within the regime itself. Here there was a sharp split between the ruling faction, the Científicos, and the two anti-Científico factions led, respectively, by General Bernardo Reyes, former minister of war and ex-governor of Nuevo León, and Dehesa. Indeed, this split came to a head over the election of 1910.

In organizing his seventh electoral campaign and selecting his running mate, Díaz was faced with a number of options. He could allow Madero to run against him and his unpopular vice-president, Científico candidate Ramón Corral, in a clean campaign, risking a political defeat. He could manipulate the election results as had always been the case and risk a revolution as Dehesa had prophesied. Or he could choose Teodoro Dehesa as his running mate. The latter choice had considerable merit. Enjoying an excellent reputation among the middle and popular classes alike as an honest and efficient administrator, Dehesa was also known throughout Mexico as an adamant enemy of the Científicos, and that ticket would have had an excellent chance of winning.[5] The choice seemed an easy one, making Díaz's ambivalent strategy all the more astonishing: he presented the electorate in 1910 with the farcical situation of the president running against himself – on one ticket he ran with Ramón Corral, and on the other with Teodoro Dehesa.

The presence of these opposing factions within the ruling group towards the end of the regime reveals the fragility of the porfirian government.[6] Factionalism was the direct result of the Porfirian system. Much could be attributed to the fact that there was one official ideology, Porfirianism, a variety of Liberalism. However, Porfirianism, or adherence to President Porfirio Díaz, masked the fact that there were these two competing factions within the official ideology, the Científicos and their opponents, sometimes called Tuxtepecanos Puros (pure Tuxtepecans) or Jacobinos (Jacobins: an utterly ironic appellation in these circumstances). In his seminal study on the Porfiriato and the Revolution, François-Xavier Guerra locates the origin of the two factions in the geo-ideological differences between region and centre. The Científicos were, in effect, the centralists, the men who wanted to and did control the lucrative contracts that came

with foreign investments and who wanted to control the hinter-
land for themselves and their clients. They were characterized
by men like Limantour, urban dwellers, intellectuals, members
of the liberal professions of the city of Mexico, knowledgeable
in international finance, who ignored the "politics of the politicians" and who would never know the world of the states.[7] The
second group, men like Reyes, Dehesa, and Díaz himself, were
provincials, drawn from the middle or lower classes, knowledgeable about the countryside, and "exercising their careers in contact with the people in the states."[8] Behind and around these two
groups there had developed a coterie of clients.

One of the major causes of the Mexican Revolution was the
inability of the Porfirian regime to bridge this division between
factions, which had been developing since the 1880s and 1890s,
and was the articulation of the deeper federalist-centralist struggle that had dogged Mexican politics since the inception of the
nation.[9] Diaz's tactic, to tolerate an opposition faction within the
ruling group, appeared from the outside to be an ambiguity in
the official position. In fact, this tolerance masked the impossible dilemma facing the president: having to choose between a
group of technocrats on whom control of the nation's financial
credit and development depended and another clientele of loyal-
ists, the men from the regions, on whom hinged invaluable control of the countryside.[10]

Although surrounding himself with the Científicos, Díaz,
therefore, allowed the Tuxtepecans to manoeuvre fairly openly.
This apparent freedom sent important signals to the discontented that Díaz might be considering replacing the Científicos.
Madero seriously entertained this possibility until June 1910,
when he was arrested and jailed. If Díaz had replaced Corral
with a candidate such as Dehesa, Madero would never have
called for revolution. After his imprisonment, however, his attitude (so noticeable in the tone of his letters) hardened as he
came to believe that replacing neither the Científicos nor Corral
would be sufficient. For Madero, the source of the evil was the
old president himself.[11] Díaz was either unable or unwilling to
recapture the ideological ground carved out by the 1876 Plan
of Tuxtepec (which was very close to Madero's own ideas and
those of the Constitution of 1857), despite a belated attempt
to heal breaches by including Dehesa. By May 1911, tempering
the Científico predominance in the cabinet by including Dehesa
would not have worked.[12] Díaz's downfall resulted from his stub-
bornness in choosing the least popular ideological position in

the last decade of the Porfiriato. In staying with the old and tried, the Científicos, but appearing to favour the more progressive forces within the ruling clique, Díaz contributed to a further fragmentation of the elite that was an important cause of the Revolution of 1910.[13] By undermining the efforts of supporters of Reyes and Dehesa, he gave Francisco Madero an opportunity to win a broad following among an exasperated and frustrated electorate. To understand this anomaly, it is necessary to recognize that the Liberalism inherent in the Plan of Tuxtepec of 1876 was gradually replaced by the Liberalism of the Científico faction.

The Científicos had their origin in the National Convention of the Liberal Union that was held in Mexico City in April 1892 and was attended by some old Porfirians living in the capital, among them Justo Sierra, Francisco Bulnes, Romero Rubio, Rosenda Pineda, and José Limantour.[14] After Díaz rejected their quasi-democratic manifesto, idealists in the Union abandoned the organization, while the rest gave up any attempt at political reforms and limited their contribution to advocating a policy that stressed material development.[15] In 1893, José Yves Limantour was named minister of finance, one of the most important and powerful cabinet positions. On the death of Romero Rubio, Díaz's father-in-law, in 1895, Limantour became the acknowledged leader of the remaining members, who were dubbed Científicos, for reasons outlined below.

The name came to signify the supporters of centralism, order, and capitalist development not social justice.[16] Judged by an analysis of economic indicators alone, Mexico prospered under their policy. Investments, mainly from abroad, increased and the middle class grew and prospered. As in most other industrializing countries, life was increasingly bitter for the masses of the population. Indeed, life expectancy actually decreased during the Porfiriato, partly due to the policies of the Científicos. Their economic ideas were based on Comtean positivism, which had been introduced into Mexico by Gabino Barreda, the brilliant minister of education under President Juárez. They believed that positivism was the only ideology that could propel Mexico into the modern scientific and technological age.[17] Impressed by the industrial development of Europe and the United States, they wished to see Mexico join the front ranks of the industrial world. And to achieve this, they advocated a long period of peace, which they thought could only be secured by keeping the *caudillo* (strong-man)-president in office for as long as possible. Second, they believed that only the upper class (aided by progressive foreigners who could provide the necessary technology and capital) could guide Mexico's destiny. Third, they wanted immigration, preferably from Europe, in order to replace the indigenous peoples, who were perceived as being too primitive to respond to modernization. The underpinnings of these ideas were the basic tenets of Social Darwinism. Limantour himself said that Mexico was "a poor country, poor in land, poor in capital resources, and poor in people."[18]

Consequently, the word "Científico" and the men associated with that group came to be regarded with suspicion by many Mexicans, and even as essentially non-Mexican. Many Mexicans considered their ideas merely a justification for the use of force against the weak or, in other words, for untrammeled capitalism.[19] No one has ever contested the exceptional ability of these men nor their tremendous influence in Mexico. They were assiduous in attempting to thwart the ambitions or opposition of those who objected to their policies. The Científicos, in other words, appear to have considered Mexico as their private patrimony.[20] Their opponents, the Jacobin/Pure Tuxtepecan faction, were united behind the basic tenets of the 1876 Plan of Tuxtepec: (1) adherence to the Constitution of 1857, (2) no re-election of the president and governors, and (3) municipal autonomy. However, the latter appear to have considered the principle of no re-election expendable for the time being, as a way of achieving order and stability. After the fall of General Reyes in 1909, their leader became Teodoro Dehesa, one of the most popular anti-Científico governors, who inadvertently contributed to the climate of opposition that eventually brought down the regime.

Dehesa agreed with the Científicos that Mexico needed peace and that President Díaz was the best person to maintain it. But as we saw in Chapter 2, Dehesa was also opposed to Científico labour policy. He was aware that the capitalist transformation of Mexico had resulted in the growing power and consciousness of the working class and believed that workers would have to be treated justly and given some voice in government if the system and its continued development were to be guaranteed. Influenced by his early religious training as well as the social concepts of his parents, his ideas were closer to those of Pope Leo XIII's *Rerum Novarum* of 1891 than to the materialism of the Científicos.

This is not to suggest that Dehesa was any more democratic in his thinking than other Porfirians. Both he and Reyes were as conservative as other Porfirians. Both believed in a limited franchise and in order of the Porfirian kind rather than decisions based on free elections. However, both had their political bases in their states, believed in state sovereignty, and resented the centralizing tendencies of the Científicos. One of Dehesa's main differences with the Científicos was his belief that social and economic problems ought to be solved by political means, not military force, as he had clearly demonstrated during the Río Blanco dispute. For these reasons, Dehesa opposed the Científicos and especially their attempt to control the executive branch, using his friendship with President Díaz to counteract their influence. And since by 1900 his own local political opposition had dwindled, Dehesa was now free to turn his attention to federal politics.[21]

President Díaz, ironically, had also come to fear the increasing power of the Científicos. So much seemed to depend on their contact with foreign financial and industrial sources.[22] To counteract their influence, he permitted other loyal supporters like General Reyes, Baranda, and Dehesa to remain close to the seat of power and protected them politically. But by occasionally permitting attacks on either group, he was trying to balance the one against the other. This struggle at the centre of government also reflected the tension between the federal government and the states, where most of the anti-Científico elements had their power bases. Nevertheless, the Científicos were the stronger group, mainly because of their important positions within the federal government, but also because the Jacobins had no specific program to offer at this time.[23]

Dehesa became extremely concerned in 1897 when the president told his minister of finance, José Yves Limantour, that he intended to propose the latter as his successor. Limantour is alleged to have declined the honour, claiming that he was unqualified for the job.[24] Díaz convinced him by pointing out that he would have the able minister of war, General Bernardo Reyes, to help him. Because Mrs. Limantour committed the indiscretion of telling lady friends at a tea party that she would soon be entertaining them in Chapultepec Castle, Díaz decided to reverse his decision. But because Limantour's skills (he had put the Mexican Treasury on a sound footing and was also responsible for the completion of a number of important public projects) were important to the government, Díaz could not do so openly.[25] While still publicly supporting Limantour's candidacy, therefore, Díaz allowed Limantour's enemies, led by Baranda and Dehesa, to unleash a powerful smear campaign against the minister of finance. Unable to challenge Limantour's ability, Baranda and Dehesa instead decided to use a little-known clause of the

Mexican Constitution: Baranda "discovered" that Limantour was not a Mexican by birth. When Limantour returned to Mexico after renegotiating Mexico's external debt, the president "sadly" informed him that due to recently discovered constitutional difficulties, and faced with enormous pressures to remain in power, Díaz would again seek re-election in 1900.[26]

In that year, President Díaz also celebrated his seventieth birthday. The realization that he would probably die in office set off a furious power struggle over the succession. Accordingly, therefore, Díaz arranged for both Reyes and Baranda to reveal their interest in the presidency without his express sanction. He was thus able to neutralize the two, while assuaging Limantour's anger at being tricked.[27] Both Reyes and Baranda were then similarly appeased. Reyes was allowed to "recapture" the governorship of Nuevo Leon, and Baranda became head of the National Bank.[28] This left Dehesa as the only Porfirian candidate who could appeal to the anti-Científico opposition. Reyes did reappear as a candidate for the presidency or the vice-presidency in 1909, but due to his own ambivalence and Díaz's energetic measures to foil his success, he was neutralized and forced to accept a military mission to Europe.[29]

Hardly had the Reyes/Limantour controversy ended when the inevitable instability of the regime, masked only by the desire of participants not to allow this political infighting to become public, began to make itself felt over the question of the 1904 election. Díaz's doubts over the problem of choosing a successor and, therefore, of selecting a vice-presidential candidate were the most important aspects of the campaign. Two lesser issues were the proposed extension of the presidential period to eight years, and the rivalry between the National Liberal Convention led by the Científicos and the older Círculo Nacional Porfirista (National Porfirian Circle, or CNP) directed by a Colonel Tovar, over who would have the honour of nominating the president for re-election.[30] The president unfortunately remained reticent about his intentions to run again, which only heightened the intrigue. Cosío Villegas argues that for the first and perhaps the only time Díaz believed it was necessary to conclude his career in 1904. His choice of successors seemed to be the same as before: Limantour as president and Reyes as minister of war. This resulted in Dehesa again taking the lead in organizing opposition to the former, eventually convincing Díaz that he had to run again.[31] In early 1903, Díaz decided to seek re-election and ordered Colonel Tovar to begin preparations. Again, he was able to assuage Limantour, this time by allowing him to choose the vice-presidential candidate.[32] Shortly thereafter, a flurry of activity commenced, instigated primarily by Dehesa assisted by Reyes supporters, with the aim of extending the presidential period to eight years. Bulnes asserts that the Jacobinos and Reyistas were trying to ingratiate themselves with the president in order to hinder the appointment of a Científico as vice-president, a charge that merits some attention. It is likely that Dehesa fervently believed, as he asserted in telegrams and letters, that Díaz's continuation in office was necessary for the public well-being and that he also sought to manoeuvre a non-Científico into office. In November, Dehesa mobilized the entire Veracruz caucus in the Congress to pilot a bill for an eight-year presidential term and asked the president of the Chamber, Leandro Alcolea, to convince Díaz.[33] The president, who received a copy of the bill, consented to meet the delegates the next day. Despite Dehesa's insistence, however, Díaz proved reticent, stating that since he had already announced his candidacy, he was the last person who could pass an opinion on the matter.[34] Obviously, the outward appearance of democracy had to be preserved.

Dehesa's attempts to influence the Chamber of Deputies are difficult to interpret. He may have wanted the longer presidential term in order to gain time to prepare for his own appearance on the federal scene. Certainly the longer Díaz remained in office, the better Dehesa's chances would be. Not only was he gaining popularity throughout Mexico, but also the dislike of the Científicos that was already manifest throughout the country was likely to increase. Despite his strenuous efforts, however, Dehesa was not able to achieve his plans, as the Chamber would only accept an extension to six years.[35]

With this partial defeat, which revealed the influence of the Científicos, Dehesa apparently began to think about the possibility of playing a role on the federal scene. He was soon to get his chance. In December 1907, Díaz granted an interview to the editor of *Pearson's Magazine*, James Creelman, who published an article in February 1908 announcing Díaz's "unchangeable" decision to relinquish power and not seek re-election in 1910. The article caused considerable consternation in Mexico's political circles. Reams of letters and telegrams flowed back and forth between governors trying to comprehend Díaz's statements.[36] The result was a unanimous demand by the governors that Díaz seek re-election in 1910.[37] The president, however, kept silent.

His silence strengthened belief in Mexico that he was indeed serious. Spurred by the apparent sincerity of the president's statement to Creelman, in which interview he had also called for a liberalization of Mexican political institutions, writings on the matter began to appear. Two in particular stirred the Mexican people to reflect on impending change: Andrés Molina Enríquez published his brilliant and influential *The Great National Problems*, calling for thorough reform, especially in the agricultural sector; and Francisco Madero penned *The Presidential Succession of 1910*, which urged Mexicans to accept the president's word and begin to organize opposition parties.[38] In October 1908, the famous publisher of the opposition paper *El Diario del Hogar*, Filomeno Mata, wrote to Díaz from Belén prison asking for an interview to discuss the Creelman allegations. Díaz's reply denied Mata an interview but included a short explanation, which said that he had "only expressed a personal desire, nothing more."[39] Simultaneously, *El Diario del Hogar* began to speculate about possible successors to Díaz. Among the possible candidates was Teodoro Dehesa, who was acclaimed as one of the genuinely popular political figures in Mexico, not least of all for his position on the Río Blanco affair which "had made him truly popular with the working class."[40]

Now a new opposition outside the Porfirian ranks began to emerge. From the beginning of that year, Madero had been playing with the idea of forming his own party and communicated his thoughts in February to the respected Dr. Vázquez Gómez. On May 22, 1909, Madero and his supporters founded the Anti-Re-electionist Centre. A manifesto was issued demanding adherence to the principle of no re-election. Madero left Mexico City on June 18 on his first political tour, which took him to twenty-two of the twenty-six states. In each state, he founded anti-re-electionist clubs, the first of which was in Veracruz port. At the meeting place, held in the Theatre Dehesa, Madero received an "unheard of ovation."[41] Dehesa was one of the few governors who had issued strict orders not to obstruct Madero in his campaign. Thereafter, however, events took a curious turn. On November 3, 1909, the National Democratic Party, a new party launched by Dr. Samuel Espinosa de los Monteros, elected Dehesa as an honorary member because of "his merits but especially his democratic tendencies."[42] A Reyes supporter, Espinosa de los Monteros had founded the party without any official candidates. Now that Reyes was no longer a feasible contender, he courted both Dehesa and Madero. Towards the end of the year, in fact,

Madero was a guest at the party's general meeting, and there were some attempts to fuse the two parties. These events raise the question of Dehesa's political stance. Was he, as the Científicos had argued, an opponent of the regime? Was he one of Madero's supporters? Or was there another explanation? Dehesa was above all a consistent supporter of President Díaz. However, he was aware that Mexico needed to reform its political life or there would be a violent upheaval, and he considered the political agitation resulting from the Creelman article injurious to the country. He was also aware of how fragile the system was, especially because of the strains of modernization. Although he did not yet support Madero's bid for power, he felt that it was Madero's democratic right to run for the vice-presidency, perhaps secretly hoping that he might undercut the Científico's influence. Consequently, he also used his influence and his power to protect Madero's right to speak and to organize.[43]

In an attempt to avert the growing political crisis, he arranged a meeting between the president and Madero. According to Dehesa, he was in Mexico City when the nomination meeting of the Anti-Re-electionist party was being held, and Madero sent an emissary asking if Dehesa would receive him. In the ensuing conversation of April 1910, Madero told Dehesa that his friends were disposed to accept Díaz for another six years but could not accept Corral as vice-president. Dehesa replied that these were also his sentiments and asked Madero why he did not communicate these thoughts to the president. Madero answered that, of course, he would go to see the president if invited. Dehesa promised to obtain an invitation. Then Madero stated that his friends were thinking of proposing Dehesa as vice-president and asked whether the governor would accept such a nomination. Dehesa answered:

> Under no condition. I am politically connected with General Díaz and I will not accept this candidacy without his agreement. Besides, I do not aspire to the position. For which reason, if as I hope, you have a conference with the president in order to share the impressions you have made about the general repugnance which exists in the country in regard to the reelection of Mr. Corral, I would ask you not to indicate in any way that I desire the post.
>
> Do not propose me in any way.... Limit yourself to telling him that he should designate some other candidate but not Mr. Corral.[44]

———————————————— XX ————————————————

Madero agreed, and Dehesa arranged a meeting with the president on April 16. What the two men discussed has never been revealed, although it has been suggested that one of the points was a guarantee by the president that Madero would be allowed to campaign freely and that the election would be fair.[45] Científico attempts to influence the campaign by having Madero arrested on a trumped-up charge were thwarted by Felix Díaz, who was chief of police for Mexico City. A few weeks later, Madero embarked on his second political journey through Mexico, this time as the official Anti-Re-electionist candidate for president. He again traveled to Veracruz, where he was well received because Dehesa had given strict orders that he was not in any way to be molested. In Veracruz port, he was received enthusiastically, and in Orizaba, scene of the Río Blanco labour dispute and massacre, 15,000 persons turned out to welcome him.[46]

By this time, Dehesa was convinced that an end to the regime was fast approaching. Still, he did not accept the suggestions being made that he declare himself as vice-presidential candidate. Among the persons urging him to do so had been Madero himself, who, in the meeting with Dehesa in April, had suggested that the Anti-Re-electionists would find him an acceptable candidate.[47] But Dehesa refused to budge from his previously stated position. On June 2, 1910, he wrote the president:

> If you in your double role as my friend and as president of the Republic were to offer me the nomination as vice-president, I would have to refuse it cordially but categorically....
>
> People have tried to suggest that I have been guilty of intrigue in aspiring to that post. I have never been an intriguer or an aspirant. I have only stated that the majority of the people of this country do not want Corral.[48]

On June 20, Dehesa arrived in Mexico City in great secrecy, having been summoned by the president. Dehesa had been urging Díaz to show greater leniency to the Maderistas, but the aging president would have none of it. In fact, Dehesa's supporters had been secretly helping them. Even the president's nephew, Dehesa's friend Félix Díaz, had been involved; he was swiftly removed as Mexico City's chief of police for having allowed the Anti-Re-electionists to put up placards in favour of Madero.[49] It is likely that at the meeting in June the president decided to counter Madero by running on another ticket with Dehesa as the vice-presidential candidate. After having communicated with Díaz, the CNP, at a meeting held June 22, 1910, proclaimed their nominations: Díaz for president and Teodoro Dehesa for vice-president. At the beginning of July, Dehesa graciously accepted the nomination at a tumultuous gathering that had been prepared for him in the Theatre Dehesa in Veracruz port.[50] How are we to explain his acceptance in the light of the letter he wrote to the president scarcely a month earlier? Some historians have seen in this a manoeuvre by the evil master politician Díaz, who was using Dehesa merely to draw fire away from the growing anti-re-electionist movement. It has also been suggested that Díaz wanted a democratic element in the campaign to impress foreign countries but that he never wavered in his support for Corral. The historian and statesman López Portillo remarks that Díaz was blind in not accepting Dehesa as his running mate. María Sodi de Pallares believed that Díaz was merely stubborn. Another historian argues that he wanted himself to look good by taking votes away from Corral through the inclusion of Dehesa as Corral's opponent in the election.[51] None of these assertions appear to be correct. The answer provided by Dr. Vázquez Gómez in his *Memoirs*, however, explains both Dehesa's acceptance and the president's actions. Vázquez Gómez had by this time been declared the nominee for vice-president by the Anti-Re-electionist party. As a friend of the president, he recorded numerous conversations with Díaz where he suggested that the president throw his weight behind Dehesa's candidacy because "*if he is elected we would accept this, perhaps avoiding the danger of a revolution.*"(italics mine). Díaz's answer was that one could not always do in political life what one wanted. In other words, the president did favour Dehesa as vice-president (as Limantour also noted), but did not feel that he, Díaz, was sufficiently powerful to oppose the wishes of the Científicos. Ironically, the latter thought otherwise. Sharing Limantour's opinion, they organized hurriedly in case the president "capriciously" decided to name Dehesa as vice-president.[52]

Dehesa must have sensed the president's dilemma, and therefore decided on a last-ditch effort – he was aware of his popularity in government circles and among independent politicians alike, as well as throughout Mexico[53] – to try and wrest the president away from the influence of Limantour and the Científicos. But was his popularity translatable into votes? Dehesa commanded a following among the middle and upper-class voters of Veracruz. In addition, he could expect to pick up the votes that would have gone to Reyes, through the Democratic Party and the National

Democratic Party (NDP).[54] Some of this support can be calcu-
lated by the multitude of followers who greeted him on his
arrival at Buena Vista station in Mexico in April, 1911, when it
was rumoured that he would be appointed minister of the interior. The NDP had many followers among the middle classes
"especially among the younger generation of professional and
businessmen, such as the lawyers and civil engineers, who resent
the monopoly of influence and patronage enjoyed by the so-
called 'scientific party.'"[55] He was also met at the station by
leading Reyistas; members of other political groups like the
Constitutional Party, the Central Félix Díaz, and the Círculo
Liberal Sufragistas (Liberal Suffragettes' Circle); and various
workers' organizations and student groups.[56] Thus, Dehesa could
count on the electoral support of those Porfirians (called the
"classical Porfirians" by François-Xavier Guerra) who desired a
change to a more democratic, although limited, political praxis;
the new economic elites in the states who were blocked at
the centre by the Científicos, and many erstwhile Reyistas.
Furthermore, he was attractive to many members of the working
classes, who knew his work on their behalf in Veracruz. He was
a civilian and, therefore, appealed to many who would not have
voted for Reyes. In short, Dehesa was popular among many of
the electorate who saw no hope for change other than adherence
to Maderismo after the election of 1910.[57]

His opponents also saw his candidacy as a serious threat.
Determined to leave nothing to either chance or "capricious-
ness," the Científicos launched a furious campaign against
Dehesa. As well, Limantour confronted the president. According
to Limantour's autobiography, Díaz told him he had limited
his interference by telling Dehesa's supporters they were free
to launch Dehesa's candidacy but without his, Díaz's, help.[58]
Vice-president Corral, who had acquired considerable political
power from his earlier post as minister of the interior and from
the vice-presidency, unleashed a separate campaign to remove
Dehesa supporters from office and diminish the chances of
victory. In any event, the president must have pressured the
Chamber of Deputies, who had the task of verifying the votes,
for the results were not unexpected – Corral received 17,177
votes to Dehesa's 1,394. On September 27, 1910, the Chamber
of Deputies declared Díaz and Corral the winners.[59] The die was
cast; the president had refused to compromise with those who
demanded a gradual liberalization of Mexican politics.

From 1904 on, one of Díaz's basic policies, that of "divide and rule," was gradually abandoned. Díaz continued to seem to allow factions to operate, permitting the Madero brand of liberalism, the appeal to the Constitution of 1857, and the policies of no re-election and municipal autonomy. The net gain for Madero was to capture an official ideological ground that was, in reality, closed to official politics. However, there was more to this position than that. Madero had come to occupy the same ideological ground that Díaz had thirty-five years earlier: he appeared to represent a challenge to centralism and re-electionism, symbolized, in most minds, by the Científicos. And by rejecting Dehesa, the only Porfirian who represented for the electorate the very principles that Madero was espousing, Díaz sealed his fate. For now, the Científicos were definitely the winners. But Madero would find support among all those anti-Científicos and federalists who considered the political options closed: the Reyistas and the Dehesistas, as well as his own followers. There was now only one possibility of changing the system.

In early October, Madero left San Luis Potosí; his destination was San Antonio, Texas. Some days later, the Plan of San Luis Potosí, declaring the recent elections null and void and calling on all Mexicans to overthrow the Díaz regime, was published and circulated.[50] The efforts of Dehesa and others had failed. The second phase of the Mexican Revolution was officially underway.

The Maderista Revolt

As was the case with the revolutionaries in southern Veracruz, those of the central region entered the fray before the Plan of San Luis Potosí was even proclaimed. One of the leading lights of this group was Cándido Aguilar, only seventeen when the revolt at Acayucan took place. Born into a family of *rancheros*, Cándido, having lost his father, went to work managing his uncle's dairy ranch, San Ricardo, in the town of Atoyac close to the city of Córdoba. Working in close contact with the farm labourers, Cándido appears to have developed a sense of social justice at a very early age. This was given a theoretical flavour through the influence of his uncle, Silvestre, who lent him books. Silvestre was a supporter of the PLM and the Magón brothers, to whom he sent money from time to time, receiving in return the newspaper *Regeneración*. Cándido was a party to these political discussions and had already come to the conclusion that the Díaz regime had to be replaced. His political ideas were further stimulated by the discussion in Veracruz newspapers of the

Dehesa: Look, General.
Diaz: The sickness has increased greatly. W'ell have to contain it

(El Dictamen, extra edition, 1 Nov. 1910)

revolt at Acayucan and the attendant denunciation of the merits
of anarcho-syndicalism.[61] In 1906, he created a mutual aid society for the benefit of his workers and even began training them
militarily. His good treatment of these workers was apparently
the reason why he could begin the revolution with a small ready-
made band when the time came.[62]

Aguilar was one of the first members of the Anti-Re-electionist
party established in Veracruz port in 1909, the president of which
was José Hinojosa, the publisher of the local newspaper, *El
Dictámen*.[63] Other opponents of the regime such as Heriberto
Jara, Gabriel Gavira, and Camerino Z. Mendoza, who also organized clubs, joined him. Aguilar himself was responsible for
establishing a branch in Atoyac. In April, he was in Mexico City
for the party convention, representing the district of Córdoba.
There he stood beside Abraham González while Madero and
Francisco Vázquez Gómez were nominated as presidential and
vice-presidential candidates, respectively. Other groups of anti-
Porfirians in Veracruz, businessmen and artisans, were joining
the new party.[64] In this heady atmosphere of political organization, the newspapers were filled with news of another sort: the
continuing activity of the PLM revolutionaries in the south commanded by Padua and Santanón, and the eventual death of the
famous bandit in October 1910.

Because of Madero's incarceration on trumped-up charges at

the beginning of June 1910, Aguilar and others correctly analyzed the political situation, reaching the conclusion that the ballot box was not going to be the way to defeat Díaz. Immediately, Cándido began organizing his political friends. These met on July 14 near the ranch at Atoyac, where they signed and issued the Proclamation of San Ricardo. Recognizing Madero as the constitutional president of Mexico, they called for the overthrow and death of Porfirio Díaz and the reversion of national sovereignty to the people of Mexico. They justified the call to arms by the fact that their attempt to change the political regime by peaceful means had been abortive.[65] That same day, with 120 peons from San Ricardo, Aguilar launched the first Maderista attack in Veracruz and, indeed, in Mexico. Twenty miles from Córdoba, at the town of San Juan de la Puente, he engaged federal troops under the command of General Gaudencio de la Llave, but was forced to withdraw to the northeast. This initial attempt having failed, Aguilar dispersed his men in the mountains and left the state in order to confer with Madero. Subsequently, he hid on the Madero *hacienda*, La Palmira, in Coahuila until Madero ordered him to return to Veracruz and begin planning for the call for a mass uprising on November 20. He returned in the third week of October and immediately began planning the campaign. On November 19, he attacked federal troops near Coscomatepec.[66]

In the south, while Padua was engaging federal forces around Acayucan, the government was made aware that a general insurrection was being planned to begin somewhere between November 18 and 30. On November 17, one day before the premature Aquiles Sérdan uprising in Puebla, the ministry of the interior ordered Dehesa to put all the *jefes políticos* on the alert. Anti-government demonstrations against the government in Orizaba, Acayucan, Cordoba, and other cantons of traditional unrest took place on November 18 but were quickly suppressed. Meanwhile, Rafael Tapia had slipped out of Córdoba, unfortunately with only twenty-four of the one hundred workers and supporters who had been supposed to go.[67] In October Gabriel Gavira went to Mexico City because he had not had any news from Madero's people after the latter's escape from San Luis Potosí. He saw Vázquez Gómez, who sent him to see Filomeno Mata. Not finding Mata, Gavira returned to Orizaba, where two secret agents sent by Madero found him. Gavira's son took them to Río Blanco to meet Rafael Tapia, and they left some copies of the Plan of San Luis with instructions. Meanwhile, in Orizaba, after a meeting with the anti-re-electionists, Gavira was elected head of the revolutionary movement in Orizaba. At the same time, revolutionaries in Puebla were trying to make contact with both Gavira and Tapia.[68]

Before any coordination could take place, however, the separate Maderista revolutionary groups – Gavira in Orizaba, Tapia at Río Blanco, Aguilar at Atoyac, and Mendoza at the Santa Rosa factory – were forced by circumstances to strike independently at the government. There had been little time between the publication of the Plan of San Luis Potosí and November 20 to prepare for an insurrection. The would-be revolutionaries had few arms and less training. Nevertheless, they believed that they had surprise on their side and would be able to at least shock the government. In addition, they were encouraged by the continuing revolution in the south of the state and by anti-U.S. riots in Mexico City.[69] Actually, they were able to produce neither surprise nor shock.

In Orizaba, the government were already on to Gavira's plans. His house was searched, revealing a number of bombs and cases of dynamite. The government was also able to obtain lists of the revolutionaries, and on the same day arrested Gavira's wife and his four sons. Gavira blamed not only their meagre armaments but also the "imprudent and clumsy conduct" of Madero's Mexico City organizer, Cosío Robelo, for allowing the authorities to get wind of the preparations.[70] He was forced to flee to Veracruz where, fortunately, he encountered Heriberto Jara from Río Blanco, who was working for a Cuban carpenter. This man was able to enlist the help of the Cuban consul, who arranged for Gavira's embarkation for Havana on November 27. There he met Camerino Mendoza, who had been equally unsuccessful in Santa Rosa.[71]

At about 6 p.m. on November 20, a group of men numbering between forty and fifty came out of the hills above Río Blanco to attack the barracks of the 15th Battalion and the 9th Rurales. Using handmade dynamite bombs (some of which failed to explode), they tried to take both barracks but were repulsed. Part of the group attacked the municipal prison, freeing eight prisoners. They also pillaged the marketplace, where many workers were shopping, urging them to join the struggle. One policeman was killed, two Rurales were injured, and two of the rebels were captured. Reinforcements were hurriedly sent out, and the rebels retreated, but not before cutting telegraph wires. Interesting is the report of the Veracruz commander-in-chief, who cabled the government that he had sent one hundred men to resist them, and that his forces were now stretched to the limit. Rumours of the impending attack had forced him to send another hundred troops to reinforce the state capital, Xalapa, where bridges and telegraph lines were guarded.[72] The authorities were especially watchful of workers around Río Blanco, as they thought the main revolutionary response would come from there. Any news of unrest or seditious activity was immediately attributed to the workers. So they kept the 15th Infantry Battalion and the 9th Rurales corps permanently stationed in Río Blanco. Samuel Ramírez, erstwhile union president at Río Blanco, and Porfirio Meneses, editor of the underground radical newspaper *Revolución Social*, both left Orizaba bound for the United States but were captured on the way. Many of the arrested revolutionaries had, indeed, been workers, corroborating the government's fears.

However, the attacks on November 20 did little damage. Only telegraph lines between Paso del Macho and Soledad were cut, the rail line and bridges were not damaged, and trains were running normally. General Poucel, in charge at Orizaba, ordered reinforcements to repair the telegraph wires. On the morning of November 21, the workers reported for work at the big factories by 10 a.m. and calm seemed to have returned; but not for long. At about 6 p.m., three hundred armed workers, organized in three columns, marched to the municipal palace firing their weapons, killing one policeman and wounding three others. Since the palace was the headquarters of the 15th Battalion and the 9th Rurales, they were able to pin these down while seventy of their number attacked the prison, releasing all the prisoners. A regiment was hurriedly ordered from Xalapa. Four workers – Darío Ruíz, Onofre García, Isabel Gómez, and Concepción Peña – planted a red flag on the mountains overlooking the town but were promptly hunted down and arrested the next day. Their leader was also apprehended after trying to hand over some documents to a female friend, who was also arrested. From the leader's testimony, the government learned that the head of the anti-re-electionist club in Nogales was the rebel leader of the group that had attacked the police.[73] The government, although taking the subversive activity seriously, nonetheless believed that the insurrection was only local, a continuation of the radical activity that had characterized the region around Orizaba since the Río Blanco events of 1906-07. From Veracruz port, the U.S. consul, William Canada, reported that all was quiet, shipping had not been impaired, rumours were exaggerated, and the government was adequate to deal with the malcontents in the interior and enjoyed the full confidence of the general.[74]

To this day, it is still commonplace among historians to insist that Maderista rebel activity in Veracruz was negligible.[75] But examination of documents from the ministry of defense, as well as the files on "Public Tranquility" in the Veracruz state archive, shows exactly the opposite. Between November 23 and 30, rebel activity took the form of troop movements, attacks on towns, and train derailments in the Tuxtlas, Minatitlán, and Orizaba, as well as Tantoyuca and Ozuluama in the far north of the state.[76] In early December, men were observed in San Antonio Tenejapam near Orizaba looking for the *jefe político* and shouting "Viva Madero" and "Death to Porfirio Díaz." Another party, reported to number one hundred and "led by a shoemaker" (probably a reference to Tapia, who was a saddler by trade) captured the towns of San Felipe de la Punta and Omealca just south of Orizaba. To the north of that town, near Manzanillo and Atoyac, Aguilar's rebels were also active. The army sent over two hundred troops from both the 15th and 19th battalions but met with little success. On December 6, Tapia also attacked a town near Orizaba, but the *jefe político* organized effective resistance. In the port of Veracruz, local rebels were able to plant a bomb in the house of the *jefe político*, Eulalio Vela, which was removed. Bombs were also placed in the homes of other officials.[77]

In December, the revolution did not make much headway, but neither had it been checked. Government response shows that even at this early date it was hardpressed to contain the rebels. Worse, although federal authorities kept capturing minor rebels and some major ones, such as Robles Domínguez, the active field commanders, including those in Veracruz, eluded them. Neither Tapia, Padua, Salas, nor Aguilar were ever captured. Meanwhile, from Havana, Gavira and Mendoza were trying to establish contact with the Maderista junta in San Antonio, Texas. Despite orders for their apprehension, other known anti-re-electionists had also not been captured; these would later become seasoned revolutionaries (e.g., Pedro and Clemente Gabay, Heriberto Jara, Agustín Millán, Miguel Alemán [father of the president], Juan Rodríguez Clara, Guadalupe Sánchez, Adolph G. García, Adalberto Palacios, Manuel H. Morales, Ramón Caracas, and Manuel and Ricardo Hernández del Moral.[78] In Orizaba, anti-government propaganda was still being circulated despite the arrests of some active Maderistas. Gómez, the *jefe político*, to intimidate *El Dictámen*, arrested one of its paperboys.[79]

The fact that the rebellion had not been crushed in Veracruz was made spectacularly obvious on December 28. Tapia's and

Aguilar's forces met at San Juan de la Puente and, together with other leading Maderista revolutionaries, issued a manifesto to the Mexican people, which they posted around the state. In it, they reiterated their support for Madero, demanded respect for the Constitution of 1857, and accused Díaz of being a usurper. Rafael Tapia, Cándido Aguilar, R. Garnica N. Jr., A. Portas, Teódulo Córdoba, Pedro Mesa, Antonio Contreras, A. Estrada, Julián Hernández, Domingo Calixto, and Fernando Cueto signed the manifesto.[80] If this meeting indicates the government's inability to defeat or even contain the rebels, its next response must be interpreted as even more indicative of the deteriorating situation. Fearing an attack on San Juan de la Puente, and lacking the necessary regular forces, the governor tried to raise a small auxiliary force for Córdoba. But these were insufficient even to defend that town, and the surroundings continued to be visited by rebels.[81]

From the end of December, there was a steady escalation of armed incidents that also engulfed the southern cantons of Cosamaloapán, the Tuxtlas, Acayucan, and Minatitlán. A group of southern rebels, probably captained by Carbajal, occupied the town of Malota, near Sayula, canton of Acayucan. A party of troops belonging to the 24th Battalion was sent after them but was ambushed at a place called Chopoapán near Cruz de Milagro, and the captain in charge of the squad was killed. Realizing that the number of rebels was higher than previously estimated, another group of soldiers in company strength was sent to reinforce Jasso's group of about two hundred. On January 24 more troops, infantry as well as mounted Rurales, were dispatched to the south from Córdoba on the Isthmian railway. The situation was exacerbated by lack of communications, since the rebels had cut telegraph wires over a distance of four kilometres between Tuxtepec, Oaxaca, and Ojitlán. Four days later, Jasso's force had another encounter near Sayula with the rebels, who were again reported to number about two hundred.[82]

By December, all rebel groups were now operating under the Maderista banner. Praxedis Guerrero had already foreseen this in September and had tried to avoid a fusion. Hilario Salas was reported to have become "enamoured" of the Maderistas by October. Guerrero warned Padua that Madero only wanted to "elevate himself, not emancipate the people."[83] One month later, this was followed by an analysis by the PLM junta of the ideological nature of the Madero revolution. Madero, they argued, wanted only a political revolution, but one in which the *hacendados* would keep their vast properties. The PLM was more than correct in both its fears. Most *hacendados* were not the losers in the Maderista phase of the revolution.[84]

As they grew in strength, rebel groups harried both the army and the general population. In January, Colmenares Rivas, the leader of the Maderista movement around Acayucan and San Juan Evangelista, was able to harass the army to such an extent that business came to a virtual standstill in that region, with people afraid to leave their homes. Colmenares Rivas also caused the first cracks to appear in the system in that area. Governor Dehesa as well as the *jefe político* complained to Díaz about the inactivity of federal troops stationed in Acayucan. There were reputedly five hundred men there, but they stayed in the garrison, afraid to go out looking for the enemy. As Dehesa explained, no sooner had Jasso's troops left one of the towns they passed through, than the rebels would drift back in.[85]

It is often asserted that there was little revolutionary activity towards the end of 1910.[86] In addition, emphasis has always been placed on activity in the north, especially Chihuahua and Durango, since the first major battles and successes of the Revolution occurred there. The latter is certainly a fact, but one cannot conclude from this that important revolutionary activity was, therefore, absent in other areas. In fact, the government's response to the revolutionary situation in Veracruz shows that even at this early date the government was having difficulty containing it. In short, we need to contest the accepted notion that the north was the "cradle of the Revolution,"[87] for there was a proliferation of small, dedicated groups of rebels, foci in the strictest sense, in Veracruz. Even in the southern cantons, there were at least five separate rebel movements plus one operating from across the border in Oaxaca.[88] Tapia, too, kept up the pressure. His tactics were to concentrate attacks around Córdoba and Orizaba, and then, as soon as troops were dispatched, to escape across the border into the state of Puebla, taking advantage of the steep hills of the Sierra Madre. As soon as the soldiers returned to barracks, he reappeared. On January 1, one hundred soldiers of the 19th Battalion were sent after him. On the next day, a party of Rurales engaged him but, holding the high ground, he was able to drive them off, albeit losing most of his horses. Reports indicated his small troop comprised only thirty men (in fact they numbered only twenty), armed, however, with Winchesters and plenty of ammunition.[89]

By the middle of January, General Poucel had to give up the chase. Tapia was nowhere to be found. Indeed, it was speculated that he had given up the fight and disbanded his force. Nothing could have been further from the truth. Secretly, the government must have believed the contrary, for the garrisons at both Perote and the city of Orizaba received reinforcements. General Poucel had to split his troops into various columns. Another general, Valle, guarded the exits to the state of Puebla. In fact, Tapia was still very close to Córdoba. On January 9, he slipped back into San Juan de la Puente, coolly went to the post office, penned a letter to the press, paid for the stamps, and left. In the letter, which he had written to a number of newspapers in Mexico City, he explained that he was no bandit, as the government had tried to make out, but a revolutionary fighting for the Anti-Re-electionist cause. As the main reason for his decision to join the revolutionary ranks, he recalled the maltreatment he had received at the hands of the porfirian *jefe político*, Miguel Gómez.[90]

From San Juan de la Puente, he slipped into Orizaba, recruited forty workers (old friends and acquaintances from the heady days of 1906-7), and took off again to join his troops. But while Poucel believed (erroneously as it turned out) that Tapia was hiding out on some neighbouring ranch or *hacienda*, Miguel Gómez felt otherwise. Tapia had, in fact, managed to evade the federal troops entirely, slip out of the region in the direction of Jalacingo to the north, and cross over into the state of Puebla, where he was heading for his birthplace, the village of Tatlauqui. The governor of Puebla had to request reciprocal permission from the state of Veracruz to have troops cross their respective borders in the hunt for the rebel. Indeed, the hunt for Tapia in January was the only revolutionary news, apart from the struggle in the north in Chihuahua, to make the headlines in most national newspapers.[91]

On February 14, Madero returned to Mexican soil – welcome news to the hardy adherents of the Plan of San Luis Potosí. More determined than ever, and despite the special volunteer force that had been formed under Gaudencio de la Llave to "exterminate" him, Tapia was able to outwit the federal army. On February 16, his small troop of sixteen men engaged federal troops outside of the town of San Cristóbal Llave. Five days later, General Poucel was on his way to Atlixco, Puebla, in search of Tapia. Meanwhile, to the south at Tlalixcoyan on the important rail connector between Veracruz port and Tierra Blanca where that line joins the Isthmian coming down from Córdoba, another group under Pecido López, allegedly part of Tapia's troop, had a skirmish with Rurales. Tapia had remained near Córdoba, and on

February 24 raided the town of San Juan de la Puente, taking the police chief's horses, two Remington rifles, and relieving the police of their pistols.[92] To the south, the other members of his band, having eluded the Rurales, were able to cut the telegraph lines for a considerable distance along the railway, making it even more difficult for the army to pursue them. Tapia himself had arrived at the railway station of Acatlán, only a few miles south of Córdoba, where he helped himself to the funds of the Isthmian railway. It was reported that he had three hundred men under his command. The figure is ridiculous, the result of imaginations stimulated by the incompetence of army intelligence and the inability of the Rurales and the "Volunteers of Córdoba" to put an end to his exploits. Tapia, in his memoirs, never claims to have had more than a few men, describing his troop as only a "mosquito disturbing the peaceful sleep of the dictator."[93]

The mosquito was metamorphosing into a wasp, for these apparently insignificant raids were accomplishing two important tasks. They were gradually providing his few men with arms and ammunition, saddles, horses, and money, the means to continue the fight. They were also slowly convincing the populace that a few men with enough grit and determination could outwit the "powerful" army of the dictator and prevent large numbers of badly needed troops from being sent to the northern frontier zone where the rebellion was stiffer. The army was seriously embarrassed that, despite its own claims that there was only "one small group" and "no others in the entire state" of Veracruz, they were unable to track this small group down and finish the business. To make matters worse, six hundred workers at Río Blanco started a strike at the end of the month, making it impossible to utilize for other purposes the battalion detailed to watch them.[94]

By January 1911, other independent groups of rebels had emerged in the central corridor of the state. One group, headed by Garrido Huerta of Xalapa, concentrated on the capital of Xalapa, and especially on the nearest station of the Interoceanic Railway, which connected Veracruz with Mexico City via Xalapa. Huerta, with about fifty rebels, raided up and down the train line, sacking municipal offices but evading federal forces, generally hiding out in the mountains to the north of Xalapa. His activity is interesting, for it sheds light on the multifarious reasons for which men and women took up arms against Díaz. Garrido Huerta was a member of the state orchestra, but because of his constant criticism of the municipal authorities, published in various newspapers, he was fired. He continued to write for a Mexico

City paper, *Gil Blas*, and was eventually arrested with some of his friends on charges of conspiracy, although nothing was proven. He was given bail and took the opportunity to escape.[95] Another group was led by Ricardo López, an Indian of the town of Alvarado, on the coast just south of Veracruz port. In early March, he left Alvarado with a small group for the hills around Tlalixcoyan, from which he could harass the Veracruz-Pacific railway with its important station at Piedras Negras. The canton of Huatusco was also the scene of rebel activity under a lawyer, Manuel Zamora (descendant of the famous Juarista Veracruz governor), although his activity was not yet impressive.[96]

These groups kept considerable numbers of federal troops occupied. At the same time, they caused damage to the railway system by blowing up or derailing trains and cutting telegraph wires. Certainly, these guerilla forces were not sufficiently strong to risk frontal encounters with regular troops or Rurales, and when they did so, the fracas usually ended in the latter's success. For example, during his first encounter with Rurales Ricardo López lost one of his demolition experts, who was unfortunately carrying important papers revealing plans for their campaign. But the guerilla forces continued to grow. They also refused to give up. By March, there was a marked increase in overall rebel activity.[97]

Because of the increase in rebel numbers, the Mexican government began looking for additional troops, falling back on the next line of defence by organizing volunteers. One such corps of one hundred men was organized to patrol the border between Veracruz and Oaxaca, in the canton of Cosamaloapan; another patrolled the Tuxtlas. Col. Gaudencio González de la Llave (scion of another famous Liberal), who had earlier formed such a volunteer corps in his birthplace, Orizaba, organized these corps.[98] In addition, in early April, Díaz ordered that each Rurales corps be expanded by a hundred men, to a total of about three hundred mounted men. This may have been a case of too little too late, and, as Paul Vanderwood has observed, the lack of success of the Rurales belied their romanticized image: recruiting practices were sloppy and most guards were entirely unsuited for serious military duty.[99] Unfortunately, too, ineptitude sometimes gave way to fatal incompetence. On April 9, a squad from the 12th Corps encountered a group of men near Mecapalapa. Without any question, they opened fire, killing five men immediately and, as they ran away, five more. Capturing the rest, they made for a nearby *hacienda*, whose owner explained that these men were not rebels but had gathered peacefully to stage a cockfight. The accurate report of the commanding officer was altered by the Rurales Inspector General to make it appear that the "rebels" had opened fire first.[100]

The month of March, too, saw increased civilian political activity in the form of growing criticism against the Científicos and Vice-President Corral. *El Dictámen* commented that Veracruz was one of the few states of the nation where there were judicial guarantees for individuals. It referred, however, to one exception, the odious conditions in the canton of Orizaba, where the hated Corralista *jefe político*, Miguel Gómez, had generated much opposition by his arbitrary arrest and incarceration of individuals. Gómez gave protection to the Científico newspaper, *El Germinal*, which consistently attacked Dehesa and his administration of the state. Because of its unfounded criticisms, the courts finally closed the paper on March 23.[101]

Some clarification is needed here about the myth, ably promulgated by some contemporary newspapers as well as modern historians, that serious revolutionary activity in Veracruz and other states began only with the defeat of federal forces at Ciudad Juárez on May 10. Gabriel Gavira also carefully nurtured that myth in his memoirs, for reasons that are not too difficult to guess. Gavira's later feud with Cándido Aguilar over the governorship, which he twice failed to secure, most probably coloured his later writing. Despite his bias, it is clear from his book that significant rebel activity – the capture of many key Veracruzan towns – occurred before the capture of Ciudad Juárez, and before the implications of this military victory had been realized. Ciudad Juárez was an important lever for bargaining between Madero and the Díaz regime, but so were the successes of Veracruzan rebels who had constantly harassed the federal forces. Can we be sure that Díaz would have been impressed by the defeat at Ciudad Juárez had his forces not been stretched past their limit in Guerrero, Morelos, Oaxaca, and Veracruz, not to speak of the northern states? Let us also not forget that the first moves towards a dialogue with the revolutionaries began before Ciudad Juárez and were probably motivated by the situation described above.[102]

The "failed revolutionaries of November 1910,"[103] Rafael Tapia and Cándido Aguilar, continued what they had started at San Ricardo. Unlike Gavira, neither of them chose exile. It was the rebels under the command of the saddler from Orizaba, Rafael Tapia, that gave the government forces the most trouble. Tapia, humble, diffident and honest as he was, has not received the homage that is his due. He was the most intrepid and dedicated revolutionary from Veracruz in this period, and by far the most audacious in the field. Tapia was one of the first Maderista revolutionaries to take up the struggle, and like the others, did not find any success on November 20. On the other hand, with few troops at his disposal, Tapia and his second-in-command, Cándido Aguilar, were to so harass the government that significant numbers of troops were kept in Veracruz state and were unable to go north to reinforce their comrades against the army of Pascual Orozco. To contain this small force, the government kept in and around Orizaba the 16th Battalion under General Poucel, part of the 15th Infantry Battalion, part of the 6th Corps of Rurales, and the 9th Volunteers, which had been formed by Colonel de la Llave.[104] What Tapia demonstrates is the effectiveness of guerrilla warfare and the *foco* before that term even officially entered the nomenclature of Latin American struggles.[105] His exploits confirm, also, that, if there was no general uprising among the people of Veracruz, there was a general attitude of support for the revolution. One of the reasons why Tapia and Aguilar were able to keep out of reach of the government forces was that no one turned them in.

Without the pressure of a general uprising, why did the Díaz government give up so easily, and what are the reasons for the hastily negotiated settlement of May 21, 1911?[106] There is one incident that might reveal the temper of the inner circle of government, the animus for its resignation; this incident underscores the explanation advanced above. There is an extremely interesting account – one that as far as this author knows has not yet come to light – requested by Teodoro Dehesa from Francisco de P. Sentíes, an Anti-Re-electionist, regarding the meeting held shortly after the fall of Ciudad Juárez in which General Huerta, the minister of war, González Cosío, Limantour, and Porfirio Díaz, Jr., discussed the military situation with the president. At the meeting, there was a confrontation between Huerta and Limantour. Huerta was adamant that the city could be recaptured. After Limantour admitted that there were 72 million pesos in the treasury, he exclaimed that with two thousand mounted troops he could clean up the north. In this, the minister of war supported him. Limantour countered that he would not be able to find sufficient horses, and in any case such an attempt was futile, as the war was already lost. At this point, Huerta reputedly exploded and told Limantour that he would find the first horses in Limantour's own stables. Díaz apparently went along with

Huerta, but before the campaign could be started, the government, allegedly on Limantour's insistence, had capitulated.[107]

One plausible reason for this capitulation is suggested by Knight, who concludes that there was fear on both sides – the government's and Madero's – of the possibility of a real social revolution. My own reading of the situation is that there is indeed ample evidence to that effect. What was the reason, for example, that Tapia, Aguilar, and others, with so few men and resources, could move around the heavily militarized zone of Veracruz with impunity? Plainly, the answer lies in Tapia's observation that, although few people wanted to join them, people were always willing to help the rebels. In other words, the rebels were safe among the people in the countryside and little towns, whom they were careful not to rob or mistreat and who, for their part, never gave intelligence of rebel movements to federal troops. This fact is an undeniable indication of the rebels' popularity. This is why, too, that Limantour refused to spend the money to buy additional horses and equipment for an army that might have won a few battles but would certainly have lost the war. The unpopularity of the old regime also extended well into the middle classes, if one can judge by the courage of newspaper editors who constantly published veiled, and not so veiled, attacks on the government.[108]

By the end of February, the determination and perseverance of the bands of rebels in Veracruz as elsewhere, in addition to the enduring siege of Ciudad Juárez in the north, had begun to take its toll of hitherto important political Porfirian figures. In mid-February, *El Dictámen* suggested that its constant attacks on Vice-President Ramón Corral and demands for his resignation had found echoes across the entire nation. A few days later, Díaz, in his address to the Congress of the Mexican Union, referred to the worsening political situation, promising reforms. Because of increasing rebel activity, constitutional guarantees were suspended. On that same day, the Científico newspaper in Orizaba was closed. The reason was the bitter dislike between the governor, Dehesa, and the vice-president, exacerbated by the action of the *jefe político*, Miguel Gómez, who was a Corralista. The two actions attest to Díaz's slow realization that the revolution had taken a serious turn. The closing of *El Germinal* was an attempt at appeasement, as had been the sacking of the governor of Puebla.[109] On April 10, Vice-President Corral departed Mexico, ostensibly on a leave of absence.

In March, there was indeed a surprising increase in the amount of revolutionary activity across the country. Troops were sent from

Veracruz by boat to Yucatán, where other revolutionaries had become active. In Morelos, Zapata and his supporters declared their support for Madero on March 11.[110] In Puebla, Camerino Mendoza and Heriberto Jara controlled the Mixtec region bordering on the states of Puebla, Veracruz, and Oaxaca. At the end of April, they were able to capture the towns of Chichapa, Tlacualpicán, Chotla, and Izucar de Matamoros. In each of these, revolutionary supporters replaced the Porfirian authorities. The ranks of the revolutionaries now began to swell. Groups that had been lying low, like those of Ricardo López, operating along the branch line of the Interoceanic between Veracruz port and Tierra Blanca, or of Garrido Huerta, operating just to the north of the state capital, Xalapa, began to capture towns, distribute revolutionary justice, and take on the army and Rurales.[111]

On March 9, with fifty men, Huerta attacked the town of Tlacolulan, a strategic point on the Interoceanic railway line just west of Xalapa, relieving the treasury of its funds, cutting the telegraph lines, and imprisoning the mayor. On March 18, he captured the small town of San José Miahuatlán, taking the direction of the larger town and cantonal seat, Misantla.[112] Every night now, the trains from the west arrived in Veracruz port with evidence (bulletholes) of running encounters with the rebels. Tapia had also returned to Córdoba. On March 12, he again raided the *hacienda* Las Palmillitas, just outside the town.[113] By this time, the government was having difficulty not only filling its ranks but also paying soldiers. The *jefe político* of Córdoba complained to the state government that he needed thirty-five pesos weekly to pay the volunteers. Criminals now had to be impressed into the ranks, causing additional problems. Some of these criminals just escaped and joined the rebels. Others caused serious problems, drinking on duty or, as in the case of one draftee during the search for Garrido Huerta, venting his displeasure by shooting his sergeant.[114]

At the end of March, all Veracruz was waiting for the cabinet changes that were supposed to reflect Díaz's reforms. Governor Dehesa was summoned to the capital, and *El Dictámen* was convinced that he would be named minister of the interior. Dehesa's role in the fall of the regime is a murky area for the researcher. *El Dictámen*'s publisher, Hinojosa, an ardent if careful Maderista, supported him, and there were accusations that Dehesa was plotting to get rid of Díaz. The latter is probably untrue, as one of Dehesa's firm qualities was loyalty. On the other hand, it was known that he despised the Científicos and identified them with the government, and with the centralism he hated. But to have rid Mexico of that group was tantamount to getting rid of Díaz, who was their main support. One is forced to conclude that this intelligent governor understood it was Díaz who was the problem. Thus, the accusation of an old Porfirista in Orizaba in a private letter to the president must be taken seriously. According to him, Ignacio Muñoz, the president's nephew, was in Veracruz port conferring with José Hinojosa and Diodoro Batalla. They apparently felt it was time for Díaz to go and that somehow only the entry of Dehesa into the cabinet, preferably as vice-president, could save the situation.[115]

That Dehesa was not appointed to the new cabinet, which still contained a majority of Científicos, now gave rise to even more rumours. No one had been named interior minister. Would Dehesa now be chosen as Corral's successor? *El Dictámen* even began speculating as to who would be his successor as governor. Accordingly, he was summoned (or chose to go) to Mexico City. Dehesa's putative appointment was certainly popular in Veracruz. Thousands of well-wishers from all sections of the population came to see him off. Likewise, on his arrival in at San Lázaro station in Mexico City, he was given a tumultuous welcome. Someone had even found the flags of the defunct National and Democratic parties which had, the previous year, supported Dehesa's candidacy for the vice-presidency. The air was full of shouts of "Viva" and "Down with the Científicos." The Spanish colony organized a demonstration of welcome. Carloads and carriage loads of dignitaries accompanied him to the Hotel Iturbide, where he was given the largest apartment. Tomorrow, exclaimed *El Dictámen*, Dehesa would be sworn in as minister. The paper even purported to have the name of the deputy minister Dehesa would appoint. The next day, it reported that if Dehesa were named minister, he would use his influence to release all political prisoners. On April 18, however, Dehesa returned to Veracruz. He was named neither vice-president nor minister of the interior.[116] There were no explanations. And it is doubtful whether, at this point, Dehesa's appointment would have made any difference.

While all Veracruz was agog at the possibility of Dehesa's appointment, Tapia was still roaming and raiding, evading the federal forces and augmenting his small force with new recruits.[117] To the west, Calixto Barbosa was also pressuring the canton of Zongólica with about four hundred "infantry and cavalry."[118] By the beginning of May, in fact, at about the time when Gabriel Gavira arrived back in Veracruz to take charge of all the revolutionary forces there, the situation in the state – probably a mirror of what was happening across the entire country – had reached the point where the government was almost helpless to intervene. The southern rebels, Manuel Paredes, Pedro Carbajal, and Guadalupe Ochoa, had re-equipped their forces and taken the offensive. Carbajal assaulted the town of Catemoco in the canton of the Tuxtlas and then marched towards the cantonal seat of San Andrés Tuxtla, outside of which there was a bloody, but indecisive engagement with federal cavalry. The rebels also continued to dismantle the railway lines and cut telegraph wires. On May 12, the 24th Infantry left Acayucan for Mexico City to reinforce the garrisons there after the fall of Ciudad Juárez.[119]

In the far north, especially the area of Veracruz bordering on the neighbouring states of Hidalgo and San Luis Potosí, the Huasteca, there were additional reasons for discontent. Containing a relatively large Indian population of Totonacs, Aztecs and Huastecas, this area had become famous for its many Indian revolts since Independence, mainly over the land issue, and especially throughout the Porfiriato. Now oil was discovered. Friedrich Katz and others have attested to the rivalry between U.S. oil companies and the British-owned Pearson trust. But the impact of the discovery of oil on ordinary citizens has hardly begun to be discussed. On February 15, Clarence Miller, U.S. consul stationed at Tuxpán, rode out to Furbero, an oil camp of the Oil Fields of Mexico Company, and sent back an intriguing report of the negative impact the oil business was having on local communities. The Porfirian *jefe político* of Tantoyuca, he declared, had just been removed for boasting that he had a thousand Indians ready to revolt against the government. That the *jefe político* could say such a thing indicated the degree of unrest among the middle classes in Tuxpán. In Miller's ride out to the countryside, however, he reported considerable unrest among Indians, whispered conversations, and the expectation that four thousand revolutionaries were about to descend on the community. Dissatisfaction was fuelled by the losses they had suffered from the wells – spills as well as gushers – which damaged crops and affected animals for miles around. For example, a huge fire occurred in the first hole dug by the Eagle Oil Company (Pearson Trust) in Dos Bocas near the Tamiahua lagoon. It lasted for three months, causing untold damage in the area. The arrogant treatment locals received from oil company officials, especially those of the Pearson Trust, which, it was alleged, controlled most officials and the courts, made such matters worse:

local citizens were unable to sue for compensation. In addition, he went on, it was rumoured that Standard Oil was financing the Maderistas because of the close relationship Pearson enjoyed with the Díaz government.[120] One of the interesting aspects of Miller's observations was his mention of Indians. Rarely had any reports appeared in the press that Indians were involved in the revolution in Veracruz. Where they do appear, the reporter went to the trouble to document the fact by describing in detail the dress of the rebel in question, as if looking for indelible proof that they were in fact Indians.

In January, the *jefes políticos* of Papantla and Chicontepec feared an uprising of some kind. Sixty men were reported crossing from Puebla into Veracruz by Teziutlán, heading for Papantla.[121] By the first week of May, the federal forces were stretched beyond their limits. There were too many groups of rebels, too many isolated raids, and too many points to protect. The army simply could not be everywhere at once. Cosío Villegas's claim in his monumental study of the Porfiriato, that by the end of April the government controlled only the cities of Veracruz, Xalapa, and Orizaba is not far from the truth. An example of this is the April 30 surprise attack on Naolinco, only a few miles from the state capital, Xalapa, carried out by Cándido Aguilar and Garrido Huerta. They succeeded in robbing the treasury as well as various businesses, then departed through the irrigation canals of a nearby *hacienda* as government forces came out after them.[122]

As more rebels entered the fray and as they increased in audacity, as did Aguilar and Huerta, it began to seem as if the government was powerless. This perception in turn led to more recruits for the rebels, increased dissatisfaction among ordinary citizens who wanted nothing more than to return to their businesses and peaceful activities, and therefore increased criticism of the regime. Even before the fall of Ciudad Juárez and the beginning of negotiations with the Maderista forces, as reported by the U.S. consul at Tuxpán, middle-class citizens were coming to the conclusion that Díaz and the Científico government had to go.[123]

Many historians have seen the fall of Ciudad Juárez as a key factor in Diaz's decision to resign. Ciudad Juárez, however, was probably one example, not the sole one, of the *de facto* collapse of the regime, for elsewhere the revolution was progressing. In Veracruz, for example, a unified command structure was created in order to coordinate attacks. The person entrusted with that task was Gabriel Gavira, who had been living quietly in exile in Havana. He was now ordered to proceed to San Antonio.[124]

There, Gavira was introduced to the junta, appointed Chief of the Revolution in Veracruz, and finally given five hundred dollars with which to finance the struggle, an amount he shared with Camerino Mendoza, who was going to Puebla. (Here lies the origins of a feud between Gavira and the active revolutionaries in the field in Veracruz, such as Aguilar and Tapia, since in fact they had been bearing the brunt of the fighting.) On April 5, Gavira embarked on a fruit steamer from New Orleans. Arriving in Veracruz port, he made his way down the gangplank disguised arm-in-arm with the Spanish consul. There, he got in touch with a Maderista sympathizer, León Aillaud. Both Aillaud and Heriberto Jara were also hiding in the port city. Since they were afraid to be seen with Gavira, another acquaintance gave him lodging and bought a Pullman ticket to the Las Vigas station, the closest station in the canton of Jalacingo in which one of his friends had a small ranch. From the ranch, Las Truchas, he made his way on horseback to the larger town of Altotonga, where he had more friends, and set about recruiting men. On May 5, he was able to capture the town. A force of Rurales sent after him stayed prudently away, and Gavira, in his memoirs, describes how the revolutionaries took part in a town council parade, at which he took the liberty of speaking and asking people to join the revolutionary cause. He was able to leave the town, his forces now grown to include thirty-four well-armed and mounted rebels.[125]

Gavira had meanwhile made contact with Aguilar. Together, they reached the mountains around Cofre de Perote, and the next day captured the towns of Xico and Teocelo. Their band continued to grow, and, on May 12, with 106 men, they captured Cosautlán, putting them only about twenty kilometres from Xalapa. Garrido Huerta had demanded the surrender of the capital on May 7 but had been rejected by Dehesa. It was reported that eight hundred rebels, commanded by the various leaders who had sprung up as out of nowhere, surrounded Xalapa.[126] Xalapa was actually guarded by General Garcia Peña, with troops of the Exploratory Geographical Commission, and the rebels did not seem to want to take them on. Consequently, Gavira divided his forces in two. Garrido Huerta made for Veracruz port, while Gavira and Aguilar advanced on the easier target of Huatusco.

By now, the government was finding it difficult to requisition horses (Huerta's opinion to the contrary). Desertions were also taking their toll. The populace around Xalapa was, to judge by the reports of the itinerant correspondent of *El Dictámen*, quite hostile to the regime. In Coatepec, the hatred of the *jefe político* was manifest. In Teocelo, commerce was dead, but coffee was being harvested, although the majority of the people supported the revolution. Cosautlán was completely quiet; no one ventured onto the streets for fear of being conscripted by the government. These people, the *El Dictámen* correspondent continued, would rather become rebels than fight for the government.[127]

Before news of the battle and fall of Ciudad Juárez reached Veracruz, Naolinco, another important town just to the north of Xalapa, fell to the insurgents. Rebels reached as far as the outskirts of Xalapa, the village of Coatepec, on May 13, taking funds from the municipal treasury. Now the encirclement of Xalapa was complete. The fall of Veracruz port was also imminent. There were practically no police left, as some had been ordered into the countryside in pursuit of rebels while others were dispatched to reinforce Mexico City. Garrido Huerta's group, having taken Medellín, only about twenty kilometres from Veracruz, was just outside the city waiting for an opportune moment. This gave them strategic control of the port city, since they controlled the municipality of Jamapa, from which the river of the same name provided water for the port. And to add to the government's difficulties, the Interoceanic Railway refused to transport soldiers between Mexico City and Veracruz port.[128]

On May 14, three days before Díaz finally bowed to the inevitable and promised to resign, Gavira and Aguilar appeared outside the city of Huatusco, demanding its surrender. In Gavira's own words, he was unable to restrain his men, who galloped into the city, securing it after a short fight. Quickly, Gavira ordered a plebiscite to choose a new cantonal mayor, a name he gave to the old position of *jefe político*. From there Gavira hurried to Córdoba, looking for Gaudencio de la Llave. In the meantime, various smaller parties of rebels joined his force, with all of Veracruz acknowledging him as the official Maderista general. Headquarters were established at Aguilar's ranch at Atoyac, an important point from which to control the Mexican railway. With Córdoba under siege, de la Lave retreated to Orizaba, seeking the protection of the 13th Battalion. On May 25, the day on which Díaz resigned, Gavira triumphantly entered Córdoba at the head of a force swollen to more than seven hundred rebels.[129] Elsewhere in the state, the picture was the same. Manuel Zamora captured Altotonga on May 20; Miguel Herrera and Miguel Domínguez took Soledad de Doblado the same day; Esteban Márquez captured various towns in the cantons of Jalacingo and Misantla, taking the cantonal seat of Misantla itself after negotiating with the *jefe político*. In Veracruz state, even before the resignation of Díaz, the cause had been won. But what cause? Certainly, considering the backgrounds of the combatants, their differing ideological positions, one could entertain serious doubts about whether this motley group would be able to cohere as a political force after the fall of the regime, to prepare and implement a common program. As we shall see, difficulties in forming common cause surfaced very quickly in Xalapa, particularly around the issue of who was to replace the governor. However, the most significant outcome of the Maderista revolution could not yet be envisaged: Madero's eventual drift to the right, to a program similar in nature to that of the Científicos.

4

The Revised Revolution

As testament to the claim of the previous chapter that the fall of Ciudad Juárez was not the sole event that triggered the demise of the Díaz regime, one need only look at the series of revolutionary events in Veracruz state, beginning around May 1, 1911. It is important to keep in mind the key role it played in the nation as one of the primary sources of government revenue, because of its port.

It was at this time that the first transfers of authority, from Porfirian to Maderista personnel, were taking place in numerous other cities and towns in the interior of Veracruz. By May 18, when Díaz's resignation was announced, only major cities such as Veracruz, Orizaba, Córdoba, Acayucan, and Minatitlán, as well as a few in the north of the state, were still in the hands of Porfirian forces, and these were now surrounded with hundreds of revolutionaries, waiting on orders to enter.

It is worth noting that, due to the growing popularity of Maderismo and the swelling ranks of the rebel forces, had the peace negotiations at Ciudad Juárez dragged on, the Porfirian army would not have been able to hold out. Increasing numbers of rebels controlled the railways and telegraphs and the approaches to the cities. A state of siege ensued. For this reason, the rebel leadership could afford to wait for the outcome of negotiations, avoiding unnecessary bloodshed. Strict orders, therefore, were issued to rebel groups to wait until the regular army had been contacted before trying to enter the cities. For example, Garrido Huerta's troops surrounded Xalapa, although it was protected by General García Peña and troops of the Geographical

Commission. Citizens there anxiously awaited the entry of revolutionary forces. Surrounding towns such as Banderilla, Xico, and Coatepec were helpless as the Rurales thought better of venturing too far from Xalapa in pursuit of rebels. On May 5, Gabriel Gavira took Altotonga, near the Puebla border.[1]

Changing the Guard

On May 6, an open town meeting of various rebels and citizens was held in Teocelo, canton of Coatepec, only two hours from Xalapa. At the meeting held by Manuel López, the townspeople agreed to accept the Plan of San Luis Potosí, adopt the motto of "Effective Suffrage, No Re-election," arm and equip ten men for the struggle, and use funds from the town's treasury for this purpose. A provisional mayor, one Felipe García, an intimate friend of Francisco Vázquez Gómez, was elected.[2] From there, López proceeded to the canton of Huatusco, just north of the Córdoba-Orizaba axis. Between May 10 (the day of the surrender of Ciudad Juárez) and May 18, most of the municipalities in this canton were visited by López's group who replaced local Porfirian government authorities with Maderista supporters in Comapa, Quimixtlán, Chichiquila, Sochiapa, Coscomatepec, and Tlacotepec.

Also in early May, Robles Domínguez, an old friend and Anti-Re-electionist supporter of Madero's and Mexico City agent for the Veracruz rebels, now fresh out of jail, was given the task of coordinating the various southern rebel groups, who separately could not take on the federal army but, acting in concert, could be more than a menace.[3] For the Maderista leadership, there were other imperatives as well. It was necessary to create order, especially because of the rapid proliferation of "last-minute" converts with their armed followers. In addition, with so many small bands of rebels, personal animosities and positioning for political spoils could threaten the revolution with chaos before it even managed to take over major cities. Second, a clarification (really a toning down of any social-revolutionary implications of the third clause of the Plan of San Luis Potosí),[4] in view of the now possible end of the revolution, was urgently needed if the cap was not to blow off the entire venture. Consequently, rebel leaders like López had to have their decisions approved by Robles Domínguez or his subordinates.

Meanwhile, the rebels in the south were getting bolder. Pedro Carbajal was still leading Gaudencio de la Llave on a merry chase around San Andrés Tuxtla, while Guadalupe Ochoa near

Acayucan kept Colonel Jasso busy. Gradually their ranks were filling with Indians from the area anxious to have their land claims filled. On May 9, the army came upon a rebel file folder containing a list of Porfirians accused of helping the government, who were to be executed. In the eastern central region, too, rebels had made considerable headway. On May 10, Gavira, with three hundred men, entered the town of Perote, commandeering the treasury, and then captured Las Vigas, an important railway station just to the north of Xalapa. Observers on the tower of the Geographic Commission just outside Xalapa claimed to have been able to see bands of Maderista troops gathering on the mountain of Macuiltepec. In Veracruz port, *El Dictámen* documented the increase in rebel bands. Jamapa, Soledad, and Medellín, the latter only a few miles from the port city, had their treasuries ransacked by well-armed rebels. Although orders from the revolutionary command restrained rebel groups, their commanders were unwilling to launch a frontal assault on the main cities. The reputation of General García Peña, not to speak of his well-organized defences, made the rebels think twice about attacking Xalapa. However, there were plans to lay siege to Veracruz port by cutting off its water supply.[5]

Negotiations between the Maderista movement and the Díaz government had begun, although Díaz had not yet decided to retire. The rebels were gaining almost complete control of the countryside and smaller towns. De la Llave, the only one of the field commanders who ventured out seeking direct confrontation with the rebels, did find a small party of rebels at Soledad, where he succeeded in killing one and taking three prisoners, but his success was confined to this one incident.

On May 15, Garrido Huerta managed to take the cantonal seat of Coatepec, a few miles from Xalapa; he released seventy prisoners, took a substantial amount from the treasury, and disarmed the Rurales. The next day, Manuel Zamora entered Jalacingo and repeated these actions. The cantonal seat of Jalacingo, another gateway to Puebla, was stripped of most of its defence force and was easily captured by Zamora. Hundreds of people came out to greet the rebels. Zamora's first official act was to review the sentences of all prisoners, setting forty free, which further enhanced his popularity.[6]

Rebels were also seen in the vicinity of Tlacotalpan and the surrounding plains of the Papaloapán River, while others had penetrated further west into the canton of Cosamaloapan. Another group was reported even closer to Veracruz, in the town of Jamapa. Ricardo López was now operating around Río Blanco, testing its defences. His forces ranged as far east as the station of Alvarado, not far from the port city, where they regularly held up trains, overpowering guards and taking weapons. Eyewitness accounts described López's band as well-armed, disciplined, and courteous. Passengers were neither robbed nor molested. Further south at the rail junction of the Isthmian Railway, 150 men under one Panuncio were threatening Tierra Blanca. On May 17, the rebels demanded the surrender of Orizaba. But the Porfirian army — bolstered by the volunteer force of de la Llave, who had decided to return, as well as one hundred Rurales who had just arrived – refused the demand.[7]

That same day, Díaz reluctantly announced his decision to resign at the end of May, together with Corral. Unfortunately, Diaz's decision was by no means the end of the Porfirian regime. John Womack has very succinctly summarized the state of affairs that characterized the transition from one regime to the other, the initial problem of the Maderista revolution:

> Since none of the national leaders whose responsibility it was to initiate change had been genuinely alienated from the old regime, none of them had any clear idea of what he hated old or craved new. In forsaking the San Luis Plan, they had lost even a crude agenda of priorities.[8]

Madero's handling of the change of executive in Xalapa illustrates Womack's analysis and reveals his own predilections. He was not a man of the people in any sense, and it is doubtful if he understood the "tiger," to use Diaz's own words, that he had unleashed. Certainly, with hindsight, he had no intention of championing a social revolution. He also completely misread the political climate in Veracruz. He would have liked to keep Dehesa on as governor. Despite the continuous ranting in *El Dictámen* about Dehesa's "popularity," however, it is apparent from other reports in that paper that Dehesa was anything but. Dehesa was popular with the upper and middle classes of the state because of his federalism. As was noted in Chapter 1, federalism was also accepted by the popular classes, but they wanted more. A majority of the people in Xalapa, and indeed Veracruz state, seemed to have grown tired of Dehesismo, a *caciquist* variant that Madero had also proselytized against. Behind the governor's anti-Científico, anti-centralist stance, sincere as that was, was still a "conservative" variant of Porfirianism.

That Madero wished to retain Dehesa is an indication of his real political attitude and a portent of things to come. He and his peace delegate to Veracruz, the well-known journalist Filomeno Mata, considered Dehesa a friend, again with hindsight not difficult to understand. Mata personally appealed to Madero to intervene with the revolutionary leaders because Dehesa, "an old friend of ours, does not deserve to be treated like this."[9] A similar case is that of Carlos Herrera, the *jefe político* of Orizaba at the time of the Río Blanco labour dispute, who had been fired by Díaz. Herrera was quickly renamed *jefe político* after the taking of that city. He was obviously Madero's choice. However, a few days later, there was a huge demonstration, calmed only by the timely intervention of Rafael Tapia. The populace demanded and obtained Herrera's immediate resignation. In the eyes of the class represented by Madero, Dehesa, and Herrera, what was taking place in Mexico was not democracy but mob rule. Ironically, some members of that same upper class were already laying the blame for this at Madero's feet, convincing themselves, with the relentless logic of their coveted social position, that Madero represented the popular classes. It was an example of the type of political analysis that would eventually lead to his assassination.[10]

However, those from the middle, lower-middle, and lower classes, those who had fought for change under the Plan of San Luis Potosí, and those who, however slowly and reluctantly, had become its adherents now looked to the new government to undertake significant reform. In the first days of victory after Diaz's resignation, revolutionary leaders all over Veracruz pursued the cause of the revolution they had fought for and believed they had won. Unlike in Puebla, Porfirian town councils were made to resign and provisional authorities were sworn in, pledging their allegiance to uphold the principles of the Plan of San Luis Potosí.[11] The struggle in Veracruz between the moderate Maderistas and the rebel leaders was more prolonged and subtle. Madero was not able to consolidate his regime immediately. The rebel chiefs, who were replacing personnel from the old regime in the countryside and some towns, were not to know that the original revolution, the one they had offered their lives for, was already being revised.

From May 18 on, numerous towns in Veracruz were captured and the local Porfirian authorities replaced with loyal Maderistas. Local authorities were also replaced in the cantons of Huatusco, Papantla, Chicontepec, Jalacingo, and Misantla. The *jefe político* of Misantla, Francisco Canovas, decided to flee Misantla, leaving the cantonal headquarters open to the rebels. Esteban Márquez's force of some two hundred rebels, consisting almost entirely of Indians from the Puebla mountains, crossed over from Puebla. As in the south, the indigenous peoples, with the uprisings at Papantla in 1891 and 1896 still fresh in their minds and interested in the restoration of lands, made up the majority of the rebel contingents here. Similar to events in Misantla, in the canton of Cosamaloapan the *jefe político* and most of the judges deemed it prudent to flee. The correspondent there for *El Dictámen* commented on the disciplined behaviour of all the rebel troops. In some towns where there were no rebel forces, such as Zontecomatlán in Chicontepec, local Maderista adherents removed the Porfirian authorities themselves, later advising the junta. In all of these transactions, the proper legal documents were drawn up, signed, and dispatched with official seals. Only in a few towns did rebel forces have to resort to violence. The observation of His Majesty's consul in Veracruz, L. C. Nunn, that there was "very little sympathy for the revolutionary party in Veracruz, due to its prosperity" was simply ridiculous.[12] In all of these towns, the new mayors and authorities began dealing with local problems and dispensing justice even before the peace negotiations were completed. All over Veracruz, with the exception of the larger cities, the Maderista revolution was effectively, secured weeks before the treaty of Ciudad Juárez was signed; and even in the larger cities, as noted previously, there existed a state of seige.[13] After the treaty was signed and with the news of Diaz's resignation on May 25, Maderista forces in Veracruz quickly moved to secure their advantage. Now, more recruits than ever flocked to the Maderista banner.

Yet there were bound to be delays and confusion surrounding the news about the armistice and peace treaty. Although the military commander of Veracruz port, General Maas, informed his field officers of the armistice on May 18, only two days later did the provisional governor, Eliezer Espinosa, inform *jefes políticos.* Maderista military actions continued in the interim with rebels derailing passenger trains and robbing passengers.[14] Railway workers in Teziutlán refused to run the trains unless the rebel forces mounted armed guards on each unit. By now, the celebrations that would erupt in the entire country were beginning. Outside Córdoba, Gavira and Aguilar held court in their hastily improvised headquarters, where a commission of leading townspeople came out to greet them. These were feted with beer and cognac well into the night.[15]

Despite the euphoria of victory, however, the revolutionary junta was confronted with a series of problems, not the least of which was the curious situation of having to convince the revolutionary army to put itself under the command of the federal army, or at best to operate alongside the Porfirian federal forces until the new government could exert its control. This was, of course, easier said than done. Another problem was getting local revolutionary leaders with small bands to acknowledge other leaders stipulated by the junta. The chosen tactic was to invest the senior local leaders with authority in the hope that they would join the moderate ranks and convince lesser leaders to do so as well. For example, Robles Domínguez suggested to Gabriel Gavira that he order all the new *jefes políticos* to recognize his authority. Robles Domínguez himself, in an effort to support Gavira, referred all queries addressed to him on to the revolutionary commander-in-chief of Veracruz. Naturally, there were some rebel leaders who, having initiated actions by themselves, were reluctant to place themselves under someone else's authority. Some of the federal forces also refused to obey the orders the new government gave in accordance with the peace treaty. Both General Maas in Veracruz and Colonel de la Llave in Orizaba tried to hinder the arrival of revolutionary forces. Gavira had to cable the government requesting the resignation of both. Even the provisional governor was worried that the hostility of the Porfirian soldiers was beginning to infect the many workers waiting for Tapia's arrival in Orizaba.[16]

Difficulties were also encountered over the entry of Maderista forces into Xalapa. Aguilar had cabled General Maas requesting that he allow Miguel Ramos, camped outside Tlacolula with several hundred men, to enter peacefully. In addition, there were other rebel groups camped just outside the capital. General García Peña, the defender, signalled that he would allow their entry if they put themselves under his command. This Gavira objected to, cabling the new secretary of war, General Rascón. The secretary upheld Gavira's objection. Manuel López was put in charge of all the groups and entered Xalapa on June 5. Simultaneously, however, Esteban Márquez entered, put himself under Garcia Peña's orders in opposition to Gavira, and ordered a banquet in honour of the federal officer. Garrido Huerta, too, blowing a trumpet, entered the city, only to be arrested and thrown in jail by Garcia Peña. Nevertheless, the takeover proceeded in a relatively peaceful manner. Members of Gavira's staff – Raúl Gabriel Ruiz, Clemente Gaballo, Manuel Jiménez – and

Adalberto Palacios were ordered to Xalapa to carry out the necessary change of government. In the south, the takeover was relatively uneventful. Ochoa was able to enter Jáltipan, Minatitlán,
on May 31, and Carbajal, on the same day, Acayucan, from which
the federals had withdrawn.[17]

In Orizaba, by contrast, the changeover had its dangerous
moments, owing to the recalcitrance of the federal army. Rafael
Tapia, who had been operating nearby in Puebla state, reached
Orizaba on May 26. Seeing his small force, generals Manzano and
de la Llave opposed his entry, despite the multitude of factory
workers who had congregated at the entrance to the city. Tapia,
not having received specific orders, decided to force entry; the
governor had to beg Rascón to intervene to ask Tapia not to
enter with his troops in parade formation in order to avoid
any incident. Again, Gavira was obliged to go there to instigate
the changes himself. With the help of the interim governor,
Espinosa, who convinced the local Porfirians to concede, elections were held for the town council and a new Maderista *jefe
político*, José María Camacho, was sworn in. Yet Espinosa also
wrote to the interim president, de la Barra, to complain that
Gavira was misusing his military authority. Espinosa's argument
was that there had to be continuity in local administration. This
appears to be a plausible argument, but beyond it one glimpses
the hard fact that the only way the old Porfirians could salvage
something from the situation was to try to maintain control using
the ruse of administrative continuity.[18]

Thus emerged the first political difficulties for the new leaders.
On the one hand were the conservative (read ex-Porfirian) politicians like Dehesa, a friend of both Madero and Filomeno Mata,
supporting Madero's apparently anti-Científico stance. There
were other moderate revolutionaries too, intelligent, capable and
dedicated, who looked to Madero to carry out his promises
of a political revolution, that is, to respect the clauses of the
Constitution of 1857. Among these were men like Raúl G. Ruiz
and Clemente Gabay, who would steadfastly maintain that ideological position, switching sides as they reacted to perceived
betrayal. On the other hand were the local revolutionary leaders
– the winners, that is – like Gavira, Tapia, and Aguilar, consistent
Maderistas and soldiers from before the San Luis Potosí declaration, inclined to real political and social change. Among them
were also the latecomers, opportunists in the main like Márquez
and Huerta, who saw a golden chance to avenge their petty grievances or advance monetarily under the new government. Then

there were the common people, some of whom had sat back to wait for the outcome, workers who wanted an end to their wage oppression, Indians who wanted their land back, and *rancheros*, especially in the north, who had already reacted, and would react again, to their mistreatment by the oil companies.

At the outset, then, all was relatively calm and civilized. Díaz's train to the port city and exile had been attacked at the Puebla–Veracruz border station of Tepeyahualco, but the rebel leadership immediately dispatched a force to avoid any further incidents. Despite Diaz's personal unpopularity in the port because of the executions of 1879, he was treated with the respect and courtesy due a president. On the afternoon of his departure, on May 31, he was guarded by a battalion of sappers and the presidential guard, from each of whom, like Napoleon Bonaparte, he took his leave, and, accompanied by dignitaries and generals, he made his way to the quay and the steamship "Ipiranga," responding graciously to the "vivas" of the large crowd. As he mounted the gangplank, cannons of the battery on the Santiago bastion, near the *malecón* (sea wall), fired a twenty-one-gun salute while the military band played the national anthem.[19]

The Immediate Struggle over the Governorship, June 1911

Díaz was bid *adieu* with all honours; not so the Porifirian machinery of state. This was retained. With Díaz gone, the immediate political problem for Veracruz was the struggle to decide who would govern the state. Because the Maderista revolution had struck deep chords of discontent and awakened a resonance of real – that is, popular – democracy, the demands for social revolution among the broader populace began to manifest themselves after the political changes of May 1911. With the freedom to express themselves politically, with no fear of the reprisals that were so much a part of the daily political reality of the Porfiriato, Veracruzans entered the political fray with gusto.

Distinct from the conservative revolutionary wing represented by Dehesa, Madero, and Mata were two main ideological currents in Veracruz after May 1911. There were, first, the lower-middle-class and middle-class elements who had helped Madero to victory and wanted a strict application of the Constitution of 1857, which meant excluding the influence of anti-democratic (in their terms), conservative liberals led, they believed, by

Teodoro Dehesa. Second, there were the lower classes – workers, *campesinos*, Indians – stirred by the perceived promises of
just working conditions and wages or the return of stolen lands
contained in the Plan of San Luis Potosí. Both of these groups
believed the revolution had been made in its name, and both
were wrong. The revolution, as we shall see, was intended to
legitimize the continued march of "modernization," of capitalism, which made a mockery of the sacrifices sustained as well
as the beliefs generated, in part, by the struggle to overthrow
the Porfirian regime. The socio-economic system inherited from
the Porfiriato would not be touched; neither would the political
system. The only real change would be the replacement of some
of the manipulators at the top of the hierarchy.

Madero and his immediate circle were faced with a situation of
near anarchy in Veracruz. There were at least three different factions clamouring to be satisfied. There were, first, the local leaders of the Maderista uprising, revolutionaries like Gabriel Gavira,
Cándido Aguilar, and Rafael Tapia, who would insist on a settlement in keeping with the aims of the Plan of San Luis Potosí, an
attitude they had already demonstrated after liberating the city
of Córdoba on May 25. This group favoured the candidacy of
León Aillaud, a known Maderista sympathizer, who had been in
contact with Gavira in April. Their heavy-handed methods, however, often at odds with the "popular will" and therefore with
democratic principles, had already caused riots in places like
Amatlán.[20] They were supported by a leading Jalapeño Maderista,
Alfredo Alvarez, who claimed to speak in the name of Madero.
Second were the people of Xalapa, who demonstrated wildly
on the night of May 20 against the new provisional governor
Delgado, a known Dehesista, but in favour of Emilio Leycegui,
supposedly a supporter of Ramón Corral. And third was the
legislature, a holdover from the Porfirian regime, constitution-
ally responsible for an appointment that would satisfy the entire
state but caught in a number of crossfires.

Filomeno Mata, just released from six months jail, who had
been nominated as the peace delegate to Veracruz, had to cable
Madero asking him to come to the state capital to "calm the spirits." In addition, there were other leaders, newly incorporated
into the Maderista ranks, who wanted a place in the new government.[21] By June 1, the rebels, impeded by the federal army,
had still not entered Xalapa. Under considerable pressure from
the new government, however, the latter withdrew their opposition. On June 5, Miguel Ramos and Manuel López were able to

reach an agreement among themselves and with the federal garrison and were allowed to enter. Ramos then negotiated Dehesa's resignation, accepting Eliezer Espinosa as interim governor.[22] The second problem for the Maderistas was pacification. Madero had hoped that a person of Mata's impeccable anti-Porfirian credentials would be able to arbitrate between the fractious rebel groups in Xalapa. Seriously ill with rheumatism, however, Mata was not able to carry out the mission. He was only able to intervene for a few weeks in the middle of June, and then retired to the port city, where he died on July 2.[23] The continuing enmity between the old Porfirian military and the revolutionaries was also difficult to settle, leading to some significant clashes, the mosty serious of which took place in Xalapa. The issue at stake was the naming of the interim governor after Dehesa's resignation on June 21, 1911.[24]

Calming the spirits was easier said than done. Obviously, in the ensuing takeover, there would be confusion, and equally obviously this would be characterized as anarchy by some observers such as U.S. ambassador Wilson. It is also clear that the Maderistas, in order to conserve order, had to appoint municipal officials on the spot and wait for calm to hold elections. Changing personnel was a delicate matter not always handled delicately. Hasty replacements caused confusion and sometimes violence, as when Gavira deposed the *jefe político* of Minatitlán, ordering him to leave Coatzacoalcos, but without replacing him. The military commander of the southern zone had to complain that the troops of the 30th Battalion would be compromised if the rebels tried to exert their authority.[25] In addition, state authorities were not always willing to accept the replacements made by the revolutionary groups.

And yet the people were themselves demanding quick and effective replacement of the old Porfirian officials. On hearing that Gaudalupe Ochoa had captured Chinameca, women from Jáltipan marched to that town demanding that he do the same for them. They lined the route with flowers for the revolutionary troops, welcoming them with "hurrahs" and pro-revolutionary slogans. Some women in Jáltipan stuck pistols in their belts and oversaw the replacement of local officials. In Orizaba, there was "immense jubilation" when the news got out that Gavira and Tapia were coming to change the personnel. However, after at least ten years of pent-up emotions, changing the guard was not to be as easy as Madero had thought. Nor was everyone satisfied. Complained *El Cosmopolita* of Orizaba: "The way in which Mr.

Gavira is governing is little short of anarchy. On the one hand he orders something, on the other he is disobeyed."[26]

On June 19, Francisco Delgado was nominated to replace Eliezer Espinosa. Delgado was well known in Xalapa, as he had a small packing business (*cajonería*) there and was well liked by the working class. Immediately, a demonstration in his favour took place but was quickly countered by another equally fervent demonstration in favour of Léon Aillaud, the choice of Gavira and Aguilar. Aillaud's supporters burst into the Palacio del Gobierno breaking windows. In the evening yet another demonstration took place, also against Delgado, but this time in favour of Emilio Leycegui. The crowd went to his house and made him accompany them in their parade around the city, and apparently forced him to accept their nomination as candidate for the provisional governorship. Mata telegraphed Madero from Xalapa that Alfredo Alvarez, in Madero's name, had urged various legislative deputies to vote for Aillaud. Mata's recommendation to Madero was that any other candidature but Leycegui's would cause "grave conflicts."[27] Part of the problem was that Delgado himself, and his appointee as *jefe político* of the canton of Xalapa, José María Camacho, were considered Dehesistas.[28]

On the night of June 21, the rivalry among the various rebel bands came to a head in Xalapa, and many innocent lives were lost. The incident started when federal army troops under General García Peña of the Federal Geographic Commission removed several cases of ammunition from the governor's palace. They were opposed by several Maderista groups, although one group, under Esteban Márquez (the first rebels to enter Xalapa), assisted them. In the evening, another group of Maderistas tried to free one of their number from the jail. They opened fire on the police, killing and wounding several. Unfortunately, that evening the park, which is beside the governor's palace, was filled with people celebrating Aillaud's nomination at a band concert. They were caught in the crossfire, and between sixty and one hundred were killed. The regular army was able to restore control eventually, and the Márquez faction hurriedly left town.[29] Alvarez sent a hurried telegram to Madero that the soldiers were firing on Maderistas. Aguilar made a similar charge. It is not clear what happened; the most even-handed and plausible account came from General Peña, who reported that one group of Maderistas had attacked the palace guarded by Márquez's men. They were shouting that they would depose Leycegui "with fire and blood" and impose Aillaud. To complicate matters, Aguilar was begging Madero to withdraw the federal forces.[30]

These events illustrate the tremendous unrest and political turmoil that the revolution had unleashed in Xalapa and other parts of Veracruz. What is most interesting, however, is how the revolutionary political problems were solved. How Veracruz was pacified, and under what political faction, tells us much about Madero's thinking, or shift in thinking, or capitulation to a particular group, however one chooses to phrase it. He has been labelled "moderately conservative" by David LaFrance,[31] a view with which I concur, although that term does not adequately capture Madero's politics, one very significant aspect of which was his shift from federalism to centralism.

For the moment, in Xalapa, he was forced to go along with the main Maderista leaders. On June 22, the legislature was still reported as favouring Leycegui, while the revolutionary troops under Aguilar, who was also acting on the orders of the chief of the revolution in Veracruz, Gabriel Gavira, were supporting Aillaud. Aillaud arrived that evening amidst a tumult. A street vendor tried to assassinate him. The perpetrator, Eucaro Huerta, local agent for the Corralista newspaper *El Debate*, was almost beaten to death. *El Diario* reported that the demonstrations in Aillaud's favour were the biggest seen in years. From the various newspaper reports, one can only conclude that there were huge groups of supporters for each candidate. Madero then decided to accept the wishes of the stronger and more insistent revolutionary forces, those led by Gavira and Aguilar. So he backtracked, assuring Aguilar that Filomeno Mata had misinterpreted his instructions, that he, Madero, did not oppose Aillaud's nomination. This meant that he had to ensure Aillaud's nomination by asking Leycegui to withdraw. He praised the latter to the hilt, explaining that Leycegui was not at all responsible for the events of June 21, that the shooting had not been instigated by Alvarez and Maderistas but by Dehesistas, and begged Leycegui to co-operate.

This latter charge that Dehesistas were at fault could not be corroborated from the documents. Violence was not Dehesa's style. On the other hand, the accusation does show that Madero was not loath to play the opportunist if it would further his goals. At the same time, he tried to cover his tracks by cabling Aguilar a copy of a telegram to Mata in which he accused Mata of not understanding his previous communication. Madero maintained that he had not opposed the decision to nominate Aillaud, but that he had had the best reports of Leycegui's ability to calm the state. With Leycegui's obliging withdrawal, however, Madero's task was made easier. He was grateful to Leycegui for this political gift and counselled Gavira to treat Leycegui well because his "situation is quite abnormal."[32] By June 23, order had been restored. Aillaud was appointed provisional governor on June 24, the assumption of power made easier by the departure of Dehesa for the port city with his family a few days later.[33] One might argue that Aillaud was not the best choice for governor since he had no experience in government. His job as an agent (*apoderado*) for the Varela railway hardly qualified him. Nevertheless, in an initial interview with *El Dictámen*, Aillaud laid out the principles under which he would govern. They were, somewhat unimaginatively, taken almost verbatim from the Plan of San Luis Potosí.

With the problem of the governorship temporarily settled, albeit in favour of the moderate revolutionary faction, the Maderista government could turn its attention to negotiating the peaceful transfer of power in those towns and municipalities that had not yet been visited by representatives of the new government. For example, Gavira had to order the *jefe político* of Minatitlán, who was supported by federal troops to resign. A petition of ordinary citizens was sent to *Gobernación* asking those troops to withdraw so the people could give a hearty welcome to the rebels, a request that was wisely approved. On July 1, Guadalupe Ochoa, after replacing the authorities in Minatitlán, continued south and was able to enter the port of Coatzacoalcos.[34] In the neighbouring canton of Acayucan, Carbajal and Paredes changed personnel in several municipalities. Both reported that in every town the new provisional authorities were welcomed by the people, who showed great support for Madero.[35] In the north, the *jefe político* of Tuxpán for many years, Arturo Nuñez was removed amid great jubilation and felt it wise to leave the city. Still, the changes could not all be made overnight. There were simply not enough qualified revolutionary personnel to go into every municipality quickly. This quite rightly troubled the revolutionaries, who feared that delays might give the Porfirians time to avoid such changes. It also troubled the state authorities who were afraid of riots. But citizens resorted to more peaceful and, indeed, more imaginative protest tactics. In Acatlán, for example, citizens refused to pay taxes to the Porfirian municiality, declaring that they only recognized Gavira's authority.[36]

The Demobilization of Rebel Forces

The next problem facing the new government was that of demo-
bilizing and paying the many rebel soldiers. These were demanding back pay dating from the signing of the Treaty of Ciudad
Juárez, but the ministry of finance did not seem to have the
money to pay them. To guarantee some semblance of order, all
revolutionary troops were put under orders of the minister of the
interior. In addition, Rafael Tapia was named state Rurales commander, with the rank of general. Aguilar himself pointed out to
Madero that the confusion of disbanding, reforming, and again
disbanding his troops was having a demoralizing effect on them.
He also pointed out that, because of continuing and dangerous
intrigues by the dehesistas, the "situation in the state is still
delicate." On July 11, the state finally paid him 2,000 pesos to
disband his troop. Younger officers such as Raúl G. Ruiz, Julio
Nájera, and Antonio Solleiro wrote to President de la Barra, complaining about Aguilar's order to disband. Their men were claiming eight days pay and needed horses and resources to get home.
Without these, they would probably be forced to rob or commit
other crimes.[37] Despite the tremendous confusion, including,
among other things, lack of precise information regarding the
exact of insurgent forces in the state, the disbandments were
notably quick and without incident. By the end of July, only 250
out of an estimated six to seven hundred men remained in the
revolutionary forces. An additional seven hundred were under
Tapia's command in the Rurales, of which only three hundred
were budgeted for.[38] By the last week in July, the new *jefes políticos*
were in place and sending in their reports.

Revising the Revolution

For the next two months, Aillaud governed the state amidst
increasing unpopularity. He was suggested for the governorship
because he had been an opponent of Dehesa and was nominated
by Aguilar. But he soon began to experience difficulty and even
open opposition. Ironically, his growing unpopularity stemmed
from the fact that he had been supported by many members of
the legislature as well as *jefes políticos*, by the de la Barra transition regime, and was therefore suspect in the eyes of the radicals. Gabriel Gavira in particular had not been happy with the
choice. Aillaud was, indeed, one of the conservative Maderistas.
He was supported by pro-Científico newspapers like *El Imparcial*

and *El Diario* and was disliked by the more democratic, populist, Maderistas. As governor, he was fairly arrogant. He did not answer the president's letters and refused to replace unpopular *jefes políticos*. Madero attempted to get him to resign; he responded with intransigence, and Madero had to exert considerable pressure to dislodge him. Aillaud did eventually resign in early December but tried to slip his very unpopular secretary of government, Huidobro de Azúa, in as interim governor. In the meantime, the legislature had called for elections on November 26, but, because of the unrest in the state, and in particular the persistent rumours that Madero was trying to impose his choice on Veracruzans, the elections were postponed until January 28.[39]

More discontent in Veracruz resulted from the removal of Aillaud, which was to earn Madero continued criticism for apparently violating his own principles of "effective suffrage."[40] De Azúa also did not last long; as his replacement Madero supported the legislature's choice of Manuel Alegre, whose specific mandate was to organize the elections for governor for the rest of the legislative period. The choice of Alegre was a logical one for the legislature. Although a Veracruzan, Alegre was better known as an organizer for the Anti-Re-electionist Party in Mexico City, yet he was sympathetic to Madero's way of thinking. He was, however, thought to have been a Dehesista, not least for his re-employment of a considerable number of Dehesa's supporters in the administration. In fact, special troops had to be sent to Xalapa because the government feared demonstrations at his inauguration.[41] Many Maderistas complained that the political clock was running in reverse: Madero was shifting his support from the moderate Maderistas to the legislature, which, as noted earlier, reflected the old regime. On January 8, 1912, in northern Veracruz, there was great unrest and threats of an uprising. These came amidst the disquietude caused by the Vázquez Gómez revolt in the north of Mexico (see below). Posters were found decrying the "hypocrisy of Madero," and federal troops had to be sent. Gavira's followers were cutting up as well, as part of the campaign for their leader, who sought the governorship. The entire state was in great turmoil due to Alegre's continued replacement of government employees with Dehesistas, and his appintment of friends as *jefes políticos*, so as to ensure his own election as governor.[42]

Others were working to ensure the continued march of the revolution. Radical Maderistas like Cándido Aguilar's brother Silvestre, *jefe político* of Córdoba, were trying to resuscitate

Cándido's armed force as well as radical Maderista politics, to which Madero himself was by this time opposed. To combat the radical Maderistas, Alegre organized a volunteer force of the middle class in the cantons, to assist the police and Rurales. The politics of this situation is obvious in a letter Alegre wrote to Madero, in which the governor remarked that in his opinion Madero never came "to do revolutionary things, but to be patriotic and work culturally." He continued by defining what he thought were revolutionary ideals, such as "respect for public liberty, compliance with the law and the dispensation of justice."[43] Obviously, social revolution was not one of his ideals, nor was anything more than a restricted electoral franchise. Very significant for our assessment of Madero is the fact that he never objected to Alegre's definition. Thus, Madero had shifted support away from the radical democrats of the revolutionary struggle to the conservative forces, the Dehesistas, the Porfirians who had run the state since 1892 and who were adamantly opposed by a majority of the people. Another shift was to take Madero into the camp of the Científicos or neo-Científicos, a shift that would soon cost him his life. In Veracruz, that shift was accomplished by a bizarre turn in local politics.

At the end of January, the elections for provisional governor were held for the remainder of the legislative term, to end in December. The two leading contestants were Gabriel Gavira, a heavyweight revolutionary, and Lagos Cházaro, a "bohemian" *hacendado*. Lagos Cházaro was a former member of the Anti-Re-electionist "Liberal Club" of Orizaba. He had worked with Gavira, Aguilar, and Tapia. From this angle, at least, he was an acceptable candidate. The election was the occasion for much abuse by both sides, but it was also a contest in which the ideological battle lines were clear. Gavira had a large following among the working classes, while Lagos was the candidate of the elites. The election results, which showed Gavira as the winner, created a dilemma for the president and were to prove disastrous in the attempt to consolidate the government and achieve order. Madero himself in a letter to Alegre concedes that the results favoured Gavira, in an official telegram that ironically also speaks of maintaining the "liberty of the process."[44] But "liberty" obviously meant the choice of the legislature, not the people, and in that august body only a certain class was represented, having been last elected while Díaz was president and Dehesa governor.

Gavira was livid at this travesty of democracy, which was in direct conflict with the principles in the name of which he had supported the revolution. He declared he would hang all the deputies from the balcony of the governor's palace if he were not conceded the victory. Then he promptly took off and "pronounced" against the state government, hoping to connect with the followers of the Emilio Vázquez Gómez rebellion, which had begun in the previous December. For a time, there were some fears that Cándido Aguilar would join him, together with Vazquistas who were now operating in various parts of Veracruz, but the fears proved unfounded. In any case, the only old revolutionary not to waver was Rafael Tapia, head of the state Rurales, who was ready to regroup forces around Córdoba in case Aguilar rebelled. Gavira was soon caught and sent to Ulúa. During February and March, Veracruz erupted with revolutionary movements, under various banners but all against Madero. The government's belated attempts at land distribution added further fuel to the fire.[45]

Lagos Cházaro took over on February 15 as provisional governor, while Veracruz continued to seethe. Gaviristas, Vazquistas, and numerous other groups as well as bandits continued to plague the state. The oil companies, for example, had to ask the state government for help in guarding their facilities. By March 1912, the newspaper *La Nueva Era* was claiming that Madero had compromised the revolution: too many of the old guard were still around; in fact, no revolution had occurred at all. On March 25, Pascual Orozco, who had been sent to put down the Vazquista rebellion, convinced the rebels to join him in a new uprising under the Plan Orozquista. In a desperate attempt to alleviate the unrest, influential Veracruzans came up with the creative solution of assembling the poorer classes and workers in the cinemas for conferences and lectures on the political situation. The governor's solution, however, was neither a political nor pedagogic but a military one. Work with the organization of volunteer forces was ordered to proceed *post haste.*[46]

To this revolutionary cauldron was added the gubernatorial campaign in June, 1912, for the new legislative period 1912-16. No fewer than nine candidates were fielded, including Guillermo Pous, Alegre, the Dehesista candidate, Hilario Rodríguez Malpica, a naval officer and chief of the presidential staff, the millionaire Tómas Braniff, who openly bought votes, and Antonio Pérez Rivera, an unknown, who had served as *jefe político* of Xalapa under Dehesa and was the candidate of the Catholic Party. From the start, the campaign was characterized by disorder and charges of meddling and corruption. By this time, Dehesa had turned against Madero and had started to campaign seriously against him. Braniff accused the president of mixing in Veracruz affairs, a charge that led to Lagos Cházaro being temporarily replaced by Manuel Levi. Lagos Cházaro was accused of taking money from Braniff in order to fix the election, ordered to Chapultepec, and sent on sick leave: it was *opera bouffe* at its best. By July 1, the unknown conservative Pérez Rivera was pulling ahead of the pack. With money that he must have received from outside sources, he had set up more political clubs than any other candidate. The obvious must also have been obvious to Cándido Aguilar, who requested and was given an unlimited leave of absence. There is every evidence that the election was rigged, a fact not lost on contemporaries.[47]

One of the most surprising turns in this catalogue of turbulent events was the behaviour of Gabriel Gavira, the erstwhile radical revolutionary. Languishing in prison, he had been consulted, and his support wooed by almost every candidate. Eventually, he threw his weight behind Pérez Rivera, whom he considered honest. Part of the truth about this election is that Pérez Rivera was Gustavo Madero's man. As was mentioned above, he also belonged to the Catholic Party (Partido Católico, or CP), which entered into an alliance with the Científicos in the Mexican Senate, after the opening of the Mexican Congress on September 14, 1912.[48]

Taken together, these facts explain ex-governor Dehesa's stance. Dehesa as well as other anti-Científicos saw Pérez Rivera as an enemy, and *vice versa*. He and his political friends tried as best they could to have Manuel Alegre named governor instead of Pérez Rivera. Possibly, Dehesa saw in Pérez Rivera, if not a Científico, then certainly a close collaborator, and he discerned futher evidence of the direction the central government was taking. Because he adamantly opposed that direction, Dehesa's attitude towards Madero changed to one of considerable hostility. However, he was not successful in persuading the legislature to appoint Alegre. His plan having failed, Dehesa, still protesting that he had not obstructed Madero but that the government was morally corrupt, went off into exile.[49]

The Nature of Maderismo

Some historians have long maintained that the murders of Madero and Pino Suárez were the result of a historical nostalgia, a desire to return to the peace and stability of the Porfirian regime. Huerta's *coup d'état* was therefore, for them, a reactionary one.[50] But the degree to which Veracruzans accepted that coup owes less to any nostalgia than to the perception that Madero not only had failed to deliver the goods but had returned to the hated centralism that had characterized the old regime. The specific feeling in Veracruz was that once again central power and, indeed, the possibility of personal gain had been concentrated narrowly, this time in the hands of one family, Madero's. Why then the at least benign support for Huerta, a military man, a member of the caste that had historically also backed centralist solutions to Mexico's political problems? For Veracruzans, the attraction of that regime did not lie with Huerta, but with Félix Díaz, the man who was identified with an adamantly anti-Científico (read: anti-centralist), political agenda.

The political climate that led to the assassinations of Madero and Pino Suárez, therefore, was by no means fortuitous. Almost from the beginning of his regime, Madero's actions, or lack of them, came under intense scrutiny and attracted considerable criticism; to blame de la Barra, as some historians have attempted, is to put the shoe on the wrong foot.[51] I wish to stress, that I am not attempting a thorough critique of Madero's politics – such a critique would necessitate an entire work in itself – but am interested mainly in the public's opinion of him, what Veracruzans and others saw as the characteristics of his government. Since it is this that in the end affords a government its legitimacy, and here as elsewhere influences the success or failure of any political venture, we need to know why Veracruzans thought and felt about Maderismo as they did, and how they reacted to the playing out of the revolution.

Even before Madero's entry into Mexico City, and the inauguration of the provisional presidency, he began to earn criticism. In the simplest of terms, he sold out the revolution before it began. In some eyes, his actions and negotiations with the Porfirian regime were the legitimization of the latter. Only thus could revolutionaries such as Zapata interpret his demand that revolutionary forces disarm and, in so doing, surrender *de jure* to the federal army they had just outmanoeuvred in the field. To other, kinder critics, he was a hostage of Porfirismo.[52]

One of the first acts to earn Madero censure was his treatment of high-ranking party officials on his left. Francisco Vázquez Gómez and his brother Emilio had supported Madero from the beginning of the anti-re-election campaign in 1909. Both had been with him in San Antonio during the heady days of the revolution. With victory, Emilio had been named secretary of the interior. However, pressured by conservatives afraid of Emilio's "radical" bent, Madero dropped him from the cabinet in August in favour of García Granados, accusing Emilio, among other things, of distributing arms to the people. David LaFrance maintains that Madero was unhappy at Emilio's handling of the crisis in Puebla over the disbandment of rebel forces. This must have been a contributing factor, but, whatever Madero's reasons, Emilio's removal from the cabinet sent serious shock waves through the revolutionary ranks, followed a short time later by a major tremor as Madero dissolved the Anti-Re-electionist Party and formed the Partido Constitutional Progresista. Francisco Vázquez Gómez was replaced as his vice-presidential running mate by the lesser known Pino Suárez.[53]

To many revolutionaries as well as ordinary citizens, Madero had not only legitimized the Porfiriato, he had also adopted its methods, foremost amongst these the hated Científico politics. In June, *La Mañana* could remark that the people wanted "Sufragio Efectivo, no el Sufragio Madero y familia." A payment of 700,000 pesos to Gustavo for expenses incurred during the revolution also earned bitter criticism. For this and other reasons, *El Ahuizote* accused Madero of outright nepotism. But nepotism was one thing, linking Madero with the Científicos quite another. Nor was this latter criticism muted. On October 17, the Mexican deputy Carlos Trejo y Lerdo de Tejada cited Rafael Hernández, Madero's cousin and both secretary of development and chairman of the National Agrarian Commission, as the chief legatee of Cientificismo. It was Hernández who blocked Luis Cabrera's appointment to the cabinet, advising his cousin that Cabrera was an enemy of capital and that his appointment would alarm foreign investors. Worse yet, Ernesto Madero, secretary of the Treasury, was overheard remarking that "nothing of Limantour's system and personal administration will be changed, because I am an admirer of his."[54] For many Mexicans, by December of 1911, there was little doubt that Cientificismo was what Madero's government was all about.[55] The core of the matter was best expressed by Mexico's most blunt, satirical, and "alternative" news organ, *El Ahuizote*. Demonstrating its almost Swiftian sense of outrage, it suggested that the only proper rhetoric to describe the political situation was that of the demonic:

> The Científico group of today, the octopus of the gustavisto hordes, which has transformed the flag of liberty into cheques, pressures

and tries to impose its governors on the states to renovate the dis-
graceful pact that, during the last regime, ended Mexico's political
life. It also imposed Manuel Alegre on Veracruz.[56]

In a brilliant and evocative cartoon, *El Ahuizote* showed the
people (*el pueblo*) being throttled by two hands, one marked
"*Sufragio Efectivo*," the other "*No Reelección*," and vomiting pesos
into a hat held by Madero. Standing watching were officials from
a company called Ojo Parado Co. (Glass Eye and Co., a reference
to Gustavo Madero); they were general manager, Gustavo Wood,
secretary F.I. Wood, and treasurer Uncle Wood. Little did most
Mexicans know at this time that Madero had apparently never
had anything much, if at all, against the Científicos. He allowed
Limantour, with whom his family was friendly, to exercise an
influence on his governmental choices that is difficult to understand, except if one accepts the previous argument.[57]

More revealing to the revolutionaries, however, was that
Madero apparently ignored their constant warnings of supposed
Científico plots. Alfredo Robles Domínguez was contacted in
early June enroute to Veracruz about Científico subversives. That
same month, he was made aware that the telegrapher in Madero's
office was in the pay of the Científicos. An insider reported
that Gustavo Madero offered a Mr. Capdevielle a lucrative post
for his services, pointing out that Capdevielle "has always blas-
phemed against Madero. He is and was a Científico." Somewhat
ironically, the informant advised that Capdevielle should not
be employed. The governor of Guerrero, Francisco Figueroa,
also warned Madero in November that he must remove all the
Porfirian elements in his cabinet as they were conspiring against
him. The last conspiracy, he warned, was hatched in Limantour's
house in Popotla." Madero should know, he continued, "that the
Científicos are your worst enemies; remove them from positions
and the management of banks and finance, if you want to liberate
yourself from the odious bourgeoisie.[58]

These charges led Robles Domínguez and other Maderista
supporters to send Madero and Pino Suárez an impassioned
and vigorous plea in October. Noting that his cabinet was to
include Rafael Hernández, Manuel Calero, and Ernesto Madero,
they counselled the president-elect that "under the banner of
'*Sufragio Efectivo* and *No Reelección*'" he "cannot appoint people
who are sympathizers and friends of José Yves Limantour,
because people will doubt your promises." The revolution, they
continued, "was made not only to destroy the dictatorship of Díaz,

but also the oligarchy and plutocracy headed up by Limantour....
The causes of most revolutions are economic; it is necessary
to destroy the financial *caciquismo*."[59] Another charge hurled at
Madero was his interference in the electoral process in various
states. We have already noted his actions in Veracruz; these methods were by no means confined to that state. A political manifesto
written in Hermosillo, Sonora, in November also accused the
federal government of trying to influence the election there.
One candidate wrote directly to Gustavo Madero complaining
that the latter's help would "resound negatively in my fight
for the fourth district of Nuevo León." Characterizing Gustavo
Madero's involvement as "undemocratic," he asked him to desist.
Commented *La Opinión* of Veracruz: "The problems all stem from
trying to establish democracy with dictatorial methods."[60]
    Madero himself was perfectly aware of the criticism. It led
him to pen a detailed explanation to Mexico's governors in the
attempt to maintain some popularity, not to speak of a semblance
of order. In this letter he blamed the press in particular, not only
for circulating "false rumours" causing "confusion" among all
classes of citizens, but even worse, for "causing alarm amongst
foreigners who have come to this country to help it grow." His
subsequent attempts to muzzle the press earned him even more
censure;[61] and his attempts at explanation did nothing to halt the
barrage of criticism. One of de la Barra's minsters even went as
far as to suggest "that the bullet that would kill Madero would
also save the Republic." De Zayas Enríquez, former critic of the
Porfiriato, rejected a post in the Madero cabinet, saying that
Madero had lost the opportunity to "establish a firm government" and accusing the new president of hypocrisy when his
supporters ended a Reyes campaign rally in Mexico City with violence, as well as over his attempts to control the press. Adding to
all this internal criticism was the hefty body of news reports from
north of the border, which made the U.S. government uneasy
about Madero's ability to protect its citizens and their property.[62]
    My own reading of Maderismo, therefore, is the opposite of
the more traditional view expressed by Meyer and Sherman
that "Madero's hands were tied and his energies diverted by a
series of revolts that broke out gainst him before he even had a
chance to make himself comfortable in the presidential chair."[63]
Perhaps Madero was as overwhelmed by the difficulty of governing Mexico as he was by the high cost of demolishing the fortress of San Juan de Ulúa.[64] Nonetheless, I believe that Madero
was the source of his own problems. He had no intention of

carrying out a revolutionary program, whatever that could be. He was besieged by the conservative elements of the new government, and could not entertain political policies that the left, his own revolutionary movement, wanted. Madero's mentality had been formed in an era in which the word "democracy" had a very limited meaning. I doubt if his understanding of it differed substantially from that of his predecessor, and this political philosophy was obvious from the first. Madero had no intention of carrying out the implied promises of the Plan of San Luis Potosí, but to avoid these he had to resort to the political trickery that characterized the Porfiriato. Unfortunately for him, he was not a Díaz. Madero's mistake was to believe naively, that he could govern with a limited democracy and fool the rest of Mexico into believing there really had been change. Many of his former political allies, however, saw through the ruse and drew the necessary consequences. The real revolution – or to put it differently, "the popular phase" of it – resumed (rather than began, as in Shadle's argument) in late 1911.[65]

The Reaction to Maderismo

From the time of Madero's inauguration, some Veracruzans began to have second thoughts about where Maderismo was taking them. Armed with the confidence of battle, shortlived as that confidence was, some former revolutionaries demanded that the government (that is, Madero) live up to the promises contained in the Plan of San Luis Potosí. Madero, whatever one mights say about his so-called idealism, his expectations, and his "apostolic"[66] qualities, could not satisfy everyone. In the end, he satisfied no one. His program appealed neither to Veracruzan conservatives and moderates, who charged him with Cientificismo, nor to many radical revolutionaries, who expected social changes.

Madero's first open break with the principles of his own Maderista movement, as well as some of his better known rebel generals, came barely two months after the installation of the interim government. Emilio Vázquez Gómez, the secretary of the interior, refused to follow up on the shooting of four Germans and one Spaniard in the Puebla textile factory, La Covadonga, and was forced to resign. Vázquez Gómez was not only considered the cabinet spokesman for the left, but he was also well known and liked in Veracruz, where his brother Francisco had a small *hacienda* outside Coatepec. As a consequence of his resignation, four famous rebel generals – Camerino Mendoza, P. A. Martínez, Ernesto Guerra, and Heriberto Jara – resigned their commands. In their open letter to Madero, they also complained about the continued incarceration of revolutionary comrades, implying that they had misunderstood Madero's stated goals and policies. Mendoza then began stockpiling arms and dynamite, mainly around his home near the Santa Rosa factory in Orizaba. An uprising to restore Vázquez Gómez planned for August 30 failed to materialize, as the government got wind of it, but all four generals were quickly arrested and sent to Mexico City for trial. Madero and the government appeared to be less interested in Mendoza's potential for rebellion than they were of his suspected allegiance to the Plan of Texcoco announced by Andrés Molina Enríquez. Since no connection was proven, by September 5, all four had regained their liberty.[67] Yet the ouster of Vázquez Gómez had serious consequences for Veracruz politics.

Other Maderistas, definitely feeling cheated of the promises of the Maderista program, did resort to arms. The Maderista leader from Minatitlán, Guadalupe Ochoa, was implicated in a plot with a group of Magonistas who were heading for Tabasco to begin an uprising there. The news was sufficiently serious for the Veracruz government to solicit security reports in September from all districts. It took no chances: troops from the 19th Battalion were ordered to protect the oil wells of Pearson's Aguila Oil Company in the south. Ochoa was arrested but nothing could be proven.[68] Another uprising in the northern part of the state was more worrisome, but was also quickly quashed. At the end of August 1911, the former chief of staff for Francisco Vázquez Gómez, Emilio Acosta, entered Pánuco with a band of about thirty-three men, disarmed the Rurales, and took about three hundred dollars from the treasury, proclaiming his dissatisfaction with the federal government. Acosta was arrested but was able to escape from prison. In January, he began another movement on behalf of the Vazquistas but was quickly captured by the townspeople of Tampico.[69]

These minuscule and abortive uprisings, if they may be called that, testified to the growing unpopularity of the Maderistas. Yet in the October 1911 presidential elections, Madero won by a large margin, and the conservative electorate chose Madero's running mate, Pino Suárez, over Francisco Vázquez Gómez. With Bernardo Reyes in San Antonio and Emilio Vázquez Gómez in El Paso, both foaming at the mouth over their defeat and plotting revolution, Madero's victory at the polls appeared pyrrhic at best. Mexico was far from pacified, and Veracruz, says Charles Cumberland, "was on the verge of rebellion."[70] Rumours of a Reyista rebellion in Veracruz were becoming stronger. Rodolfo Reyes disembarked from Veracruz at the beginning of November, ostensibly to join his father. General Peña was reported at the head of Reyista groups in Catemaco; from Papantla in the north and Coscomatepec, canton of Huatusco, there were reports of a buildup of arms and supplies; and some former Maderista officers were resigning their positions in order, it was thought, to be free to join an insurrection.[71]

Because of the continuing unrest in Veracruz and Aillaud's inability to pacify the state, but also because of his alleged administrative incompetence, not to speak of corruption, the Veracruz legislature relieved him of the governorship, appointing Manuel Alegre in his place. On December 11, three hundred additional troops were sent to Xalapa under the orders of General Peña. Observers immediately concluded that the central government had interfered.[72] Why? Both Madero and the legislature represented the class that had the most to fear from a radical interpretation of the revolution. These men were not only all property owners, the privileged of Veracruzan society; they were mainly holdovers from the previous regime. It is no accident, then, that an old supporter of Madero's with revolutionary credentials reaching back to the formation of the Anti-Re-electionist party, who was a vice-president of the new Partido Constitucional Progresista, was appointed as the new interim governor.[73]

Alegre's instructions were clear: pacify the state. To this end, two means, one political and one military, were utilized. Alegre asked that a reserve commander Major Benito Vargas Barranco, ex-secretary of the revolutionary junta in Puebla, be sent to Veracruz on a special mission around Coatepec, the nature of which I could not ascertain. Since this was the area in which the Vázquez Gómez brothers had property, there is a possible connection. Barranco was named visitador (inspector) of *jefes políticos* in the state and, in March, commander of the 36th Rurales Corps. Second, with Madero's express agreement, a regional armed force consisting of three hundred infantry and two hundred mounted soldiers was set up. That this was a conservative Maderista coup was unmistakeable. Madero explicitly ordered Alegre to make sure there was no trouble with the Aguilar brothers, especially Silvestre, the *jefe político* of Córdoba. Both of the latter had imposed Aillaud on the state in June 1911. But

Cándido Aguilar himself had been fighting Zapata in the state of Morelos since August and was thus temporarily out of the way.[74] In December 1911, the Plan of Tacubaya, announcing Emilio Vázquez Gómez as provisional president, was proclaimed. By January 1912, a number of uprisings on his behalf had begun in Zacatecas, Sinaloa, and Chihuahua. In Veracruz, too, the movement, albeit small, had its adherents. Although General Villar, officer in command in Veracruz, declared in an interview with *La Nueva Era* that all was absolutely quiet in the state, rebels of unknown affiliation had appeared on the western border with the state of Puebla, in the canton of Zongólica. The *jefe político* frantically requested that troops be stationed between the area and the cantonal seat as a precaution.[75] While these plans and plots were taking shape, Gabriel Gavira was also fuming over his defeat in the December election. Deciding that his only choice was an armed struggle against the state government he, and a few supporters, launched a rebellion. They were soon caught and jailed in Misantla. In December and January, Cándido Aguilar showed his disenchantment by trying to discredit both Manuel Alegre and Lagos Cházaro. For him, both represented the return of Dehesismo, against which he had fought so ardently. But Madero would hear none of it and on February 10 shipped him off to the north as commander of the 38th Rurales, to fight against Orozco.[76]

The first real threat occurred in the north. In January, Emilio Acosta threatened the oil fields around El Ebano in San Luis Potosí, attempting to link up with an obscure revolutionary in Veracruz, Ramón R. Berrenedea. Known mainly in his canton of Tantoyuca, Berrenedea had been appointed military chief in the failed Reyista invasion a few months before but was worrisome to the government because of the region in which he was operating. In addition, Higinio Aguilar was supposed to have troops near the El Potrero oil field of the El Aguila Company.[77] Cándido Aguilar himself was suspect; this was one of the reasons he was posted far away from Veracruz. Even his old friend General Tapia suspected that he might be so disillusioned with events in the state that he was considering rebellion. Another former comrade and stalwart Anti-Re-electionist, Robles Domínguez, had just accused Madero of selling out the revolution, so there might just have been some truth to Tapia's suspicions.[78]

By the first week of February, there were isolated armed uprisings throughout the state. There was no coordinated rebellion, yet the presence of so many different groups in so many places spoke of a deep discontent in the state. Between February and June, bands of between twenty to two hundred men roamed Veracruz, in the north around Tampico, Tuxpán, and Tantoyuca, in the centre around the capital as well as the Orizaba-Córdoba axis, and in the south in the Tuxtlas, Acayucan, and Minatitlán. There were also reported Indian uprisings. Foreigners were alarmed as *haciendas* were a favourite target. Telegraph wires were continuously being cut, trains derailed, and the treasuries of small towns removed. Taking no chances, the government began arresting whomever they suspected of remotely qualifying as rebels on the mere grounds of being related to someone who was. However, the government did not have sufficient forces to patrol the countryside as well as the towns, nor the resources to do so. At a time when he needed rifles and ammunition, the governor of Veracruz was forced into an argument with the secretary of finance over how much money the state owed the central government.[79]

By the last week of February, shortly after the new provisional governor, Lagos Cházaro, was inaugurated, rebels were making their presence felt all over Veracruz. Some of these supported Gabriel Gavira; others were Vazquistas, aided by some Zapatistas in the state. The government did not know on whom it could count. Pedro and Clemente Gabay were in prison for expressing unfavourable sentiments about the state government, and an ex-*jefe político* of Orizaba, Angel Juarico, as well as the popular Maderista leader Manuel Zamora were arrested for complicity with the rebels. A rebel of unknown affiliation, Jesús Marín, appeared around Altotonga at the head of eighty men. At the same time, Cecilio Baez, a known Zapatista, was cornered by a federal force and killed at Mazomba, in the centre of the state. Another revolutionary, this time the Vazquista leader in Veracruz, Daniel Herrera, began his uprising on behalf of the Plan of Tacubaya, attacking the railway town of Santa Fé near the Veracruz port.[80]

The combined revolts caused serious problems for commercial and passenger traffic, as well as for the state security forces. Train crews, warned by the Gaviristas, refused to staff the trains if troops were to be transported. Various rebels were so audacious as to demand the surrender of small towns around Xalapa. The situation was aggravated by the impossibility of transmitting orders, since telegraph lines were systemtically destroyed.[81] Lamented His Britannic Majesty's consul in Veracruz:

> It is difficult to understand the inertia of the great mass of the people in connection with these bands of robbers, as extraordi-

nary as it may seem, my opinion is that a great majority of the people would rather be robbed and killed than fight... Five or six bandits armed with machetes and old guns can walk into a village of 800–1000 and rob at will. People won't even give information to the troops.[82]

Consul Nunn's opinions are arrogant. It did not occur to him that the people were not giving information to the troops for the same reason they did not during the Madero revolution: they probably approved of the rebel activity.

On March 8, Herrera was able to join forces with the Gaviristas on his march north, after the failure of his attempt to join forces with another rebel, Esteban Bañuelos. The latter had been repulsed in an effort to capture the Rurales garrison in Misantla. Entering one of the doors to the garrison after killing a sergeant and some of his men, they were repulsed by the sergeant's wife, who, angered at the shooting of her husband, picked up his pistol and returned such heavy fire that the Gavirista attackers were forced to retreat.[83] From Misantla, Herrera proceeed south with his band of now only twenty-four men, but after a battle with some volunteers south of the port of Veracruz, he decided to withdraw. Herrera's position was desperate; his band was reduced to robbing *ranchos* and *haciendas* on the way south in order to sutain themselves. Considering the Vazquista–Gavirista movement vanquished, Herrera petitioned for amnesty and was granted on April 12, 1912.[84]

Because armed uprisings continued to erupt most of them uncoordinated with each other and appealing to different factions or grievances, the government's task of pacification was onerous if not impossible. Not even the regular troops could be counted on. Soldiers guarding the textile facilities at Orizaba had to be rotated regularly in order to avoid "ideological" contamination by the militant workers. To add to the more or less regular depredations by an emerging "left-wing" backlash, several hundred Indians in the south, in Acayucan and Minatitlán, were venting their anger and frustration that nothing had been done about the return of their lands by raiding towns and *haciendas*.

Another serious area of revolt was the Huatusco, to which General Tapia had been sent. There, the self-taught tactician did have some success against the rebels, who were making use of the frontier with Puebla state to carry out raids. Ostensibly organized by the Vazquista "army," these rebels under Panuncio Martínez were routed by Tapia and regular army troops. Paso del

Macho was threatened by Clemente Gabay, brother of Pedro, who was in jail awaiting trial. Bañuelo and Panuncio Martínez joined forces to attack the canton of Cosamaloapan, while Gaviristas under Rafael Loyo harassed the area around Córdoba. Further to the south, the rail line to Santa Lucrecia was under constant surveillance by rebels, while Acayucan continued in a state of general unrest.

In order to forestall the emergence of real disorder in the south, Hilario Salas, the erstwhile PLM-anarchist, was named *jefe político* of Acayucan. Now the new governor, Lagos Cházaro, decided it was opportune to take the offensive. With the express encouragement of Madero, Lagos Cházaro decided to put himself at the head of an armed force, visit various municipalities across the state, and see that justice was enforced. His other purpose was to carry out a complete reform of the administration. In effect, he wanted to remove everyone from aldermen to judges, who had been involved with the Porfirian administration. There may have been more to the governor's actions than meets the eye. The local Rurales commander in Xalapa, Luis Castillo, complained to Madero that Lagos Cházaro was planning a "conspiracy" against him. Why was it necessary, he asked, for the governor to put together a force of two hundred men, depositing arms in his house and those of his friends?[85] Whatever Lagos Cházaro's motivations were, it is quite probable, given his background, that he was thinking of a coup against the Dehesista elements that continued to dominate the adminsitration of the state. Before he could carry it out, however, he was overtaken by the next surge of the Vazquista rebellion, which appeared to be gathering momentum in the state, even as it was ignored in the rest of Mexico.

On April 1, 1912, Madero gave his "state-of-the-nation" address to the Congress. In it he, mentioned the continuing violence in Morelos and the north (according to him, because of impatience over agrarian questons); the suspension of civil rights in Morelos, Guerrero, Tlaxcala, Puebla, and Mexico; and the successful elections in other states. There was no mention of Veracruz, in which the elections were not remotely successful, and in which there was serious armed unrest. Unlike Morelos, this unrest was uncoordinated, but in terms of extension, it indicates the complete lack of trust in the Madero government. Neither the president's appeal for calm nor the resignation of the cabinet had any marked effect on Veracruz or the nation. In April, rebel activity reached a crescendo in Veracruz.

5

Revolution and Counter-Revolution

From Orozco to Díaz

A summary of events in Veracruz during 1911 and 1912 demonstrate that the "revolution" did not end, *pace* Madero, with Porfirio Díaz's departure in June. There was a short hiatus in revolutionary activity, as many Veracruzans stood witness to the unfolding of events. But by August 1911, that period was over. Many Veracruzans had formed a judgment as to the political trajectory of the interim government and watched, with growing dismay, as Madero's perceived promises came to naught. In August 11, dismay gave way to anger. In small groups, in out-of-the-way places, men began to talk and to plan. Yet there was no clear statement of principle that would serve as the catalyst for action. Nor was there any leader of sufficient stature behind whom one could mobilize; both Vázquez Gómez and Gavira had tried and failed. The most impressive leader was about to make his second debut.

If the Vázquez Gómez fiasco had ignited the flame and the Gavira uprising had been the fan, it was Pascual Orozco's Plan of March 25, 1912, that provided the additional fuel. One month after the declaration of the Plan Orozco, Veracruz began to come apart. Rebellions began in all areas of the state, the most serious in the centre and south. What were the reasons? To view the uprisings as spontaneous, ideologically benign, or opportunistic belies the nature of the sources of discontent in Veracruz. It is tempting to accept Knight's characterization of the Orozquista movement as neo-Maderista.[1] Certainly there is much to this label. Many Veracruzans were no doubt disappointed by the failure to restore the Constitution of 1857, to return to a "democratic"

145

electoral system. But others wanted more. The people who rallied around Vázquez Gómez and Gavira were from the industrial and rural working classes, joined by some petite bourgeois elements. With the Plan Orozco, however, and the prominent and clear exposition of agrarian reform that had only been hinted at in Madero's Plan of San Luis Potosí, other parts of society were mobilized. To the preceding would now be added Indians and all those who had waited, some not too patiently, for the extension of the revolution to include their main interest: land. That this sentiment existed as a revolutionary expectation can be documented. A succinct statement of these aims was found in the town of Ayahualulco, near to Coatepec, in the house of a Vazquista supporter. It had been signed by one of the first rebels to enter Xalapa in June 1911, who was later declared military leader of the Vazquista revolt in Veracruz, Miguel M. Ramos.[2]

Much of the Vazquista and later, Orozquista activity was based in the centre of Veracruz, near the capital, Xalapa. In the town of Paso del Macho, for example, followers of Gabriel Gavira fortified themselves in a garment shop and shot it out with Rurales on April 24. Several small arms, a dynamite bomb, and machetes were found after the encounter. In nearby Xico on April 29, a group of men entered the town proclaiming the Plan of Tacubaya and denouncing Madero. The mayor, knowing that there were only ten Rurales some five kilometres away did not bother to call them. Perhaps he also knew, as the *jefe político* of Coatepec noted, that, although the townspeople did not accept the rebels' invitation to join them, they had considerable sympathy for the cause. The leader of the rebel group was Crescencio L. Villarauz of Misantla, who had taken part in the Gavirista uprising in that town. From there, they went to Coatepec, Ayahualulco, and Las Vigas, where they cut the telegraph lines and levied forced loans from the inhabitants. Villarauz and his second-in-command, Carlos Díaz, raided towns as far as Perote until the end of June. Although pursued by federal troops, they were not caught. Considerable evidence – including the ease with which they came and went, knowing exactly where to look for arms and money – indicates that they had the support of the *jefe político* of Coatepec, Lauro Ramírez, who was subsequently removed from office.[3] In the months of June and July, there were disturbances all over Veracruz. To add to this list of troubles, the workers in Orizaba were once again on strike. The state's military forces were inadequate to ensure order in Veracruz, which meant that federal troops had to be sent. Yet, the volunteer battalion of Xalapa was sent to Morelos to lend a hand there. The conclusion that must be drawn is that the situation in Veracruz was so volatile even its own local forces could not be trusted, and hence the necessity of using federal troops. All this, of course, came on the heels of, and was certainly to some extent motivated by, the election.[4]

However, the threat around Xalapa could be contained. So could the odd raid that took place close to the port as well as in the canton of Zongólica, which almost fell to Panuncio Martínez's forces at the end of April. In mid-May, most of the northern cantons reported calm.[5] But in the south, in the cantons of Acayucan and Minatitlán, the PLM propaganda of 1906-07 had found fertile ground among the lower middle class as well as Indians. The seedbed of the Acayucan revolt of 1906, this area remained unquiet. People there, especially the Indian Popolucas, had been waiting for inclusion in the agrarian reform they thought had been promised by the Plan of San Luis Potosí. Like that of the Morelenses to their east, their patience had run out. With the promulgation of the Plans of Tacubaya and Orozco, they had been given new hope. In February a local teacher, José Leyva, accompanied by Guadalupe Ochoa and a number of Popolucas from Acayucan, travelled to Xalapa to interview the governor over the business of their stolen lands. They left, certain that their claims would be adjudicated.[6]

By mid-April, disappointed, they decided on revolt and gathered a formidable force of over two hundred men, captained by Manuel Flores, who supported the Plan of Tacubaya. In its name, they levied justice, executing those whom they claimed had been traitors to Madero's Plan of San Luis Potosí. Further to the east, another hundred and fifty men under Nicanor Pérez attacked the important town of San Juan Evangelista with its railway connection to the Isthmian railway. After taking the town, they levied loans, then left in complete discipline. In March, a rebel named Bañuelos, fresh from exploits in the northern canton of Cosamaloapan, had come down to Acayucan. Another well-known rebel and ex-Maderista, Manuel Paredes, also began operating in the region after declaring against Madero.[7] The actions of these groups forced families to leave the towns and seek refuge in either Xalapa or Veracruz port. U.S. employees of the Interoceanic railway also decided to escape the danger by leaving their employment and returning to the United States.[8]

By the beginning of May 1912, southern Veracruz was in a full-fledged state of insurrection. Most, if not all, of the former Maderista revolutionaries, with the exception of Aguilar, Jara, and Tapia, and possibly Salas, had been caught up in the mael-strom emanating from the Vázquez Gómez movement. In general, these were the left wing of the former Maderista movement, allied with and supported by Indians all over the southern cantons, who had desired the implementation of the "radical" tenets of the Plan of San Luis Potosí. It is interesting, but quite understandable as well as indicative of the state government's bias, that the *hacienda* Corral Nuevo, owned by the Cházaro Soler family, was singled out for special protection.[9]

For the moment, at least, the government and security forces appeared to be able to withstand the threats. But with thirty well-armed and mounted men under Juan Sandoval camped outside Puerto México, and with Pavón Flores and his lieutenant with another three hundred threatening Sayula, the situation looked bleak. Cantonal guards with federal troops, Rurales, and volunteers left Acayucan in three columns. Led by regular army colonel Villegas and Miguel Alemán, the battle was joined on April 23, and, despite being outnumbered, the federal troops were able to inflict a serious defeat on the rebels. Two of Nicanor Pérez's lieutenants, Rafael Ortiz and Melecio Méndez, were killed. The group was unable to link up with Sandoval's forces, which in any case retreated towards the southern part of the state. There, in the town of Pajapan, canton of Minatitlán, Sandoval shot up the town, burnt the municipal archives, and went looking for the mayor to settle grudges dating from the days with Santanón.[10]

In May, the situation was so precarious that the army had to resort to creative reporting to justify its lack of success. Unable to deal with the pressure from the different rebel groups (whom it was difficult to locate and pin down in open combat), it proferred a unique explanation of its failure to prevail. The entire municipal council of San Juan Evangelista was accused of supporting the rebels, as was the *jefe político* of Acayucan, Hilario Salas, himself. These were supposed to be planning a general uprising in the southeastern mountains, which bordered on the state of Oaxaca. The corporal in charge of Rurales, Luis Castillo, reported to Madero that Guadalupe Ochoa, Daniel Herrera, and Raúl Ruiz were all also plotting against the president with the collaboration of the newly elected governor, Lagos Cházaro.[11]

Adding to the revolutionary ferment, some rebels were now identifying with Zapatismo. Sandoval and his group belong in this category. So does another revolutionary, Honrato García, who, also exploiting the difficulties facing the army, created havoc in the villages around Minatitlán in mid-May, where his main activity consisted in burning archives. On May 9, García raided Cosoleacaque and, two days later struck at Jáltipan.[12] Thus, while one cannot speak of concerted military action against Madero, one can assert that in Veracruz both moderates like Ruiz and the left wing, represented by older revolutionaries like Ochoa, had come to the identical conclusion that the government was not going to implement any of its promises. They therefore considered themselves justified in taking up arms to remove the president. This coalition of forces, if one can call it that, was not very different from that which had come into existence in the north, united by the Orozco campaign.[13]

Together, they kept up a constant harassment of the government and army. In early May, the troops belonging to Manuel Pavón Flores had established their headquarters on the *hacienda* El Central. Salas, the *jefe político*, begged the government for fifty additional troops for a few days in order to dislodge those troops. But it was the regular army, apparently in an effort to prevent this group from derailing trains on the Tehuantepec railroad, that sent a significant force to engage Pavón Flores's three hundred rebels. That force was completely routed, leaving behind many dead as well as documents. In the Tuxtlas too, there were significant groups of Zapatista rebels who, because of the concentration of regular troops further south, were able to raid *ranchos* and small towns with impunity.[14]

It was in Minatitlán, however, that rebel activity was fiercest. Activity there was so worrisome that the owner of the oil fields, Lord Cowdray, together with his general manager John Body, felt it necessary to visit the area, arriving by the *Princess Cecilia* from London and escorted by a British warship, the cruiser, *Melpomene*. The action there began with an attack on the cantonal seat of Minatitlán on May 17. With over one hundred men, Joaquín Marañon, Alvaro Alor, Juan Sandoval, and Alejandro Torres entered the town to cries of "Viva Orozco," forcing the prison gates and setting prisoners free. The troops that recently been sent to Acayucan were force-marched back to Minatitlán, but not before the fifteen local Rurales and some citizens had driven off the rebel attackers, numbered now at about one hundred and sixty. According to the military reports, the motive for the attack was solely local politics. The commander of the ninth military zone reported that there was only "discontent at some appointments by the government against the wish of the citizens who are Gaviristas."[15] Such local politics were exactly of the nature we have been describing. But the government was doubly concerned because of the effects the rebellion could have on the local economy. The two consuls at Veracruz kept constant vigilance over the course of events, reporting regularly to their governments. The U.S. consul, William Canada, reported the arrival of numerous U.S. citizens, mainly managers and accountants of various plantations, fleeing this zone of rebel activity.[16] Accordingly, the town was now reinforced by an additional one hundred regular troops, and the gunboat *Veracruz* was dispatched up the Coatzacoalcos River to take up a position opposite the town. On May 25, General Victoriano Huerta defeated Orozco's forces at Rellano, and the government managed some minor victories in Veracruz.[17]

Despite the fact that the Orozquista movement seemed to be losing its momentum, local rebel bands, fed by local problems and politics, continued their isolated activity. Nor was the government (i.e., the army) able to defeat them decisively and pacify the southern cantons. Eighty men entered Minatitlán one evening in an unsuccessful bid to free their jailed leader, Marañon, but were not pursued by government troops.[18] Throughout July, the situation remained the same. Rebel raids continued with frequency in Minatitlán. An expedition mounted in the ninth military zone, reaching into Oaxaca, which was believed to give haven to the Veracruz rebels, yielded nothing. Sandoval, for example, continued to dominate the countryside around the town of Acayucan, the security forces of which, for lack of mounted troops, were unable to join in pursuit.[19] Further to the east, in Playa Vicente, rebel activity was so strong that Rafael Tapia had to lead a special force of Rurales to retake the town of that name. Despite being seriously outnumbered, Tapia was able to recapture the town, killing five of the rebel leaders and capturing fifty horses as well as a large amount of ammunition, while suffering the loss of only one Rurales guard.[20]

The federal soldiers were also hampered by frequent desertions. The army offered at least a fairly stable existence for poorer Mexicans, but this was not always enough to ensure loyalty. In moving about the country or even the state, soldiers became exposed to ideas that induced them to leave the relative security of life in the armed forces. For example, in May a number of Rurales stationed at the rail junction of Tierra Blanca mutinied, opting for the life of the bandit before joining up with a rebel outfit. This was a different kind of security, but one presumably more in keeping with the social ideas of these mutineers. The Rurales who deserted in Tierra Blanca were soon part of a larger outfit of over two hundred rebels, known to the manager of the huge U.S. sugar plantation near Tierra Blanca, J.C. Dennis, who noted how disciplined they were. Thirty-eight of them "visited" the plantation and told him their chief had warned them to behave. But the reception given rebels was not always as benign as at this U.S. plantation. In Estanzuela, a small town near Tierra Blanca, citizens resisted attempts to be intimidated, killing the rebel – or bandit – leader, Federico García.[21] Yet, in nearby Naranjo rebels penetrated the town, and, because the authorities there were in league with them, volunteers sent from Tierra Blanca could not dislodge them. At the beginning of August, the *jefe político* of the canton of Cosamaloapan cabled the government that he would need reinforcements to drive them out.[22]

Further north of Tierra Blanca, the canton of Zongólica witnessed running battles between Rurales and the local rebel leader, Panuncio Martínez. Martínez, careful to distinguish himself as a rebel and not a bandit, wreaked havoc on the *haciendas* of that region, leaving many in bankruptcy. Attempts to persuade him and others in that canton to lay down their arms and avail themselves of a government amnesty failed. Although he was never defeated, and later joined the anti-Constitutionalist Felicista movement, Martínez was also not spectacularly successful against the regular troops. Instead, his was a type of guerrilla warfare bent on ruining as many of the plantation companies in the canton as possible. In this, he was quite successful, a feat which must have increased the already considerable dissatisfaction with the Madero government.[23]

Even the central cantons became more active in May. As elsewhere, many of the ex-Maderista leaders appeared as rebels. For the most part, these were men who had joined the Maderista revolution only in the spring of 1911, when victory seemed certain, and they were as quick to jump ship as they had been to enlist. Manuel López, Ricardo López, and others thus resumed familiar activity in their old stomping grounds. More will be said of their motives later; that they were disappointed with the Madero government is obvious, although what they actually stood for – an ideology, or social principle – is difficult to discern.[24]

From the central region, rebel activity was extended into the north. By July, Manuel Díaz, a relative newcomer to the anti-Madero cause, was carrying out raids from Soledad, Huatusco. In Misantla, too, scene of the Gavirista rebellion, rebel activity remained strong. The arrest of Gavira had obviously not calmed the situation. Now, in June, the Márquez brothers, apparently in league with the *jefe político*, attacked the town. Taking over the town square, they fired shots and then left as federal troops went after them. But Misantla was not only a Gavirista but also a Vazquista stronghold, and there were not sufficient troops to deal with both. The *jefe político* complained that there would be disturbances if the government did not send reinforcements, since no orders had been issued to the treasury official, and a volunteer force could not be sustained. He was under no doubt that the nature of these movements was political, not inspired social banditry, as has been suggested elsewhere. In addition, the unrest was so widespread that one cannot describe this region as being largely quiescent.[25]

In fact, regardless of topography, social ecology, or economic activity, in Veracruz anti-Madero rebellion was endemic. To the east of Misantla, the canton of Jalacingo was under attack in July. In Papantla, the government asked ex-Porfirista major Simón Tiburcio to organize volunteer forces in March. Tiburcio, who was from the region, had intimate contact with the Totonac Indians in some of the municipalities and could be counted on to enlist their help, or at least guarantee their neutrality. For this purpose, he was equipped with eight hundred Marlin rifles and eight Hockiss cannons. From Papantla, he could roam north into the neighbouring canton of Tuxpán, and thus protect the Mexico Oilfields Company, which was being harassed by rebel groups.[26] Rebel activity ranged as far north as the canton of Chicontepec, where Indians had refused to pay taxes since the previous June and had been in open rebellion since October.[27]

With Tapia and the federal army mopping up small rebel bands around Córdoba and elsewhere, and despite some disturbances in Minatitlán, the government had the upper hand against the neo-Maderista rebels. One of the greatest successes of the state forces was the surrender of Panuncio Martínez under an offer of amnesty. These negotiations were so delicate that the government withdrew its protection from a large British plantation so as not to anger Martínez. With his acceptance of amnesty, he was then commissioned by the government to police the area he knew so well with a force of Rurales.[28] However, the biggest news of all came in August 1912, with the federal government's victory in the north over the Orozquista forces.[29]

Nevertheless, the general unrest in the state was not dissipated. Among the most alarming reports were those from the *jefe político* of Córdoba, Francisco Urrutia, that General Tapia had been seen conferring with the well-known rebels Mario Vázquez,

Pedro Gabay, and Teódulo Córdoba. Tapia's recent behaviour on being sent to put down an uprising in the Huatusco – he delayed his arrival and diverted part of his forces to Omealca instead – lent credence to these charges. Yet they were never proven; and although the Veracruz interim governor, Manuel Leví, asked that Tapia's forces be replaced with another Rurales unit, Madero could not bring himself to organize an investigation and the whole matter disappeared from their correspondence. Moreover, on August 24, the Rurales severely mauled Pedro Gabay's unit, seriously wounding Gabay himself in the skirmish: hardly proof that Tapia was conspiring with him. The truth is that Leví, a conservative Veracruzan, had little faith in the self-made Rurales general, and asked that the Veracruz army commander, General Durán, be given the command of the state's security forces in place of Tapia. Leví represented those Veracruzans who were genuinely upset by Madero's attempts to manipulate Pérez Rivera into the governor's chair. He thus mounted a last-ditch effort to hamper the governor-elect's assumption of office.[30]

The situation Madero had created was confusing to all factions. He had rejected his most dedicated and long-standing allies, such as Aguilar, Jara, and Gavira and had thrown himself on the mercy of the discontented and divided conservatives. Because of his uneven politics, he was no longer trusted. Consequently, his sources of information were suspect, as different groups appealed to him, usually with differing stories about the situation. Madero was placed in the unenviable situation of not knowing which faction to believe. For example, an attack on the Veracruz train on August 31 resulted in the death of the bandit leader Santiago Boquiño, on whose body was found a letter supposedly from Pérez Rivera. But Madero would not countenance any slur on the governor-elect's reputation. He decided it was better to continue on the course he had chosen. In fact, Leví was replaced in early September as the provisional governor. Lagos Cházaro resumed office to pave the way for Pérez Rivera's smooth inauguration.[31]

On September 9, a meeting was held between Lagos Cházaro, Pérez Rivera, and the Veracruz military commander, General Vega, to arrange the takeover. The new secretary of government, J. Domínguez, was sworn in. An editorial in the Mexico City daily *La Nueva Era* cynically exclaimed that the revolution had eaten itself: "The same Científicos we revolted against are now back in power."[32] A few days later, troops were sent into the Veracruz legislature to intimidate reluctant deputies into confirming the election "victory" of Pérez Rivera. In an unprecedented move, Lagos Cházaro handed over his executive responsibilities to Pérez Rivera on September 26, although the legislature did not declare the new governor the official winner until October 10.[33] The machinations and manipulations, as well as the breach of state sovereignty, were obvious for all to see.

Now the situation in Veracruz really began to deteriorate. To the anti-Maderistas were added a second rebel force, consisting for the most part of the Porfirian reactionaries who wanted a return to the old order. In the Huasteca, a revolutionary movement emerged, still in the shadows of ideology, its leaders unknown to the government. The Veracruz governor appealed to the president for arms and ammunition. In addition, he proposed a hurried plan to create police forces in each municipality and village, the latter to have one police chief and five constables, making at least thirty for each municipality and about two hundred for each canton. Three thousand rifles were requested from the central government, in addition to which Tapia was asked to raise an additional troop of three hundred Rurales to be stationed in the Huasteca permanently.[34] Around Orizaba, a rebel force under a new Orozquista leader, Maximo Bello, appeared, and in the south Sayula was taken by Nicanor Pérez and his group, who emptied the treasury before departing.[35]

Old Porfirian general, Higinio Aguilar, however, posed the greatest threat. Hardly out of jail, Aguilar launched his movement from Tehuacán, Puebla, crossing over into Veracruz at the head of a group of ex-Rurales that he had convinced to follow him. His field headquarters was established at the *hacienda* San Diego close to Orizaba, from whence troops of the 12th Regiment were sent after him. Another part of his troop was also attacked by General Tapia at La Perla and Texmalaca, equally unsuccessfully, because by October Aguilar's forces apparently numbered over one thousand and had occupied a considerable part of central Veracruz. Simultaneously, one of his old underlings, the Orizaban, Gaudencio de la Llave, together with his two sons, Gaudencio Jr. and Porfirio, also raised a rebel force. Although it is not clear whether he and Aguilar worked in concert, they were soon able to mount a considerable threat to the Madero government.[36]

As during the former Maderista phase of the revolution, parts of the countryside were fairly calm as people went about their business. Unrest in those areas, where it did break out, was usually due to local conditions or grievances. Some of these can be gleaned from the many reports commissioned by the U.S. consul from fellow citizens managing various plantations in Veracruz. We already know that Higinio Aguilar's conservative movement did not impress the working class in the textile mills around Orizaba. Nor were plantation workers interested in joining any rebel movement so long as they were fairly paid, as on the rubber plantations at Tula, in the canton of the Tuxtlas. In Tierra Blanca, however, the U.S. manager noted the quiet conditions but remarked on the independent feeling of the local people, who had refused to pay taxes. In the south, on the other hand, J. W. Abrahams, manager of the plantation Bella Vista near San Juan Evangelista, noted the potential unrest. The point of contention was the government's returning lands to the huge *hacienda* Corral Nuevo owned by the Cházaro Soler family (one of the sources of the Acayucan rebellion in 1906). And U.S. citizens were very wary of the volatility of working-class Veracruzans, always expecting violent anti-U.S. outbursts of anger at the slightest provocation. They were right to be vigilant, despite Cumberland's claims that fear of anti-U.S. sentiment in Mexico was highly exaggerated, for in Veracruz such feeling was not far below the surface. For example, the previous May the arrival of a steamer in Veracruz port with one hundred Black workers going to the electric plant at Necaxa in Puebla state caused considerable concern: local citizens thought they were U.S. soldiers in disguise, an advance invasion party.[37]

Even within a relatively calm larger picture, Higinio Aguilar and Gaudencio's movements nevertheless caused well-founded concern in government circles. At the beginning of October, trains were again coming under attack, and Aguilar's political supporters were all about. Four columns of federal troops had to be deployed to Veracruz under the command of General Beltrán in order to attempt to contain the situation, without much result. Nor could the government even ascertain the source of Aguilar's movement: whence, for example, was he obtaining the funds to supply and pay such a large force of men? From Orizaba, Aguilar's rebels pushed north into the Huatusco, passing close by Xalapa, then doubled back, crossing over into the state of Puebla and re-entering Veracruz in the first week of October. From San Salvador, Puebla, where his force had their headquarters, they roamed almost unopposed deep into the Sierra Madre around Tequila and Xoxocotla, near to the cantonal seat at Zongólica. Protected by the terrain, they were joined by other forces loyal to Félix Díaz (the ex-president's nephew; see below), commanded by a General Muñoz. On October 28, twenty-five Rurales arrived from Orizaba under Captain Vega, hardly sufficient to comb the mountains or protect Zongólica from a frontal attack. The defensive tactic of maintaining a strict watch of the main roads, while perhaps comforting to those who did not understand the real situation, was useless. The rebels were not taking the main roads, but travelling through the mountains, and the federal forces were neither able nor sufficiently courageous to search for them there.[38] In the south, too, ranches and *haciendas* in Acayucan continued to be assaulted by anti-government forces.

In Veracruz, the Porfirian ex-governor, Teodoro Dehesa who had returned in April, accepted the advice of his friend Ignacio Muñoz and decided he had suffered enough blame from the Maderistas: he went into another self-imposed exile.[39] In a conversation with the British consul in Mexico City, ex-president de la Barra remarked that he was expecting further trouble, and that the defection and uprising of Higinio Aguilar should be taken seriously.[40] Dehesa's departure at the end of September also indicated that something was seriously wrong. Whether Dehesa himself knew what that something was is not possible to ascertain. Madero certainly did not blame Dehesa for what followed. But since the ex-governor's brother, Francisco, was an intimate friend of Félix Díaz's, what occurred a few days later must have made many contemporaries, including Madero's secretary De los Rios, believe that Dehesa must have played a role in the upcoming disaster.

That disaster was, of course, the Félix Díaz revolt of October 16, 1912. Díaz, frustrated by being constantly outmanoeuvred in the Mexican Chamber of Deputies, realized that there was no place for him in a Mexico of the Maderista stamp. By August of 1912, he had concluded that he and other disgruntled members of the Porfirian elite could only exert political influence if they ousted Madero as president. There were, moreover, sufficient grounds to believe this was possible. North American as well as Mexican newspapers had continuously been portraying Madero as weak and incapable of governing the country. Madero had hardly been successfuly in pacifying the country, as events in Veracruz alone had shown; and his methods, a combination of integrity and casuistry, had removed the moral advantage with which he had been elected. The left was dissatisfied with the slowness of social reforms and the right harboured a combined hatred of what had by now been recognized as a renewed Cientificismo and the potential for a class-based attack on property. For non-propertied members of the middle classes, the elevation of people from the lower and lower-middle classes into positions of authority (such as Tapia) was a symbol of what the future would hold. For Díaz, then, it appeared that the time was ripe to cash in on the discontent, through an appeal to the dignity of the armed forces, hardly celebrated and honoured under the new government.

The Félix Díaz Revolt

All the revolts mentioned so far, the Vazquista, Gavirista and Orozquista, may be said to have emanated from the same political source: the feeling of betrayal of the principles for which these individuals had involved themselves in the Maderista movement. The same cannot be said of the Félix Díaz revolt, which began on October 16 with the capture of the city of Veracruz and the mutiny of the garrison there. Ostensibly to restore the honour of the army, Diaz's revolt was first against Madero and then against the state government. However, Díaz was a well-known anti-Científico and a close friend of Teodoro Dehesa. Although John Womack Jr. alleged Científico organization behind his revolt, I could find no evidence to support this claim. Alan Knight only calls the revolt conservative, which it obviously was. But it was much more than that. The real idea behind the revolt was anti-Cientificismo. It is highly unlikely that Dehesa would have supported it otherwise. Not coincidentally, he returned hurriedly from exile in New York when he heard about the Díaz uprising, although, prudently, he did not take an active part.[41]

On October 13, rumours began to circulate that something was developing, although the police went out of their way to issue a denial.[42] Henderson has ably depicted the reasons for Díaz's choice of Veracruz as the place from which to launch his revolution. Veracruz was associated with another revolution (the Revolution of Ayutla and the Reform wars) and another Díaz, his uncle, and had the aura of the success of 1876 attached to it. His cousin enjoyed an important command in a town with an important rail connection to the port. The port was also an important shipping point through which arms could be obtained and would provide links to the outside world, especially since the U.S. border had been closed to munitions shipments the previous March.[43] Finally not only the Díaz name, but also that of "Liberalism," was connected with Veracruz. Long considered a quintessential liberal city in the sense of its support of the federalist clauses of the Constitutions of 1824 and 1857,

Veracruz – both the city and the state – had long harboured animosities towards Cientificismo, or the centralist policies that many Veracruzans saw emerging with the Madero government. Díaz, with long connections to the group of anti-Científicos headed by ex-governor Dehesa, must have considered Veracruz the ideal place from which to launch his movement.[44]

In addition, other anti-Maderistas such as Aguilar and de la Llave were already heading a significant military movement in the state, which the government was having difficulty quelling. Another important factor was that Diaz's movement could be spearheaded from the north as well as from the port and the centre of the state. In the area of Tuxpán, Manuel Peláez (who was subsequently to play such a significant part in the revolution in Veracruz) was ready to second Díaz, although the evidence that the latter knew this at the time is scanty. Certainly, middle and upper-middle-class families were known to have been followers of Díaz and were ready for an anti-Madero revolution. Peláez's brother, Ignacio, was also a "longtime Felicista." Both brothers, like many of their class, resented the unrest and banditry that the Madero government had been unable to control. Again, in the neighbouring canton of Ozuluama, an old Dehesista stronghold, there was considerable dislike of the government.[45]

It was not farfetched, therefore, for Díaz to consider Veracruz the ideal place from which to launch his movement. On the morning of October 16, Díaz and Díaz Ordaz with the 21st Battalion entered Veracruz and were joined by the Rurales of Orizaba under their commander, Manuel Mallín. Quickly, they convinced the local commander to join the movement. Simultaneously, Peláez in Tuxpán, a Colonel Ortega y Rivera in Ozuluama, Guillermo Pous in Tlacotalpan, and Pastor López in the mountains of the Tuxtlas raised the flag of revolt, seconding the Veracruz movement.[46] The Madero government thought it was all over. Their reports from Xalapa indicated that General Beltrán had gone over to the movement and was preparing to move into Oaxaca and Puebla, that the police chief of Veracruz had done likewise, and that contraband arms were moving into the port. Much of this was rumour. Of the three main military elements in Veracruz, only one, the Veracruz garrison, had joined the Díaz rebels. Neither the navy in the port nor the second garrison in the old fortress of San Juan de Ulúa had followed suit. In fact, the old commander in the fortress, General José M. Hernández, had fortified himself in the structure and was organizing resistance. The next day Governor Lagos Cházaro confirmed that only a few soldiers had deserted and that the rest of the state was quiet. From Córdoba, generals Vega, Beltrán, and Valdés also reported that they had no news of any further uprising.[47]

That was exactly the case. Although foreign observers reported strong feelings for Díaz, the opposite for Madero, and pleasure among U.S. residents at the prospect of the government's overthrow by a pro-U.S. faction, nothing much happened. Everyone in Mexico seemed to be waiting for somebody else to take action. A perfect example is the behaviour of ex-governor Dehesa. He returned to Veracruz from self-imposed exile at the exact time of the coup. Remarks Henderson: this was "a coincidence some members of the government, including Madero's private secretary, found impossible to believe." Because Dehesa had been a close personal friend of Díaz, and Dehesa's brother, Francisco, was Díaz's political organizer in Veracruz, it was quite logical that Dehesa would be suspect. He was even arrested and sent to Mexico City for investigation, although nothing could be proven against him. There was nothing to prove.[48]

The Veracruz governor, however, read the general situation very clearly. He advised the president to send troops immediately to retake Veracruz, after which the rest would be easy. He also counselled sending the loyal warships to Tampico and Tuxpán, as they would get there faster than infantry would.[49] By October 23, it was all over. General Beltrán had marched troops down to Veracruz, dug in carefully, and then indicated his intention of attacking. Díaz and his forces surrendered almost without firing a shot. Díaz was arrested and imprisoned in San Juan de Ulúa. General Blanquet with the main federal force at Orizaba hurriedly wrote the president a letter of unconditional support. An equally hastily compiled list of loyal military and civilian followers was sent to Madero by one of his secret agents. However, despite an accusation that Beltrán had sold Díaz to Madero for sixty thousand pesos, the danger seemed to have passed – the military danger, that is.

The defeat of Díaz did not mean that Madero had won either sympathy or praise. Mexico had turned away from any belief in the promised magic of Maderismo. In the eyes of the U.S. consul general in Mexico City, Madero was "absolutely impotent to bring about even a semblance of peace and order." The feeling apparently extended even into the halls and offices of the national palace where the president earned the derogatory nickname, "Pobre Panchito" (poor, little Francisco).[50]

This impotence seemed to dog the government in all sectors.

Perhaps it was caused by knowledge of the government's unpopularity. Furthermore, the port city, if not the entire state, supported Díaz. U.S. newspapers reported how quickly troops in the port went over to Díaz. Other observers remarked on the obvious Felicista affiliation of *El Dictámen*, as well as almost the entire civil service. In other parts of Mexico, too, officers openly toasted Díaz, and the governors of Oaxaca and Colima offered their allegiance should the movement be successful. More importantly, even non-Felicistas supported the attempted coup, all perhaps united behind the idea of getting rid of Madero.[51]

Díaz was an important catalyst behind whom many different anti-Maderista elements could rally. Madero obviously did not understand the extent to which his political legitimacy had been undermined. He actually believed that, with the collapse of the revolt in Veracruz, Oaxaca, for example, would lapse into "complete tranquility."[52] And his decision to spare Díaz's life appears ridiculous in the extreme. But the manner in which he came to that decision reveals that impotence, that indecisiveness, which many Mexicans saw as his *modus operandi*. Raúl Dehesa overheard a telephone conversation between his father-in-law, General García Peña, and Madero in which the president congratulated the general for having ordered Díaz's immediate execution after his court martial. Certainly his closest collaborators advised Madero that his continued leniency towards such rebels was weakening his political position.[53] In the meantime, however, Rodolfo Reyes prepared an *amparo* (stay of judicial procedure) arguing that Díaz's court martial was illegal because he had resigned from the military before embarking on his revolutionary course. Then the petitioners began to gather at the national palace. First to arrive was ex-president de la Barra with a delegation, followed by a coterie of the capital's aristocratic ladies; as well, a petition containing over six hundred signatures was received. Under this much pressure Madero capitulated, despite the fact that the unrest in Veracruz was not over. The *amparo* was deliberated by the Supreme Court, which commuted the death sentence to life imprisonment.[54] And not only did Madero accept Díaz's reduced sentence, he extended the same leniency to many others as well.

This is not to be construed as evidence of Madero's inclination to "work within the law." On numerous other occasions, he had behaved in the opposite way. In fact, his methods were that of a desperate politician who wanted to avoid creating any additional excuses for opposition to his government. In particular, he did not wish to make enemies among the upper classes, whose political support was crucial. He refused, for example, a young officer's offer to apply the Ley Fuga (a method of execution "while trying to escape") to Díaz, remarking that he would rather leave Mexico if that was the kind of system Mexicans wanted. He also refused to censure the most obvious supporters of Díaz, such as Teodoro Dehesa, who, although probably blameless in regard to the coup, was certainly a Díaz supporter.[55]

Nevertheless, the Díaz revolt was shortlived, as it did not appeal to the people at whom it was directed, the army leaders, nor did it capture the hearts of many people outside of Veracruz. But the end of the Díaz revolt was not the end of problems either in that state or the country. Attention became fixed on Mexico City where the political battle for high stakes was being fought. It was obvious to both foreign and local observers that it was just a matter of time before the extremely unpopular Madero government would be replaced.

The result of the failed coup was not a strengthening, but a serious weakening of the government's and especially Madero's prestige. All classes of people seemed now to share the same opinion: Madero had to go. Just when and how, nobody knew. They were also not to know that the failed *coup* was only the violent continuation of a more serious movement that was eventually to involve the entire army. Henderson's judgment of the lessons the military as well as the Porfirians learned from the Veracruz fiasco is apt: while the army would sit back and await the results of a movement in one of the provinces, it would probably not hesitate to support one in Mexico City.[56] Gaudencio de la Llave had actually proposed just such a tactic. Already active in the field since September, after the taking of Veracruz, he had sent his son to confer with Díaz. His suggestion was that Díaz should leave the city immediately, uniting with Aguilar's and de la Llave's forces to move against Puebla, where they had considerable support and then advance on Mexico City. But Díaz would not budge from Veracruz, firm in his arrogant belief that the army would come over to him without his having to fire a shot.[57]

The Counter-Revolution Continues

Not all of Díaz's forces had surrendered with him. In addition to his allies Higinio Aguilar and Gaudencio de la Llave, a junior officer, Captain Odorico, succeeded in escaping with his company into the Sierra Negra. There they were able to continue in

rebellion until the *cuartelazo (coup)* in February 1913. Together
with the forces of Aguilar and de la Llave, they caused havoc
in the canton of Zongólica. General Tapia ordered federal
troops down from Orizaba, splitting the garrison there in half.
Unfortunately for the canton, the army required the city to provide forage for the horses, and, as it had not fully complied, only
a small force of twenty-five Rurales could be sent.[58]

From the beginning of November, then, and despite the failure of the short-lived Díaz rebellion, the counter-revolution in
Veracruz was already well underway with a federal army unable
or unwilling to crush it. It was also reported that Zapatistas had
joined Aguilar's force. As incomprehensible as this may seem,
there is more than circumstantial evidence to support these
reports.[59] In any case, Aguilar and de la Llave roamed freely
through the canton, raiding municipal offices, freeing jailed prisoners, and taking whatever funds they could find from treasuries
or businesses. The government forces were stretched to the limit.
No help could be expected from the nearest military garrison at
Orizaba.[60]

In the north as well, there was evidence of continued anti-
government agitation. There were more than eight hundred
rebels concentrated around Temapache, about twenty miles from
Tuxpán. These had availed themselves of more than 100,000
pesos of "forced loans" taken from banks and businesses and
were now demanding, in return for submission, that the government cover the loans. The gunboat *Bravo* had to be sent from
Veracruz, and with the reinforcement of three hundred troops
under Colonel Ocaranza, the revolutionary activity was brought
to an end – not that this ended anti-government feeling or rebel
activity. Isolated bands remained in Papantla as well as Tuxpán,
and were never altogether subdued.[61] On November 13, it was
discovered that in October a Rurales corporal, Ismael Rosete,
calling himself commander of the Sotavento (southern coast),
had issued a proclamation exhorting the army to part company
with the Madero government because of personal and political
corruption. Specifically, Rosete charged the Madero family with
enriching themselves at the expense of the country and the state
of Veracruz. Here was additional proof of the evils of centralism.
It was a charge similar to that levelled against the centralist
Porfirian Científicos. Worse, Rosete accused the Madero government of rigging the elections of the vice-president, the state governor and the state deputies or, in other words, for having made
a mockery of the slogan by which the Maderista movement had

justified its rebellion against Porfirio Díaz.[62] Here was the clearest proof of the hatred of the centre, of Cientificismo.

The military situation in Veracruz was indeed precarious, and the political situation was no better. The armed counter-revolutionary movement of Aguilar and Zapatista allies was paralleled by a counter-revolutionary political movement among the old Porfirian order, which, however, displayed the old divisions between Dehesistas and Científicos. For the president, the situation in Veracruz was extremely confusing. He did not know whom to believe. The interim governor, Lagos Cházaro, continually warned Madero to consider exiling Dehesa, who, even if he had had no connection with the Félix Díaz uprising, was certainly a symbol behind whom his old political cronies could organize. And Dehesa's hackles were up because, as previously indicated, he was convinced that Pérez Rivera represented the new Científico forces of the Madero family.[63]

To reiterate one of the themes of this work, a theme clearly seen in this latest political battle in Veracruz towards the end of 1912, Dehesa and the people for whom he was the spokesman and leading advocate wanted the state for themselves, as guaranteed by the Constitution of 1857. They resented and opposed the encroachments of the central government on their turf. If they supported Félix Díaz, it was because he was known to be an adherent of the Constitution of 1857, a friend of Dehesa's, and an equally adamant enemy of the Científicos.

The confusion over whom to believe and whom to support is illustrated by the case of the appointment of a new *jefe político* for Ozuluama. As was stated earlier, this canton was one in which Dehesa had considerable influence, as he and his wife owned large *haciendas* there. With Dehesa residing in his home state, that canton would continually be a trouble spot for any governor who happened not to be on Dehesa's side. That was the case for Lagos Cházaro, as it would be for Pérez Rivera. On November 1, Lagos Cházaro appointed Juan Quintal Gea as *jefe político*. Promptly, residents of Ozuluama wrote to the president complaining that certain other parties who had supported the Félix Díaz uprising were behind the nomination of Quintal Gea. He was, they asserted, not only illiterate and of bad character, but had supported the Reyista movement and the Braniff gubernatorial candidature. Lagos Cházaro countered with the fact that Quintal Gea, at the moment of the Felicista uprising, had offered his services to the governor and had remained loyal. Furthermore, he continued, Efren Reyna, the supposed "tiger" of Chicontepec, had also opposed his nominee, Melo y Téllez, for the same post in that canton. And Reyna was, in fact, an intimate friend of the governor-elect, Pérez Rivera.[64]

By mid-November, in this climate of political uncertainty, not to speak of intense intrigue, Madero was made aware of the beginnings of a new revolutionary movement against him in Veracruz, a more serious undertaking to which the Felicista uprising was allegedly the prologue. The "ghost" – Teodoro Dehesa – was supposedly behind this new plot; the suspicion had been aroused by the frequent visits he received from Manuel Calero, the ambassador to the United States, as well as Rodolfo Reyes. Another supposed indicator was that Félix Díaz was to be moved to the municipal jail, from which it would be easy to escape. Both *jefe político* and district judge were involved in this plan. The U.S. consul in Veracruz had also been apprised of the situation by General Beltrán and from other sources acknowledging the possibility of the uprising. Most of the federal forces, he noted with alarm, were in the north, and the rest of the state was without protection.[65]

Consequently, the newly installed governor, Pérez Rivera, decreed the conscription of all able-bodied males between the ages of eighteen and twenty-two (except for a few specific categories) and had the legislature pass a law of amnesty for all political prisoners and former rebels. The amnesty was also intended to boost the new governor's popularity, since his inauguration had attracted anything but spontaneous outbursts of support, despite (or because of) the appearance of Gustavo Madero at his inauguration. There was further a more serious reason: the amnesty allowed the governor to compensate one of the men who had eased his gubernatorial victory, Gabriel Gavira. Gavira was subsequently freed and given a great welcome in Altotonga, as well as a substantial state pension but, for security, he was invited by Madero to take up residence in Mexico City at Pérez Rivera's behest. Madero himself did not understand the reason for the governor's manoeuvre. Pérez Rivera had to explain to him that Gavira still represented the lower classes of the state, that these class divisions were fairly sharp, and that he was working to make the people forget them, or at least not add to his political troubles by organizing demonstrations. With Gavira in Mexico City, Pérez Rivera might be able to breathe a little easier.[66]

In addition, Pérez Rivera hastened to secure his own followers in sensitive political posts. Municipal elections were about to be held in the port city, and the governor worked feverishly

Inaugural Parade for Pérez Rivera in Xalapa.

to assure that the outcome favoured his candidates. He counter-manded an order by Madero to replace the *jefe político* of the port city, Joaquín Lagos, with P. Leal Milán. It was essential to retain Lagos, he explained, to ensure that elections resulted in people who "were sane and loyal, our people"; in other words, rigged. To that end, it was "indispensable to have as *jefe político* someone who can work discreetly and with full knowledge of the election procedures."[67] Madero concurred. On the military front, the governor requested the immediate dispatch of three hundred extra Rurales to the state. Although claiming that the revolutionary foci in Veracruz had been easy to keep in check until then, he spoke of an emerging alliance between Orozquistas, Felicistas, and Zapatistas, as well as a new plot to assassinate Madero.[68] Since these forces were needed elsewhere, it was not possible for the president to grant Pérez Rivera's request. The governor then asked Madero to at least remove General Tapia, with whom he could not work, and replace him with Camerino Mendoza.

This latter request is interesting. Tapia was not only an excellent soldier, but also had been unswervingly loyal to Madero. His name had been mentioned a few months before in connection with some anti-government plans, but nothing had been proven.

His removal must then be seen as the governor's political house-cleaning, that is, the removal of any political opponent who could question his actions. It must also be seen in the light of the revolution, whose goals and praxis had, with this gubernatorial election, been completely revised. The request was granted, and a week later Tapia was ordered to Tlaxcala.[69] For good measure, and to ensure that the slate was entirely clean, the governor also had a theatre and street that had been named after Dehesa revert to their original names of "Teatro Principal" and "Calle de la Paz" (Peace Street). That peace was made manifest on December 26 by the arrival of old revolutionary Daniel Herrera in the port with thirty-eight rebels, seeking amnesty. Another old revolutionary, the "converted" Panuncio Martínez, was busy near Tierra Blanca chasing other rebels.

But the atmosphere was charged, despite Pérez Rivera's energetic measures to control the political situation. Ominously, Teodoro Dehesa returned to the port city at the end of December, expecting to confer with his old supporters, all, of course, enemies of the new governor. And the violence continued. The presence of the army in the north was not sufficient to maintain that "peace." U.S. citizens around Tampico were constantly being robbed and threatened, as were the oil companies around Tuxpán, British and U.S. alike, which prompted the U.S. consul in Tampico to seek additional protection from the federal government.[70] The propaganda Madero circulated through his agent in the U.S., J.J. Fitzgerrell, in an effort to reassure President Taft but primarily to avoid any U.S. intervention – that he had everything under control – and that there was no threat to the lives and property of U.S. citizens – rings rather hollow in the light of these facts.[71]

Nevertheless, faced with a deteriorating political situation, the president did try to shore up his position. He had finally, and erroneously, been convinced that Dehesa was behind the political unrest in Veracruz. Dehesa's protestations that he was merely asserting his right to free speech among his friends failed to convince. Already, in the first week of January, Dehesa was preparing for a sudden departure, his daughter Emma in Havana making the preparations for the journey to New York. Fearing an order for his arrest, he departed Veracruz port on January 17 with his eldest son, Raúl, for Havana.[72] His main detractor was ex-interim governor Lagos Cházaro who, even though retired from politics and running a restaurant in the port, was in close contact with Madero. Lagos Cházaro believed that Dehesa was behind the social unrest in the state, a position that Madero was to adopt.

With Dehesa's departure, as well as the removal of Félix Díaz to a Mexico City jail, Madero felt that the situation would normalize.[73] But Madero was wrong. Both Dehesa and Díaz were only symbols; the unrest went much deeper. There was no peace in Veracruz, nor in Mexico, and the president had almost no control. The Madero government was running out of time, as it had run out of political options. Whatever moral authority Madero had engendered with his victory over Porfirio Díaz had been completely dissipated. From one end of Veracruz to the other, there was serious unrest. In the countryside, revolutionary groups of various stripes abounded, and politics showed the unmistakable turning away from the president. The governor was unable even to control the election of local authorities, which would support his government. Such was the resentment against Madero that local authorities and citizens openly rejected his government and officials. His political enemies were protected in every municipality by local authorities, who were themselves also suspect: these were the people who were closely allied with the Felicista cause or who supported some other, allied movement. Towards the end of January, it was obvious that the days of the regime were numbered.

In addition to "exiling" Dehesa and removing Díaz to what was considered a more secure jail, Madero initiated other methods to contain his opposition. In the northern cantons of Veracruz, special agents, called Federal Agents of Public Tranquility, were appointed. These were nothing less than spies charged with informing on "suspicious" persons, that is, those who might be harbouring arms or who had connections with rebels. Yet former loyals, such as Cándido Aguilar, who might have been a positive force, were not allowed to return to Veracruz. Aguilar, who had requested a return to civilian life, was asked to stay on to help in the pacification of Durango and Chihuahua. Nevertheless, on sick leave recovering from an attack of pneumonia, he returned to Córdoba, from where he was asked to come to Mexico City as Madero's adjutant.[74]

It is doubtful whether Cándido Aguilar could have done any better in pacifying Veracruz. Between the beginning of January and February 10, when the revolt of the Ciudadela commenced, Veracruz was in the throes of a conservative rebellion. The major force there was the group under Higinio Aguilar and Gaudencio de la Llave, operating around Córdoba and the Huatusco. The federal army lacked both men and horses to take them on. In Orizaba, only six Rurales could be spared to go after Aguilar's band. From the Huatusco, Aguilar crossed over into Puebla and back again to Perote, joining battle with Rurales at El Potrero. He was too strong and his force too agile to be captured.[75] One hundred and fifty of his men had been sent to harass the railway near Camerón, Paso del Macho, and Soledad del Doblado. Other alarming news was that U.S. citizens had been captured at El Potrero and held hostage. Worse, the Rurales that were sent after them ran out of ammunition and had to retreat. Lack of ammunition again allowed one of Aguilar's units to take the town of Paso del Macho a month later without resistance.[76]

Pressure on the military establishment was also obvious in the north. General Ocaranza, headquartered at Papantla with the mission of guarding the oilfields, was obliged to send part of his forces to Puebla, specifically Teziutlán, to try to contain the attempt by Aguilar and de la Llave to overthrow the Maderista government there. The attempt failed, but the re-assignment of troops left the north without protection.[77] In the municipality of Zontecomatlán, canton of Chicontepec, Otomí Indians revolted against the administration, captured the *conservador* (government agent), and declared that they were going kill all the "Aztecs" resident there. In the mountains of Zongólica, there were also reports of uprisings of the hill people. Despite the general amnesty proclaimed on January 24, however, the revolts continued. Rebel movements were also reported in Minatitlán and Acayucan as well as in Córdoba and Orizaba. On February 7, rebels under one Manuel Oceguera succeeded in capturing Acayucan. Madero's cable to Pérez Rivera on February 10 that he was sending troops from Morelos, that the main rebel force was locked up in the Ciudadela, and that the government was in complete control has the air of tragi-comedy. Not even Madero's closest advisers believed this.[78]

Antonio Pérez Rivera hardly had two months to settle into office before the vortex known as the Battle of the Ciudadela in Mexico City broke out. Both old General Bernardo Reyes and Félix Díaz were released from prison and began an uprising in the capital. Reyes was killed immediately in the attempt to capture the national palace; Díaz and troops ensconced themselves inside the barracks called the Ciudadela, a few miles from the palace. The ensuing bombardment has gone down in history as the *Decena Trágica*, the tragic ten days. While General Huerta, commissioned by Madero with the task of capturing Díaz, diddled (or planned), hundreds of people were killed in the useless crossfire. Cándido Aguilar, in the national palace at Madero's side, warned him about the probability of Huerta's treason. The president foolishly disregarded his advice. By choosing Huerta against the advice of his advisers, Madero had "signed his death warrant."[79] Within a few days, the Pact of the Ciudadela, a deal between Díaz and Huerta, was signed. On February 18, 1913, Madero and Pino Suárez were arrested in the palace and imprisoned. On the night on February 21, under the ruse of being transferred to another prison, they were both shot. The man responsible was none other than Captain Francisco Cárdenas, the soldier credited with the victory over Santanón, although the intellectual author of the crime was U.S. ambassador Henry Lane Wilson.

Immediately on hearing the news of the president's arrest, anti-Madero rebels in the field moved to take over the towns in their immediate vicinity, or cabled their supporters to do so. Most of Veracruz was taken over this way, without any shots being fired. Shortly after the coup, General Huerta let it be known that he was about to send the ex-president and the ex-vice-president to Veracruz on their way into exile. He then changed his mind, stating that the military commander of the garrison there was a Maderista. Actually, the port city harboured a few more influential sympathizers. In addition to the garrison commander, General Velasco, there was General Valdéz, the administrator of the customs house, the *jefe político*, the inspector of police, commanding officers of some of the gunboats in the harbour and the district judge. In the field, part of the 38th Rurales under Major Agustín Millán deserted, apparently in touch with Ernesto Madero.[80]

Madero may have been the only member of the government who thought things were under control. His own private secretary, De los Ríos, writing to a friend in Xalapa, expressed his doubts about the efficacy of Madero's policies: "if the center follows a policy of pardon and benignity, all government is impossible."[81] Yet in San Juan de Ulúa, there were at the time almost four hundred sentenced military prisoners. I suggest that it is this contradiction in policy – to appear as liberal and benign, yet simultaneously wield a big stick – that may have been Madero's greatest liability. In a political climate in which Porfirismo had not been forgotten, Madero's lack of consistency unsettled everyone in a Mexico that needed a firm but fair hand. Possibly Cumberland is right that the problems of governing an intractable Mexico were insurmountable within the political praxis of the Madero government.[82]

In any case, the game was up well before the end of 1912.

By January 1913, Madero's lack of perspicacity had come to plague his government. The results were obvious in Veracruz. If, in mid-1912, Manuel Alegre could plead that he needed civil servants from the *ancien régime* to be able to run the state, now, at the beginning of 1913, these were already bent on returning to the *status quo ante*. Citizens, such as those in the municipality of La Antigua, canton of Veracruz, could well complain that they were being molested by the local authorities, who "are contrary to revolutionary precepts."[83] But the state government could or would do nothing to help them. Even minor employees, such as a postal worker in Córdoba, could put about their insurrectionary anti-Maderista propaganda with impunity. The government seemed unable to distinguish between free speech and sedition. Two days before the final treachery in Mexico City, a band of Felicista rebels under Facundo Tello entered the cantonal seat of Zongólica where they were well received by the townspeople. The mayor, P. Rodríguez, who was still loyal to Madero, frantically cabled his *jefe político* asking for advice: the advice was to flee with the state Rurales.[84]

Madero's last-ditch attempts to shore up his support in Veracruz by appointing new *jefes políticos* in the cantons of Veracruz, Córdoba, and Coatepec were abortive. Too many officials – those that had been reinstated by Alegre and retained by Pérez Rivera – blocked any manoeuvre that would help the Maderista government. In the February municipal elections, ballots were withheld from those constituencies that would have voted in Maderista candidates.[85] Before Madero's arrest and resignation, therefore, Veracruz, in both the military and civil senses, was practically in the hands of the anti-government, conservative (i.e., pro-Porfirian forces). One day before the arrests of the president and vice-president, the commander of the municipal police in Zongólica handed over all the municipality's arms and a horse to the "leader of the expeditionary force," Facundo Tello. He also cabled the governor that he had done so. Does this indicate that Pérez Rivera was either aware of or supported the Pact of the Ciudadela? There is other evidence indicating that, whether aware or not, he did not go out of his way to help the government. He certainly did not show much energy in investigating the complaints of electoral fraud that had been made a few weeks earlier.[86]

With such weak support from the administration of a key state, Madero had no chance of serving out his constitutional term. There were too many people who wanted a return to the

Porfirian system, but with a difference. That system had to be clean of any Científico influence; that is, it had to be federalist in nature. In Veracruz, the symbolic leader of the anti-Madero forces was certainly Teodoro Dehesa, from his self-imposed exile in New York. Despite his denials, no one believed that he was not wielding his considerable influence against Madero. As we have noted, even the president himself, who had refrained from voicing suspicions about Dehesa, came to accept this accusation. And there is ample other evidence that Dehesa was involved in undermining the government. Writing to Dehesa the day after the *cuartelazo*, an old political friend, Senator Manuel Calero, thanked Dehesa for supporting his campaign in the Congress "against the weak Madero government."[87] In the same letter, he also refers to the reasons for this campaign. Calero was, like Dehesa, an old enemy of centralism and Cientificismo, which according to them had been re-established by the former president. It was an inexcusable policy that had to be excised, whatever the cost. As Calero explained: "I also think that the double Cuartelazo was a very sensitive matter and constituted a dangerous precedent; but there was no other way of washing the new administration of their original sin."[88] Dehesa's answer is equally chilling. He fully approved, he said, of the military solution, the "rooting out of the evil". This man, who had always believed sincerely in peaceful solutions to political problems, not only fully supported the military overthrow of the government, he also appears to have seen Madero's murder as the only way out. Out of what? For Dehesa, the main problem was again the concentration of power in the hands of the *camarilla* (political clique) surrounding the president – in other words, the problem of Cientificismo. And the saviour for them both was Félix Díaz, the nephew of the old dictator, the one leading politician who had impeccable anti-Científico credentials. Dehesa immediately hurried back from New York, arriving in March. In the meantime, his brother, Francisco, was given a "lucrative office" and set about organizing Díaz's political campaign in Veracruz.[89]

If the situation in the capital was clear, albeit tragic, in the state government it was murky. We are left with the enigma of Pérez Rivera's affiliation. Pasquel writes that he found himself between two "fires," the Huertistas who wanted him to leave and the Maderistas who wanted him to stay on as governor, giving them whatever aid he could. He did stay on for as long as he could. It soon became obvious to Huerta that Pérez Rivera was not pursuing the opposition very energetically. He was thus forced to ask for a leave of absence for three months. His replacement was Eduardo Cauz Cervantes, of a well-known, aristocratic Xalapa family. Cauz Cervantes was a military man, a former staff officer of general and governor Juan de la Luz Enríquez. The appointment caused considerable consternation in the legislature, whose members complained at this violation of state sovereignty. The three most vociferous opposition deputies, Adolfo Domínguez, Enrique Llorente and Armando Deschamps were advised to flee Huerta's wrath; but they had made their point. Not willing to antagonize Veracruzans any further, Huerta asked the legislature to choose a replacement, and Enrique Camacho was appointed provisional governor. For his part, Pérez Rivera, aided by Huertista general Blanquet, considered it prudent to hide in the plantation of an old Veracruzan friend, José de Landero y Cos, remaining there until Huerta was overthrown. He then decided to flee the country, going into self-exile with his family in the United States and not returning to Mexico until 1920.[90]

Coincidentally, while the battle of the Ciudadela was raging, Cándido Aguilar, summoned to Mexico City as Madero's adjutant, had been specifically ordered to give the president military reports on the situation. Aguilar warned Madero countless times of Huerta's possible treason, commenting on the fact that loyal soldiers were ordered into positions that amounted to certain death (Aguilar, himself, had been one of the luckier ones). Madero, of course, ignored the warning to his own detriment. On the morning of February 18, Aguilar, with a friend, Lieutenant García de la Cadena, heard shots from inside the palace and were able to witness the arrest of Madero. Cleverly, they made a hasty retreat, escaping through a back door of the palace, disarming the guard on the way. Aguilar departed immediately for Córdoba.[91]

Another loyal Maderista, Rafael Tapia, was not to be so lucky. Tapia had apparently decided to support the new regime, although the truth about his attitude is difficult to ascertain. His earlier support of Maderismo would have made him suspect in the eyes of the new president; remaining in Mexico would have been dangerous. It is claimed that he arranged for his family to flee to Havana. He himself was arrested in July 1913, on a pretext, and was confined to Santiago Tlatelolco prison. In December, he fell victim to the Huerta regime by way of the *Ley Fuga*.[92]

6

The Neo-Porfirian Experiment

While it is generally accepted that Victoriano Huerta possessed a supreme self-confidence,[1] there is less agreement regarding the nature of his regime. Alan Knight has seriously challenged Michael Meyer's conclusion that the regime was progressive. Based on evidence gathered in the course of this research, I would argue strongly in favour of Knight's position that the Huerta regime was indeed reactionary.[2] Part of the evidence for this argument is the way Mexicans viewed the regime and reacted to it.

By 1913, there was evidence of significant changes in the Mexican mentality. Mexicans did not wish to return to the conditions of the Porfiriato. For example, if in the previous revolution of 1910 rural employees frequently displayed a cowed attitude towards authority, by 1913, when the fight against Huerta began, they seemed less apt to do so. Increasingly, rural workers began to complain about their conditions of work. Farmers and fishermen, too, as for example those around the Coatzacoalcos River, complained about the oil spillage from ships belonging to the El Aguila Oil Company. Ships literally opened their valves in the river after discharging oil to the refinery.[3] Here are the first signs, not only of a concern for the environment, but the waning of any awe in which foreign companies and technology were held. In different language, one can say that here was the appearance of a genuine revolutionary mentality.[4]

In the first place, we must note the rebellious behaviour of *hacienda* contract workers (*enganchados*). Workers were still being lured to the Valle Nacional by deceptive promises of good pay and working conditions. Complaints to the governor of Veracruz, and from there to the governor of Oaxaca, produced no results. In fact, the governor of Oaxaca argued that since the contracts had already been signed, he could do nothing. In response, workers at the Vista Hermosa Sugar Mercantile Company in southern Veracruz reacted to the horrible conditions by planning a revolt.[5] The realization on the part of foreign managers that such working conditions had driven the workers to plan violence brought continued requests to the Mexican government for protection of life and property, especially, but not uniquely, from United States owners of Mexican property.[6] The situation was indeed serious, as workers-turned-rebels usually burnt down entire *haciendas* after removing arms and other valuables. The subsequent Constitutionalist struggle in Veracruz, therefore, had a different character from that of the previous revolution. Now there was an increasing demand for a social revolution. Another historian has also concluded that there was "sufficient evidence of genuine rural (and specifically) agrarian revolt in Veracruz."[7]

In addition to the popular nature of the revolution after 1913, there is another important element: the combination of middle-class popular, and even some conservative, elements in a common battle for federalism. Although each pursued federalism for its own reasons, there were times when they merged in opposition to the central government. There was evidence of this in 1913 in clashes between federal and state forces, in the attempts by governor and legislature to assert their authority against the centre, in the emergence of "landlord" revolts, and in the enmity between Constitutionalists and Manuel Peláez in the Huasteca after 1915. Whatever the nature of these alliances, federalism (or the lack of it), which had played a role in Madero's downfall, came back to haunt the Huerta regime and would be an integral theme in the ongoing revolutionary war.

The Huerta Regime

In deciding whether or not to support Huerta, Veracruzans first divided along class lines. Members of the upper class, such as Dehesa, hoping that Félix Díaz would gain the upper hand, went along with the coup. Moderate former Maderistas of the middle class, such as Raúl G. Ruiz, bided their time to see what would happen. As soon as Huerta began what appeared to be a return to the policy of centralism, they would look for the nearest opponent who seemed to support federalism. However, those Maderistas who had come from the lower-middle or working class, such as Aguilar, and Gavira, knew exactly what their position would be. They were more concerned with the reactionary nature of the new regime, so they tried to flee in order to begin resistance immediately. They were wise, considering what followed: the continued drift of the Huerta regime towards militarism.

Huerta's first move was to ascertain which of the governors was loyal, cabling them for expressions of support. We have already noted Pérez Rivera's refusal to distribute arms to Gavira, this governor being one of the few who failed to cable Huerta to affirm, or deny, his support. Huerta's request was, however, affirmed by the commander of the garrison in Veracruz, General Velasco, who nevertheless was instrumental in arranging Gavira's escape.[8] Next, a general amnesty was offered to all anti-Huerta forces if they laid down their arms within fifteen days. In addition, political prisoners in San Juan de Ulúa, especially those sentenced after the Díaz revolt in October, were released, among them, Díaz Ordaz, Zárate, and other officers.[9]

Naturally, Huerta was keen to pacify the country and to pre-empt any further rebellion. Faced with the announced opposition of three key states initiated by Venustiano Carranza, and the appearance of various foci of opposition all over Mexico, it was necessary for him to proceed *post haste*. As *El Dictámen* indelicately put it, "Madero the Martyr weighs more in the hearts of revolutionaries than Madero the Apostle."[10] To the tactic of amnesty, therefore, was added that of outright suppression of opposition; here Huerta evidenced in the first days of his presidency the true mettle of his political methodology.

One of the first victims of this policy of suppression was a man who had supported Madero from the left, and who was intimately connected with the struggles in the textile region of Orizaba, Camerino Mendoza. Mendoza was dangerous to Huerta precisely because he enjoyed an excellent reputation among the workers of Santa Rosa and Río Blanco. On hearing of Madero's murder, Mendoza immediately resigned his command in the Rurales and was imprisoned in Mexico City. Released on the objections of Heriberto Jara and Francisco Arias, both deputies for Veracruz in the Mexican Congress, Mendoza was cautioned not to leave the city, an order that he disobeyed immediately, thus drawing more suspicion on himself. He returned to his house in Santa Rosa and quickly became the object of a rumour that he was planning revolutionary action against the new government.[11] The new interior minister, Alberto García Granados, ordered Gaudencio de la Llave, commissioned with reorganizing the canton of Orizaba after the Huerta takeover, to take measures against that possibility.

On their way to Mendoza's house, the soldiers marched through Santa Rosa, where they were met by a throng of workers who began insulting them and throwing stones. Reports have it that shots were fired and a dynamite bomb was thrown. Whatever the details, the workers' hatred of de la Llave and their opposition to the new regime were obvious.[12] Soldiers surrounded the building and ordered him to submit to arrest. De la Llave's report insists that shots were fired from the interior of the house, which he answered from his own ranks. The building was set on fire; Mendoza made an exit firing as he walked and was immediately killed. After the fracas was over, the troops discovered the bodies of Vicente and Cayetona Mendoza, brothers of Camerino, together with the bodies of twenty-three other men and one woman. The house also contained dynamite bombs, arms, and a good quantity of ammunition of various types.[13]

Certainly, because of his actions, Mendoza's intentions were suspect, and the evidence does point to his revolutionary intentions; yet the precipitous response of the government was typical not only of Gaudencio de la Llave, but of the manner in which the new regime intended to treat any opposition. It is no coincidence that in the early hours of that same day, another militant and dedicated Maderista, Abraham González, governor of Chihuahua, was murdered at the behest of the government.[14]

Of the other leading Maderistas in Veracruz, another was eliminated, while three were able to escape. Rafael Tapia, sent to Tlaxcala to help the governor, Antonio Hidalgo, against Felicista rebels there, was quickly arrested and confined in the military prison of Santiago Tlatelolco, from which he was taken on December 2, 1913, and executed, his body buried without a marker in Coyoacán.[15] Heriberto Jara, Cándido Aguilar, and Gabriel Gavira were luckier. Jara, a deputy in the Mexican Congress, displayed considerable courage in remaining in Mexico City, using his influence in the Congress to help friends, such as Camerino Mendoza. His last political act in the capital was to participate in a meeting of the Liberal Party, in view of the approaching elections. Since the decision of the party executive, of which Jara was a member, was not to participate in the elections (indeed, in their manifesto they cited the "praetorian" nature of the regime, as well as its militarization), its members came to be viewed with some suspicion by the authorities. It was suggested, and this is probably true, that Jara was one of the main Constitutionalist propagandists in the capital. He therefore felt it necessary to make himself scarce. He hid in the capital for a while, then made his way to Xalapa, where he once again tried to convince governor Pérez Rivera to join the anti-Huerta movement, only to be rejected. With the aid of political friends, he was able to get to Veracruz port, and thence, with old Maderista ally, León Aillaud, made his way to Havana. Once there, he contacted the Constitutionalists, embarking in July for New Orleans. Later, he reentered Mexico through Matamoros, Tamaulipas, where he contacted Constitutionalist general Lucio Blanco and was given command of a regiment.[16]

Gabriel Gavira was even luckier. General Velasco delayed the order for his arrest, allowing him to evade it, embarking on the steamer *Monterrey*. Evading capture once more when the U.S. consul in Progreso, Yucatán, refused to order his arrest on the ship, and protected by the sympathetic captain of the vessel, he reached Havana unharmed. After four months, he also returned to Mexico via Matamoros, where he was incorporated into the Constitutionalist army.[17]

The luckiest of all was Cándido Aguilar, present as an aide to Madero during the battle of the Ciudadela. At one point, he was attached to General Huerta's staff in order to furnish the president with accurate information on the military situation. Huerta, obviously annoyed that his plans were being questioned, asked Madero to lend him Aguilar. He then sent the young officer on a reconnaissance mission to the front of the line, where the chances of survival were slim. Luckily Aguilar survived, returning to the palace where he again tried to get the president to understand Huerta's treason and to flee. Madero, as we saw, insisted on staying, sealing his fate. Shortly after, General Blanquet appeared and arrested him. Aguilar and two lieutenants managed to escape out a back door of the palace where they disarmed the guard, and got to Córdoba, where Aguilar hid for a short time. From there, he went to Guatemala, embarking at Puerto Barrios for the U.S. and thence to Monclova where he also joined the Constitutionalist army. Aguilar was the first Veracruzan officer to be accorded the rank of general, to which Madero had promoted him. After several months of fighting in Jalisco and Nayarit, he was sent on July 30 with orders to organize the battle against Huertismo in his home state. His staff included two other famous Veracruzan revolutionaries, Gabriela Gavira and Heriberto Jara, as well as others who would become famous. Among these was

Agustín Millán, the Rurales colonel who had deserted with his troops, as well as Adalberto Palacios, Antonio Portas, Guadalupe Sánchez, and Adalberto Tejeda.[18]

These weren't the only Veracruzan Maderistas who declined to recognize Huerta. In the region of Ixhuatlán, canton of Chicontepec, Alfonso Polanco and Vicente Salazar, the latter soon to be incorporated into Aguilar's First Division of the East, declared against Huerta, as well as General Antonio Medina in the Huasteca. In the south, the old grouping of PLM supporters came together again to carry the struggle against Huertismo into the plains around the Tuxtlas, Acayucan, and Minatitlán. On June 7, 1913, they issued a manifesto from the mountains around San Martín in the Tuxtlas, under the banner of the red flag, declaring as their principles the Plan of San Luis Potosí, reformed by the plans of Tacubaya and Ayala. P.A. Carbajal, Hilario C. Salas, Miguel Alemán, and ten others signed this document.[19]

It took time, however, for this military opposition to become organized, and not until the end of April 1913 did physical assaults on federal garrisons and various towns in Veracruz begin. In an effort to offset this eventuality, the government had secured whatever advantages it could by appointing Huertista or pro-Porfirian officials as mayors, aldermen, and *jefes políticos*. Next were plans to undertake the complete militarization of Mexican society. Everyone, including women, was ordered to wear military uniforms at work and to undertake three hours of military training one day per week. In addition, ten new divisions of infantry were created for the Rurales. Although Veracruz was supposedly in a state of peace, General de la Llave was ordered to create a force of one thousand troops. By the middle of April, the garrison at Veracruz contained the 18th and 19th Infantry Battalions, each with 460 men and machine guns, 111 mounted Rurales, four large and eleven smaller field guns, 250 foot and thirty-five mounted police, plus 1,500 volunteers – a formidable force. This contingent was large but not extraordinary, considering that Veracruz contained the country's most important port.[20] The problem now was how to deploy them effectively in containing the gathering opposition.

The key to a vigorous pursuit of this military goal was the governor. Pérez Rivera had only confirmed his support of the new government on March 1. Huerta, for his part, needed the backing of as many states as possible, especially one as strategically important as Veracruz. But he also needed the appearance of legality or constitutionality, and was therefore, loath to part with anyone – in this case a "legally" elected governor – who could lay claim to such legitimacy.[21] Admittedly, Pérez Rivera's credentials were somewhat shaky: there was considerable opposition to his remaining in office, for it was openly contended that his had been an illegal election, manipulated by the former president. However, the governor, backed by Huerta, refused to resign.[22]

Huerta's next major political move was to outmanoeuver Félix Díaz in the upcoming elections. The tactic he adopted was to flirt with the Maderistas in Congress, who had begun to organize Diaz's campaign.[23] Teodoro Dehesa had returned from exile, while his brother Francisco was already hard at work organizing political clubs to work on Félix Díaz's behalf in the presidential election. In early March, Francisco organized and was elected president of the Veracruz Liberal Club. In addition to these clubs, which sprang up all over Veracruz, there was external help for Díaz. Other clubs were organized in Havana and New Orleans, the first with five hundred members.[24] The Dehesas supported the candidacy of Félix Díaz precisely because of his anti-Científico stance.[25] Yet they could not be sure that Huerta would honour the agreement made in the Ciudadela. Second, they could not be certain whether Huerta intended to allow Félix Díaz a fair chance in the presidential elections.

From the Dehesas' standpoint, the election would be the key to returning the country to normalcy. If it was fair, then Díaz would be sure of winning, and the country would be saved from bloodshed. If not, then Huerta would continue in power. In Teodoro Dehesa's opinion, this would mean governing "with the use of the most terrible force in order to achieve his goals."[26] Although Dehesa did not know it, his judgment of the political situation would soon be proven correct. In the meantime, the two could only wait. Soon, there were rumours of dissension in the Huerta cabinet, and García Granados, a Felicista, was forced to resign. Dehesa expected that the new minister would be a Felicista, if Huerta remained loyal to the Pact of the Ciudadela. But an attempt by some friends to have Teodoro Dehesa named to this position was met with a curt "*requaquam*" (no way!).[27]

By May, the situation was no better; Huerta's political directions were still not clear. The only change was in the revolutionary movement, which appeared to be flourishing. In a feeble attempt to bolster his own position, but also to calm the political uncertainty in the state, Pérez Rivera approached Dehesa through a mutual friend, González Mena, to assure him that he harboured no enmity. Dehesa could only remind González Mena that, while he did not consider the governor a bad person, Pérez Rivera was still shielding former Maderistas who were Dehesa's sworn political enemies. In addition, Dehesa did not think that the governor had any legitimacy, because of his support from Maderistas and Gaviristas. Taking the initiative, Dehesa suggested that the only action that would legitimate the governor in the eyes of Veracruzans was to publicly disassociate himself from Maderismo.[28]

Dehesa's suggestion has the ring of naïveté. What he couldn't know was that Pérez Rivera was playing a double game. At the same time as the governor was offering his hand to Dehesa, his minions in the state were carrying out an active persecution of Felicistas who were organizing for the forthcoming elections. The Dehesas were, in fact, organizing for a candidate who, through intention or omission, had allowed the governor's friend and former mentor, Gustavo Madero, to be murdered in the most brutal way. One should not be surprised, then, that Díaz's campaign was blocked from the beginning in Veracruz. Nor can one accuse Huerta of ordering the harassment. The president just had to sit back and allow events to take their natural, vengeful, course. Still, a semblance of fairness had to be maintained. The ministry of the interior warned Pérez Rivera to issue clear instructions to his *jefes políticos* not to antagonize Felicistas or those who availed themselves of the amnesty.[29]

Still the harassment continued. One Felicista was followed so closely that, as he put it, the police agents "were almost stepping on my heels."[30] In Xalapa, where there appeared to be considerable Felicista support from factory workers, artisans, and the middle class, delegates of the Club Patria were forced to report to the army commander, General Paredes, on a daily basis. Some were prevented from travelling to carry out political work, while others were called in by the *jefe político* and harangued over their political affiliation. Every petty excuse to haul in a Felicista campaigner was utilized. By the latter part of April, it was obvious what was happening. Dehesa's hopes for a clean campaign were dashed. Díaz, too, saw the writing on the wall. On April 25, he and De la Barra both renounced their candidacies.[31]

In the meantime, the house-cleaning took a new turn. With the continued advance of Carrancismo, especially in the north but also in Veracruz, and the continued resistance in Morelos, Huerta decided to get rid of the last vestiges of the former government. There were still deputies to the Mexican Congress who were direct in their criticism, guarded as it had to be. In mid-June, Heriberto Jara openly accused General de la Llave of responsibility in the shooting of Camerino Mendoza and members of his family the previous February.[32] Then the governor and the legislature confirmed the election of magistrates carried out on February 9. This was too much for Huerta. Maderistas occupying various positions of authority, whether or not they had committed any crime, let alone that of "treason," were denounced and removed from office. Pérez Rivera himself became suspect. Feeling the pressure, he asked for and was given a leave of absence. He was replaced on July 2 by General Eduardo Cauz Cervantes, an appointment that caused some consternation because it was unconstitutional. Five deputies in the Veracruz legislature complained and resigned in protest. Others followed. They were promptly arrested.[33]

The Constitutionalist Struggle

Huerta's increased use of repression was due, not only to his desire to neutralize any political opposition, but also to his deteriorating military position in the state of Veracruz. Scarcely two months after the coup, the first armed attack was launched against his government there. On April 24, Tamiahua was taken by a party of rebels led by Agustín Blanco, assisted by local citizens. Having taken the town, the rebels left for Tuxpán, which was guarded by only twenty-five men.[34] The second attack followed hard on the first. Vicente Salazar, Francisco de P. Mariel, and Daniel Cerecedo Estrada, having begun their rebellion in Huejutla, in the state of Hidalgo, crossed over into Veracruz on April 25. They quickly captured the cantonal seat of Tantoyuca, which they held for four days before being dispersed.[35]

From the very beginning of resistance, the tactical hand of Venustiano Carranza, named First Chief of the Constitutionalist Army, was evident. The attack on Veracruz came from a region that was almost under the command of the Constitutionalist army and was carried out in a way that threatened the strategic interests not only of the Mexican government, but also of foreign nationals. Carranza's main aim was to gain control of the important oil fields in the north of Veracruz, so as to be able to exercise as much leverage as possible as well as to fund his campaign. Then he planned to isolate Veracruz in order to starve the federal government of funds and supplies. He first ordered León Aillaud in Havana to return to Veracruz immediately and to begin disrupting rail traffic on the Mexican Railway as well as the Interoceanic. Aillaud reportedly left Havana with dynamite a few weeks later. Carranza's next tactical move was to commission Cándido Aguilar to head for the south and be given command of the 38th Regiment.[36] On May 1, federal forces engaged the well-organized, well-armed, and coordinated attackers in Ixhuatlán. This encounter, one of the first battles in the northern region of Veracruz, marked the appearance of Manuel Peláez, who was the Constitutionalist commanding officer there. More will be said of this *hacendado-cum-military cacique*, but it is interesting to note the causes, and timing, of his involvement in the revolution. Peláez was one of many small and large landowners who had leased their land to oil companies. The archive of the Veracruz Notary Public, which recorded such land transactions, is replete with the signing of property leases and sub-soil concessions to oil companies in the north of Veracruz, especially around Tantoyuca. Intense oil exploration was taking place, and companies did not have long to wait for their returns. On May 23, an oil gusher ten feet high was registered just over a kilometre from Tuxpán.[37] The importance of the area, so obvious to the Constitutionalists, would soon increase significantly.

The fighting there lasted for over a month and comprised the cantons of Tantoyuca, Ozuluama, Tuxpán, and Papantla. The rebels numbered well over five hundred and consistently, although narrowly, defeated the federal troops, causing numerous casualties. People deserted the town of Ixhuatlán and sought shelter in the countryside. Despite concerted attempts by the government troops, the rebels not only resisted defeat but seemed to gather adherents wherever they went. On June 6, they decimated the federal force near Ixhuatlán and then took the direction of Furbero, where there was a large U.S. oil field. On June 24, Papantla fell to the rebels. By this time, it was reported that there were at least two thousand rebels under arms in the region. Pérez Rivera's speech at a banquet on May 6, at which he spoke of having driven out rebels and put an end to banditry, may have sealed his fate. The army command knew differently.[38]

Between June and September, various groups continued to operate in Veracruz, more or less in touch with the headquarters of the Constitutionalist army in Piedras Negras, or with Luis Blanco in Matamoros. Rebel activity also emerged in the centre of the state, around Orizaba as well as in the canton of Zongólica. Gaudencio de la Llave was reconfirming his reputation by hanging anyone suspected of being a sympathizer.

Even people named as "agitators" were summarily executed by hanging from the nearest tree, as was the unhappy end for four workers from Orizaba.[39] In mid-June, about three hundred rebels led by Melesio Cabanzo reduced the *hacienda* Xonotipam, canton of Zongólica, to ashes. Indeed, the entire canton was overrun with "bandits," who crossed the border into Puebla with impunity, taking advantage of the low state of the rivers.[40] Because federal troops had been sent to Puebla, by November 1913, Veracruz rebels could roam as close to the state capital as Teocelo.[41] There were too many rebels, and not enough soldiers or supplies to keep them constantly in the field.[42]

In the south, the situation was similar, except that here there were two distinct groups engaged in attacking the government. Not much has been written about Zapatista activity outside of Morelos, but in Veracruz there were frequent raids by groups supporting the Plan of Ayala. The majority of these attacks occurred around the Tuxtlas and Acayucan. The manager of Campamento Sewanee, a British-owned sugar plantation, complained of raids at the end of May by Zapatistas who were ensconced in the hills at Cerro Grande. In Jáltipan, there was action as well, and in July uprisings of Zapatistas were reported in Minatitlán, Las Vigas, and Córdoba.[43] The other group in the south was that of Hilario Salas and Miguel Alemán, successors to the PLM revolutionaries of Acayucan in 1906, which comprised about six hundred men divided into groups of between fifty and sixty, who operated from the mountains of the Tuxtlas. The British embassy requested protection for the El Palmar rubber estate at Tezonapa, canton of Acayucan, but the government could do no more. It couldn't even help its own corps of engineers engaged in mapping territory in the area. Another section of the southern rebel army led by Pedro Carbajal attacked Jáltipan, while Hilario Salas concentrated on the area around San Andrés Tuxtla.[44]

In August, Captain Sotomayor put together an expedition to relieve the situation. Arriving in mid-August, this force began a sweep mainly around the canton of Acayucan, where they helped repulse a raid by Salas on the town of Acayucan. By December, the regular army was having slightly more success. On December 8, Carbajal and four hundred men were repulsed. Two weeks later, they encountered a federal corps in the Soteapan and were given a considerable drubbing, leaving behind sixty-seven horses and much ammunition.[45] In war, strange things happen, some of them unexplainable, as in the appearance of a ship painted black with a yellow funnel that appeared off the coast of San

Andrés Tuxtla at a place called Roca Partida. Men from this ship captured ten fishermen, shot off its cannon undisturbed, and then made off towards the south. No flag was flown, nor did the vessel appear to have a name. Judging from the correspondence, it caused quite a furour within the government, who believed that the rebels now had their own navy.[46]

Confusion is, however, only one element in war. Others include audacity, perseverance, and logistics. Superior numbers also help. Unfortunately, they did not help Huerta's government. As González Mena had revealed to Dehesa in May, the government was at a disadvantage: "Presently [it] has eighty thousand men under arms but lacks tactical officers to command it. Of these eighty thousand men 75 percent lack military training.... The rebels are now thirty-three thousand strong. In order to defeat them we need ten soldiers for every one rebel."[47] Despite superior numbers, the government was fighting a well-organized and coordinated guerilla war. For those rebels not associated with the Carrancistas there was still a common cause: get rid of Huerta. The rebels therefore controlled one factor that in war can be decisive: the moral ground. Even where there was nostalgia for the Porfiriato, there was also repugnance at serving a regime that owed its existence to usurpation and murder. Madero had also, as González Mena pointed out, instilled dreams, and these were not going to disappear easily. They fuelled the relentless attacks on the system, which kept the federal army hopping from one place to another. For example, in September, there were twenty-four separate but indecisive skirmishes in Veracruz, in fifteen out of the eighteen cantons. Carbajal attacked the town of Acayucan on September 2 and 3. He then broke away to the south, while Salas entered the town of Pato del Agua nearby on September 4, taking eleven horses, regrouping, and marching north where he attacked and captured the town of Catemoco in the Tuxtlas on September 20. In San Juan Evangelista, a large town in the centre of Acayucan, Tomás Agramonte and Guadalupe Ochoa, (the latter also a veteran of the 1906 Acayucan revolt) were openly recruiting men.[48]

In addition to the difficulties of any regular army fighting against guerilla forces, we need to factor in the constant enmity between the state of Veracruz and the central government. This tension is a constant and underlying theme of this work, as it was a recurring feature of Veracruz history. Rurales forces deeply resented the presence of federal troops in Orizaba, despite a supposed commonality of interest, so much so that the two clashed in June, stopping just short of an outright and bloody skirmish. The antagonism between the governor and legislature on the one hand, and the federal government in Mexico on the other, can also be discerned in Pérez Rivera's decision to take a leave of absence one month later. This was another ironic victory of sorts for the federalist-minded Veracruzans who had earlier identified Pérez Rivera with the neo-Científicos of the Madero family.[49]

Another factor supporting the rebel forces was the extremely thorough strategic planning emanating from Constitutionalist Army headquarters in Piedras Negras, overseen by Carranza himself. Carranza may not have been a military man, but the evidence suggests he was a master of tactical and strategic planning. While Gavira was on a mission in Havana, raising money from rich supporters in Mexico City with which to buy supplies for entry into Veracruz, and before Cándido Aguilar was dispatched to the Huasteca, the Constitutionalist army set out to unite the various factions existing in the north of Veracruz. These would become the nucleus of the Division of the East. The plan was to be put into effect by Demetrio Bustamante, the Constitutionalist agent in Havana. Gavira was then to proceed to Matamoros, from whence he and Heriberto Jara would enter Veracruz from the north. Two so-called public women, Luz Gil and Esperanza Ramires, carried money from Mexico City to Havana. Luz Gil was said to have at least two thousand pesos on her person. At the same time, León Aillaud had purchased three hundred carbines and dynamite and was preparing to ship these to the state.[50]

In the meantime, Lucio Blanco in Matamoros coordinated Veracruz operations. Runners were sent into the Huasteca to contact the rebels there. Orders were given to try to cut the railway linking San Luis Potosí to Tampico, and to interrupt all traffic to the oil fields at El Ebano.[51] With revolutionary ranks growing daily, bolstered by Huastecan Indians who were operating in the Chintipán hills around Chicontepec, the oil companies found themselves in a worsening situation. U.S. diplomatic requests notwithstanding, rebels had discovered how easy it was to extract forced loans and supplies, including horses from vulnerable companies. By August, Carrancista rebels were headquartered permanently in Ixhuatlán (canton of Chicontepec). And the first desertions from the federal forces were reported.[52]

Further to the south, the Márquez brothers from Puebla together with Alejandro Vega, nephew of Huertista General Celso Vega, attacked the cantonal seat of Papantla, and, in a torrential rain, after a ten-hour battle, captured it.[53] One of the reasons for the rebel victory was that the Indians fighting with the federals under Major Simon Tiburcio refused to continue after twenty-four of their comrades were killed. But there were other reasons. Vega, an ex-Rurales officer and a firm Maderista, harboured his own resentments. The Márquez brothers, also former Maderistas were part of that growing rural protest – at first localized, but of a socio-economic content that was generalized throughout Veracruz, and perhaps all Mexico – that gave a distinct character to this phase of the Mexican Revolution.

The pressure on Tuxpán and the surrounding oil fields in the north was stepped up in July, when both the town and nearby Temapache, as well as Chontla, canton of Tantoyuca, were captured and held for a while. Many U.S. citizens fled the area for the port of Veracruz, which was considered safer. And Esteban Márquez continued his march across the northwest corner of the state, now commanding some eight hundred troops. In the meantime, Papantla was recaptured, and the federal commander could claim that the canton was free of rebels except for one small band, under Julio Arroyo.[54] In July, too, Cándido Aguilar commenced his march south, through the states of San Luis Potosí and Tamaulipas, arriving at the border of Veracruz on September 2.

There, he incorporated various rebel forces under his command and proceeded to establish his headquarters at Ixhuatlán. He then divided Veracruz into a northern and southern region, naming commanders for each canton. In October, the combined force became the Division of the East, and Aguilar prepared for an attack on Tuxpán. The federal government, recognizing the imminent, reorganized and strengthened its forces in the north. Among the new commanders was Manuel Peláez who was given command of forces covering the heights above Ixhuatlán. The attack on Tuxpán was carried out from November 14 and 15, but was broken off, as the rebels were not able to dislodge the federals, who on the other hand could not pursue them.[55]

For the next few months, Aguilar had to content himself with replenishing his forces. Like others before him, he forced money and supplies from the oil companies, which eventually led to an interesting confrontation, one that displayed a singular departure in policy from that of both the Porfiriato and the Maderista government.[56] Both Porfirio Díaz and Madero had considered foreign property sacrosanct. Not much effort had been made to either levy or collect taxes from the oil companies, who were carting off the nation's subsoil heritage, literally by the barrel.

However, in the ensuing years and with a new generation of young politicians, that liberal trade ideology was about to change. Cándido Aguilar, now wiser and more experienced in politics as well as war, was about to put his own stamp on the revolutionary struggle. He would now attempt to exert the state's sovereignty in an effort to have the companies pay taxes to Veracruz.

For the moment, he had a free hand as the Constitutionalist government was in no position to force commanders to adhere to any given policy. Aguilar's actions in regard to the oil companies of the region first brought him into conflict with U.S. admiral Fletcher, whose naval forces, some thirteen to fourteen ships had been deployed to protect the oil fields. At the end of December, Fletcher sent Aguilar a note demanding that, since the rebel general was incapable of protecting life and property in the zone, he withdraw from the area within twenty-four hours or the fleet would land its own forces for that purpose. After conferring with his officers, who gave him carte blanche to resolve the situation as he saw fit, Aguilar replied to Fletcher's note:

> I refer to your insolent note of today's date. The life and interests of all foreigners has had, has, and will have the utmost guarantees of my forces in this military zone. If you carry out your threat to disembark United States troops on Mexican territory, *I will be obliged to fight them, to set fire to all the oil wells in this region, and to execute all Americans encountered here.* (emphasis added)

To implement his threat, he had defensive trenches dug and issued orders to his officers to round up all Americans and, at the first burst of cannon fire, to light the wells and execute the hostages. Faced with this audacious response, Admiral Fletcher was forced to back down, requesting that Aguilar meet with the captain of the *Nebraska.*[57] Chagrined, the U.S. government could only resort to intrigue and lies, accusing Aguilar of taking hostages and threatening to light the wells if he was not given fifty thousand dollars by the oil companies. The matter was referred to Carranza, who ordered Aguilar's court martial before becoming aware of the truth.[58]

Fletcher ought not to have been too worried at this time. The setback at Tuxpán coincided with an ebb in the fortunes of the Constitutionalists. By the end of December, the federal army had recovered most of the captured cities in northern Veracruz. And despite a successful attack on Pánuco, also in the oil area, on December 24, Aguilar's army was facing a resurgent federal force. At the end of November, General Joaquín Maas with over eight hundred troops from Mexico City had arrived by train in Veracruz. By mid-December, it was reported, he had reached Tuxpán and had re-fortified the area, bringing the oil fields again under the protection of the federal government. These troops were then reinforced by the two gunboats, *Veracruz* and *Zaragoza* which took up positions off Tampico.[59]

Despite this improvement in the overall military situation, Huerta decided to tighten his control on the republic. In Veracruz, *El Dictámen*, whose director, Juan Malpica Silva, had published an editorial distancing Veracruz from the government "because of its origin, its system, and the men who are at the pinnacle of power" and calling for Huerta's resignation, was closed down. He was promptly sent to San Juan de Ulúa, although later released through the auspices of the director of *El Imparcial*, the Xalapan poet Díaz Mirón.[60] Two other papers, *La Opinión* and *El Grito del Pueblo,* were also shut. What worried the government most, however, was not the internal struggle, but the considerable enmity emanating from Washington and the consistent rumours of, and among foreigners, the wish for U.S. intervention.[61]

At the end of October, Huerta dissolved Congress and arrested 110 deputies, most of whom had been Maderistas.[62] Ex-governor Dehesa was also ordered to Mexico City. Fearing an assassination attempt (there is apparently some basis to this worry), his daughter-in-law, Emma García Peña, whose father was a minister in Huerta's cabinet, accompanied him. In Mexico City, he stayed in the house of an English friend under house arrest. His interview with Huerta took place in a restaurant, where apparently the only conversation was Dehesa asking the reason for his summons, and Huerta replying that he was free to go. Huerta also told Dehesa that a special train had been ordered for his departure, but when Dehesa declined, the General told him he could either take it or go to jail. Dehesa returned to Veracruz, where he lived until the success of Carrancismo was certain and then embarked for exile yet again, along with many former Huertistas, in September 1914.[63]

January 1914 was a significant month for the Huerta regime because its greatest fear materialized: isolation from former supporters in Europe. It began with European bankers' decision not to renew their option on a loan. Huerta's response was to suspend interest payments on the national debt. Isolated financially, he was now desperate to end rebel activity. A renewed effort was undertaken, despite which or perhaps because of it, revolutionary activity increased dramatically. In addition to rebel activities in the north and south of Veracruz, well-organized and officered groups replaced the bandits who were coursing through the central area of the state. The revolutionary struggle had also turned strategic. An English oil company, for example, had been supplying the Mexican railroads with oil for its locomotives. Cándido Aguilar warned *El Aguila* that if the supplies continued he would set fire to the large well at El Potrero in the north. That would have been a disaster for the British, as Mexican oil also supplied the Royal Navy at a time of increasing problems in the international arena. The Mexican government attempted to convert its locomotives to coal burning, but that also produced difficulties, for the U.S. consul at Veracruz, William Canada, advised his government that if asked it should not supply coal to Mexico.[64]

At the start of the New Year, the rebels were now raiding as close to ten miles from Veracruz port.[65] A third front was opened in the centre of the state, with well-known leaders from the Maderista revolution such as Raúl G. Ruiz and Teódulo Córdoba. Ruiz attacked Zongólica in early January, causing considerable damage to the hospital and garrison, while Córdoba concentrated his small force around Atoyac. Ruiz was supposed to have about 150 ex-federal soldiers under his command. Throughout January, these groups engaged federal and state forces without any decisive result. Where the federals were able to engage rebels in open combat, it seems they got the upper hand. But since rebels rarely engaged in such combat, the federal forces were quite ineffective. Rebel tactics consisted of raiding cantonal seats, such as Zongólica, or foreign plantations such as the El Palmar Rubber Company in the Tuxtlas, and building up their forces.[66]

The tactics of the rebels, especially those of Aguilar, continued to show very innovative qualities. Aguilar was beginning to develop the strategic and tactical sense that he would later employ as governor. For instance, he planned to take a small town that lay between the Cofre de Perote and the Orizaba volcano because it was a coffee centre, from which he could obtain funds, probably in the form of taxes, so as to maintain his troops. Two Spaniards, Antonio and Félix Cosío, had set up shops there in Altotonga, from which, financed with the help of the coffee trade, they were supplying rebels with arms and ammunition.[67]

In the south, the situation also see-sawed between rebel attacks and government counter-attacks.[68] A quarrel between the rebel leaders, however, led to the murder of Hilario Salas by Carbajal, early in March. Although this deprived the southern rebels of the support of those Popolucas who had fought with Salas, it did not diminish rebel activity. Indeed, federal troops had to be dispatched from here to there with haste. As soon as one army detachment had cleared out bandits near the state capital, Xalapa, they were dispatched to the canton of Minatitlán to prevent the unloading of Felicista troops and arms. The mention of Felicista troops in a report is strange and could not be verified from other sources. The only direct corroborating evidence was an order by the local authorities to set a curfew in Puerto México from 11 p.m. for anyone not possessing a special pass.[69] Clearly the government was expecting some trouble, Felicista or otherwise.

Faced with the regime's increased efforts, Aguilar began to wield a potent political weapon. In order to gain support among the population, particularly the landless and lower classes, he issued a proclamation invoking the principles of humanity, exhorting everyone to cease support for the "spurious government." "Come to our ranks, he asked, "to the ranks of reason and legality." This was followed by the first political action of the revolutionary government in Veracruz, and provided a foretaste (as had his threat to Admiral Fletcher) of Aguilar's style of governorship after Huerta's defeat. On April 30, he published a decree confiscating the properties of prominent Veracruzans José and Gonzalo Trinidad Herrera, on grounds of having cooperated with Huerta, and declared that the properties would revert to the Constitutional government until they could be returned to the original owners from whom they had been stolen.[70] Aguilar's action does not appear insincere. He was known for his progressive social ideas, which, as will be argued later, did not always to conform with those of his First Chief. His proclamation given time, might have had the desired effect; before it could, the entire revolution was thrown onto a new path by events that were not known to the revolutionaries until the morning of April 21.

On that morning, United States forces under Admiral Fletcher invaded Mexico at Veracruz for the stated purpose of preventing a shipment of arms on the German ship *Ipiranga* from reaching Huerta's forces. Ironically, the ship had at the last minute been diverted to Puerto México, where it was able to discharge its cargo. Invasion was the tactic that many U.S. citizens with property in Mexico had asked of their government months before President Wilson took the actual decision. Lord Cowdray, too, favoured an invasion. The same was true of the U.S. citizen with perhaps the greatest investments in Mexico, Edward Doheny. In

November 1913, the U.S. government had advised Doheny of the threat to the substantial oil wells of the American Huasteca Petroleum Company at Juan Casiano, Veracruz.[71] The orders to the U.S. forces were to carry out a full-scale occupation of the port. General Mass, the Huertista commander in the port city, withdrew his forces outside of the city, which he ringed with trenches in an attempt to forestall a march on the capital. Others, however, resisted, including women and students of the Naval School. The U.S. forces were surprised: they had expected a kind of holiday outing, and instead Veracruzans fought from house to house for four days before the invaders could secure the city. Wilson was apparently appalled at the number of dead. In all, some nineteen blue-jackets had been killed and over seventy wounded.[72]

Of course, taking and holding a city is quite a different thing from governing it. From the very first, Veracruzans for the most part refused to cooperate with the invaders. The city council resigned en masse, and many families left the port rather than remain there under foreign rule. For those who remained, life was difficult.[73] Both Huerta and Carranza demanded nothing short of a complete withdrawal of the United States forces. Veracruzans, Carranza warned, should not collaborate with the enemy, nor accept positions in the city government or any other official capacity.

While the "ABC Conference" (Argentina, Brazil, and Chile were asked to be the mediators) at Niagara Falls debated the situation, Huerta was faced with the threat of the United States attacking the capital. He therefore withdrew many of his forces to protect Mexico City. Into this vacuum slipped the Constitutionalists and others, such as Zapata.[74] Their decision regarding Veracruz was to remove the oilfields from Huertista control as soon as possible. The reason was obvious. Huerta's main source of government revenue had been cut off at Veracruz. His order forbidding any commerce with that city and rerouting everything through Puerto México in the south of the state, which he still controlled, would prove ineffective. The only other source of income would be from the oilfields.[75]

So while Huerta tried to control the collapsing situation, the Constitutionalists continued their advance. Torreón had fallen in early April, Matamoros a few days after the U.S. invasion. Just before the U.S. invasion Cándido Aguilar had recaptured the important city of Tantoyuca, in the north of Veracruz. On May 13, Tampico fell, putting Tuxpán in the centre of a pincer movement. With reserves of only 120,000 bullets, Lieutenant Colonel Guillemín was hard put to resist the 1,500 to 2,000 rebels who pressed on him. By May 12, Aguilar's forces had taken the towns of Tantima, Tamalín, and Amatlán. Tamiahua was taken after a bitter fight, lasting eleven days. A few days later, Tuxpán fell to Gabriel Gavira, almost without a fight.[76] After its fall, the Division of the East set up headquarters there, declaring the city the provisional capital of Veracruz. Aguilar then reorganized his forces in a line from the coast stretching into Teziutlán, Puebla, and began the march south for Xalapa, driving the federal troops under General Roberto Carranza (no relation to the First Chief) before him. On May 29, Carranza named Aguilar provisional governor of Veracruz. At his side was Heriberto Jara, named secretary to the governor.[77]

After the taking of Tuxpán, Aguilar sent Gavira south to attack Papantla. With Papantla in Constitutionalist hands, not only would the new state capital of Tuxpán be protected, but also the road to the south would be accessible. Papantla fell on June 8, as did the nearby towns of Gutiérrez Zamora and Ixhuatlán. This was another strategic victory, as these towns afforded Aguilar's forces access to the mountains of Puebla, an additional advantage in the Constitutionalist advance.[78] A heavy column next attacked and captured Teocelo and Coatepec, in preparation for the attack on Xalapa, guarded by General Medina, while Aguilar and another force roamed into the Huatusco dispensing "revolutionary" justice. Again, combining political with military strategy, he induced fifteen hundred Indians in Santa Ana Atzacán to rebel against Huertismo, causing the federal forces in Orizaba to reduce the garrison there as they went after these latest adherents to the Constitutionalist cause.[79] Zongólica, too, was captured, placing almost the entire northern and central part of the state in Constitutionalist hands. From this canton, the revolutionary force then prepared to make the assault on Xalapa.[80] Federal troops made one last-ditch effort to regroup and counterattack: reinforced troops attacked the revolutionaries at Misantla on July 1. But already the first rumours of Huerta's resignation were about. Reporters of *La Opinión*, back in business, broke the story that Huerta's family were making preparations to depart via Puerto México. The newspaper's tone also changed, from quite guarded reporting to stories favouring the Constitutionalists in general and Aguilar in particular.[81] At other points in the state, the revolution continued its forward march. By July 8, two thousand rebels surrounded Orizaba, while the Indians of Santa

Ana Atzacán, numbering around 1,800, had allied with Aguilar's forces. On July 5, Carbajal attacked and took Acayucan, the most important town to fall in the south. With its strategic location, affording it control of the surrounding countryside, Acayucan was the equivalent of Tuxpán in the north.[82]

These successful attacks threw the state government in Xalapa into confusion. Pérez Rivera, hiding in Pachuca, Hidalgo, did not appear in Xalapa at the appointed time to renew his leave of absence from the governorship. The legislature therefore declared the state without an executive and swore in Cervantes Cauz as interim governor. At the moment of swearing in, the lights went out, giving a menacing symbolic undertone to the proceedings.[83] On July 13 came news of the fall of Teziutlán in Puebla, a key strategic point on the western flank. That same day, Cauz resigned for reasons of health. On July 15, General Huerta also resigned, leaving Francisco S. Carbajal to negotiate the inevitable. Huerta was given an escort of one hundred men to take him to Puerto México and thence into exile.

7

Constitutionalists, Conventionists, and Félix Díaz

tterly disappointed and chagrined, Teodoro Dehesa wrote his old friend, ex-president Díaz, a disparaging summary of the political events of the last sixteen months: "Huerta has resigned and left the country. Only his discredited regime could have made the revolutionaries succeed. Possibly history will record him as the most execrable president Mexico ever had."[1] This was an accurate assessment by an astute politician, who must have rued the day he returned to Mexico after the coup.

On August 13, General Obregón signed the Treaty of Teoloyucan, and on August 20, Carranza made his triumphal entry into Mexico City. On August 25, Aguilar entered Xalapa, also to a tumultuous welcome; the next day, Cervantes Cauz handed over power legally to him. Jara was appointed secretary of government, and José E. Domínguez sub-secretary. Accompanying Aguilar were about five thousand troops, among them many women, soldaderas of the Huasteca (one of them an "amazon" dressed as a man). These women were not camp followers, but regular soldiers who had taken part in the battles of the north.[2]

In Xalapa, the new government prepared to get down to business. León Aillaud was named head of the Custom's House, whose new headquarters was established in Orizaba. Carranza's decree not to subject goods to charges if they had been levied in the port by the occupation forces brought welcome relief and was necessary to revive trade and give the central government revenue. One of Aguilar's first acts as governor was to expel all foreign clergy from Veracruz territory. In addition, he stipulated the exact ratio of each clergyman for the population (in towns of 1,500 to 10, 000, one clergyman, and so on). Then he declared all laws, decrees, and circulars passed by the previous regime null and void. On entering Orizaba, Jara had done similarly, closing all Catholic schools as well.[3] Carranza had meanwhile entered into negotiations with the United States for the withdrawal from the port, raising hopes that this could occur by October. In Veracruz state, a return to a normal, peaceful life seemed to be just around the corner.

   With the capture of Xalapa, and the rest of the state, the Constitutionalists had won. But had they? Or in what sense? Cándido Aguilar had carried the struggle in Veracruz through his reputation made in the hills of Atoyac in 1910 and thereafter. He had garnered the support of workers, both rural and urban, *rancheros*, and some of the middle classes through his intrepid actions and sense of the political. His nationalism, focused on the sub-soil rights of his own state, and his energy in protecting them for his fellow Veracruzans had earned him, even among the most skeptical, grudging admiration. The same can be said of his efforts to protect agricultural and urban workers from the exploitation they had been accustomed to from the Porfiriato up to the present. But the fight was not yet over. Veracruzans were not thoroughly convinced. Aguilar was above all loyal to the man he had served, and to the continuation of the government under which he had first taken up arms as a very young man. His friendship with, and 1917 marriage to, Carranza's daughter would seal that connection. Aguilar, however, had one vision, and Carranza another. And the latter did not appear, at least convincingly, to want to deliver the very prescription that many Veracruzans held dear: a federal constitution. And it resulted in yet another phase of this revolution, much more clearly fought over the issue of federalism. Indeed, the victory over Huertismo was more than a mere military one, passing power back to the constitutional regime that Madero had represented. It was also a victory over Porfirismo, the end of an era, one to which there would and could be no return. The old Porfirians making their way to the safety of Veracruz and on into exile knew this. On September 22, Teodoro Dehesa, his brother, two sons, and his old friend Carlos Herrera, *jefe político* at the time of the Río Blanco massacre, were among many who boarded the Norwegian steamer, *City of Tampico*, bound for a long exile.[4] They were representative of the old guard, the Veracruzan and Mexican "aristocracy," and their departure was symbolic of the end of one phase of the revolution.

Unfortunately, the ensuing vacuum, which was primarily an ideological one, would confound the legatees of the system and introduce the bloodiest and most intransigent period the revolution was to witness. The seal on this phase was the split into opposing factions that became codified at the Sovereign Revolutionary Convention of Aguascalientes on October 22. On October 26, the Zapatista speaker, Paulino Martínez, signalled the real meaning behind the Convention. First, it would be a Villa-Zapata alliance against Carranza. Second, it would seek to implement the social goals of the revolution, those of the Plan of Ayala, "the first official commitment to a policy of rural welfare in the nation's history."[5]

Carranza had begun preparing for this ideological eventuality and a possible rift with Villa even before the Convention had begun. First, he had designated Aguilar, of whose loyalty he was sure, as his delegate receiving the port of Veracruz once the U.S. invaders had withdrawn. Then he made plans for removing the capital to Veracruz port. The state capital was to be moved to nearby Orizaba, as was the Custom's House. From this position, Carranza would have a number of advantages. He would control one of the richest states, its oil wealth waiting to be tapped by the government. He could ensure government revenue through control of the national Custom's House and control two major rail centres linking him to north and south, as well as east. Veracruz port was, without doubt, an excellent strategic position.

On November 23, the last United States troops withdrew from Veracruz. Out of the hills surrounding the town came Aguilar's troops to take command. On November 26, Carranza, accompanied by loyal generals and staff, among them, Alvaro Obregón, Salvador Alvarado, Heriberto Jara, Agustín Millán, Luis Cabrera, Jesús Urueta, Luis Manuel Rojas, Gerzayn Ugarte, and Alberto Pani, was received by Cándido Aguilar.[6] Almost all the officers were members of the staff of the Division of the East. In a sense, Veracruzans controlled the fortunes of Mexico at this end. The port city was, for a time at least, to be the capital of the nation. It was the second time the city had been so honoured. [7]

The Constitutionalist-Conventionist Civil War

Almost from the entry of the Constitutionalists into Veracruz, opposition appeared. The Huatusco canton was supposedly still a hotbed of Huertistas. But Zapatistas, too, now appeared in Veracruz, recruiting mainly among the Indian people. On October

28, two hundred Indians of the "Volcano Volunteers" rose against the Constitutionalist government and were put down after a short fight. In the south, dissension took a more serious form. Pedro Carbajal, true to his PLM ideas, sided with the Convention and tried to replace the authorities in the canton of Acayucan with his own followers. Attacked by Jesús Carranza (the First Chief's brother), Carbajal was killed. His death, however, was not the end of the affair, but the beginning. Obviously, this area of Veracruz, with its anarcho-socialist background, was not going to be satisfied with anything but the ideas that emanated from the Convention.[8] In the north, Gavira was fighting Zapatistas whom he thought he had expelled for good from Veracruz.

Opposition to the Constitutionalists also appeared from within the ranks of the former moderate Maderistas, who went all out in their attempt to extirpate the centralism inherent in Carranza's policies. This tendency was articulated first through an alliance with Villa, but later gave way to support for Félix Díaz. In Veracruz port, on November 15, General Raúl G. Ruiz, the young lawyer from the Huatusco, who had been a member of Gavira's staff in 1911, deserted the Constitutional ranks with fifteen hundred men and joined the Villistas,[9] It was the second time Ruiz had turned his back on the party he had fought for. Why? Ruiz was a well-educated lawyer from an upper-middle-class family. It seems plausible that Ruiz and others who constantly switched sides were disenchanted with Carrancismo, precisely because they began to see it as another form of centralism. Ruiz and others like him wanted a renewed federalism and would support anyone who seemed to offer this option. At this point, the likely contenders for them were the Conventionists.[10]

To counter this new development, Carranza, on December 12, issued his first decree. It was a recapitulation of his Plan of Guadalupe, stating his intentions to resign and convoke elections once the revolution had triumphed.[11] In December, however, other forces were gathering that would fester the wounds of war for the next few years. While Villa and Zapata were trying to develop a strategy, with Félix Díaz waiting in the background for the right time to strike, Felicistas were again beginning to appear all over Veracruz. Felicista troops had appeared around Zongólica, and Higinio Aguilar had already gathered a neo-Porfirista force of one hundred to two hundred men just across the border in Puebla. He had others, too, massed just across the border in Oaxaca. On November 15, they were camped around Paso del Macho; by mid-December, they were attacking. The 38th Regiment had been sent north to reinforce the line there, and only 469 troops were left in Córdoba. The commander of the front desperately asked for reinforcements. He received two hundred men whom he dispersed around Coscomatepec. In Cosamaloapan, Panuncio Martínez, apparently supporting the Convention, operated around the railway station of Tierra Blanca. In December, too, it was discovered that Felicista support was also to be found in Tuxpán, curiously in the person of Antonio G. Azuara, personal secretary to Luis Cabrera, a member of Carranza's government.[12] By December 1, General Jesús Carranza had to warn his brother, the president, that the entire southern flank was open, the way to the Isthmus from Santa Lucrecia in dire need of protection.[13]

However, the expected Villista attack on the centre of Veracruz did not materialize. Instead, Villa decided to concentrate on the north of the state, for two reasons. First, he did not want to extend his supply lines too far south; and, second, he wanted to avail himself of the oil revenue, the same tactic Carranza had successfully used. At the beginning of December, Villa set up headquarters in Tantoyuca. By December 16, the entire line throughout the north was under fire, and Ozuluama and Huejutla fell quickly. On the 15th, the attack began on Tuxpán, without success, and although Villistas were able to overrun San Luis Potosí and capture the oilfields around Ebano, the Constitutionalists in Veracruz managed to recapture the three northern cantons and drive them out.[14]

During the fighting, no damage was done to the oilfields: neither side wanted to destroy this lucrative source of revenue. Later during the battle for the area, there was much turmoil, but even this did not manifest itself in physical damage. Instead, the problem was one of collecting revenue from the companies. The U.S. consul, William Canada, complained that the authorities in Temapache were requesting a second contribution from the companies at Tampico and asked Carranza to send a force for their protection. Aguilar quickly replied with the ascerbic charge that the oil companies "are the first ones to give help to the rebels like Manuel Peláez and others who disturb the public peace. Their observed actions are patent proof of their hostility to this government."[15] This antagonism between Aguilar and the oil companies was to increase over time and would become a major difficulty for the Mexican nation, especially for the Carranza government. At root was the issue, to whom did the riches of the Mexican sub-soil belong? Embroiled in the controversy, too, was the question of whether the nation or the state should control this important source of revenue.

For the moment, however, other problems had to be tackled, precisely in the awakened mood of rural and industrial workers. Amidst the ideological warfare that ensued between Conventionists and Constitutionalists, there were renewed claims for land distribution. Faced with an advancing Villa-Zapata alliance that militarily, seemed to have the upper hand, Carranza and Aguilar – really the masters only of a Mexico now centred in Veracruz – had to move quickly if they were not to lose popular support. Lands stolen from Indians and poor mestizos had not been returned after Madero's victory, nor during Huerta's regime. William Canada was in no doubt that "this agrarian question, in fact, has always been the cause of most of the unrest in this state."[16] Neither had working conditions on *haciendas* changed since the Porfiriato. Reporting to the U.S. Foreign Relations Committee Investigation of Mexican Affairs, John Lind, visiting Mexico in 1914, observed that Emery Sloane employed only contract labourers on his sugar plantation in Veracruz. These worked in gangs watched over by guards with guns and were locked up at night in a huge shed (*tejabán* [sic]).[17]

Consequently, Carranza was forced (much against his will, as hindsight has shown) to promise redress of these horrific social conditions in order to keep the poorer, now expectant classes, from joining the Conventionists. At his opening address to the Convention of Aguascalientes in October, Carranza had promised municipal freedom. In addition, he indicated that it was his intention to rectify the land problem by an immediate *reparto* (redistribution of land to peasants), by reducing the hours of work to nine per day, by decreeing a Sunday rest day, and in general by improving the conditions of work.[18] In Veracruz, the campaign was two pronged. Already in October, Cándido Aguilar had passed Decree 8, establishing an Agrarian Commission, whose task was to survey, divide, and adjudicate lands to those who were without. One local historian, Olivia Domínguez Pérez, has viewed this initiative as one of advances and retreats. Aguilar, she maintains, did little to stimulate land redistribution "with the exception of some provisional land endowments, which he conceded near to Xalapa and in the municipality of La Antigua." Nevertheless, there are reports that an engineer had been hired to initiate a *reparto* of lands belonging to the huge *hacienda*, Corral Nuevo," the proceeds going to twenty-seven towns (*congregaciones*) in the canton of Acayucan. Equally as important was the restoration of lands to Indians in the town of Binigno

Ríos, canton of Jalacingo.[19] Now Carranza stepped in. Legislation adopted January 6, 1915, created a National Agrarian Commission to which those of the states were subordinate. Instead of garnering support, as might have been expected, this law was viewed as further proof of his centralist motives, further alienating anticentralists and sending them into the arms of the self-appointed champion of the Constitution of 1857, the federalist Félix Díaz.

Despite the closure put on land reform by the central government, Aguilar legislated other reforms. For example, he addressed the problem of working conditions. Echoing Carranza's promises from October, he decreed the closing of all commercial business and a Sunday rest day for all workers. Decree 9 established the nine-hour workday and ordered an increase of twenty per cent over the minimum wage. In addition, workers were allowed to elect councils (juntas directivas) to handle grievances.[20] The decree was certainly of a progressive nature, but it was of little help to the workers of Orizaba, who, for lack of supplies from Mexico City, were only working three days per week. In Veracruz port on December 7, a huge demonstration of workers gathered to deliver a petition to Carranza. Other workers, such as the Union of Conductors and Motorists, struck against the tram company seeking a raise. A thirty per cent increase was thus achieved, but only at the expense of a ten cent increase in the ticket price.[21] Workers, restless throughout the Madero as well as Huerta periods, wanted to catch up. Unfortunately, the government was itself in a fiscal crisis of some magnitude and found itself in a difficult position. It could not afford to alienate the workers, for these represented a potential opposition; nor could it afford to anger the bourgeoisie, from whose industrial activity revenues could be obtained. It resorted, therefore, to the lever of propaganda, invoking nationalism and socialism through a series of lectures held in the Dehesa Theatre. Dr. Atl, author and radical socialist, spoke on the negative influence of foreign governments a few days after the U.S. forces had left. He and Jesús Urueta also lectured on "the social, revolutionary actions" of the present government. The popular series, was repeated two weeks later.[22]

The next phase of the revolution was about to begin, in which these concerns over social and economic policies were about to become paramount. The key actor was a man who had joined the Constitutionalists only at the last minute: Alvaro Obregón. Militarily, he was aided by a tactical blunder on Villa's part. Despite the urgings of General Felipe Angeles, Villa decided not to attack Veracruz, which was indeed vulnerable at the time.

Instead he abandoned Veracruz to the Zapatistas, who also did not seem eager to press their advantage, even though supporters were already engaging Constitutionalists there.[23] At the beginning of the year, Obregón went on the offensive. Utilizing the railroads, he quickly recaptured Puebla, putting into effect the agrarian decree of January 6, 1915, the first of its kind promulgated in the revolution, promising the restoration of *ejido* (communal farm) lands.[24]

Because of the drain on troop reserves from Veracruz, the state of Veracruz was continuously under attack from various revolutionary groups, especially in 1915. At the beginning of January, for example, there were reports of only between five hundred to two thousand troops in the port city.[25] Towards the end of March, a proclamation was posted around this area of Veracruz promising summary execution to anyone making payments of taxes, even under the threat of force, to the Constitutionalist government and declaring all loans and taxes decreed by that government null and void. It was signed by Raúl Ruiz, as Brigadier General and Chief of Villista-Zapatista operations in the state of Veracruz, and in agreement with Brigadier General Nicanor Pérez, Colonel Toribio Gamboa, and Captain Samuel Carvallo Tejeda.[26] All of these men were to join in the next phase of the revolution in Veracruz, heralded by the return of Félix Díaz the following year. Manuel Peláez, who had defected from the Constitutionalist ranks on November 10, 1914, also joined the Villistas. Peláez represented small landowners, oil lessors, and small business in the region and is another example of a Veracruzan fighting for regional control against the forces of centralism.

On January 30, General Obregón re-entered Mexico City, where he set about wooing the Casa del Obrero Mundial (House of the Workers of the World). By March, he could count on significant support from this sector, which in Orizaba translated into a new battalion of worker-soldiers at Río Blanco. This added help came just in time as Villa had ordered an all-out assault at Ebano in the Huasteca, in order to gain control over the oilfields.[27] Carranza and Obregón therefore decided engage Villa and attack his main force so as to ease the pressure on the area.

While the struggle for the Huasteca was raging, another and equally significant threat appeared in the north-central region of the state. One of Carranza's first acts on leaving Mexico City, before breaking with the Convention, was to have Aguilar return the state capital back to Xalapa, it's historic seat, from Orizaba. He then appointed the unpopular General Marcelino Murrieta as commander of the city. The arbitrary acts of Murrieta's staff, apparently committed in his absence, upset Xalapans. Murrieta's or his staff's actions in Xalapa are examples of a general trend observed among the Constitutionalist forces, in Veracruz and beyond: that of increasing corruption and lack of discipline.[28] Murrieta's behaviour, as well as the general disgust of Veracruzans at the corrupt and immoral behaviour of many officers and officials of the Constitutionalist army in Veracruz, would spark a rebellion led by extremely wealthy Veracruzan coffee planter from Misantla, Manuel Armenta, in April.[29]

Armenta's resentments of the Constitutionalists stemmed from several arbitrary arrests as well as extortion. His lands were also threatened, and in an attempt to save them, he decided to join the opposition. Armenta, Pedro Gabay from the Huatusco, and an ex-federal officer, Colonel Roberto Cejudo, all placed themselves under the Zapatista banner. In fact, shortly thereafter Zapata named Armenta governor of Veracruz. Armenta's was no mere landlord rebellion, as Knight has described it. Similar to the Pelaecista movement in the north, Armenta represented small landowners, farmers working leased land (*arrendatarios*), and people of various occupations, not least of all rural and urban workers. Very quickly, therefore, Armenta's army grew to number over five thousand and controlled the cantons of Xalapa, Misantla, Coatepec, Jalacingo, Huatusco, and part of Papantla.[30] These men all harboured the perception that the Constitutionalists were a new type of Científico in disguise. That they were not more successful in 1915 was due, in part, to the eroding alliance between Villistas and Zapatistas, a vacuum that would be filled by Félix Díaz, even now preparing for his comeback.

All over Veracruz, the Constitutionalists were under attack. The three main regions were the north under Peláez, the centre under Armenta, and the near south under Raúl Ruiz. But there were also other smaller bands, operating with anywhere up to five hundred men, in various parts of the state. Confidently, the Conventionist newspaper *El Radical* could report that there were five thousand Conventionist rebels operating in the state. Besides the three just mentioned, there were Pedro Gabay, Constantín Galán, the Cervantes brothers, the Lagunes brothers, Panuncio Martínez, Teódulo Córdoba, Colonel Jesús Ramírez, and Ramón López, and the so-called Córdoba Brigade.[31] Part of the problem in Veracruz was the lack of recruits; many had been sent to help Obregón, and the activities of the numerous rebel bands made recruiting difficult. Government forces were simply starved of personnel. General Millán had to complain to the governor that in the combat at Ometusco in May he had only six hundred troops, although Carranza had promised him two to three thousand.[32]

July and August were months of fierce attacks by Zapatista forces. It was obvious that their target was to disrupt rail communication between Veracruz and the Constitutionalists fighting in the north. The toll on civilians was terrible. In three weeks in September, over seven hundred lives were reported lost due to the work of Zapatista sappers.[33] It took sharp reminders from Carranza – and a threat to replace Aguilar – before the latter would act. He was called to the First Chief's office and given a proper dressing down. Apparently Obregón threatened to enter the state to rid it of "bandits" if Aguilar was unable to. Carranza, therefore delayed his own departure from Veracruz for several months; he could have returned to Mexico City in August but did not do so until October 11. Meanwhile, Aguilar commenced the campaign in September.[34] Additional troops were sent south to guard the Isthmian railway and to reinforce Córdoba. By September, there were five thousand soldiers guarding the railroad between the port city and Orizaba.[35]

Before we consider the turn of events beginning in 1916, which constituted the most serious opposition to Constitutionalism in Veracruz, not to speak of the nation, we should briefly consider the accomplishments of the civil government in Veracruz under Aguilar, and, later, Millán. This will convey a sense of what Veracruzans felt was most important. It is my contention that efforts to address the serious problem of the control of land as well as to improve working conditions in rural areas were token – never seriously undertaken. The population was by and large dissatisfied with the state government. Despite Aguilar's "socialist" face, he was committed to the policies of Carranza, to whom that appelation could never be made. The flirtation that was allowed with socialism, preached by Dr. Atl and practised by Obregón in Mexico City, and Aguilar in parts of Veracruz was in my view only a subterfuge, a pretense made necessary by the strategic situation and the necessity of gaining the support of the working class. The *reparto* of lands in the south of Veracruz was also necessitated by the potential appeal of Zapatismo. The Veracruz government never succeeded in breaking the back of the dominant *hacienda* system established during the Porfiriato.[36] Aguilar carried out a few *repartos*, such as that in Medellín and on the enormous estate of Corral Nuevo, but even these were subject to counter-attacks by large landowners, who managed to slow down if not reverse some of the work of the Comisión Agraria Mixta (Mixed Agrarian

Commission, known as CAM). In any case, the CAM was placed under the authority of the federal government, another example of the attenuation of state sovereignty.[37]

In the field of labour relations, Aguilar's work reveals more thought and concern. Here he tried to implement his liberal ideas. Yet there is also evidence of cynicism. In a September address to 5,000 textile factory workers in Orizaba who had come to indicate their allegiance to the Constitutionalist cause, Aguilar "reminded" them that they should fight the common enemy: capital. No evidence exists, however, that Aguilar really believed capital was the enemy. No businesses were attacked or taken over by the state. On the other hand, he did try to improve working conditions and allowed unions the right to exist and to negotiate. In October, Millán, now the interim governor, decreed that unions had the right not only to exist but also to have business negotiate with them. The favourable climate towards labour in Veracruz induced the Federación de Sindicatos Obreros del DF (Federation of Unionized Workers of the Federal District), a non-partisan union, to hold its meeting in the port.[38] And as we have noted, laws regulating or addressing terrible working conditions and establishing equitable hours and minimum wages were passed.

The most difficult nut to crack here was the oil companies. The oilfields around Tuxpán, for example, were in the hands of two companies, El Aguila (Pearson and Sons) and the Mexican Oil Company (Doheny). Doheny's company alone had storage facilities of over ten million barrels. The problem was that these companies were so big they could ignore the government with impunity. Efforts to control working conditions were difficult at best, even when government inspectors were allowed in. El Aguila was especially notorious for its arbitrary conduct. Since the days of the Porfiriato, it had forcibly occupied the lands of one woman, without compensation, building storage tanks at will. In the circumstances, it was impossible to police let alone enforce laws against the oil companies.[39]

In another legislative area, education, the government showed its intention to begin constructing a program without which a civilized and progressive country cannot exist. Veracruz considered itself one of the most enlightened of the Mexican states in regard to education. Boasting educators such as Laubscher and Rebsamen, it had been a model for Mexico throughout the Juárez and Díaz eras. In February 1915, Aguilar allowed the principal of the Preparatory College in Xalapa, Dr. Enrique Herrera

Moreno, to organize the Third Pedagogical Congress, which met in the port city. Educators from all over the state as well as the nation met to discuss the problems facing education in the future and to draw up plan, for its renewal. One of these was put into effect by Governor Millán in January 1916, when he decreed that any *hacienda* having thirty or more children must construct and maintain a school building, which would become the property of the municipality, who would provide the teacher.[40]

In another area, the government achieved even more success. This was the area of surveillance or, to put it differently, a sort of Veracruzan or Mexican political *Gleichschaltung*. Obviously, in time of war, extraordinary measures are called for, and governments do not always observe the niceties of justice. In the case of Carranza and Veracruz, however, repression and arbitrary arrest were the order of the day. On one occasion, the secretary of government, Heriberto Jara, ordered the expulsion of all Spaniards merely on suspicion, or accusations of treason. There are reams of files with the names of apprehended citizens, and an equal number of individual petitions in the Carranza archives, asking for justice, that is, release from jail. Some of these people were kept incommunicado and at the pleasure of the government. Ninety per cent of one box from the Veracruz State Archive contains orders for the arrest of various citizens suspected of opposing the Constitutionalists. Furthermore, the Supreme Court was given the right to intervene directly in all administrative and judicial matters. Thieves were to be executed if caught red-handed, regardless of the value of the goods stolen. These were rough times, and keeping order while trying to fight a bitter revolution called for drastic measures.[41] Carranza's spies were everywhere, but were nowhere as active as in the port of Veracruz, because of its connection with the outside world. Veracruz–Havana–New Orleans–San Antonio was a path that for various reasons had been trodden in both directions for at least a century.

Anti-Carranza political movements are known to us, because of the manoeuvrings of their backers primarily in the United States, whose letters appear in the State Department records. In mid-July, for example, someone with an unreadable signature sent a report to U.S. Secretary of State Robert Lansing, advising him of the formation of a Nationalist Army, the head of which was a Mr. Yturbide (a name with a particular, not necessarily happy, resonance in Mexican history, recalling the first Emperor of Mexico). He was backed by numerous ex-federal officers with a clean past, – that is, not associated with the revolt of the

Ciudadela – who would be supported mainly by small landowners and who would provide the "best democratic solution" for Mexico. Some of these opposition groups were noting the growing rift between Obregón and fellow general Pablo González, or the coolness that existed between Obregón and Carranza. By December, this so-called Nationalist Army had not made any headway, but another group was about to rear its head with considerable menace for the not-yet-established Constitutional government: the reborn Félix Díaz party.

At this time, the Félix Díaz party, with heavy backing in New York and connected to the Madero family (the best of a bad situation?) was apparently making overtures to Pancho Villa, who was still licking his wounds in Chihuahua.[42] There is some truth to this latter report. The movements of the Felicistas were already known to the Constitutionalists, who watched their every move keenly. Spies accounted for the movements of all Felicistas, especially in the port city. They were so adept that they were able to find incriminating documents in the shoes of Mrs. Teresa Mier as she stepped off the Spanish steamer *Antonio López*. They knew, too, about the Felicistas' connections with the Roman Catholic Church, and the manner in which information was communicated. They knew which towns harboured Felicista sympathizers, and which rebels would probably join Díaz in his adventure. They must also have known that Díaz would probably try a comeback. It is all the more surprising, then, that harsher measures were not taken against these potential political enemies, given the crackdown in the port city. Díaz was incredibly lucky to make it back into Mexico alive. But in Veracruz, his second choice as a staging area, he eventually found a situation that he probably could only have dreamt of.[43] In any case, his return advanced the revolution to its next stage, the final struggle of the remnants of the Porfirian committed armed with a weak appeal to federalism. That battle would be primarily waged in Veracruz.

The political comeback of Félix Díaz, and the intensity of his movement from 1916 to 1919, cannot be accounted for merely as the last gasp of the Porfiriato or the attempt by Veracruzan "aristocrats" to restore the "ancien regime."[44] Certainly there was nostalgia for the Porfiriato. However, as Henderson and Knight have shown, the Félix Díaz movement encompassed people from all classes. His Plan of Tierra Colorado discussed below, included the restoration of the *ejido* and the confiscation of lands from big *haciendas* in order to alleviate the land hunger of poor rural inhabitants. In addition, the support of the Roman Catholic

Church contributed to Diaz's success in building a multi-class, broad-based following.[45]

Yet land hunger alone was not the only force motivating rural inhabitants, nor was the reactionary bent of "aristocratic" Veracruzans the only inducement to support Díaz. He was able to unite various loosely associated groups, such as those from the Villista-Zapatista camp, with men like Cástulo Pérez in the south and Peláez in the north, into a formidable force, because he was fighting for the restoration of federalism and an end to the Cientificismo of the Porfiriato, of Madero, Huerta and, latterly, Carranza.[46] In Veracruz at least, the chord that was struck with the appearance of Díaz and his rallying detail was, as others have observed, the Constitution of 1857. But what made this document so attractive? Obviously, it was not that it represented a reactionary return to a pristine economic liberalism that was already dead; Díaz had been careful to distance himself from this ideological trace of the Porfiriato in the Plan of Tierra Colorada. Rather, he gained such a tremendous following, mounting an offensive that was perhaps the most serious the Constitutionalist regime would face, precisely because he bore impeccable anti-Científico credentials. This is the reason why many if not all Veracruzan rebels already in the field – some associated with the Zapatistas, some with the Villistas, others maintaining a wary, precarious independence – turned to Díaz en masse when news of his landing broke.

At the time of his return, Veracruz was in turmoil. Misantla, for example, was under constant attack from anti-Constitutionalist rebels, the garrison there unable to leave the town to combat them. The mayor complained that the municipality was unable to collect taxes and pay wages to state employees. The state of siege in Misantla was complete. Towns close to Misantla such as Juchique de Ferrer, Colipa, and Yecautla were in the hands of Diaz's followers.[47] In Huatusco, Constantín Galán had two hundred men under his command and completely controlled agricultural production.[48] In the far north, Coscomatepec, Papantla, and Tuxpán were the main pressure points, the latter, of course, constantly under the threat of Peláez.[49] In the south, there were three main groups, commanded by Ruiz, Nicanor, and Cástulo Pérez and Alvaro Alor. Ruiz was active around San Andrés Tuxtla, Nicanor Pérez around Acayucan, while his cousin Cástulo and Alor operated around Hidalgotitlán, situated between Acayucan and the Oaxacan border.[50]

Yet not all of these groups had officially declared for Felicismo.

Felicismo

In the midst of this turmoil, Félix Díaz tryed to put his movement together on Mexican soil. The Plan of Tierra Colorado, named after a small ranch south of the port city of Veracruz, was signed on February 29, creating the Ejército Reorganizador Nacional (National Reorganizing Army).[51] Shortly thereafter, Díaz was arrested on suspicion of being a rebel. Henderson has depicted Díaz's dramatic landing on the coast of Veracruz as something out of "a romantic tale by Sir Walter Scott." Truly, Díaz – disguised only by his beard – showed incredible courage and presence of mind. Moreover, he was blessed with luck, especially in having his case dismissed by a Matamoron court and in his subsequent journey to Mexico City and then Oaxaca.[52] Yet he would initially face considerable difficulties since his former allies in Oaxaca, now committed to Zapata, refused to join his movement. He therefore made his way to Veracruz, where he already had some connections as well as cells operating in his name in various towns and the countryside.[53] In Oaxaca, Díaz was joined by Higinio Aguilar, and subsequently in Chiapas by ex-Huertista Gaudencio de la Llave. Apart from these, he could as yet count on little support. In March, there were rumours that Pancho Villa would join his movement, but this possibility came to naught.[54] And despite Díaz's attempts to court Washington, the crucial factor, support of the United States, came also to nothing. Woodrow Wilson was polite but firm in informing the Roman Catholic Church, which had consistently lobbied in favour of the Díaz movement, that the United States could not condone any activity in opposition to the Carranza government, which it had recognized in October, 1915.[55]

Thus, between March and October, the Díaz movement was without much success in gaining adherents. Neither Gabay nor the Galáns went over to the movement immediately but continued fighting against Constitutionalists under whatever banners they had struck in 1915. One of the rebels who did switch sides was Raúl Ruiz, operating in the canton of Cosamaloapan. On October 10, he, Lagunes, and Ricardo Chávez,\ attacked the station at Piedra Negras, shooting a number of suspected Constitutionalists. In both Piedras Negras and nearby Tlalixcoyan, posters and handbills urging the people to support the Díaz movement, signed by Díaz and Higinio Aguilar, circulated freely.[56]

By the end of October, Díaz had managed to incorporate most if not all of the Veracruz anti-Constitutionalist rebels under his command. Captured documents reveal the command structure as impressive, at least on paper. However, all of the rebels encountered in this study (except two: Gaudencio de la Llave and Cástulo Pérez) found a place in the so-called Army of the East, supposedly one arm of the National Reorganizing Army under Díaz. The Army of the East was further divided into the Army of the Gulf and the Army of the Mountains. Higinio Aguilar was, of course, the general in command. Panuncio Martínez commanded the first division of the Army of the Gulf, Constantín Galán the second, Pedro Gabay the third (in which Raúl Ruiz and Clemente Gabay officered brigades), Roberto Cejudo the fourth, and Manuel Peláez the fifth. Medical units with doctors were also attached.[57] Cástulo Pérez assumed command of the region where he lived, and Gaudencio de la Llave also supported the cause.

The sudden success enjoyed by the rebels, in Veracruz now mainly Felicistas (the exceptions were the bands of Zapatistas still operating across the border from Puebla), was not primarily due to this new alignment of rebel forces in the state, but to a withdrawal of regular Constitutionalist soldiers which had been occurring since May.[58] This withdrawal from the interior of Veracruz was ordered in order to fortify the port city: Mexico was expecting another invasion by the U.S. By mid-1916, it was becoming obvious that the probability had become a certainty. The United States would enter World War I on the Allied side. The government expected another U.S. invasion through Veracruz fuelled by the excursions of a frustrated Pancho Villa across the northern border in March, which indeed resulted in the Pershing expedition.[59] The entire arsenal at Veracruz plus all the rolling stock were removed from the city. Mexican warships in the harbour were dismantled, their guns being placed on railway cars. All government offices packed their documents for removal, and soldiers were withdrawn to a perimeter around the city.[60] The crisis lasted until January 1917, when Pershing withdrew his force from Mexican territory.

The preoccupation with the expected invasion from the north gave Félix Díaz the time and space needed to propagandize his movement, to recruit troops, and to plan his campaign. By January 1917, his movement had grown considerably and was headquartered in Veracruz state, from whence most of his military support came. Knight has characterized Díaz's movement as "fissiparous." Yet it was not more so than the Constitutionalist movement: the two bore similar features. The Constitutionalists were seen as northerners and were resented as such. The common bond of region and regionalism united Veracruzans. The main ideological program of these Veracruzan rebels was the call by Félix Díaz for the restoration of the Constitution of 1857, which was interpreted as a federal constitution, giving significant powers to the states. Raúl Ruiz was not merely a "perennial local rebel," as Knight has characterized him. His was an ideological battle for state sovereignty. The movement, therefore, appealed to people of all classes whose loyalties and traditions lay with their state, whose existence they thought was best protected by the old constitution. It appealed particularly because the Carrancistas, besides being hated as corrupt and callous interlopers, appeared to want to replace that constitution with a more centralist document, which Veracruzans would view with antipathy. The apparent defeat of this attempt is the reason for the eventual evaporation of Felicismo in 1919, and the switch of these local rebels to Obregón.[61]

In the meantime, however, the Felicistas carried out an intensive and harrowing campaign against the remnants of the Constitutionalist forces in Veracruz. The main tactical targets, as before, were the railways, which were relentlessly destroyed, rebel soldiers employing the tactic of routing trains down a steep incline where they could crash into others. The train escorts were usually executed. To achieve maximum effect, Higinio Aguilar issued a manifesto warning passengers of the attacks, emphasizing that they used the trains at their own peril. Naturally, civilian casualties could not always be avoided. In November, General Millán's own father and brother were victims, their bodies brought naked to Xalapa, having been relieved of their clothes by Millán's own troops.[62]

In addition to assaults on the railway, in July the Felicistas launched a series of attacks on main garrisons. Medellín, only ten kilometres from the port, was attacked on July 19 and again on July 22. In August, Tlacotalpan was taken. In each case, the garrison was either put to flight or the unhappy prisoners were executed. Pedro Gabay now completely controlled the cantons of Huatusco, Córdoba, and Veracruz, except, of course, the major towns and the railway. At the end of July, he was joined by another rebel group numbering over one thousand men, led by Arturo Solache, a former assistant director of the Mexican Naval School. Further to the south, Raúl Ruiz kept up the pressure on the towns around San Juan Evangelista, while Alvaro Alor, second-in-command to Cástulo Pérez, captured Hidalgotitlán, where the two appointed new town councilors and distributed propaganda for the Felicista cause. In Chinameca, old revolutionary

Donato Padua could report that Lieutenant Colonel Genaro Sulvarán, an accomplished turncoat, allowed Cástulo Pérez and his men to enter and leave the town at will.[63]

The reason for the successes of these rebels has received little attention, due no doubt to the paucity of reliable records. But it seems highly likely that one of the significant factors was corruption among the Constitutionalists. Among the only sources are the regular reports of U.S. consul for Veracruz, William Canada. He relied on reports on conditions by U.S. residents and estate managers in the countryside and was privy to the many charges of corruption leveled at Constitutionalist officers. There might be substantial truth to reports that Cándido Aguilar and other officers spent a good part of the time chasing around after rebels but never actually inflicting much damage on them, primarily because they were doing a good business together.[64]

On September 3, the Constitutionalists turned to the tactic of elections in order to make good one of their promises. Eligibility to vote in the municipal elections was granted any male who had not in any way served other anti-Carranza governments, or who had not opposed the Constitutionalist cause. In other words, few people were eligible to vote. In Veracruz, moreover, few people appeared to want to. Carrancismo was definitely not the party of choice there, and the elections did not always favour the candidates of Carranza's choosing. In the port city, with an estimated population of 60,000, only 654 people voted, electing an ex-brick mason as mayor. It was reported that governor Jara would later nullify the entire election. To be fair, citizens in other parts of Veracruz petitioned for nullification due to irregularities committed by local authorities.[65]

Indeed, the general living conditions in the state were atrocious. Workers could not live on their wages, the paper money they were compensated with was virtually worthless, and government attempts to stabilize monetary policy after the years of debilitating fighting made the situation worse. Foremost in this endeavour was Carranza's currency devaluation, the issuing of the *infalsificables* (unfalsifiables) in May 1916, which brought the old peso crashing down, soon followed by the new currency itself. Workers demanded payment in gold, the first such demand appearing during a strike in Veracruz at the beginning of 1916 that was quickly suppressed with bayonets.[66] The year 1916 appears to have been the watershed for labour, which, now that Carranza had won his major battles and could turn to establishing civil government, was no longer needed.

The government thus intervened to curb active propaganda on the part of the workers. Jara arrested Salvador González García, the leader of the Casa de Obrero Mundial in Veracruz. In February, Luis Morones convened the First Preliminary National Workers Congress in Veracruz port instead of the Federal District, because of the less hostile climate. But Jara declined to attend, accusing the workers of abandoning the government that had protected them. All in all, the year 1916 was a bad one for unionized workers. Labour would get the help of government if it conformed to the government's desires, but not as a freely organized, independent group.[67] Nevertheless, the Carranza government did not simply abandon workers. Because of increasing numbers of strikes in Veracruz from October 1916, the major cause of which was high inflation, Carranza passed a decree on October 23 that half the workers' salaries would henceforth be paid in gold or its equivalent. The other half would be covered by *infalsificables*, whose value would be announced every ten days. In addition, the government also intervened to arbitrate settlements, not all of which resulted in setbacks for workers. But not all demands were met. A request for a raise by conductors and drivers of the government-owned tram company was refused.[68]

There were other developments on the labour front, very tentative at this time that would in coming years transform the Veracruz labour scene. Labour in Veracruz had neither envisioned nor accepted the position that the Carranza government was formulating, that would eventually be characteristic of modern Mexico: co-optation. In March 1916, Herón Proal was elected Veracruz secretary general of the Confederación del Trabajo de la Región Mexicana (Confederation of Work of the Mexican Region). In December of that year, renters were beginning to organize themselves against crushing increases by landlords. The call was for a renters' union, and its organizers included another name that would soon make Veracruzan labour history, Ursulo Galván.[69]

In the face of these challenging political and military circumstances, a meeting of leading generals was called in Veracruz. Aguilar, now Minister of Foreign Affairs, Jara, Millán, and five leading staff officers met to discuss measures. One of the problems confronting the Constitutionalists was the lack of harmony among these leading figures, resulting from friction caused by the pettiness of inflated vanities. However, they managed at this meeting to agree on a tactic whereby "flying columns" would be established to go on the attack across the state. To facilitate the endeavour, Carranza decided to ship an entire cavalry of defected Villista troops to Oaxaca, in order to bring that rebel state back into the Constitutionalist fold, but more importantly, to put pressure on Félix Díaz, whose home state it was and who had a considerable following there. That the tactic might work was the hope of William Canada, who reasoned that Aguilar, now out of the field and having made his fortune, would not be against pursuing the war in a more rigorous manner. By December, the flying columns were in position, at least around the municipality of Tlalixcoyan, and the authorities there were hoping for some relief.[70] Just the opposite, however, was in store.

The Constitutionalist government could barely hold the line against the National Reorganizing Army. In addition, as the chief U.S. information gatherer, Carothers, reported, the "country is teeming with revolution again; there is little or no connection between the different bands; they have only one real object in common, the overthrow of Carranza." The Huasteca, for example, was almost completely under the control of Peláez. He frequently made levies of between five hundred to five thousand pesos on the oil companies.[71] Zapatistas were also on the march. For two years, these maintained control just north of the city of Xalapa, at Plan de las Hayas, until government forces were sent to dislodge them. The problem was that the Zapatistas were aided and supported by the small farmers and *campesinos*, who had no difficulty identifying with the ideology of the Plan de Ayala. Right into June, Zapatistas were a particular nuisance to the government. They enlisted the help of Indians mainly, distributing propaganda that attracted other *campesinos* and made it difficult for *hacendados* to harvest crops.[72]

Due to the consolidation and coordination of his movement, the progress of Díaz's revolt was relentless in the rest of the state. By March 1917, there were pitched battles between the Constitutionalists and the Felicistas. In April, there was a huge battle between the two sides near Tierra Blanca.[73] Panuncio Martínez attempted to take this strategic rail junction with twelve hundred men but was repulsed by the federals there. For, although the Felicistas were growing stronger, government forces were realizing that they could fight the rebels and win, that hiding in barracks was not the best way to carry out the fight. Yet with Díaz himself in Veracruz, and a successful mission by Gaudencio de la Llave to unite the various smaller groups under the flag of the National Reorganizing Army, the fight became more difficult for the government. Díaz personally moved his headquarters from Chiapas and made regular trips throughout Veracruz directing operations.[74] In November, a massed attack on Veracruz was prepared by Higinio Aguilar but was called off by Díaz, who wanted the enemy engaged wherever it could be found. It is important to note that in these exceedingly fierce engagements between June and December, the government was not always the loser. Even though the National Reorganizing Army had superior forces, the government could and did inflict serious losses on the Felicistas. For example, returning from Tuxtepec on a campaign, General Miguel Alemán (father of the future president), on hearing of a rebel encampment at the *hacienda* Guerrero near Chiltepec belonging to former governor Lagos Cházaro, decided to attack it. The camp, one of the field headquarters of Raúl Ruiz, was well fortified with two machine guns. Despite the element of surprise, the rebels were able to mount a stiff resistance for five hours, after which they were forced to withdraw, leaving behind many guns and horses and much ammunition. The government suffered only eleven dead and a number of seriously wounded soldiers.[75]

As in the south, one of the reasons why the Felicistas achieved success in the north was because of the way they treated local people, gaining their support. In contrast, the Constitutionalists were a burden to the locals, "using their authority to acquire crops, especially maize, at reduced prices."[76] The government therefore went all out in its efforts to counter with force the popularity enjoyed by the Felicistas. Four thousand additional troops were sent to Veracruz. At the end of November, additional troops were sent to the fortress at Perote under General Castro, bringing the number there, it was reported, to ten thousand. Small naval vessels were sent up the Papaloapán river to chase rebels away from Cosamaloapán, a tactic which was quite successful in reducing the pressures on the many foreign and domestic sugar plantations along the river.[77]

Alongside the military campaigns, primarily against Díaz in the south and centre and against Peláez in the north, the Constitutionalist government in 1917 also attempted to restore and emphasize civilian rule, or the appearance of it. Carranza was determined to cut the ground out from under the feet of the major rebels, Villa, Zapata, and Díaz, and indeed the minor ones as well. He called for a constituent assembly to create a new constitution, and then for a general election for president, state governors, senators, and deputies. On October 22, 1916, the elections were held for assembly delegates, the plan being for the assembly to prepare the new constitution by January 31.[78] Only a minority of voters turned out, and many of the electoral districts were unable to hold elections due to rebel activity. Nevertheless, Veracruz port returned two of the most important members of the Veracruz delegation, Cándido Aguilar and Heriberto Jara, to the assembly, although Aguilar was not able to take full part due to his continuation as minister of foreign affairs.[79]

This is not the place to debate the negotiations of this assembly, which produced the Constitution of 1917 or to enter into a full discussion of the nature of that document. However, one must remark that a number of important signals emanated from this Constitution that would profoundly affect the outcome of the revolution in Veracruz, and indeed in Mexico.

The first was the obvious partisanship of the delegates, divided into two camps: for Carranza or for Obregón. Aguilar was a firm Carrancista, never wavering in his loyalty to the First Chief (he would marry Carranza's daughter Virginia in August of that year).[80]

The other signal (or problem, as it would become) appeared almost surreptitiously, unrecognized for the importance it would subsequently have. It appeared first as a dispute over the official name that Mexico would adopt. Cumberland correctly identifies the issue as one of "federalism." In the end, of course, the official name chosen was "The United States of Mexico," manifesting the federal nature of the constitution, in imitation of the Constitution of 1857.[81] Yet the principle of federalism was simultaneously attenuated by the relegation of all rights to sub-soil deposits to the nation, removing one of the most powerful weapons that the states could have been given in the exercise of their putative sovereignty. It is ironic that Article 27, in which this national right was enshrined, merited little debate and was accepted unanimously. This means that Heriberto Jara would have voted for it, a decision, perhaps scarcely even considered, that would come to haunt him with ferocious irony in 1927.[82] No wonder that, reading between the lines, the Felicista rebels continued their clamour against this constitution. The abolition of the cantons on September 4, 1916, and the declaration of the free municipality reinforced their opinions. Henceforth, there would be direct communication between the central government and the municipality, creating a balkanization of political power that would strengthen the hand of the former and weaken the power of the state government.

Moreover, the fears of the federalists were confirmed

immediately after the signing of the new constitution, when it became absolutely clear how Carranza intended to implement it. Porfirio Díaz had governed closely from Chapultepec, and everyone knew where the seat of power was, although the dictator had tried to maintain a semblance of constitutionality. Carranza appears to have copied Díaz's tactics: his praxis in the election campaign was completely at odds with the spirit of the 1917 Constitution.[83] Probably he was too used to leading Mexico as First Chief, perhaps it was his personality, which could not brook opposition. In any case, as soon as elections under this new constitution were called for March 11, 1917, it became apparent that Carranza was going to throw his weight and influence about in order to have his own men elected. One may argue that there is, from the point of view of democracy, nothing wrong in this. From the perspective of the Mexican electoral scene, however, it was too reminiscent of the past, too heavy a manoeuvre for a country whose history was marked with controversies over federalism, too obviously centralist, nay, even Científico by nature. No matter how one may justify the principle, the fact is that it was perceived in Veracruz and elsewhere as centralist, a return to the past, and therefore a threat.[84]

In Veracruz, amidst rumors of a developing rift between Carranza and the two leading generals, Obregón and González, political clubs (formed already for the election of delegates) continued organizing for the expected national elections. While there was no dispute that Carranza was the favourite for president, the electoral rift in Veracruz articulated itself as a gubernatorial battle between Cándido Aguilar and Gabriel Gavira, the latter being supported by General Obregón. Amidst the charges and countercharges of the campaign, Carranza, the local Partido Liberal Constitucionalista (Liberal Constitutional Party, or PLC), and numerous clubs of the Partido Obrero (Workers' Party, or PO) supported Aguilar. Especially important was Herón Proal's decision to support Aguilar rather than Gavira. On June 23, the legislature declared Aguilar the winner with forty-three thousand votes to Gavira's thirteen thousand.[85] Immediately, the electoral commission was charged with fraud. The question of government tampering in the election in Veracruz will never be solved, although one historian has pointed to figures for each district printed in *El Universal* which do not add up to the stated total.[86] One wonders how fair it could have been with almost the entire countryside excluded and with Aguilar in control of the legislative electoral commission. In one district, the fifteenth, the election of the leading candidate was declared null and void, and a Doctor Loyo chosen in his place; Loyo was a member of the PLC. Even *El Dictámen*, avidly pro-Aguilar, had to remark that this was hardly fair given that the legislature consisted of Aguilaristas. Aguilar's victory seems to have been fairly popular, tainted, as it was by charges of tampering. It represented a victory of the towns over the countryside, if not a victory for the middle class. Gavirismo was reported to have been strong, but even on his own turf, Orizaba, Gavira supposedly gained only one thousand votes over Aguilar.[87] Also of note in this election was the victory of Adalberto Tejeda, who won the senatorial seat in the Mexican Congress. Tejeda had been also supported by the PLC and the PO, which latter he would shape in the coming decade into a formidable weapon, far beyond Jara's dreams and Aguilar's desires.

Municipal elections were also held in Veracruz in December. In the port city, there was a slight scandal: the winner there, José Mercado Alarcón, a Gavirista, was accused of having served as a troop instructor in the Huertista army. As any civil servant or military person of that regime was disallowed from running in elections, the matter had to be adjudicated by the legislature.[88] These adjudications tell a story of these municipal elections, as they do the intention of the Veracruz government. Carranza obviously wanted to have his own men in the gubernatorial seats and exercised his influence where he could. But in the municipalities, at least in Veracruz, the elections seem to have been fairly clean. With the exception of the south, for example Acayucan, and the north, which was controlled by Peláez, elections were verified in a perfectly fair manner, whether the result was for or against the government. These municipal elections were also a portent of things to come. In Tuxpán, for instance, although the PLC tried to block the victory of the "Red formula," the legislative committee upheld the latter. The same was true in Papantla, only in this case the electoral fight was between two parties: the Liberal Constitución, the government party; and the Regional Papanteco (Papantla Regional Party), called reactionary in the dispatches. The latter received official verification as the winner. Demonstrations against the legislature's decision were ordered suppressed by the military command.

The tendency on the part of the Veracruz government to foster and maintain the support of working-class, "socialist," movements was noticeable at this time. An example of this, in addition to the favourable electoral outcome for "Red" parties, was the support of the initial renters' movement. This movement had grown out of conflicts between renters and landlords in early 1917. Because landlords had succeeded in availing themselves of favourable judicial decisions, renters took it upon themselves to organize. In October, at the initiative of the Confederation of Workers' Unions, the Liga de Inquilinos (Renters' League) was formed. With the approaching election, the Veracruz government of Cándido Aguilar was quick to champion this group in its search for votes. Victory in hand, the government rewarded the renters with a new law that reflected their interests and that, it was hoped, would put an end to the strife. The hoped-for peace did not last for long. In January, renters in Orizaba went on "strike," refusing to pay rents because landlords had not complied with the law requiring them to maintain dwellings and apartments in a decent condition.[89] The renters' movement, in addition to the formation of "Red" parties and the continued growth of the labour movement, was evidence of the radicalization of labour as well as some sectors of the general population in Veracruz. Initially, this trend, as noted, was supported by the Aguilar government, which would make this state one of the few to give a militant, leftist, tone to the revolutionary movement.

The intention of the Constitutionalist government to hold "constitutional" elections and support the working classes while satisfying some people failed to convince others. It is obvious that the major support for the Veracruz government came from the towns. In the rest of the state, in the countryside, that support did not materialize; the political equivalent of the working-class movements in the towns was an increase in activity on the rebel front. During 1917 and the first months of 1918, the Felicista movement reached its zenith. In November 1917, there were eighteen engagements between Constitutionalist and Felicista forces in which eleven victories were scored by the latter. All in all, Díaz commanded between sixteen thousand to eighteen thousand troops, and "about 25 cannon and 60 rapid-fire guns," facing only eight thousand Constitutionalist. In the north of Veracruz, Manuel Peláez commanded fifteen hundred to twenty-five hundred men continuously in the field. Efforts to dislodge him militarily or to co-opt his movement failed. Apart from Morelos, which the Zapatistas controlled, numerous states in the Mexican federation were the scene of rebellions, but Veracruz was perhaps the state with the second most serious and successful rebel offensive.

In this general situation of assumed electoral fraud and

military frailty, not to speak of the spectre of "socialism" (read: rule of the masses), still influential Mexican exiles tried assiduously to convince the United States to switch its support from Carranza to Félix Díaz. They argued the line of peace and reconciliation, based firmly on the principles of the Constitution of 1857, but modified to include references to the working and rural *campesino* classes. This group was headed be León De la Barra and appealed not only to the old constitution but was anchored in the conviction that both the Madero family and the Carranza government represented a return to Cientificismo, in addition to a pro-German attitude. They therefore called for the support of the United States in defeating Carranza and the Constitutionalists.[90]

There were also reports that some businessmen preferred the Felicistas. With Peláez in command of the oilfields, however odious the business of "protection" payments might be, the oilfields and the delivery of oil were assured.[91] Despite his occasional threats to blow up the oilfields if the companies failed to make their payments, Peláez and the Felicista movement were seen as the better deal by businessmen in particular because of their adamant opposition to Articles 27 (restoration of lands stolen from Indians in the Porfiriato and restrictions on foreign ownership of land) and 123 (the eight-hour workday and recognition of unions) of the Constitution of 1917.[92] Local Veracruzans, too, those of course outside the cities and towns controlled by the Constitutionalists, seemed very favourable towards the Felicista movement. One U.S. businessman, wandering through southern Veracruz in search of lumber, was taken prisoner and kept at Díaz's headquarters. He reported:

> Economic conditions are fairly good, the crops were good, corn very cheap. The general public sentiment of the inhabitants of the territory occupied by these revolutionists are in favour of said revolutionists winning and talk a lot about being in favour of this old regime and they control a vast amount of Mexican territory in eastern Mexico outside the railroads and big cities and towns.

Furthermore, he noted, Felicistas were supporters of the Allied cause in the World War and were well armed and equipped.[93] The United States government under President Wilson, however, was not about to support Díaz. Neither was Wilson convinced by the Committee on Foreign Relations of the U.S. Senate, chaired by Senator Albert Bacon Fall, which began its deliberations on Mexico in January 1919.

With business support for the Felicistas growing, and because of the counterproductive behaviour of Constitutionalist officers and soldiers, Cándido Aguilar was sent back to Veracruz to clean up the state and rid it of the Felicistas.[94] The results were not long in coming. Aguilar's first tactic was to attempt to reduce political support for Díaz in the towns. To this end, he addressed a stiff letter to the Spanish ambassador, accusing most Spanish subjects in Veracruz of supporting the Díaz cause. Since agents of the Felicista network in Mexico City and Veracruz had inadvertently divulged this information, the secret police were able to ascertain that some of these supporters were indeed Spaniards.

Next, Aguilar took his campaign to the field, aggressively seeking out Felicista encampments. At the end of November, Gaudalupe Sánchez raided the rebel headquarters in the Huatusco commanded by Pedro Gabay, leaving one hundred of the enemy dead, and capturing a quantity of rebel archives. Sánchez's attack was followed up further south at Cañada Blanca near Amatlán, one of Díaz's new headquarters; and in the hills above Orizaba he was able to rout the forces of Cástulo Pérez. Because of his successes, in January of 1919, he was promoted to divisional general.[95]

Cándido Aguilar not only carried the fight successfully to the Felicistas, he also began a campaign to weed out corruption among the Constitutionalist elements in Veracruz. This earned him the admiration of his fellow Veracruzans, as well as support which now began to ebb away from the Felicista cause.[96] In February and March the Felicista movement suffered a series of setbacks that sounded its death knell. On March 19, Roberto Cejudo surrendered to the Constitutionalists and was given a command as divisional general, fighting against his former friends. Panuncio Martínez and Arturo Arellano, the latter operating in the Huasteca, also sought amnesty. In addition, Manuel Peláez came under increasing pressure from the Constitutionalist army. In early 1920, after a failed attack by Higinio Aguilar on the town of Gutíerrez Zamora, Gaudencio de la Llave was captured and taken to Mexico City. Then Marcelo Caraveo, campaigning with Peláez in the north, surrendered, and Constantino Galán died.[97] In April, General Zapata was ambushed and killed by federal troops. This was an important achievement for the Carrancistas. And the disasters multiplied. In Veracruz, with Félix Díaz attempting to shore up his movement, to capture the eagerly sought, anxiously awaited, but never promised and never achieved United States backing, another disaster occurred and Díaz's last-ditch effort to lend his movement some inspiration was dashed. The aged General Blanquet, convinced to leave his retirement and return to the field, was killed when the small force he was with, commanded by Pedro Gabay, was cornered on the edge of a cliff where the only retreat was to jump over. The fall killed Blanquet instantly. In an act of barbarism, Sánchez had his head severed with a machete and displayed in Veracruz port. It was reported that as retribution Díaz ordered Gabay executed, and in retaliation Peláez had General Eduardo Martínez, a Felicista emissary trying to negotiate a unification of the two movements, shot.[98] True or not, the attempted rapprochement between the Díaz and Peláez movements did not materialize.[99]

8

Experiment
with Socialism

As the revolutionary struggle ebbed and flowed, another battle began to loom: the political one over the presidential candidate for the 1920 election. Despite Carranza's efforts to forestall campaigning as long as possible, his two opponents for the presidency, Obregón and Pablo González, had begun manoeuvring, seeking out allies and supporters for the coming election, with the former having the upper hand. Ever since, if not before, the constitutional convention held at Queretaro in 1917, the battle lines had been hardening. In the subsequent period, Obregón began to be looked upon as "the champion of the masses who would unseat Carranza as president in 1920."[1] Indeed, his support seemed to come solidly from the organized and militant working class, especially those in the oilfields in Veracruz and Tamaulipas. A socialist convention held in Mexico City of about twenty thousand worker delegates solidly gave their support to Obregón, denouncing Carranza and his official candidate, Bonilla.[2]

With desertions in Felicista ranks caused by Obregón's campaign strategy, things were coming to a head with Felicismo. Reduced to between five and six thousand men, now not as well-armed or supplied as before, they were faced by an equal number of Constitutionalists, who were better armed and coordinated by a determined Aguilar and a ruthlessly efficient Guadalupe Sánchez. These forces were supplied from the arms factory in Mexico City, heavier ammunition being manufactured in the fortress of San Juan de Ulúa.[3] Throughout central and southern Veracruz the Constitutionalists went on the offensive. In order to increase the pressure on the Felicistas, in early July another veteran revolutionary, General Miguel Alemán, was given the command of southern Veracruz, the Isthmian railway, and Oaxaca. His headquarters was at the rail junction of Tierra Blanca. Not a week later, it was reported that Félix Díaz decided he had had enough and bid his generals goodbye at his headquarters in Cotaxtla, although he did not leave the country until after the defeat of Carranza. By the end of 1919, it was obvious that his movement had been trumped by both the renewed Constitutionalist military campaign, and Obregón's politics.[4]

Díaz's decision to end his military foray and then retire from Mexico after Carranza's death was based on the realization that Obregón's ascension had changed the political constellation. He was seen by many Veracruzans as promising to adhere to the very principles that had accounted for their choice of Félix Díaz. Diaz's feeble accusation that the Constitution of 1917 was a "Bolshevik" document failed to ignite the expected response from the United States, nor did a last-minute effort in September to unite all the revolutionary movements under one banner and revive his flagging fortunes.[5] Obregón's political platform, heavily weighted in favour of social reforms – that is, those enunciated in the new constitution – also appealed to many who resented Carranza's centralist politics. The drafters of the new constitution had, in fact, opted for a framework that would give ample room for the realization of local control, through state and municipal autonomy for Carrancismo was not popular.[6] It was reckoned that at best a minority supported it in 1919. Federalism, in Veracruz still a potent unifying force, was ever strong. Díaz may have been bested, but the forces supporting his movement were still virile, especially in the north. The key was Obregón's explicit commitment to federalism.[7] And it was this policy that drew Felicista political groups directly into his camp.[8]

Carranza and Centralism

Faced with the mounting opposition to Ignacio Bonilla, his candidate, Carranza committed the ultimate mistake, which would end his career and his life. He tried to impose Bonilla on the nation. Mexicans had fought too long and too hard to allow such domination by the centre, considered a return to neo-Porfirismo. To suffocate any further opposition, in March, Carranza formulated a plan together with Aguilar, who had recently resigned from the cabinet to conduct Bonilla's campaign. It was a desperate attempt to achieve Carranza's desires. Knowing that the state of Sonora was the source of Obregón's support, naval forces were dispatched to Guyamas in early April, supposedly to fight Yaquis (who were, in fact, not in revolt) but really to engineer a coup against the governor, Adolfo de la Huerta.[9] Challenged by de la Huerta as to the real reason for the dispatch of troops, Carranza declared that he would not offer an explanation and, further, that the matter had to do with state versus federal authority. The state legislature agreed with the last statement but gave the matter an entirely different interpretation. For the next day, it gave the governor "special powers to protect the state against what was described as a 'deliberate challenge to its independence and sovereignty.'"[10]

It is interesting that at almost the very moment when Obregón was challenging Carranza for having used Porfirian methods of interference in state and local elections, Carranza should have been preparing an action that would earn him the opprobrium of almost the entire nation. It was another and blatant example of a breach of state sovereignty. On April 10, the state of Sonora broke off relations with the federal government.[11] Within a few days, General Calles had seized the gunboat *Guerrero* and arrived in Mazatlán with eight hundred marines. All the customs houses were seized and federal employees imprisoned. As Governor de la Huerta was ill, Calles assumed the governorship, and within the next few days worked assiduously to ensure the maximum cooperation. Telegrams flew back and forth as support for Sonora grew. In the Huasteca, the federal general, Gómez, joined Manuel Peláez, who had declared support for Obregón on April 21. Together, they captured Tuxpán. Rumours of the desertions of numerous small interior garrisons in Veracruz began to reach the capital. In addition, Guadalupe Sánchez was rumoured to have been fired for harbouring pro-Obregón sympathies.[12] Within a few days, Calles had organized a movement in support of state sovereignty, which most of the states joined. Adolfo de la Huerta was declared the supreme chief of the Revindicating Movement, and, on April 23, the Plan of Agua Prieta was announced.

Within a few weeks, Obregón was in almost complete control of the country. Carranza could count on the help of only a few leading generals, among them Cándido Aguilar, Manuel M. Diéguez, and Cesáreo Castro. In territory, he controlled a small portion of Veracruz (Guadalupe Sánchez there joined the Obregón rebellion on May 7) and the valley of Mexico under Francisco Murguía. That small bit of Veracruz territory he controlled was the fortress of San Juan de Ulúa, to which the state government had been transferred.[13] But by the next day Guadalupe Sánchez was in firm control of the rest of the port city, and negotiations were underway for Aguilar to leave the country. In the north, Peláez was also in control. The revolution, shortlived and relatively free of bloodshed, did claim one important victim. The previous night, Carranza, fleeing from Mexico City, was forced to take to the hills at Aljibes, where he was murdered while he slept.[14] De la Huerta assumed the presidency and set about organizing elections for the coming September. In Veracruz, a professor, Antonio Nava García, a man of "good character and modern ideas," was appointed provisional governor by the legislature.[15]

One of the most interesting aspects in the study of revolutions is how sometimes, as if without explanation, they rapidly come to an end. Can one speculate that after ten years of almost continuous war, Mexicans were tired of fighting? This is surely part of the answer. But another element has to be considered. The stand at Agua Prieta had certainly been initiated because of the attack on state sovereignty in Sonora. But underlying this was Mexicans' desire for effective democracy. Wasn't the idea of "democratic" election, Madero's initial call for *sufragio efectivo,* one for which the revolution had after all been fought? Thus, with Agua Prieta two important goals of the revolution had been acknowledged: democracy and federalism. The clincher was the reformist attitude of the man most Mexicans felt would be the sure winner, designed to affect the fortunes of *campesino* and worker alike.

Mexico under de la Huerta

One by one, former revolutionaries and anti-Constitutionalists sought to make their peace with the new government and Alvaro Obregón. First in line, and the most difficult to explain, was old Porfirista general Higinio Aguilar, who in the last few years had had considerable contact with the Zapatistas. Not that Aguilar had changed his ideology. He had seen his forces reduced to only fifty men; his motive for switching sides and supporting the Aguaprietistas was probably opportunistic.[16] But others came across, too, most prominently Pancho Villa. And Félix Díaz now considered it was finally time to lay down arms, asking only for sufficient guarantees to be able to leave the country.[17] By the third week in May, most of the states had recognized the Aguaprietistas.

On May 30, de la Huerta arrived in Mexico City to take the oath of office, without much fuss. In Veracruz, too, the change-over was relatively smooth, if somewhat earlier. The new governor was sworn in.[18] Elections were set by the interim president for September 5. The tranquillity and satisfaction in the country was more than skin deep. There was a general approval of the outcome of this latest phase of the revolution. It seemed to offer something to everyone, especially since with Carranza's death there seemed to be, outside of General Pablo González, no major figure to present a nucleus from which a new revolution could originate. Even the U.S. appeared to be content with the outcome, despite some voices critical of Obregón's "Bolshevikism." Writing from Progreso, Yucatán, U.S. consul Gayland Marsh expressed the sentiments of many foreigners: "Americans generally express satisfaction at what they recognize as a greatly improved attitude toward citizens of the United States and foreigners in general." Speaking of the new leaders in Yucatán, he continued: "I know all of these men very well. They may have Socialistic [sic] political tendencies but at the same time they favour more social and educational reforms which are good and much needed in Mexico."[19] Despite the hysterical demands for intervention from some quarters, Mexico in May 1920 seemed in a better position to protect foreigners and foreign interests than ever before. Certainly, the oilfields, now completely under Peláez's control because of his adherence to Obregón, would be safer than they had been for the last six years.

Manuel Peláez, too, had accepted the Plan of Agua Prieta, with its promise of state sovereignty, which could be used to protect his oil interests. Neither foreigner nor Mexican wanted to see him leave for Mexico City. But he did, and the victory parade held in Mexico City on June 8, in which Peláez rode, gave a symbolic sense of the unity that had been achieved. Even the bubonic plague, raging in Veracruz for some time, appeared to have run its course.[20] The revolution seemed at last to have come to an end.

Nothing was further from the truth. At the end of June, the bubonic plague returned and so did another plague. The essential battle of the revolution, the question of state sovereignty, was not laid to rest at Aljibes.[21] Within a few months, it returned in a dispute between Veracruz and the central government. On August 8, the interim president, Adolfo de la Huerta published a decree refusing to recognize any acts passed by the state of Veracruz. He also deposed the acting provisional governor, Carlos Méndez (acting for Antonio Nava García), and annulled local elections held on August 8, after the presidential decree, and only ten per cent of the registered voters participated. The reason for the president's actions, he stated, was to give the people and political parties sufficient time to campaign, a reasoning that seems to have been approved by the voters. However, when de la Huerta removed the acting provisional governor and appointed Gabriel Garzón Cossa in his place, the people turned against him, because removing the constitutional governor was seen to be as undemocratic as the hasty elections. It was also seen as a breach of state sovereignty. Faced with this united opposition, de la Huerta backed down, leaving the ultimate decision in the hands of the legal authorities. When the district judge rejected Nava García's *amparo*, however, the latter refused to leave office and prevented the newly appointed governor from beginning his work. In this, Nava García was supported by a majority of Veracruzans, although Garzón Cossa eventually did act for a short period in order to convoke the elections.[22]

Veracruz under Tejeda

We saw in the previous chapter how the central government reacted to the first attempts by Cándido Aguilar at implementing social justice, feeble though they were. Carranza had shown little patience with those initiatives of the state government as had his predecessors. It remained to be seen how the new governor, Tejeda, and his successor, Jara, would fare with, respectively, Obregón and Calles.

The 1920s were, ironically, a period of extreme unrest in Veracruz amidst a clamour for change. The decade saw the rise of powerful and militant mass organizations supported by the state governor, Adalberto Tejeda. These groups were generated by the masses of Veracruzan society and included unionized workers, *campesinos*, and other citizens organized around the renters' union. Their demands were for no less than revolutionary social and economic changes. It would be no exaggeration to speak here of an outbreak of "class warfare."

By placing himself at their head and affording them not only the protection but the co-operation of the state government, Tejeda was continuing a trend that had been set six years earlier by Cándido Aguilar. In both his intent and reach, however, Tejeda's social and economic policies surpassed what even Aguilar had envisioned. They included land redistribution as well as restrictions on capitalist exploitation. They were, therefore, based on Tejeda's unabashed adhesion to "socialism." And they were to be funded on a tax policy aimed primarily at the oil companies but resting on the political principle of state sovereignty. To this end Tejeda wrote to the governors of Nuevo León, Oaxaca, Coahuila, Tabasco, and susequently to all other governors, requesting their support for the reactivation of Article 27 of the Constitution of 1917. In addition, he asked them to clarify the roles of the federal and state governments "*vis-à-vis*" the petroleum industry, especially in the fiscal domain."[23] This position was destined to bring the state of Veracruz into open conflict with the federal government, yet because of circumstances in the early 1920s the time was not ripe for such a confrontation.

On September 5, general elections were held throughout the republic. In Veracruz, there was a stiff gubernatorial battle between the two candidates: the representative of the landlords, Jacobo Rincón, and Adalberto Tejeda. Confusing the whole scene was that intrepid political figure, Gabriel Gavira. Not surprisingly, he threw his support and that of the workers from Orizaba connected with the CROM, on Rincón's side. Tejeda, whose star had risen during the revolutionary years due to his friendship with Aguilar (and no doubt to his capability), had been with Aguilar during the first battles with the petroleum companies in 1916. Subsequently elected as a Veracruz delegate to the Queretaro Convention, Tejeda had also been one of the elected senators for Veracruz. Later, he had helped Aguilar clean up corruption among Constitutionalist officers, especially in the north of the state. He was thus no neophyte politically and had had time to foster his own political connections.[24] In 1920, he decided to support Obregón for the presidency, a fact of which the latter had to be reminded on more than one occasion. Supported by a majority of the deputies and with pressure from Obregón, Tejeda was able to win the election and began work within a week.[25]

Fortunately, the central government was not yet in a position of strength. Obregón had not had sufficient time for consolidation. He could not yet renege on the policy that had carried him to power, state sovereignty. Tejeda could therefore begin his term with social reforms, the legislative groundwork for which had already been laid in 1914 by Aguilar. He was aided by the volatile situation in Veracruz characterized by class tensions.

The later social reforms of the 1920s would never have been realized had the peasantry and working class not been radicalized by the two major events that set off the Mexican Revolution in Veracruz: the Acayucan uprising of 1906 and the Río Blanco

labour dispute of 1907. These two events produced a class consciousness further aroused by labour conditions between 1907
and 1920 and by the concern showed by Cándido Aguilar, Pérez
Romero, and Agustín Millán. It was also influenced by the
rhetoric that poured first from the Convention, then from the
Constitution of 1917, not to speak of agitation by Zapatistas and
the entire revolutionary struggle.

In other words, when Adalberto Tejeda stepped into the saddle
in December 1920, the ground had already been well prepared
for a complete radicalization of the state, for a profound overhaul
of social conditions in regard to the twin pillars of hierarchy
and class domination. Never before or perhaps anywhere else in
the republic, apart perhaps from Morelos, had there been such
radical consciousness griping thousands of workers, *campesinos,*
and artisans.[26] What was new was that now the governor and the
state government, instead of representing the upper and middle
classes exclusively as in Dehesa's, Madero's, and Carranza's day,
were now solidly on the side of the working and rural classes.
And the political weapon used to accomplish social changes
would be the emphasis on the sovereignty of the state, a tactic
wielded skillfully by Tejeda.

Tejeda was born in 1880 in Chicontepec, in the north of the
state, completing his education in Mexico City, where he grad-
uated as a topographical engineer. Employed by the state of
Veracruz to work on the construction of a drinking water source
for the port city, he was exposed as a young man to the problems of unrestricted growth of a large urban complex. In 1910,
he joined the Maderistas, rising quickly to the rank of captain.
He then met Cándido Aguilar, and during the Constitutionalist
struggle served him as chief of staff in the Division of the East.
Named chief of operations for the Huasteca, he resigned in 1916
to run for election as a delegate to the Queretaro constitutional
convention. Thereafter, he served the state as a senator, becoming fully aware of the problems with the oil companies, an experience that animated the nationalist in him.[27] In 1920, switching
his allegiance from Carranza to Obregón, and rejecting former
political associate Cándido Aguilar, Tejeda was in the perfect
position to become the new governor. From all the evidence,
it appears that Obregón was hesitant but was swayed by the
support Tejeda could bring from important sectors of the state;
Tejeda was duly elected governor. Nevertheless, his ideological
stance was not entirely acceptable to Obregón.

The reason was the continuing unrest in the state as well as other parts of Mexico due to the political backlash of Veracruz landlords, who were already showing a "tenacious resistance" to any ideas of land reform. In December 1920, they were confronted by a restless peasantry, as well as a state government intent on proceeding with the stated goals regarding agrarian policy of the Constitution of 1917. Obregón's problem was that he had campaigned as the champion of workers' and *campesinos'* rights, believed firmly in these himself, but was faced not only with the resistance of landlords but also the intractable problem of organizing the recovery of agriculture in the national interest.[28]

Obregón's solution was simply to buy time. Tejeda, however, in his attempt to satisfy the social and economic demands of an aroused populace, had none to lose. At issue was not simply the question of land redistribution, but also a contest, emanating from the time of Carranza's presidency, between the state and the central government over the question of constitutional power in this area of legislation. Under the federal Agrarian Law of 1915, committees of peasants had been set up in some communities in order to petition either for lands or to demand restitution of lands alienated from their rightful owners. As previously noted, a small distribution of lands had taken place during Aguilar's governorship. Between 1917 and 1920, thirty-seven resolutions of land conflicts had been concluded.[29] But Aguilar had been careful not to exceed the parameters set by Carranza.[30] Tejeda followed a different path.

Using the Comisión Local Agraria (State Agrarian Commission), he responded quickly to the first demands for land. These came from the central region of Veracruz between the capital Xalapa and the port city. Here the majority of people lived off the land, the only problem being that most of it was in the hands of a few families. Salmoral, an impoverished area in the municipality of La Antigua, can be credited with the initiation of the movement which grew quickly. José Cardel, the man destined to become a noted peasant leader, and a number of Salmoral's inhabitants filed a request for lands in April 1921, which were duly allocated by the CLA, but augmented by the governor. The same occurred in the municipality of Puente Nacional, whose lands were owned by two huge *haciendas*. In the south, too, near San Andrés Tuxtla, redistribution was carried out. The landlords were quick to act. At first, their measures were peaceful, withdrawing rented lands from their lessees and importing day workers from outside the state. In addition, they utilized the forces of a local army commander, Colonel Pascual Casarín, to impede the work of the commission. Very quickly, though, they turned to violent methods. "White guards" were employed to protect property and intimidate peasants and new *ejidatarios*, as well as to assassinate "recalcitrant" leaders. Tejeda was compelled to deploy the civil guard in those communities and to commence arming peasants for their self-defence.[31] His actions drew the opposition of the Veracruz military commander, Guadalupe Sánchez, friend of the landowners, who protested constantly to the president.

Tejeda also used his power to help the working class (indeed, the working classes, for this term must include the artisans as well). Radicalized by the labour dispute in Río Blanco in 1906-7, workers had continued to demonstrate and demand better working conditions and wages. In fact, it was the revolution itself that gave great stimulus to the workers' movements. The reasons are obvious. Although business continued almost unaffected during the revolution, except for the years 1914-16, when there was "a major downturn in industrial production," during its course there was rampant inflation. This was caused, *inter alia,* by a diminution in the supply of essential goods, especially foodstuffs, as well as the circulation of various kinds of paper money, which very quickly lost value.[32] Between 1916 and 1919, therefore, workers continued to build and expand their own organizations. Chambers of labour were created in the industrial area of the state comprising not only textile but also tobacco and railroad workers, while the advancing oil industry in the north and south provided the conditions for militant labour organization. In 1919, the oil workers brought oil production to a halt, necessitating the use of federal troops.[33] This militant and determined organization had its roots in the history of labour militancy in Veracruz. But with the Constitution of 1917, which enshrined basic labour laws, especially the right to unionize and to strike, workers now felt they had the legal underpinnings that gave new promise of better working conditions.

For its part, the government of Veracruz had attempted, since the Constitutionalist recovery of Veracruz in 1914, to use its legislative power to ameliorate the economic situation. Laws had been passed controlling the price of basic foods such as maize and other grains, but there was no mechanism to ensure that commodities would not be shipped for sale in areas where prices were higher. Anticipating the new Constitution, the Veracruz government had already in 1914 legalized trade unions as the bargaining elements between workers and capital and had legislated the nine-hour working day. And as noted above, in

1915, Veracruz was chosen as the site for the Congress of the Labour Confederation of the Mexican Region because of its progressive labour climate. (This organization, the precursor of the Confederación Regional de Obreros Mexicanos [Regional Confederation of Mexican Workers, or CROM] was under the leadership of Herón Proal.) In October 1915, a commission was created by the Veracruz government and charged with the inspection of factories.[34] As a futher measure in 1918, with the Labour Law, a Junta Central de Conciliación y Arbitraje (Central Commission for Conciliation and Arbitration) was established to handle labour disputes.

These legislative initiatives, carried out mainly by Cándido Aguilar, had produced a firm basis on which Tejeda could build a progressive labour policy.[35] However, the actual collusion between state and workers, initiating a new and radical chapter in the socio-political struggle, did not really emerge until the victory of Obregón as president, and that of Tejeda in Veracruz in 1920. This governor (from 1920 to 1924, and again from 1928 to 32) joins other famous radical governors such as Salvador Alvarado and Carillo Puerto, both of Yucatán, Garrido Canabal in Tabasco, and Emilio Portes Gil in Tamaulipas, as examples of state radicalism in action.

At the outset, one must recognize that the radical movements in Veracruz did not emanate from above. Instead, they were the spontaneous class reactions of various sectors of the population, emboldened by the revolution and inspired by the radical promise of the Constitution of 1917, as well as the Bolshevik revolution in Russia in the same year. And they grew to fruition *before* Tejeda or any government official had taken their side. As in Río Blanco, workers, peasants, artisans, renters – all those who came to represent the "radical" side of the revolution in Veracruz – were not the products of some manipulation from above. They had carried through an analysis of their own objective conditions and had begun to act in opposition to them years before Tejeda. In fact, one can find a parallel between the creation of the first union in Río Blanco in 1906 and the founding of the Communist Party in Veracruz in 1919. Both were the result of reading circles. The Communist Party was founded by a tobacco worker, Manuel Díaz Ramírez, in the port city towards the end of the year. It included other soon-to-be prominent social organizers such as Ursulo Galván, Herón Proal, and Manuel Almanza García.[36]

Haber is partially correct to speak of the Mexican Revolution as a "class war," and this aspect of it, I believe, found its most profound expression in Veracruz, especially after the so-called revolutionary settlement of 1920.[37] Yet it was more than that. This specific class war was organized and fought under the auspices of the state government of Veracruz, free for the moment due to the weakness of the central government. Undoubtedly, the state government helped to push the process along. It armed peasants and passed laws to protect or enhance the workers' position. One of Tejeda's first acts, in fact, was to finalize a Ley de Participación de Utilidades (Profit Sharing Law), setting off a furious battle by capitalists to have it rescinded by the courts, a move supported by president Obregón.[38] The following year, yet another challenge to the traditional social order appeared. A movement that had been brewing for some years now in Veracruz port appeared as full-fledged rebellion: the renters' strike. Carranza's use of the port city as the national capital had strained housing capacity and demand, enabling landlords, with an avaricious eye for profits, to increase rents. Where housing was available, sanitary conditions were almost non-existent.

Such conditions spurred increasing militancy among the poorer and working classes. Yet the rise of the renters' movement, and Tejeda's subsequent help for it, was also the product of a conjunction of political forces.[39] The port city had been and still was the source of the most concerted opposition to the governor, and he for his part took advantage of the movement to consolidate his political support there. This was no cynical politics at work: the renters' movement was precisely the kind to which Tejeda wanted to apportion state support. Unfortunately for Tejeda, the movement itself was removed from his hands by Herón Proal, activist with the Veracruz Communist Party, who wanted to mold it for his own political ends. In the spring of 1922, the movement made use of the strike tactic. Prostitutes were the initiators, threatening to burn the rented accoutrements of their trade, their mattresses.[40] On March 5, over forty thousand tenants participated in a march and demonstrations, which paralyzed the city.

Tejeda attempted to intervene, enlisting the help and support of the minister of the interior, Plutarcho Elías Calles. But the problem was much larger than a mere fight over rents. Foreigners, Spaniards, and U.S. citizens especially owned many of the dwellings. Sensitive to complaints from the representatives of those countries, the president threatened armed intervention with federal troops if there was no solution. Indeed, the federal commander of Veracruz, Guadalupe Sánchez, forbade any more demonstrations and arrested the leader of the renter's union,

Proal. Tejeda tried to improve the situation by having the legislature pass a rent law. Despite the massive opposition press campaign mounted throughout the state as well as in Mexico City, where Tejeda was continuously accused of "Bolshevism" and of attacking private property, the law was passed. To appease tenants and to tackle the deplorable housing situation, it ordered that rents be reduced "to slighlty more than 1910 levels" and stipulated that the government "donate land for the construction of new housing, and provide for the supervision of landlord-tenant relations."[41] Now the forces were clearly aligned. The federal government would back private property, and the state government the people.[42] Federal forces intervened against the renters, in which confrontation some renters were killed, but the renters' union was not broken.[43] It was able to continue on into the late twenties. More important, the movement had shown the strength and vehemence of popular protest.

Thwarted in this area, Tejeda redirected his efforts to the rural sector. But the organization of *campesinos*, via aggressive ideological propagandizing backed by the power of the governor's office, and demanding that land not only be returned, but distributed to those who had none, was the straw that began to break the camel's back. Ursulo Galván and Juan Andreu Almanza, who had left for the countryside in 1923, coordinated these efforts. There they organized meetings of *campesinos*, the aim being to gather delegates for a state peasant congress. In the villages, they attempted to mobilize peasants by singing revolutionary songs. *Hacendado* reaction was not long in coming. In Tlacotepec de Mejía, for example, the agitators were arrested by federal troops. Tejeda immediately cabled the president and used a detachment of soldiers stationed in Córdoba to release Galván and others. Five days later, Tejeda invited Galván to Xalapa for talks, and with his help the congress became a reality. The two hundred agrarian committees, which had been formed in various parts of the state, were invited to send delegates to a congress in Xalapa, which was convened on March 23, 1923. Thus did the Liga de Comunidades Agrarias y Sindicatos Campesinos de Veracruz (Veracruz Peasant League) come to be.[44]

Nor were their efforts without success. Between 1920 and 1924, Tejeda distributed about forty per cent more lands than had Aguilar, benefiting almost twenty-four thousand people (nearly double the number for the period 1917-20). In addition, he established a regional bank to finance the agricultural work of the new peasant landowners, facilitated the formation of

El Camarada —
Manuel Almanza
Pasando el Rio —
"El Faisán" para
ir a saludar a los —
campesinos de la
Region de Salmoral.
lleva en
ancas al
C. Diputado
Ursulo Galván.

Julio 15 de 1925,

a.D. Vázquez.
for. —

Galván and Almanza riding to Salmoral for a peasant meeting

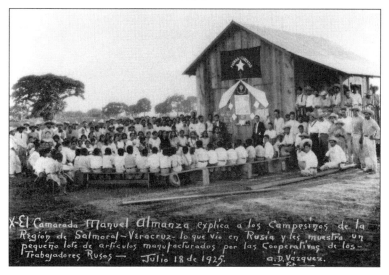

Almanza lecturing to villagers after visiting the Soviet Union, 1925

co-operatives, and initiated an irrigation scheme.[45] For this, he faced mounting opposition from the *hacendados* as well as the president. Throughout 1923, Tejeda was the object of a vitriolic campaign of denunciation in the Veracruz (*El Dictámen*) and national press (*Excelsior, El Demócrata*), amidst personal denunciations from *hacendados* and businessmen in the port city. Resistance to his policies from the federal army commanded by Guadalupe Sánchez in Veracruz, and the presidential order to disarm the Veracruz Civil Guard as well as all *agraristas*, brought the class war to a fever pitch. In March, federal troops killed eight people and injured six in a confrontation in the municipal building at Puente Nacional forcing the president to make a fact-finding tour of Veracruz in September.

One day after his meeting with the Veracruz bourgeoisie, and now fully cognizant of the tremendous popular support for the governor, Obregón changed tactics one hundred and eighty degrees and began to court Tejeda.[46] His reasons were entirely political. Obregón felt he was loosing control in the battle for the presidency. His choice of an "official" candidate, Calles, had put him in the same boat as, earlier, Carranza had been, and it was necessary for him to consolidate as much political support as he could muster. Again, he needed the help of the urban and rural working classes. In October, the situation worsened as he became aware of the nation's precarious finances. The new minister of finance, Alberto Pani, found a deficit much larger than had been reported by Adolfo de la Huerta.[47] But this knowledge came to light only after de la Huerta, angry over what he considered Obregón's interference in the state politics of San Luis Potosí and Nuevo León, resigned from the cabinet. The break with de la Huerta boded ill for Obregón.

The Delahuertista Rebellion

It is interesting to see a decisive but logical shift in political ideology that had been taking shape over the last few years now shoot forth with as much fury as the oil gushers in the north. Although I have not encountered the label in any historical work dealing with this period, in Veracruz there was growing interest in fascism in order to combat the radical socialist policies of Tejeda.[48] Copies of the newspaper *El Fascismo* were circulating in the state and were collected by the government for distribution to various workers' organizations. Who were these 'fascists'? They were the *hacendados*, capitalists, and industrialists, concentrated in Veracruz, among whom were many ex-Felicistas. Also included were members of the Roman Catholic clergy. Names such as Gabay, Galán, Panuncio Martínez, Peláez, and Medina Barrón were included in a report to Tejeda. Lagunes, of the rich family from a huge *hacienda* near Piedras Negras, was also specifically mentioned. The leader of this group was said to be General Guadalupe Sánchez, whose frequent denials would soon prove him a liar. The report also gave an indication of some of the political origins of this group. They had earnestly believed that Obregón was their man but, confronted with the two most salient facts of his presidency, the attempt to strengthen the central government, and his alliance with the workers' and *campesinos'* ideological challenge, they had decided otherwise and shifted their allegiance to de la Huerta.[49]

A rebellion was declared on December 6, 1923, in the port city, where ex-president de la Huerta launched a manifesto to the nation explaining its reasons.[50] In it, he argued that the president had violated the sovereignty of the states, specifically in Michoacán, San Luis Potosí, Zacatecas, and Nuevo León. Further, he accused the president of electoral fraud in Veracruz (he was referring to elections for the legislature held that year) in order to support the "tyranny" of Tejeda, of imposing the "unpopular" candidate Calles on the nation, and in general of annihilating various freedoms. With this declaration, many old state-sovereignty and Felicista revolutionaries jumped out of the woodwork. Raúl G. Ruiz, for example, who had settled down to a quiet life in Mexico City, quickly made his way to Veracruz.[51] What surprised the state and federal governments was not the declaration of a rebellion, but the magnitude of the movement and the rapidity with which the rebels took over territory. Fortunately for Obregón and the government, they retained the loyalty of over sixty per cent of the officer corps. Although its cities were almost completely overrun by the Delahuertistas, Veracruz, too, was able to offer significant help. One million dollars of the Veracruz treasury was remitted by the Bank of Montreal, which Tejeda now placed at the disposal of the federal government.[52] As a pre-emptive measure, Obregón also ordered the immediate arrest and seclusion of Manuel Peláez.[53] Despite the immediate successes of the Delahuertistas, especially the defection of so many troops, the government was in a better position than the rebels. One of the fundamental factors in its favour was the support of the United States. Another was that the majority of the population of Mexico and of Veracruz, composed of workers and *campesinos*, were on the government's side, despite de la Huerta's belated attempt to make his Plan of Xilitla palatable to them. These were now too well prepared ideologically to swallow the shallow promises of "democracy" and "liberty" that they had heard before. They knew that the people behind de la Huerta were those who wanted a free hand to exploit them, to deprive them of the precious little land that had been distributed. It was also their firm belief that Calles, the chosen, was the man who would continue to govern in the style and with the policies of Obregón and Tejeda.[54]

In all, over eighteen thousand *agraristas* from Veracruz alone were estimated to have remained loyal to Obregón. But they were too late to prevent the capture and executions of agrarian leaders, Cardel, Caracas, and Rodríguez Clara (a veteran of the Acayucan uprising of 1906). Proal and Galván were able to escape.[55] The governor himself, with old cohorts Adalberto Palacios and Heriberto Jara, took the field, joined by numerous *agraristas* recruited by Tejeda on the spot.[56] In this struggle, they were decisive. On February 16, a column of six hundred *campesinos* recaptured the town of Papantla. So decisively did Veracruz *campesinos* react to the rebellion that federal troops were able to leave the state in order to fight elsewhere. On February 11, the port city was recaptured.[57] The government continued its advance in Veracruz, the final battle in the state

being fought at San Francisco de las Peñas (later renamed
Cardel) on March 22, where Sánchez was given his last drubbing.
Interestingly, one of the inveterate fighters for federalism, Raúl
G. Ruiz, was captured along with 185 other prisoners.[58] By June,
discouraged by the defeat at Esperanza, the losses in Veracruz,
and the failure to capture Tampico, the Delahuertista movement
had collapsed. The whole episode had lasted hardly one year but
had cost over six thousand lives.[59]

The Delahuertista rebellion had important consequences for
both the state and the nation. On the national level, it consoli-
dated the victory of the Sonoran duo, Obregón and Calles. It
also cleansed the army of untrustworthy elements, an important
factor in the next phase of the revolution. On the other hand,
it strengthened the *agrarista* forces in Veracruz.[60] This allowed
Tejeda to continue his work in distributing land. Ironically, this
very fact weakened the state in an unforeseeable way. Tejeda's
success was the state's loss in that the next governor would find it
difficult if not impossible to achieve the backing of the *agraristas*,
weakening his own ability to stand up to the central government.

Calles versus Jara

The year 1924 was also the occasion of national and gubernatorial elections. These were viciously contested, and the outcome in Veracruz was far from certain. The official candidate was
Heriberto Jara, but, since some workers' political clubs did not
support him, Tejeda had to pull some hefty political strings and
even use violence to get his way.[61] Tejeda saw clearly what others
like Galván and Cardel had foreseen earlier: that Jara, because
of his impeccable revolutionary past, but also because of his support by the CROM and the industrial workers, was the logical
candidate to run on the slate with Calles. Not that his agrarian
roots were negligible. He had consistently supported Tejeda, had
helped organize and lead the 86th Battalion, and had supported
the *agraristas* during the Delahuertista revolt.[62] So, with official
help at the national and state levels, Jara was duly elected governor for the term 1924 to 1928.

His short term in office, however, was not characterized by
great success. Shortly after his inauguration, he began running
into trouble. In the first place, Jara could not muster the type of
solid support that Tejeda had been able to command. Despite his
support for the Peasant League, his real political base was with
the industrial workers, hardly a significant block of bodies within

the entire state. Then again, Tejeda, for a brief time minister of communications and then minister of the interior, kept firm control of the peasant organizations in order to ensure a political base for his re-election. Galván, whom Tejeda tried to encourage in becoming a federal deputy, instead became the head of the state Civil Guard and legislative deputy for Córdoba. So the Peasant League at best showed coolness towards Jara's administration. Second, Jara's record in land redistribution was uninspiring. Each year his administration redistributed less land, a fact that did not endear him to the League.[63]

What finally destroyed even the semblance of backing by the Peasant League was the fatal shooting of Francisco Moreno, a peasant leader and state deputy from San Andrés Tuxtla. He was shot by the commander of the Civil Guard in the governor's palace, where he was threatening to kill Jara. "A wave of indignation swept the state as the League and its leaders began to protest the unwarranted shooting of the *agrarista* deputy." When Galván pressed for an investigation, Jara's answer was to end the state subsidy paid to the League.[64]

Jara even had trouble with his own supporters. The secretary general of the Workers' Party of Veracruz complained bitterly to Tejeda that Jara's political praxis lacked revolutionary commitment. For example, he appointed a former Dehesista, Atenógenes Pérez y Soto, director of education in the state. The appointment brought this emphatic reminder from the Workers' Party: "Taking into consideration that Governor Jara was elected by the working classes of this state, not by the competents of the Public Administration, this party thinks that only those addicted to the proletariat should be helping the government. Competence is a strategy of the reactionaries."[65]

Jara succeeded in damaging relations with practically every powerful group "inside or outside Veracruz."[66] One of these gruops was headed by a man who knew how to consolidate and use power: Luis Morones, the leader of the powerful CROM union. Nevertheless, these alienations would have meant nothing had Jara kept the support of the president. Part of his failure to do so is due to ineptitude: in labour affairs, he went head on against Morones, who was key to the implementation of the president's new policy of conciliating foreign investors, above all, the United States.

In 1925, Morones, at Calles's behest, began a policy of what must be dubbed class collaboration. The policy was intended to pacify foreign businesses and to ward off both criticism and intervention from the United States. Morones's means of achieving this end was to break the independent unions and to make the CROM the only viable alternative.

In 1924, workers at the famous Río Blanco factory had protested at the salary reductions of certain categories of employees. This led to a twenty-two day strike and immobilized all the factories in Orizaba. In response, Morones inveigled the ministry of industry, commerce and work (SICT) to organize a convention for the purpose of standardizing wage levels in the textile industry. The Convención Industrial Obrero del Ramo Textil was convoked and inaugurated October 6, 1926. Despite the formal agreements, however, many industrialists refused to pay the prescribed wages.[67] The federal government reduced taxes to the industry to allow the salary commitments to be met.[68] Yet the workers still awaited improvements, although Jeffrey Bortz argues that the episode was an important gain for the workers in the revolution, since it made it "legally very, very difficult to discipline a worker without consent of the union."[69] The union, by contrast, clearly gained a great deal as it received the important right to hire and fire workers, and thus gave immense power to the CROM.

That the CROM used this power to strengthen its position by attacking other unions can be seen in its actions during the subsequent labour dispute among railroad workers. The railroad workers were the most numerous group that had managed to remain independent of the CROM. As Jara was trying to cope with the CROM's inroads into the textile unions, he was faced with a crippling strike by railroad workers of the Veracruz-Isthmus, Tehuantepec, and Pacific railroads, and once again the CROM's intention of breaking the railroad union and bringing the workers into its fold.

The union in question was the Confederación de las Sociedades Ferrocarrilleras (CSF). It bears remembering that this union was the one utilized by Obregón in his fight against Huerta, when he formed the Red Brigades. Complicating matters was an older conflict between this union and the Morones-led Liga de Trabajadores de la Zona Maritima (LZM) going back to 1922.[70] In that year, the CROM began its campaign to control the CSF or have it decertified. Its primary tactic was to replace the CSF with its own Unión de Obreros Ferrocarrileros del Puerto (UOFP).[71] In 1925, the CROM again attempted to take over the CSF by creating its own railway union, the Federación Nacional Ferrocarrilera (FNF). This attempt failed because the CSF workers, true to their reputation for independence, held fast to their union.[72]

But the *casus belli* of the railroad strike were those actions consequent on the privatization of the national railroads. Refurbishing of the railroad network had become one of the main tragets of the government's policy. Because of the ravages of the revolution, the railroad was saddled with an enormous debt, its equipment needed repair or repacing, and there were continous labour disputes that affected the rehabilition of the roadwork. Consequently, the finance minister, Alberto Pani, drew up a plan to resuscitate the railway system, in such a way that its debt could be reduced. He proposed handing over the management to a private firm, in return for which they would guarantee the payment of cash warrants to cover the interest on the debt.[73] In 1926, with the assumption of management by private interests, this plan was put into effect. In order to meet its requirements, the company set about restructuring the railroad network, which meant laying off numerous personnel. Thus began the conflict that was to escalate into a strike by a majority of railroad workers across Mexico.

In February 1926, the CSF received a setback. The Liga was able to win the legal battle for reincorporation of its members into the CSF. At the same time, the president issued a decree declaring the railroad workers essential personnel and employees of the federal government, under the Ministry of Communications and Public Works. Then, the restructuring began, and with it the plan to discredit and ultimately destroy the CSF. A slur campaign started, accusing the CSF of being in league with the Communist Party, a charge that was vehemently denied. Then, in Buena Vista station in Mexico City, the CROM tried to have six of its members reinstated in a workshop controlled by the CSF. A shoot-out ensued. Calles responded by sending in the army, dispatching one hundred soldiers to each workshop ostensibly to keep the peace, but really to intimidate the CSF. In addition, six new CROM unions were recognized within the railway system. By July, almost the entire network had come to a standstill, and there was open battle between Cromistas and the CSF.[74] In December, trains ground to a halt in the entire northeast. Calles's response was to send in soldiers and scabs. Workers who resisted were arrested, amidst the continuing campaign to cite them as communists. Finally, on Fenbruary 23, 1927, the government withdrew recognition from the CSF and jailed its leaders. Neverteless, the strikes not only continued but spread to other states or other industries, such as with the telephone workers and textile spinners in the Federal District.

In the end, the strength of the government, with Calles's

willingness to deploy troops and scabs, was too much for the CSF and its affiliates. In September, Calles had recourse to the legal system as well. He turned the matter of the CSF strike over to the Junta Federal de Conciliación y Arbitraje, controlled by Morones, which delivered the verdict of illegality. This changed the nature of the whole proceeding. Suddenly, the workers could be accused of dereliction of duty and, since they were federal employees, be arrested and charged. To make matters worse, the Supreme Court upheld the decision. The strike was broken.[75]

But it had been costly, not only for the railroad workers and the CSF, but for the company as well as the national economy. More importantly, the whole episode implicated the governor of Veracruz, Heriberto Jara, who had consistently supported the railroad workers. Equally important was the tactic of shifting the arbitration of labour disputes from the state to the federal level. Similar to the removal of the agrarian boards from the hands of the state, as had been accomplished under Aguilar, the federal government took advantage of the unrest in the railroad and petroleum sectors to control arbitration, and thus stifle any hint of independence among the workers. Since 1918, the Juntas de Conciliación of Veracruz had been the arbitrators in disputes between petroleum workers and the companies. In the disputes of 1924-25, it was these that adjudicated grievances. In March 1927, however, the petroleum industry was placed under the Ministry of Communications and Works, and, in September, by presidential decree, the Juntas were raised to federal rank and charged with adjudicating in five *sectrores*: mines, oilfields, electricity, railway, and the textile industry. Since the CROM exercised its influence to staff the Juntas, any semblance of impartiality was lost.[76] Henceforth, the Juntas would do the bidding of the government.

The End of Federalism

This success of the CROM and Morones notwithstanding, Jara was in little trouble as long as he went along with the central government. It was his unwillingness to do so that cost him his position and the state so dearly.[77] The source of the trouble this time was the foreign oil companies. That fight was to bring the state government into outright conflict with the federal government: at stake was the issue of state sovereignty.

Oil was discovered in Mexico in the nineteenth century, but not until the beginning of the twentieth was exploration and serious exploitation of the oil-bearing areas undertaken. Veracruz was the area most favoured with underground resources, and thus bore the brunt of the impact of development of this industry, in the social well as the economic sense. The revolution of 1910 had almost no negative effect on the continued development of the industry, which expanded exponentially to become the most lucrative in Mexico. However, the revolution did sound a note to the oil companies that differed markedly from the tone of its predecessor, the Porfiriato. The first revolutionary president, Madero, had ordered the registration of all oil companies in 1912, also imposing the first tax on shipments of crude oil. It was under Carranza, however, that Mexico began to take note of the revenue potential as well as exert its national right to control its patrimony. In opposition to the dominant policy in the Porfiriato, Article 27 of the Constitution of 1917 re-invoked the ancient Spanish law of claiming sub-soil rights for the nation.[78]

The state government had also attempted to exert its rights vis-à-vis the oil companies. In 1915, Cándido Aguilar had cancelled the concessions given to El Aguila by Governor Manuel Leví, levying a charge of two cents per barrel for the benefit of the state and municipalities. This policy of exerting state control over businesses, not just the oil companies, was continued by Aguilar's replacement, Heriberto Jara. Other decrees were passed regulating administrative procedures for registering and operating businesses in general. The Supreme Court, moreover, under legal attack by the oil companies, finally upheld the decrees of 1915.[79] With the promulgation of the Constitution of 1917, control of Mexico's patrimony was enshrined at the highest legal level. Here was a declaration that the nation would no longer do business in the manner of the Porfiriato. Business and investments were welcome but would have to pay for the right to make money out of the nation's resources. Obviously, the oil companies felt differently and explored every possible legal procedure to avoid paying taxes. Worse for Mexico, the government of the United States supported those companies.

Despite the passage of the laws necessary to implement the Constitution, both Carranza and his successor, Obregón, were constrained in their ability to employ these, as they had to second-guess the attitude and possible intervention of the United States.[80] The agenda of the United States in its relationship with Mexico after the First World War was to secure oil reserves as an element in its quest for power. And with the election of Republican president Harding, the man at the helm was not only a more aggressive leader, but one whose ear was acutely attuned.[81] Since Mexico produced 22.7 per cent of the world's oil, it is not difficult to see its strategic importance.[82]

The Mexican government itself, even if it wished to be more moderate, was facing the demands of a populace awakened by the social promises of the revolution. In the cases of Aguilar, Tejeda, and Jara, there was no such wish for moderation. All three were nationalists and state sovereignists. They were intent on development through positive acts of the state government and by utilizing the federal rights entrenched in the Constitution. These had facilitated Aguilar in the passage of Decree 9, mentioned above. Veracruz was in need of the tax revenue to ensure its own development and to begin the task of reconstruction. Nor were the tax payments excessive, considering that El Aguila was returning over forty-five per cent profit on its operations.[83] But even more than Aguilar and Jara (in his first administration), Tejeda, who had been a member of the Petroleum Commission in the Senate, was determined to secure the payment of taxes and royalties for the benefit of the state.

The passage of the federal Petroleum Law in 1926, which gave the companies one year in which to present their applications for the confirmation of property rights, drove Mexico and the United States to the brink of war. The United States planned to invade Mexico once again in an attempt to overturn that law. These plans emanated from the highest level: involved were the secretary of state, Frank Billings Kellogg; Andrew W. Mellon, secretary of the treasury, and himself a shareholder in some of the major oil companies; and James R. Sheffield, ambassador to Mexico. Sheffield consistently painted the worst possible picture of Mexico for his government in Washington.[84] In 1993, documents found in the U.S. embassy in Mexico City reveal, the intensity of the crisis as well as President Calles' indomitable determination to protect the nation's patrimony. These documents, correspondence between Kellogg and Sheffield, reveal plans for an invasion. A Mexican spy working in the U.S. embassy, whose code name was Agent 10B and whose identity has never been revealed, sent these plans to Calles. Calles then threatened the new U.S. president, Calvin Coolidge, by revealing that he had given copies to every foreign ambassador in Mexico, and, in the event of war, the plans and their motives would become known throughout the world. His strategy worked. Cooler heads prevailed, and with the appointment of a new ambassador to Mexico, Dwight W. Morrow, the tone (although not the thrust) of U.S. policy towards Mexico changed.[85]

Just at this moment Jara dug in his heels, demanding payment of taxes withheld by the oil companies. The taxes, however, were not the main problem. The oil companies had considered themselves the *maîtres chez nous* (masters in their own house) in the north. They refused to recognize the authority of state or municipality. Roads going through their properties were frequently blocked; they refused to respect the article of the state constitution requiring the construction and maintenance of schools; and companies drilled on lands they had not legally acquired. They consistently employed foreigners as "white guards," again in defiance of the nation's sovereignty, throwing their weight around with impunity.[86]

When Jara took over the governorship in 1924, he was already considered an enemy by the oil companies because of his attitude and policies during his previous term as interim governor and because he was a collaborator of both Aguilar and Tejeda.[87] Another and related problem of Jara's was his relationship with Luis Morones, the union boss of the CROM. Ths relationship suffered partly because of the relative weakness of the CROM, especially in the coastal plains of the state. But Morones also seized the opportuinty by opposing Jara and his "Red" unions, hoping to get rid of this governor and thus have a free hand in the port city, in the countryside, and among the petroleum workers.[88] Although Jara had always supported the union, Morones, now the minister of industry and commerce, adhered to the praxis that was developing as part of the revolutionary settlement. This policy promoted the complete co-optation of various sectors of the nation, the unionized working class, *campesino* organizations, even businesses, by the ruling party or, to put it simply, by the president. When, for example, a strike was called in 1925 against the El Aguila and the Huasteca oil companies, Jara supported the strikers, but Calles and Morones "arranged with the oil companies to suspend the strike and to withdraw recognition from union factions refusing to go back to work." This government trend in favour of business was observable in other parts of Mexico as well. To achieve the desired effect, in March 1927, the president had given exclusive rights to the ministry of industry, commerce and labour to intervene in labour conflicts in the petroleum and mining industries.[89]

To be fair, Calles, in 1927, was confronted with dealing with the avaricious needs of the emerging and belligerent imperialist power to the north, for which the state was merely a tool of big business. Calvin Coolidge's famous dictum "The business of America is business" can be seen clearly in U.S. diplomatic dealings with Mexico. Moreover, the Coolidge administration had shown its hostility to labour and, in 1926, had demonstrated, with its dispatch of marines to put down Nicaraguan revolutionaries, how it would deal with any attempt to change the social and economic structure in the hemisphere. Calles, to judge by his voluminous correspondence with the ex-president, Obregón, was trying to find the safest path to tread between realizing the goals of the revolution (demanded stridently by a militant working class and *campesinos*) and protecting the nation's patrimony. At issue were the Regulating Laws of Article 27, which the oil companies were loath to recognize since they did not want to concede the nation's right to legislate in commercial matters, let alone to assume ownership of the sub-soil.[90]

In Veracruz, Jara confronted the central government with consistent and firm action on two policy fronts: the right of the state government to deal with the companies and the right to receive taxes and royalties from them. This position put him on a collision path with the president, the minister of industry and commerce, and, ironically, the interior minister, former Veracruz governor, Adalberto Tejeda. The initial issue was a court case involving the inheritance rights of a woman, in which the local judge at Amatlán had ordered the oil wells capped until the case could be resolved. The companies complained to Tejeda, who reminded Jara that the petroleum industry came under his ministry, and therefore the judge had exceeded his jurisdiction. Jara explained that the wells were actually in reserve and were not pumping, but also told Tejeda that he expected the federal government to back the state when businesses broke the law, and asked that the minister of industry and commerce not intervene in favour of the companies.[91]

The fight between the two sides continued from April until September 1927, with the company, El Aguila, resorting to lies to get the backing of the federal government. It complained that the capping of the wells would cause them to explode; upon hearing this, Morones as the responsible minister immediately ordered them re-opened. Jara complained that the federal government was taking away his only weapon to force the companies to pay their back taxes, but Morones would not back down. After April, he intervened several other times, most notably in another legal battle over the inheritance of a property, the *hacienda* of Chapacao, claimed by the Huasteca Company. The case is complicated and cannot be discussed here; suffice to say that Morones

sent agents of his ministry to Veracruz in order to change decisions of the courts there, in direct violation of the sovereignty of
the state. Jara complained to Calles but did not receive his support.[92] His efforts to have the Huasteca Oil Company pay its royalties were obviously going to be foiled by the federal government.

Now other factors entered into the relations between Jara and
the central government. Seizing their chance, a small group of
deputies in the Veracruz legislature began to intrigue against Jara,
with federal support. Military and political figures descended
on Jara in Xalapa, asking for his co-operation in rescinding the
judgment of the Veracruz courts. Jara, obstinate sometimes to
the point of rudeness, refused to back down. Interestingly, he
received support only from the commander of military operations in the Huasteca, General Lazaro Cárdenas.[93] Not even the
murder of the presiding judge, Francisco Méndez, ostensibly
on the orders of the oil company, would change the policy of
the federal government. Morones then entered into negotiations
with the companies, working out a deal whereby they paid eight
million pesos to the federal government instead of to Veracruz.

On the night of September 29, a military train arrived in
Xalapa with troops from the port city, under the command of
the military commandant there, General Jesús Aguirre. The next
day, they assaulted the governor's palace and called an extraordinary session of the legislature. Those deputies who refused to
obey were replaced by their seconds (*suplentes*). The governor was
replaced, as well as the president and vice-president of the chamber. Jara's protest to Calles went unanswered. Despite the fact
that the majority of the deputies supported Jara, he was deposed.
After a few days of uncertainty, the Mexican Senate declared the
executive and legislative powers of Veracruz null and void, and
named Abel S. Rodríguez interim governor. Thus was the sovereignty of the state of Veracruz violated by the federal government
in an utterly unconstitutional manner.[94] More importantly, this
violation of the state was much more than the abrogation of a
legal principle. It meant, in effect, the end of an experiment in
state power, whose object had been the termination of capitalist
exploitation of the workers and peasants of Veracruz. State sovereignty had been the means; social and economic power for the
working classes and peasants had been the end.

—— XX ——

The End of the Experiment

Jara's ouster in 1927 came not because of his bad relations with labour and the *agraristas* but because of the oil situation and *raisons d'état* as perceived and practised by President Calles. The problem was one of constructing a viable nation, by eliminating the issue of state sovereignty. But that necesitated a power base from the regions to support the centre. Carranza had failed to achieve this, especially against regional power bases such as that of Peláez. Obregón's presidency, on the other hand, was the *interregnum* that allowed pacification of the individual states through an apparent federalism. Here Tejeda's politics in Veracruz were crucial. By backing the social and economic demands of the armed working and peasant classes of the state, he was able to deliver a numerically powerful political instrument to the centre. His policies (and those of others) allowed the Sonorans a breathing space, time to consolidate. By the time Calles came along, this political army was ready to back whichever political level promised them support against the *hacendados*. Plagued by the oil situation, threatened by a recalcitrant state government and a hostile United States, Calles was able to enlist their help in pulling the plug on federalism in order to save the nation.

Thus was the oil question settled, at least for the time being. Meetings, which had taken place in March 1916 in El Paso, Texas, between the representative of Phelps Dodge and other U.S. oil companies and Luis Cabrera, it has been argued, "set the agenda and the tone for interaction between the Mexican revolutionary elite and American banks and corporations for the next decade."[95] They did more than that; they set the agenda for relations between U.S. business and the Mexican nation into the 1930s until Cárdenas decided that enough was enough.

The final word is not yet out on the revolution. In terms of Veracruz, Stephen Haber's words ring true in the symbolic sense: the revolution, "rather than tearing down the industrial structure of the Porfiriato, reinforced it."[96] And not just the industrial structure: the revolution retained the class basis of Mexican society by reinforcing the bourgeoisie and large landowners.[97] Via the tactic of co-optation, it thoroughly deprived peasants and workers of any real participation.

What also changed and has held until the present was the relationship between the central government and the state. The oil issue and the pressure from the United States in 1927 dashed all hopes of a real federalism. The states would now be completely subordinated to the central government in order to appease U.S. business interests. One can also argue that the defeat of federalism in 1927 ushered in the formation of the Mexican post-revolutionary state. At least, the central government's ability to treat with foreign powers was now unhampered by the claims of the regions.[98] Was this the real meaning behind the revolution? If it was, then the later actions of Cárdenas make more sense. Without the subordination of Veracruz, without the enforced principle that the sub-soil wealth of Mexico belonged to all Mexicans, and not the particular state in which it was found, Cárdenas's action in 1938 of nationalizing the entire oil industry would have been impossible.

However, one can well ask what other options Calles had. Faced with the needs of an aggressive, expanding U.S. economy, and its demands for oil to fuel the industrial engine, Calles's choices were limited. He could not risk intervention over oil production at a time when the republic was just settling down from the protracted violence of a bloody revolution. The nation came before the states. It is ironic that Jara, a proud supporter of Article 27 (which also gave the nation the right to regulate natural resources) during the constitutional talks at Queretaro, failed then to understand that it was this question, not the agrarian one, that would be the origin of the demise of state sovereignty.

In any case, and for whatever reason, state sovereignty was a dead issue. Centralism and the centralists had vanquished – regionalism had almost vanished. It would reappear in divers forms, especially in 1994 with Chiapas. The revolution destroyed the promise of democracy, and it finally, ironically, after one hundred years of hope, put paid to the promise of federalism.

9

Conclusion

Tomorrow Never Comes

The answer to the question of what changed in Veracruz as a consequence of the Mexican Revolution is a complex one. The very fact that the struggle was prolonged over decades and that the costs were exorbitant in human terms makes one want to answer that there had to be significant changes that would not have occurred through a "normal" course of development. But this is not necessarily so. As Simon Schama reminds us in his history of the French Revolution, many of the changes occurring in France by 1814 would have happened anyway.[1] Might this have been the case with the Mexican Revolution from the perspective of Veracruz? Counterfactual arguments are only speculative, but they have a place in historical thinking, if only as reminders that human affairs and the march of history are not predetermined outcomes.

To answer the question posed above, we need to reflect briefly on where and why a revolution broke out in the first place. In 1876, Porfirio Díaz, an astute politician, oversaw the creation of a state the reins of which he held tightly in his hand. With the intention of modernizing Mexico in the fastest possible way, he ruled as absolute dictator. He allowed the establishment of powerful *caciques* in the states and played the game of federalism as long as they controlled these states in the interest of the nation, that is to say, according to his way of thinking. In short, Díaz developed a political structure that had little flexibility. The *jefe político*, the key Porfirian appointee in the states with an enormous array of administrative and legal powers, was utilized to enforce the president's will at the cantonal level, at times bypassing the governor.

Enforcing that will was not a simple task. And Veracruz during the Porfiriato was by no means a peaceful state. The successful application of the Ley Lerdo during the Porfiriato brought about a forceful rejection by two native groups, in Papantla and then Acayucan. In addition, the modernizing policies of the Porfirian regime promoted the establishment of the first giant factories, and the concomitant rise and resistance of the working class.

Both at Acayucan and a few months later at Río Blanco, Indians and textile workers responded violently to the oppression they had endured for decades. Armed with the radical anarcho-socialist ideology of the Partido Liberal Mexicano, Indians, peasants, and workers erupted in what were the first violent outbursts of the Mexican Revolution aimed at replacing the system. One may argue about the extent of the PLM's influence; certainly an investigation of this topic is overdue. Unarguably, its influence was sufficient to inform the analysis of some workers, Indians, and others into the 1920s and beyond.[2]

The first alliances against the Porfirian regime were then made manifest with the link between the erstwhile lower-middleclass and Indian fighters of Acayucan and workers who had fled Río Blanco after the massacre of January 1907. Having failed to ignite a full-scale regional conflict, these marginalized Veracruzans decided to support Francisco Indalecio Madero's 1910 call to arms against Porfirio Díaz. Middle- and upper-class Veracruzans then entered into a crucial alliance with the veterans of the PLM movement in Veracruz, and together supported Madero's call for the ouster of Porfirio Díaz (even, it seems, one of the most devoted Porfirians, the Veracruz governor Teodoro Dehesa). So successful was this cross-class alliance that it brought down the old dictator in less than six months. But this was not the end, only the beginning of the entire drama.

The literature on the revolution has generally accorded Francisco I. Madero the accolade of "apostle of democracy" in Mexico. But the ouster of Díaz did not mark the beginning of democracy. Unseating a regime and implementing revolutionary ideas are not the same thing — not that Madero had any intention of doing the latter. When it became apparent that Madero was willing to use tactics reminiscent of his predecessor, and as a new clique of Científicos[3] arose, many Veracruzans were willing to accept his overthrow and even murder by General Victoriano Huerta.

Madero's brief period as president and his political interference in that state, especially his attempts to manipulate elections, indicate his betrayal of democratic principles in Veracruz and his rapid drift to more centralist, manipulative, indeed Científico, politics. In 1912, the revolution was, indeed, 'revised.' Madero's political praxis produced a series of reactions both in Veracruz and in Mexico in general. Yet these resulting uprisings were not mere reactions against the undemocratic drift of the regime, for they incorporated elements designed to address the grievous social inequalities of the country.

In 1911 and early 1912, there were three rebellions, that promised an implementation of the "social" principles of the Plan of San Luis Potosí: the revolts of Emilio Vázquez Gómez, Gabriel Gavira, and Pascual Orozco. Because of these, Madero and his government began to recognize the need for a social policy, especially for land reform. The first tentative steps, begun in the autumn of 1912, produced a conservative backlash: two known Porfirian soldiers, Higinio Aguilar and Gaudencio de la Llave, took to the field in Veracruz, rebelling against the government. In October 1912, Félix Díaz also attempted a counter-revolution from the port city. It was the beginning of the disaster that led to Madero's assassination. Some Veracruzans were glad to get rid of him because he had not fulfilled his promises of land reform and social justice. Others welcomed the coup against a president who seemed to be adopting a path of centralism they abhorred and, moreover, using the central government to promote reform. Instead, Veracruzans turned to Victoriano Huerta, who had promised to respect the Constitution of 1857.

The results of the coup were not entirely what people had expected. Huerta's was at best a feeble attempt to maintain or reintroduce a neo-Porfirian government. The country was swift to respond, turning towards the movement headed by Venustiano Carranza. But Carrancismo was soon perceived to be another attempt at the autocratic centralism that had been characteristic of the Díaz regime. Even though in this Constitutionalist phase there was a stated intention to carry out social reforms, the pace was slow, if not negligible. Opposition to Carranza's policies brought about the second attempt at revolution by Félix Díaz, from a base in Veracruz, which gave him tremendous support for a time. His rallying cry was the Constitution of 1857 with its guarantee of state autonomy.

By 1919, the most violent phases of the revolution had been left behind, and Mexicans turned to the task of rebuilding their lives. Since this included the efforts of marginalized Mexicans to realize their social and political expectations, the essential problem for Mexican governments from the 1920s on was how to defuse and deflect the demands for representation and participation in government that had given the revolution its essential character. In other words, the challenge to the national government now was how to orchestrate an outcome that would allow the revolutionary state to continue with business as usual: the continued capitalist development, or modernization, of Mexico.

For with the revolution had come a change in the basic mentality of lower-class Mexicans.[1] The lower class in Veracruz, comprising renters, peasants, and workers, were demanding essential rights such as land reform as well as social justice. In Veracruz in particular, they were now abetted by the governor and the state government, which saw federalism as a vehicle through which to attain those rights. What the central government needed, therefore, was a plan to incorporate the protest of the rural, peasant, and Indian sectors into the emerging post-revolutionary state, which wanted to get on with developing Mexico along what, one must readily admit, were traditional lines. But can one even speak of a plan? And was the outcome the result of a carefully devised policy of state? Or was it the result of haphazard searching for a solution, one that was perhaps offered by fortuitous circumstances.

The 1920s were a confusing and contradictory decade for Veracruz. On the one hand, it witnessed the most radical and promising phase of the Mexican Revolution for the ideological descendants of the original Indian, peasant, and working-class protesters of the initial years. On the other hand, it saw the successful harnessing of these energies by an increasingly confident centralizing national government, against the very interests of those participants. So the question remains, did anything change?

In late 1914, Cándido Aguilar passed Decree 8 establishing an Agrarian Commission to tackle the land question. A little land was surveyed and given out, especially in Acayucan canton, but that effort was curtailed when Carranza subsumed the commission under a federal one. Aguilar, however, went further. Unions were legalized, and a Junta Central de Conciliación y Arbitraje was established and charged with arbitrating labour disputes. The next year (but in accordance with Carranza's speech to the Convention in 1914), he decreed a nine-hour workday, increased the minimum wage, and set aside Sunday as a day of rest. To those workers in the textile mills who were used to working twelve-hour shifts, it was a little, but because the depression had reduced their workweek to three days, it was not much. It was a start, but, since the government's idea of development was the free enterprise model, it could not conciliate workers for fear of offending foreign investors.

Under Tejeda's leadership, the attempt at social reforms gained momentum. By 1929, just over fifty-one thousand *campesinos* had received land. During his second term in office, his success at land redistribution was even more impressive, certainly when compared with that of the nation.[5] In addition, Tejeda oversaw some of the most radical social reforms in Mexico. He passed a profit-sharing law, backed the Renters' Union, and was instrumental in welding separate agrarian committees into the Liga. But were these changes enduring?

Despite the fact that Tejeda and the agrarians backed the central government during the de la Huerta rebellion, the president who succeeded Obregón had come to the conclusion that the only developmental path for the nation was that promoted by capitalists. Consequently, even though some peasants received land under Tejeda, their movement was finally brought to heel and stripped of "its military, political, and economic powers as a social institution by the central government during the 1930's."[6] It ceased to function as a mass-based organization capable of withstanding oppression.

And what of the working class? Due to their continued militancy, textile workers in Veracruz achieved some very real gains in working conditions. Working hours were reduced from twelve hours to eight per shift, seven for night work. Moreover, workers were no longer forced to put up with "despotic and intransigent" bosses.[7] State and federal laws recognized their challenge to factory owners. Yet workers' freedom to bargain over their own conditions were severely restricted. For in the eyes of the government, workers and their unions simply had to be curtailed. Workers were forced, cajoled, and bullied into joining the officially recognized umbrella union, the CROM, which was established to carry out the president's wishes. The independent craft union, therefore, was a short-lived phenomenon in post-revolutionary Mexico. As Bortz puts it, "after the revolution, unions hired and unions fired."[8] Workers, therefore, merely exchanged the powers to which they deferred. And the new bosses were now armed with the power of the state. With these changes, Calles succeeded in devising the system that was to rule Mexico successfully until the present.

What of the other marginalized Veracruzans, those, for example, who had formed the Renters' Union? Did the urban reform movement achieve any success? There was at least a temporary rollback of rents. Did it last? Wood demonstrates that it did not. "After the dust had settled," he remarks, "state intervention offered at least the promise of significant housing reform even if never fully realized." In fact, when summing up the importance of the strike, Wood admits that the importance of the tenant movement lay in its providing "an important example of collective action by urban popular groups"[9]: nothing more.

I would argue that the revolutionary settlement, that emerged after 1927 was the outcome of a challenged regime undergoing a learning process, but this time one that had to take into account the changes of modern life and produce a settlement that would allow exploitation to continue in other forms. Unfortunately, Veracruz governors Tejeda's and Jara's attempts to employ the state's sovereignty to further the social aims of the revolution were in conflict with this unstated goal. In sum, I think one is forced to conclude that there were some changes in the mode of imagining politics and social affairs between 1906 and 1927, but these were minor. More importantly, to re-invoke the counter-factual question posed above, it seems likely they would have come about anyway, without a revolution.

In Veracruz, the tendencies that were crushed in 1927 were of two very different yet intimately related kinds. In the first place, federalism was defeated because the central government could not permit a revolutionary project to continue that might have elevated the working classes, rural and urban, to power through the mediation of the state government.

The cause of centralism, therefore, and the victory of the national elite were part of the same process whose content was, to invert a well-known phrase, "Power to the Revolutionary Bourgeoisie." In any case and for whatever reason, state sovereignty shortlived as it had been, was a dead issue. Centralism had conquered. (Not that regionalism had vanished; it would reappear in divers forms, especially in 1994 in Chiapas).

The revolution destroyed the promise of democracy, and, it finally, ironically, put paid to the promise of federalism. But it had a more serious effect. My argument is that the new revolutionary leaders actually continued a project that had been started earlier in the Porfiriato, utilizing various political tactics (co-optation is the obvious one) in order to maintain power against a group of ruled people who wanted more change.[10] But now Mexico had found the system that was to guide it into the new century. The entry of federal troops into Veracruz, their occupation of the gubernatorial palace in 1927, and the ousting of the governor was a symbol that the brief period of social reform was at an end.

Notes

Notes to Preface

1. The idea of these movements as "precursors" to the Mexican Revolution is best presented by James Cockroft, *Intellectual Precursors*.
2. See Adolfo Gilly, "Chiapas and the Rebellion of the Enchanted World," in Nugent, *Rural Revolt*.
3. See Wells and Joseph, *Summer of Discontent*, p. vi.

Notes to Chapter 1

1. Southworth, *El estado de Veracruz-Llave*, p. 5; see also Siemens, *Between the Summit*, for a general discussion of central Veracruz geography from travellers' perspectives.
2. Politically and administratively Veracruz entered the Mexican federation of 1824 as a sovereign state with the territory it had inherited as an intendancy of the Viceroyalty of New Spain. Constitutional power was vested in a governor elected by the 'people,' and the state was sub-divided into eleven cantons grouped under four departments. With the promulgation of the state constitution on June 3, 1825, the name *canton* was changed to *partido*, reflecting an earlier Spanish usage. With the temporary defeat of federalism in 1836, Veracruz was subdivided into five districts each with a number of *partidos*. In 1848 there was some return to the earlier system when the cantons and municipalities were reintroduced. In 1853 the territory was rationalized: the district of Tuxpán was detached from Puebla and added. With the restoration of federalism through the Constitution of 1857, the district of Huimangillo was ceded to Tabasco, whereby Veracruz assumed its present borders, and thus territorial contiguity. The new federal constitution also determined the division of the state into eighteen cantons, that continued to exist until the Constitution of 1917 did away with them and introduced the Free Municipality.

3. Pérez Miliucía, *Compendio de geografía del estado*, p. 20; Keremitsis, *La industria textil mexicana*, p. 101; Chávez Orozco and Florescano, *Agricultura y industria textil*, pp. 93-96. This potential was recognized shortly after independence, and the exploitation of hydro-electric power in Veracruz for industrial purposes is an early example of Mexican national industrial policy; Wieners, "Agriculture and Credit in Nineteenth-Century Mexico," p. 522.

4. Velasco, *Geografía y estadística del estado*, pp. 9, 13-15, 35; Pérez Miliucía, *Compendio de geografía del estado*, p. 35.

5. Ibid., p. 28; Zilli, *Historia sucinta*, p. 10.

6. See Siemens, *Between the Summit*, pp. 32, 73, for a description of these storms and the entertainment they occasioned Veracruzans.

7. Zilli, *Historia sucinta*, p. 11; Pérez Miliucía, *Compendio de geografía del estado*, p. 29; Pérez Hernández, *Estadística en la República Méxicana*, p. 149.

8. Pérez Miliucía, *Compendio de geografía del estado*, p. 29; Mar Olivares, "Estudio histórico y económico de Chicontepec," p. 177; De Bassols Batalla, *Las Huastecas en el desarrollo regional*, pp. 332-333.

9. Blázquez Domínguez, *Veracruz*, pp. 13-14.

10. Cárdenas, "A Macroeconomic Interpretation of Nineteenth-Century", pp. 70-71.

11. Tenenbaum, *The Politics of Penury*, pp. 108-113; Cárdenas, "A Macroeconomic Interpretation of Nineteenth-Century," pp. 71-74.

12. Orizaba, Córdoba, Huatusco and Zongólica were the only areas allowed to grow tobacco under the vice-regal *estanco* (monopoly). See González Sierra, *Monopolio del Humo*, p. 48; Walker, "Business as Usual," p. 677.

13. Potash, Robert A., *El Banco de Avío de México*, pp. 219-20, cited in Cárdenas, "A Macroeconomic Interpretation of Nineteenth-Century," p. 88n.

14. Wells and Joseph, *Summer of Discontent*, esp. Chapter 2; Knight, *The Mexican Revolution;* LaFrance, *The Mexican Revolution.*

15. Wells and Joseph define *camarillas* as regional elite political factions, arguing that in Yucatán, the president's tactic was to try to keep these in balance. See Wells and Joseph, *Summer of Discontent*, pp. 4, 22.

16. For a discussion of this strong regionalist sentiment, see Blázquez Domínguez, *Veracruz liberal*, pp. 24-25; Hamnett argues that this regional sentiment was crucial in the outcome of the Reform Wars. He writes, "In many respects, the real power within the Liberal party lay with the political chieftains in the regions. They effectively decided that Juárez should lead the Liberal cause during the civil war of the Reform." See Hamnett, *Juárez*, p. 116; Cadenhead, *Benito Juárez*, pp. 138-139.

17. The biographical details are found in "De mis recuerdos," ATD, but were also published in De Pallares, *Dehesa*, p. 4.

18. Teodoro A. Dehesa, "De mis recuerdos," ATD; Scholes, *Política mexicana*, p. 215, makes the somewhat ambiguous statement that. "The revolt reached the culmination at the beginning of *November* with the Plan of La Noria, which was published in Mexico on November 13." See also Roeder, *Hacia el México Moderno*, v. 1, pp. 34-35; and Lopez-Portillo y Rojas, *Elevación y Caída*, pp. 89-90, who sees the revolt as having no basis besides the desire for power.

19. Cosío Villegas, *Historia Moderna*, v. 1, pp. 641-642; Roeder, *Juárez*, v. 2, p. 720. These historians disagree on the date for the beginning of the revolt and give different justifications for choosing it. For Cosío

Villegas, it is the date on which a letter bearing the letterhead "Popular Revolutionary Army," was written by Luciano López (one of the men leading the revolt in the Ciudadela in Mexico City) to Porfirio Díaz, who is addressed as General-in-Chief of the revolt. For Roeder, it is early November, the date on which Díaz actually rides out of Oaxaca.

20. This colourful episode was the subject of a number of local newspaper articles as well as some shorter monographs. See *El Imparcial*, 17 Dec. 1933; Cosío Villegas, *Porfirio Díaz en la revuelta de La Noria*; Domínguez Castilla, *Ensayo crítico*; Domínguez, *Cómo salió el General Díaz*.

21. Dehesa, "De mis recuerdos," ATD.

22. See Cosío Villegas, *Historia Moderna*, v. 1, p. 720, for a discussion on the date of departure. Dehesa's memoirs contain the date 1 Sep. 1871, which was an error, probably due to the fact that the memoirs were written in the 1930s. Later research established the date as 1 Feb. 1872. Dehesa's date is impossible as the insurrection did not begin until October/November 1871. See also González Sempé, *Evolución política y constitucional*, p. 210.

23. Roeder, *Juárez*, v. 2, p. 729. Juárez died 18 Jul. 1872; Cosío Villegas, *Historia Moderna*, v. 1., p. 305.

24. Cosío Villegas, *Historia Moderna*, v. 1, pp. 766, 305; Lopez-Portillo y Rojas, *Elevación y caída*, p. 100.

25. De Pallares, *Dehesa*, pp. 24-25; Dehesa, "El General Mier y Terán," ATD; cf. *El Reproductor*, 20 Feb. 1908, which gives the date as 1873. 1872 is the correct one.

26. Díaz to Dehesa, 21 Oct. 1873, reprinted in *La Patria*, 7 Jun. 1904. A copy of the letter was given to the paper by Dehesa; De Pallares, *Dehesa*, p. 25; Valadés, *El porfirismo*, v.1, p. 14; Dehesa, " De mis recuerdos," ATD; Pérez, *Dehesa*, p. 13; De Pallares, *Dehesa*, p. 33; cf. Perry, *Juárez and Díaz*, p.18, who cites numerous newspaper sources claiming that Dehesa was elected to a seat in the Mexican Congress. In fact it was Díaz who was elected.

27. Salmerón Castro, *Dehesa*, p. 85.

28. Ibid., p. 770; Parkes, *A History of Mexico*, p. 285, observes: "Ignacio Ramírez and Riva Palacio both felt that Díaz was the embodiment of Mexican democracy."

29. Cosío Villegas, *Historia Moderna*, v. 1, p. 816.

30. Cosío Villegas, *Historia Moderna*, v. 1., pp. 771-72, 774; Dehesa, "El General Mier y Terán," ATD. Dehesa's account appears to be incorrect in regard to the timing and motivation for the revolt. He writes: "The presidential election looming on the horizon did not appear to be in Don Sebastian's favour, and the persistent Porfirians clung to Díaz's candidature, which, whatever one might say, was popular. The result of said elections was the election of Don Sebastian, and, considering it fraudulent, General Díaz decided to resort to arms." It was not the fraudulence that motivated Díaz, but Lerdo's intention to seek re-election.

31. Dehesa, "El General Mier y Terán," ATD; *El Reproductor*, 20 Feb. 1908.

32. Dehesa, "El General Mier y Terán," ATD.

33. Pasquel, *Cronológica ilustrada de Xalapa*, pp. 86-87; Zilli, *Historia sucinta*, pp. 120-121; for additional information on Luis Mier y Terán, including the discovery that his was an assumed name, see Pasquel, ed., *Mátalos en Caliente*.

34. Salmerón Castro, *Dehesa*, p. 77; *El Reproductor*, 20 Feb. 1908. Pérez, *Dehesa*, p.13; Trens, *Historia de Veracruz*, v. 6, p. 336; De Pallares, *Dehesa*, p.53; Cosío Villegas *Historia Moderna*, v. 8, pp. 693-694.

35. Zilli, *Historia sucinta*, pp. 122-123.
36. Reina Aoyama, *Las rebelliones campesinas*, pp. 358-59; Ramírez Caloca, *Geografía del Estado*, p. 62. Tutino affirms that the implementation of the *Ley Lerdo* was a pretext by some landowners to avail themselves of communal land. They were not always successful as Indians fought back, enlisting even Díaz's help. Tutino estimates that many communal villages hung onto their lands until 1910 or beyond. See Tutino, *From Insurrection*, pp. 260, 276.
37. *El Reproductor*, 17 Dec. 1891; Cosío Villegas, *Historia Moderna*, v. 9, p. 103.
38. Baranda to Dehesa, 31 Jan. 1892, ATD; Dehesa to Díaz, 24 Feb. 1892, CPD, L17:2043; Martínez to Díaz, n.d., CPD, L17:2437.
39. Dehesa to Díaz, 24 Feb. 1892, CPD, L17:2043; Martínez to Díaz, n.d., CPD, L17:2437.
40. Cosío Villegas, *Historia Moderna*, v. 9, p. 442; Dehesa to Díaz, 17 Mar. 1892, CPD, L17: 3699.
41. Castillo to Díaz, 9 Mar. 1892, CPD, L17:3654.
42. Dehesa to Díaz, 17 Mar. 1892, CPD, L17:3799; *El Monitor Repúblicano*, 20 Mar. 1892; Leví to Díaz, 21 Mar. 1892, CPD, L17:4028.
43. *El Monitor Repúblicana*, 30 Mar. 1892; Díaz to Leví, 20 Mar. 1892, L17:4030, CPD; Díaz to Dehesa, 18 Mar. 1892, CPD, L17:5499.
44. Dehesa to Díaz, 22 Mar. 1892, CPD, L17:5509.
45. The public support for Dehesa was, indeed, widespread. It extended even to students in the Preparatory College (pre-university) in Xalapa, who, apparently against the wishes of their teachers, who were *Enriquistas*, gave spontaneous demonstrations on the campus in favour of Dehesa; *El Monitor Repúblicano*, 30 Mar. 1892; Manuel Leví was replaced by Alejandro Alcolea, a wealthy and influential Veracruzan, on 1 Apr. 1892. See Leví to Díaz, 28 Mar. 1892, CPD; *El Monitor Repúblicano*, 30 Mar. 1892.
46. CPD, L17:10 & 11; also Dehesa to Díaz, 15 Apr. 1892, CPD, L17:5505-07; Canseco to Díaz, 20 Apr. 1892, CPD, L17:5404, informing the President of his nomination as *jefe político* on Dehesa's recommendation.
47. Díaz to Dehesa, 12 Apr. 1892, CPD, L17:5492; Dehesa to Díaz, 1 May 1892, CPD, L17:7204.
48. Díaz to Dehesa, 4 May 1892, CPD, L17:7206.
49. *Leyes, Decretos y Circulares del Estado de Veracruz-Llave*, p. 142; Pasquel, *Cronología ilustrada de Xalapa*, v.1, p. 104; letter to the Editor from "Club Liberal," Veracruz, 10 Dec. 1892, in *El Diario del Hogar*, 14 Dec. 1892, Dehesa to Editor, *El Diario del Hogar*, 27 Dec. 1892.
50. Wells and Joseph, *Summer of Discontent*, p. 22.
51. As an instrument of centralization, for example, Díaz retained the Mexican Senate. See Hale, "Political Ideas and Ideologies," p. 142.
52. This is not to say that he did not utilize other techniques. But a distinction is made here between political and purely administrative tactics, which would include the use of the army or the *Rurales*. *El Diario de Hogar*, 8 Mar. 1892; Ankerson, *Some Aspects*, p. 19; Braderman, *A Study of Political Parties*, p. 10.
53. Frank Tannenbaum, *Peace by Revolution*, pp. 98-99; Parkes, *A History of Mexico*, p. 286; Wells and Joseph, *Summer of Discontent*, Ch. 2, demonstrate the device of *divide et impera* at the state level in Yucatán, where *camarillas* were allowed to operate so as to provide an outlet for elite rivalry.
54. Braderman, *A Study of Political Parties*, p.10.

55. Stevens, "Agrarian Policy and Instability." Díaz had aided the Indians of
    Tamazunchale in retaining their traditional lands against the governor
    who had tried to expropriate them; De Zayas Enríquez, *Porfirio Díaz*,
    p. 207; the Articles in question are Nos. 104 and 105, Cap. I, 31 May 1896
    in AGN-GOB, L1666-1a.
56. Beals, *Porfirio Díaz*, pp. 276, 288, 372; Bryan, "Political Power;" *El Monitor
    Republican*, 8 Apr. 1896; De Pallares, *Dehesa*, p. 168; Cosío Villegas, *Historia
    Moderna*, v. 5, p. 493; *El Diario del Hogar*, 1 Dec. 1908. It should be noted
    that this paper was hostile to the regime, and its famous editor, Filomeno
    Mata, was continuously in jail. On this occasion, it referred to Dehesa as
    that "exceptional governor" who "has the attention of all the republic"; see
    also *La Patria*, 1 Jan. 1903.
57. For a discussion of the origin and role of the *jefe político* see Falcón, "The
    Force and Search for Consent," in Joseph and Nugent, eds., *Everyday
    Forms of State Formation*.
58. Vanderwood, *Disorder and Progress*, p. 86; Ankerson, *Some Aspects*, p. 19.
    They could also be subject to the President's personal investigation. In
    July 1900, Díaz went to Ozuluama to investigate the victimization of a
    young man by the *jefe político*; see Díaz to Dehesa, 28 Jul. 1900, ATD, #30;
    Orozco Espinosa, "El sistema agrario," p. 47.
59. Various to Díaz, 5 Jun. 1908, CPD, l33:8197-98; Dehesa to Díaz, 12 Jun.
    1908, CPD, L33:8195.
60. Díaz to Dehesa, 21 Feb. 1902, Dehesa to Díaz, 11 Mar. 1902, ATD, File #3;
    Díaz to Dehesa, 18 May, 1898, CPD, L23:6258; Dehesa to Díaz, 20 May,
    1898, CPD, L23:6259; Dehesa to Díaz to 31 May, 1898, CPD, L23:8651-52;
    Dehesa to Díaz, 16 Mar. 1905, CPD, L3570.
61. *El Monitor Repúblicano*, 4 Jan. 1893, Díaz to Dehesa, 14 Dec. 1895, CPD,
    L20 C39; Dehesa to Díaz, 15 Dec. 1895, CPD, L20 C39; Medel y Alvarado,
    Historia de San Andrés Tuxtla, pp. 439-440; *El Cosmopólita*, 21 Aug. 1898.
62. Dehesa to Díaz, 25 Oct. 1901, CPD, L26:10359; various to Díaz, n.d.,
    L33:2893-2915, CPD; *El Monitor Repúblicano*, 19 Jan. 1893. In Acayucan,
    Rontilla was replaced with José Beltran, brother of General Joaquín
    Beltran; Dehesa to Díaz, 14 Jul. 1897, L22:8908-09, CPD.
63. *El Paladín*, 7 Feb. 1901; the Valle Nacional was an infamous place to which
    people could be sent without charge and where they were forced to work
    under horrible conditions from which there was rarely any escape. See
    Turner, *Barbarous Mexico* for a vivid description of the Valle Nacional. *El
    Paladín*, 3 Mar. 1901.
64. *El Monitor Repúblicano*, 30 Apr. 1892; *El Nacional*, 7 Oct. 1903; Díaz to
    Dehesa, 26 Jan. 1893, CPD, L18:302.
65. Díaz to Dehesa, 21 Oct. 1899, CPD, L24:15288; Dehesa to Díaz, 25 Oct.
    1899, CPD, L24:15285; *El Paladín*, 11 Apr., 1901, 24 Nov. 1901. The refer-
    ences here were to the new *jefes políticos* of Papantla and Tuxpán; *El
    Nacional*, 17 Jan. 1895; *La Patria*, 17 Feb. 1906.
66. *El Nacional*, 21 Mar. 1895, 4 Jun. 1895; Dehesa to Díaz, 6 Dec. 1895, CPD,
    L20:19179,; *El Cosmopólita*, 21 Mar. 1897.
67. Díaz to Dehesa, 18 Oct. 1910, CPD, L35:15344; Dehesa to Díaz, 25 Oct.
    1910, CPD, L35:15331. He was accused of tolerating revolutionaries in
    his canton and of having amorous relations with the wife of a Madero
    supporter who was in San Juan de Ulúa prison, ATD, File #16.
68. Camacho to Dehesa, 2 Dec. 1910, ATD; Dehesa to Díaz, 2 Dec. 1910,
    ATD; Díaz to Dehesa, 3 Dec. 1910, ATD; Camacho to Dehesa, 3 Dec.

1910, ATD; Dehesa to Camacho, 5 Dec. 1910, ATD; Díaz to Dehesa, 8 Dec.1910, ATD.

69. For a full discussion of the origins and definition of this group, see Chapter 3.

70. Beals, *Porfirio Díaz*, pp. 281, 287, 357; Iturribaría, *Porfirio Díaz ante la historia*, p. 121; Parkes, *A History of Mexico*, p. 292.

71. Beals, *Porfirio Díaz*, p. 289; Cosío Villegas, *Historia Moderna*, v. 9, p. 423; Dehesa to Díaz, 9 Jan. 1893, CPD, L18:296; Dehesa to Díaz, 9 Aug. 1905, CPD, L20:12535; Dehesa to Díaz, 9 Feb. 1897, CPD, L22:1767; Dehesa to Díaz, 11 Nov. 1899, CPD, L24:16497; Dehesa to Díaz, 9 Aug. 1905, CPD, L30:10874; Dehesa to Díaz, 11 May 1907, ATD.

72. *El Diario del Hogar*, 20 May 1894, 23 May 1894, 5 Dec. 1897; Melgarejo Vivanco, *Breve historia*, p.184; Carlo de Fornaro, *México tal cual es*, p. 107; Paz to Díaz, 25 Mar. 1911, CPD, L36:4372; *La Patria*, 1 Feb. 1905; Paz, *Algunas campañas*, prologue by Ortíz Vidales, p. x.

73. Dehesa to Díaz, 27 Mar. 1903, CPD, L28:3595; Cosío Villegas, *Historia Moderna*, v. 9, p. 594. Dehesa was a friend of the owner, Juan Malpica Silva. See interview conducted by Rodney Anderson with Gabriel Cházaro in Anderson, *Outcasts in their own Land*, p. 209.

74. Dehesa to Díaz, 21 Apr. 1902, ATD; González Meña to Alvarez Soto, 21 Sep. 1902, ATD, File #10.

75. *El Paladín*, 17 Jan. 1901, 16, 20 Jun. 1901, 5 Jun. 1902; *El Paladín*, 11 Jul. 1901; Díaz to Dehesa, 15 Apr. 1902, ATD.

76. Díaz to Dehesa, 29 May 1905, ATD, File #11; Dehesa to Díaz, 3 Jun. 1905, ATD, File #11; *Basler Nachrichten*, 30 Oct. 1892, and *Le Matin*, Paris, 29 Jul. 1906, in CPD, L17:17069, L31:9749-50. Díaz also had Zayas Enríquez send him articles from various newspapers in the United States, CPD, L31, C24.

77. Beals, *Porfirio Díaz*, p. 225 remarks that Díaz "set faithful men to watch doubtful men." The opposite was also the case. On one occasion, Heriberto Barrón was sent to Xalapa to spy on Dehesa; De Pallares, *Dehesa*, p. 175.

78. Cárdenas, "A Macroeconomic Interpretation of Nineteenth-Century," pp. 76-77; Keremitsis, *La industria textil mexicana*, p. 112; *El Imparcial*, 23 Aug. 1893, p. 1.

79. Alamán was a noted conservative politician and historian in the early years of the Mexican republic; Chávez Orozco and Florescano, *Agricultura y industria textil*, pp. 93, 98-99; *El Imparcial*, 23 Aug. 1893, p. 1; Keremitsis, *La industria textil mexicana*, p. 144.

80. Keremitsis, *La industria textil mexicana*, pp. 144, 149; *El Cosmopólita*, 29 Aug. 1897, p. 1.

81. Ibid., p. 112.

82. Bazant, *Historia de la deuda exterior*, p. 138. In 1875, the peso was on a par with the U.S. dollar, but by 1891 had fallen to 1.27 pesos to the dollar. In 1905 it took two pesos to buy a dollar. See Velasco, *Geografía y estadística*, p. 197.

83. Ankerson, *Some Aspects of Economic Change*, p. 17.

84. Falcón, *El agrarismo en Veracruz*, p. 29.

85. *El Diario del Hogar*, 3 Feb. 1897, p. 1; *La Patria*, 14 Jun. 1905, p. 1.

86. *La Patria*, 27 Sep. 1905, p. 1.

87. *La Patria*, 17 Nov. 1905, p. 1; 8 Feb. 1906, p. 1.

88. Mariscal to Dehesa, 6 Mar. 1906, AGVC-ATD, Dehesa to Mariscal, 7 Mar. 1906, AGVC-ATD, and Dehesa to Santibañez, 7 Mar. 1906, AGVC-ATD, requesting information on the suitability of the hacienda "Oaxaqueña" for growing sugar cane for a William Todd of Omaha. Cf. Harrer, *Raíces económicas de la revolución Mexicana*, pp. 51-52. Mexico was one of the preferred areas for foreign, mainly European, investment, receiving about twenty-five percent of the entire investment for Latin America during this period. Weetman Pearson, for example, invested US$1.8 million over a seven-year period and paid seven percent of earnings from oil to the federal treasury, and three percent to the state of Veracruz. See Aston, "The Public Career of José Yves Limantour," p. 201.

89. Corral to Dehesa, 8 Feb. 1905, Dehesa to Corral, 14 Mar. 1905, AGVC-ATD, C1. See also Dehesa to Díaz, 24 May 1901, CPD, L226:3986-3987, and Díaz to Dehesa, 24 May 1901, CPD, L26:3989 on a similar request for a subsidy from the New York Bureau of Information and Commercial Agency.

90. Keremitsis, *La industria textil mexicana*, p. 93.

91. Chávez Orozco and Florescano, *Agricultura y industria textil*, pp. 89, 98-99. Large coal seams had also been discovered and were being worked. See *La Patria*, 2 May 1905, p. 1.

92. Ochoa C. And Velasquez O., *Volumen, dinámica y estructura*, p. 7; Maldonado Aguirre, *Poder regional*, p. 163.

93. Maldonado Aguirre, *Poder regional*, p. 164; Olvera R., *La estructura económica*, p. 12

94. On the Olarte rebellion, see Reina Aoyama, *Las rebeliones campesinas*. Despite the pioneering studies by Reina Aoyama, Katz, *Riot, Rebellion and Revolution*, and Tutino, *From Insurrection to Revolution*, much work needs to be done on the phenomenon of rural revolt before the 1840s. For example, neither Katz not Tutino mention the Olarte rebellion. Costeloe, *The Central Republic*, p. 24, maintains that scholars are "hard-pressed" to find any examples before that date. Land and local control were the core demands in Veracruz Indian uprisings between 1845-49, the Totonac uprising of 1853, the Plan of Tantoyuca in 1856, Acayucan, 1881-84 and 1906, and Papantla, 1891,1896 and 1906. See Reina, *Las rebeliones campesinas*, pp. 341-59. Michael Ducey, studying nineteenth-century liberal land policies and peasants in the Huasteca, comes to the conclusion that peasants were able to retain much land into the 1880s because they were dealing at the local level. It is only with the political centralization of the Porfiriato that their lot worsened. See Ducey, "Liberal Theory and Peasant Practice," p. 85. Womack, *Zapata*, pp. 7-8, has demonstrated the vivid recollection by the people of Anenecuilco of their history. Other Indians would also have been clear about their history and the origins of their land problems.

95. Ramírez Lavoignet, *Misantla*, pp. 247-49.

96. Kourí, *The Business of the Land*, pp. xi-xii.

97. Ibid., p. 193.

98. Kouri agrees that Totonac natives were the largest group adversely affected by the *reparto*. See pp. 194, 274. Yet his point, that "to see the behavior of Papantla's Totonacs solely or essentially as resistance – even as diverse forms of resistance – is to obscure the complexity of their roles as historical actors," needs to be applied to other discussions of land tenure patterns in Mexico. See p. 265.

99. Hart, "Agrarian Precursors of the Mexican Revolution;" Katz, "Labor Conditions on Haciendas in Porfirian Mexico;" Stevens, "Agrarian Policy;" Helen Phipps, *Some Aspects of the Landholding Question*, pp. 128-130. Cf. Meyer, *Problemas campesinas y revueltas agrarias*, p. 225, who estimates that overall "in Oaxaca, Jalisco, Veracruz, Morelos, Tlaxcala, part of Puebla and the Federal District, there were not a few rural communities that had kept their land." His estimate is that about forty per cent succeeded in doing so. González Navarro, "Tenencia de las tierras," pp. 67-70, agrees that about forty per cent of the Indian villages in central Mexico held onto their land; Stevens, "Agrarian Policy;" Díaz Soto y Gama, *La revolución agraria del Sur*, p. 54, cites President Díaz's letter of September 10, 1889, warning officials to be just and ensure that the "disinherited classes of the people" were given land. In the latest work on the land question, Robert Holden asserts that, "In conflicts between large landowners and the rural poor, Díaz may have preferred to provide more protection to the latter than he actually succeeded in doing, as John Tutino has specualted." See Holden, *Mexico and the Survey of Public Lands*," p. 134.

100. De Vore, "The Influence of Antonio Díaz Soto y Gama," pp. 5-6; Díaz Soto y Gama, *La revolución agraria*, p. 53; Bellingeri and Gil Sanchez, "Las estructuras agrarias bajo el porfiriato," p. 315; Blázquez Domínguez, *Miguel Lerdo de Tejada*, pp. 87-88; Hart, *Anarchism and the Mexican Working Class*, p. 14.

101. Bellingeri and Sanchez, "Las estructuras agrarias," p. 317.

102. Dehesa to Díaz, 19 Sep. 1905, ATD, File # 11.

103. Ministerio de Justicia, *Colleción de Leyes*, p. 63; Orozco, *Legislación y jurisprudencia*, p. 576; *El Nacional*, 3 Apr. 1894; De Vore, "The Influence of Díaz Soto y Gama," p. 10; González and Covarrubías, *El problema rural*, p. 89.

104. CAM, "Juchique de Ferrer," #33, pp. 1, 34-35; interview with Engineer Melgarejo y Vivanco (CAM), 8 March, 1984; CAM, "Juchique de Ferrer," #861; De la Peña, *Veracruz económico*, v.1, p. 217.

105. Falcón, *El agrarismo en Veracruz*, p. 28; Aston, *Limantour*, p. 190; Gobierno del Estado de Veracruz-Llave, *Leyes y Decretos (1894)*; Redondo Silva, "La cuestión agraria," p. 23; Díaz Soto y Gama, *La revolución agraria*, p. 23.

106. Orozco, *Legislación y jurisprudencia*, v.1, p. 658; Lara y Prado, *De Porfirio Díaz a Francisco Madero*, cited in Phipps, *Some Aspects*, p. 116; Quirk, *The Mexican Revolution*, p. 16; Díaz Soto y Gama, *La revolución agraria*, p. 55; Stevens, "Agrarian Policy;" Tannenbaum's assertion that "Díaz thought the regeneration of Mexico lay in the destruction of Indian communal organization" is over simplified. See Tannenbaum, *The Mexican Agrarian Revolution*, pp. 14-15; Dehesa to Díaz, 10 Jun. 1895, CPD, L20:10053.

107. From today's vantage point, with the December massacre of 45 Indians in Chiapas by paramilitary forces in 1997, this assertion is not subject to question. See *La Jornada*, 26 Dec. 1997, p. 1.

108. Hart, *Anarchism*, p. 15; Aston, *Limantour*, p. 190. This point has been consistently overlooked. See Stevens, "Agrarian Policy;" Braniff, "Observaciones sobre el fomento agricola," p. 36, ATD. Braniff was a member of a commission studying the feasibility of founding an agricultural credit bank for loans to small farmers.

109. Audiras to Díaz, 1 Nov. 1892, CPD, L17:16732; Dehesa to Díaz, 22 Oct. 1900, CPD, L25:13294-95; Dehesa to Díaz, 22. Oct. 1900, ATD, File #30; Dehesa to Díaz, 27 Oct. 1900, ATD, File #30.

110. Dehesa to Díaz, 22 Dec. 1892, CPD, L17:19093.
111. Herrera was to be named interim governor of Veracruz when Dehesa returned to the Customs in the port. See Dehesa to Díaz, 21 Jul. 1892, CPD, L17:8937-40.
112. Dehesa to Díaz, 25 Feb. 1896, CPD, L21: 1061; Díaz to Dehesa, 28 Feb. 1896, CPD, L21: 1062; Díaz to Dehesa, 27 Apr. 1894, CPD, L19:4881; Díaz to Dehesa, 19 May 1896, CPD, L21: 6931; Dehesa to Díaz, 30 May 1896, CPD, L21: 9957-58.
113. Chacón Caporal, *El balance de la Reforma Agraria*, p. 96; Vázquez Vela to CAM, 21 Nov. 1919, CAM, #14, "Papantla", pp. 16-17.
114. Kourí, *The Business of the Land*, p. 255.
115. Ibid., pp. 265-66.
116. Ibid., pp. 293, 310, 318.
117. Beals, *Porfirio Díaz*, pp. 301-02; González Navarro, *Historia Moderna*, v. 4, p. 204; Meyer, *Problemas campesinas*, p. 24; Melgarejo Vivanco, *Breve Historia*, p. 190; Enríquez to Díaz, 4 Jan. 1892, CPD, L17:477; Enríquez to Díaz, 9 Feb. 1892, CPD, L17:2070.
118. Díaz to Dehesa, 26 Jul. 1892, CPD, L17:10453; Díaz to Dehesa, 10 Aug. 1892, CPD, L12324; Dehesa to Díaz, 18 Aug. 1892, CPD, L17:12338; Díaz to Dehesa, 22 Aug. 1892, CPD, L17:12340.
119. Bellesteros to CAM, 8 Oct. 1919, CAM, #14, "Papantla;" *El Reproductor*, 26 Sep. 1895; a transcription of Dehesa's speech opening the new session of the legislature is in *El Reproductor*, 26 Sep. 1895; Díaz to Dehesa, 22 Sep. 1894, CPD, L19:14481.
120. Kourí, *The Business of the Land*, pp. 351-52.
121. This Victoriano Huerta is the man who became president in 1913 after the murder of Madero and Pino Suárez; Huerta to Díaz, 21 Nov. 1892, CPD, L17:17265; Díaz to Dehesa, 29 Nov. 1892, CPD, L17:17026. A *ranchero* is a small farmer with less than 1,000 hectares of land; Cambas's report is in CPD, L17:19084-85.
122. Díaz to Dehesa, 27 Dec. 1892, CPD, L17:19089; Dehesa to Minister of the Interior, 7 Nov. 1895, AGN, Gob 1a, L545:4.
123. Cambas to Herrera, 13 Apr. 1893, CPD, L18:5066; Dehesa to Díaz, 22 May 1893, CPD, L18: 6690; Díaz to Dehesa, no date, CPD, L18:6691; Dehesa to Díaz, 7 Mar. 1893, CPD, L18:7638; Veléz's report, 27 May 1893, CPD, L18:7639.
124. Díaz to Dehesa, 23 Sep. 1893, CPD, L18:13851.
125. Dehesa to Díaz, 14 Oct. 1893, CPD, L18:14552.
126. Díaz to Dehesa, 22 Sep. 1894, CPD, L19:14481; Dehesa to Díaz, 27 Sep. 1894, CPD, L19:14497; Dehesa to Díaz, 28 Sep. 1894, CPD, L19:16119-20; Díaz to Dehesa, 28 Sep. 1894, CPD, L19:16121; Dehesa to Díaz, 7 Nov. 1894, CPD, L19:16961-62; Mendizabal to Dehesa, no date, CPD, L19:16965-67; Dehesa to Díaz, 7 Nov. 1894, CPD, L19:16962-63.
127. Unsigned report to Dehesa, no date, CPD, L19:17015-36.
128. Dehesa to Díaz, 25 Nov. 1894, CPD, L19:17008-11.
129. Díaz to Dehesa, 26. Nov. 1894, CPD, L19:17037; Dehesa to Díaz, 21 Dec. 1894, CPD, L19:20024; Díaz to Dehesa, 22 Dec. 1894, CPD, L19:20025; Dehesa to Díaz, 22 Dec. 1894, CPD, L19:20038; Dehesa, *Memoria, 1892-94*, ATD, pp. 41-43.
130. *El Diario del Hogar*, 17 Dec. 1894.
131. *El Diario del Hogar*, 4 Jan. 1895; Dehesa to Díaz, 22 May 1895, CPD, L20:10060.

132. *Leyes y Decretos, 1892- 1910*; *Leyes y Decretos, 1894*, p. 129; Díaz to Dehesa, 19 May 1896, CPD, L21: 6931; *El Monitor Repúblicano*, 23 Jan. 1896, 25 Feb. 1896.
133. Various to Díaz, 31 Mar. 1896, CPD, L21:5056-57; see also García Cantú, *El pensamiento de la reacción mexicana*, pp.17-18.
134. Dehesa to Díaz, 16 May 1896, CPD, L21:6936-37; *El Hijo de Ahuizote* (Papantla), 28 Jun. 1896; Ramírez Lavoignet, *Soteapan: Luchas agrarias*, p. 23; *El Monitor Repúblicano*, 3 Jul. 8 Jul. 11 Jul. 14 Jul. 26 Jul. 1896; *El Diario del Hogar*, 10 Jul. 1896.
135. For a detailed discussion of the historical background and complexity see Kourí, *The Business of the* Land; El *Diario del Hogar*, 21 Jul. 1896; Melgarejo Vivanco, *Breve historia*, p. 190; Ramírez Lavoignet, *Soteapan*, p. 23; González Navarro, *Historia Moderna*, v. 4, p. 244; Dehesa, *Memoria, 1894-96*, p. 5; Dehesa to Díaz, 16 Jul. 1896, CPD, L21:12013; in Veracruz there were six Totonac revolts in the nineteenth century and four by the Popolucas of the south.
136. Kourí, *The Business of the Land*, p. xi.
137. For a compilation of these rebellions in Veracruz, see Reina Aoyama, *Las rebelliones campesinas*, pp. 325-59; Dehesa, *Memoria 1894-96*, p.14; *El Nacional*, 13 Jul. 1896; *El Monitor Republicano*, 3 Jul. 1896.
138. *El Reproductor*, 10 May 1900; McBride, *The Land Systems of Mexico*, p. 147; Falcón, *El agrarismo en Veracruz*, p. 29; Ochoa Contreras, "Cambios estructurales en la actividad," pp. 70-71.

Notes to Chapter 2

1. For an account of this congress and the founding of the PLM, see Albro III, *Always a Rebel: Ricardo Flores Magón and the Mexican Revolution*, Ch. 1.
2. Frank Tannenbaum, *Peace by Revolution*, is the originator of the 'social revolution' thesis. The most recent major return to this interpretation is Knight, *The Mexican Revolution*. See v. 1, pp. x-xi; for a discussion of other interpretations see Hart, "Historiographical Dynamics"; Knight, "Peasant and Caudillo," p. 19 ; Knight, "The Mexican Revolution: Bourgeois? Nationalist? Or just a 'Great Rebellion'?"; Knight, *Mexican Revolution*, v. 1, pp. ix-xi; Vanderwood, "Resurveying the Mexican Revolution"; Wasserman, "The Mexican Revolution."
3. The rural population was 71.47% of the total population. See Olvera R., *La estructura económica y social*, p. 8. See Katz, *Riot, Rebellion and Revolution*, pp. 46-62 for a discussion of causes and theories of rural revolt, and Knight, *Mexican Revolution*, v. 1, pp. 150-70, for "Thoughts on the Causes of Peasant Discontent."
4. See Rodríguez O., *The Revolutionary Process*, p. 3; MacLachlan and Beezeley, *El Gran Pueblo*, pp. 198-199.
5. For example, Knight, *Mexican Revolution*, v. 1, refers to the Acayucan uprising alternatively as "caste war," p. 9, "serious conflict", p. 106, "protest", p. 107, and a "dispute centered on land ownership," p. 114; on the other hand, Cosío Villegas, *Historia Moderna*, v. 9, does not refer to it at all.
6. Strictly speaking it was not the first shot. That occurred on 26 Sep. 1906 in Jiménez, Coahuila, although with only sixty men. See Albro III, *To Die on Your Feet*, p. 24; Acayucan must be considered the first seriously organised uprising. See Barrera Fuentes, *Historia de la revolución mexicana*, p. 204.

7. Revolt and rebellion are synonymous. They are both uprisings against a particular ruler or government for a particular reason. Revolution, however, is more than that. It is an attempt to change the entire *system* of government as well.

8. These statistics are from Southworth, *El estado de Veracruz-Llave*, p. 60.

9. Velasco, *Geografía y estadística*, p. 10; Zilli, *Historia sucinta*, p. 10; Pérez Miliucía,*Compendio de geografía*, p. 37. The Popolucas are the descendents of the ancient Olmec peoples; Arroniz, *La costa de Sotavento*, pp. 18-19; Ramírez Lavoignet, *Soteapan: Luchas*, p. 49; Medel y Alvarado, *Historia de San Andrés Tuxtla*, p. 349.

10. The region under discussion remained in the hands of the Cortés family for about three hundred years. Azaola Garrido, *Rebelión y derrota*, p. 30.

11. Ibid., pp. 32-33. For a discussion of the railroad see Glick, "The Tehuantepec Railroad", pp. 373-82. The railroad was Mexico's unsuccessful attempt to preempt the competition from an eventual canal across Panama.

12. See Azaola Garrido, *Rebelión y derrota* for a detailed history of the successive alienation of these lands into private hands over the preceding centuries; Pasquel, *La rebelión agraria*, p. 13; Azaola Garrido, *Rebelión y derrota*, p. 78. Azaola's work is based primarily on information in the CAM archives in Xalapa. This archive contains a wealth of information on land transactions and consist to a great extent of accounts given by peasants after the Revolution while attempting to benefit from the land reform. There is doubtless a great deal of truth to their accounts, but one cannot help thinking that there must be some embellishments if not distortions in them. Some of the pages in these files are numbered, others are not.

13. CAM, Exp. 35, pp.154-55, cited in Azaola Garrido, *Rebelión y derrota*, p. 80.

14. Azaola Garrido, *Rebelión y derrota*, pp. 80-81.

15. Ramírez Lavoignet, *Soteapan: Luchas*, pp.18, 22, 49; interview with the Veracruz historian, Melgarejo Vivanco, who knows the region well, 12 Mar. 1984, Museo Antropólogo, Xalapa,Veracruz; Foster, *A Primitive Mexican Economy*, p. 11; Ramírez Lavoignet, *Soteapan*, p.18; Azaola Garrido, *Rebelión y derrota*, p. 92; cf. Ramírez Lavoignet, *Soteapan*, p. 46, who gives the number as 120,035. Romero Rubio was then Minister of the Interior; *El Nacional*, 4 Oct. 1895. Very few people apparently lamented his passing as he was an absolute materialist. See García Granados, *Historia de México*, v. 2, p. 271; *El Monitor Republicano*, 2 Jan. 1896.

16. Díaz to Dehesa, 9 Jan. 1897, CPD, L22:1065.

17. Ramírez Lavoignet, *Soteapan*, pp. 38, 40-42, 33.

18. John Body to Dehesa, 26 Jul. 1907, ATD; Cott, *Porfirian Investment Policies*, p. 176. Ironically the PLM also thought the possibility existed. See Novoa to Magón, 26 Jan. 1906, AGN-GOB, 1a 906(8) 1.52, p. 40; see also Katz, *Deutschland, Díaz*, pp. 64-70 for a discussion of this all-too-prescient Mexican fear.

19. Katz, *Deutschland, Díaz*, p. 66; Calvert, *The Mexican Revolution*, pp. 23-24; *Leyes, Decretos y Circulares, 1904*, pp. 7-9. Decree #4, 13 Jan. 1903 ceded to Pearson all the taxation rights to certain properties in the municipalities of Jáltipan, Minatitlán and Acayucan for twelve thousand pesos. Cf. Novoa to Flores Magón, 26 Jan. 1906, AGN-GOB, 1a 906(8)1.52, p.29, who calls Pearson a snake and Dehesa a bandit because of this sale; Díaz to Dehesa, 22 Jan. 1903, CPD, L28:951; Díaz to Dehesa, 22 Jan. 1903, ATD, File #3.

20. Díaz to Dehesa, 2 Oct. 1903, ATD, File #30.
21. Dehesa to Díaz, 5 Oct. 1903, CPD, L28:13903-04; Dehesa to Díaz, 5 Oct. 1903, ATD, File #30.
22. CAM, Exp. 1432. In the Canton of Acayucan ca. 102,861 hectares were sold to Pearson and Co. See CAM, Exp. 29 for similar information on the Canton of Minatitlán; Dehesa to Díaz, 5 Mar. 1906, CPD, L31:1859; Camara de Diputados de México, *Diario de Debates, 1906*, p. 186 gives the details of the contract with Pearson regarding land expropriation rights.
23. Stevens, "Agrarian Policy," pp. 153-66. In 1901, Art. 27 of the Constitution of 1857 was revised to permit corporations to again hold land communally; Zayas Enriquez, *Porfirio Díaz*, p. 222.
24. Arriaga was the grandson of a famous social liberal, Ponciano Arriaga, who had been involved with the Revolution of Ayutla and the subsequent Liberal government in the 1850s.
25. Cockroft, *Intellectual Precursors*, pp. 117-20.
26. Ibid., p. 92; Barrera Fuentes, *Historia de la Revolución*, p. 21; Meyers, "The Mexican Liberal Party 1903-1910," pp. 99-100, 115; Padua, *Movimiento revolucionario*, pp. 5, 84ff; Cumberland, "Precursors of the Mexican Revolution," pp. 344-356; Agetro, *Las luchas proletariadas*, pp. 25-26.
27. Martínez Hernández, *Tiempos de Revolución*, p. 28. Martínez Hernández was only fourteen months old at the time of the attack on Acayucan, but subsequently related the account he had heard from his parents. It was written in his Zoque-Popoluca language and then translated into Spanish by two young men from his group. The memory of this revolution is still fresh in the minds of his people.
28. See CPD, L31:9325 for a copy of the newspaper *Regeneración* in which the party program was printed; Meyers, "Mexican Liberal Party," p. 176; Agetro, *Las luchas proletariadas*, p. 26; Albro III, "Ricardo Flores Mágon," p. 98.
29. Meyers, "Mexican Liberal Party," p. 124. Ramírez Lavoignet, *Soteapan*, p. 55; Cockroft, *Intellectual Precursors*, p. 119ff; in AGN-GOB, 1a 906, there is a considerable amount of material on the PLM; Díaz to Dehesa, 7 Jun. 1906, ATD, File #32.
30. Ramírez Lavoignet, *Soteapan*, p. 55; Novoa to Magón, 26 Jun. 1906, ATD, File #C-33. This letter was sent from a "mountain near Chinameca"; Magón to Marín, 1 Sep. 1906, AGN-GOB, 1a 906(8) 1-52; Magón to Tolentino, no date, AGN-GOB, 1a 906(8) 1- 52; Magón to Peniche, 14 Sep. 1906, AGN-GOB, 1a 906(8) 1-52. This reference to an "uprising" is to the famous Cananea strike which began 1 Jun. 1906. These incriminating letters were all sent by ordinary mail, which appears relatively naive in retrospect. Novoa, for example, remitted party dues to Magón by Wells Cargo Express!
31. Sixto to Magón, 19 Jun., 1906, AGN-GOB, 1a 906(8) 1-52.
32. Agetro, *Luchas proletaiadas*, p. 25; Hart, *Anarchism*, p. 93; Padua, *Movimiento revolucionario*, pp. 5-6, 8; the general consensus is that the rebels numbered about one thousand. See also Meyers, "Mexican Liberal Party," p.143. The report from the *Washington Times*, 23 Sep. 1906, of 10,000 men seems to be highly exaggerated. Meyers, "Mexican Liberal Party," p. 143; Thompson to Secretary of State, Washington, D.C., 3 Oct. 1906, CPD, L31:13347-48; De Vore, *The Influence of Díaz Soto y Gama*, p. 67; Agetro, *Luchas proletariadas*, p. 26; González Sempé, *Evolución política*, p. 234.

33. Padua, *Movimiento revolucionario*, loc. cit.; Dehesa to Minister of Interior, 13 Oct. 1906, AGN-GOB, 1a 906(8) 1-52; Araíza, *Historia del movimiento obrero*, p. 144; Agetro, *Luchas proletariadas*, p. 30; Barrera Fuentes, *Historia de la Revolución*, p. 205; Meyers, "Mexican Liberal Party," p. 151.

34. Thompson to Secretary of State, Washington, D.C., 3 Oct. 1906, CPD, L31:13347. *La Patria* did not report the news; *El Diario*, 16 Nov. 1906 spoke of "some disorders"; *El Dictámen* (Veracruz), 2 Oct. 1906, said that the situation was not as grave as first believed. Unfortunately this attitude by contemporaries toward the Acayucan uprising has been accepted as correct by many historians. For example, García Granados, *Historia de México*, v. 2, does not mention it. Albro III, *Ricardo Flores Magón*, p. 98, says that the reason it received so little publicity was that it took place deep inside Mexico instead of at the border. This explanation is vague. The real reason is that since it took place deep inside the country it could be more easily hushed up!

35. *El Dictámen*, 8 Oct. 1906; E. Novoa to Dehesa, 6 Oct. 1906, CPD, L31:12347. This Novoa was a relative of the man who led the group against Minatitlán; Goyri to Minister of Interior, 10 Nov. 1906, AGN-GOB, 1a 906(8) 1-52; *El Diario*, 16 Oct. 1906; A. González to Dehesa, 17 Oct. 1906, ATD, C33:D107; Dehesa to González, 5 Nov. 1906, ATD, C33:D107.

36. Sentíes to Díaz, 16 Oct. 1906, CPD, L31:12919-20; Padua, *Movimiento revolucionario*, p.11 asserts that it was widely believed that one of the leaders was poisoned on Sentíes's orders. Sentíes's claim of the danger of epidemic may not be at all a cover-up. I visited that jail in 1981 and it was still not the most edifying of places. He also probably feared attempts to engineer their release.

37. Novoa, Pérez, Salas and Padua were still at large. See Padua, *Movimiento revolucionario*, p.11; Díaz to Dehesa, 6 Oct. 1906, CPD, L31:13133.

38. Camacho to Dehesa, 2 Nov. 1906, ATD, C33:D107; Camacho to Dehesa, 2 Nov. 1906, CPD, L31:15460. Not until the following year was this causal connection thought to be confirmed by the discovery of a letter from Hilario Salas to the PLM Junta in Missouri. See Goyri to Díaz, 8 Jun. 1908, CPD, L33:6947-48. Document #6948 is a copy of Salas's letter.

39. Novoa to Magón, 26 Sep. 1906, CPD, L31:15460.

40. District Judge (no name) to Dehesa, 22 Nov. 1906, ATD, C33:D107; Camacho to Dehesa 25 Nov. 1906, ATD, C33:D107; Díaz to Dehesa, 27 Nov. 1906, ATD, C33:D107; Dehesa to Díaz, 28 Nov. 1906, ATD, C33:D107; Dehesa to Fernández, 19 Dec. 1906, ATD, C33:D107; Dehesa to Camacho, 18 Dec. 1906, ATD, C33:D107.

41. Dehesa to Díaz, 25 Feb. 1907, CPD, L32:3548; Canseco to Sec. Gob. (Veracruz), 12 May 1907, CPD, L32:5317-18.

42. Beltrán to Dehesa, 24 Sep. 1907, ATD, File #B26. This entire file is devoted to the correspondence concerning Beltrán's nomination and subsequent actions. Canseco was active in other matters of justice too. In July 1907, he used his power to order the manager of the Miller Plantation Co., George Anderson, to pay forty pesos owing to some plantation workers. After his removal, the company unsuccessfully tried to get the government to reimburse them for the payment. See Dehesa to Muñoz, 25 Jul. 1907, CPD, L32:6892-95.

43. Dehesa to Muñoz, 27 Sep. 1907, ATD, File #B26.

44. Beltrán to Sec. Gob. (Veracruz), 14 Oct. 1907, ATD, File #B26; Dehesa to Muñoz, 21 Oct. 1907, ATD, File #B26.

45. Dehesa to Muñoz, 21 Oct. 1907, ATD, File #B26.
46. Dehesa to Díaz, 20 Oct. 1907, ATD, File #B26.
47. Francisco Dehesa to Dehesa, 26 Oct. 1907, ATD, File #B26; Cartas to Francisco Dehesa, 23 Oct. 1907, ATD, File #B26; Agramonte to Dehesa, 24 Oct. 1907, ATD, File #B26; López to Francisco Dehesa, 27 Oct. 1907, ATD, File #B26.
48. Gómez to Dehesa, 18 Nov. 1907, ATD, File #3; Dehesa to Gómez, 21 Nov. 1907, ATD, File #3; Dehesa to Díaz, 7 Jul. 1908, CPD, L33:9037-38.
49. This interpetation regarding the trend of exploitation seems to have been accepted. See Cumberland, *Mexican Revolution*, v. 1, pp. 24-25; see also Knight, *The Mexican Revolution*, v. 1, pp. 23, 36, who refers to the *Científico* programme of development as "unjust" and at the same time "economically progressive, developmentalist and forward-looking."
50. Lubasz, "Introduction" in Lubasz, ed., *Revolutions*, p. 4.
51. There is little agreement about the nomenclature for the events that culminated at Río Blanco on January 7, 1907. Most historians have used the word "strike." This is a serious misrepresentation as the events of that day were not preceded by a strike, but by a company, wide lockout.
52. *El Dictámen*, 17 July, 1906; *El Reproductor*, 19 Aug. 1909; *La Patria*, 5 Jun. 1907; *El Diario del Hogar*, 24 Oct. 1908; *El Reproductor*, 3 Aug. 1911; Knight, *The Mexican Revolution*., v.1, 136-137; Anderson, "Mexican Workers and the Politics of Revolution, 1906-11," Anderson, *Outcasts in Their Own Land*; James D. Cockfort, *Precursores intelectuales*; Anderson, "Textile Labor Movement"; Hart, *Anarchism and the Mexican Working Class*; Salvador Hernández, "Tiempos libertarios"; Albro III, "Ricardo Flores Magón;" for early revolutionary activities in Orizaba and the connections between socialists, Magonistas and workers, see Zapata Vela, *Conversaciones con Heriberto Jara*. Jara worked as an accountant in the Río Blanco factory, clandestinely distributed *Regeneración*, in Orizaba, and was a reader at workers' reading clubs.
53. Haber, *Industry and Underdevelopment*, p. 56.
54. For the history of the textile industry, see Keremitsis, *The Cotton Textile Industry*; Chávez Orozco and Florescano, *Agricultura y industria textil*, pp. 98-99, 278.
55. Anderson, "Textile Labor Movement," p. 57; Chávez Orozco and Florescano, *Agricultura y industria*, p. 279. The towns were Nogales, Necoxtla and Río Blanco; Haber, *Industry and Underdevelopment*, p. 57; *El Reproductor*, 12 Jan. 1905. The inauguration of the factory was a national event attended by the president, ministers, and hosts of foreign dignitaries. See also Peña Samañiego, *Río Blanco*, p. 12, and Anderson, "Textile Labor Movement," pp. 12-13, 58-60.
56. Rosenzweig," El desarrollo económico de México"; Cockcroft, Frank and Johnson, *Dependency and Underdevelopment*, p. 69; Anderson, "Textile Labor Movement," p. 44; see also Cott, *Porfirian Investment Policies, 1876-1910*, p. vi, who argues that "although the importance of promoting foreign investment was recognised, Porfirian development policies did not surrender the Mexican economy to foreign states."
57. In Veracruz, with the increased employment by the textile industry and the development of large estates, this was particularly the case. See *La Patria*, 17 Dec. 1902, 12 Jul. 1905; Dehesa to Díaz, 21 Feb. 1899, CPD, L24:2531; El Colegio de México, *Estadísticas económicos del Porfiriato*, pp. 149-150; Rosenzweig "El desarrollo," has shown that mortality rates in

Mexico actually increased after 1877. In that year, Veracruz had a mortality rate of eight per thousand which subsequently rose to thirty in the following year. Basurto, *El proletariado industrial*, p. 123; De Pallares, *Dehesa*, p. 126; Keremitsis, *La industria textil*, p. 203.

58. Basurto, loc. cit. When the workers left the factory on Saturday afternoons with their pay, they had to beg for credit at the company store, pledging the next week's pay in order to cover their purchases; Keremitsis, *La Industria textil*, p. 220; Anderson, "Textile Labor Movement," p. 218; Moisés González Navarro, "La Huelga de Río Blanco."

59. Idem. "Las huelgas textiles," p. 94; Cockcroft, *Mexico: Class Formation*, p. 94; Gilly, *La formación de la conciencia*, p. 6; Basurto, *El proletariado*, pp. 102-103. In addition to external factors, there was also pressure from over-production as the textile industry saturated the internal market. See Knight, *The Mexican Revolution*, v.1, p. 134; Acevedo to Sec. Gob., Veracruz, 21 Nov. 1891, CPD, L17:470.

60. Medel y Alvarado, *Historia de San Andrés Tuxtla*, pp. 399-400; Peña Samaniego, *Río Blanco*, p. 19.

61. Walker, "The Empresa del Tabaco."

62. Díaz to Dehesa, 13 Jun. 1903, ATD, C33 #D107; Herrera to Dehesa, 15 Jun. 1903, ATD, C33 #D107; Peña Samañiego, *Río Blanco*, p. 21; Dehesa to Díaz, 17 Jun. 1903, ATD, C33 #D107.

63. Pasquel, *El conflicto obrero*, p. 120; Melgarejo Vivanco, *Breve historia de Veracruz*, p. 192; *La Patria*, 21 Nov. 1905.

64. *El Paladín*, 4 Mar. 1906; Hart, *Anarchism*, p. 105.

65. *El Repdroductor*, 7 Jun. 1906; *El Paladín*, 23 Aug. 1906.

66. Dehesa requisitioned reports from the various textile factories on the feasibility of reducing working hours from fifteen to twelve per day for the same remuneration. See Dehesa to various, 26 Jun. 1906, CPD, L31:8659; Keremitsis, *La industria textil*, p. 219.

67. De Zayas Enríquez, *Porfirio Díaz*, p. 223; Dehesa to Díaz, 13 Jul. 1906, CPD, L31:8718;. Hartington to Reynaud, 17 Nov. 1906, ATD, C33 D#107; *El Reproductor*, 20 Sep. 1906, 4 Oct. 1906, 1 Nov. 1906. In September the new manager of the jute factory ordered a reduction in workers' pay of five centavos per roll which caused a strike that lasted for six weeks and almost bankrupted the factory. The workers were able to sustain themselves with strike pay from the Union Mexicana de Obreros, which could have lasted for ten months. On November 1, they returned to work at their old pay rate.

68. Hart, "Nineteenth Century Urban Labor Precursors"; Walker, "Porfirian Labor Politics"; Valadés, *Sobre los orígenes*, p. 13; Agetro, *Las luchas proletariadas*, p. 41; González Sempé, *Evolución política y constitutional*, p. 235. No exact date could be found for the founding of this society.

69. García Díaz, "Apuntes;" Bastian, "Metodismo y clase obrero;" see also Ojeda, *Ricardo Flores Magón*, p. 39; De Pallares, *Dehesa*, p. 121; Walker, "Porfirian Labor Politics"; Hart, *Anarchism*: p. 103; Peña Samañiego, *Río Blanco*, p. 26; Albro III, "Magón," p. 76; the paper had, apparently in a short time, been successful in stirring up the workers and causing short work stoppages. See Dehesa to Díaz, 4 Jul. 1906, CPD, L31:8668-70; Hart, *Anarchism*, p. 105-06; Anderson, "Textile Labor Movement," p. 93.

70. Hart, *Anarchism*, p. 107; Cosío Villegas, v. 9, p. 721; Dehesa to Díaz, 13 Jul. 1906, CPD, L31:8704-08, includes the report from Ramón Rocha.

71. Rocha to Dehesa, 13 Oct. 1906, CPD, L31:13171-74.

72. Díaz to Dehesa, 23 Oct., 1906, CPD, L31:13175.

73. The report is entitled "Breves apuntes relativos a los antecedentes de la cuestión obrera en Orizaba, etc." See Rocha to Dehesa, 10 Jan. 1907, CPD, L32:931-936; Ramírez to Hartington, 23 Nov. 1906, CPD, L31:16060; Dehesa to Díaz, 14 Dec. 1906, CPD, L31:16056.

74. This Ramírez was the same person who fled Orizaba and signed the pact with Salas, Padua et al. in 1908. Hartington to Reynaud, 17 Nov. 1906, CPD, L31:16062-66.

75. Anderson, "Textile Labor Movement," p. 157; see Walker, "Porfirian Labor Politics," who argues against the stereotyped portrayal of porfirian policy as one of "unrestrained violence and wickedness," and that neither the brutally repressive picture, nor the neutral laissez-faire one of the porfirian regime is correct. He also sees continuity in labour politics from the Porfiriato through the Revolution.

76. Anderson, "Textile Labor Movement," p. 20; Katz, *Deutschland, Díaz und die mexikanische Revolution*, pp. 42-43, 169; De Pallares, *Dehesa*, pp. 125-126.

77. After the strike at Cananea, Dehesa sent one hundred pesos to the families of workers killed in the violence. See Hart, *Anarchism*, p. 209; Anderson, "Textile Labor Movement," p. 166; Araiza, *Historia del movimiento obrero*, pp. 115, 121.

78. Pasquel, *El conflicto obrero*, pp. 29-30; De Pallares, *Dehesa*, pp. 72, 132; Aragón, *Porfirio Díaz*, pp. 30-31. A search of the debates of the Chamber of Deputies did not reveal any discussion of such a law. It never reached the floor of the Chamber for discussion. This information came from Raúl Dehesa, the governor's son and friend of Veracruzan author Leonardo Pasquel. Interview with Pasquel held in Mexico City, February, 1983.

79. Hart, *Anarchism*, p. 209; Anderson, "Textile Labor Movement," p. 166; Dehesa to Herrera, 28 Nov. 1906, CPD, L31:16061; Araiza, *Historia del movimiento obrero*, p. 115; *El Imparcial*, 4 Jan. 1907.

80. *El Imparcial*, 30 Oct. 1906; Díaz to Dehesa, 12 Dec. 1906, CPD, L31:16025; *El Imparcial*, 17 Sep. 1906; De Pallares, *Dehesa*, pp. 133, 136; *El Cosmopólita*, 24 Jun. 1906; De Pallares, *Dehesa*, p. 139; Dehesa to Díaz, 4 Aug. 1906; Dehesa to Tron, various dates, ATD.

81. Keremitsis, *La industria textil*, p. 219; Dehesa to Díaz, 6 Nov. 1906, CPD, L31:15455; Cosío Villegas, *Historia Moderna*, v. 9, p. 733; Díaz to Dehesa, 7 Nov. 1906, CPD, L31:15456; Araiza, *Historia del movimiento obrero*, v. 2, p. 103; Basurto, *El proletariado industrial*, p. 125.

82. Basurto, *El proletariado industrial*, p. 125.

83. Araiza, *Historia del movimiento obrero*, v. 2, p. 104; *El Imparcial*, 8 Dec. 1906; Basurto, *El proletariado industrial*, loc. cit.

84. *El Diario*, 6 Dec. 1906; De Pallares, *Dehesa*, p. 149. The increase was from 15 to 25 centavos weekly.

85. *El Imparcial*, 16 Dec. 1906; Dehesa to Díaz, 6 Nov. 1906, CPD, L31:15455.

86. Araiza, *Historia del movimiento obrero*, p. 105; the date given, December 28, is not accepted by other historians. Dehesa, in his famous correspondence with Limantour after the fall of the regime, accused the government of advising the factory owners to take this measure. But he did not accuse Limantour personally. See Dehesa to Limantour, 30 Jul. 1911, ATD; Anderson, *Outcasts*, p. 144; García Díaz, "Apuntes;" Walker, " Porfirian labor politics."

87. Dehesa to Díaz, 25 Dec. 1906, CPD, L31:16090; *El Diario*, 27 Dec. 1906; *El Reproductor*, 27 Dec. 1906; *El Diario*, 28 Dec. 1906; *La Patria*, 29 Dec. 1906.

88. For the full text of the *laudo*, see Koth, "Not a Mutiny," Appendix I; Walker, "Porfirian labor politics"; Anderson, *Outcasts*, p.151.

89. Araiza, *Historia del movimiento obrero*, pp. 108-110; Cosío Villegas, *Historia Moderna*, v. 9, pp. xxiii-xxiv; Anderson, *Outcasts*, p. 151 conflicts with an earlier assessment of the *laudo* as "a substantial victory for the Mexican textile labor movement." See Anderson, "Textile Labor Movement," p. 222. See also Walker, "Porfirian Labor Politics," who is much less sanguine about the *laudo*.

90. Araiza, *Historia del movimiento obrero*, pp. 110-11; Basurto, *El proletariado industrial*, p. 133; Walker, "Porfirian Labor Politics."

91. Ibid. p. 113; *El Reproductor*, 10 Jan. 1907. This Orizaban newspaper did not report the shouts, but documents the agitation of the workers and their total rejection of the *laudo*. Another historian claims that the workers voted to continue the strike, but as there was no strike to begin with, this is questionable. No verification of this statement could be found. See List Azurbide, *Apuntes sobre la prehistoria*, p. 93. Morales himself, in a letter to *El Diario* claims that he left the theatre because of the growing tumult against the *laudo*. *El Diario*, 11 Jan. 1907.

92. Walker, "Porfirian Labor Politics"; Basurto, *El proletariado industrial*, p. 130; Agetro, *Las luchas proletariadas*, p. 43; *El Diario*, 11 Jan. 1907.

93. Some of this is based on the report by the local newspaper, *El Reproductor*, 10 Jan. 1907; *El Diario*, 8 Jan. 1907; Basurto, *El proletariado industrial*, p. 134; *El Diario* claims that he discounted up to twenty five percent. See *El Diario*, 10 Jan. 1907; Rocha to Dehesa, 7 Jan. 1907, CPD, L32:925.

94. *El Reproductor*, 10 Jan. 1907. There is a picture printed in both Anderson, *Outcasts*, p. 158 and Araiza, *Historia del movimiento obrero*, v. 2, p. 114, showing a group of mounted men, presumably Rurales, quietly watching the store burn. Herrera later accused the Rurales of not doing anything to prevent the disturbances. See *El Dictámen*, 14 Jan. 1907.

95. Herrera's report to Dehesa was printed in *El Reproductor*, 10 Jan. 1907. It was also printed in the official state paper, *Periodico del Estado de Veracruz-Llave*, 12 Jan. 1907; Rocha to Dehesa, 7 Jan. 1907, CPD, L32:924; *El Reproductor*, 10 Jan. 1907.

96. List Azurbide, *Apuntes sobre la prehistoria*, p. 94, estimates that some four thousand soldiers were mobilized; *El Reproductor*, 10 Jan. 1907. It has been asserted that Díaz sent Martínez because the general was a political opponent of Dehesa. See Anderson, *Outcasts*, p. 165. Others thought so as well. See unsigned to Dehesa, 25 Jan. 1907, ATD, C33 #D107; Anderson, *Outcasts*, pp. 163-165, contains the best account of the executions and the controversy surrounding the responsibility for their summary nature; the telegrams are contained in CPD, L66:109,111,133-36 &182.

97. *El Dictámen*, 14 Jan. 1907; *El Reproductor*, 17 Jan. 1907; Dehesa to Díaz, 12 Jan. 1907, CPD, L32:928; Dehesa to Díaz, 15 Jan. 1907, ATD, C33 #D107; Rocha to Dehesa, 7 Jan. 1907, CPD, L32:925-925; report from Rocha to Gen. Martínez, no date, CPD, L32:933-36.

98. Circulars #2 & #5, 16 Jan. 1907, 16 Feb. 1907, in AGN-GOB, 1a 907(17)1; Anderson, *Outcasts*, p. 147, is wrong when he says that Dehesa charged

Limantour specifically with the blame. See Dehesa to Limantour, 30 Jul. 1911, ATD, C33 #D107 where Dehesa explained that he had not even mentioned Limantour's name in an interview with *El Diario* and that the newspaper had incorrectly quoted him. In fact, he assured Limantour that he had no specific evidence of the former finance minister's culpability.

99. Trens, *Historia de Veracruz*, v. 6, p. 402; De Pallares, *Dehesa*, p. 154; Pérez, *Teodoro A. Dehesa*, p. 14.

100. Herrera to Dehesa, 16 Oct. 1929, ATD, C33 #D107. There is agreement that Dehesa had nothing to do with the massacres. His positive role and efforts to secure justice for the workers has received recognition among labour historians. See Araiza, *Historia del movimiento obrero*, pp. 115, 121.

101. *El Diario*, 15 Jan. 1907. A copy of this report was found in Dehesa's papers, ATD, C33, #D107; Pasquel, *Río Blanco*, p. 122; For a discussion of the responsibility see Anderson, *Outcasts*, p. 164, who suggests that the evidence is clear, though not conclusive, that Díaz himself was the source of the orders; Herrera to Dehesa, 1 Mar. 1907, ATD, C33, #D107; the resentment caused by the repression and executions made it comparatively easy to recruit volunteers in Orizaba for the Revolution in 1910-1911. See Zapata Vela, *Heriberto Jara*, p. 29.

102. Dehesa to Díaz, 13 Jan. 1907, CPD, L32:937-38; Ruiz to Díaz, 15 Jan. 1907, CPD, L32:419; Corral to Dehesa 16 Jan. 1907; Dehesa to Corral, 20 Feb. 1907, ATD, C33 #D107; Gómez to Dehesa, 22 Feb. 1907, ATD, C33 #D107; Dehesa to Díaz, 19 Feb. 1907, CPD, L32:2266.

103. *El Tiempo*, 26 May 1907, AGN-GOB, 1a "Revoltosos Magonistas," C 4, exp. 2; *Ideas Nuevas*, #48, 24 May 1907, in CPD, L32:5222; AGN-GOB, 907(17) 1; various to Dehesa, 24 May 1907, CPD, L32:5216-17.

104. Tron to Dehesa, 28 May 1907, CPD, L32:5218; Dehesa to Tron, 28 May 1907, CPD, L32:5219; Dehesa to Gómez, 28 May 1907, CPD, L32:5220; Gómez to Dehesa, 28 May 1907, CPD, L32:5221; Cosío Villegas, *Historia Moderna*, v. 9, pp. 729, 737-38; Anderson, *Outcasts*, p. 207.

105. Anderson, *Outcasts*, pp. 207-8; De Pallares, *Dehesa*, pp. 158-160

106. In Cananea, Sonora, the U.S.-owned Cananea Copper Co. was the scene of the first PLM-sponsored and bloody labour dispute of the Porfiriato. See Cosío Villegas, *Historia Moderna*, v. 9, pp. 707-15.

107. Padua, *Movimiento revolucionario*, p. 14.

108. Martínez Hernández, *Tiempos de revolución*, p. 44.

109. Ibid., p.37; Padua, *Movimiento revolucionario*, p. 28.

110. For a discussion of the Robin Hood myth and social banditry, see Vanderwood, *Disorder and Progress*, pp. xix, 94; Santanón was from the canton of Acayucan, where he had been a soldier in the 24th Battalion. About six years earlier, he had gone AWOL because of a personal incident and swore vengeance on the government. His mother lived on a plantation "El Laurel" in San Andrés Tuxtla where she cultivated some land. Jasso to Minister of War, 17 Oct. 1910, AHSDN XI/481, 5/310 C 144.

111. These included the famous Veracruzan poet Salvador Díaz Mirón, who had vowed to kill Santanón himself and insisted on joining the *Rurales* in their search. Cpl. E. Téllez to Com. 6 Rurales, 7.VII.10, AGN-CR, 6/109.

112. JP Cosamaloapán to Dehesa, 27 May1910, AGVC-TP C2; JP Los Tuxtlas to Dehesa, 28 May, 1910, AGVC-TP C2.

113. JP Acayucan to Espinosa, 31 May1910, AGVC- TP, C2.

114. Rafael Rebollar to Supreme Court, 26 Jul. 1910, AGN-SC 195/15.

115. Martínez Hernández, *Tiempos de revolución*, p. 38.
116. Cpl. Téllez to Com. 6 Rurales, 3 Aug. 1910, AGN-CR, 6/109; Fco. Cárdenas
      to Inspector General Rurales, 10 Oct. 1910, AGN-CR, 1/5; Jasso to Minister
      of War, 17 Oct. 1910, AHSDN, XI/481, 5/310 C 144.
117. Martínez Hernández, *Tiempos de revolución*, p. 38; these women may well
      have been the first *soldaderas*.
118. Padua, *Movimiento revolucionario*, p. 79. This Captain Cárdenas was the
      same man responsible for the murders of Madero and Pino Suárez.
119. Minister of the Interior to Inspector General Rurales, 15 Oct. 1910,
      AGN-CR, 1/5, 6/109.
120. Jasso to Minister of War, 17 Oct. 1910, AHSDN, XI/481, 5/310 C 144;
      Martínez, *Tiempos de revolución*, p. 42.
121. Cpl. Gutíerrez to Inspector General Rurales, 17 Oct. 1910, AGN-CR, 1/35.
122. Jasso to Minister of War, 17 Oct. 1910, AHSDN XI/481, 5/310 C 144.
123. Cárdenas to Inspector General Rurales, 21 Oct. 1910, AGN-CR, 1/5; Sgt.
      Rodolfo S. Furlong to Inspector General, AGN-CR, 6/109.
124. Martínez Hernández, *Tiempos de revolución*, p. 44; M. A. Pretelín to Dehesa,
      Catemaco, 7 Nov. 1910, AGVC-AMI, C 2; Camacho to Gob., Xalapa, 10
      Nov. 1910, AGVC-AMI, C 2.

Notes to Chapter 3

1. Hamnett, "Liberalism Divided," p. 662.
2. For a discussion of the problems surrounding municipal autonomy, see
    Hale, *Mexican Liberalism*, chap 2.
3. Hamnett, "Liberalism Divided," pp. 687-88.
4. Huntington, "Revolution and Political Order," p. 45; Tutino, *From
    Insurrection*, p. 326; Skocpol, *States and Social Revolutions*, p. 112;
    Goldstone, *Revolutions*, p. 12.
5. Guerra, *Le Mexique de l'Ancien Régime*, v. 2, pp. 149, 207; Daniel Cosío
    Villegas, *Historia Moderna*, v. 9, pp. 493; Alan Knight, *Mexican Revolution*, v. 1,
    p. 75; Avila, " '¡Así se gobierna señores!'," p. 15.
6. Goldfrank, "Theories of Revolution." The definition of "faction" and
    "party" follow the meanings established by Sartori, *Party and Party
    Systems*, pp. 3-38. Consequently, only Madero's Anti-re-electionist Party
    can be viewed as a political party rather than a faction.
7. Guerra, *México*, v. 2, pp. 85-87.
8. Ibid.
9. Hart, *Revolutionary Mexico*, p. 349.
10. Guerra, México, v. 2, p. 93.
11. Madero to Calderón, 27 Jul. 1909, AM, R. 9; Sánchez Azcona, *Apuntes*,
    p. 47; Madero to Vázquez Gómez, 18 Aug. 1910, AM, R. 10, F 60-63.
12. Dehesa was proposed as minister of the interior by Limantour. Díaz is
    supposed to have rejected the nomination. See Prida, *From Despotism
    to Anarchy*, p. 29; Baerlein, *Mexico the Land of Unrest*, p. 251. Limantour
    himself claims that it was Díaz who wanted Dehesa in the Cabinet.
    He (Limantour) opposed this move since it meant serving with Dehesa.
    Instead, he wanted Díaz to make a clean sweep and remove all the
    Científicos. Limantour, *Apuntes sobre mi vida pública*, pp. 242-47.
13. Smith, *Labyrinths of Power*.
14. Rice, "The Porfirian Political Elite," p. 19. The Convention was held
    at the behest of veteran politician Rosenda Pineda for the purpose of
    nominating Díaz for the presidency; see Cosío Villegas, *Historia moderna*,

v. 9, pp. 655, 663; cf. Roeder, *Hacia el México*, v. 2, p. 97, who sees the
Convention as an "economic conference disguised as a political one;"
Breyman, "The Científicos."

15. Rice, "The Porfirian Political Elite," p. 22; for the Manifesto, see Manero,
El antiguo régimen, pp. 286-96, and Díaz Dufoo, *Limantour*, p. 229. Knight,
Mexican Revolution, v. 1, p. 24, argues that the Científicos were dependent
on Díaz and not the other way around. This argument is partially true, but
does not explain Díaz's stubborn adherence to the Díaz-Corral formula
in the 1910 election. There is still considerable controversy as to whether
the Científicos were a political group or not. For a discussion of them,
see Cosío Villegas, *Historia moderna*, v. 9, pp. 335-338; Breyman, "The
Científicos," pp. 91-97, and Limantour, *Apuntes*, pp. 21-22. Limantour,
Apuntes, pp. 14-17, discusses their ideology.

16. Cockroft, *Intellectual Precursors*, p. 59; cf. Manero, *El antiguo régimen*, p. 299,
who gives the date of its demise as 1893, and Limantour, *Apuntes*, p. 21,
who claims little participation in the Union as well as with the Científicos.
Lopez Portillo y Rojas, *Elevación y caída*, p. 212. It has been asserted that
there were in essence two groups: the larger group of supporters and
those close to power, such as Limantour. See Breyman, "The Científicos,"
pp. 91-97.

17. Breyman, "The Científicos," pp. 91-97. See Zea, *Positivism in Mexico*, and
Hale, *The Transformation of Mexican Liberalism*, for a discussion of Barreda.

18. Cumberland, *Mexican Revolution*, v. 1, p. 11.

19. Zea, *Positivism*, pp. 236-37.

20. Bryan, "Mexican Politics," p. 47; Trens, *Historia de Veracruz*, v. 8, p. 339;
Reyes, *De mi vida*, v. 1, pp. 20-21. Foreign observers are of the opinion
that this feeling was widespread in Mexico. See Macleay to Grey, 6 Jan.
1910, FO, 371/926:40.

21. Cosío Villegas, *Historia moderna*, v. 9, p. 434; Roeder, *Hacia el México*, v. 2.,
p. 111. Roeder argues that actual power passed to Limantour in 1896
with Díaz's dependency on Limantour's financial wizardry. Cf. Valadés, *El
porfirismo*, v. 1, p. 53, who claims that Díaz was upset by the death of
his father-in-law, who had been his guiding hand and was so fearful of
Mexico's future after his own death that he began to concern himself with
the problem of a presidential successor.

22. Beals, *Porfirio Díaz*, p. 330, remarks that "into their hands fell the contracts
for paving, lighting, local railways, roads. Mostly lawyers, they were the
legal representatives of the powerful foreign companies; they arranged
the banking and industrial concessions, secured special favours, expedited
legal procedures and milked all the teats of the cow."

23. López Portillo, *Elevación y caída*, pp. 20, 212; Sánchez Garrito Murquía,
El antireeleccionismo, p. 67. Garrito's assertion that "situation and adequate
persons seemed to appear just when Díaz needed them "and that "he
developed the perfect plan" to oppose Limantour with Baranda and
Dehesa smack too much of fate as well as conspiracy to be acceptable;
Cosío Villegas, *Historia moderna*, v. 9, p. 853; Anderson, *The Mexican
Textile Labour Movement*, p. 27. Anderson argues that Díaz relied on the
Científicos only for economic and not for political decisions. Why he
makes this distinction is not clear, since both areas are closely allied.
The statement also does not appear to be correct; Anderson, *The Mexican
Textile Labour Movement*, pp. 23-24.

24. Limantour, *Apuntes*, pp. 105-17; cf. Valadés, *Historia de un régimen*, v. 1, p. 55, who claims that Limantour was so certain that he would be named successor that he went to Europe on a trip.
25. Bellingeri and Gil Sánchez, "Las estructuras agrarias," p. 312.
26. Braderman, *A Study of Political Parties*, p. 20; Valadés, *El porfirismo*, v. 1, p. 57.
27. Beals, *Porfirio Díaz*, p. 353; Roeder, *Hacia el México*, v. 2, p. 202.
28. Cosío Villegas, *Historia Moderna*, v. 9, pp. 434, 505; *El Diario del Hogar*, 20 Oct. 1908, p. 3.
29. Cumberland, *Mexican Revolution*, v. 1, pp. 69, 85.
30. Ibid., pp. 433, 753.
31. Cosío Villegas, *Historia moderna*, v. 9, p. 615; De Fornaro, *México tal cual es*, pp. 23, 128.
32. Dehesa to Díaz, 18 Mar. 1903, CPD, L28:3611-12; Cosío Villegas, *Historia moderna*, v. 9, p. 615. For parts of Bulnes's speech see Roeder, *Hacia el México*, v. 2, p. 146ff; Bulnes, quoted in Roeder, *Hacia el México*, v. 2, p. 155.
33. Díaz to Dehesa, 21 Sep. 1903, AGVC-ATD; Dehesa to Díaz, 21 Sep. 1903, AGVC-ATD; Alcolea to Dehesa, 18 Nov. 1903, AGVC-ATD, File #14; Muñoz to Sentíes, 19 Nov. 1903, AGVC-ATD, File #14; Sentíes to Muñoz, 19 Nov. 1903, AGVC-ATD, File #14; Dehesa to Alcolea, 21 Nov. 1903, AGVC-ATD, File #14.
34. Alcolea to Dehesa, 22 Nov. 1903, AGVC-ATD, File #14; Díaz to Dehesa, 23 Nov. 1903, AGVC-ATD, File #14.
35. Alcolea to Dehesa, 1 Dec. 1903, AGVC-ATD, File #14; Dondé to Dehesa, 1 Dec. 1903, AGVC-ATD, File #14; Dehesa to Díaz, 1 Dec. 1903, AGVC-ATD, File #14; Díaz to Dehesa, 2 Dec. 1903, AGVC-ATD, File #14; Muñoz et al. to Dehesa, 2 Dec. 1903, AGVC-ATD, File #14; Alcolea to Dehesa, 3 Dec. 1903, AGVC-ATD, File #14.
36. Cosío Villegas, *Historia moderna*, v. 9, pp. 767-68; cf. Roeder, *Hacia el México*, v. 2, p. 382; Dehesa to Baranda, 4 Mar. 1908, AGVC-ATD, File #16.
37. Baranda to Dehesa, 10 Mar. 1908, AGVC-ATD, File #16; Dehesa to Díaz, 4 Apr. 1908, AGVC-ATD, File #16; Dehesa to Miguel Cárdenas, 12 May 1908, AGVC-ATD, File #15; Dehesa to Obregón González, Enrique Creel et al., 12 May 1908, AGVC-ATD, File #15; Creel to Dehesa, 29 Jun. 1908, CPD, L33:9100; González to Dehesa, 29 Jul. 1908, CPD, L33:11027; Cosío Villegas, *Historia moderna*, v. 9, p. 772.
38. Roeder, *Hacia el México*, v. 2, p. 406.
39. Ibid., p. 404; *El Diario del Hogar*, 20 Oct. 1908, republished the "controversial" part of the interview.
40. *El Diario del Hogar*, 27 Oct. 1908; *El Diario del Hogar*, 20 Oct. 1908.
41. Váquez Gómez, *Memorias políticas*, pp. 20-21; Zilli, *Historia sucinta*, p. 130; Beals, *Porfirio Díaz*, p. 409.
42. De los Monteros to Dehesa, 3 Nov. 1909, CPD, File #15.
43. De Pallares, *Dehesa*, p. 181; see especially her interview with José Vasconcelos, who was a member of the Anti-Re-electionists, p. 176.
44. Dehesa, "April de 1910," AGVC-ATD.
45. Ibid.; Madero to Díaz, 26 May 1910, *La Opinión* (Texas), 18 Feb. 1934, pp. 1, 8, cited in Cumberland, *Mexican Revolution*, v. 1, p. 105.
46. Cumberland, *Mexican Revolution*, v. 1, p. 105; Beals, *Porfirio Díaz*, p. 415, goes as far as asserting that Félix Díaz and Dehesa gave Madero a timely warning. As far as could be ascertained, it seems that Díaz merely refused

to serve the warrant for Madero's arrest. See Licéaga, *Félix Díaz*, p. 33, who claims that Corral ordered Félix Díaz to apply the *Ley Fuga* and that Díaz refused, telling Corral to give him the order in writing; De Pallares, *Dehesa*, p. 181; the bulletin announcing Madero's meeting in Orizaba, May 1910, is in CPD, L35:6601; García Granados, *Historia de Mexico*, v. 4, p. 97.

47. Dehesa to Díaz, 2 Jun. 1910, CPD, L35:8655. A type written account of the interview that was published in *El Imparcial of Texas*, 19 Feb. 1915, is to be found in the AGVC-ATD; García Granados, *Historia de México*, v. 4, p. 109, cites a letter from Madero to Váquez Gómez dated 15 Jun. 1910, in which Madero stated that if Díaz ran with an independent candidate rather than with a Científico, he would win and the revolution would not occur. Cumberland, *Mexican Revolution*, v. 1, p. 113, and Knight, *Mexican Revolution*, v. 1, p. 75, both assert that it was Váquez Gómez's idea to promote Dehesa because of the former's fears after Madero's arrest. Knight concludes that "Madero would have none of it." This was true after Madero's arrest. It certainly does not reflect Madero's stance prior to that event.

48. Dehesa to Díaz, 2 Jun. 1910, CPD, L35:8652-59.

49. Henderson, *Félix Díaz*, p. 22; cf. Limantour, *Apuntes*, pp. 167-68, who also felt that Dehesa was the president's favourite; Tower to Grey, 20 Jun. 1910, FO, 371/928:9-15. Other observers agree. See Pedro Mora Beristain in *El Dictámen*, 8 May 1944, in AGVC-ATD, "Memorias"; Tower to Grey, 24 Jun. 1910, FO 371/926:42-46.

50. Manifesto of the NPC printed in González Ramírez, Prologue to *Epistolario y textos*, pp. 86-90.

51. García Granados, *Historia de México*, v. 4, p. 100; the British Embassy agreed, adding that Dehesa's candidature was "treated with levity from the start." They don't, however, say by whom. See Tower to Grey, 31 Dec. 1910, FO 371/1149:380; López Portillo, *Elevación y caída*, p. 453; De Pallares, *Dehesa*, p. 186; Manero, *El antiguo régimen*, pp. 315-16.

52. Váquez Gómez, *Memorias políticas*, p. 57; Luther Ellsworth (U.S. Consul General) to Minister of State, 20 Sep. 1910, USDS, 812.00:406.

53. *México Nuevo*, 18 Apr. 1910, p. 1; Cumberland, *Mexican Revolution*, v. 1, p. 113.

54. Cumberland, *Mexican Revolution*, v. 1, p. 113; López Portillo, *Elevación y caída*, p. 453.

55. Macleay to Grey, 6 Jan. 1910, FO, 371/926:40; *El Diario*, 6 Apr. 1911, p. 1.

56. *El Heraldo Mexicano*, 4 Apr. 1911, p. 1, in AEM, Tomo 1, #141.

57. Guerra, *México*, v. 2, pp. 149, 207; *México Nuevo*, 4 Apr. 1910, p. 2; 12 Apr. 1910, p. 3; Sánchez Azcona, *Apuntes*, p. 47.

58. *El Debate*, 2, 6, 16 Jul. 1910, p. 1; Elsworth to Minister of State, 20 Sep. 1910, USDS, 812.00:406; Limantour, *Apuntes de mi vida*, p. 168.

59. Dehesa to Muñoz, 3 Oct. 1910, CPD, L35:15355-57; García Galván to Pineda, CPD, L35:15358-59; Zugasti to Dehesa, 24 Sep. 1910, CPD, L35:13412; Dehesa to Muñoz, 3 Oct. 1910, CPD, L35:13413; *El Diario* (Mexico City), 28 Sep. 1910.

60. Cumberland, *Mexican Revolution*, v. 1, p. 121.

61. For these biographical details see Corzo Ramírez, González Sierra and Skerritt, *...nunca un desleal*, pp. 13-16. For Madero's campaign tours, see Cumberland, *Mexican Revolution*, v. 1, pp. 70-100; Estrada Reynoso, *La revolución*, pp. 141-87, 217-29; Palavicini, *Mi vida revolucionario*, pp. 25-42, and Ross, *Francisco I. Madero*, pp. 65-94. Pasquel, *La revolución*, pp. 159-162.

62. Katz, *The Secret War*, p. 133.
63. Cumberland, *Mexican Revolution*, v. 1, pp. 71-72. Pasquel, *La revolución*, p. 159, claims that the first Veracruz Anti-Re-electionist club was founded by Gavira and Tapia.
64. Francisco Vázquez Gómez had a small ranch near Coatepec and was well known in this area of Veracruz. See Pasquel, *La revolución*, p. 159.
65. Manzur Ocaña, *La revolución permanente*, pp. 40-42; The other signatories were either already or were to become important Veracruzan revolutionaries: Rafael Tapia, Miguel Aguilar, Enrique Bordes Mangel, Miguel Alemán, José Tapia, Pedro Gabay, Severino Herrero Moreno, Vicente F. Escobedo, Petronilo O.García, Marcelino L Caamaño, Clemente Gabay, and Miguel Contreras. The intellectual author of this somewhat vague but enthusiastic document was Enrique Bordes Mangel. See Pasquel, *La revolución*, p. 161.
66. Manzur Ocaña, *La revolución permanente*, p. 43; Corzo Ramírez et al., *...nunca un desleal*, pp. 19-20.
67. Macedo to Dehesa, 17 Nov. 1910, AGN-GOB 4a/911/(22)/4; Pasquel, *La revolución*, p. 156; *El Heraldo Mexicana*, 19 Nov. 1910, p. 5. Tapia was a saddler from Orizaba who had worked in the textile factory. He was one of the original Anti-Re-electionists and founder of a Maderista political club there.
68. Gavira, *Su actuación*, pp. 24-25; del Castillo, *Puebla y Tlaxcala*, p. 47.
69. Cumberland, *Mexican Revolution*, v. 1, chap. 6.
70. Cicular signed and dated La Punta, 28 Dec. 1910, AGVC-GOB/TP, C1, #29; Gómez to Dehesa, 20 Nov. 1910, AGVC-SP/TP, C2; Gavira, *Su actuación*, pp. 28-29; Zilli, *Historia sucinta*, p. 122.
71. Hernández to Minister of Defence, Veracruz, 21 Nov. 1910, AHSDN, XI/481.5/310, C144; Manzano to Minister of War, Orizaba, 21 Nov. 1910, AHSDN, XI/481.5/310, C144; Figueroa to Dehesa Córdoba, 22 Nov. 1910; and Maas to Dehesa, Veracruz, 25 Nov. 1910, AGVC-AMI, C1; Rocha to Dehesa, Orizaba, 22 Nov. 1910, AGVC-AMI, C2; Gavira, *Su actuación*, p. 30.
72. Tamayo to Manzano, Río Blanco, 20 Nov. 1910, AHSDN XI/481.5/310, C144; Mayor of Tezango to Secretario del Gobierno, Tezango, 21 Nov. 1910, AGVC-SP/TP, C2; Amézquita to Ramírez, Río Blanco, 21 Nov. 1910, AGN-GOB 4a/911/22:4; Maas to Gobenación, Veracruz, 20 Nov. 1910, AHSDN, XI/481.5/310, C 144; Dehesa to War, Xalapa, 20 Nov. 1910, AGVC-SP/TP, C 2; Lt. Col. Tamayo to Col. Manzano, 20 Oct. 1910, AHSDN, XI/481.5/310, C 144; Mayor of Tezango to Dehesa, 21 Oct. 10, AGVC-SP/TP, C 2; *El Heraldo Mexicano*, 21 Oct. 1910, p. 1; Cabo Amézquita to Gen. Ramírez, 21 Oct. 1910, AGN-GOB/PR, 4/15:359; Dehesa to JP Huatusco, 21 Oct. 1910, AGVC-SP/TP, C2. Dehesa was trying to reassure the JP because of rumours that Huatusco to the south was going to be attacked as well. He attributed the rumours to a nervous telephone clerk in Orizaba; Gen. Maas to Minister of War, 20 Oct. 1910, AHSDN, XI/481.5/310, C 144.
73. Tower to Grey, Mexico, 23 Nov. 1910, FO, 371/928:210-212; the arrested workers were Darío Ruíz, Onofre García, Isabel Gómez, and Concepción Peña. See Luque to Minister of War, Orizaba, 23 Nov. 1910, AHSDN XI/481.5/310, C144; the arrested Maderista was Enrique Cipriano. The woman was not identified. See Luque to Minister of War, Orizaba, 23 Nov. 1910, AHSDN, XI/481.5/310, C 144. The U.S. consul in Veracruz reported that the attacks had not disrupted commerce or shipping and that the government was coping adequately. See Canada to Minister of State, Veracruz, 23 Nov. 1910, USDS, 812.00:539.

74. Army HQ, Veracruz to Minister of War, 21 Oct. 1910, AHSDN, XI/481.5/310, C 144; Col. Manzano to Minister of War, 21 Oct. 1910, AHSDN, XI/481.5/310, C 144; *El Heraldo Mexicana*, 22 Nov. 1910, p. 1; Tower to Grey, 23 Nov. 1910, FO, 371/928:210-12; Gen. Luque to Minister of War, 23 Nov. 1910, AHSDN, XI/481.5/310, C 144; Gen. Luque to Minister of War, 23 Nov. 1910, AHSDN, XI/481.5/310, C 144; Canada to Minister of State, 23 Nov. 1910, USDS, 812.00:539.

75. Skerritt Gardner, *Rancheros sobre tierra fértil*, p. 68; Kight, *Mexican Revolution*, v. 1, Ch. 4, concentrates too much on the north, neglecting what was happening in Veracruz. In addition, he jumps from November 1910 to December or even January, thus distorting the picture of the increasingly popular revolution.

76. Gómez to Sec. Gob, Orizaba, 30 Dec. 1910, AGVC-AMI, C 2; *El Heraldo Mexicano*, 30 Dec. 1910, p. 4; Dehesa to Figuerao, Xalapa, 30 Dec. 1910, AGVC-AMI, C 1; General Maas to Dehesa, Veracruz, 31 Dec. 1910, AGVC-AMI, C 1; Various to Dehesa, 23-30 November, "Novedades," AGVC-AMI, C. 2.

77. Ministry of Communications and Public Works to Dehesa, 3 Dec. 1910, AGVC-SP/TP, C 2; Félix González to Porfirio Díaz, 6 Dec. 1910, CPD, L 36, C 1:000097; Gen. Maas to Porfirio Díaz, 10 Dec. 1910, CPD, L 35, C 42:02083.

78. Zilli, *Historia sucinta*, p. 122; on December 14 the Interior ministry sent orders to Chicontepec to arrest Pedro Gambay (this is a misspelling for Gabay) and others for rebellion. See JP Chicontepec to Gob., 14 Dec. 1910, AGVC-SP/TP, C 3.

79. Rocha to Dehesa, Orizaba, 3 Dec. 1910, AVC-GOB/AMI, C 2; *El Diario*, 4 Dec. 1910, p. 6; Maas to Díaz, 10 Dec. 1910, CPD, L 35, C 42:020833; *El Diario*, 11 Dec. 1910, p. 4; *El Diario*, 9 Dec. 1910, p. 8; *El Heraldo Mexicano*, 6 Dec. 1910, p. 1; Hinojosa to Dehesa, 5 Dec. 1910, AGVC-Q, C 12.

80. Manifesto signed by Rafael Tapia, 28 Dec. 1910, CONDUMEX, cited in Corzo Ramírez et al., *...nunca un desleal*, p. 20; AGVC-SP/TP, C 1:29. The others were R. Garnica N. Jr., A. Portas, Teódulo Córdoba, Pedro Mesa, Antonio Contreras, A. Estrada, Julián Hernández, Domingo Calixto, Teófilo Medina, Juan Ramírez, Miguel Contreras, H. Cárdenas, and Fernando Cueto. Some of these men would later be engaged in the attempt to overthrow the Huerta regime.

81. Dehesa to Maas, Xalapa, 29 Dec. 1910, AGVC-AMI, C 1; Gómez to Gobernación, Orizaba, 30 Dec. 1910, AGVC-AMI, C 2; *El Heraldo Mexicano*, 30 Dec. 1910, p. 4.

82. Cosío to Commander, 9th Zone, Mexico, 13 Jan. 1911, AHSDN, XI/481.5/311, C144:4; Merodio to Gobernación, Juchitan, 24 Jan. 1911, AHSDN, XI/481.5/311, C144:51; *El Diario*, 11 Feb. 1911, p. 3.

83. Agetro, *Luchas proletarias*, pp. 34-35.

84. Meyers, "Mexican Liberal party," p. 337; Sánchez Lamego, *Historia militar*, v. 2, p. 292.

85. *La Patria*, 28 Jan. 1911, p.4; 30 Jan. 1911, p.1; Dehesa to Díaz, Xalapa, 12 Feb. 1911, CPD, L36, C7:3304-6.

86. Cumberland, *Mexican Revolution*, v. 1, pp. 125-126; LaFrance, *Mexican Revolution*, p. 59; Knight, *Mexican Revolution*, v. 1, pp. 174-75.

87. Knight *Mexican Revolution*, v. 1, p. 175, resserts this traditional interpretation.
88. Knight, *Mexican Revolution*, v. 1, p. 175, uses the term *foco* in regard to the rebel groups in Chihuahua and Durango. Cosío to Commander, 9th Zone, Mexico, 13 Jan. 1911, AHSDN, XI/481.5/311, C144:4; Camacho to Dehesa, Acayucan, 13 Jan. 1911, CPD, L36. C3:1012-13.
89. González Molina, *Catálogo*, p. xv; Figueroa to Dehesa, 2 Jan. 1911, AGVC-AMI, C. 1; *El Diario*, 3 Jan. 1911, p. 1; 6 Jan. 1911, p. 1; Dehesa to Figueroa, 3 Jan. 1911, AGVC-AMI, C 2; Dehesa to Figueroa, 4 Jan. 1911, AGVC-AMI, C 1. Tapia was actually operating around the village of San Juan de la Puente, just outside Córdoba, where he had lived as a young saddler's apprentice. He therefore knew the area and its inhabitants well. See Tapia, *Mi participación*, pp. xiii-xiv and pp. 19ff.
90. *El Diario*, 15 Jan. 1911, p. 1; *El Heraldo Mexicano*, 11 Jan. 1911, p. 1; 12 Jan. 1911, p. 1; 14 Jan. 1911, p. 1.
91. Tapia, *Mi participación*, p. 35; *El Diario*, 14 Jan.1911, p. 1; Gómez to Díaz, 21 Jan. 1911, CPD, L36, C1:158; Rojón to Corral, Teziutlán, 19 Jan. 1911, AGN-GOB/PR; Dehesa to Gómez, 23 Jan. 1911, AGVC-AMI, C2; for example, see *El Diario*, *El Heraldo Mexicano*, *El Imparcial*; for local newspapers see *El Dictámen* of Veracruz.
92. Sánchez Lamego, *Historia militar*, v. 1, p. 288; *El Diario*, 21, 22 Feb. 1911, p. 1; Portepetit to Dehesa, 24 Feb. 1911, AGVC-AMI, C1.
93. Dehesa to Vela, 21 Feb. 1911, AGVC-AMI, C1; Portepetit to Gobernación, 24 Feb. 1911, AGN-GOB, 4a/911(22)4; *El Diario*, 25 Feb. 1911, p. 3; 26 Feb. 1911, p. 3; Tapia, *Mi participación*, pp. 29-30.
94. Maas to Díaz, 27 Feb. 1911, CPD, L36, C8:3890; Maas to Sec. Gob., 28 Feb. 1911, AHSDN, XI/481.5/311, C144:74.
95. Unsigned to Sec. Gob., Xalapa, 1 Jan. 1911, AGVC-SP/TP, C 4; Dehesa to Castillo, Xalapa, 13 Mar. 1911, AGVC-SP/TP, C 4; Com. Mil. to Sec. Gob., Veracruz, 17 Mar. 1911, AHSDN, XI/481.5/311, C 144:83; Maas to Sec.Gob., Veracruz, 1 May 1911, AHSDN, XI/481.5/311, C144:123; *El Dictámen*, 6 Mar. 1911, p. 1.
96. *El Dictámen*, 25 Feb. 1911, p. 1; *El Heraldo Mexicano*, 7 Mar. 1911, p. 2; *El Diario*, 28 Mar. 1911, p. 3; Robles Domínguez to Zamora, Mexico, various letters, AGN-ARD, T5, E25.
97. *El Heraldo Mexicano*, 7 Mar. 1911, p. 2; there were only eighteen armed events in the whole of Mexico in January, a number that increased to forty-one by March. There was, however, an increase in the extension of territory. Veracruz and Durango joined Sonora and Coahuila, the only other non-northern states to register significant revolutionary activity in January. See Instituto Nacional de Estudios Históricos de la Revolución Mexicana, *Triunfo de la Revolución Maderista*, p. 22.
98. Unsigned to Díaz, Veracruz, 18 Feb. 1911, CPD, L36, C5:002098; see Garciadiego, "Gaudencio de la Llave," for a study of this colourful, porfirian soldier.
99. See Vanderwood, *Disorder and Progress*, pp. 101-2 for a discussion of recruitment practices.
100. Inspector General to corps commanders, Mexico, 4 Apr. 1911, AGN-CR, Insp. Gen:472; Lozano to Ramírez, Mexico, 10 Apr. 1911, AHSDN, XI, 481.5/311, C144:84-86; Ramírez to Sub. Sec. *Despacho*, Mexico, 21 Apr. 1911, AGN-CR, Insp. Gen. 472.
101. *El Dictámen*, 10 Mar. 1911, p. 4; 22 Mar. 1911, p. 1; 24 Mar. 1911, p. 1.

102. *La Patria* and *El Diario*, April and May, 1911; Knight, *Mexican Revolution*, v. 1, p. 204; Gavira, *Su actuación*, pp. 32-39; González Marín, *Heriberto Jara*, p. 77.
103. Technically, Knight, *Mexican Revolution*, v. 1, p. 205, is correct. They failed to overthrow the regime on November 20, 1910. But why emphasize this unimportant fact?
104. Tapia, *Mi participación*, pp. 25-30; Sánchez Lamego, *Historia militar*, v. 1, p. 286.
105. The term *foco* was first popularized by French journalist Regis Debray in regards to Che Guevara's 1960s operation in Bolivia.
106. Until this date, and despite the extensive military activity, there had been no general uprising. That only occurred on May 24 after Díaz announced his resignation. See Cosío Villegas, *Historia moderna*, v. 9, p. 907.
107. The account was written by Sentíes and verified by Huerta. It was Dehesa's attempt to pin the blame for the government's capitulation on Limantour, the leader of the Científicos. The correspondence on this exchange is in the Dehesa archive. See letters between Sentíes and Dehesa, 20 Jan. 1912, AGVC-ATD, #350; 8 Feb. 1912, AGVC-ATD, #351-52; 11 Feb. 1912, AGVC-ATD, #353. The account itself is from 24 Mar. 1912, AGVC-ATD, #355-60; Limantour apparently owned a large number of fine horses.
108. Tapia, *Mi participación*, p. 29; Tapia engaged seventy-five Rurales at Peña Blanca on January 2, 1911. General Poucel chased him thereafter, with over three hundred federals, without luck. See Sánchez Lamego, *Historia militar*, v. 3, pp. 287-88; de la Llave to Díaz, Orizaba, 31 Jan. 1911, CPD, L36, C6:2566.
109. *El Diario*, 27 Feb. 1911, p. 1; LaFrance, *Mexican Revolution*, pp. 66-67; *El Dictámen*, 24 Mar. 1911, pp.1, 2.
110. Instituto Nacional de Estudios Históricos de la Revolución Mexicana, *Triunfo de la revolución*, p. 22; Womack Jr., *Zapata*, p. 75.
111. In Izucar de Matamoros the JP and his family were forced to flee under the threat of a popular tribunal. See *El Heraldo Mexicano*, 7 Mar. 1911, p. 2; *El Diario*, 28 Mar. 1911, p. 3.
112. *El Dictámen*, 6 Mar. 1911, p. 1; Melgarejo to Sec. Gob., 9 Mar. 1911, AHSDN, XI/481.5/311, C 144:77; *Gil Blas*, 15 Mar. 1911, p. 4, reports the number as only fourteen; Dehesa to JP Jalacingo, Xalapa, 10 Mar. 1911, AGVC-SP/TP, C 3; Castillo to Dehesa, Tlacolulam, 10 Mar. 1911, AGVC-SP/TP, C 4; *El Dictámen*, 17 Mar. 1911, p. 1; Dehesa to Castillo, Xalapa, 13 Mar. 1911, AGVC-SP/TP, C 4; JP Jalacingo to Dehesa, Jalacingo, 14 Mar. 1911, AGVC-SP/TP, C 3; *El Dictámen*, 19 Mar. 1911, p. 1.
113. *El Diario*, 3, 5 Mar. 1911, p. 6; Arroyo to Gobernación, Cordoba, 12 Mar. 1911, AHSDN, XI/481.5/311, C 144:81.
114. Figueroa to Sec. Gob., Cordoba, 16 Mar. 1911, AGVC-AMI, C 1; Macedo to Dehesa, Mexico, 28 April, 1911, AGVC-AMI, C 1; Castillo to Dehesa, Naolinco, 14 Mar. 1911, AGVC-SP/TP, C 4; *El Dictámen*, 17 Mar. 1911, p. 1.
115. Manuel García to Díaz, Orizaba, 16 Feb. 1911, CPD, L36, C6:2943-44.
116. *El Dictámen*, 8 Apr. 1911, p. 1; 7 Apr. 1911, p. 1
117. *El Diario*, 26 Mar. 191, p. 2; Maas to Díaz, Veracruz, 16 Apr. 1911, CPD, L36, C15:7227; for some time the authorities had been wondering why they were unable to get information regarding Tapia's whereabouts. On March 21, a number of inhabitants were arrested in Manzanillo near San Juan

de la Punta, among them a police adjutant. See *El Dictámen*, 23 Mar. 1911, p. 1; 2 Apr. 1911, p. 1; 18 Apr. 1911, p. 4; 20 Apr. 1911, p. 4.

118. *El Dictámen*, 5 May 1911, p. 1; Espinosa to Gob., Xalapa, 27 Apr. 1911, AHSDN, XI/481.5, C 144:113-116; Espinosa to Gob., Xalapa, 24 Apr. 1911, AHSDN, XI/481.5/311, C 144:105-07; JP Zongólica to Espinosa, Zongolica, 28 Apr. 1911, AGVC-SP/TP, C 4. Espinosa was the acting governor of Veracruz.

119. Haskell to Sec. State, Mexico, 31 Mar. 1911, USDS 812.00:1157; Maas to Gob., Veracruz, 25 Apr. 1911, AHSDN, XI/481.5/311:103; JP, Los Tuxtlas to Espinosa, San Andrés. 26 Apr. 1911, AGVC-SP/TP, C4; Maas to Díaz, Veracruz, 27 Apr. 1911, CPD, L36, C15:7216; *El Diario*, 3 May 1911, p. 3; 6 May 1911, p. 2; Merodio to Gobernación, Juchitan, 6 May 1911, AHSDN, XI/481.5/311, C144:126; Haskell to Sec. State, Mexico, 12 May 1911, USDS 812.00:1786.

120. Katz, *The Secret War*, v. 1, p. 46; see Kuecker, "Land, Oil and Space," for an penetrating discussion of some of the political anomalies surrounding the development of oil fields in northern Veracruz; Secretaría del Patrimonio Nacional, *El petróleo de México*, p. 13, cited in Carillo Dewar, *Industria petrolera*, p. 33; Miller to Sec. State, Tuxpán, 15 Feb. 1911, USDS, 812.00:846.

121. *El Dictámen*, 18 Mar. 1911, p. 1; 5 May, p. 3. The description was "typical dress of Indians, i.e., *huaraches*, white trousers, large white shirt, and a cape, 'tilma'"; Alc. Mun. to Dehesa, Papantla, 17 Jan. 1911, AGVC-SP/TP, C4; JP Chicontepec to Dehesa, 29 Dec. 1910, AGVC-SP/TP, C 3; Cosío to Macedo, Mexico, 20 Jan. 1911, AGN-GOB. 4a/911/22:4.

122. Cosio Villegas, *Historia Mexicana*, v. 9, p. 896; Lieuwen, *Mexican Militarism*, pp. 9-10, reaches a similar conclusion; Castillo to Dehesa, Naolinco, 30 Apr. 1911, AGVC-SP/TP, C. 4.

123. Miller to Sec. State, Tuxpán, 15 Feb. 1911, USDS, 812.00:846.

124. Gavira, *Su actuación*, pp. 32-33.

125. Ibid. pp. 34-35; Dehesa to Maas, Xalapa, 5 May 1911, AGVC-SP/TP, C 3. It is interesting to note the different perceptions that resulted from both fear and lack of information. Dehesa thought that Gavira had three hundred men; the mayor of Altotonga reported twenty-five with sixty others guarding the entrance to the town. In reality, Gavira entered Altotonga with only twelve but left with thirty-four. Dehesa to governor of Puebla, Xalapa, 4, 5 May, 1911, AGVC-SP/TP, C 3; Dehesa to Maas, Xalapa, 5 May 1911, AGVC-SP/TP, C 3.

126. Gavira, *Su actuación*, pp. 35-36; JP, Xalapa to Gob., 10 May, 1911, AGVC-SP/TP, C 4; Gavira, *Su actuación*, p. 36, only mentions Aguilar. Other reports indicate that Garrido Huerta was also present with his men. See *El Dictámen*, 7 May 1911, p. 1; 9 May 1911, p. 2. *El Diario*, 6 May 1911, p. 3, carried a report that a certain Domínguez, nicknamed "El Gallito," with one hundred men, was part of this group.

127. JP Jalacingo to Dehesa, Jalacingo, 6 May 1911, AGVC-SP/TP, C 3; Mayor of Perote to Dehesa, Perote, 9 May 1911, AGVC-SP/TP, C 3; *El Dictámen*, 10 May 1911, p. 2.

128. JP Xalapa to Sec. Gob., Xalapa, 11 May 1911, AGVC-SP/TP, C 6; Dehesa to Maas, Xalapa, 13 May 1911, AGVC-SP/TP, C 3; *El Diario*, 13 May 1911, p. 6; 14 May 1911, p. 3; Mayor of Perote to Dehesa, 15 May 1911, AGVC-SP/TP, C 3;

129. Gavira, *Su actuación*, p. 39-40; *El Dictámen*, 20 May 1911, p. 1.

Notes to Chapter 4

1. Cosío Robelo to Tapia, Orizaba, 26 May 1911, AGN-ARD, T5 E25:65; Alvarez to Cosío Robelo, Xalapa, 1 May 1911, AGN-ARD. T5, E25:3; *El Dictámen*, 2 May 1911, p. 4.

2. López to Madero, Teocelo, 6 May 1911; various to Madero, Teocelo, 6 May 1911; López to Robles Domínguez, Teocelo, 9 May 1911, AGN-ARD, T5, E25:nn, E25:7; *El Diario*, 12 May, 1911, p. 3.

3. Manuel López to Robles Domínguez, 10, 11, 16 May 1911, AGN-ARD, T5, E25:8-28. Knight, *Mexican Revolution*, v. 1, p. 231, implies that Robles Domínguez was given this task at the end of May, or at best after the fall of Ciudad Juárez. The ARD archive, however, indicates that said activity began much earlier.

4. On this point see Womack Jr., *Zapata*, pp. 89-90.

5. *El Dictámen*, 5 May 1911, p. 3; 10 May 1911, p. 2; 13 May 1911, p. 3; *El Dictámen*, 11 May 1911, p. 1, 4; 12 May 1911, p. 1; *El Dictámen*, 13 May 1911, p. 4; 14 May 1911, p. 1; *El Diario*, 28 May 1911, p. 1.

6. Maas to Gob., Veracruz, 15 May 1911, AHSDN, XI/481.5/311, C444:161; *Gil Blas*, 16 May 1911, p. 4; JP Jalacingo to Dehesa, Jalacingo, 16 May 1911, AGVC-TP, C3; *El Dictámen*, 17 May 1911, p. 1.

7. *El Dictámen*, 16 May 1911, p. 4; 17 May 1911, p. 1.

8. Womack Jr., *Zapata*, p. 91.

9. *El Dictámen*, 8 Jun. 1911, p. 1, 14 Jun. 1911, p. 1; 15 Jun. 1911, p. 1, thought that Dehesa was so popular he would be nominated minister of finance in Madero's cabinet; Mata to Madero, Xalapa, 11 Jun. 1911, AFM R18:264.

10. *El Dictámen*, 4 Jun. 1911, p. 4; 6 Jun. 1911, p. 4; for this view, see García Granados, *Historia mexicana*, p. 177, and Prida, *From Despotism*, p. 77. Not only Mexico's upper class but foreign observers also misread the mood of the populace. See Hohler to Grey, Mexico City, 8 Jun. 1911, FO 371/1148:185-86. The other point of view was expressed by *El Sufragio Libre*, 21 Jun. 1911, p. 1, which saw Dehesa as "deceitful, friend and enemy of porfirismo, follower and opponent of Reyismo; deceitful with De la Barra, servile and humble with Madero. He ought to disappear from national politics."

11. LaFrance, *The Mexican Revolution*, chap. 4.

12. López to Robles Domínguez, Comapa, 18 May 1911, AGN-ARD, T5, E25:8-44; *El Dictámen*, 21 May 1911, p. 1; 24 May 1911, pp. 1, 4; 25 May 1911, p. 1; León and others to Madero, Zontecomatlán, 22 May, 1911, AGN-ARD, T5, E25:46-49; in Ixhuatlán, Córdoba, rebels took the town, burning the archives and naming a provisional mayor. See Maas to Gob., Veracruz, 18 May 1911, AHSDN XI/481.5/311, C144:162; Nunn to Embassy, Veracruz, 16 May 1911, FO 371/1147:282.

13. Josefa López to Zamora, Teziutlán, 20 May 1911, AGN-ARD, T5 E25:42-43; Carlos Zavala to Zamora, Teziutlán, 20 May 1911, AGN-ARD, T5 E5:42; *El Dictámen*, 16 May 1911, p. 4.

14. Maas to Gob., Veracruz, 19 May 1911, AHSDN XI 481.5/311 C144:163; Espinosa to Gob., Xalapa, 20 May 1911, AGN-GOB, PR, 5:50; Maas to Gob., Veracruz, 23 May 1911, AHSDN XI 481.5/311 C144:175.

15. Macottla to Zamora, Teziutlán, 22 May 1911, AGN-ARD T5 E25:46; C.W. to Zamora, Teziutlán, 23 May 1911, AGN-ARD T5 E25:55; *El Dictámen*, 24 May 1911, p. 1.

16. Robles Domínguez to Gavira, Mexico, 29 May 1911, AGN-ARD T5 E25:94,95,99,113; López to García, Teocelo, 30 May 1911, AGN-ARD T5 E25:140-41; Espinosa to War, Xalapa, 28 May 1911, AGVC-AMI C2; Gavira to Robles Domínguez, Córdoba, 31 May 1911, AGN-ARD T5 E25:169-71.

17. Maas to Gob., Veracruz, 30 May 1911, AHSDN XI 481.5/311 C144:1998; "Ego" to Cosío Robelo, Xalapa, 30 May 1911, AGN-ARD T5 E25:145; Cerdán to Robles Domínguez, Xalapa, AGN-ARD T5 E25:117; Aguilar to Robles Domínguez, Córdoba, 5 Jun. 1911, AGN-ARD T5 E25:197; Gavira, *Su actuación*, pp. 40-41; *El Diario*, 31 May 1911, p. 2; Carreón to Robles Domínguez, Jaltipan, 31 May 1911, AGN-ARD T5 E25:154; Ochoa to Robles Domínguez, Jaltipan, 31 May 1911, AGN-ARD T5 E25:158; Carbajal to Gobernación, Hixhuapan, 30 May 1911, AHSDN XI 481.5/311 C144:180-82; Carbajal to Robles Domínguez, Hixhuapan, 30 May 1911, AGN-ARD T5 E25:136.

18. Espinosa to Secretary of War, Xalapa, 26 May 1911, AGVC-AMI C2; Cosío Robelo to Tapia, Mexico, 26 May 1911, AGN-ARD T5 E25:65; Gavira, *Su actuación*, p. 39; Espinosa to De la Barra, Veracruz, n.d., AHUNAM-DLB C19/3:58.

19. Ramón Prida, a former Veracruz judge, and apparently no friend of Dehesa's, argues that Dehesa had full knowledge of the attack, a charge that seems unlikely. See Prida, *From Despotism*, p. 40. The rebel leadership made every effort to protect the old president. See Márquez to Robles Domínguez, Xalapa, 27 May 1911, AGN-ARD, T5 E25:85. For the ceremonies surrounding Diaz's departure, see *El Dictámen*, 1 Jun. 1911, p. 1.

20. Corzo Ramírez et al., *...nunca un desleal*, p. 23. *El Diario*, 5 Jun. 1911, p. 1, noted the "immense jubilation" of the people at the notice that Gavira and Tapia were coming to change the authorities; the local newspaper, *El Cosmopólita*, 4 Jun. 1911, pp. 1–2, however, cites the disgust of Maderistas who saw the old Porfirian authorities removed but arbitrarily replaced by others who did not enjoy the support of the people; Gavira, *Su actuación*, p. 35; Ramírez P. to Gob., Xalapa, 15 Jun. 1911, AGN-GOB 4a 911 (4)1.

21. Mata to Madero, 20 Jun. 1911, AFM, R18:264; Gavira, *Su actuación*, p. 41.

22. Alvarez to Cosío Robelo, Xalapa, 1 Jun. 1911, AGN-ARD T5 E25:176; López to García, Xalapa, 1 Jun. 1911, AGN-ARD T5 E25:175; Aguilar to Robles Domínguez, Córdoba, 5 Jun. 1911, AGN-ARD T5 E25:197; *El Diario del Hogar*, 5 Jun. 1911, p.1.

23. Mata, *Filomeno Mata*, pp. 89-90; Espinosa to Gob., Xalapa, 14 Jun. 1911, AGVC-TP C4, assuring the central government that Mata would be treated as a guest of Veracruz state.

24. Neri to Gob., Oaxaca de Juárez, 1 Jun. 1911, AHSDN XI/481.5/311, C144:199; Circular #21, 21 June, 1911, Estado de Veracruz-Llave, *Leyes y Decretos*, 1912).

25. Wilson to Secretary of State, Knox, 11 July, 1911, U.S.DS, 812.00/2219; Gen. Merodio to Secretary of Government, Xalapa, 21 Jun. 1911, AHSDN, XI 481.5/311, C144, #224-25; Merodio to Sec. Gob., 9 Jun. 1911, AHSDN, XI 481.5/311, C144, #200-201.

26. Guaripo to Robles Domínguez, Orizaba, 1 Jun. 1911, AGN-ARD T5 E25:178; Francisco Tellez et al. to Gob., 5 Jun. 1911, AGN-GOB 911 (22) 4; Tapia to Robles Domínguez, 4 Jun. 1911, AGN-ARD T5 E25:194; *El Diario*, 2 Jun. 1911, p. 4; *El Cosmopólita*, 4 Jun. 1911, p. 1.

27. *El Imparcial de Texas*, 19 Feb. 1919, p. 1; *El Dictámen*, 6 Jun. 1911, p. 1; *El Dictámen*, 20 Jun. 1911, p. 1; Mata to Madero, 20 Jun. 1911, AFM, R18, #264; *El Dictámen*, 21 Jun. 1911, p. 1.

28. Madero to Mata, 20 Jun. 1911; Madero to Aguilar, 21 Jun. 1911, AFM, R18:263, 265.

29. "Events in Xalapa," 21 Jul. 1911, AGN-SC 149/2; Nunn to Hohler (Ambassador), 3 July, 1913, FO, 371/1148:310-13.

30. Alvarez to Madero, 21 June1911, AFM, R18:85; Aguilar to Madero, 22 Jun. 1911, AFM, R18:267; Prida, *From Despotism*, p. 44; Peña to Secretary of Government, 22 Jun. 1911, AHSDN XI 481.5/311 C14:27-31; Aguilar to Madero, 22 Jun. 1911, AFM, R18:265.

31. LaFrance, *Mexican Revolution*, p. 99.

32. *El Dictámen*, 22 Jun. 1911, p. 1; *El Diario*, 23 Jun. 1911, p.1; Madero to Leycegui, 22 Jun. 1911, AFM, R18:266; Madero to Aguilar, 22 Jun. 1911, AFM, R18:267; Madero to Gavira, 23 Jun. 1911, AFM, R22:3692-93.

33. *El Diario*, 28 May 1911, p. 4.

34. Merodio to Gobernación, Juchitan, 9 Jun. 1911, AHSDN, XI/481.5/311, C144:200-201; Elena C. de Rocha et al. to Gob., Minatitlán, 15 Jun. 1911, AHSDN, XI/481.5/311, C144:211-214; Merodio to Gob., Juchitan, 1 Jul. 1911, AHSDN XI/481.5/311, C133:252.

35. Mercades to Robles Domínguez, Oluta, 1 Jun. 1911, AGN-ARD, T5 E25:185; Reyes to Robles Domínguez, Sayula, 1 Jun. 1911, AGN-ARD, T5 E25:183-84; Aguirre to Cosío Robelo, Coatzacoalcos, 1 Jun. 1911, AGN-ARD, T5 E25:177; Ochoa to Robles Domínguez, Jaltipan,, 1 Jun. 1911, AGN-ARD, T5 E25:172; Carbajal and Paredes to Robles Domínguez, Acayucan, 3 Jun. 1911, AGN-ARD, T5 E25:189. This was generally true in Acayucan. See Patraca to Robles Domínguez, Texixtepec, 5 Jun. 1911, AGN-ARD, T5 E25:192-93.

36. Miller to Sec. State, Tuxpán, 8 Jun. 1911, USDS, 812.00:2128; Aguilar to Robles Domínguez, Córdoba, 6 Jun. 1911, AGN-ARD, T5 E25:207; JP Tuxtepec to Aillaud, Veracruz, 25 Jun. 1911, AGN-GOB, 4a 911 (25)1.

37. Tapia was first named Chief and Inspector of Liberation Forces in Veracruz, then Rurales commander. Chávez to Aillaud, Mexico City, 5 Jun. 1911, AGVC-M, C1; Gobernación to Tapia, Mexico City, n.d., AGN-GOB, 4a 911 (22) 4; Circular, signed by Vázquez Gómez, 6 Jun. 1911, AGN-GOB, 1a 911 (1) 6; the army commander in the south, General Merodio, had to make a special request that original Rurales not be disbanded because of the banditry, possible caused by ex-revolutionaries, around San Juan Evangelista. In Xalapa, Governor Aillaud managed to delay the disbanding of Manuel López's men for the same reason. See Merodio to Gob., Juchitan, 13 Jun. 1911, AHSDN, XI 481.5/311 C144:205; Aillaud to Gob., Xalapa, 14 Aug. 1911, AGVC-GOB/M, C1; Aguilar to Madero, Xalapa, 30 Jun. 1911, AFM, R18:269; "Agreement," signed 11 Jul, 1911, Xalapa, AGVC-GOB/M, C1; Ruiz et al. to De la Barra, Huatusco, 30 Jun. 1911, AHUNAM-DLB, C21/7:597.

38. Vázquez Gómez to Aillaud, Mexico City, 3 Jul. 1911, AGVC-M, C1; Aillaud to Gob., Xalapa, 13 Jul. 1911, 13 Jul. 1911, AGVC-M, C1; Vázquez Gómez to Aillaud, "Estado de Fuerzas," Mexico City, 3 Jul. 1911, AGN-GOB, 4a 911-12 (12):251, 350. A complete list of the state of disbandments in all the cantons is contained in AGVC-GOB/M, C1; Chávez to Aillaud, Mexico City, 28 Jul. 1911, AGVC-M, C1.

39. Pasquel, *La revolución*, v. 1, p. 20; *La Nueva Era*, 15 Oct. 1911, p. 1; Madero to Aillaud, Mexico City, 22 Nov. 1911, AGN-FMCA, C32:24353; *El Siglo Veinte*, 29 Oct. 1911, p. 2; *La Nueva Era*, 16 Oct. 1911, p. 1; *La Nueva Era*, 13 Oct. 1911, p. 6; 10 Dec. 1911, p. 1.

40. Aillaud was petitioning the permanent Commission of Congress to convoke a special session of the Senate to deal with his removal. Aillaud to Permanent Commission, 15 Dec. 1911, AGN-GOB, 1a, 911 (22) 4; Madero to Alegre, 5 Jan. 1912, AGN-FMLC, #180. See Henderson, *In the Absence of Don Porfirio*, pp. 109-111, for a discussion of electoral practices in 1911.

41. Gen. García Peña to Veracruz governor, Xalapa, 12 Dec. 1911, AGVC-EE, C2.

42. Miller to Sec. State, Tampico, 8 Jan. 1912, U.S.DS, 812.00; *El Siglo Veinte*, 7 Jan. 1912, p. 3.

43. Alegre to Madero, Xalapa, 9 Jan. 1912, AGN-FMCA, C32 E865:24093-95.

44. Canada to Sec. of State, Veracruz, 25 Jan. 1912, USDS, 812.00:2722; Madero to Alegre, Mexico City, 29 Jan. 1912, AGN-FM, LC1:301-02. Contemporary observers and mayors and later historians felt the same. See Enrique Lobato to Madero, 29 Jan. 1912, AGN-FMCA, C21, E554-1:16697-98; Melgarejo Vivanco, *Breve historia de Veracruz*, p. 197.

45. Raúl Argudín to Alegre, Misantla, 31 Jan. 1912, AGN-FMCA, C32 E865:24143; Miller to Secretary of State, Tampico, 8 Jan. 1912, USDS, 812.00; *El Siglo Veinte*, 7 Jan. 1912; Tapia to Alegre, Córdoba, 3 Feb. 1912, AGN-FMCA, C32 E865:24145; *La Nueva Era*, 1 Mar. 1912, p. 2.

46. Cantonal reports, 23 Feb. 1912; 28 Feb. 1912, AGVC-TP, C6; Lagos Cházaro to Madero, Xalapa, 2 Mar. 1912, AGN-FM, C32 E865:24175; *La Nueva Era*, 24 Feb. 1912, p. 3; 29 Feb. 1912, p. 6; Lagos Cházaro to Madero, Xalapa, 2 Mar. 1912, AGN-FMCA, C32 E865:24175.

47. Madero to Lagos Cházaro, Mexico City, 7 Jun. 1912, AGN-FMCA, C32 E865:24200-02; *La Nueva Era*, 23 Jun. 1912, p.6; 23 Jul. 1912, p. 3; Bonilla, Jr., *El regimen maderista*, p. 24; Cantonal reports to Sec. Gob., 1 Jul. 1912, AGVC-PP, C1; Report, 12 Jul. 1912, AGN-CR, 38:429; the U.S. consul felt the same way. He relates the incident in the northern part of the state where the JP shot several citizens who were claiming the right to elect their own candidate. See Canada to Secretary of State, 23 Aug. 1912, USDS, 812.00:4779; *La Nueva Era*, 29 Jul. 1912, p. 1.

48. Gavira, *Su actuación*, p. 68; Pasquel, *La revolución*, v. 2, p. 54; Womack Jr., "The Mexican Revolution, 1910-20," p. 91.

49. Salazar to Madero, Veracruz, 20 Aug. 1912, AGN-FMCA, C20 E504:15686; Dehesa to García Peña, 11 Nov. 1912, ATD, C1:2148-50; Dehesa to García Peña, Veracruz, 26 Sep. 1912, ATD, C1:2126-28.

50. Knight, v. 2, p. 63, challenges the view proposed by Meyer about the progressive nature of Huerta's regime. See Meyer, *Huerta*, chap. 8.

51. For a thorough discussion of de la Barra's interim presidency, see Henderson, *In the Absence of Don Porfirio*.

52. Pani, *Mi contribución*, p. 22; Melgarejo Vivanco, *Breve historia*, p. 207.

53. Hohler to Grey, Mexico City, 3 Aug. 1911, FO 371/1149:34-39; Prida, *From Despotism*, p. 44; LaFrance, "Madero and the Interim Governorship"; Fernández Rojas, *La revolución mexicana*, p. 20. For a detailed discussion of this move, see also Cumberland, *Mexican Revolution*, v. 1, p. 159ff.

54. *La Mañana*, Tomo I, 9 Jul. 1911, p. 14; 22 Jun. 1911, p. 9; see Cumberland, *Mexican Revolution*, v. 1, pp. 153-154, for the details; Carlos Trejo y Lerdo

de Tejada in a speech to the Mexican Congress, 17 Oct. 1911, AGN-CREV, C2 CA24 E585; González Roa, *El aspecto agrario*, p. 273; Pani, *Mi contribución*, p. 26.

55. Fortino B. Serrano, a well-known Anti-Re-electionist, in an interview with *El Imparcial*, claimed that Madero was surrounded by "a camarilla of neo-Científicos, influenced by his family, headed up by Gustavo." See Fernández Rojas, *La revolución mexicana*, pp. 38-41.
56. *El Ahuizote*, 16 Dec. 1911, p. 7.
57. *El Ahuizote*, 2 Dec. 1911, p. 5; Madero to Palavicini, Mexico City, 16 Aug. 1909, quoted in Palavicini, *Mi vida revolucionaria*, p. 51; Licéaga, *Félix Díaz*, p. 41; De la Barra, *Memoria*, UNAM-ADLB, C3:258.
58. Unsigned to Robles Domínguez, 1 Jun. 1911, AGN-ARD, T6 E28:32; unsigned to Robles Domínguez, 20 Jun. 1911, AGN-ARD, T6 E28:60; Figueroa to Madero, 11 Nov. 1911, AGN-C.Rev., C1 CA.11 E248; unsigned to Robles Domínguez, n.d., AGN-ARD, T6 E28:165.
59. Robles Domínguez et al. to Madero, Mexico City, Oct. 1911, AGN-ARD, T7 E36:1.
60. Manifesto, Hermosillo, 30 Nov. 1911, AGN-CREV, C1 CA.12 E304; Crespo to Metra, Mexico City, 2 Aug. 1911, AGN-ARD, T6 E28:109; De la Garza Jr. to Madero, Nuevo León, 28 Jun. 1912, AGN-C. Rev., C2 CA.22 E539; *La Opinión* in *El Mañana*, Tomo 1, 20 Feb. 1912, p. 107.
61. Madero to governors (draft letter), Mexico City, n.d., AGN-RRFM, C1 E15:358.
62. Vasconcelos, *Ulíses Criollo*, p. 379; Zayas Enríquez, *The Case of Mexico*, pp. 13-32; there are numerous letters explaining Madero's agent's attempts to reassure President Taft. See Fitzgerald to Madero, Nov. 1911 to Nov. 1912, AGN-RRFM, C3 E71:2099-2125; Barrón to Madero, New York, Dec. 1911, various clippings of U.S. news reports on the Mexican situation, AGN-RRFM, C26 E680.
63. Meyer and Sherman, *The Course of Mexican History*, p. 514.
64. The estimated cost of the demolition was over one million pesos, a cost that surprised even General Durán, commanding officer of the Veracruz military garrison. See Durán to Madero, Veracruz, 6 Jul. 1912, AGN-RRFM, C15 E367-1:11879.
65. Shadle, *Andrés Molina Enríquez*, p. 59.
66. For the beginning of the myth of Madero's apostolic qualities see O'Malley, *The Myth*, chap. 2.
67. For a full discussion of this incident, including its connection to Madero's planned change of vice-presidential running mate, see LaFrance, *Mexican Revolution*, pp.120-21. LaFrance also calls Emilio Vázquez Gómez an opportunist, a charge with which there can be little disagreement; *El Dictámen*, 12 Aug. 1911, p. 1; 15 Aug. 1911, p. 1; Meraz to Insp. Gen. of Rurales, Tehuacan, 30 Aug. 1911, AGN-CR, 9/186; Rojas to Villaseñor, Tehuacan, 30 Aug. 1911, AGN-CR, 9/186; Del Pozo to Villaseñor, Puebla, 11 Sep. 1911, AGN-CR, 9/186; LaFrance, *Mexican Revolution*, p. 121; *El Dictámen*, 6 Sep. 1911, p. 1. The only connection to Molina Enríquez's Plan of Texcoco was the inclusion of Rafael Tapia's name in the so-called revolutionary tribunal that was to have been set up. See Shadle, *Andrés Molina Enríquez*, p. 46.
68. Zozoya to Sec. Gob., San Geronimo, 2 Sep. 1911, AHSDN, XI/481.5/311 C144:264; Gob. to Sec. Gob., Mexico City, 7 Sep. 1911, AHSDN,

XI/481.5/311 C144:274; Sec. Gob. to Merodio, Xalapa, 6 Oct. 1911,
AHSDN, XI/481.5/311 C144:285; Adm. del Timbre to Sec. Gob., Orizaba,
22 Sep. 1911, AGN-GOB, 1a 911(1) 12; Adm. del Timbre to Sec. Gob.,
Tuxpán, 22 Sep. 1911, AGN-GOB, 1a 911 (1) 12; Zozoya to Sec. Gob.,
San Geronimo, 2 Sep. 1911, AHSDN, XI/481.5/311 C144:265; Ambielly to
Madero, Minatitlán, 14 Nov. 1911, AGN-RRFM, C10 E249:7248; Merodio to
Sec. Gob., San Geronimo, 21 Dec. 1911, AHSDN, XI/481.5/311 C144:300.
69. Miller to Sec. of State, Tampico, 29 Aug. 1911, USDS, 812.00:2315; 10
Sep. 1911, USDS, 812.00:2359; *La Nueva Era*, 23 Sep. 1911, p. 1; *El
Dictámen*, 2 Sep. 1911, p. 1; 26 Sep. 1911, p. 1; *La Nueva Era*, 21 Jan.
1912, p. 6.
70. Cumberland, *Mexican Revolution*, v. 1, p. 170.
71. *La Nueva Era*, 26 Oct. 1911, p. 5; Hinojoso to Sánchez, Veracruz, 9
Nov. 1911, AGN-FM, C17 E414-1:13572; Acura to Madero, Xalapa, 27
Nov. 1911, AGN-FM, C25 E666:18848-50; Domínguez to Madero, Veracruz,
2 Dec. 1911, AGN-FM, C28 E801:22364; Díaz to Madero, AGN-FM, Xalapa,
C15 E371-1:12015; Aguilar to Alegre, Córdoba, 21 Dec. 1911, AGVC-TP,
C4; *The Sun Newspaper*, 20 Dec. 1911, in AGN-FM, C26 E680:19407.
72. Corzo Ramírez et al., *... nunca un desleal*, pp. 28, 30.
73. *El Dictámen*, 16 Dec. 1911, p. 1; 11 Dec. 1911, p. 1; 16 Dec. 1911, p. 1; 12
Dec. 1911, p. 1; 13 Dec. 1911, p. 1.
74. Alegre to Gobernación, Xalapa, 26 Dec. 1911, AGN-CR, 36:426; the pro-
motion of Barranco to major is found in AGN-CR, 36:426, dated 16
Nov. 1911; Alegre to Barranco, Xalapa, 5 Jan. 1912, AGN-CR, 36:426;
Gobernación to Barranco, 30 Mar. 1912, AGN-CR, 36:426; Alegre to Sec.
War, Xalapa, 2 Jan. 1912, AGN-FMCA, C32 E865:24090; Madero to Alegre,
Mexico City, 12 Jan. 1912, AGN-FMLC, 1:208; Corzo Ramírez et al.,
...nunca un desleal, p. 28.
75. General Villar sought to assure the interviewer that with the 19th and 21st
Battlions in Veracruz, and the 15th in Orizaba, a total of 2,000 soldiers,
there wasn't much to worry about. See *La Nueva Era*, 3 Jan. 1912, p. 3;
jefe político to Sec. Gob., Zongólica, 3 Jan. 1912, 4, 5 Jan. 1912, INAH-AZ,
R25 187:51, 54, 55.
76. Corzo Ramírez et al., *...nunca un desleal*, pp. 30-31.
77. *La Nueva Era*, 16 Jan. 1912, p. 6; Carranco to OC Veracruz, El Potrero, 11
Jan. 1912, AHSDN, XI/481.5/312, C145:2-5; Pérez Rivera to OC Veracruz,
Xalapa, 12 Jan. 1912, AHSDN, XI/481.5/312. Whether Aguilar himself led
this group is unclear. He was supposed to be in prison at the time for his
part in a plot to assassinate Madero. See Garciadiego, "Higinio Aguilar."
78. Alegre to Madero, Xalapa, 4 Feb. 1911, AGN-FMCA, C32 E865:24144;
Tapia to Alegre, Córdoba, 3 Feb. 1911, AGN-FMCA, C32 E865:24145; in an
article sent to *Mexico Nuevo*, dated 5 Feb. 1911, Robles Domínguez gave his
reasons. See AGN-ARD, T8 E41:1.
79. Wilson to Sec. State, Mexico City, 7 Feb. 1912, USDS, 812.00:2755,
2768, 2798; CO Veracruz to Sec. War, Veracruz, 16 Feb. 1912, AHSDN,
XI/481.5/312, C145:9; *La Nueva Era*, 20 Feb. 1912, p. 2; Wilson to Sec.
State, Mexico City, 21 Feb. 1912, USDS, 812.00:2862; Miller to Sec. State,
Tampico, 23 Feb. 1912, USDS, 812.00:2995; Durán to Sec. War, Veracruz,
24 Feb. 1912, AHSDN, XI/481.5/312 C145:12; Micaela de Gabay to Alegre,
Paso del Macho, 21 Feb. 1912, AGVC-Q, C14.

80. *La Nueva Era*, 25 Feb. 1912, p. 4; 5 Mar. 1912, p. 6; *El Dictámen*, 24 Feb. 1912, p. 1; *El Dictámen*, 20 Feb. 1912, p. 1; *La Nueva Era*, 26 Feb. 1912, p. 6.

81. Van der Goot to Nunn, Xalapa, 1 Mar. 1912, FO 371/1392:275; *La Nueva Era*, 3 Mar. 1912, p. 6.

82. Nunn to Stringer, Veracruz, 4 Mar. 1912, FO 371/1392:272-74.

83. There are few references to women in the revolution in Veracruz, not to speak of *soldaderas*. Yet women were directly involved, among other things, as soldiers. For example, one of the bands operating at this time, under the *cabecilla* (leader) José María Danantes, included among the troops five women dressed as men. See Rincón to Ramírez, Xalapa, 14 Mar. 1912, AGN-CR, 36/426; *La Nueva Era*, 5 Mar. 1912, p. 6; 8 Mar. 1912, p. 6; *El Dictámen*, 4 Mar. 1912, p. 1.

84. *La Nueva Era*, 12 Mar. 1912, p. 6; *El Dictámen*, 27 Mar. 1912, p. 1, 9 Apr. 1912, p. 1; *La Nueva Era*, 12 April, p. 6.

85. Lagos Cházaro to Madero, Xalapa, 6 Apr. 1912, AGN-FM, C32 E865:24190-91; Madero, Mexico City, 9 Apr. 1912, AGN-FM, LC2 E43; Castillo to Madero, Xalapa, 5 May 1912, AGN-FM, C27 E736-2:20893.

Notes to Chapter 5

1. Knight, *Mexican Revolution* v. 1, p. 294.

2. JP Coatepec to Sec. Gob., Coatepec, 6 May 1912, AGVC-TP C6.

3. *La Nueva Era*, 25 Apr. 1912, p. 6, 21 Jun. 1912, p. 6; Attorney General to Supreme Court, Mexico City, 25 Apr. 1912, AGN-SC, 150/58; Ramírez to Sec. Gob., Coatepec, 3 May 1912, AGVC-TP, C6; Ramírez to Sec. Gob., Coatepec, 6, 7 May 1912, AGVC-TP, C6; Maldonato to Com. Mil., Perote, 20 May 1912, AHSDN, XI/481.5/312, C145:65, 71; Com. Mil. to Sec. Gob., Veracruz, 21 Jun. 1912, AHSDN, XI/481.5/312, C145:73.

4. Canada to State Dept., Veracruz, 27 Jul. 1912, USDS, 812.00:4499.

5. Cruz Ramora to Sec. Gob., San José de Hule, 27 Apr. 1912, AGVC-Q, C13; *La Nueva Era*, 29 Apr. 1912, p. 6; reports of various *jefes políticos* to Sec. Gob., 15 May 1912, AGVC-TP, C6.

6. *El Dictámen*, 24 Feb. 1912, p. 2. Leyva soon joined the rebels as well. See *La Nueva Era*, 30 May 1912, p. 6.

7. *La Nueva Era*, 6 Mar. 1912, p. 6; 4 Apr. 1912, p. 6; Guillén to Gob., Puerto México, 13 Apr. 1912, AHSDN, XI/481.5/312, C145:510. Nicanor Pérez, from Veracruz port, was a follower of the bandit Santanón and then joined Donato Padua in the uprising at Acayucan in 1906. He was well acquainted with the area around Acayucan. See INAH, *Diccionario histórico y biográfico*, v. 7, p. 463.

8. *El Dictámen*, 16 April, 1912, p. 4; 18 Apr. 1912 p. 4; 21 April, 1912, p. 1.

9. Delgado to Sec. Gob., San Geronimo, 25 Feb. 1912, AHSDN XI/481.5/312, C145:504-06.

10. Guillén to Gob., Puerto México, 13 Apr. 1912, AHSDN XI/481.5/312, C145:510; Villegas Moreno to Gob., Acayucan, 23 Apr. 1912, AGVC-TP, C6; JP Acayucan to Sec. Gob., Acayucan, 26 Apr. 1912, AGVC-TP, C6; *El Dictámen*, 24 Apr. 1912, p. 1; 28 Apr. 1912, p. 1. Miguel Alemán was to be the father of the Mexican president of that name; JP, Minatitlán to Sec. Gob., Minatitlán, 26 Apr. 1912, AGVC-TP C6; *La Nueva Era*, 27 Apr. 1912, p. 6.

11. Castillo to Madero, Acayucan, 10 May 1912, AGN-FMCA, C27 E736-2:20894

12. Nájera y Olivier to Villegas Moreno, San Juan Evangelista, 2 May 1912, AGVC-TP, C6; Alarcón to Sec. Gob., Acayucan, 8 May 1912, AGVC-TP, C6; Castillo to Madero, Acayucan, 10 May 1912, AGN-FM, C27 E736-2:20894; *El Dictámen*, 15 May 1912, p. 1; *La Nueva Era*, 9 May 1912, p. 6; Head of Public Security to Sec. Gob., Xalapa, 10 May 1912, AGVC-TP, C6.

13. For a discussion of the make-up of Orozco's rebellion, see Knight, *Mexican Revolution*, v. 1, pp. 289ff. In general, I agree with Knight's assertion, p. 333, of the popular, not, "counter-revolutionary," nature of this unrest.

14. Salas to Sec. Gob., Acayucan, 8 May 1912, AGVC-TP, C6; Hernández to Sec. Gob., Juchitán, 12 May 1912, AHSDN XI/481.5/312,C145:21; Justice to Levi, Los Tuxtlas, 26 Jul. 1912, AGVC-M, C1.

15. Puig to Camacho, Minatitlán, 15 May 1912, AGVC-TP, C6; Camacho to HQ, 9th military zone, Xalapa, 15 May 1912, AGVC-TP, C6; Commander, 9th military zone to Sec. Gob., San Geronimo, 17 May 1912, AHSDN XI/481.5/312,C145:41; Benítez to Camacho, Minatitlán, 18 May 1912, AHSDN XI/481.5/312, C145:516-17; *El Dictámen*, 17 May 1912, p. 2. The "Melpomene" had originally been sent to Tuxpán, shipping port for El Aguila oil, and was meant to indicate British intentions to protect the interests of the W. Pearson Company For a discussion of British diplomacy during this era , see Meyer, *Su Majestad Británica*.

16. Nunn to Stringer, Veracruz, 21 May 1912, FO 371/1393:301; Canada to State Dept., 26 May 1912, USDS, 812.00:1955.

17. *La Nueva Era*, 29 May 1912, p. 6; Commander, 9th military zone to Sec. Gob., San Geronimo, 3 Jun. 1912, AHSDN XI/481.5/312, C145:48; Vivero to Sánchez Azcona, Minatitlán, 13 Jun. 1912, AGN-FMCA, C4 E101-3:2932.

18. Haskell to Sec. State, Mexico City, 20 Jun. 1912, USDS, 812.00:4254; 22 Jun. 1912, USDS, 812.00:4336.

19. Benítez to Sec. Gob., Minatitlán, 29 Jul. 1912, AHSDN XI/481.5/312, C145:119, 123, 129; Commander, 8th. military zone to Sec. Gob., Tuxtepec, 29 Jul. 1912, AHSDN XI/481.5/312, C145:95; Krauss to Sec. Gob., Acayucan, 31 Jul. 1912, AGVC-M, C1.

20. Flores Magón to Camacho, Mexico City, 17 May 1912, AGVC-TP, C6; Camacho to Flores Magón, 17 May 1912, AGVC-TP, C6; Tapia to Flores Magón, Orizaba, 17 May 1912, AGVC-TP, C6.

21. *La Nueva Era*, 11 May 1912, p. 6; Canada to Sec. State, Veracruz, 18 May 1912, USDS, 812.00:4048; *La Nueva Era*, 5 Jun. 1912, p. 6. Sometimes it was difficult to decide whether armed groups were rebels or bandits, since both existed, especially in the south. García was considered a rebel but led only a small troop of ten men. See *La Nueva Era*, 18 May 1912, p. 6.

22. *La Nueva Era*, 29 Jul. 1912, p. 6; Camacho to JP Cosamaloapan, Xalapa, 2 Aug. 1912, AGVC-M, C1.

23. *La Nueva Era*, 1, 18, 22, 31 May 1912, p. 6; Gob. to Sec. Gob., Mexico City, 14 May 1912, AGVC-TP, C6; García Bravo to Sec. Gob., 30 Jul. 1912, AGVC-M, C1.

24. Camacho to Sec. Finance, Xalapa, 30 Jul. 1912, AGN-PR, C38, E 16; Urutia to Camacho, Córdoba, 31 Jul. 1912, AGVC-M, C1.

25. Landa to Camacho, Huatusco, 31 Jul. 1912, AGVC-M, C1; Melén to Camacho, Soledad, 31 Jul. 1912, AGVC-M, C1; Dardón to Huerta, Xalapa, 21 Jun. 1912, AGVC-Q, C15; Gamargo to Madero, Misantla, 20 Jun. 1912, AGN-FM, C12, E291-1:9196-99; JP, Misantla to Camacho, Misantla, 18, 22 May 1912, AGVC-TP, C6; cf. Knight, *Mexican Revolution*, vol.1, pp. 365-66,

who remarks "that the region gave no support to Gavira's rebellion
in the spring of 1912," a statement that is largely true but induces a
generalization of subsequent quiescence for the canton of Misantla, which
is misleading.

26. Grajales to Camacho, Jalacingo, 31 Jul. 1912, AGVC-M, C1; Lagos Cházaro
to Madero, Xalapa, 9, 14 Mar. 1912, AGN-FM, C32, E865:24181-82, 24186;
Canada to State Dept., 8 Apr. 1912, USDS, 812.00:1247; Vázquez to
Camacho, Tuxpán, 2 Jun. 1912, AHSDN XI/481.5/312, C145:52-53.

27. JP Chicontepec to Camacho, Chicontepec, 29 Apr. 1912, 24 May 1912,
AGVC-TP, C6.

28. Urrutia to Sec. Gob., Córdoba, 1, 2, 3 Aug. 1912, AGVC-M, C1; Leví
to Gob., Xalapa, 1, 2 Aug. 1912, AGVC-M, C1; Leví to Celso Vega, 3
Aug. 1912, AGVC-M, C1; Van der Groot to Stronge, Xalapa, 29 Jul 1912,
FO 371/1394:60; 3 Aug. 1912, FO 371/1394:47-49; 14 Aug. 1912, FO
371/1394:78; Sec. Gob., Xalapa to Gob., 5 Aug. 1912, AGVC-M, C1.

29. *La Nueva Era*, 2 Aug. 1912, p. 1.

30. Urrutia to Leví, Córdoba, 21 Aug. 1912, AGN-FMCA, C32, E865:24287-88;
Leví to Madero, Xalapa, 21 Aug. 1912, AGN-FMCA, C32, E865:24282;
Duran to Leví, Veracruz, 21 Aug. 1912, AGN-FMCA, C32, E865:24284; Leví
to Madero, Xalapa, 22 Aug. 1912, AGN-FMCA, C32, E865:24283; Leví to
Madero, Xalapa, 23 Aug. 1912, C32, E865:24286.

31. Vallejo to Insp. Gen. Rurales, Orizaba, 24 Aug. 1912, AGN-CR, 29/405; Leví
to Madero, Xalapa, 29 Aug. 1912, AGN-FMCA, C32, E865:24290.

32. *La Nueva Era*, 14 Sep. 1912, p. 3.

33. Madero to Lagos Cházaro, Mexico City, 9 Sep. 1912, AFM, R12:337;
Domínguez to Madero, Xalapa, AGN-FMCA, C32, E865:24165; *La Nación*,
17 Sep. 1912, p. 1; Cumberland, *Mexican Revolution*, v. 1, p. 199; Lagos
Cházaro to Madero, Xalapa, 26 Sep. 1912, AGN-FMCA, C23, E608-2:17695;
La Nación, 11 Oct. 1912, p. 1.

34. Canada to State Department, Veracruz, 31 Oct. 1912, USDS, 812.00:5387;
Lagos Cházaro to Madero, Xalapa, 6 Sep. 1912, AGN-FMCA, C32
E865:24211-13.

35. Alcantra to Gob., Orizaba, 21 Sep. 1912, AGN-PR; Canada to Sec. State,
Veracruz, 30 Sep. 1912, USDS, 812.00:5191; Cejudo to Sec. Gob., San
Geronimo, 24 Sep. 1912, AHSDN, XI/481.5/312, C145:534.

36. *La Nación*, 28 Sep. 1912, p. 4; Garciadiego, "Higinio Aguilar", p. 446;
Garciadiego, "Gaudencio de la Llave," p. 17.

37. *La Nación*, 28 Sep. 1912, p. 4; Cumberland, *Mexican Revolution*, v. 1,
pp. 201-02; Canada to Sec. State, 30 Sep. 1912, USDS, 812.00:5191, 4 May
1912, 812.00:3802.

38. Sec. Gob. to Altamirano, Xalapa, 7 Oct. 1912, AZ, R25/187:15; Mayor
of Xoxocotla to Altamirano, Xoxocotla, 26 Oct. 1912, AZ, R25/187:22;
Altamirano to Sec. Gob., Zongólica, 26 Oct. 1912, AZ, R25/187:12, 28
Oct. 1912, R25/187:29; Mayor of Atlahuilco to Altamirano, Atlahuilco, 28
Oct. 1912, AZ, R25/187:25. Lagos Cházaro was not very impressed with
Altamirano's capabilities and begged Madero to replace him with a more
aggressive JP, but to no avail. See Lagos Cházaro to Madero, Xalapa, 3 Oct.
1912, AGN-FMCA, C32, E865:24225; Cejudo to Sec. Gob., San Geronimo,
9 Oct. 1912, AHSDN XI/481.5/312, C145:538.

39. *La Nueva Era*, 1 Oct. 1912, p. 1; 4 Oct. 1912, p. 1; Camacho to Madero,
Río Blanco, 2 Oct. 1912, AGN-FMCA, C12, E295-2:9353; Stronge to Grey,
Mexico City, 4 Oct. 1912, FO, 371/1394:291; Canada to Sec. State, Veracruz,

2 Oct. 1912, USDS, 812.00:5143; Dehesa to García Peña, Veracruz, 26 Sep. 1912, ATD, C1:2126-28.

40. Stronge to Grey, Mexico City, 4 Oct. 1912, FO, 371/1394:291. De la Barra knew Aguilar well and did not think he would risk his life unless he had substantial backing. What that source was has, however, never been determined.

41. Henderson, *Félix Díaz*, p. 50; *La Nueva Era*, 12 Nov. 1912, p. 3; Womack Jr., "The Mexican Revolution," p. 91. Some contemporary observers obviously felt so as well, although there is no clear evidence. See Léon to Sánchez Azcona, 18 Nov. 12, AGN-FM, C2, E22-23:775-80; Knight, *Mexican Revolution*, v. 1, p. 475; Henderson, *Félix Díaz*, p. 66; "Basis and Opinions of Gen. F. Díaz's Revolt in Veracruz," no name, AFD, C1:82.

42. *La Nueva Era*, 13 Oct. 1912, p. 1.

43. Madero to Lagos Cházaro, Mexico City, 29 Oct. 1912, AGN-FMCA, C32, E865:24255; Henderson, *Félix Díaz*, pp. 52-53.

44. For a discussion of Díaz's anti-Científico credentials, see Liceaga, *Félix Díaz*, p. 62, and Knight, *Mexican Revolution*, v. 1, pp. 473-74.

45. Brown, *Oil and Revolution in Mexico*, p. 255; Garciadiego, "Revolución Constitutionalista y Contrarevolución," pp. 99-100; Madero to Lagos Cházaro, Mexico City, 29 Oct. 1912, AGN-FM, LC3:320.

46. "Basis y orígen," AFD, C1; Henderson, *Félix Díaz*, p. 54; Knight, *Mexican Revolution*, v. 1, p. 474; *La Nación*, 17 Oct. 1912, pp. 2-3; JP the Tuxtlas to Sec. Gob., San Andrés Tuxtla, 30 Oct. 1912, AGVC-TP, C6.

47. Henderson, *Félix Díaz*, p. 54; León to Madero, 16 Oct. 1912, AGN-RR/FM, C2 E22-3:751; Lagos Cházaro to Madero, Xalapa, 17 Oct. 1912, AGN-FMCA, C32, E865:24233-34; *La Nueva Era*, 17 Oct. 1912, p. 6.

48. Henderson, *Félix Díaz*, p. 66; García Granados, *Historia mexicana*, p. 403; Madero was apparently quite convinced that Dehesa was in on the plot, but did nothing because he had no proof. See De los Ríos to Muñoz Pérez, Xalapa, 4 Nov. 1912, INAH-FM, R11:259-60.

49. Schuyler to Sec. State, Mexico City, 17 Oct. 1912, USDS, 812.00:5255; Stronge to Grey, Mexico City, 19 Oct. 1912, FO 371/13988:85; Canada to State Dep., Veracruz, 20 Oct. 1912, USDS, 812.00:5281; Lagos Cházaro to Madero, Xalapa, 18 Oct. 1912, AGN-FMCA, C32, E865:24235-36.

50. Nunn to Stronge, Veracruz, 24 Oct. 1912, FO, 371/1398:112-17; Blanquet to Madero, Orizaba, 26 Oct. 1912, AGN-FMCA, C26, E682:19794; León to Madero, 27 Oct. 1912, AGN-RR/FM, C2, E22-3:748-50; various to Blanquet, Orizaba, 25 Oct. 1912, AGN-FMCA, C26, E682:19797; Schuyler to Sec. State, Mexico City, 23 Oct. 1912, USDS, 812.00:5333; "Basis y origen," CONDUMEX, AFD, C1.

51. Palavicini, *Mi vida revolucionaria*, p. 124; *Mexican Herald*, 16 Oct. 1912, p. 1 in INAH-AEM, T II:50; clipping from a U.S. newspaper, 19 Dec. 1912, AGN-FIM, C3, E61-1:1848; León to Azcona, Veracruz, 28 Oct. 1912, AGN-FIM, C2, E22-3:753-54; Fernández Rojas, *La revolución mexicana*, p. 250; Prida, *From Despotism*, pp. 114-15; Henderson, *Félix Díaz*, p. 56; Madero's secret agent in Veracruz, Domingo León, claimed that Corralistas and Científicos were also involved. See León to Azcona, Veracruz, 18 Nov. 1912, AGN-FIM, C2, E22-3:775-80.

52. Madero to López, 2 Nov. 1912, AGN-FM, LC3:335.

53. Licéaga, *Félix Díaz*, p. 59; Vasconcelos, *Ulíses criollo*, p. 409.

54. Ignacio Muñoz, Juicio de Amparo, Mexico City, 25 Oct. 1912, AGN-SC, C729:4483; Henderson, *Félix Díaz*, pp. 64-66. A study of the legal

implications of the court martial may be found in Melgarejo, *Breve estudio*, p. 12.

55. Vasconcelos, *Ulíses criollo*, p. 409; De los Ríos to Muñoz Pérez, Xalapa, 17 Oct. 1912, INAH-FM, R 11:237; Calero to Dehesa, Mexico City, 31 Oct. 1912, ATD, C1:2145; Henderson, *Félix Díaz*, p. 66.

56. Espinosa et al., *La decena roja*, pp. 4-9; Henderson, *Félix Díaz*, pp. 66-67.

57. Prida, *From Despotism*, pp. 120-21.

58. Ibid., pp. 117-118; Tapia to *jefe político*, Zongólica, Orizaba, 1 Nov. 1912, AZ, R25, 187:45, 46.

59. Muñoz to Altamirano, Tihuipango, 2 Nov. 1912, AZ, R25/187:38, 39. For discussions on Aguilar's dealings with Zapata, see Garcaidiego, "Higinio Aguilar," p. 451, and Womack Jr., *Zapata*, pp. 167, 212.

60. Mayor of Tlaquilpa to Altamirano, 2 Nov. 1912, AZ, R25/187:38; Altamirano to Sec. Gob., Zongólica, 2, 3 Nov. 1912, AZ, R25/187:48, 49, 52; Alfonsín to Altamirano, Orizaba, 3 Nov. 1912, AZ, R25/187:53.

61. Miller to Secretary of State, Tuxpán, 6 Nov. 1912, USDS, 812.00:5428; Beltrán to Sec. Gob., Veracruz, 11 Nov. 1912, AHSDN, XI/481.5/312, C145:1475.

62. Proclamation signed by Ismael Rosete, Acayucan, October, 1912, in AGVC-TP, C6:1830; JP the Tuxtlas to Sec. Gob., San Andrés Tuxtla, 13 Nov. 1912, AGVC-TP, C6.

63. Lagos Cházaro to Madero, Xalapa, 1 Nov. 1912, AGN-FMCA, C32 E865:24237-38.

64. Sánchez Azcona to Lagos Cházaro, Mexico, 5 Nov. 1912, AGN-FMCA, C32 E865:24240-41; Lagos Cházaro to Sánchez Azcona, Xalapa, 8 Nov. 1912, AGN-FMCA, C32 E865:24242-43.

65. Domínguez to Madero, Xalapa, 17 Nov. 1912, AGN-FMCA, C32 E865:24167-68; Canada to State Department, Veracruz, 27 Nov. 1912, USDS, 812.00:5662, 6 Dec. 1912, USDS, 812.00:5655.

66. AVISO, Xalapa, 24 Nov. 1912, AHMVC, C366 V496:35; Circular 9265, signed by Pérez Rivera, Xalapa, 7 Dec. 1912, AGVC-TP, C6; Canada to State Dept., Veracruz, 6 Dec. 1912, USDS, 812.00:5655; Pérez Rivera to Madero, Xalapa, 3 Dec. 1912, AGN-FMCA, C32 E865:24313; López to Pérez Rivera, Altotonga, 25 Dec. 1912, AGVC-Q, C14; Pérez Rivera to Madero, Xalapa, 11 Dec. 1912, AFM, R21:2629; Pérez Rivera to Madero, Xalapa, 16 Dec. 1912, AFM, R21:2631.

67. Pérez Rivera to Madero, Xalapa, 7 Dec. 1912, AFM, R21:62632.

68. Ibid.

69. Madero to Pérez Rivera, Mexico City, 10 Dec. 1912, AFM, R11:231; Pérez Rivera to Madero, 17 Dec. 1912, AFM, R21:2635; Madero to Pérez Rivera, Mexico City, 21 Dec. 1912, AFM, R21:2652.

70. *La Nueva Era*, 22 Dec. 1912, p. 5; 26 Dec. 1912, p. 5; Valle to Sec. Gob., Veracruz, 31 Dec. 1912, AHSDN XI/481.5/312, C145:503; AGN-FMCA, C18 E457-1:14601; Gob. to Pérez Rivera, Mexico City, AGVC-Q, C14.

71. Fitzgerrell to Madero, Washington, Nov. 1912, AGN-FMCA, C3 E71:2099-2125. There are countless letters between the two in this file between November 1911 and November 1912.

72. Dehesa to Calero, Veracruz, 6 Jan. 1913, AGVC-ATD, #2180; Emma Dehesa to Raúl Dehesa, Hotel Telegrafo, Havana, 6 Jan. 1913, AGVC-ATD, #22; *El Imparcial*, 18 Jan. 1913, p. 1. Teodoro Dehesa obviously had his own secret informers. From Veracruz, he was advised to proceed without delay to the U.S. His personal archive even contains the ticket for the Pullman coach from Key West to New York City, where he stayed in the Hotel Seville. See

Márquez to Dehesa, Havana, 28 Jan. 1913, AGVC-ATD, #22.
73. Lagos Cházaro to Madero, Veracruz, 19 Jan. 1913, AGN-FMCA, C23 E608-2:17714-16; Madero to Lagos Cházaro, Mexico, 23 Jan. 1913, AGN-FMCA, C23, E608-2: 17717.
74. Ocaranza to Gob., Papantla, 3 Jan. 1913, AHSDN XI/481.5/314, C146:3-6; Madero to Aguilar, Mexico City, 3 Jan. 1913, INAH-AFM, R11, C19:340; Corzo Ramírez et al., ...*nunca un desleal*, p. 36.
75. Valdés to Gob., Veracruz, 7 Jan. 1913, AHSDN XI/481.5/3144, C146:8; Canada to State Department, Veracruz, 10 Jan. 1913, USDS, 812.00:5845; Velasco to Sec. Gob., Veracruz, 17 Jan. 1913, AHSDN, XI/481.5/314, C146:55.
76. Valdés to Sec. Gob., Veracruz, 9 Jan. 1913, AHSDN, XI/481.5/314, C146:9; García Peña to Sec. Gob., Mexico City, 11 Jan. 1913, AHSDN, XI/481.5/314, C146:11; Valdés to Sec. Gob., Veracruz, 11 Jan. 1913, AHDN, XI/481.5/314, C146:12; Moreno to Velasco, Córdoba, 11 Feb. 1913, AHSDN, XI/481.5/314, C146:159. Since the beginning of January, Gaudencio de la Llave and Higinio Aguilar had joined forces. Gaudencio's son, Gaudencio Jr., was appointed Aguilar's Chief-of-staff. See Garciadiego, "Gaudencio de la Llave," p. 17.
77. Querol y Gómez to Velasco, Papantla, 3 Feb. 1913, AHSDN, XI/481.5/314, C146:129; Velasco to Min. War, Veracruz, 3, 6 Feb. 1913, AHSDN, XI/481.5/314, C146:127, 147; Ocaranza to Velasco, Papantla, 13 Jan.1913, AHSDN, XI/481.5/314, C146:35, 45.
78. JP Chicontepec to Pérez Rivera, Chicontepec, 21 Jan. 1913, AGVC-TP, C7; Ocaranza to Velasco, Papantla, 26 Jan. 1913, AHSDN, XI/481.5/314, C146:96; Valdés to Sec. Gob., Veracruz, 16 Jan. 1916, AHSDN, XI/481.5/314, C146:53; Gob. to Pérez Rivera, Mexico, City, 24 Jan. 1913, AGVC-TP, C7; Pérez Rivera to Ocaranza, Xalapa, 7 Feb. 1913, AGVC-TP, C7; Madero to Pérez Rivera, Mexico City, 10 Feb. 1913, AGVC-TP, C7.
79. Cumberland, *Mexican Revolution*, v. 1., p. 234.
80. Yeria to Pérez Rivera, Zongólica, 22 Feb. 1913, AZ, R11, 71/10; Mayor of Soledad Doblado to *jefe político*, Veracruz, 20 Feb. 1913, AHSDN, XI/481.5/314, C146:186; Cumberland, *Mexican Revolution*, v. 1, p. 240; Canada to State Dept., Veracruz, 20 Feb. 1913, USDS, 812.00:6279; De Zaldo to Inspector General, Córdoba, AGN-CR, C38:431.
81. De los Rios to Muñoz Pérez, Mexico City, 30 Jan. 1913, AFM, R11:491.
82. Commander, Military Prison of Veracruz and Ulúa to Sec. Gob., Veracruz, 31 Jan. 1913, AHSDN, XI/481.5/314, C146:134-41; Cumberland, *Mexican Revolution*, vol. 1, p. 244.
83. Various to Sec. Gob., La Antigua, 22 Jan. 1913, AGN-PR, C 1 E 18-7:1-7.
84. Pérez Rivera to JP, Xalapa, 22 Jan. 1913, AGN-PR, C 1 E 18-7:1-7; Uriarte to Sec. Gob., Córdoba, 12 Feb. 1913, AVC-GOB (Correos), C1; Rodríguez to JP, Zongólica, 16 Feb. 1913, AZ, R 11:71/7.
85. *El Imparcial*, 5 Jan. 1913, p. 1; 7 Jan. 1913, p. 1; Lagos to del Toro, Veracruz, 3 Jan. 1913, AHMVC, C367 V500:33; Lara to Gob., Veracruz, 4 Feb. 913, AGN-GOBPR, C1, E60-4:3; Domínguez to JP Orizaba, Xalapa, 8 Feb. 1913, AGVC-EE, C4; Domínguez to Hernández, 8 Feb. 1913, AGVC-EE, C4.
86. García to Pérez Rivera, Zongólica, 18 Feb. 1913, INAH-AZ, R11:71/9; Gob. to Pérez Rivera, Mexico City, 9 Jan. 1913, AGN-PR, C64 E18.
87. González Mena to Dehesa, Mexico City, 4 Jan. 1913, ATD, C 2; Dehesa to González Mena, New York, 6 Jan. 1913, ATD, C 2; Madero to Lagos Cházaro, Mexico City, 23 Jan. 1913, AGN-FMCA, C23, E608-2:17717; Calero to Dehesa, Mexico City, 21 Feb. 1913, ATD, C 1.

88. Calero to Dehesa, Mexico City, 21 Feb. 1913, ATD, C 1.
89. De Pallares, *Dehesa*, p. 234; Henderson, *Félix Díaz*, p. 93. Henderson is wrong about the relationship. Francisco was Dehesa's brother, not his son. Francisco had been, and would be, one of Díaz's chief campaign organizers in Veracruz; Dehesa's exact words were: "Los procedimientos militares subsecuentes, eran indispensible para satisfacer la aspiración nacional. Por otros medios no era posible desarraigar el mal y fue así como pudo realizarse el anhelo de todos." See Dehesa to Calero, Veracruz, 14 Mar. 1913, ATD, #2243.
90. Pasquel, *La Revolution*, v. 2, pp. 65-66; INAH, *Diccionario histórico y biográfico de la Revolución Mexicana*, pp. 463-64.
91. Manzur Ocaña, *La revolución permanente*, pp. 59-60.
92. Pasquel, "Prologo," pp. 37-38, in Tapia, *Mi participación*; *El Imparcial*, 24 Feb. 1913, p. 1.

Notes to Chapter 6

1. Meyer argues for Huerta's self-confidence. In view of Huerta's constant appeals to Díaz to return, this is doubtful. See *El Imparcial*, 7 Mar. 1913, p. 1; Dehesa to González Mena, Veracruz, 15 Mar. 1913, ATD, C2.
2. Knight provides a cogent rebuttal to Meyer's argument that the Huerta regime was "progressive." See Meyer, *Huerta*, p. 129, chap. 8; Knight, *Mexican Revolution*, v. 2, pp. 94-103.
3. Branbilla to Gob. (VC), Minatitlán, 13 Apr. 1913, AGN-GOB/PR, C95:5.
4. For a discussion of the question of "revolutionary mentality," see Koth, "People, Products and Protests."
5. Valencia to Gob. (VC), San Andrés Tuxtla, 28 Aug. 1913, AGVC-AL, C2; Huerta to Cauz, Mexico City, 9 Aug. 1913, AGVC-Q, C15.
6. Brown and Fletcher, (U.S. senators) to Gob., Washington, 23 Jun. 1913, AGN-GOB/PR, C39 E17; in August two French citizens had been murdered in Jicaltepec. See Min. of War to Gob., Mexico City, 1 Sept. 1913, AGN-GOB-PR, C83 E16.
7. Knight, *Mexican Revolution*, v. 2, p. 53. Knight's comments are meant to correct the impressions left by Heather Fowler Salamini, *Agrarian Radicalism in Veracruz*, and Romana Falcón, *El agrarianismo*, that the vigorous peasant movements of the 1920s and 1930s do not have a rural but a working-class origin.
8. Pérez Rivera to Velasco, Xalapa, 21 Feb. 1913, AHSDN XI/481.5/314, C146:192; *El Dictámen*, 22 Feb. 1913, p. 1.
9. *El Imparcial*, 27 Feb. 1913, p. 1.
10. *El Dictámen*, 11 May 1914, p. 6.
11. *El Imparcial*, Mar. 1913, p. 1; Garciadiego, "Gaudencio de la Llave," p. 21; see also González Marín, *Heriberto Jara*, p. 129.
12. Velasco to Mondragón, 2 Mar. 1913, AHSDN, XI/481.5/314, C146:196. Another version of this story relates De la Llave's attempts to recruit some workers for his corps, which backfired, causing the incident. See González Marín, *Heriberto Jara*, p. 129.
13. Canada to Sec. of State, Veracruz, 10 Mar. 1913, USDS, 812.00:6862; Garciadiego, "Gaudencio de la Llave," p. 19; González Marín, *Heriberto Jara*, p. 129; Velasco to Mondragón, Veracruz, 10 Mar. 1913, AHSDN, XI/481.5/314, C146:198-99.

14. Beezley, *Abraham González*, p. 158.
15. *El Imparcial*, 24 Feb. 1913, p. 4; 27 Feb. 1913, p. 4; Tapia, *Mi participación*, pp. 35-36.
16. Zapata Vela, *Conversaciones con Heriberto Jara*, pp. 42-43; González Marín, *Heriberto Jara*, p. 139; Martínez De la Vega, *Heriberto Jara*, p. 53.
17. Gavira, *Su actuación*, pp. 72-75; Gavira to Supreme Court, Veracruz, 27 Feb. 1913, AGN-SC, 782:928. Gavira was arrested awaiting charges on a "military" matter from Mexico City. His request for an *amparo*, based on his argument that he had never been in the army and was a civilian, was granted, ironically, on 3 Oct. 1913. He also didn't know that the U.S. consul at Veracruz, William Canada, blocked his arrest in Progreso. See Canada to Sec. of State, Veracruz, 10 Mar. 1913, USDS, 812.00:6909.
18. Manzur Ocaña, *La revolución permanente*, pp. 58-60, 69, 72; Corzo Ramírez et al., *...nunca un desleal*, pp. 38-39.
19. Pasquel, *La revolución*, pp. 71-72; Corzo Ramírez et al., *...nunca un desleal*, pp. 38-39.
20. Mayor, Zongólica to Mayor, Papantla, Zongólica, 4 Mar. 1913, AZ, R11, 71:18; *El Imparcial*, 5 Apr. 1913, p. 4; Presidential Decree #435, AGN-CR, IG:501; *El Imparcial*, 20 Mar. 1913, p. 1; Altamirano to JP, Córdoba, 30 Mar. 1913, CONDUMEX-AVC, C1/152:90; *El Imparcial*, 10 Apr. 1913, p. 4; Canada to Sec. of State, Veracruz, 8 Apr. 1913, USDS, 812.00:7054; 19 Apr. 1913, USDS, 812.00:7359.
21. *El Imparcial*, 1 Mar. 1913, p. 1.
22. Canada to State Dept., Veracruz, 16 Mar. 1913, USDS, 812.00:6707; *El Imparcial*, 12 Mar. 1913, p. 4; 6 Apr. 1913, p. 1, Mexico City, 7 Mar. 1913, AGN-GOB/PR, C82 E39:4; JP, Córdoba to Gob., Veracruz, 13 Apr. 1914, AGVC-SP/TP, C1; Citizens of Chicayán to Gob., 4 Mar. 1913, AGN-GOB/PR, C95 E11; *El Imparcial*, 23 Apr. 1913, p. 4.
23. Dehesa to Calero, Veracruz, 17 Apr. 1913, ATD, #2247; Dehesa to Rodríguez Talavera, Veracruz, 20 Apr. 1913, ATD, #32.
24. *El Imparcial*, 5 Mar. 1913, p. 4; Canada to Sec. State, Veracruz, 19 April, 1913, USDS, 812.00:7359.
25. Henderson, *Félix Díaz*, p. 93.
26. Dehesa to Rodríguez Talavera, Mexico City, 13 Apr. 1913, ATD, C2.
27. Dehesa to Rodríguez Talavera, Veracruz, 19 Apr. 1913, ATD, C2; Rodríguez Talavera to Dehesa, Mexico City, 26 Apr. 1913, ATD, C2; Dehesa to Rodríguez Talavera, Veracruz, 27 Apr. 1913, ATD, C2. An analysis of the resignation of Huerta's first cabinet is contained in Meyer, *Huerta*, pp. 141-143.
28. González Mena to Dehesa, Mexico City, 24 May 1913, ATD, C1:2296; Dehesa to González Mena, Veracruz, 28 May 1913, ATD, C1:2296; González Mena to Dehesa, Mexico City, 29 May 1913, ATD, C1:2297; Dehesa to González Mena, Veracruz, 2 Jun. 1913, ATD, C1:2392.
29. León et al. to Sehar, Cosamaloapan, 12 Mar. 1913, AGN-GOB/PR, C57:82; various to Sec. Gob., Huatusco, 21 Mar. 1913, 10 Apr. 1913, AGN-GOB/PR, C1, E26-3:1-3; AGN-CR, 36:426; Dardón to unknown, Misantla, 28 Mar. 1913, AGN-GOB/PR, C57, E82:11-12; JP Los Tuxtlas to Sec. Gob., San Andrés Tuxtla, 1 Apr. 1913, AGVC-SP/TP, C7; Gob. to Pérez Rivera, Mexico City, 1 Apr. 1913, AGVC-SP/TP, C7.
30. Carvallo to unknown, Xalapa, 2 Apr. 1913, AGN-GOB/PR, C57, E82.
31. See complaint to JP Xalapa, signed by a delegate of the Club Patria, Leoncio Cabañas Delgado, and complaints by other party workers, 2, 3 Apr. 1913, AGN-GOB/PR, C57 E82 ; *El Imparcial*, 25 Apr. 1913, p. 1.

32. *El Imparcial*, 16 Jun. 1913, p. 5; Decree 7 of the Legislature, Xalapa, 12
    Jun. 1913, AGVC-EE, C4; Pasquel, *La revolución*, p. 75.
33. Law 12, Xalapa, 26 Jun. 1913, AHMVC, C367 V499:355; Camacho to
    JP Veracruz, Xalapa, 22 Sep. 1913, AGVC-SP/TP, C7:1440; the five
    were Delfino Victoria, Silvestre Aguilar, Armando Deschamps, Adolfo
    Domínguez, and Tomás Piñeiro. See *acuerdo* of the Legislature, dated
    Xalapa, 8 Nov. 1913, AGVC-EE, C4; Cauz to Attorney General of Veracruz,
    Xalapa, 18 Nov. 1913, AGVC-EE, C4; see also Pasquel, *La revolución*, p. 75.
34. Canada to Sec. State, Veracruz, 24 Apr. 1913, USDS, 812.00:7255;
    Domínguez Milián, *Tuxpán*, p. 33.
35. *El Imparcial*, 26 Apr. 1913, p. 4; 1 May 1913, pp. 1, 5; Domínguez Milián,
    Tuxpan, p. 34.
36. Carranza to Aillaud, Piedras Negras, 18 May 1913, CONDUMEX-AVC,
    XXI C2:208; Min. of Finance to Min. of War, Mexico City, 7 Jun. 1913,
    AHSDN XI/481.5/314, C147:266; Carranza to Jesús Carranza, Piedras
    Negras, 13 May 1913, AVC, XXI C2:152.
37. *El Imparcial*, 1 May 1913, pp. 1, 5; Numerous leases to various oil compa-
    nies, notarized by Ricardo Arguelles, Tantoyuca, 19-22 May 1913, ANPVC,
    19-27; *El Imparcial*, 21 May 1913, p. 4.
38. Pérez Rivera to Gob., Xalapa, 7 May 1913, AHSDN, XI/481.5/314,
    C146:227, 228; *El Imparcial*, 8 May, 1913, p. 4; 9 May 1913, p. 4; 14 May 1913,
    p. 1; Quintanar to Gob., Ixhuatlán, 10 May 1913, AHSDN, XI/481.5/314,
    C146:224; Velasco to Gob., Veracruz, 16 May 1913, AHSDN, XI/481.5/314,
    C144:134-135; 18 May 1913, AHSDN, XI/481.5/314, C146:244-245; *El
    Imparcial*, 6 Jun. 1913, p. 4; Cordova y Gómez to Min. of War, 9 Jun. 1913,
    AHSDN, XI/481.5/314, C147:266; Miller to Sec. State, Tampico, 7 Jun. 1913,
    USDS, 812.00:7886; Canada to State Dept., Veracruz, 2 Jul. 1913, USDS,
    812.00:7950; *El Imparcial*, 6 May 1913, p. 4.
39. *El Imparcial*, 1 Jun. 1914, p. 4; 4 Jun. 1914, p. 4.
40. Velasco to Min. of War, Veracruz, 16 Jun. 1913, AHSDN, XI/481.5/314,
    C147:267; Allende (Subregidor) to JP Zongólica, Caxapa, 22 Jul. 1913, AZ,
    R11:20-21; Allende to mayor, Zongólica, Caxapa, 9 Aug. 1913, AZ, R11,
    71/22; JP Zongólica to mayor, 13 Aug. 1913, AZ, R11, 71/25.
41. *El Imparcial*, 10 Jul. 1913, p. 4; 15 Jul. 1913, p. 4; Canada to State Dept.,
    Veracruz, 20 Jul 1913, USDS, 812.00:8094; JP Coatepec, to Cauz, 30
    Nov. 1913, AGVC-SP/TP, C8.
42. Camacho to JP Zongólica, Xalapa, 1 Sep. 1913, AZ, R16, 109:9; Camacho
    to JP Zongólica, Xalapa, 28 Aug. 1913, AZ, R16, 109:2.
43. Kirby-Smith to Pérez Rivera, Cuatotolapam, 7 Jun. 1913, AGVC-SP/TP,
    C6; *El Imparcial*, 11 Jun. 1913, p. 4; report dated 11 Jul. 1913, Mexico City,
    AGN-CD/INEHRM, Anexos IX-32, Acciones de Guerra.
44. Canada to State Dept., Veracruz, 18 Aug. 1913, USDS, 812.00:8446; Gob.
    to Sec. Gob., Mexico City, 9 Jun. 1913, AHSDN, XI/481.5/314, C146:263,
    264; British Embassy to Gob., Mexico City, 22 Jul. 1913, AGN-GOB-PR,
    C412:290; Palomino, Sixth Exploration Corps to Min. of War, Acayucan, 29
    Jul. 1913, AHSDN, XI/481.5/314, C146:306; *El Imparcial*, 30 Jul. 1913, p. 4;
    16 Aug. 1913, p. 4.
45. Cejudo to Min. of War, Acayucan, 20 Aug. 1913, AHSDN, XI/481.5/314,
    C147:314; JP Acayucan to Sec. Gob., 28 Aug. 1913, AGVC-SP/TP, C7;
    Merodio to Min. of War, Chiapas, 8 Dec. 1913, AHSDN, XI/481.5/314,
    C147:539; Corona to Min. of War, Soteapan, 18 Dec. 1913, AHSDN,
    XI/481.5/314, C147:608.

46. Cauz to Gob. Xalapa, 1 Sep. 1913, AGVC-SP/TP, C7.
47. González Mena to Dehesa, Mexico City, 17 May 1913, ATD, C1:2252-2253.
48. This information comes from various reports and letters to the governor, Cauz, found in AGVC-SP/TP, C7.
49. Sherwell to Canada, Orizaba, 13 Jun. 1913, USDS, 812.00:8005; Embassy to State Dept., Mexico City, 31 Jul. 1913, USDS, 812.00:8203.
50. Gavira, *Su actuación*, pp. 76-77; Bustamante, Gavira et al. to Carranza, Havana, 7 Oct. 1913, in Fabela, *Documentos Históricos*, v. 1, pp. 125-126; Heredia (a Huerta spy) to Min. of War, Veracruz, 18 Jun. 1913, AHSDN, XI/481.5/314, C147:276; Vara (a Mexican residing in Havana) to Min. of Communication and Public Works, Havana, 4 Jun. 1913, AHSDN, XI/481.5/314, C 147:272.
51. Santos to Carranza, Matamoros, 9 Jun. 1913, AVC, C3:423; Blanco to Carranza, Matamoros, 10 Jun. 1913, AVC, C3:428.
52. Mello y Tellez to Min. of War, Chicontepec, 13 Jun. 1913, AHSDN, XI/481.4/314, C147:268; Miller to Sec. State, Tampico, 17 Jun. 1913, USDS, 812.00:7863; U.S. embassy to Gob., Mexico City, 18 Jun. 1913, AGN-GOB/PR, C39:18; Maas to Min. of War, Veracruz, 9 Jun. 1913, AHSDN, XI/481.5/314, C147:292; Canada to Sec. State, Veracruz, 25 Jun. 1913, USDS, 812.00:7871; petition by citizens of Ixhuatlán to Cauz, 3 Aug. 1913, AGVC-SP/TP, C6; for the first time, the rebels, instead of being referred to as bandits, were now called Carrancistas. See *El Imparcial*, 2 Aug. 1913, p. 4.
53. *El Imparcial*, 26 Jun. 1913, p. 4; 6 Jul. 1913, p. 4; for a humorous description of the battle, see Knight, *Mexican Revolution*, v. 2, p. 57; for the words of the *corrido* written to commemorate the battle, see Trigos, *El corrido veracruzano*, pp. 120-123.
54. Canada to Sec. State, Veracruz, 7 Jul. 1913, USDS 812.00:7974; 31 Jul. 1913, 812.00:8308; captured documents of the Constitutionalist Army, no name, AHSDN, XI/481.5/314, C147:298; 21 Jul. 1913, C147:302; Villar to Cauz, Papantla, 1 Sep. 1913, AGVC-SP/TP, C7.
55. Circular, 1 Oct. 1913, AGN-CD/INEHRM, Anexos IX-32, Acción de Guerra; Estado Mayor, Tuxpán, to Min. of War, 24 Oct. 1913, AHSDN, XI/481.5/314, C147:386; Canada to Sec. State, Veracruz, 11 Nov. 1913, USDS 812.00:9670; Perdo Vázquez to Min. of War, Tuxpán, 15 Nov. 1913, AHSDN, XI/481.5/314, C147:425-427.
56. Rodríguez to Min. of War, Tuxpán, 17 Nov. 1913, AHSDN, XI/481.5/314, C147:513-514.
57. The incident is recorded in Pasquel, *La revolución*, v. 2, pp. 88-90 and was based on a newspaper article by Isidro Fabela published in the newspaper *Excelsior*, April, 1960.
58. Manzur Ocaña, *La revolución permanente*, pp. 97-100; cf. González Marín, *Heriberto Jara*, p. 149 who gives the amount as $10 million.
59. *El Imparcial*, 10 Nov. 1913, p. 1; 12 Dec. 1913, p. 1; Canada to Sec. State, Veracruz, 27 Dec. 1913, USDS, 812.00:10323; 27 Nov. 1913, USDS, 812.00:9943; *El Imparcial*, 28 Nov. 1913, p. 4; 16 Dec.1913, p. 5; Canada to State Dept., Veracruz, 12 Dec. 1913, USDS, 812.00:10158.
60. *El Imparcial*, 16 Jul. 1913, p. 4; Huerta to Cauz, Mexico City, 11 Nov. 1913, AGVC-SP/TP, C5; Vivanco to Cauz, Orizaba, 21 Nov. 1913, AGVC-SP/TP, C5; Pasquel, *La revolución*, v. 2, pp. 77-79. This Díaz Mirón was the same person who had chased unsuccessfully after the bandit and revolutionary Santanón in 1910.

61. Doblado, *Mexico para los mexicanos*, p. 170; Miller to State Dept., Tampico, 19 Jul. 1913, USDS 812.00:8085; De la Barra to Min. of External Affairs, Mexico City, 9 Aug. 1913, UNAM:ADelB, C24:303; *El Imparcial*, 29 Aug. 1913, p. 1.

62. Meyer, *Huerta*, pp. 147-48.

63. Huerta to Gabriel Huerta, Mexico City, 25 Jan. 1914, ATD, E22; De Pallares, *Dehesa*, pp. 249-51; Huerta to Min. of Communication, 31 Jan. 1914, ATD, E22. Dehesa was very shaken up by these events. When he arrived back in Veracruz, he cabled Huerta his arrival. In the draft telegram in his archive, he crossed out the word "*afectuosamente*" and replaced it with "*atentamente.*" See Dehesa to Huerta, Veracruz, 1 Feb. 1914, ATD, E22.

64. Canada to Sec. State, Veracruz, 5 Jan. 1914, USDS, 812.00:10432; 8 Jan. 1914, USDS, 812.00:10588.

65. Canada to Sec. State, Veracruz, 1 Jan. 1914, USDS, 812.00:10461; Canada to State Dept., Veracruz, 3 Jan. 1914, USDS, 812.00:10400.

66. Mayor, Texhuacan to JP Zongólica, 15 Jan. 1914, AZ, R9:46/16; JP Zongólica to Cauz, 10 Jan. 1914, AZ, R9:46/2-5; *La Opinión*, 6 Jan. 1914, p. 1; Camacho to JP Xalapa, 27 Jan. 1914, AZ, R9:46:14; Canada to Sec. State, Veracruz, 15 Jan. 1914, USDS, 812.00:10768; 22 Jan. 1914, USDS, 812.00:10664; Cerisola to Min. of War, AHSDN, XI/481.5/315, C148:14; Muñoz to Gob., Paso del Macho, 19 Jan. 1914, AHSDN, XI/481.5/315, C148:28; Various to Cauz, Cotaxtla, 16 Jan. 1914, AGVC-SP/TP, C8.

67. Segundo to Huerta, 19 Jan. 1914, AHSDN, XI/481.5/315, C148:34; Camacho to JP Xalapa, 13 Jan., 27 Jan. 1914, AZ, R6:25/2, 9.

68. In this encounter, the rebels lost thirty-nine men and eighteen horses. See *La Opinión*, 8 Jan. 1914, p. 1, 4; Mil. Command, Veracruz to Cauz, 17 Jan. 1914, AGVC-SP/TP, C9; various to Cauz, 30 Jan. 1914, AGVC-SP/TP, C8; *La Opinión*, 31 Jan. 1914, p. 4.

69. Pérez Castro to War, 18 Feb. 1914, AHSDN, XI/481.5/315, C148:108; *La Opinión*, 15 Mar. 1914, p. 4; Maas to War, 16 Feb. 1914, AHSDN, XI/481.5/315, C148:98; *La Opinión*, 5 Mar. 1914.

70. Corzo Ramírez et al., *...nunca un desleal*, p. 41; this speech as well as the proclamation is quoted in Manzur Ocaña, *La revolución permanente*, p. 75.

71. Cowdray had offered the exiled president permanent use of his estate Paddockhurs. See Cowdray to Lady Cowdray, 26 Jun. 1911, UTBC-SP&S, Selected Records, #20, R161 A3; Body to Cowdray, 28 Jun. 1911, UTBC-Sp&S, Selected Records, #20 R161 A3; Meyer, *Su majestad Británica*, pp. 156-157; La Botz, *Edward Doheny*, pp. 49-50. Fabela argues that the animosity of the United States towards Mexico was grounded in the privileged treatment U.S. interests had come to expect from the Porfiriato. The same was true of other foreigners, such as Lord Cowdray. See Fabela, *Documentos históricos*, v. 2, p. 194.

72. A prostitute nicknamed, ironically, América, draped herself with a cartridge belt and fired on the advancing soldiers from the roof of her dwelling. Two other *señoritas*, shielded behind venetian blinds, kept up constant rifle fire, killing two soldiers. They were trapped inside a garage, raped, and left for dead. See Martínez, *La intervención norteamericana*, p. 38. The invasion cost 126 Mexican lives. Nineteen Yankees were killed. See AGN-CD/INEHRM, Anexos IX-32, Acciones de Guerra. For an account of the defence see report by General Maas to War, 22 Apr. 1914, AHSDN, XI/481.5/315, C148:241-244; Haverstock, "Waiting in Veracruz, 1914," p. 35.

73. Pasquel, *La revolución*, chap. 8; *El Dictámen*, 17 Jul. 1914, p. 1; for conditions in Veracruz under the U.S. occupation, see Donnell, "The United States Military Government at Veracruz, Mexico," in *Essays in Mexican History*.

74. Meyer, *Huerta*, p. 207.

75. Barragán to Chief of Staff, 1st Infantry Brigade, Mexico City, 9 May 1914, AHSDN, XI/481.5/315, C149:751.

76. Carranza (no relation to Venustiano) to War, Tuxpán, 12 May 1914, AHSDN, XI/481.5/315 C149:501-502; Gavira, *Su actuación*, pp. 89-91; González Marín, *Heriberto Jara*, p. 153.

77. *La Opinión*, 9 Jun. 1914, p. 1; Domínguez Milián, *Tuxpán*, p. 67; Corzo Ramírez et al., *...nunca un desleal*, p. 44.

78. Corzo Ramírez et al., *...nunca un desleal*, p. 44; Gavira, *Su actuación*, pp. 93-94; Millán to Odorica, 8 Jun. 1914, AGVC-SP/TP, C10; Cauz to Gov. Puebla, Xalapa, 12 Jun. 1914, AGVC-SP/TP, C10; Odorica to Cauz, Papantla, 11 Jun. 1914, AGVC-SP/TP, C10; *El Dictámen*, 25 Jun., 1914, p. 1; Velasquez to Cauz, Nautla, 8 Jun. 1914, AGVC-SP/TP, C10.

79. *El Dictámen*, 11 Jun. 1914, p. 1; Velasquez to Cauz, Jicaltepec, 9 Jun. 1914, AGVC-SP/TP, C10; JP, Córdoba to Cauz, 11 Jun. 1914, AGVC-SP/TP, C10; *La Opinión*, 18 Jun. 1914, p. 2.

80. Hernández to JP Zongólica, Tlaquilpa, 15 Jun. 1914, AZM R17:123/17; *La Opinión*, 27 Jun. 1914, p. 1.

81. *La Opinión*, 1 Jul. 1914, p. 1; 3 Jul. 1914, pp. 1, 4; 5 Jul. 1914, pp. 1, 4; 7 Jul. 1914, p. 1.

82. *La Opinión*, 9 Jul. 1914, p. 2; 11 Jul. 1914, p. 3.

83. *La Opinión*, 9 Jul. 1914, p. 2; 11 Jul. 1914, pp. 1, 4.

Notes to Chapter 7

1. *La Opinión*, 13 Jul. 1914, p. 1; 14 Jul. 1914, p. 1; 21 Jul. 1914, p. 1; Guevara to War, Mexico City, 18 Jul. 1914, AHSDN, XI/481.5/315, C149:547; Dehesa to Díaz, Veracruz, 22 Jul. 1914, ATD, C2.

2. *El Dictámen*, 23 Aug. 1914, p. 1; 28 Aug. 1914, p. 1; Galván to War, 27 Aug. 1914, AHSDN, XI/481.5/315, C148:565-567; Report, 28 Aug. 1914, AGN-CD/INEHRM, Anexos IX-32, Acciones de Guerra; *La Opinión*, 28 Aug. 1914, p. 3.

3. *El Dictámen*, 2 Sep. 1914, p. 1; 3 Sep. 1914, p. 1; Jara to Gob., Xalapa, 11 Sep. 1914, AGN-GOB/PR, C33 E32; *El Dictámen*, 13 Sep. 1914, p. 1; 17 Sep. 1914, p. 1; *La Opinión*, 1 Sep. 1914, p. 2; 4 Sep. 1914, p. 1.

4. *La Opinión*, 22 Sep. 1914, p. 1; Knight, *Mexican Revolution*, v. 2, p. 173.

5. Womack, *Zapata*, p. 218; the standard treatment of the Aguascalientes Convention is Quirk, *The Mexican Revolution*.

6. *La Opinión*, 14 Nov. 1914, p. 1; *El Dictámen*, 12 Nov. 1914, p. 1; Hall, *Obregón*, p. 99; Womack, *Zapata*, p. 219.

7. Ulloa, *Veracruz*, pp. 43-44, 47. On December 24, the port city was officially designated the national capital.

8. HQ to Domínguez, Puerto México, 30 Nov. 1914, AVC, C21:2167; Domínguez to J. Carranza, 30 Nov. 1914, AVC, C21:2164; HQ to Domínguez, Puerto México, 30 Nov. 1914, AVC, C21:2163.

9. Gavira, *Su actuación*, pp. 105-6; *El Dictámen*, 28 Nov. 1914, p. 3; 30 Nov. 1914, p. 1.

10. For a full discussion of Ruiz's political behaviour, see Koth, "Cameleón o tigre pintido"; the conventional wisdom has it that Villa and Zapata were

the reactionaries (a term first used by Carranza; see "Mexican Letter," New York, 13 Nov. 1914, AVC, C20:2039), and that Carranza was the progressive. Part of this argument is based on Carranza's address to the Convention when it was still based in Mexico City, in which he guaranteed, *inter alia*, municipal freedom. See Córdova, *La ideología*, p. 199f; this whole business needs more extensive treatment. However, if Villa was not a reactionary, there were real reactionaries, the Científicos who thought they could use him to their advantage, that is, to turn back the clock. There is an interesting letter from ex-president Díaz to Felipe Angeles, 18 Jun. 1913, urging him to "save the army and the nation by listening to Limantour," in Fabela, *Documentos históricos*, v. 1, pp. 89-90. What was he to listen to? In late May, Limantour wrote to De la Barra saying: "Everyone knows that Huerta will soon fall, and with him all the noble and good institutions of the country; we cannot stay aloof from these events. You know that the Division of the North had no political ambitions, but is commanded by an ambitious individual who wants power; on the other hand one of our men is serving in his ranks in a high position. It is impossible that Felipe Angeles forget the great services he owes to Gen. Díaz. We can satisfy the ambition of the first with gold, and use Angeles' gratitude to our advantage. Then we will advise Villa to approach Zapata, and thus give our new order a revolutionary aspect, and thus reclaim all, which we now need. We will honor the Plan of Ayala, distributing lands only in the state of Morelos, and compensate his generosity with concessions and lands in other states which are less populated.... *By this method we will return to govern Mexico in a definitive and energetic way* (emphasis added)." In Fabela, *Documentos históricos*, v. 1, pp. 90-91, another observer referred to Zapata's "radical socialism." See Silliman to Sec. State, 22 Dec. 1914, USDS, 812.00:14070; none other than the famous Dr. Atl, found Zapatismo truly revolutionary and antithetical to Villismo. See Atl, "The Mexican Revolution and the Nationalization of Land: The Foreign Interests and Reaction," in USDS, 812.00:23141a.

11. The Plan of Guadalupe, signed in late March of 1913, was Carranza's call to arms against the Huerta regime. "Program of the First Chief, Venustiano Carranza, Pending the Suppression of the Villista Rebellion," in Villareal, *Immediate Causes of the Present Conflict*, p. 19.

12. OC Isthmus to J. Carranza, Tehuantepec, 8 Oct. 1914, AVC, C17:1700; Aguilar to War, 25 Oct. 1914, AHSDN, XI/481.5/315, C149:588; 1 Nov. 1914, AHSDN, XI/481.5/315, C149:601; Barrera to War, 1 Nov. 1914, AHSDN, XI/481.5/315, C149:593; *El Dictámen*, 11 Nov. 1914, p. 1; 20 Nov. 1914, p. 1; Machuca to Carranza, 12 Dec. 1914, AHSDN, XI/481.5/315, C149:685-688, 696-697. For a discussion of the Díaz attempts at a comeback, his failure to woo Villa, and the occupation of the state of Oaxaca by Felicistas, see Henderson, *Félix Díaz*, pp. 113-17; Higareda to Carranza, Tuxpán, 23 Dec. 1914, AVC, C23:2247.

13. *La Opinión*, 23 Oct. 1914, p. 1; J. Carranza to Carranza, Puerto México, 1 Dec. 1914, AVC, C22:2170. It is the standard view that it was impossible to unite the various elements at Aguascalientes. Both Villa and Zapata were determined to have their own way. See Villareal, *The Real Story*, pp. 3-4.

14. Beva (vice-consul) to Sec. State, Tampico, 7 Dec. 1914, USDS, 812.00:14102; Aguilar to Carranza, 16 Dec. 1914, AVC, C23:2218; Jara to Carranza, 16 Dec. 1914, AHSDN, XI/481.4/315, C149:709; Canada to Sec. State, 19 Dec. 1914, USDS, 812.00:14052; 25 Dec. 1914, USDS, 812.00:14082; *El Dictámen*, 24

Dec. 1914, p. 1; Alamina to Carranza, 18 Dec. 1914, AHSDN, XI/481.5/315, C149:711; Jara to Carranza, 18 Dec. 1914, AHSDN, XI/481.5/315, C149: 716-720; *El Dictámen*, 23 Dec. 1914, p. 3.

15. Beva to Sec. State, 7 Dec. 1914, USDS, 812.00:14102; Ext. Rel. to Aguilar, 28 Dec. 1914, AGVC-SP/TP, C8; Aguilar to Ext. Rel., 28 Dec. 1914, AGVC-SP/TP, C8.

16. Canada to Sec. State, 4 Sep. 1913, USDS, 812.00:8851.

17. Quoted in Katz, *Condiciones de trabajo*, pp. 31-32 ; Chief of Arms, Los Tuxtlas to Aguilar, 31 Oct. 1914, AGVC-AL, C2.

18. Carranza's address to the Convention is quoted in Córdova, *La ideología*, p. 199.

19. *El Dictámen*, 7 Nov. 1914, p. 1; Aguilar to González, (President of Indigenous Community of Jalacingo), 19 Dec. 1914, AVC, C23:2226; Domínguez Pérez, *Política y movimientos sociales*, p. 16.

20. Decree 9, Dec. 1914, AVC, C32:2303. This labour law has been cited as "the most complete of all those decreed by Constitutionalist governors at this time," and thus is an important stimulant to the radical labour movement of the 1920s. See Domínguez Pérez, *Política y movimientos sociales*, p. 16.

21. *El Dictámen*, 7 Dec. 1914, p. 1; 19 Dec. 1914, p. 2.

22. *El Dictámen*, 5 Dec. 1914, p. 1; 17 Dec. 1914, p. 2. For the origins of the radical wing of Constitutionalism, the group known as the Confederación Revolucionaria, see Hall, *Obregón*, p. 101. Hall's work is an excellent and balanced biography of this important Mexican politician.

23. Womack, *Zapata*, p. 223; Knight, *Mexican Revolution*, v. 1, p. 310; Hall, *Obregón*, p. 99.

24. Hall, *Obregón*, p. 107; Pasquel, *La revolución mexicana*, v. 2, p. 201.

25. Canada to Sec. State, 5 Jan. 1915, USDS, 912.00:14145; cf. *El Radical*, 9 Jan. 1915, p. 1, which gives the number as two thousand, a figure which seems more realistic.

26. Proclamation, HQ Axochíc, Canton of the Tuxtlas, 26 Mar. 1915, AVC-GOB/SP/TP, C 10; Aguilar to Carranza, 17 Feb. 1915, AVC, C28:2922.

27. Hall, *Obregón*, p. 116; Silliman to Sec. State, 18 Mar. 1915, USDS, 812.00:14624.

28. An example was Companía Mexicana Importadora y Exportadora. It was a general commercial as well as merchandising company and was owned by Agustín Diez (a Spaniard), a Mr. Rabelo, Silvestre Aguilar, Cándido Aguilar, and Luciano Leycegui. Their main export commodity was cattle, obtained sometimes by force with Constitutionalist soldiers. See report by Canada to Sec. State, 22 Jan. 1915, USDS, 812.00:14332.

29. Constitutionalist troops were in the habit of taking everything. In one town, they even stole the musical instruments of the populace. See petition of citizens of Santa Ana Atzacan to Aguilar, 3 Jul. 1915, m AGVC-SP/TP, C10; Perkins to Canada, 15 May 1915, USDS, 812.00:15560; Ulloa, *Veracruz*, pp. 126-27; *El Radical*, 17 Apr. 1915, p. 1; Silliman to Sec. State, 17 Jun. 1915, USDS, 812.00:15258.

30. Canada to State Dept., 12 Jul. 1915, USDS, 812.00:15578; 7 Jun. 1915, USDS, 812.00:15156; *El Radical*, 17 May 1915, p. 1; *El Dictámen*, 23 Apr. 1915, p. 1.

31. *El Radical*, 4 Jun. 1915, p. 1.

32. Consular reports as well as military reports submitted by the U.S. Fleet speak of daily attacks against trains all over the state. See Scudder, "Brief Statement of Present Political Situation in Mexico Based on Official

Reports," 6 Oct. 1915, USDS, 812.00:16962; *El Demócrata*, 17 Jun. 1915, p. 3; Canada to Sec. State, 1 Jul. 1915, USDS, 812.00:15350; Millán to Aguilar, 11 May 1915, AHSDN, XI/481.5/316, C149:159.

33. Canada to Sec. State, 14 Jul. 1915, USDS, 812.00:15446; 19 Jul. 1915, USDS, 812.00:15487; Gemmill (British vice-consul) to Canada to Sec. State, 14 Jul. 1915, USDS, 812.00; Canada to Sec. State, 6 Aug. 1915, USDS, 812.00:15672; 13 Sep. 1915, USDS, 812.00: 16139; 16 Sep. 1915, USDS, 812.00:16201; 24 Sep. 1915, USDS, 812.00:16381; Scudder to State Dept., 6 Oct. 1915, USDS, 812.00:16962.

34. Canada to Sec. State, 8 Sep. 1915, USDS, 812.00:16080; Silliman to Sec. State, 10 Sep. 1915, USDS, 812.00:16101; Commander, Detached Squadron to Sec. Navy, 24 Sep. 1915, USDS, 812.00:16368.

35. Ulloa, *Veracruz*, p. 161; Canada to Sec. State, 26 Aug. 1915, USDS, 812.00:15949; 13 Sep. 1915, USDS, 812.00:16140.

36. Domínguez Pérez, *Política y movimientos*, pp. 11-12; Gavira, *Su actuación*, p. 154; for a balanced assessment of Aguilar's intentions, see Corzo Ramírez et al., *...nunca un desleal*, pp. 83-96, who argue that Aguilar's intentions were never to carry out a general land redistribution and, in any case, at this time he was concerned to not break up producing estates whose products were essential to the state's well-being. This may be true, but it is still a fact that there were estates concerned only with exporting for profit; their products did not benefit Veracruzans, who would have been better off utilizing these large estates for cash crops. Was so much sugar needed, for example, when corn and beans were in such short supply? This is an age-old controversy, the outcome of which depends on benefits from agricultural production.

37. *El Dictámen*, 16 Jul. 1915, p. 1, Corzo Ramírez et al., *...nunca un desleal*, p. 85.

38. *El Dictámen*, 20 Sep. 1915, p. 1; 17 Oct. 1915, p. 1; Zubarán Capmany to Aguilar, 4 May 1915, AGVC-GOB/AL, C2; López Jiménez to Sec. Gob., 2 Dec. 1915, AGN-GOB/PR, C31 E11; Basurto, *El proletariado industrial*, pp. 185-186.

39. Stewart, *The Petroleum Industry*, p. 22; Mayor of Minatitlán to Aguilar, 21 Oct. 1915, AGN-GOB/PR, C27 E12; García Jurado (interim governor) to Casilles, 30 Dec. 1915, AGN-GOB/PR, C27 E12; Castán to Carranza, 1 May 1915, AHSDN, XI/481.5/316, C149:137; Sec. Gob. To Rouaix, 3 Jan. 1916, AGN-GOB/PR, C27 E12.

40. Pasquel, *La revolución Mexicana*, pp. 215-220; Decree #14, 12 Jan. 1916, signed A. Millán, AGN-GOB/PR, C9 E23.

41. Urueta to Zubarán Capmany, 10 Jun. 1915, AGN-GOB/PR, C100 E33; Decree #41, 25 Sep. 1915, Decree #53, 24 Dec. 1915, Decree #14, 12 Jan. 1916, AGN-GOB/PR, C9 E23; numerous arrest and detention orders are contained in AGN-GOB/PR, C93; the same are found in AGVC-SP/TP, C11; *El Dictámen*, 29 Dec. 1915, p. 1.

42. Unknown to Lansing, 31 Jul. 1915, USDS 812.00:17538; Canada to Sec. State, 6 Sep. 1915, USDS, 812.00:16274; Carrothers to Sec. State, 12 Dec. 1915, USDS, 812.00:16938.

43. A list of people to be investigated or watched in 1915 was prepared by the secret service of the Rurales in Veracruz. Raúl Ruiz was listed as chief of the Felicistas in the port city. See AGN-CR, Fuerza Auxiliares/529. Security also kept watch on Consuelo Tejedor, daughter of Enrique

Tejedor Pedroses, who was in exile in Havana. Consuelo's sister was married to Leandro Alcolea, brother-in-law of Félix Díaz. The report states that an older lady visited her from a religious association. See Security Chief, Veracruz to Sec. Gob., 19 Apr. 1915, and the police report dated 9 May 1915, AGN-GOB/PR, C99 E18. Another suspect, also a woman, Mrs. Carmen Ruiz Seco, lived in Orizaba before moving to the port city and was an avid follower of Díaz. She had been watched in Orizaba, where many secret meetings were held in her house. She also supposedly had an affair with an engineer, Ricardo Ortíz, an intimate friend of Diaz, who was active on his behalf during the coup attempt in October 1912. See memo to Carranza's private secretary, 31 Jul. 1915, AVC, C46/152:5133.

44. Henderson, *Félix Díaz*, pp. 123, 125.

45. "Manifesto a la Nación Mexicana," especially clauses 8 and 9, referring to the Plan of Tierra Colorado, signed Veracruz, 23 Feb. 1916, in AVC, C71/152:7715. For a discussion of the multi-class nature of Felicismo, see Henderson, *Félix Díaz*, pp. 129-133; Knight, *Mexican Revolution*, v. 2, pp. 383-385.

46. Knight, *Mexican Revolution*, v. 2, p. 383, asserts that "the common denominator which loosely united the varied Felicista forces – was a rejection of alien, northern interlopers (whose generals were callous and whose troops ill-behaved) and an assertion of local opposition and resistance. There was clearly more to Felicismo than this. Díaz was consistent in his anti-Científico stance. Henderson, *Félix Díaz*, pp. 92-93 attests to this: "Many Mexicans believed that General Díaz would reincarnate the old Porfiriato without the influence of the hated Científicos."

47. Domínguez (Sec.Gob.) to Chief of Staff, Division of the East, 4 Jan. 1916, AHSDN, XI/481.6/317, C150:1; Rodríguez to Gov., Misantla, 14 Jan. 1916, AGVC-SP/TP, C12.

48. Hernández, a Carrancista spy, to Urquizo, 16 Jan. 1916, AHSDN, XI/481.5/317, C150:10; Sánchez to Millán, 19 Jan. 1916, AHSDN, XI/481.5/317, C150:42.

49. Herrera to Chief of Arms, Córdoba, 9 Jan. 1916, AHSDN, XI/481.5/317, C150:7-8; Herrera to Millán, 19 Jan. 1916, AHSDN, XI/481.5/317, C150:59-60; Herrera to Millán, 20 Jan. 1916, AHSDN, XI/481.5/317, C150:77.

50. Castro to Sec. War, 8 Jan. 1916, AHSDN, XI/481.5/317, C150:3; Nincanor Pérez commanded about 350 men, not an inconsiderable number. At the end of January, his main camp was surprised by the army. They retreated but left two captains, two lieutenants, and fourteen soldiers of the federal Usumacinta Brigade dead. See Castro to Pesqueira, 3 Feb. 1916, AHSDN, XI/481/317, C150:141; Chief of Staff, Division of the East to Sec. Gob., 11 Jan. 1916, AGVC-SP/TP, C12; Hernández (mayor of Hidalgotitlán) to HQ, Division of the East, 24 Jan. 1916, AHSDN, XI/481.5/317, C150:134.

51. Translated copy in USDS, 812.00:17418. Henderson gives the date as February 23, but his reference is Liceaga, *Félix Díaz*, not the original document.

52. Henderson, *Félix Díaz*, pp. 125-26.

53. For an account of Díaz's peregrinations, see Henderson, *Félix Díaz*, pp. 127-29; Chief of Security to Gob., 2 May 1916, AGN-GOB-PR, C3, E15; documents captured on Mrs. Teresa Mier, which were found in her shoe as she stopped of the boat from New Orleans, contained a list of Felicista adherents. See Aguilar to Jara, 21 Jul. 1916, AGN-GOB/PR, C81, E26.

54. Garciadiego, "Higinio Aguilar", p. 459; Garciadiego, "Gaudencio de la Llave", p. 26; Carothers to Sec. State, 7 Mar. 1916, USDS, 812.00:17417.
55. The U.S. government was well aware of Díaz's plans before he even left New Orleans. See Bielaski (Dept. of Justice) to State Dept., 25 Jan. 1916, USDS, 812.00:17220; one of the principal backers was Cardinal Farley of New York City. See Silliman to Sec. State, 10 Mar. 1915, USDS, 812.00:14554; Bryan to Wilson, 16 Mar. 1915, USDS 812.00: 14554. Wilson, commenting on the requests by the Catholic Church to support the movement, referred to it as "a pig in a poke"; Bryan to Bishop Currier, 19 Mar. 1916, USDS, 812.00:16810.
56. Pacheco (mayor) to Sec. Gob., Tlacotepec de Mejía, 31 Jul. 1916, AGVC-SP/TP, C12; M. Aguilar to Manzano, 5 Sep. 1916, AHSDN, XI/481.5/317, C150:340-342; Jara to Gob., 7 Oct. 1916, AHSDN, XI/481.5/317, C150:350; M. Aguilar to Gob. 17 Oct. 1916, AGN-GOB-PR, C34 E14.
57. The documents contained a manifesto written by H. Aguilar, as well as the structure of the armies and their officers. See "Manifesto to the Mexican People," 26 Nov. 1916, AHSDN, XI/481.5/317, C150:384-386, 394-395.
58. Canada to Sec. State, 6 May 1916, USDS, 812.00:18077.
59. For details of the diplomacy between Mexico, the United States, Germany, and Great Britain during the war years, see Katz, *The Secret War*.
60. Telegram to Sec. State, 4 May 1916, USDS, 812.00:18071; U.S.S. Kentucky to Sec. Navy, 30 Apr. 1916, USDS, 812.00:18110; the Constitutionalist soldiers promised "looting, rapine, murder and even the demolishment [*sic*] of the town," as reported by Canada to Sec. State, 24 Jul. 1916, USDS, 812.00:18871. Whatever might be said about him, Carranza was nothing if not determined. He was not averse to using the vilest means of propaganda to get his message across. Perhaps one of the least known *corridos* of the revolution is the one entitled "La cucaracha gringa: Piropos a Mister Wilson," which Carranza allowed to be printed and circulated in Chihuahua at five cents a copy. It was a warning to President Wilson, couched in the most vulgar terms. The actual text was translated with a detailed explanation of all the nuances and allusions that would be lost in translation by the U.S. Embassy in Mexico City. One of the most insulting of the verses calls Wilson the son of a whore:

Oh, Mr. Wilson; Oh, Mr. Wilson,
You believe that brute strength,
Will make the Mexicans bow down to you.
Be careful with your hands,
You son of – Lady Canuta.

"Lady Canuta" was the name commonly applied to a woman who ran a brothel. It was sung to the tune of *La Cucaracha*. See Cobb to Sec. State, 7 Jun. 1916, USDS, 812.00:18362.
61. Zarauz López, "Rebeldes istmeños," *Boletín*, 22 (APEC); Henderson, *Félix Díaz*, p. 131; Knight, *Mexican Revolution*, v. 2, pp. 381-85.
62. Trains were usually halted, the passengers, after a lecture on Felicismo, were allowed to take their baggage and go and then the train was either blown up or burned. Usually the *felicista* did not harm or rob the passengers. The same cannot be said for the Carrancista troops, who even robbed the dead of ear-rings, watches, and the like. There are too many

reports in the USDS to mention them all. However, see Canada to Sec. State, 4 Jul. 1916, USDS, 812.00:18638; 25 Jul. 1916, USDS, 812.00:18791; 4 Aug. 1916, USDS, 812.00:18859; 29 Aug. 1916, USDS, 812.00:19047; 19 Nov. 1916, USDS, 812.00:19983.

63. Canada to Sec. State, 19 Jul. 1916, USDS, 812.00:18750; 22 Jul. 1916, USDS, 812.00:18772; 12 Aug. 1916, USDS, 812.00:18927; 1 Aug. 1916, USDS, 812.00:18987; Mayor of San Juan Evangelista to Commander, 9th. Military Zone, 15 Nov. 1916, AGVC-SP/TP, C12; Hernández to Sec. Gob., 26 Aug. 1916, AGVC-GOB/SP/TP, C 12; Padua to Sec. Gob., 27 Oct. 1916, AGVC-SP/TP, C 12.

64. Canada to Sec. State, 11 Sep. 1916, USDS, 812.00:19256.

65. Canada to Sec. State, 4 Sep. 1916, USDS, 812.00:19221; Mendizábal to Gob., Orizaba, 5 Oct. 1916, AGN-GOB/PR, C 34 E14.

66. Knight, *Mexican Revolution*, v. 2, p. 409; Basurto, *El proletariado industrial*, p. 177.

67. Ulloa, *Historia de la Revolución Mexicana*, pp. 293-94; Knight, *Mexican Revolution*, v. 2, pp. 433-34.

68. *El Dictámen*, 11 Nov. 1916, p. 1; Office of Information and Propaganda, Veracruz, to Carranza, 20 Jan. 1916, AVC, C66/152:7274; Consejo to Gob., 17 Apr. 1916, AGVC-GOB/AL, C2; *El Dictámen*, 20 Nov. 1916, p. 1; unsigned letter to Conductors' and Motorists' Union, 26 Dec. 1916, AGN-GOB/PR, C91 E24.

69. *El Dictámen*, 19 Dec. 1916, p. 1; 25 Dec. 1916, p. 1; 29 Dec. 1916, p. 1.

70. Canada to Sec.State, 24 Aug. 1916, USDS, 812.00:19089; 11 Sep. 1916, USDS, 812.00:19256; mayor to Aguilar, Tlalixcoyan, 13 Dec. 1916, AGN-GOB/PR, C36 E72.

71. "Carothers "Memo for Gen. Pershing," 25 Mar. 1917, USDS, 812.00:20732; Dawson to Sec. State, Tampico, 23 Jan. 1917, USDS, 812.00:20474.

72. Perkins to Canada, 6 Jan. 1917, USDS, 812.00:24450; Mayor to M. Aguilar, 5 Jan. 1917, AGVC-GOB/SP/TP, C13; mayor of Perote, to Sec. Gob., 21 May 1917, AGVC-SP/TP, C13; mayor, Altatonga, to Sec. Gob., 25 Jun. 1917, AGVC-SP/TP, C13.

73. Canada to Sec. State, 14 Mar. 1917, USDS, 812.00:20650; *El Dictámen*, 6 Apr. 1917, p.1;

74. Mayor of Hidalgotitlán, to Sec. Gob., 18 May 1917, AGVC-SP/TP, C 13. This is the first mention of Félix Díaz in this file.

75. Canada to Sec. State, 2 Apr. 1917, USDS, 812.00:20740; Canada to Sec. State, 8 Jun. 1917, USDS, 812.00:20997; 18 Oct. 1917 USDS, 812.00:21376; 8 Dec. 1917, USDS, 812.00:21572; it was estimated that the rebels had sixteen to eighteen thousand men, the Constitutionalists, at the most, eight thousand. See Canada to Sec. State, 6 Dec. 1917, USDS, 812.00:21583; *El Dictámen*, 15 Nov. 1917, p. 1.

76. Cámara Agricola, Córdoba, to Aguilar, 15 Nov. 1917, AGVC-GOB/SP/TP, C13; Canada to Sec. State, 4 May 1917, USDS, 812.00:20917. This was also the openly expressed views of delegates to the 10th Veracruz Agricultural Congress held at Córdoba in December. See Canada to Sec. State, 18 Dec. 1917, USDS, 812.00:21611. This should not be construed as if the rebels did not participate in theft, forced loans, or other criminal acts. But their targets were either municipal offices, or *haciendas*. They left the small farmers and *campesinos* alone, which accounts for a good deal of their support.

77. *El Dictámen*, 21 Nov. 1917, p. 1; Canada to Sec. State, 4 Apr. 1917, USDS, 812.00:20752.
78. Cumberland, *Mexican Revolution*, v. 2, pp. 328-31. Chapter 9 of this work contains one of the most accurate summaries of the work of the assembly.
79. A complete list of the Veracruzan delegates may be found in Ramírez Lavoignet, *Los constituyentes federales veracruzanos* and Ulloa, *Historia de la Revolución Mexicana*, v. 6, p. 528; for Jara's work at the assembly, see González Marín, *Heriberto Jara*, pp. 184ff.
80. Corzo Ramírez et al., ...*nunca un desleal*, pp. 177, 204.
81. Cumberland, *Mexican Revolution*, v. 2, pp. 343, 353.
82. Jara's main objective and interest was Article 123, concerned with workers' rights. See González Marín, *Heriberto Jara*, chap. 9. Where Article 27 was concerned, Jara was blinded to these implications by his own nationalism. See Zapata Vela, *Conversaciones con Heriberto Jara*, pp. 70, 77.
83. Cumberland, *Mexican Revolution*, v. 2, p. 362-63.
84. Cumberland, *Mexican Revolution*, v. 2, p. 370, says that Carranza "frequently made a mockery of his oft-repeated principle of state sovereignty"; see also Knight, *Mexican Revolution*, v. 2, p. 435-54 on the Carranza 'machine', and provincial opposition to centralism.
85. *Excelsior*, 27 Apr. 1917, p. 4; Club "Aquiles Serdán" to Carranza, 24 Jan. 1917, AVC, C109/152:12536; Workers' Party, Alvarado to Carranza, 25 Dec. 1917, AVC, C108/152:12329. The details of the campaign, in which it is impossible to ascertain who insulted who first, are in Corzo Ramírez, et al., ...*nunca un desleal*, pp. 185-200; *El Universal*, 1 Feb. 1917, p. 5; *El Dictámen*, 23 Jun. 1917, p. 1.
86. Corzo Ramírez uses the figures from *El Universal*, 16 May 1917, 23,413 for Aguilar against 8,025 for Gavira. However, on May 18 the paper reported 23,962 for Aguilar against 14,067. These figures also differ from those presented in *El Dictámen* that same day: 27,920 against 11,861; see Corzo Ramírez et al., ...*nunca un desleal*, p. 199; *El Universal*, 18 May 1917, p. 4;
87. *El Dictámen*, 10 Jun. 1917, p. 1; 14 June, 1917, p. 1; 26 May 1917, p. 1.
88. *El Dictámen*, 17 Dec. 1917, p. 1; El Universal, 17 Dec. 1917, p. 4; Canada to Sec. State, 18 Dec. 1917, USDS 812.00:21590; Decree #20, 6 Dec. 1917, AGN-GOB/PR, C91 E24; the AGN-GOB/PR, Exp. 82-91 contain the charges, countercharges, and results of the elections. The trial and suspension of Alarcón were reported in *El Dictámen*, 18 Oct. 1918, p. 1; 28 Nov. 1918, p. 1.
89. *El Universal*, 17 Apr. 1917, p. 4; 28 Oct. 1917, p. 4; 29 Nov. 1917, p. 4; *El Dictámen*, 1 Dec. 1917, p. 1; various to Governor, Santa Rosa, 9 Jan. 1918, AGVC-SP/TP, C14; Mayor, Santa Rosa to Governor, 31 Jan. 1918, AGVC-GOB/SP/TP, C14.
90. The group included Pedro Lascurain, Manuel Calero, David De la Fuente, Pedro del Villar, and Gen. Blanquet. See Rascón to Lansing, 5 Dec. 1918, USDS 812.00:21647; Del Villar to Polk, 12 Dec. 1918, USDS 812.00:22432; report by a prominent U.S. businessman taken captive by the Felicistas in southern Veracruz, in Hanna to Sec. State, 26 Nov. 1918, USDS, 812.00:22395.
91. Dawson to Sec. State, 29 Jun. 1918, USDS, 812.00:22098; Commander, Mexican Patrol, to Navy Dept., 8 Oct. 1918, USDS, 812.00:22337; one of the people pushing the support of Díaz was Henry Lane Wilson. See Wilson to Knox (Senator), 15 Jun. 1918, USDS, 812.00:22857.

92. Dawson to Sec. State, 19 Jan. 1918, USDS, 812.00:21689; Commander, U.S.S. Annapolis to Navy Dept., 28, USDS, 812.00:22345; *El Dictámen*, 23 Nov. 1918, p. 1; there is much doubt that one should include Peláez in this opposition to U.S. intervention. See unsigned memo to State Dept., 4 Oct. 1918, USDS, 812.00:22356.
93. Hanna to Sec. State, 26 Nov. 1918, USDS, 812.00:22395.
94. *El Dictámen*, 15 Oct. 1918, p. 1; 28 Oct. 1918, p. 1; Fletcher to Sec. State, 30 Oct. 1918, USDS, 812.00:22343; Aguilar to Gob., 21 Nov. 1918, AGN-GOB/PR, C91 E30.
95. *El Dictámen*, 23 Nov. 1918, p. 1; 27 Nov. 1918, p. 1; 9 Dec. 1918, p. 1; 27 Dec. 1911, p. 1; Stewart to Sec. State, Veracruz, 5 Jan. 1919, USDS, 812:22523; Memorandum, 7 Jan. 1919, AVC, C1129/152:14721; Corzo Ramírez et al., *...nunca un desleal*, p. 228.
96. Corzo Ramírez et al., *...nunca un desleal*, p. 227; Henderson, *Félix Díaz*, p. 140.
97. Weekly Report No. 363, 27 Mar. 1919, USDS, 812.00:21890; Weekly Report No. 364, 3 Apr. 1919, USDS 812.00:22890; Sánchez to Oficial Mayor, 9 Feb. 1920, AHSDN, XI/481.5/321, C152:68-70, 200-201, 258; Henderson, *Félix Díaz*, pp. 142-43. The charge that Obregón was in cahoots with Cejudo was denied vehemently by him, although it is plausible. See Hall, *Obregón*, p. 237.
98. Womack, *Zapata*, pp. 322ff; Henderson, *Félix Díaz*, p. 143; Corzo Ramírez et al., *...nunca un desleal*, p. 229; Deschamps to Aguilar, 19 Mar. 1919, AVC, C132/152:15024; Weekly Report No. 518, 17 May 1919, USDS 812.00:22726.
99. For a discussion of these attempts see Womack, *Zapata*, chap. 8.

Notes to Chapter 8

1. Hall, *Obregón*, p. 183.
2. Weekly Report No. 364, 3 Apr. 1919, USDS, 812.00:22890.
3. "Certain Information Concerning the Territory Embraced in the State of Veracruz, Northern Tabasco, Northern Chiapas and Eastern Oaxaca," 10-13 Aug. 1919, USDS, 812.00:23011; Corzo Ramírez et al. conclude that Aguilar's campaign in Veracruz effectively reasserted Constitutionalist control in many areas of the state. See Corzo Ramírez et al., *...nunca un desleal*, p. 231.
4. *El Dictámen*, 13 Jun. 1919, p. 6; 25 Jun. 1919, p. 6; 3 Jul. 1919, p. 6; 12 Jul. 1919, p. 6.
5. Stokes to Lansing, 4 Apr. 1919, USDS, 812.00:22604; "Memorandum" presented by Pedro del Villar to the U.S. Senate Subcommittee of the Committee on Foreign Relations, 6 Dec. 1919, USDS, 812.00:23262; "Memorandum to the President, and the People of the United States of America, our Neighboring Republic," signed by Amezcua, Díaz, Meixueiro, Angeles, Villa, and Peláez, 3 Sep. 1919, USDS, 812.00:23060; Henderson, *Félix Díaz*, p. 142.
6. Hall, *Obregón*, p. 183; *El Monitor Republicano*, 14 Mar. 1920, cited in Cumberland, *Mexican Revolution*, v. 2, p. 406.
7. Gavira, *Su actuación*, p. 139.
8. See Summerlin to Sec. State, 21 Jan. 1920, USDS, 812.00:23358, and Hall, *Obregón*, pp. 229-32, for Carranza's attempt to eliminate Obregón from the presidential race.

9. Weekly Report No. 361, 13 Mar. 1920, USDS, 812.00:23524; talks between the state government and the Yaquis had just been successfully completed. See Weekly Report No. 363, 27 Mar. 1920, USDS, 812.00:23539.

10. Law #30 in Rivera, *La Revolución*, pp. 522-23, cited in Hall, *Obregón*, pp. 235-36.

11. Obregón made this charge during his campaign speech in Tampico on March 28. See Dawson to Sec. State, 1 Apr. 1920, USDS, 812.00:23594; Dyer to Sec. State, 10 Apr. 1920, USDS, 812.00:23557.

12. Hanna to Sec. State, 13 Apr. 1920, USDS, 812.00:23686; Dawson to Sec. State, 21 Apr. 1920, USDS, 812.00:23693; Foster to Sec. State, 28 Apr. 1920, USDS, 812.00:23752.

13. Hall, *Obregón*, p. 242; the Plan of Aguaprieta makes specific mention of Carranza's violation of state sovereignty in para. 2 of the preamble. See translation of the plan in Dispatch No. 3149, Summerlin to Sec. State, 13 May 1920, USDS, 812.00:24098; Foster to Sec. State, 1 May 1920, USDS, 812.00:23793; 6 May 1920, USDS, 812.00:23857; 7 May 1920, USDS, 812.00:23865; Davidson Obrien to All America Cables, 7 May 1920, USDS, 812.00:23867; Castro Martínez, *Adolfo de la Huerta*, p. 44.

14. Foster to Sec. State, 8 May 1920, USDS, 812.00:23880; Dawson to Sec. State, 10 May 1920, USDS, 812.00:23955.

15. Foster to Sec. State, 19 May 1920, USDS, 812.00:24027; INEH, *Diccionario histórico y biográfico*, pp. 454-55.

16. Summerlin to Sec. State, 11 May 1920, USDS, 812.00:24093; Garciadiego, "Higinio Aguilar," p. 472.

17. Summerlin to Sec. State, 18 May 1920, USDS, 812.00:24134; "The Mexican Anarchy" by H. Grahame Richards, *The Pall Mall Gazette*, 12 May 1920 in USDS, 812.00:24132.

18. Summerlin to Sec. State, 31 May 1920, USDS, 812.00:24136; Foster to Sec. State, 8 May 1920, USDS, 812.00:24154; there is no resolution to the question of where Aguilar was between May 8 and June 1 when he reappeared in Veracruz port to embark on the first ship for Havana. See Corzo Ramírez et al., *...nunca un desleal*, pp. 244-45.

19. Marsh to Sec. State, 8 Jun. 1920, USDS, 812.00:24123.

20. Dawson to Sec. State, 30 May 1920, USDS, 812.00:24142. In fact, Peláez was at the head of the military parade with Obregón on the occasion of the swearing in of de la Huerta. See Summerlin to Sec. State, 8 Jun. 1920, USDS, 812.00:24124; 15 Jun. 1920, USDS, 812.00:24232.

21. Forces commanded by Guadalupe Sánchez attacked Carranza's train at Aljibes, a Pueblan town, forcing him to take to the hills, where he was later assassinated.

22. Summerlin to Sec. State, 29 Jun. 1920, USDS, 812.00:24335; 10 Aug. 1920, USDS, 812.00:24474.

23. Tejeda to Juan M. García et al., Jalapa, 8 Sep. 1921, AGVC-AAT, 1/6:26410-13.

24. Domínguez Pérez, *Política y movimientos sociales*, p. 17; Corzo Ramírez et al., *...nunca un desleal*, p. 227.

25. Pérez Díaz to Tejeda, 20 Aug. 1920, AGVC-AAT, 2/2:86; Foster to Sec. State, 13 Oct. 1920, USDS, 812.00:24786; Sandoval to Obregón, 12 Sep. 1920, AGVC-AAT, 2/2:54; Tejeda to Gutiérrez Reyes, 20 Sep. 1920, AGVC-AAT, v. 1:58; Tejeda to Márquez, 27 Sep. 1920, AGVC-AAT, v. 1:47.

26. Corzo Ramírez et al., *...nunca un desleal*, p. 58; Domínguez Pérez, *Política y movimientos sociales*, pp. 16-17, 24; García Díaz, *Textiles del Valle de Orizaba*, p. 131, 203; García Morales, *La rebelión delahuertista*, p. 17.

27. Domínguez Pérez, *Política y movimientos sociales*, p. 18.
28. Unnamed U.S. representative of General Meixueiro to Pedro del Villar, 1 April1919, AJA, VIII-2, C4:358; Bravo to Carranza, 5 Dec. 1919, AVC, C143/152:16529; Domínguez Pérez, *Política y movimientos sociales*, p. 24; Hall, *Obregón*, p. 252; García Morales, *La rebelión delahuertista*, pp. 9-11.
29. Domínguez Pérez, "Del sueño regional a la experiencia nacional," p. 24.
30. Corzo Ramírez, et al., *...nunca un desleal*, pp. 94-96.
31. Domínguez Pérez, *Política y movimientos sociales*, pp. 24-26; Domínguez Pérez, "Del sueño regional a la experiencia nacional," pp. 24-25.
32. Haber, *Industry and Underdevelopment*, p. 137; Corzo Ramírez et al., *...nunca un desleal*, p. 97; García Díaz, *Textiles*, p. 206.
33. Oil production in January 1921, for example, was the highest yet in Mexico. See Summerlin to Sec. State, 3 Mar. 1921, USDS, 812.00:24885; Fowler-Salamini, *Agrarian Radicalism*, pp. 27-28.
34. Basurto, *El proletariado industrial*, p. 185; Fowler-Salamini, *Agrarian Radicalism*, p. 26; Corzo Ramírez et al., *...nunca un desleal*, pp. 114-15.
35. Corzo Ramírez et al., *...nunca un desleal*, p. 111.
36. Falcón and García Morales, *La semilla en el surco*, p. 133; Fowler-Salamini, *Agrarian Radicalism*, p. 29-30.
37. Basurto, *El Proletariado Industrial*, p. 196; Haber, *Industry and Underdevelopment*, p. 123.
38. This law had been passed in 1918 but had not been implemented after an appeal to Carranza. See Lagarda to Carranza, Orizaba, 27 Dec. 1918, AVC, C128/152:14606; García Díaz, *Textiles del Valle de Orizaba*, p. 207; Domínguez Pérez, *Política y movimientos*, pp. 42-43; *El Demócrata*, 20 Jul. 1921, and *Excelsior*, 21 Jul. 1921, in USDS, 812.00:25119.
39. See Wood, *Revolution in the Street*, for an exhaustive treatment of this significant urban reform movement.
40. Gill, "Veracruz: Revolución y extremismo," p. 623, cited in Domínguez Pérez, *Política y movimientos*, p. 59.
41. Wood, *Revolution in the Street*, p. 150.
42. Fowler-Salamini, *Agrarian Radicalism*, p. 32; Domínguez Pérez, *Política y movimientos*, pp. 60-61.
43. Wood, *Revolution in the Street*, p. 207.
44. Domínguez Pérez, "Del sueño regional," p. 27; Acosta Díaz, *Lucha agraria en Veracruz*, p. 21.
45. García Morales, *La rebellión delahuertista*, pp. 17-18; Fowler-Salamini, *Agrarian Radicalism*, p. 38.
46. Acosta (mayor of Puente Nacional), to Tejeda, 14 Apr. 1923, AGVC-AAT, C15/82:1; Commission of the Veracruz Legislature to Obregón, 16 Apr. 1923, AGVC-AAT, C15/82:6-14; Falcon and García Morales, *La semilla en el surco*, p. 153; García Morales, *La rebellión delahuertista*, pp. 18ff; Domínguez Pérez, *Política y movimientos*, p. 63; Fowler-Salamini, *Agrarian Radicalism*, p. 39.
47. Falcon and García Morales, *La semilla en el surco*, p. 160; Castro Martínez, *Adolfo de la Huerta*, p. 92; Pani, *Mi contribución*, p. 299.
48. The use of the term "fascism" is problematic. See Sherman, *Mexican Right*, pp. xv-xvi, who argues for a stringent use of the term. Here, I use it in a generic sense. It is unarguable that certain elements in Veracruz were looking at fascism as a model to emulate.
49. Cortes to Ortega (Tejeda's secretary), Pánuco, 20 Jan. 1923, AGVC-AAT, C17/88:116; unsigned, report to Tejeda, n.d., AGVC-AAT, C15/82:3; Sánchez to Calles, 18 Aug. 1922, APEC, 77.2/2-5277:101.

50. In his second work on de la Huerta, Castro Martínez explains with more detail his conclusion that de la Huerta was coerced into a revolutionary position by Prieto Laurens. See Castro Martínez, *Adolfo de la Huerta: La Integridad*, pp. 209-10.

51. Castro Martínez, *Adolfo de la Huerta*, p. 104; García Morales, *La rebellión delahuertista*, pp. 190-11; Memo to Sec. Finance, 31 Jan. 1922, AGN-O/C, 241-H-R-129.

52. Castro Martínez, *Adolfo de la Huerta*, p. 105; García Morales, *La rebellión delahuertista*, p. 135.

53. Peláez was apparently involved in a scheme to declare the Huasteca independent of Mexico and then attach it to the United States. He had an agent in the U.S. inquire about the purchase of aircraft, two of which had already been shipped to him. Other conspirators in the de la Huerta rebellion were supposedly Senator Fall, Doheny, and St. Clair. See telegrams from Pelaez to John Camp in Venice, California, and San Antonio, Texas, 29 Nov. 1923, AGN-O/C, 101-R2-D-2, and Chief of the Federal Judicial Police to Attorney General, 12 Mar. 1924, AGN-O/C, 101-R2-D-2; Obregón to Lorenzo Muñoz, Mexico, 7 Dec. 1923, AGN-O/C, 101-R2-D-2.

54. Castro Martínez, *Adolfo de la Huerta*, p. 107; García Morales, *La rebellión delahuertista*, p. 113; García Rodríguez and other legislative deputies to Tejeda, 24 Aug. 1923, AGVC-AAT, C16/85:195.

55. Fowler-Salamini, *Agrarian Radicalism*, p. 42; Domínguez Pérez, "Del sueño regional," pp. 28-29.

56. García Morales, *La rebellión delahuertista*, p. 136.

57. Castro Martínez, *Adolfo de la Huerta*, p. 114; García Morales, *La rebellión delahuertista*, pp. 149-51; Calles to Tejeda, Mexico, 16 Feb. 1924, APEC, 26.6/15-5558:286; Calles to Tejeda, Torreón, 16 Feb. 1924, APEC, 26.6/15-5558:284.

58. García Morales, *La rebellión delahuertista*, p. 153.

59. Castro Martínez, *Adolfo de la Huerta*, pp. 120-21.

60. Because of the help received from the Veracruz *campesinos* in suffocating the rebellion, Tejeda was able to convince Obregón not to disarm them. See Falcón and García Morales, *La semilla en el surco*, p. 167.

61. Gen. Palma to Tejeda, Xalapa, 6 Jun. 1924, AGVC-AAT, 20/97:196; some campaign workers were also murdered. See Gen. Sec., Veracruz Workers' Party to Tejeda, 24 Jun. 1924, AGVC-AAT, 20/99:271.

62. Fowler-Salamini, *Agrarian Radicalism*, p. 55.

63. Falcon and García Morales, *La semilla en el surco*, p. 172; Tejeda to Obregón, Orizaba, 14 Aug. 1924, AGVC-AAT, 19/94:433; Fowler-Salamini, *Agrarian Radicalism*, p. 55.

64. El Dictámen, 15-16 Sep. 1925, cited in Fowler-Salamini, *Agrarian Radicalism*, p. 56; Domínguez Pérez, "Del sueño regional," p. 31.

65. Ponce to Calles, Orizaba, 17 Dec. 1924, AGVC-AAT, 21/102:340.

66. Falcón, *La semila en el surco*, p. 174.

67. Gamboa, "Los momentos de la actividad textil," pp. 257, 260-61.

68. Meyer et al., *Historia de la Revolución Mexicana*, v. 11, p. 158.

69. Bortz, "The Revolution of the Labour Regime," pp. 688-89.

70. Aguilar Sánchez, "Cronología de cuatro conflictos," *Anuario 6*, p. 277.

71. Ibid., p. 266.

72. Carr, *El movimiento obrera*, p. 168; Krauze et al., *Historia de la revolución Mexicana*, v. 10, p. 89.

73. Krauze et al., *Historia de la revolución Mexicana*, v. 10, p. 83-84.
74. Meyer, et al., *Historia de la Revolución Mexicana*, v. 11, pp. 159-62; Aguilar Sánchez, "Cronología de cuatro conflictos," *Anuario* 6, p. 285; Carr, *El movimiento obrera*, p. 169.
75. Meyer, et al., *Historia de la Revolución Mexicana*, v. 11, p. 166.
76. Benitez Juárez, " La organización sindical," *Anuario* 5, pp. 28-29; Reyna Muñoz, "150 conflictos en la industria textil," *Anuario* 7, p. 165; Carr, *El movimiento obrera*, p. 173.
77. Weddell to Sec. State, Mexico City, 6 Jul. 1926, USDS 812:278129; Schoenfeld to Sec. State, Mexico City, 3 Oct. 1927, USDFS 812:28819.
78. See Ivonne Carillo Dewar, *Industria petrolera y deasrrollo capitalista*, chap. 1, for a discussion of the antecedents to Article 27. See also Brown, *Oil and Revolution*, pp. 224-29; Knight, *Mexican Revolution*, v. 2, pp. 470-76.
79. Hermida Ruíz, *La batalla por el petroleo*, pp. 95-97; Manzur Ocaña, *La revolución permanente*, p. 251.
80. Meyer, *México y los Estados Unidos*, p. 154.
81. For a discussion of this development see ibid., pp. 155-57.
82. Ibid., p. 160.
83. *The Mexicanist*, 21 Jul. 1921, in USDS 812.00:25057.
84. Malpica Uribe, "Y 'la bola empezó,'" p. 1; Meyer, *México y Estados Unidos en el conflicto*, p. 222.
85. Malpica Uribe, "Y 'la bola empezó,'" p. 2; Hermida Ruíz, *La batalla por el petroleo*, pp. 124-25.
86. Alafita Méndez, "La administración privada"; Hermida Ruíz, *La batalla por el petroleo*, p. 137: Summerlin to Sec. State, 30 Jul. 1921, USDS, 812.00:25130.
87. Basurto, *El proletariado industrial*, pp. 245-47; Hermida Ruíz, *La batalla por el petroleo*, p. 139; O'Brien, *The Revolutionary Mission*, p. 271.
88. Meyer et al., *Historia de la Revolución Mexicana*, v. 10, p. 157.
89. Fowler-Salamini, *Agrarian Radicalism*, p. 57; O'Brien, *Revolutionary Mission*, p. 278; Benítez Juárez, "La organización sindical," p. 28. Coolidge's instructions to the new ambassador, Morrow, which, of course, Calles had no way of knowing, were to "avoid a confrontation with Mexico: he [Morrow] succeeded in obtaining important modifications in the Petrol legislation, and in return, helped Calles to consolidate his power internally. With these acts the revolutionary thrust of Calles' first years were attenuated, but his survival and the implementation of a new political system was ensured." See Buchenau, "Calles y el movimiento liberal en Nicaragua," *Boletín*, 9, Mar. 1992, p. 14.
90. Calles to Obregón, 20 Jan. 1927, APEC, 14.4/7:189-198; 10-B (a Calles spy, whose identity has never been revealed) to Calles, 15 Dec. 1926, APEC-ANEXO Fondo Plutarcho Elias Calles, Informaciones Confidenciales emitida por 10-B; Hermida Ruíz, *La batalla por el petroleo*, p. 124.
91. For the flow of telegrams between the various ministries, see Hermida Ruíz, *La batalla por el petroleo*, chap. 9; Jara to Calles, 11 Apr. 1926, APEC, E 11-Inv. 2960:42.
92. For details of the case see Hermida Ruíz, *La batalla por el petroleo*, pp. 147-58.
93. Pasquel, *Veracruzanos en la Revolución*, p. 75; Falcon and García Morales, *La semilla en el surco*, p. 174; Corzo Ramírez et al, *...nunca un desleal*, p. 265; Fowler-Salamini, *Agrarian Radicalism*, p. 57.

94. Memo, unsigned, n. d., AHUNAM-HJ, C33/1227:24155-24156; Fowler-Salamini, *Agrarian Radicalism*, p. 57; Falcon and García Morales, *La semilla en el surco*, p. 174; Hermida Ruíz, *La batalla por el petroleo*, pp. 166-69.
95. Obrien, *The Revolutionary Mission*, p. 252.
96. Haber, *Industry and Underdevelopment*, p. 124.
97. Katz, *The Secret War*, p. 321.
98. Loyola Díaz, *La crisis Obregón-Calles*, p. 14, argues that the regional situation was an impediment to constructing the national state. And Hall credits Obregón and Calles with establishing and maintaining a "powerful central government." See Hall, *Obregón*, pp. 255-59.

Notes to Chapter 9

1. Schama, *Citizens*, pp. 854-55.
2. Wood, *Revolution in the Streets*, p. xvi.
3. These were actually called neo-Científicos by contemporaries, who were referring mainly to members of Madero's own family.
4. Henderson, *In the Absence of Don Porfirio*, p. 191.
5. Falcón, *La semilla en el surco*, pp. 165, 225.
6. Fowler-Salamini, *Agrarian Radicalism in Veracruz*, p. 140.
7. Bortz, "The Revolution, the Labour Regime and Conditions of Work," pp. 697, 701.
8. Ibid.
9. Wood, *Revolution in the Street*, p. 215.
10. In this, Veracruz is probably similar to other areas of Mexico. In his study of Nuevo León, Cerutti uses the city of Monterrey to illustrate the limited impact of the revolution on the entrepreneurial class, which continued to dominate regional political and economic life. See Cerutti, " Monterrey: From Reform to Revolution," p. 58.

Glossary

Alcabalas	an internal sales tax
Amparo	a judicial order restraining the authorities, Mexican equivalent of *habeas corpus*
Cabildo	town council
Cacique	literally a chief, usually a strongman with a large following
Campesinos	peasants
Castas	people of mixed race
Caudillo	a leader, usually of national importance
Científico	literally scientist, but a derogatory name given to a political group in the Porfiriato
Conservatism	in Mexican terms a political ideology based on adherence to the monarchy, Church and army
Cuartelazo	a coup, usually refers to the Díaz-Huerta coup of February 1913
Ejido	a communal farm
Ejidatarios	members of a communal farm
Gachupines	a derogatory name for Spaniards
Gobernación	Interior ministry
Hacendado	large landowner with more than one thousand hectares of land
Infalsificable	currency issued by Carranza that was suposedly immune to counterfeiting
-ismo	suffix referring to the policies of a president or political movement, e.g. Huertismo (Huerta)
-istas	the suffix means followers of. For example, Maderistas, followers of Madero
Jefe político	political boss, usually magistrate in charge of a state canton
Ley Lerdo	one of the Reform Laws (1856), which prohibited ecclesiastical and civil institutions form owning property. The law affected Indian communal properties.
Ley Fuga	literally, Law of Flight, a method of executing prisoners by shooting them in the back, claiming they were trying to escape

Ley Lerdo	a law passed in the Reforma (1850s) oulawing communal land-holding
Liberalism	a political ideology whose main tenets were federalism and secularism
Mestizo	mixture of Spanish and Indian
Morelense	person from Morelos
Porfiriato	the period from 1876-1911 under President Porfirio Díaz
Puros	"pure" liberals, initially a term designating the radical liberals of the early nineteenth century, who were mostly opposed to the Roman Catholic Church
Ranchero	small landowner with less than one thousand hectares of land
Reforma	the period of Liberal reforms under President Juárez in the 1850s
Reparto	redistribution of land to peasants
Rurales	a mounted police corps deployed mainly in the countryside
Sierra	mountain
Soldadera	female camp follower, but recently given recognition as soldiers in the revolution
Tienda de Raya	company store, used as a means to bind pesants and workers to their place of employment
Veracruzano	person from Veracruz
Zapatistas	followers of Emiliano Zapata, the peasant leader from Morelos. Between 1911 and 1919, when he was murdered, Zapata led a peasant army in the state of Morelos claiming the return of lands stolen during the Porfiriato. Zapata went on to oppose succesively, Madero, Huerta, and Carranza, who paid him as little heed as had Porfirio Díaz.

Abbreviations

AEM	Archivo Espinoso de los Monteros, Instituto Nacional de Antropología e Historia, Mexico City
AFD	Archivo Félix Díaz, CONDUMEX, Mexico City
AFM	Archivo Francisco Madero, Instituto Nacional de Antropología e Historia, Mexico City
AGN-ARD	Archivo General de la Nación, Archivo Robles Domínguez, Mexico City
AGN-CD/INEHRM	Archivo General de la Nación, Colleción Documental, Instituto Nacional de Estudios Históricos de la Revolución Mexicana
AGN-CR	Archivo General de la Nación, Cuerpo Rurales
AGN-CREV	Archivo General de la Nación, Collecion Revolución
AGN-FMCA	Archivo General de la Nación, Francisco Madero, Catálogo alfabético
AGN-FMLC	Archivo General de la Nación, Francisco Madero, Libro Copiador
AGN-O/C	Archivo General de la Nación, Gobernación, Obregón/Calles
AGN-PR	Archivo General de la Nación, Gobernación, Periodo Revolución
AGN-RR	Archivo General de la Nación, Gobernación, Ramo Revolución
AGN-RRFM	Archivo General de la Nación, Ramo Revolución, Francisco Madero
AGN-SC	Archivo General de la Nación, Suprema Corte
AHMVC	Archivo Histórico Municipal de Veracruz
AHSDN	Archivo Histórico de la Secretaría de la Defensa Nacional, Mexico City
AHUNAM-DLB	Archivo Histórico de la Universidad Nacional Autónoma de México, Archivo De la Barra, Mexico City
AHUNAM-HJ	Archivo Histórico de la Universidad Nacional Autónoma de México, Archivo Heriberto Jara

AGVC-AAT	Archivo General del Estado de Veracruz-Llave, Archivo Adalberto A. Tejeda
AGVC-AMI	Archivo General del Estado de Veracruz-Llave, Gobernación, Administración Municipal, Informes, Xalapa
AGVC-ASC/BM	Archivo General del Estado de Veracruz-Llave, Gobernación, Actividades Sociales y Culturales, Banda Musical
AGVC-ASC/DP	Archivo General del Estado de Veracruz-Llave, Gobernación, Actividades Sociales y Culturales, Diversones Públicas
AGVC-C	Archivo General del Estado de Veracruz-Llave, Gobernación, Comunicaciones
AGVC-EE	Archivo General del Estado de Veracruz-Llave, Gobernación, Elecciones Estatales
AGVC-M	Archivo General del Estado de Veracruz-Llave, Gobernación, Milícia (Destacamentos Federales)
AGVC-PP	Archivo General del Estado de Veracruz-Llave, Gobernación, Partidos Políticos
AGVC-Q	Archivo General del Estado de Veracruz-Llave, Gobernación, Quejas
AGVC-SP/TP	Archivo General del Estado de Veracruz-Llave, Gobernación, Seguridad Pública (Fuerzas Cantonales)/ Tranquilidad Pública
AJA	Archivo Jenaro Amexcua, CONDUMEX
ANPVC	Archivo Notaria Pública de Veracruz, Xalapa
APEC	Archivo Plutarcho Elías Calles, Mexico City
ATD	Archivo General del Estado de Veracruz-Llave, Archivo Teodoro Dehesa
AVC	Archivo Venustiano Carranza, CONDUMEX
AZ	Archivo Zongólico, Instituto Nacional de Antropología e Historia, Mexico City
CAM	Archivo General del Estado de Veracruz, Archivo Comisión Agraria Mixta
CPD	Colección Porfirio Díaz, Universidad Iberoamericana, Mexico City
FO	Public Records Office, Foreign Office (Great Britain), México, El Colegio de México, Mexico City
SP&P	Sir Weetman Peerson Archive, The Nettie Lee Benson Latin American Collection, The University of Texas
USDS	United States, Department of State, México, El Colegio de México; The Nettie Lee Benson Collection, The University of Texas, Austin

Bibliography

A. *Newspapers*

El Ahuizote (Mexico City), 1911
Basler Nachrichten, 1892
El Cosmopólita (Orizaba), 1897, 1898, 1905
El Debate (Corralista), July 1910–Sept. 1910
El Demócrata, Sept–Nov. 1914, 1915, March–April 1919
El Diario, 1906–1907, 20 Nov. 1910–28 May 1911
El Diario del Hogar, 1893, 1895, 1897, 1910–1912
El Dictámen (Veracruz), 1904–1920
Excelsior (Constitutionalist), 28 March 1917– 27 April 1917, 1960
Germinal (Orizaba), 1909
Gil Blas, June 1910–June 1911
El Heraldo Mexicano, Oct. 1910–April 1911
El Hijo de Ahuizote, 1896, March–Dec. 1913, Jan.–March 1914
Ideas Nuevas, 1907
El Imparcial of Texas, 1915
El Imparcial (Científico), 1901, 2 Jan. 1913–31 Dec. 1913, 1933
La Jornada, 1997
La Mañana, 1911–1912
Le Matín, 1906
Mexican Herald, 1912
The Mexicanist, 1921
Mexico Nuevo, April–Dec. 1910
El Monitor Republicano, 1892, 1896, Sept.–Oct. 1919, Nov. 1920
La Nación (Mexico City), 1912
El Nacional, March–April , 1893, 1896, Dec. 1917, Feb.–Dec. 1918, April–June
   1919
La Nueva Era (Mexico: Organ del Partido Constitucional Progresista), 1911–1912
La Opinión (Veracruz), 1914
La Opinión (Texas), 1934

El País, Jan.–Nov. 1910, Jan.–June 1911
El Paladín, 1901–1902
Pall Mall Gazette, 1920
La Patria, 1904, 1905, 1906, 1911
El Periodico del Estado de Veracruz, 1924–1927
El Radical, 1915
El Reproductor, 1893, 1895–1897, 1899, 1900, 1906–1908
El Siglo Veinte, 1911
Los Sucesos (Veracruz), 1903
El Sufragio Libre, 1 Feb. 1911–19 July 1911.
The Sun Newspaper, 1911
El Tiempo, 1907
El Universal (Constitutionalist), 1 Jan. 1917–

B. Published Government Documents

Camara de Diputados de México. *Diario de debates, 1906*. Mexico City: Imprenta del Gobierno Federal, 1907.
Comisión de Investigaciones Históricos de la Revolución Mexicana. Edited by Isidro Fabela. *Documentos Históricos de la Revolución Mexicana: Revolución y Régimen Constitucionalista, II*. Mexico: Fondo de Cultura Económica, 1962.
Estado de Veracruz-Llave. *Leyes, decretos y circulares del estado de Veracruz-Llave, 1855–56*. Xalapa: Imprenta del Gobierno del estado, 1889.
Estado de Veracruz-Llave. *Leyes, decretos y circulares, 1892- 1912*. Xalapa: Imprenta del Gobierno del estado, 1892–1912.
Estado de Veracruz-Llave. *Peridodico oficial, 1907*. Xalapa: n.p., 1908.
Ministerio de Justicia, Fomento y Instrucción Pública, Sección de Fomento. *Colleción de Leyes,1900–1911*. Mexico City: n.p., 1912.
Secretaría de Gobernación. *Memoria de la Secretaría de Gobernación, comprendido entre el 1 de Julio de 1911 y el 20 de Febrero de 1913*, Vol. 1. Mexico City: Diario Oficial, 1913.
———. *Memoria de la Secretaría de Gobernación, correspondiente al periodo revolucionario comprendido entre el 19 de febrero de 1913 y el 30 de noviembre de 1916*. Mexico City: n.p., 1916.

C. Monographs, Theses, and Chapters

Acosta Díaz, C. P. Vladimir. *La lucha agraria en Veracruz*. 3 vols. Xalapa: Gobierno del Estado de Veracruz, 1989.
Agetro, Leafar. *Las luchas proletarias en Veracruz: historia y autocrítica*. Jalapa: Editorial Barricada, 1942.
Aguilar Camín, Héctor. *La frontera nómada: Sonora y la revolución mexicana*. Mexico: Siglo XXI, 1986.
Albro III, Ward Sloan. *Always a Rebel: Ricardo Flores Magón and the Mexican Revolution*. Fort Worth: Texas Christian University Press, 1992.
———. *Ricardo Flores Magón: An Inquiry into the Origins of the Mexican Revolution 1910*. Ph.D. diss., University of Arizona, 1967.
———. *To Die on Your Feet: The Life, Times, and Writings of Práxedis G. Guerrero*. Fort Worth: Texas Christian University Press, 1996.
Anderson, Rodney. *Outcasts in Their Own Land: Mexican Industrial Workers, 1906-1911*. DeKalb: Northern Illinois University Press, 1976.

———. *The Mexican Textile Labor Movement, 1906–07: an Analysis of a Labor Crisis.* Ph.D. diss., University of Arizona, 1967.

Ankerson, Dudley. *Agrarian Warlord: Saturnino Cedillo and the Mexican Revolution in San Luis Potosí.* DeKalb: Northern Illinois University Press, 1976.

———. *Some Aspects of Economic Change and the Origins of the Mexican Revolution, 1876–1910: Working Papers #12.* Cambridge: Cambridge University Press for the Center for Latin American Studies, n.d.

Aragón, Augustín. *Porfirio Díaz.* 2 vols. Mexico City: Editorial Intercontinental, 1962.

Araíza, Luis. *Historia del movimiento obrero mexicano.* 4 vols. Mexico City: Editorial Cuauhtémoc, 1964.

Arroniz, Joaquín. *La costa de Sotavento.* Mexico: Editorial Citlaltepetl, 1961.

Aston, B.W. *The Public Career of José Yves Limantour.* Ph.D. diss., Texas Technical University, 1972.

Avila, Ricardo. "¡Así se gobierna señores'!: El gobierno de José Vicente Villada." In *The Revolutionary Process in Mexico; Essays on Political and Social Change, 1880–1940,* edited by Rodríguez O., Jaime E. Los Angeles: UCLA Latin American Center Publications, 1990.

Azaola Garrido, Elena. *Rebelión y derrota del magonismo agrario.* Mexico City: Fondo de cultura económica, 1982.

Baerlein, Henry. *Mexico the Land of Unrest.* London: Herbert and Daniel, 1913.

Baldwin, Deborah J. *Protestants and the Mexican Revolution: Missionaries, Ministers, and Social Change.* Chicago: University of Illinois Press, 1990.

Barragan Rodríguez, Juan. *Historia del ejército y de la revolución constitucionalista,* 2 vols. Mexico City: n.p., 1946.

Barrera Bassols, Jacinto. *El bardo y el bandolero: La persecución de Santanón por Díaz Mirón.* Puebla: Universidad Autónoma de Puebla, 1987.

Barrera Fuentes, Florencio. *Historia de la revolución mexicana: La etapa precursora.* Mexico: Talleres Gráficos de la Nación, 1955.

Bastian, Jean-Pierre. *Los disidentes: Sociedades protestantes y revolución en México, 1872–1911.* Mexico: Fondo de cultura económica, 1989.

Basurto, Jorge. *El conflicto internacional en torno al petroleo de Mexico.* Mexico: Siglo XXI, 1976.

———. *El proletariado industrial en Mexico, 1850–1930.* Mexico: Universidad Nacional Autónoma de México, 1981.

Bazant, Jan. *Historia de la deuda exterior de México (1823-1946).* Mexico City: El Colegio de México, 1968.

Beals, Carleton. *Porfirio Díaz: Dictator of Mexico.* Philadelphia: J.B.Lippincott, 1932.

Beezley, William H. *Insurgent Governor: Abraham González and the Mexican Revolution in Chihuahua.* Lincoln: University of Nebraska Press, 1973.

Bellingeri, Marco, and Isabel Gil Sanchez. "Las estructuras agrarias bajo el porfiriato." In *Mexico en el siglo XIX: Historia económica y de la estructura social,* edited by Ciro Cardoso. Mexico City: Editorial Nueva Imágen, 1930.

Belmonte Guzmán, Maria de la Luz. *La organización territorial de Veracruz en el siglo XIX.* Xalapa: Seminario de Historia, Universidad Veracruzana, 1987.

Benjamin, Thomas, and Mark Wasserman, eds. *Provinces of the Revolution: Essays on Regional Mexican History, 1910–29.* Albuquerque: University of New Mexico Press, 1990.

Bernstein, Harry. "Regionalism in the National History of Mexico." In *Latin American History: Essays on Its Study and Teaching, 1898–1965,* edited by Howard F. Cline. Austin: University of Texas Press, 1967.

Blázquez Domínguez, Carmen. *Miguel Lerdo y Tejada: Un liberal veracruzano en la política nacional*. Mexico City: El Colegio de México, 1978.

———. *Políticos y comerciantes en Veracruz y Xalapa, 1827–1829*. Jalapa: Gobierno del Estado de Veracruz, 1992.

———. *Veracruz*. Jalapa: Gobierno del Estado de Veracruz, 1988.

———. *Veracruz Liberal, 1858–60*. Mexico: El Colegio de México, 1986.

———. ed. *Veracruz: Textos de su historia*. Jalapa: Gobierno del Estado de Veracruz, Instituto veracruzano de cultura, Instituto de investigaciones Dr. José María Luis Mora, 1988.

Bonilla, Manuel, Jr. *El régimen maderista*. Mexico: Biblioteca histórico de El Universal, 1922.

Braderman, Eugene M. *A Study of Political Parties and Politics in Mexico since 1890*. Urbana: University of Illinois, 1938.

Brading, D.A. *Caudillo and Peasant in the Mexican Revolution*. Cambridge: Cambridge University Press, 1980.

Braniff, Oscar J. "Observaciones sobre el fomento agricola considerando como base para la ampliación del credito agricola en Mexico." In *La cuestión de la tierra 1910-1911*, edited by Jesus Silva Herzog. 2 vols. Mexico City: Instituto Mexicano de Investigaciones Económicas, 1960.

Brown, Jonathan. *Oil and Revolution in Mexico*. Berkeley: University of California Press, 1993.

Bryan, Anthony T. "Mexican Politics in Transition 1900-13: The Role of General Bernardo Reyes." Ph.D. diss., University of Nebraska, 1969.

Buisson, Inge, Günther Kahle, Hans-Joachim König, Horst Pietschman. *Problemas de la formación del estado y de la nación en Hispanoamerica*. Köln: Böhlau Verlag, 1984.

Bulnes, Francisco. *El verdadero Díaz y la revolución*. Mexico City: Gómez de la Puente, 1920.

Cadenhead, Ivie E., Jr. *Benito Juárez*. New York: Twayne, 1973.

Calvert, Peter. *The Mexican Revolution 1910-14: the Diplomacy of Anglo-American Conflict*. Cambridge: Cambridge University Press, 1968.

Cárdenas, Enrique. "A Macroeconomic Interpretation of Nineteenth-Century Mexico." In *How Latin America Fell behind: Essays on the Economic Histories of Brazil and Mexico, 1800–1914*, edited by Stephen Haber. Stanford: Stanford University Press, 1997.

Carr, Barry. *El movimiento obrero y la política en México, 1910–1929*. Mexico City: Ediciones Era, 1981.

Carrillo Dewar, Ivonne. *Industria petrolera y desarrollo capitalista en el norte de Veracruz, 1900–1970*. Xalapa: Universidad Veracruzana, 1993.

Castro Martínez, Pedro. *Adolfo de la Huerta: La integridad como arma de la revolución*. Mexico City: Siglo veintiuno editores, 1998.

———. *Adolfo de la Huerta y la Revolución Mexicana*. Mexico City: Instituto Nacional de Estudios Historicos de la Revolución Mexicana, 1992.

Cerutti, Mario. "Monterrey: From Region to Revolution." In Wil Pansters and Arij Ouweneel, eds. *Region, State and Capitalism in Mexico: Nineteenth and Twentieth Centuries*. Amsterdam: CEDLA (Centre for Latin American Research), 1989.

Chacón Caporal, Adolfo. *El balance de la Reforma Agraria en el estado de Veracruz*. Mexico City: Universidad Nacional Autónoma de México, 1958.

Chávez Orozco, Luis, and Enrique Florescano. *Agricultura y industria textil de Veracruz: Siglo XIX*. Xalapa: Universidad Veracruzana, 1965.

Círculo Nacional Porfirista, Convención Nacional Porfirista, April de 1909. Mexico City: La Helvetia, 1909.

Cockroft, James D. *Intellectual Precursors of the Mexican Revolution 1900-13*. Austin: University of Texas Press, 1968.

————. *Mexico: Class Formation, Capital Accumulation and the State*. New York: Monthly Review Press, 1983.

Cockcroft, James, Andre Gundar Frank, and Dale H. Johnson. *Dependency and Underdevelopment: Latin America's Political Economy*. New York: Doubleday, 1972.

Córdova, Arnaldo. *La ideología de la revolución mexicana: La formación del nuevo régimen*. Mexico: Ediciones Era, 1973.

Corzo Ramírez, Ricardo, José G. González Sierra, and David A. Skerritt *...nunca un desleal: Cándido Aguilar, 1889–1960*. Mexico City: El Colegio de Mexico, 1986.

Cosío Villegas, Daniel, ed. *Historia moderna de México*. 10 vols. Mexico City: Editorial Hermes, 1957.

————. *Porfirio Díaz en la revuelta de La Noria*. Mexico City: Editorial Hermes, 1953.

Costeloe, Michael A. *The Central Republic in Mexico, 1835–46: Hombres de bien in the Age of Santa Anna*. Cambridge: Cambridge University Press, 1993.

Cott, Kenneth S. *Porfirian Investment Policies, 1876-1910*. Ann Arbor: Michigan University Press, 1982.

Cumberland, Charles C. *Mexican Revolution*. 2 vols. Austin: University of Texas, 1974.

De Bassols Batalla, Angel. *Diódoro Batalla: huella de su pasión y de su esfuerzo*. Mexico: n.p., 1957.

————. *Las Huastecas en el desarrollo regional de México*. Mexico City: Editorial Tritles, 1977.

De Fornaro, Carlos. *México tal cual es: Comentarios*. Philadelphia: n.p.,1909.

Dehesa, Teodoro A. *Memoria,1894–96*. Xalapa: Estado de Veracuz-Llave, 1897.

De la Peña, Moisés. *Veracruz económico*. 2 vols. Mexico: Gobierno del Estado de Veracruz, 1946.

Del Castillo, Porfirio. *Puebla y Tlaxcala en los días de la revolución*. Mexico: Zavala, 1953.

De María y Campos, Armando. *La revolución mexicana a través de los corridos populares, Tomo I*. Mexico: Biblioteca del Instituto Nacional de Estudios Históricos de la Revolución Mexicana, 1962.

De Pallares, Sodi. *Teodoro A. Dehesa: una época y un hombre*. Mexico City: Editorial Citlaltepetl, 1959.

De Vore, Blanche. *The Influence of Antonio Díaz Soto y Gama on the Agrarian Movement in Mexico*. Ph.D. diss., University of Southern California, 1963.

De Zayas Enriquez, Rafael. *Porfirio Díaz*. Translated by T. Quincy Bourne, Jr. New York: Appleton, 1908.

————. *The Case of Mexico and the Policy of President Wilson*. Translated by Andre Tridon. New York: A. and C. Boni, 1914.

Díaz Dufoo, Carlos. *Limantour*. Mexico City: Editorial Eusebio Gómez de la Puente, 1910.

Díaz Soto y Gama, Antonio. *La revolución agraria del sur y Emiliano Zapata, su caudillo*. Mexico City: Talleres Policromía, 1960.

Didapp, Juan Pedro. *Gobiernos militares*. Mexico City: Librería Español, 1904.

————. *Partidos políticos de México: La política del dinero y la política del patrio- tismo*. Mexico City: Librería Española, 1903.

DiTella, Torcuato S. *National Popular Politics in Early Independent Mexico, 1820–1847*. Albuquerque: University of New Mexico Press, 1996.

Doblado, Manuel. *México para los Mexicanos: El Presidente Huerta y su Gobierno*. Mexico City: Antonio Enríquez, 1913.

Domínguez, Miguel. *Cómo salió el General Díaz al fracasar la revolución de La Noria*. Mexico City: n. p., 1947.

Domínguez Castilla, José M. *Ensayo crítico histórico sobre la revolución de La Noria*. Mexico City: El Cuadratín, 1934.

Domínguez Milán, Carlos. *Tuxpán: Capital provisional del primer gobierno constitucionalista*. Xalapa: Universidad Veracruzana, 1964.

Domínguez Pérez, Olivia. "Del sueño regional a la experiencia nacional." In *Agraristas y agrarismo*, edited by Olivia Domínguez Pérez and Feliciano García Aguirre. Xalapa: Consejo Técnico Consultiva de la Liga de Comunidades y Sindicatos Campesinos del Estado de Veracruz, 1992.

———. *Política y movimientos sociales en el tejedismo*. Xalapa: Universidad Veracruzana, 1986.

Domínguez Pérez, Olivia, and Feliciano García Aguirre, eds. *Agraristas y agrarismo*. Xalapa: Consejo Técnico Consultiva de la Liga de Comunidades y Sindicatos Campesinos del Estado de Veracruz, 1992.

Donnell, Guy R. "The United States Military Government at Veracruz, Mexico." In *Essays in Mexican History*, edited by Thomas E Cohner and Carlos E. Castaneda. Austin: University of Texas Press, 1958.

Ducey, Michael T. "Liberal Theory and Peasant Practice: Land and Power in Northern Veracruz, Mexico, 1826–1900." In *Liberals, The Church, and Indian Peasants: Corporate Lands and the Challenge of Reform in Nineteenth-Century Spanish America*, edited by Jackson, Robert H. Albuquerque: University of New Mexico Press, 1997.

El Colegio de México. *Estadísticas económicas del Porfiriato*. Mexico City: El Colegio de México, 1956.

Espinosa, Gonzalo N., Joaquín Pina and Carlos B. Ortíz. *La decena roja*. Mexico City: n. p., 13.

Estrada, Roque. *La Revolución y Francisco I. Madero*. Guadalajara: Imprenta Americana, 1912.

Estrada Reynoso, Roque. *La revolución y Francisco I. Madero*. Mexico City: Instituto Nacional de Estudios Históricos de la Revolución Mexicana, 1985.

Fabela, Isidro, ed. *Documentos históricos de la Revolución Mexicana*. Mexico City: Fondo de Cultura Económica, 1960.

Falcón, Romana. *El agrarismo en Veracruz: La etapa radical*. Mexico City: El Colegio de México, 1977.

———. *Revolución y caciquismo: San Luis Potosí, 1910–1938*. Mexico: El Colegio de Mexico, 1984.

Falcón, Romana, and Soledad García Morales. *La semilla en el surco: Adalberto Tejeda y el radicalismo en Veracruz, 1883–1960*. Mexico City: El Colegio de México, 1986.

Fernández Rojas, José. *La revolución mexicana: De Porfirio Díaz á Victoriano Huerta*. Mexico City: F.P. Rojas, 1913.

Flores, Jorge D. *La revolución de Olarte en Papantla (1836-38)*. Mexico City: Imprenta Mundial, 1938.

Flores Magón, Ricardo. *1914: La Intervención Americana en Mexico*. Mexico City: Antorcha, 1981.

Foster, George McClelland. *A Primitive Mexican Economy*. Seattle: University of Washington Press, 1966.

Fowler-Salamini, Heather. *Agrarian Radicalism in Veracruz, 1920–38.* Lincoln: University of Nebraska Press, 1971.

Friedrich, Paul. *Agrarian Revolt in a Mexican Village.* Chicago: University of Chicago Press, 1977.

Gamboa, Leticia. "Los momentos de la actividad textil." In *La industria textil en México,* edited by Aurora Gómez-Galvarriato. Mexico City: Instituto de Investigaciones Dr. José María Luis Mora, 1999.

García Cantú, Gastón. *El pensamiento de la reacción mexicana: historia documental 1810-62.* Mexico City: Empreson Editoriales, 1965.

García Díaz, Bernardo. *Textiles del Valle de Orizaba, 1880–1925.* Xalapa: Universidad Veracruzana, 1990.

———. *Un pueblo fabril del Porfiriato: Santa Rosa, Veracruz.* Mexico: Fondo de Cultura Económica-Secretaría de Educación Pública/80, 1981.

García Díaz, Bernardo and Laura Zevallos Ortíz. *Orizaba-Veracruz: Imágenes de su historia.* Xalapa: Gobierno del Estado, 1989.

Garciadiego Dantán, Javier. *Revolución constitucionalista y contrarevolución: Movimientos reaccionarios en México, 1914–20,* Ph.D. diss., El Colegio de México, 1981.

García Granados, Ricardo. *Historia de México desde la república en 1867 hasta la caída de Porfirio Díaz.* 4 vols. Mexico City: A. Botas y hijos, 1912.

García Morales, Soledad. *La rebelión delahuertista en Veracruz (1923).* Xalapa: Universidad Veracruzana, 1986.

García Mundo, Octavio. *El movimiento inquilinario de Veracruz, 1922.* Mexico City: SepSetentas, 1976.

Gavira, Gabriel. *Su actuación político-militar revolucionaria.* Mexico City: A. del Bosque, 1933.

Gilly, Adolfo. "Chiapas and the Rebellion of the Enchanted World." In *Rural Revolt in Mexico: U.S. Intervention and the Domain of Subaltern Politics,* edited by Daniel Nugent. Durham: Duke University Press, 1998.

———. *La formación de la conciencia obrera en México.* Xalapa: Universidad Veracruzana, 1979.

Goldstone, Jack A., ed. *Revolutions: Theoretical, Comparative, and Historical Studies.* Fort Worth: Harcourt Brace, 1994.

Gómez-Galvarriato, Aurora, ed. *La industria textil en México.* Mexico City: Instituto de Investigaciones Dr. José María Luis Mora, 1999.

González, Fernando and José Covarrubías. *El problema rural de Mexico.* México City: Secretaría de Hacienda, 1917.

González Cossío. *Xalapa: Breve reseña histórica.* Mexico City: n.p., 1957.

González Garza, Federico. *La revolución mexicana: Mi contribución político-literaria.* Mexico City: A. del Bosque, 1936.

González Marín, Silvia. *Heriberto Jara, luchador obrero en la Revolución Mexicana, 1879–1917.* Mexico City: Sociedad Cooperativa Publicaciones Mexicanas, S.C.L., 1984.

González Molina, José Ignacio. *Católogo de documentos: Carta de la Colección Porfirio Díaz.* Mexico: Universidad Ibero Americana, 1987.

González Navarro, Moisés. *Historia Moderna de México. El Porfiriato. La vida social.* Vol. 4 of *Historia moderna de México.* Edited by Daniel Cosío Villegas. 9 vols. Mexico City: Editorial Hermes, 1957.

González Ramírez, Manuel. *La huelga de Cananea.* Mexico: Fondo de Cultura Económica, 1956.

———. Prologue to *Epistolario y textos de Ricardo Flores Magón.* Edited by Manuel González Ramírez. Mexico City: Fondo de Cultura Económico.

González Roa, Fernando. *El aspecto agrario de la Revolución Mexicana*. Mexico City: Liga de Economistas Revolucionarios de la República Mexicana, 1975.

González Sempé, Aurelio. *Evolución política y constitucional del estado de Veracruz-Llave*. Mexico City: Seminario de derecho constitucional, 1965.

González Sierra, José. *Monopolio del humo: Elementos para la historia del tabaco en México y algunas conflictos de tabaqueros veracruzanos: 1915–1930*. Xalapa: Universidad Veracruzana, 1987.

González y González, Luis. *La República restaurada: La vida social*. Vol. 3 of *Historia moderna de México*. Edited by Daniel Cosío Villegas. 9 vols. Mexico City: Editorial Hermes, 1957.

Guerra, Francois Xavier. *Le Mexique de l'ancien régime a la Révolucion*. 2 vols. Paris: L'Harmattan, 1985.

Haber, Stephen H. *Industry and Underdevelopment: The Industrialization of Mexico, 1890–1940*. Stanford: Stanford University Press, 1989.

———, ed. *How Latin America Fell Behind: Essays on the Economic History of Brazil and Mexico*. Stanford: Stanford University Press, 1997.

Hale, Charles A. *Mexican Liberalism in the Age of Mora, 1821–1853*. New Haven: Yale University Press, 1968.

———. "Political Ideas and Ideologies in Latin America, 1870–1930." In *Ideas and Ideologies in Twentieth Century Latin America*, edited by Leslie Bethell. Cambridge: Cambridge University Press, 1996.

———. *The Transformation of Mexican Liberalism in Late Nineteenth-Century Mexico*. Princeton: Princeton University Press, 1989.

Hall, Linda B. *Alvaro Obregón: Power and Revolution in Mexico, 1911–1920*. Austin: Texas A&M University Press, 1981.

———. *Oil, Banks and Politics: The United States and Post-revolutionary Mexico, 1917–1924*. Austin: University of Texas Press, 1995.

Hamnett, Brian R. "Factores Regionales." In *Problemas de la formación del estado y de la nación en Hispanoamerica*, edited by Inge Buisson et al. Köln: Böhlau Verlag, 1984.

———. *Juárez*. London: Longman, 1994.

Harrer, Hans Juergen. *Raíces económicas de la revolución mexicana*. Translated by Ingrid Geist. Mexico City: Taller Abierto, 1979.

Hart, John Mason. *Anarchism and the Mexican Working Class, 1860-1931*. Austin: University of Texas Press, 1978.

———. *Revolutionary Mexico: The Coming and Process of the Mexican Revolution*. Berkeley: University of California Press, 1987.

Henderson, Peter V. N. *Félix Díaz, the Porfirians, and the Mexican Revolution*. Lincoln: University of Nebraska Press, 1981.

———. *In the Absence of Don Porfirio: Francisco de la Barra and the Mexican Revolution*. Wilmington: Scholarly Resources, 2000.

Hermida Ruiz, Angel J. *La batalla por el petroleo en Veracruz*. Xalapa: Gobierno del Estado de Veracruz, 1991.

Hernández, Salvador, "Tiempos libertarios: El Magonismo en México; Cananea, Río Blanco y Baja California." In *La Clase Obrera en la Historia de México: De la dictadura porfirista a los tiempos*, edited by Ciro F. S. Cardoso, Francisco G. Hermosillo, and Salvador Hernández. Mexico City: Siglo veintiuno editores, 1991.

Hernández Chávez, Alicia. *La tradición republicana del buen gobierno*. Mexico City: El Colegio de México, 1993.

Holden, Robert H. *Mexico and the Survey of Public Lands: The Management of Modernization*. DeKalb: Northern Illinois University Press, 1994.

Huerta, Adolfo de la. *Memorias*. Mexico City: Editorial Guzmán, 1957.

Huerta, Victoriano. *Memorias del General Victoriano Huerta*. Barcelona: Librería de Quiroga, 1915.

Huntington, Samuel P. "Revolution and Political Order." In *Revolutions: Theoretical, Comparative and Historical Studies*, edited by Jack A. Goldstone. Fort Worth: Harcourt, Brace, 1994.

Instituto Nacional de Estudios Históricos de la Revolución Mexicana. *Diccionario histórico y biográfico*, vol. 7. Mexico City: n.p., 1992.

———. *Triunfo de la Revolución Maderista: del Plan de San Luis Potosí á la renuncia de Porfirio Díaz*. Mexico City: n.p., 1985.

Iturribaría, Jorge Fernando. *Porfirio Díaz ante la historia*. Mexico City: n.p., 1967.

Jacobs, Ian. *Ranchero Revolt: The Mexican Revolution in Guerrero*. Austin: University of Texas Press, 1982.

Joseph, Gilbert M. *Revolution from Without: Yucatán, Mexico and the United States, 1880–1924*. Cambridge: University of Cambridge Press, 1982.

Joseph, Gilbert M., and Daniel Nugent, eds. *Everyday Forms of State Formation: Revolution and the Negotiation of Rule in Modern Mexico*. Durham: Duke University Press, 1994.

Katz, Friedrich. "Condiciones de trabajo en las haciendas de Mexico durante el Porfiriato: Modalidades y tendencias." In *La servidumbre agraria en Mexico en la época porfiriana*, edited by Friedrich Katz and translated by Antonieta Sánchez Mejorada. Mexico City: SepSetentas, 1976.

———. *Deutschland, Díaz und die mexikanische Revolution: Die deutsche politik in Mexico, 1870–1920*. Berlin: VEB Deutscher Verlag der Wissenschaften, 1964.

———. *The Secret War in Mexico: Europe, the United States, and the Mexican Revolution*. Chicago: University of Chicago Press, 1983.

———. ed. *Riot, Rebellion, and Revolution: Rural Social Conflict in Mexico*. Princeton: Princeton University Press, 1988.

Keremitsis, Dawn. *La industria textil mexicana en el siglo XIX*. Mexico City: Secretaría de Educación Pública, 1973.

Knight, Alan. *The Mexican Revolution*. 2 vols. Lincoln: University of Nebraska, 1986.

———, "Peasant and Caudillo." In *Caudillo and Peasant in the Mexican Revolution*, edited by David A. Brading. Cambridge: Cambridge University Press, 1980.

Koth, Karl B. *Teodoro A. Dehesa and Veracruz in the Porfiriato 1892–1913: A Case Study in Mexican Federal Relations*. Ph.D. diss., University of Manitoba, 1986.

Kouri, Emilio H. *The Business of the Land: Agrarian Tenure and Enterprise in Papantla, Mexico, 1800–1910*. Ph.D. diss., Harvard University, 1996.

Krauze, Enrique. *Historia de la Revolución Mexicana, 1924–1928: La reconstrucción económica*. Mexico City: El Colegio de México, 1977.

La Botz, Dan. *Edwin L. Doheny: Petroleum, Power, and Politics in the United States and Mexico*. New York: Praeger, 1991.

LaFrance, David. *The Mexican Revolution in Puebla, 1908–1913*. Wilmington: Scholarly Resources, 1989.

Lara y Prado, Luis. *De Porfirio Díaz a Francisco Madero: La sucessión dictatorial de 1911*. New York: n.p., 1912.

Leal, Juan Felipe, and José Villaseñor. *La clase obrera en la historia de México*. Vol. 5. *En la revolución 1910–1917*. Mexico City: Siglo Veintiuno Editores/ Instituto de Investigaciones Sociales, Universidad Nacional Autónoma de México, 1988.

Licéaga, Luis. *Félix Díaz*. Mexico City: Editorial Jus, 1958.

Lieuwen, Edwin. *Mexican Militarism: The Political Rise and Fall of the Revolutionary Army*, New Mexico: University of New Mexico Press, 1968.

Limantour, José Yves. *Apuntes sobre mi vida pública 1892–1911*. Mexico City: Editorial Porrúa, 1965.

List Azurbide, Armando. *Apuntes sobre la prehistoria de la revolución*. Mexico City: n.p., 1958.

Lopez-Portillo y Rojas, José. *Elevación y Caída de Porfirio Díaz*. Mexico City: Librería Español, 1921.

Loyola Díaz, Rafael. *La crisis Obregón-Calles y el estado mexicano*. Mexico City: Siglo Veintiuno Editores, 1980.

Lubasz, Heinz. "Introduction." In *Revolutions in Modern European History*, edited by Heinz Lubasz. New York: Macmillan, 1966.

MacLachlan, Colin M., and William H. Beezley. *El Gran Pueblo: A History of Greater Mexico*. Englewood Cliffs: Prentice-Hall, 1994.

Madero, Francisco I. *The Presidential Succession of 1910*. Translated by Thomas B. Davis. American University Studies, series IX, History, vol. 89. New York: Peter Lang, 1990.

Maldonado Aguirre, Serafín. *Poder regional y poder nacional: El movimiento agrarista en Veracruz, 1920–34*. Master's thesis, Institución de Investigación Dr. José Maria Luis Mora, 1989.

Mallon, Florencia. *Peasant and Nation: The Making of Postcolonial Mexico and Peru*. Berkeley: University of California Press, 1995.

———. "Reflections on the Ruins: Everyday Forms of State Formation in Nineteenth-Century Mexico." In *Everyday Forms of State Formation: Revolution and the Negotiation of Rule in Modern Mexico*, edited by Gilbert M. Joseph and Daniel Nugent. Durham: Duke University Press, 1994.

Manero, Antonio. *El antiguo régimen y la revolución*. Mexico City: n.p., 1911.

———. *Qué es la revolución*. Veracruz: n.p., 1915.

Mata, Filomeno I. *Su vida y labor (ensayo biográfico)*. Mexico City: Secretaría de Educacción Pública, 1945.

Manzur Ocaña, Justo. *La revolución permanente: Vida y obra de Cándido Aguilar*. Mexico City: Costa-Amic, 1972.

Mar Olivares, Hector Manuel. *Estudio histórico y económico de Chicontepec, Veracruz*. Ph.D. diss. Escuela Normal de México, 1981.

Marichal, Carlos. "Obstacles to the Development of Capital Markets in Nineteenth-Century Mexico." In *How Latin America Fell Behind: Essays on the Economic Histories of Brazil and Mexico, 1800–1914*, edited by Stephen Haber. Stanford: Stanford University Press, 1997.

Martínez, Andrea. *La intervención norteamericana: Veracruz, 1914*. Mexico City: Cultura/Secretaría de Educacción Pública, 1982.

Martínez de la Vega, Francisco. *Heribeto Jara: Un Hombre de la revolución*. Mexico City: Ediciones Dialogo, 1964.

Martínez Hernández, Santiago. *Tiempos de Revolución*. Mexico City: Premia Editora de Libros, S.A., 1982.

McBride, George McCutchen. *The Land Systems of Mexico*. New York: Octagon Books, 1971.

Medel y Alvarado, Len. *Historia de San Andrés Tuxtla, 1532-1950*. Mexico City: Editorial Citlaltepetl, 1963.

Melgarejo Vivanco, Jose Luis. *Breve Historia de Veracruz*. Xalapa: Universidad Veracruzana, 1960.

Menéndez, Gabriel Antonio. *El cacique de las Huastecas*. Mexico: Secretaría de Educación Pública, 1957.

————. *Doheny el cruel*. Mexico City: Ediciones Bolsa Mexicana del Libro, 1958.

Mexican Petroleum Co. Ltd. of Delaware. *Annual Report*. 1914.

Meyer, Jean. *Problemas campesinas y revueltas agrarias, 1821–1910*. Mexico City: Secretaría de Educación Pública, 1973.

Meyer, Jean, Enrique Krauze, and Cayetano Reyes. *Historia de la Revolución Mexicana, 1924–1928: Estado y sociedad con Calles*. Mexico City: El Colegio de México, 1981.

Meyer, Lorenzo. *México y los Estados Unidos en el conflicto petrolero, 1917–1942*. Mexico City: El Colegio de México, 1972

————. *Su Majestad Británica contra la Revolución Mexicana, 1900–1950*. Mexico City: El Colegio de México, 1991.

Meyer, Michael C. *Huerta: A Political Portrait*. Lincoln: University of Nebraska Press, 1972.

Meyer, Michael C., and William L. Sherman. *The Course of Mexican History*. New York: Oxford University Press, 1979.

Meyers, Ellen Howell. *The Mexican Liberal Party 1903-1910*. Ph.D. diss., University of Virginia, 1970.

O'Brien, Thomas F. *The Revolutionary Mission: American Business in Latin America, 1900–1944*. New York: Cambridge University Press, 1996.

Ochoa Contreras, Octavio A. *Cambios estructurales en la actividad del sector agrícola del Estado de Veracruz, 1870–1900: causas y consecuencias*. Ph.D. diss., Universidad Veracruzana, 1974.

Ochoa Contreras, Octavio, and Flora Velásquez Ortiz. *Volumen, dinámica y estructura de la población total del estado de Veracruz, 1793–1980*. Xalapa: Instituto de Investigaciones y Estudios Superiores Económicos y Sociales de la Universiadad Veracruzana, 1986.

Ojeda, Abelardo *Ricardo Flores Magón: Su vida y su obra frente al orígen y las proyecciones de la Revolución Méxicana*. Mexico: Secretaria de Educación Pública, 1967.

Olvera R., Alberto J. *La estructura económica y social de Veracruz hacia 1930*. Xalapa: Centro de investigaciones históricos, Universidad Veracruzana, 1981.

O'Malley, Ilene V. *The Myth of the Revolution: Hero Cults and the Institutionalization of the Mexican State, 1920–1940*. New York: Greenwood Press, 1986.

Orozco, Winstano Luis. *Legislación y jurisprudencia sobre Terreños Baldios*. 2 vols. Mexico City: El Tiempo, 1895.

Orozco Espinosa, Rodolfo. *El sistema agrario del régimen porfirista y la reforma agraria de la revolución de 1910*. Ph.D. diss,, Universidad Nacional Antónoma de México, 1963.

Padua, C. Donato. *Movimiento Revolucionario 1906 en Veracruz: Relación cronológica de las actividades del PLM en los ex-cantones de Acayucan, Minatitlán, San Andrés Tuxtla y Centro del país*. Cuernavaca: n.p., 1936.

Palavicini, Felix F. *Mi vida revolucionario*. Mexico City: Ediciones Botas, 1937.

Pani, Alberto J. *Mi contribución al nuevo régimen, 1910–33*. Mexico City: Editorial Cultura, 1936.

Pansters, Wil, and Arij Ouweneel, eds. *Region, State and Capitalism in Mexico: Nineteenth and Twentieth Centuries*. Amsterdam: CEDLA (Centre for Latin American Research), 1989.

Parkes, Henry Banford. *A History of Mexico*. Boston: Houghton-Mifflin, 1938.

Pasquel, Leonardo. *Cronología ilustrada de Xalapa, 1178-1911*. 2 vols. Mexico City: Editorial Citlaltepetl, 1978.

———. *El conflicto obrero de Río Blanco en 1907*. Mexico City: Editorial Citlaltepetl, 1976.

———. *La rebelión agraria de Acayucan en 1906*. Mexico City: Editorial Citlaltepetl, 1976.

———. *Veracruzanos en la Revolución*. Mexico City: Instituto Nacional de Estudios Históricos de la Revolución, 1985.

———. ed., *Matalos en Caliente*. Prologue by Leonardo Pasquel. Mexico City: Editorial Citlaltepetl, 1965.

Paz, Ireneo. *Algunas campañas*. Prologue by Salvador Ortíz Vidales. Mexico City: SepSetentas, 1944.

Peña Samañiego, Heriberto. *Río Blanco: El gran circulo de oberos libres y los sucesos del 7 de enero de 1907*. Mexico City: Centro de Estudios Históricos del Movimiento Obrero Mexicano, 1975.

Pérez, Abel R. *Teodoro A. Dehesa: Gobernante Veracruzano*. Mexico City: Imprenta Talleres Stylo, 1950.

Pérez Hernández, José María. *Estadística en le República Méxicana*. Guadalajara: Tipografía del Gobierno, 1862.

Pérez Miliucía, Luis. *Compendio geográfico del Estado de Veracruz*. Xalapa: Tipografía del Gobierno del Estado, 1902.

Pérez Olivares, Porfirio. *Memorias: Un dirigente agrario de Soledad de Doblado*. Prologue by Olivia Domínguez Pérez. Xalapa: Universidad Veracruzana, 1992.

Perry, Laurens Ballard. *Juárez and Díaz: Machine Politics in Mexico*. Chicago: Northern Illinois University Press, 1978.

Phipps, Helen. *Some Aspects of the Landholding Question in Mexico: A Historical Study*. Austin: University of Texas Press, 1925.

Potash, Robert A. *Mexican Government and Industrial Development in the Early Republic: The Banco de Avío*. Amherst: University of Massachusetts Press, 1983.

Prida, Ramón. *From Despotism to Anarchy*. El Paso: El Paso Printing, 1914.

Quirk, Robert. *The Mexican Revolution, 1914–15: The Convention of Aguascalientes*. Bloomington: Indiana University, 1960.

———. *The Mexican Revolution and the Catholic Church 1910-29*. Bloomington: Indiana University Press, 1973.

Ramírez Caloca, Jesús. *Geografía del estado de Veracruz*. Mexico City: Herrero Hermanos Sucesores, 1962.

Ramírez Lavoignet, David. *Los constituyentes federales veracruzanos, 1917*. Xalapa: Gobierno del estado libre y soberano de Veracruz-Llave, 1979.

———. *Misantla*. Mexico City: Editorial Citlatepetl, 1959.

———. *Soteapan: Luchas agrarias*. Xalapa: Seminario de Historia, Universidad Veracruzana, 1971.

Redondo Silva, Jesús. *La cuestion agraria en el estado de Veracruz durante el siglo XIX*. Ph.D. diss. Universidad Iberoamericana,1971.

Reina Aoyama, Leticia. *Las rebeliones campesinas en México (1819–1906)*. Mexico: Siglo veintiuno, 1988.

Reyes, Rodolfo. *De mi vida: Memorias políticas, 1899–1913*. 2 vols. Madrid: Biblioteca Nueva Madrid: 1929.

Reyes Heroles, Jesús. *El liberalismo Mexicano*. 3 vols. México City: Fondo de Cultura Económica, 1974.

Rice, Jacqueline Ann. *The Porfirian Political Elite: Life Patterns of the Delegates to the 1892 Union Liberal Convention*. Ph.D. diss., Los Angeles: University of California, 1979.

Rivera, Antonio. *La Revolución en Sonora*. Mexico City: Imprenta Arana, 1969.

Rodríguez O, Jaime E. *The Revolutionary Process in Mexico; Essays on Political and Social Change, 1880–1940*. Los Angeles: UCLA Latin American Center Publications, 1990.

Roeder, Ralph. *Hacia el México moderno: Porfirio Díaz*. 2 vols. Mexico City: Fondo de cultura económica, 1973.

———. *Juárez y su México*. Mexico City: Fondo de Cultura Económica, 1980.

Romero Flores, Jesús. *Annales históricos de la revolución mexicana*, vol. 1: *Del porfirismo a la revolución constitucionalista*. Mexico City: Libro Mexicano, 1960.

Ross, Stanley R. *Francisco I. Madero: Apostle of Mexican Democracy*. New York: Columbia University Press, 1955.

Salmarón Castro, Alicia. *Teodoro A. Dehesa y el partido porfirista veracruzano en su lucha por el poder*. Master's thesis, Universidad Autónoma Metropolitana-Iztapalapa, 1992.

Sánchez Azcona, Juan. *Apuntes para la historia de la revolución mexicana*. Mexico City: Instituto Nacional de Antropología e Historia, 1961.

Sánchez Garrito Murquía, Cecilia. "El antireeleccionismo en México 1867-1910. Ph.D. diss., Universidad Nacional Autónoma de México, 1964.

Sánchez Lamego, Miguel A. *Historia militar de la revolución mexicana en la época maderista*, 3 vols. Mexico: Instituto Nacional de Antropología e Historia, 1976.

Sartori, Giovanni. *Party and Party Systems*. New York: Cambridge University Press, 1976.

Schama, Simon. *Citizens: A Chronicle of the French Revolution*. New York: Alfred A. Knopf, 1989.

Secretaría de Patrimonio Nacional. *El petróleo de México*. México City: n.p., 1963.

Shadle, Stanley F. *Andrés Molina Enríquez: Mexican Land Reformer of the Revolutionary Era*. Tucson: University of Arizona Press, 1994.

Sherman, John W. *The Mexican Right: The End of Revolutionary Reform, 1929–1940*. Westport: Praeger Publishers, 1997.

Scholes, Walter V. *Política mexicana durante el régimen de Juárez, 1855–1872*. Mexico City: Fondo de Cultura Económica, 1976.

Siemens, Alfred H. *Between the Summit and the Sea: Central Veracruz in the Nineteenth-Century*. Vancouver: University of British Columbia Press, 1990.

Sims, Harold Dana. *The Expulsion of Mexico's Spaniards, 1821–36*. Pittsburg: University of Pittsburg Press, 1990.

Skerritt Gardner, David. *Rancheros sobre tierra fertil*. Xalapa: Biblioteca Universidad Veracruzana, 1993.

Skocpol, Theda. *States and Social Revolutions: A Comparative Analysis of France, Russia and China*. Cambridge: Cambridge University Press, 1980.

Smith, Peter H. *Labyrinths of Power: Political Recruitment in Twentieth-Century Mexico*. Princeton: Princeton University Press, 1979.

Southworth, John. *El estado de Veracruz-Llave: Su historia, agricultura, comercio e industria*. Xalapa: Gobierno del Estado, 1990.

Stewart, P.C.A. *The Petroleum Industry of Mexico*. London: Crowther and Goodman, 1915.

Tannenbaum, Frank. *Peace by Revolution: Mexico after 1910*. New York: Columbia University Press, 1966.

———. *The Mexican Agrarian Revolution*. Hamden: Anchor Books, 1968.

Tapia, Rafael. *Mi participación revolucionaria*. Mexico City: Editorial Citlaltépetl, 1967.

Tennenbaum, Barbara A. *The Politics of Penury: Debts and Taxes in Mexico, 1821–1856*. Albuquerque: University of New Mexico Press, 1986.

Trens, Manuel B. *Historia de la ciudad de Veracruz y de su ayuntamiento*. Mexico City: n.p., 1955.

———. *Historia de Veracruz*. 6 vols. Mexico: n.p., 1950.

Trigos, Georgina. *El corrido veracruzano*. Xalapa: Universidad Veracruzana, 1990.

Turner, John Kenneth. *Barbarous Mexico*. London: Cassell, 1911.

Tutino, John. *From Insurrection to Revolution in Mexico: Social Bases of Agrarian Violence, 1750–1940*. Princeton: Princeton University Press, 1986.

Ulloa, Berta. *Historia de la Revolución Mexicana, 1914–1917: La Constitución de 1917*. Mexico City: El Colegio de Mexico, 1983.

———. *Historia de Mexico: La lucha armada, 1911–20*. Mexico City: Secretaría de Educación Pública, 1978.

———. *La encrucijada de 1915*. Mexico City: El Colegio de México, 1979.

———. *Veracruz: capital de la Nación, 1914–15*. Mexico City: El Colegio de México, 1986.

Un Maderista. *El maderismo en cueros: Apuntes íntimos escritos en el año de 1912 por un maderista decepcionado (lease avergonzado)*. Havana: n.p., 1913.

Valadés, José C. *El porfirismo: Historia de un régimen: el crecimiento*. 2 vols. Mexico City: Editorial Patria, 1948.

———. *Sobre los orígenes del movimiento obrero en Mexico*, Mexico: C.E.H.S.M.O (Conferencia de Estudios Históricos sobre el movimiento Obrero), 1979.

Vanderwood. Paul J. *Disorder and Progress: Bandits, Police and Mexican Development*. Lincoln: University of Nebraska Press, 1986.

Van Young, Eric, ed. *Mexico's Regions: Comparative History and Development*. San Diego: Centre for U.S.-Mexican Studies, University of California, 1992.

Vasconcelos, José. *Ulíses criollo: La vida del autor escrita por él mismo*. 9th. ed. Mexico City: Ediciones Botas, 1945.

Vázquez Gómez, Francisco. *Memorias políticas 1909–1913*. Mexico City: Imprenta Mundial, 1933.

Velasco, Alfonso Luis. *Geografía y estadística del estado de Veracruz*. Mexico City: T. González Sucesores, 1895.

Villareal, Antonio I. "The Real Story of the Aguascalientes Convention." In *Immediate Causes of the Present Conflict in Mexico*. n.p., n.d.

Wasserman, Mark. *Capitalistas, Caciques, and the Revolution: Elite and Foreign Enterprise in Chihuahua, 1854–1911*. Chapel Hill: University of North Carolina Press, 1985.

———. *Persistent Oligarchs: Elites and Politics in Chihuahua, Mexico, 1910–1940*. Durham: Duke University Press, 1993.

Wells, Allen, and Gilbert M. Joseph. *Summer of Discontent, Seasons of Upheaval: Elite Politics and Rural Insurgency in Yucatán, 1876–1915*. Stanford: Stanford University Press, 1996.

Womack, John, Jr. *Zapata and the Mexican Revolution*. New York: Vintage, 1968.

Wood, Andrew Grant. *Revolution in the Street: Women, Workers, and Urban Protest in Veracruz, 1870–1927*. Wilmington: Scholarly Resources, 2001.

Zapata Vela, Carlos. *Conversaciones con Heriberto Jara*. Mexico City: Costa-Amic Editores, 1992.

Zea, Leopoldo. *Positivism in Mexico*. Austin: University of Texas, 1974.

Zilli, Juan. *Historia sucinta del estado de Veracruz*. Xalapa: n.p., 1943.

D. Articles

Aguilar Sánchez, Martín Gerardo and Martha Cortés Rodríguez. "Cronología de cuatro conflictos ferrocarrrileros en Veracruz, 1920–26," *Anuario* 6 (1989): 263–86.

Anderson, Rodney. "Mexican Workers and the Politics of Revolution, 1906–11." *Hispanic American Historic Review* 54, no. 1 (1974): 94–113.

Arreola, Daniel D. "Nineteenth-Century Townscapes of Eastern Mexico." *The Geographical Review* 72, no. 1 (Jan. 1982): 1–19.

Bastian, Jean-Pierre. "Metodismo y clase obrero en el Porfiriato." *Historia Mexicana* 33, no. 1 (July-Sept., 1983): 39–71.

Benítez Juárez, Mirna. "La organización sindical de los trabajadores petroleros en la hustaeca veracruzana, 1917–1931." *Anuario* 5 (1988): 13–33.

Berquist, Charles. "Latin American Labor History in Comparative Perspective: Notes on the Insidiousness of Cultural Imperialism." *Labor/Le Travail* 25 (Spring 1990): 189–98.

Bortz, Jeffrey. "The Revolution, the Labour Regime and Conditions of Work in the Cotton Textile Industry in Mexico, 1910–1927." *Journal of Latin American Studies* 32 (2000): 671–703.

Breyman, Walter N. "The Científicos: Critics of the Díaz Regime, 1892-1903", *Proceedings of the Arkansas Academy of Science* 7 (1955): 91–97.

Bryan, Anthony T. "Political Power in Porfirio Díaz's Mexico: A Review and Commentary." *The Historian* 38 (August 1976): 648–68.

Buchenau, Jürgen. "Calles y el movimiento liberal en Nicaragua." *Boletín* (APEC) 9(1992): 1–15.

Buve, Raymond Th. J. "Peasant Movements, Caudillos and Land Reform during the Revolution (1910–1917) in Talaxcala, Mexico." *Boletín de estudios Latinoamericanos y del Caribe* 18 (June 1975): 112–52.

Chevalier, François. "Un facteur décisif de la Révolution agraire au Mexique: Le soulevement de Zapata (1911–1919)." *Annales; economies, societés, civilisations*, 16, no. 1 (January 1961): 67–82.

Contreras Utrera, Julio. "Los comerciantes del puerto de Veracruz en la Era del progreso." *Anuario* 9 (1994): 57–78.

Cumberland, Charles C. "Precursors of the Mexican Revolution of 1910." *Hispanic American Historical Review* 22 (1942): 344–56.

Díaz, María Elena. "The Satiric Penny Press for Workers in Mexico, 1900–1910: A Case Study in the Politicization of Popular Culture." *Journal of Latin American History* 22, no. 3 (October 1990): 497–517.

Ducey, Michael. "Village, Nation, and Constitution: Insurgent Politics in Papantla, Veracruz, 1810–1821." *Hispanic American Historical Review* 79, no. 3 (August 1999): 463–93.

Florescano Mayet, Sergio "El tránsito a la manufactura en la región de Orizaba y el surgimiento de su primera fábrica textil: Cocolapan, 1837–1845." *Anuario* 7 (1990): 35–54.

Fowler, Will. "Valentín Gómez Fárias: Perceptions of Radicalism in Independent Mexico, 1821–1847." *Bulletin of Latin American Research* 15, no. 1 (1996): 39–62.

Fowler-Salamini, Heather. "Los orígenes de las organizaciones campesinas en Veracruz: raíces políticas y sociales." *Historia Mexicana* 22, no. 1 (1972): 52–77.

————. "Revuelta popular y regionalismo en Veracruz, 1906–1913." *Eslabones* 5 (Jan.–June 1993): 99–117.

García Díaz, Bernardo. "Apuntes sobre la huelga de Río Blanco." *Anuario* 2 (1981): 183–207.

Garciadiego, Javier. "Gaudencio de la Llave: de porfirista a 'contrarevolucionario.'" *Estudios* 34 (1993): 7–32.

————. "Higinio Aguilar: Milicia, rebelión y corrupción como modus vivendi." *Historia Mexicana* 16, no. 3 (1992): 437–88.

Gill, Mario. "Veracruz: Revolución y extremismo," *Historia Méxicana* 2, no. 4 (April–June 1953): 618–36.

Glick, Edward B. "The Tehuantepec Railroad; Mexico's White Elephant." *Pacific Historic Review* 32 (November 1953): 373–82.

Goldfrank, Walter L. "Theories of Revolution and Revolution Without Theory: The Case of Mexico." *Theory and Society* 7 (1979): 135–65.

González Navarro, Moisés. "La Huelga de Río Blanco." *Historia Mexicana* 6 (April-June, 1957): 510–33.

————. "Las huelgas textiles en el porfiriato." *Historia Mexicana* 6 (Oct.-Dec., 1956): 201–16.

————. "Tenencia de las tierras y población agricola." *Historia Mexicana* 19 (July-Sept. 1969): 67–70.

Haber, Stephen, "The Worst of Both Worlds: The New Cultural History of Mexico." *Mexican Studies/Estudios Mexicanos* 13, no. 2 (Summer 1997): 363–83.

Hamnett, Brian. "Liberalism Divided." *Hispanic American Historical Review* 76, no. 4 (1996): 659–89.

Hart, John Mason. Agrarian Precursors of the Mexican Revolution: The Development of an Ideology." *The Americas* 29 (October 1972): 131–50.

————. "Dynamics of the Mexican Revolution: Historiographical Perspectives." *Latin American Research Review* 19, no. 3 (1984): 223–31.

————. "Nineteenth Century Urban Labor Precursors of the Mexican Revolution: The Development of an Ideology." *The Americas* 30 (January 1974): 297–318.

Haverstock, Mike. "Waiting in Veracruz, 1914." *Américas* 35, no. 6 (1983): 34–39.

Katz, Friedrich. "Labor Conditions on Haciendas in Porfirian Mexico: Some Trends and Tendencies." *Hispanic American Historical Review* 54, no. 1 (February, 1974): 1–47.

Knight, Alan. "El liberalismo mexicano desde la Reforma hasta la Revolución (una interpretación)." *Historia Mexicana* 35, no. 1 (July–Sept.): 59–61.

————. "The Mexican Revolution: Bourgeois? Nationalist? Or just a 'Great Rebellion'?" *Bulletin of Latin American Research* 4, no. 2 (1985): 1–37.

Koth, Karl B. "Camaleón o hijo de tigre pintito: Raúl G. Ruiz and the Mexican Revolution in Veracruz." Paper presened at the Rocky Mountain Conference on Latin American Studies, Santa Fe, New Mexico, March, 1996.

————. "Crisis Politician and Political Counterweight: Teodoro A. Dehesa in Mexican Federal Politics, 1900–1910." *Mexican Studies/ Estudios Mexicanos* 11 no. 2 (Summer 1995): 243–71.

————. " Madero, Dehesa, y el cientificismo: el problema de la sucesión gubernamental en Veracruz, 1911–1913. *Historia Mexicana*, 46 no. 2 (1996): 397–424.

————. "'Not a Mutiny but a Revolution': The Río Blanco Labour Dispute, 1906–1907." *Canadian Journal of Latin American and Caribbean Studies* 18, no. 35 (1993): 39–65.

————. "People, Products and Protest." Paper presented at the Ninth Conference of Mexican Historians, Mexico City, October 1994.

Kuecker, Glenn David. "Mapping Creative Destruction: The Discursive Practice of Space in Tampico, 1890–1910." Paper presented at the Rocky Mountain Council for Latin American Studies, Santa Fe, New Mexico, March, 1996.

LaFrance, David. "Francisco I. Madero and the 1911 Interim Governorship in Puebla." *The Americas* 42, no. 3 (January 1986): 311–31.

León Fuentes, Nelly Josefa "Los antagonismos empresariales de Xalapa en el siglo XIX." *Anuario* 9 (December 1994): 79–97.

Macías, Anna. "Women and the Mexican Revolution." *The Americas* 37, no. 1 (July 1980): 53–82.

Monsiváis, Carlos. "La aparición del subsuelo. Sobre la cultura de la Revolución Mexicana." *Historias* 8–9, (Jan.–June 1985): 159–77.

Reyna Muñoz, Manuel. "150 conflictos en la industria textil, 1928–32" *Anuario* 7, (1990): 161–212.

Rosenzweig, Fernando. " El desarrollo económico de Mexico de 1877-1911." *El Trimestre Económico* 32 (July-Sept. 1965): 405–53.

Stevens, Donald Fithian. "Agrarian Policy and Instability in Porfirian Mexico." *The Americas* 39 (October 1982): 153–66.

Vanderwood, Paul J. "Mexico's Rurales: Reputation vs. Reality." *The Americas* 34 (July 1977): 102–12.

————. "Resurveying the Mexican Revolution: Three Provocative New Syntheses and their Shortfalls." *Mexican Studies/Estudios Mexicanos* 5, no. 1 (Winter 1989): 145–63.

Walker, David W. "Business as Usual: The Empresa del tabaco in Mexico, 1837–44." *Hispanic American Historical Review* 64, no. 4 (1984): 675–705.

————. "Porfirian Labor Politics: Working Class Organization in Mexico City and Porfirio Díaz, 1876-1902." *The Americas* 37, no. 3 (January 1981), 257-89.

Wasserman, Mark. "The Mexican Revolution: Region and Theory, Signifying Nothing?" *Latin American Research Review* 25, no. 1 (1990): 231–42.

Wieners, Eugene L. Jr. "Agriculture and Credit in Nineteenth–Century Mexico: Orizaba and Córdoba." *Hispanic American Historical Review* 65, no. 3 (1985): 519–46.

Zarauz López, Héctor Luis. "Rebeldes Istmeños." *Boletín* (APEC) 22(1996): 1–21.

Index

*A*BC Conference, 191
Abrahams, J. W., 155
Acapulco, 10
Acatlán, 102
Acayucan, 17, 19, 48–52, 65, 117, 148–49,
    184, 193, 208, 263, 265, 288
  anti-Díaz demonstrations, 95
  municipal elections, 218
  rebels enter, 122
  surrounded by rebels, 115, 150
Acayucan canton, 2, 18, 29, 41, 45–46,
    51–52, 55, 71, 74, 76–77, 99–100,
    178, 279, 276, 292, 296, 300
  Conventionists, 198
  land distribution, 256
  local authorities changed, 128
  PLM activity, 147
  Popolucas, 40
  Porfirian revolts, 10
  rebel activity, 142–44, 168
  Zapatista attacks, 183–84
Acayucan municipality, 269
Acayucan uprising, 3, 41, 42–44, 50,
    54–55, 65, 77, 79, 93–94, 147, 155,
    184, 229, 239, 254, 268, 270, 271
  survivors, 80
Acosta, Emilio, 139, 147
Agent 10B, 246
Agramonte, Tomás, 184
Agrarian Commission (Veracruz state),
    200. See also Comisión Agraria
    Mixta.
Agrarian Law of 1915 (Ver.), 231

Agraristas, 237, 239–41, 250
Agua Prieta, 226
Aguaprietistas, 226
Aguilar, Cándido, 111, 197, 204, 223, 226,
    285, 287, 288, 291, 294, 295, 296,
    297, 300, 304, 305, 306, 308, 309,
    310, 311, 312
  appointed general, 177
  attacks Felicistas, 221
  background, 93
  backs Carranza and Bonilla, 225
  backs Aillaud, 126
  corruption, 212
  court martial, 187
  demobilization, 129
  entry into Xalapa, 121
  escape, 172, 177
  establishes State Agrarian
    Commission, 200
  expels foreign clergy, 195
  events of June 21, 1911, 126
  initial revolutionary activity, 94–96
  marriage to Virgina Carranza, 196,
    216
  Minister of Foreign Affairs, 213
  named Madero's adjutant, 167
  named provisional governor, 192
  progressive social ideas, 190
  reforms, 201, 204–5
  state sovereignty and, 187
  suspected of treason, 141
  military tactics, 189
  ultimatum to Admiral Fletcher, 187

unites forces with Gavira, 111
warns Madero, 168
Aguilar, Higinio, 141, 167, 175, 198, 215,
    221, 308, 312
    joins Felicistas, 209–11
    leads counter-revolutionary forces,
        158, 161–63
    organizes neo-Pofirian forces, 198
    raises rebel force of ex-Rurales, 154–56
    supports Obregón, 226
Aguilaristas, 218
Aguilar, Miguel, 281
Aguilar, Silvestre, 93, 130, 140
Aguirre, Jesús, 249
Aillaud, Léon, 111, 118, 124, 126–30, 141,
    177, 181–82, 185, 195, 288, 289, 300
Alamán, Lucas, 5, 264
Alcabalas, 11
Alcolea, Alejandro, 14, 87, 262
Alegre, Manuel María, 130–33, 136,
    140–41, 170, 289, 291
Alemán, Miguel, 98, 148, 178, 183, 215,
    224, 281, 292
Alfonso, Juan, 49
Aljibes (Pueb.), 227, 312
Almanza García, Manuel, 233
Alor, Alvaro, 149, 208, 211
Altotonga, 111–12, 116, 164, 189, 285, 296
Alvarado, 2, 103, 118
Alvarado, Salvador, 197, 310
Alvarez, Alfredo, 124, 126–27, 145, 154,
    286, 287, 288
Alvarez Soto, Ramón, 21
Amamaloya, 76
Amatlán, 124, 192, 221, 248
Ambielle, Genaro, 52
Anarchism in labor movement, 47, 61–62
Anarcho-syndicalism, 94
Anderson, George, 271
Anderson, Rodney Dean, 56
Andreu Almanza, Juan, 235
Anenecuilco (Mor.), 265
Angeles, Felipe, 201, 304
Anti-Científicos, 84–86, 93, 208, 307
Anti-reelectionism, 15, 91, 101
Anti-reelectionist Center, 88
Anti-reelectionist Party, 80–81, 89–91,
    135, 140
Anti-U.S. Riots, 96
Anti-U.S sentiments, 155
Apa rancho, 76
Araiza, Luis, 66

Arias, Francisco, 175
Armenta family, 29
Armenta, Manuel, 203
Army of the East (felicista), 210
Army of the Gulf (felicista), 210
Army of the Mountains (felicista), 210
Arrellano, Arturo, 221
Arriaga, Camilo, 41, 47, 270
Arriaga, Ponciano, 270
Arrendatarios, 203
Arroyo Grande, 39
Article 27 (Constitution of 1857), 251,
    254, 258
Article 27 (Constitution of 1917), 216,
    220, 229, 245, 248, 251, 315
    Regulating Law of, 248
Article 123 (Constitution of 1917), 220
Artisans, 94, 180, 230, 232, 233
Atl, Dr. (Gerardo Murillo), 201, 204, 304
Atlixco (Pueb.), 101
Atoyac, 93–97, 98, 112, 189, 196
Autonomous municipality, 79
Avíla, Manuel, 61
Ayahualulco, 146
Aztec Indians, 109
Azuara, Antonio G., 199

Baez, Cecilio, 142
Baldíos, 28, 32, 34, 37, 45
Banco de Avío, 5, 57
Banderilla, 116
Bandits, 132, 143, 183, 189, 190, 204, 301
Bañuelos, Esteban, 143
Baranda, Joaquín, 20, 85–86, 278
Barbosa, Calixto, 108
Barreda, Gabino, 83
Barrón, Heriberto, 264
Batalla, Diodoro, 108
Battle of Puebla, 6
Battle of Tecoac, 10
Belén prison, 88
Bello, Maximo, 154
Beltrán, Joaquín, 155, 158, 159, 164, 263,
    296
Beltrán, José, 53, 54, 263, 271
Beltrán, Marcelino, 53
Berrenedea, Ramón R., 141
Betancourt, Ignacio, 17
Binigno Ríos, 200–201
Blacks, 155
Blanco, Agustín, 181

Blanco, Lucio, 177, 182, 185, 301
Blanquet, Aureliano, 159, 172, 177, 222, 295, 310
Body, John, 149
Bolshevik Revolution, 233
Bolshevism, 235
Bonilla, Ignacio, 223, 224
Boquiño, Santiago, 153
Bordes Mangel, Enrique, 281
Bortz, Jeffrey, 242, 257
Braniff, Tomás, 132–33, 163
Brownsville, Texas, 9
Bubonic plague, 227
Buena Vista railway station, 92
Bullé Goyri, Judge, 50
Bulnes, Francisco, 83, 87
Bustamante, Demetrio, 185

*C*aamaño, Marcelino L., 281
Cabanzo, Melesio, 183
Cabrera, Luis, 135, 197, 199, 250
Caciques, 253
Calero, Manuel, 136, 164, 171, 179, 296, 298
Calixto, Domingo, 99, 282
Calle de la Paz, 166
Calles, Plutarcho Elías, 225, 234, 237–40, 246–51, 257, 313, 314, 315, 316
Camacho, José María, 19, 51–52, 122, 126
Camacho, Odón, 75
Camarilla politics, 6, 14–15
Camarillas, 171, 260, 262
Cambas, Lucido, 33–34, 36, 267
Camerón, 168
Campamento Sewanee Plantation, 183
Campesinos, 124, 214, 220, 226, 230–31, 235,238–39, 247–48, 257, 309, 314
Cañada Blanca, 221
Canada, William, 97, 150, 189,199, 200, 212, 214, 292, 293, 294, 295, 296, 297, 299, 308, 309, 310
Cananea, 73–74
Canseco, Ignacio, 18, 52–53
Cantons. See also Acayucan, Chicontepec, Coatepec, Córdoba, Cosamaloapan, Huatusco, Jalacingo, Minatitlán, Misantla, Orizaba, Ozuluama, Tantoyuca, Tuxpán, The (Los) Tuxtlas, Papantla, Veracruz, Zongólica
Canovas, Francisco, 119

Capdevielle, Mr., 136
Caracas, Ramón, 98, 239
Caraveo, Marcelo, 221
Carbajal, Francisco S., 193
Carbajal, Pedro A., 74, 109, 116, 122, 128, 178, 183–84, 189, 193, 198, 287, 288
Cardel, José, 231, 239–40
Cárdenas, Francisco, 65, 169, 277
Cárdenas, H., 282
Cárdenas, Lazaro, 249, 250, 251
Carillo, Marcos, 9
Carillo Puerto, Felipe, 233
Carothers, Mr., 214, 308, 309
Carrancismo, 180, 188, 198, 212, 224, 255
Carrancistas, 185, 211
Carranza, Jesús, 198–99
Carranza, Roberto, 192
Carranza, Venustiano, ix, 196, 199, 202, 208, 234 255–56, 300, 301, 303, 304, 305, 306, 307, 310, 311, 312, 313
  Aguascalientes Convention, 197, 200
  anti-Carranza political movements, 206
  assassination, 226
  centralism, 198, 224
  Cientificismo, 220
  Constitution of 1917, 215–17
  co-optation, 213
  currency devaluation (*infalsificables*), 212
  creates National Agrarian Commission, 201
  establishes national capital in Veracruz, 197
  failure to achieve regional power base, 250
  named First Chief Constitutionalist Army, 181
  names Aguilar provisional governor, 192
  opposes Huerta, 175
  opposes U.S. invasion, 191
  orders Aguilar's court martial, 187
  pro-German attitude, 220
  repressive measures, 206
  rift with Obregón, 217
  tactical and strategic plans, 185
Carranza, Virginia, 196, 216
Carvallo Tejeda, Samuel, 202
Casa del Obrero Mundial, 202, 213
Casarín, Pascual, 231

Castas, 4
Castillo, Apolinar, 11
Castillo, Luis, 144, 148, 182, 292, 293
Castillo, Pedro, 13
Castro, Cesáreo, 225
Castro, General, 215, 252, 307
Catemoco, 50, 74, 109, 140, 184
Catholic Church, 207, 208, 209, 308
Catholic Party, 132–33
Catholic schools, 196
Caudillo, 6, 83
Cauz Cervantes, Eduardo, 172, 181
Cejudo, Roberto, 203, 210, 221, 300, 311
Central Félix Díaz, 92
Central Plain, 3
Centralism, 81, 83, 127, 134, 162, 171,
    174, 198, 202, 211, 217, 224, 251,
    255, 258
  opposition to, 80
Centralist politics, 80
Centralist trend, 79
Centralizing processes, x
Centro Industrial Mexicana (Mexican
    Industrial Centre, CIM), 64–66, 68
Cerecedo Estrada, Daniel, 181
Cerro Grande, 183
Cervantes brothers, 203
Chamber of Deputies, 20, 64, 87, 92, 274
Chambers of Labor, 232
Chapacao *hacienda*, 248
Chapultepec Castle, 53, 85, 217
Chávez, Ricardo, 209
Cházaro Soler family, 11, 29, 44, 54, 148,
    155
Chiapas state, 2, 29, 209, 215, 251, 258,
    266, 311
Chichapa, 107
Chichiquila, 116
Chicontepec, 110, 119–20, 185, 230
Chicontepec canton, 28, 31, 3, 121, 152,
    164, 168, 178, 185, 282, 294, 297, 301
Chihuahua, 48
Chihuahua state, 100–101, 141, 167, 176,
    207, 283
Child labor/employment of, 58
Chiltepec, 215
Chinameca, 47, 49, 74, 77, 211, 270
Chintipán hills, 185
Chontla, 186
Chotla, 107
Chopoapán, 99
Cientificismo, 135, 138, 208, 220

Científicos, 135, 136, 153, 158, 162–63,
    254–55, 277, 278, 284, 295
  blamed for deceiving president, 71
  blamed for unrest in Mexico, 80
  Catholic Party, 133
  centralism, 77, 93
  critiqued in de Zayas Enríquez report,
    46
  definition of, 82–87, 91
  headed by Romero Rubio, 20
  Madero's shift, 131
  opponents of Dehesa, 24
  policies, 26–27, 41, 54
  weight of influence, 73, 89–90
Cipriano, Enrique, 281
Círculo Liberal Sufragista, 92
Círculo Nacional Porfirista, 86
Citlaltepec, 31
Ciudad Juárez, 104–6, 109–10, 115–16
Ciudadela, Battle of the, 177, 261
Ciudadela revolt, 167–68, 172
Civil Guard, 232, 237, 241
Class alliance, 80
Class war, 233–34, 237
Club Patria, 180, 299
Coahuila, 95
Coatepec, 112, 116–17, 139, 140, 146, 192,
    203, 281, 292, 300
Coatepec canton, 116, 170
Coatzacoalcos, 3, 43, 47, 49, 51, 74. See
    also Puerto México.
Coatzacoalcos River, 150, 173
Cocatapán factory, 57
Cockroft, James, D., 56
Cofre de Perote, 2
Cofre de Perote mountain, 111, 189
Colipa, 208
Colonization Law, 28
Colmenares Rivas, 100
Comapa, 116, 286
Comisión Agraria Mixta, 200, 204–5, 256
Comisión Local Agraria, 231
Committee on Foreign Relations of the
    US Senate, 220
Communist Party of Mexico, 233, 243
Communist Party (Ver.), 234
Compañía Industrial de Orizaba
    (CIDOSA), 57–58, 60, 73, 77
Compañía Industrial Veracruzana (CIV),
    23, 58, 60
Compañía Mexicana de Petroleo, 23
Conduveñazgos, 32–33

Condueños, 32
Confederación del Trabajo de la Región
    Mexicana, 213
Confederation of Workers' Unions, 219
Congress of the Labor Confederation of
    the Mexican Region, 233
Conquistadores, 2
Constitution of 1824, 157
Constitution of 1857, 6, 27, 30, 41, 55,
    56, 79, 82, 84, 122–23, 157, 163, 201,
    208, 211, 216, 255, 259, 270
Constitution of 1917, 216, 217, 220, 224,
    230–33, 245
Constitutionalist Army, 181, 185
Constitutionalists, 174, 177, 182, 185,
    187, 191, 192, 196–215, 219–21,
    223–24, 229–30, 232, 252, 255, 301,
    305, 308, 309, 311
    as Científicos, 203
Constitutional Party, 92
Contreras, Antonio, 99, 282
Contreras, Miguel, 281
Convention of Aguascalientes, 197–200,
    202, 256, 303, 304, 305
Convention of Queretaro, 223
Coolidge, Calvin, 246, 315
Co-optation, 258
Córdoba, 25, 112, 167, 183, 235 , 283, 286,
    287, 288, 289, 291, 293, 294, 297,
    299, 303
    anti-Díaz demonstrations, 95
    auxiliary force, 99
    climate, 5
    garrison in, 77
    Isthmian Railway, 101
    liberation of, 124
Córdoba canton, 159,168, 211, 260, 307,
    309
    hydro-electric plant, 23
Córdoba Brigade, 203
Córdoba, Teódulo, 99, 153, 189, 203, 282
Córdoba-Orizaba axis, 116, 142
Corral, Ramón, 24, 72, 80–82, 89, 91–92,
    104, 106, 118, 124, 278, 280
Cortés, Fermín, 75
Cosamaloapan, 31, 299
Cosamaloapan canton, 17–18, 99, 103,
    117, 120, 144, 147, 151, 215
Cosautlán, 111
Coscomatepec, 7, 10, 95, 116, 140, 199, 208
Cosío, Antonio, 189
Cosío, Félix, 189

Cosío Robelo, Mr., 96
Cosío Villegas, Daniel, 7, 86, 110
Cotaxtla, 224
Coyoacán, 176
Creelman interview, 73, 87–88, 89
CROM, 229, 233, 240, 247, 257
Cruz de Milagro, 99
Cruz, Felipe, 75
Cueto, Fernando, 99, 282
Cumberland, Charles, 140, 155, 169, 178,
    216, 252, 289, 291, 310, 311
Customs House (Veracruz port), 11, 169,
    195, 197

*D*antón (pseudonym of Enrique
    Novoa), 51
De la Barra, Francisco Léon, 122, 129,
    134, 137, 156, 160, 180, 220, 286,
    287, 288, 290, 295, 302, 304
De la Huerta, Adolfo, 225, 227, 228,
    238–39
De la Llave, Gaudencio, 95, 294, 297, 298,
    308
    attacks Camerino Mendoza, 176
    attempts to hinder rebels, 121–22
    brutality, 182
    captured, 221
    forms volunteer force, 101, 103, 118
    leads conservative rebellion in
        Veracruz, 167
    militarization of Veracruz city, 178
    proposes attacking Mexico City, 161
    rebels against Madero, 154, 158
    unites smaller groups under felicista
        banner, 214
De la Llave, Jr.,Gaudencio, 154
De la Llave, Porfirio, 145, 154
De la Luz Enríquez, Juan, 11–13, 30, 39,
    263, 264
De Landero y Cos, José, 172
De los Ríos, Mr., 156, 159, 297
De P. Mariel, Francisco, 181
De Zayas Enríquez, Rafael, 46–47, 60,
    137
Decena Trágica, 168
Decree # 9, 201
Decree #8, 200
Dehesa, Emma, 296
Dehesa, Francisco, 20, 54, 156, 159, 171,
    179, 298
Dehesa, Raúl, 20, 160, 166, 274, 296

Dehesa, Teodoro A., 100, 118–19, 127,
    161, 163, 261, 262, 264, 267, 273,
    274, 275, 276, 277, 278, 280, 281,
    283, 284, 285, 286, 287, 289, 295,
    296, 297, 298, 299, 301, 302, 303
  Acayucan Rebellion, 50–57
  arranges Díaz-Madero meeting, 89
  arranges Diaz's escape, 1872, 7
  assessment of Madero government, 133
  as vice-presidential candidate, 89,
    91–92
  attempts to solve the Popoluca-Rubio
    dispute, 45–46
  background, 6
  builds Veracruz dike, 3
  campaigns for governorship, 22
  champion of conservatives, 122–25
  condemns Científico policies, 77, 80
  disregards Acayucan commission
    findings, 44
  election of 1910, 81 passim
  events of June 21, 127
  exile, 166, 196
  Félix Díaz coup, 159
  involvement with Porfirian Party, 7–9
  land policy, 21–32
  leads Díaz campaign against Lerdo, 8
  named Administrator of Customs, 13
  named Inspector of Maritime
    Customs, 12
  opinion of Huerta, 195
  opinion on Madero's overthrow, 171
  orders Liberal Clubs closed, 48
  Papantla revolts, 33 passim
  press relations, 21
  relations with Díaz, 17–18
  reaction to breach of state sovereignty
    at Río Blanco, 70
  report on 1911 meeting between Díaz,
    Limantour and Huerta, 105
  rift with Díaz's policies, 41
  Río Blanco Labour Dispute, 59–65, 67,
    70–74
  rumoured as next Minister of Interior,
    107
  supports Huerta-Díaz coup, 174, 179
  threatened by Huerta, 188
Dehesa Theatre, 88, 91, 201
Dehesismo, 118, 141
Dehesistas, 93, 124, 126–27, 129, 130–32,
    144, 163, 241
Delahuertistas, 239

Delgado, Francisco, 124, 126
Democratic Party, 91
Dennis, J. C., 151
Deschamps, Armando, 172
Díaz, Alvaro, 53
Díaz, Carlos, 146
Díaz, Carmen, 45
Díaz, Eduardo, 75–76, 81
Díaz, Félix, 280, 295, 296, 298, 299, 301,
    303, 304, 307, 308, 309, 310, 311,
    312, 313, 316
  campaign encounters reverses, 221
  decides to leave Mexico, 224, 226
  federalism, 201
  moves headquarters to Veracruz, 215
  National Reorganizing Army, 210, 219
  presidential candiate, 179
  protects Madero, 90
  release from prison, 168
  reputation as anti-Científico, 134, 171
  signs Pact of the Ciudadela, 169
  success in Veracruz, 209
  U. S. connections, 207
  Veracruz revolt (1912), 155–64
Díaz, Manuel, 151
Díaz, Porfirio, 1, 41, 253, 261, 262,, 263,
    264, 266, 273, 275, 276, 277, 278,
    280, 287, 290, 291
  and Científicos, 83
  and the press, 21
  camarilla politics, 14
  choosing a successor, 86
  commission's report from De Zayas
    Enríquez, 46
  Dehesa's complaints re Río Blanco, 71
  disagreements with Dehesa, 55–56
  departure from Veracruz, 123
  discusses maderista situation with
    Huerta and Limantour, 105
  expansion of Rurales, 103
  fears regarding U. S. intentions in the
    south-east, 45
  federalism, 14
  foreign property, attitude to, 186
  ideological preferences, 82
  laudo presented, 68
  labour policy, 64, 73
  labour situation, 60
  land policy, 27–28, 30–31, 35, 37, 52
  "matalos en caliente," 10
  political tactics, 15, 20, 54, 82
  reaction to Acayucan uprising, 50

receives notices of PLM rebellion
    plans, 48
re-elected 1910, 92
relationship with Dehesa, 13
resignation, 115, 118, 120
revolt of La Noria, 7
revolution of Tuxtepec, 9–10
Romero Rubio's estate, 44
sugar planter, 8
use of *jefes políticos*, 16
vice-presidential choice 1910, 91
victory over French at Puebla, 6
Díaz Mirón, Salvador, 12, 188, 276
Díaz Ordaz, José, 158, 175
Díaz Ramírez, Manuel, 233
Diéguez, Manuel M., 225
Díez Gutiérrez, Carlos, 15, 30
Division of the East (Cándido Aguilar),
    178, 185–86, 192, 197, 230, 307
Doheny, Edward, 190–91, 205, 302
Domínguez, Adolfo, 172
Domínguez, José E., 153, 195
Domínguez, Honrato, 7
Domínguez, Miguel, 113
Domínguez Pérez, Olivia, 200, 305, 306
Dos Bocas, 109
Durán, General, 153
Durango state, 100, 167, 283

*E*agle Oil Co. See El Aguila Oil Co.
Eastern Revolutionary Army (Santanón),
    76
Ejército Reorganizador Nacional
    (National Reorganizing Army), 209,
    214-215
Ejidatarios, 232
Ejidos, 27–29, 44, 202, 207
El Aguila Oil Co. (Eagle Oil Co.), 139,
    146, 173, 189, 194, 205, 245, 246–47
El Destino tobacco factory, 59
El Ebano oil field, 141, 185, 199, 202
Election of 1910, 80, 92
Ellsworth, Luther, 280
El Palmar Rubber Co, 183, 189
El Paso, Texas, 250
El Potrero oil field, 141, 168, 189
El Tajín, 32
El Valle Nacional tobacco factory, 59
Enganchados, 173
Enganche, 43
English, 36

Enriquistas, 14
Escobedo, Vicente F., 281
Esperanza, 240
Espinosa, Eliezer, 120, 122, 125–26, 286,
    287
Espinosa, José, 76
Espinosa de los Monteros, Samuel, 88
Estanco (monopoly), 260
Estanzuela, 151
Esteva, Guillermo A., 14
Estrada, A., 99, 282
Europe, 2, 83–84, 188, 279
Exploratory Geographical Commission,
    111, 116

*F*all, Albert Bacon, 220, 314
Fascism, 238, 313
Federación de Sindicatos Obreros del
    DF, 205
Federación Nacional Ferrocarrillera, 242
Federal Agents of Public Tranquility, 167
Federal District, 213
Federal Geographic Commission, 34
Federalism, 6, 253, 256, 258, 259
    attenuation of principle in Const. of
        1917, 216
    Dehesa's use of, 73
    Diaz's use of, 14–15, 79
    end of, 244, 251
    'ideology' of Veracruz rebels, 174, 198,
        208
    Madero's shift from, 127
    Obregon's commitment to, 224
    Obregon's misuse of, 250
    popularity with upper and middle
        classes, 118
Federalist system, 3
Felicismo, 211, 223, 307, 308
Felicistas, 167, 170, 176, 190, 238–39, 304,
    306, 308, 310
    Aguilar's campaign against, 221, 224
    alliance with Orozquistas and
        Zapatistas, 165
    attempts to unite with Pelaecistas, 222
    businessmen attracted to, 220
    in Huerta's cabinet, 179
    in Tuxpán, 199
    in Veracruz, 198, 210
    persecution of, by Huerta, 180
    reasons for initial success, 215
    remnants attracted to De la Huerta, 239

spied on, 207
strength of, 214
zenith of, 219
Figueroa, Francisco, 136, 290
First Preliminary National Workers
　　Congress, 213
Fishing industry, 2
Fitzgerrell, J. J., 166, 296
Fletcher, Frank, 187, 190, 194, 298
Flores Magón brothers, 42, 48
Flores Magón, Ricardo, 42, 48, 49, 51
Flores, Manuel, 147
Flores, Pavón, 293
Flying columns, 213–14
Foco, 105, 283
Fraccionamiento, 30
France, 16
Franyutti family, 54
Free Municipality, 216, 259
Free Trade, 5
French business community, 57
French invasion of Mexico, 6, 11
French Revolution, 1789, 253
Furbero oil field, 109, 182

*G*aballo, Clemente, 121
Gabay, Clemente, 98, 122, 142, 144, 150,
　　152, 209, 210, 238, 281, 291
Gabay, Pedro, 98, 150, 153, 203, 210, 211,
　　221, 222
Galán brothers, 209
Galán, Constantín, 203, 208, 210, 221, 238
Galván, Pedro A., 7
Galván, Ursulo, 213, 233, 235, 239–41
Gamboa, Toribio, 202
García, Adolf G., 98
García, Federico, 151
García, Felipe, 116
García, Honrato, 148–49
García, Manuel, 9
García, Onofre, 97
García de la Cadena, Lieutenant, 172
García Granados, Alberto, 135, 175, 179,
　　286
García, Honrato, 293, 295, 297
García, Onofre, 281
García Peña, Angel, 111, 115, 117, 121,
　　124, 126, 140, 160, 288 289
García Peña, Emma (Dehesa), 188
García Petronilo O., 281
García Torres, Vincente, 10

Garcín, Victor, 69
Garnica N., Jr., R, 99, 282
Garrido Canabal, Governor, 233
Garzón Cossa, Gabriel, 228
Gavira, Gabriel, 98, 108, 120–22, 145, 229,
　　281, 285, 287, 288, 289, 294, 299,
　　301, 303, 306
　　adherence to Plan of San Luis Potosí,
　　　　124
　　amnestied, 164
　　appointed chief of revolution forces in
　　　　Veracruz, 111
　　arrested, 132, 151
　　captures Altotonga, 116
　　captures Huatusco, 112
　　captures Perote, 117
　　captures Tuxpán, 192
　　cheated of governorship, 131
　　choice of interim governor, 126–29
　　class background, 146, 175
　　enters Córdoba, 112
　　enters Las Vigas, 117
　　feud with Cándido Aguilar, 104
　　flees to Havana, 177
　　ideological background, 79
　　in Havana, 98
　　joins Anti-reelectionists, 94–96
　　joins Constitutionalists, 185
　　joins forces with Aguilar, 111
　　loses gubernatorial race to Aguilar,
　　　　217–18
　　rebels against Madero, 132, 141
　　rejected by Madero, 153
　　replaces local authorities, 125
　　returns to Veracruz, 108
Gavirismo, 218
Gaviristas, 146, 149, 151–52, 157, 161, 218
Gaw, Alex M., 24
Gente de razón, 26, 43
Gil, Luz, 185
Gil Blas, 103
Gleichschaltung, 206
Gobernación (Ministry of Interior), 128,
　　287, 288, 291
Gómez, General, 225
Gómez, Isabel, 97, 281
Gómez, Lorenzo, 18
Gómez, Martin, 54
Gómez, Miguel, 72, 98, 101, 104, 106
Gómez, Pedro, 53–54
González, Abraham, 94, 176, 298, 299,
　　301, 303, 305

González, Eduardo, 52
González, Manuel, 1, 9
González, Pablo, 207, 213, 217, 223, 227, 310
González Cosío, General, 105
González García, Salvador, 213
González Mena, Mr., 179, 184
Gorostiza Theatre, 63
Granada, Antonio, 31
Gran Círculo de Obreros Libres (Great Circle of Free Workers [GCOL]), 61–63, 66, 68, 74
Great National Problems, 88
Guasutlán, 76
Guatemala, 177
Guerra, Ernesto, 139
Guerra, François-Xavier, 81, 92
Guerrilla warfare, 151
Guerrero hacienda, 215
Guerrero state, 104, 136, 144
Guerrero Theatre, 68
Guerrero, Praxedis, 48, 99
Guerrilla warfare, 105
Guillemín, Lieutenant-Colonel, 192
Gulf of Mexico, 1, 2
Gutiérrez, Ignacio, 76
Gutiérrez Zamora, 192, 221
Guyamas, 225

*H*aber, Stephen, 233, 250, 313, 316
Hacendados, 18, 40, 99–100, 214, 237–38
Haciendas
  Bella Vista, 75, 155
  Corral Nuevo, 11, 44, 54, 56, 75, 148, 155, 200, 204
  El Central, 149
  La Candelaria, 8, 9
  La Noria, 8, 261
  La Palmira, 95
  Las Palmillitas, 107
  Oaxaqueña, 265
  San Diego, 154
Harding, Warren, 245
Hart, John Mason, 56
Hartington, George, 60, 65
Havana, 7, 110, 172, 177, 179, 185, 206, 296, 301, 307
Hearst family, 40
Henderson, Peter V. N., 157, 159, 207, 209, 295, 296, 298, 307, 308, 311
Hermosillo (Son.), 137

Hernández, José M., 158, 293, 297
Hernández, Julián, 99, 282
Hernández, Rafael, 135
Hernández del Moral, Manuel, 98
Hernández del Moral, Ricardo, 98
Hernández, Salvador, 57
Herrera, Carlos, 59–60, 63, 65–67, 69–70, 72, 119, 275
Herrera, Daniel, 142–43, 148, 166
Herrera, Julian, 31
Herrera, Miguel, 112
Herrera Moreno, Enrique, 206
Herrera Moreno, Severino, 281
Hidalgo, Antonio, 176
Hidalgo state, 2, 31,109, 181, 193
Hidalgotitlán, 208, 211, 307, 309
Hinojoso, José, 94, 107–8
Hotel Iturbide, 10, 108
Huamantla, 30
Huasteca, 3, 25, 109, 174, 178, 185, 195, 202, 214, 221, 225, 230, 249, 265, 314
Huasteca Oil Co., 191, 247–49
Huastecan Indians, 109, 185
Huatusco, 111–12
Huatusco canton, 10, 18, 153, 155, 192, 211, 221, 260, 281, 288, 293, 299
  Constantín Galán in, 208
  Pedro Gabay in, 221
  huertista activity, 197
  rebel activity, 103, 116, 140, 151, 167
  Vazquistas in, 143
Huazuntlán, 76
Huejutla, 181, 199
Huerta, Eucaro, 127
Huerta, Garrido, 102, 107, 113, 115, 117, 121–22, 285
Huerta, Victoriano, 184, 190, 254, 267, 282, 284, 293, 298, 299, 301, 302 303, 304, 312, 313, 314
  and Cientificismo, 208
  Battle of the Ciudadela, 168–69
  coup d'état of 1913, 133–34
  defeats Orozco at Rellano, 150
  discusses maderista situation with Díaz and Limantour, 105
  muzzles press, 188
  prorogues Congress, 188
  regime, 174–81
  resignation and departure, 195
  surveys Papantla, 33–34
  U.S. invasion of Veracruz, 190–91
Huertismo, 177, 178, 192, 196

Huertistas, 171, 178, 188, 209, 218
Huidobro de Azúa, Miguel Angel, 130
Huimangillo, 259
Hydro-electric power, 2

Independence, 5, 109, 260
Indians, x, xi, 12, 44, 79, 185, 262, 263, 265,
    266, 285. See also Aztec, Huasteca,
    Otomí, Popoluca, Totonac-Huasteca
    and Yaqui Indians
  in Acayucan, 18, 55, 254
  in the Huasteca, 109
  in Santa Ana Atzacán rebel against
    Huerta, 192
  in Veracruz, nineteenth century, 4
  land claims, 53, 117, 200
  marginalized, 11
  of Lomo Larga, 74
  Papantla, 25–40
  PLM supporters, 147
  revolutionaries, 110, 143
  supporters of Plan of San Luis Potosí,
    124
  "Volcano Volunteers," 198
Indian lands, 41, 42–55
Infalsificables, 212–13
Intendant, 16
Inter-Oceanic Railway, 11, 102, 107, 112,
    147
Isthmian Railway, 101–2, 118, 147, 224
Isthmus of Tehuantepec, 43, 199, 304
Ixhuatlán, 178, 182, 186, 192, 198, 300, 301
Izucar de Matamoros, 107

Jacobinos, 81, 84–85, 87
Jalacingo, 10, 18, 32, 117
Jalacingo canton, 16, 101, 111, 152, 266,
    286, 294, 305
  Armenta's army in, 203
  change of local authorities, 119
  complaints of cruelty of jefe político, 16
  maderistas capture towns in, 112
Jalisco state, 24, 177, 266
Jáltipan, 122, 125, 183, 287, 288
  municipality, 269
Jamapa, 112, 117–18
Jara, Heriberto, 96, 111, 147, 185, 197,
    244–51, 258, 298, 299, 301, 303, 304,
    305, 308, 310, 315

accuses De la Llave for Mendoza's
    death, 181
  and Article 27 (Constitution of 1917),
    216
  backs railroad workers against
    Morones, 244
  Catholic schools in Orizaba closed,
    196
  conflict with federal government, 244
  confronts federal government, 248
  considered enemy by oil companies,
    247
  controls Mixtec region in Puebla, 107
  courage of, 176
  elected governor, 240
  expells Spaniards, 206
  ideological background, 79
  joins Aguilar's staff, 177
  joins Anti-reelectionists, 94
  named secretary to governor, 192
  named Veracruz delegate to Queretaro
    Convention, 216
  nullifies election results 1915, 212
  obtains Mendoza's release, 175
  ousted from governorship, 249
  refuses to attend labour congress, 213
  rejected by Madero, 153
  relations with central government,
    249–51
  resigns commission, 139
  state sovereignist, 245, 258
  supports Obregón, 239
Jasso, Manuel (Colonel), 19, 75, 77,
    99–100, 117
Jefes políticos, 141, 146, 170, 178, 262, 263,
    284, 286, 288, 289, 291, 292, 293,
    294, 295, 296, 297
  anti-government actvity of, 151,
    164–65
  changed by maderistas, 119–22, 125,
    128–30
  definition and role in Porfiriato,
    15–19, 253
  Cambas's role in Papantla, 33–39
  role in Acayucan uprising, 44–46, 48,
    50–54
  role in Río Blanco labour dispute,
    59–61, 63–64, 69–70
  Salas named to Acayucan, 144, 148
  visitador (inspector) for Veracruz
    named, 140

Jiménez (Coah.), 49, 85, 268
Jiménez, Manuel, 121
Josephs, Gilbert, 15
Juan Casiano, 191
Juárez, Benito, 6–7, 26–27, 83, 205, 260, 261
Juárez, Manuel, 63, 68
Juarico, Angel, 142
Juchique de Ferrer, 29, 208
Junta Central de Conciliación y Arbitraje (Federal), 233
Junta de Conciliación y Arbitraje (Ver.), 244, 256
Juntas Directivas, 201

*K*atz, Friedrich, 109
Kellogg, Frank Billings, 246
Kerlegand, Teodoro, 6
Knight, Alan, 56, 106, 145, 157, 173, 203, 207, 210–11, 280, 293, 294, 295, 298, 301, 303, 305, 307, 308, 309, 310, 315
Kourí, Emile, 26, 32

*L*a Antigua, 170, 200, 231, 297
Labour movement, 63, 64, 275
La Covadonga textile factory, 138
LaFrance, David, 127, 135, 288, 289, 290
Lagos Cházaro, Francisco, 131–33, 141–42, 144, 148, 153–54, 158, 163, 166, 174, 215, 289, 292, 294, 295, 296, 297, 298
Lagos, Joaquín, 165
Lagunes brothers, 203
Lagunes, Manuel, 209, 238
Lake Tamiahua, 23
Land conflicts, 32, 231
Land distribution, xi
Land redistribution, 231, 241
Land reform, 231, 255
Landero y Cos, Francisco, 8
Landlords, 213, 219, 229, 231, 234
    revolts, 174
La Noria Revolt, 7, 14
Lansing, Robert, 206
La Perla, 154
La Reforma, 56
Las Truchas, 111
Laubscher, Enrique, 205
Laudo, 68–69, 72–73, 275

Las Vigas, 111, 146, 183
Laws of Disamortization, 28
Leal Milán, P., 165
Lerdistas, 9–10
Lerdo de Tejada, Sebastian, 7–9, 10, 26, 261, 266
Leví, Manuel, 13, 153, 245, 262, 294
Leycegui, Emilio, 124, 126–28, 288
Ley de Participación de Utilidades, 234
Ley Fuga, 161, 172
Ley Lerdo, 11, 27, 55, 254, 262
Leyva, José, 147, 292
Liberals, 16, 47
    radical, 79
Liberal Clubs, 47
Liberal Congress of 1901, 41
Liberal Constitución party, 218
Liberal Party, 176, 260
Liberalism, 41, 79, 81, 83, 93, 157
Liberal Union, 83
Liga de Comunidades Agrarias y Sindicatos Campesinos de Veracruz, 235, 257
Liga de Inquilinos, 219
Liga de Trabajadores de la Zona Marítima, 242
Limantour, José Yves, 66, 82–87, 91–92, 135–37, 274, 276, 277, 278, 279, 284
    discusses maderista situation with Díaz and Huerta, 105
Limantour, Mrs., 85
Lind, John, 200
Llorente, Enrique, 172
Local elites, x
Lomo Larga, 74, 76
López, Manuel, 116, 121, 124, 151, 286, 287, 295, 296
López, Pecido, 101
López, Ramón, 203
López, Ricardo, 103, 107, 118, 151, 280
López Portillo y Rojas, José, 91
Lord Cowdray. See Sir Weetman Pearson.
Los Angeles (Calif.), 76
Los Tuxtlas canton, 43, 97, 99, 103, 109, 142, 149, 155, 158, 163, 178, 183–84, 189, 295, 296, 305
Lower class, 79, 82
Lower-middle class, 79, 254
Loyo, Rafael, 144
Lumber industry, 3, 23

*M*aas, Joaquín, 120, 121, 191, 286, 287, 301, 302
Macuiltepec mountain, 117
Maderismo, 92, 115, 134, 137–38, 159, 172, 180
Maderistas, 174, 186, 281, 287, 289
  attracted to Vázquez Gómez movement, 147–48
  betrayal of principles, 157
  control countryside, 115–31
  disappointment with Madero, 151
  eliminated by Huerta regime, 176
  flee Mexico, 177
  ideological split in ranks, 140
  initial rebel activity of, 98–100
  successes, 109–10
Madero, Ernesto, 135, 169
Madero family, 163
Madero, Francisco I, 116, 122, 129, 140, 143, 165, 170, 277, 280, 286, 287, 288, 289, 290, 291, 292, 293, 294, 295, 296, 297
  accepts Aillaud as interim governor, 127
  accepts Alegre as interim governor, 130
  accused of Cientificismo, 135-136
  accused of compromising the revolution, 132
  accused of electoral interference, 137
  Alegre assesses Madero's politics, 131
  and foreign property, 186
  arrested by Huerta, 169
  assassination, 169
  assessment of Madero's government, 169–72, 254–55
  assesses political situation, 167–68
  bargaining levers with Díaz regime, 104
  benefits from elite fragmentation, 83
  breaks with stated principles, 138
  calls for revolution 1910, 25
  centralist shift, 127
  changing the guard, 125
  Cientificismo of, 208, 220
  complaints by field generals, 139
  conservative bent, 118–19, 123
  Dehesa's opposition, 132–33
  dissatisfaction leads to revolt, 145–49, 151–54
  dreams instilled by, 184
  drift to the right, 113
  Emilio Vázquez Gómez replaced, 135

  enters the breach opened by Dehesa, 80
  Félix Díaz revolt, 156–61
  ideological ground, 82, 93
  incarceration, 95
  Mata recommends Leycegui, 126
  meetings with Dehesa, 71
  mentality, 138
  nominated presidential candidate, 94
  orders registration of oil companies, 245
  promulgates Plan of San Luis Potosí, 93
  propaganda efforts in U.S.A., 166
  protected by Dehesa, 89
  publishes *The Presidential Succession*, 88
  returns to Mexico, 101
  'state of the union' address, 144
  suggests Dehesa as vice-president, 89
  urges Aillaud to resign, 130
  warned about Científicos, 136
  warned about Dehesa's opposition, 163–64
Madero, Gustavo, 133, 135–37, 164, 180, 290
Magón brothers, 42, 47, 93
Magón, Ricardo Flores, 42, 270
Mallín, Manuel, 158
Malota, 99
Malpica Silva, Juan, 188, 264
Manzanillo, (Ver.), 98, 284
Manzano, General, 122
Marañon, Joaquín, 149, 150
María Mena, José, 9
Marín, Jesús, 142
Marín, Román, 49
Márquez brothers, 151, 185
Márquez, Esteban, 112, 120–21, 122, 126, 186, 287
Marsh, Gayland, 227, 312
Martell, Felipe, 40
Martínez, Eduardo, 222
Martínez, P. A., 139
Martínez, Panuncio, 144, 147, 151–52, 166, 199, 214, 221, 238, 312, 313, 314
Martínez, Paulino, 197, 299, 302
Martínez, Rosalino, 20, 39, 70, 72, 275
Mata de Canela, 74
Mata, Filomeno, 88, 95, 119, 122–27, 263, 286, 287, 288
"*Matalos en caliente*", 10

Matamoros, 177, 182, 185, 301
Mazatlán, 225
Mazomba, 142
Mecapalapa, 103
Mecayapán, 76
Medellín, 112, 203, 211
Medina, Antonio, 178, 192
Medina, Cipriano, 47
Medina, Teófilo, 282
Mellon, Andrew W., 246
Melo y Téllez, Macario, 164
Méndez, Carlos, 227, 315
Méndez, Francisco, 249
Méndez, Melecio, 148
Mendoza, Camerino, 94, 96, 107, 111, 139, 165, 175, 176, 181
Mendoza, Cayetona, 176
Mendoza, Estanislao (Teodoro Dehesa's nom de plume), 10
Mendoza, Julio, 75
Mendoza, Vicente, 68, 176
Meneses, Porfirio, 97
Mercado Alarcón, José, 218
Merino, Captain, 9
Mesa, Pedro, 282
Mestizo(s), 28, 43, 49
Mexican Congress, 7–8, 10, 20, 65, 106, 133, 171, 175–76, 179–80, 188, 193, 218, 261, 290
Mexican Naval School, 211
Mexican Railway, 181
Mexican Revolution, x, xi, 151, 154, 192, 269, 274, 276, 286, 288, 289, 290, 291, 293, 294, 295, 297, 298, 301, 303, 304, 305, 307, 308, 309, 310, 311, 315
    Agua Prieta and goals of, 226
    Alegre's understanding of, 131
    as "class war," 233
    compromised by Madero, 132, 134, 136
    conservative fears of radical interpretation of, 140
    continuity of, 145
    demands for social revolution, 174, 186
    democratic and social goals of, ix, 248
    differing expectations of, 119, 124, 156
    effect on industry, 245
    end of phase one, 196
    factionalism as cause of, 82
    felicista phase, 207
    Indians' interpretation of, 146
    publication of Plan of San Luis Potosí, 93
    periodization, 42
    phase two, social revolution, begins, 201
    policies of, 29
    results of, 253–58
    social reforms of, 229
    turmoil unleashed by, 127
Mexican Senate, 20, 133, 249, 262
Mexican Tropical Planter Co., 40
Mexico, x, 1, 5–6, 10, 14, 22, 25–27, 44–45, 47, 55, 60–61, 71, 80–81, 83–84, 86, 90, 92, 108, 160, 257
Mexico City, ix
    completion of railway to Veracruz, 11
Mexico Oilfields Co, 152
Meyer, Michael, 173, 194, 298, 299, 302, 303
Middle class, 11, 28, 30, 42, 46, 50, 80–82, 92, 118, 254
Mier, Teresa, 207
Mier y Terán, Luis, 8, 10, 261
Militarism, 175
Militarization, 176, 178
Military College, 30
Millán, Agustín, 169, 178, 197, 203–6, 211, 213, 230, 303, 306, 307
Miller, Clarence, 109–10
Minatitlán, 49, 77, 115, 122, 139, 142–43, 149–50, 152, 288, 291
Minatitlán canton, 2, 17, 19, 25, 40, 43, 45, 98–99, 125, 128, 148–52, 168, 178, 183, 190, 192, 270, 271, 292, 293, 298, 306
Minatitlán municipality, 269
Mining industry, 22
Ministry of Communication and Public Works, 243
Misantla, 10, 26, 107, 112, 141, 143, 146, 208, 307
Misantla canton, 10, 17, 112, 119–20, 151–52, 203, 289, 293, 294, 299
Missouri, 47, 271
Mixtec region, 107
Moctezuma, 32
Moctezuma beer factory, 66
Molina Enríquez, Andrés, 88, 139, 290
Monclova (Coah.), 177
Montera, Isidro, 54
Monterrey, 16
Morales, José, 61, 63, 66, 68, 70–71, 275
Morales, Manuel H., 98
Morelos state, 104, 107, 141, 144, 147, 168, 176, 180, 183, 219, 230, 266, 304

Moreno, Francisco, 241
Moreno, Rafael, 63
Moreno Cora, Silvestre, 64, 72
Morones, Luis, 213, 247–49
Morrow, Dwight W., 246, 315
Muñoz, General, 155–56, 295, 296, 297
Muñoz, Ignacio, 37–38, 53, 108, 271
Murguía, Francisco, 225
Murrieta, Marcelino, 202, 203
Mutual Savings Society, 61

*N*ájera, Julio, 129
Naolinco, 110, 112
Napoleon Bonaparte, 123
Naranjo, 151
National Agrarian Commission, 135, 201
National Bank, 86
National Democratic Party, 88, 91–92
National Liberal Convention, 86
National Reorganizing Army (felicista),
  209, 214–15
Nationalist Army, 206
Nava García, Antonio, 226–28
Nava, Margarito, 47
Naval School (Veracruz city), 191
Nayarit state, 177
Necaxa electrical plant, 155
Necoxtla, 23, 58
Neo-Científicos, 185
Neo-Porfirismo, 224
New Orleans, 111, 177, 179, 206
New Spain, 4, 16
Newspapers
  Diario Oficial, 70
  El Ahuizote (Mexico City), 135, 143, 290
  El Ahuizote (Papantla), 9
  El Ciudadano Libre (Veracruz city), 13
  El Cosmopolita (Orizaba), 125
  El Debate (Mexico City), 127
  El Demócrata (Mexico City), 237, 313
  El Diario (Mexico City), 66–67, 72, 127,
    129, 154, 275, 276, 286, 287, 288
  El Diario del Hogar (Mexico City), 15,
    39, 88
  El Dictámen (Veracruz city), 188, 194,
    218, 237, 252, 284, 286, 287, 288,
    290, 291, 292, 293, 298, 303, 304,
    305, 306, 309, 310, 311, 314
    calls for Ramón Corral's
      resignation, 106

  convinced of Dehesa's
    appointment to cabinet, 107–8
  denounces Tejeda, 237
  editorial comment on Madero, 175
  felicista affiliation, 160
  Huerta criticized, 188
  intimidated by *jefe político* Gómez,
    98
  interviews Aillaud, 128
  protected by Dehesa, 21
  supports Aguilar, 218
  touts Dehesa's popularity, 118
  El Fascismo (Ver.), 238
  El Germinal, 104, 106
  El Grito del Pueblo (Ver.), 188
  El Imparcial (Mexico City), 66, 129,
    188, 288, 290, 298, 299, 300, 301, 302
  El Imparcial (Veracruz city), 13
  El Monitor Repúblicano (Mexico City),
    10
  El Nacional (Mexico City), 12, 18
  El Padre Cobos (Mexico City), 9
  El Paladín (Mexico City), 17–18, 21
  El Paladín (Orizaba), 60
  El Radical (Mexico City), 203, 305
  El Reproductor (Orizaba), 12, 67, 70
  El Universal (Mexico City), 217, 310
  Excelsior (Mexico City), 237, 310, 313
  La Mañana (Mexico City), 135, 289
  La Nueva Era (Mexico City), 132, 141,
    153, 182, 289, 291, 292, 293, 294,
    295, 296
  La Opinión (Veracruz), 137, 188, 192,
    302, 303, 304
  La Patria (Mexico City), 16, 19, 20, 67
  La Voz de Lerdo, 47
  Periódico Oficial, 76
  Revolución Social (Orizaba), 57, 61, 71,
    97
New York, 7, 23, 157, 171, 296, 297
Neyra, José, 60–61
Niagara Falls, 191
Nogales, 69, 72, 97, 272
Nogales factory, 59
Nopalapám, 76
Nortes, 3
Novoa, Enrique (alias Dantón), 47–49,
  51–52, 270
Nuevo León state, 81, 86, 238, 290
Nunn, L. C., 120, 143, 154, 286, 288, 292

*O*axaca state, 2, 7, 9, 18, 75, 99–100,
103–4, 107, 148, 150, 158, 160, 174,
198, 209, 214–15, 224, 261, 266, 304,
311
Obregón, Alvaro, 197, 303, 305, 311, 312,
313, 314, 315, 316
agraristas remain loyal, 239
breaches sovereignty of San Luis
Potosí and Nuevo León, 238
changes tactics to support Tejeda, 237
Delahuertista rebellion, 238
events leading to Agua Prieta, 223–26
Fifteenth Battalion stationed in, 72, 77
oil policy, 245, 248
Pelaez's support of, 227
political tactics, 231
presidency evaluated, 250
rift with Carranza, 107, 116–17
signs the Treaty of Teoloyucan, 195
supports Veracruz capitalists, 234
takes offensive against Convention,
202
Tejeda's support of, 229
Ocaranza, General, 162, 168, 297
Oceguera, Manuel, 168
Ochoa, Guadalupe, 109, 116, 122, 125,
128, 139, 147–49, 184, 287, 288
Odorico, Captain, 161
Oil, 3, 23, 25, 265
Oil companies, 123, 132, 166, 173, 182,
185–87, 199, 205, 214, 230, 244–48,
250, 300
Oil fields, 181, 185–88, 191, 197, 205, 223,
227
Oil Fields of Mexico Co., 109
Oil revenue, 199
Oil workers, 232
Ojitlán, 99
Olarte rebellion, 25, 265, 267
Omealca, 98, 153
Ometusco, 204
Orizaba, 9, 19, 90, 110, 276, 280, 281, 282,
284, 286, 287, 291, 293, 294, 295,
296, 297, 301, 307, 309, 312, 313, 314
anti-Díaz demonstrations, 95
Córdoba-Orizaba axis, 116, 142
Customs House moved to, 195
Gavirismo, 218
geography, 5, 25
inauguration of new textile factory, 22

odious conditions, 104
rebels demand surrender of, 118
Red Brigades, 202
renters' strike, 219
replacing local authorities, 122
state capital, 197
textile labour unrest in, 55–70, 143
Xalapa-Mexico City corridor, 4
Orizaba canton, 96, 98, 104, 119, 260
Orozco, Pascual, 105, 132, 141, 145–47,
149–50, 182, 293
Orozquistas, 145–46, 150, 152, 154, 157,
165
Ortega y Rivera, Colonel, 158
Ortíz, Colonel, 17
Ortíz, Francisco, 52
Ortíz, Rafael, 148
Otomí Indians, 31, 168
Ozuluama canton, 31, 98, 158, 163, 182,
199, 263

*P*achuca (Hdgo.), 193
Pact of the Ciudadela, 169, 170, 176, 179
Padua, Cándido Donato, 48, 50, 74–75,
77, 94–95, 98–99, 212, 271, 309
Pajapan, 148
Palacio del Gobierno, 126
Palacios, Adalberto, 98, 122, 178, 239
Pani, Alberto, 197, 238, 313
Pánuco, 139, 187
Pánuco River, 2
Papaloapán River, 2, 3, 43, 75, 117, 215
Papantla, 39, 44, 45, 46, 168, 175, 182,
185–86, 192, 198, 208, 218, 239, 263,
299, 301, 303
Papantla canton, 10, 11, 23, 29, 31–34,
36–37, 39, 42, 47, 110, 119–20, 140,
152, 162, 182, 203, 297
Papantla Uprisings/Rebellions, 26, 32, 43,
55, 254
Paredes, General, 180
Paredes, Manuel, 109, 147
Partido, 259
Partido Constitucional Progresista, 135, 140
Partido Liberal Constitucionalista, 217–18
Partido Liberal Mexicana. See PLM.
Partido Obrero, 217
Paso del Macho, 97, 146, 168, 175, 198,
291, 302
Pasquel, Leonardo, 171, 274

Patino, Manuel, 39
Pavón Flores, Manuel, 148–49
Paz, Ireneo, 9, 20
Pearson company, 46
Pearson, Sir Weetman, 23, 45–46, 149, 265
Pearson's Magazine, 87
Peasant League, 235, 240–41
Peasants, x, 42–43, 47, 79–80, 231–35, 256, 265, 269
peasant rebellion, x
Pelaecista, 203
Peláez, Ignacio, 158, 295
Peláez, Manuel, 208, 215, 222, 250,311, 312, 314
affiliation with Félix Díaz, 158
cited as "fascist," 238
commander Fifth Division, Army of the Gulf (felicista), 210
commander of Constitutionalist forces, 182, 186
controls the Huasteca, 214, 218
enmity with Constitutionalists after 1915, 174
favoured by businessmen, 220
federalist (regionalist) sentiments, 202
joins delahuertistas, 239
joins Pancho Villa, 199, 202
pressured by Constitutionalist army, 221
size of forces, 219
supports Obregón, 225–27
Peña, Concepción, 97, 281
Peons, 24
Pérez, Cástulo, 208, 210–12, 221, 307, 312, 313, 314
Pérez, Espiridion, 75
Pérez, Nicanor, 75, 147–48, 153–54, 175, 177–82, 185, 193, 199, 202, 292, 295, 296, 297, 298, 299, 300, 302
Pérez Rivera, Antonio, 132, 133, 153–54, 163–66, 168, 170–71, 175, 177–82, 185, 193, 199, 291, 298, 299, 300
Pérez Romero, Manuel, 230
Pérez y Soto, Atenógenes, 241
Perote, 101, 117, 146, 168, 175, 182, 215, 292, 309
Pershing, J. J., 210, 309
Petroleum Commission (Mexican Senate), 246
Petroleum Law of 1926, 246
Phelps Dodge Oil Co., 250

Pico Orizaba, 2
Piedras Negras, 103, 182, 185, 209, 300
Pineda, Rosenda, 83
Pino Suárez, José María, 133–36, 139, 169, 177, 277
Plan de las Hayas, 214
Plan of Agua Prieta, 225, 227
Plan of Ayala, 178, 183, 197, 214, 304
Plan of Guadalupe, 198
Plan of La Noria, 260
Plan of Palo Blanco, 38
Plan of San Luis Potosí, 93, 95–96, 101, 116, 118–19, 124, 128, 138, 146, 147–48, 178, 255
Plan of Tacubaya, 141–42, 146–47, 178
Plan of Texcoco, 139, 290
Plan of Tierra Colorado, 207–9, 307
Plan of Tuxtepec, 9, 12, 38, 79, 82–84
Plan of Xilitla, 239
Plan Orozquista, 132, 145
Playa Vicente, 150
PLM (Partido Liberal Mexicana), 42–43, 47–48, 55–57, 61–62, 65, 74, 76–77, 80–81, 93–94, 99, 147, 178, 183, 198, 254, 268, 269, 270, 271
anarchist ideas of, 61
Ponce, Isauro, 75
Polanco, Alfonso, 18, 178
Popoluca Indians, 11, 40, 42–44, 47, 49, 55, 147, 190, 268, 270
Popotla, 136
Porfirian Movement, 7–10
Porfirianism, 81
Porfirian system, 6
Porfiriato, x, 28, 254, 274, 302, 307
Cientificismo, 208
Científicos, 82–85
hacienda system, 204
ideology of, 41
industrial structure of, 250
jefe político in, 16–20
land problems, 26–27, 29–30
limits to presidential authority, 26
nostalgia for, 184
oil discoveries, 109
paradox of, 80
political structure, 22
re-election as principle, 12
social conditions in, 56–57
strikes in, 59
tiendas de raya in, 67–68

Portas, Antonio, 99, 178, 282
Portes Gil, Emilio, 233
Positivism (Comtean), 83
Poucel, Emilio (General), 97, 100–101,
  105, 284
Pous, Guillermo, 132
'Precursor' uprisings, xi
Preparatory College (Xalapa), 205
Prescotte and Co., 23
Presidential Succesion of 1910, 88
Prieto, Angel, 19
Proal, Herón, 213, 217, 233–35, 239
Proclamation of San Ricardo, 95
Progreso (Yuc.), 177, 227, 299
Prostitutes, 234
Puebla, 63, 65, 73, 95–96, 100–101, 106–7,
  110–11
Puebla state, 2, 74, 95, 100, 161, 168, 259,
  266, 290, 303
  Aquiles Serdán uprising, 95
  frontier raids into Veracruz, 123, 141,
    143, 154
  labour unrest among textile workers,
    65–69
  La Covadonga shooting, 138
  recaptured by Obregón, 202
  retention of porfirian personnel, 119
  revolutionaries, 96
  Puente Nacional, 231, 237, 313
Puerto Barrios, 177
Puerto México, 49, 190–93 303, 304. See
  also Coatzacoalcos.

Queretaro Convention, 223, 229–30, 251
Quimixtlán, 116
Quintal Gea, Juan, 163
Quintana Roo state, 65, 73

Rabasa, Emilio, 44
Railways, 22, 242–44
Ramíres, Esperanza, 185
Ramírez, Jesús, 203
Ramírez, Juan, 282
Ramírez, Lauro, 146
Ramírez, Samuel A., 63, 71, 74, 97
Ramos, Miguel, 121, 124–25, 146
Rancheros, 47, 123, 196
Rascón, Eugenio, 121–22
Ravelo, María, 75
Rebsamen, Enrique, 11, 205

Red Brigades, 242
"Red" parties, 218, 219
Reform Laws, 26–27, 43
Reform Wars, 157, 260
Regeneración, 47, 56, 93, 270
Regional Papanteco party, 218
Regionalism, 211, 251, 258
Rellano, 150
Renters, 213, 219, 233–35
Renters' League, 219
Renters' Union, 213, 257
Reparto, 26, 200, 204
Republican Club of Veracruz, 7
Rerum Novarum (1891), 84
Revindicating Movement, 225
Revolution of Ayutla, 157, 270
Revolution of Tuxtepec, 1, 9–10, 14
Reyes, Bernardo, 16, 81–86, 88, 91, 137,
  139–40, 168, 288
Reyes, Rodolfo, 160, 164
Revistas, 92–93, 140–41, 163
Reyna, Efren, 163
Reynaud, Antonio, 58, 63
Rincón, Jacobo, 229
Rincón Grande hydro-electric plant, 23
Río Blanco, 41, 51, 57, 69–74, 77–80,
  95–97, 102, 118, 175, 202, 254, 272
Río Blanco factory, 22–23, 58–61
Río Blanco Labour Dispute, 20, 79, 84,
  88, 90, 229–30, 232–33
Riva Palacio, Vincente, 9
Robles Domínguez, Alfredo, 98, 116, 121,
  136, 141, 286, 287, 288, 290, 291
Roca Partida, 184
Rocha, Ramón, 62–63, 70
Rodríguez, Abel S., 249, 307, 314
Rodríguez, Antonio Mateo, 52
Rodríguez, P., 170
Rodríguez, Santana (alias Santanón). See
  Santanón.
Rodríguez Clara, Juan, 98, 239
Rodríguez Malpica, Hilario, 132
Rojas, Luis Manuel, 197
Romero Rubio, Manuel, 20, 44–46, 83, 269
Rosete, Ismael, 162
Royal Navy, 189
Ruíz, Darío, 97, 281
Ruíz, Francisco, 70, 72
Ruiz, Raúl G., 121–22, 129, 148–49,
  174, 189, 198, 202–3, 208–11, 215,
  239–40, 288, 303, 306, 307
Rumbía, José, 61

Rurales, 111, 117, 137, 143–44, 148, 153, 262, 275, 276, 284, 288, 290, 294, 306
  arrest GCOL leaders, 61
  attacked by maderistas, 96, 107
  Benito Vargas Barranco named *visitador*, 140
  efforts against counter-revolution, 165–69
  engage maderistas, 99–101
  expansion by Huerta, 178
  fail to locate Tapia, 102
  lack of supplies, 162
  Ninth Corps stationed in Río Blanco, 97
  Orizaba garrison joins Félix Díaz, 158
  romanticized image, 103
  Santanón killed, 75–76
  Tapia named Veracruz commander, 129, 132
  Totonac rebellion 1890, 33
Russia, 233

*S*aint Louis, Missouri, 48
Salas, Hilario, 47–50, 79, 98–99, 144, 148–49, 178, 183–84, 189–90, 271, 293
Salmoral, 231
San Anastasio hacienda, 75
San Andrés Tuxtla, 17, 50, 59, 75, 109, 116, 183–84, 208, 231, 241, 298, 299
San Antono, Texas, 93, 98, 110, 134, 139, 206
San Antonio Tenejapam, 98
San Carlos sugar plantation, 75
San Cristóbal Llave, 45, 101
San Felipe de la Punta, 98
San Francisco de las Peñas. See Cárdel
San Gertrudis jute factory, 59
San José Miahuatlán, 107
San Juan de la Puente, 95, 99, 101–2, 283, 285
San Juan de Ulua, 51
  fortress, 51, 132, 137, 169, 175, 188, 193, 223, 226
  garrison, 158
San Juan Evangelista, 2, 18, 53, 147–48, 155, 184, 211
San Juan Michapán River, 2, 75
San Lorenzo factory, 60
San Lázaro station, 108
San Luis Potosí, 93, 95

San Luis Potosí state, 2, 15, 30, 47, 109, 141, 185, 199, 238, 311
San Martín, 178
San Martín Mountains, 75
San Pedrito, 31
San Ricardo rancho, 93, 104
San Salvador (Pueb.), 155
Sánchez, Guadalupe, 98, 178, 221–22, 223, 225–26, 232, 234, 237–38, 240, 307, 311, 312, 313
Sandoval, Juan, 148–50
Santa Ana Atzacán, 192
Santa Fé, 142
Santa Lucrecia, 199
Santa Rosa, 175, 176
Santa Rosa factory, 23, 63, 70, 96, 139
Santaella, Demetrio, 17–18
Santanón (Santana Rodríguez), 74–75, 94, 148, 169, 292
Santasa factory, 58
Santiago bastion (Ver.), 123
Santiago Tlatelolco prison, 176
Santibañez, Demetrio, 19, 48
Sarabía, Juan, 48
Sayula, 18, 99, 148, 154
Schama, Simon, 253
Scott, Sir Walter, 209
Sentíes, Francisco de P., 50, 105
Sérdan, Aquiles, 95
Sheffield, James R., 246
Sierra, Justo, 83
Sierra Madre Oriental, 1, 2, 100, 155
Sierra Negra mountains, 161
Sierra of Zongólica, 7
Silva, P., 48
Sinaloa state, 141
Sloane, Emery, 200
Sochiapa, 116
Social Darwinism, 84
Socialism, 71, 201, 204, 220, 304
Socialist Convention (Mexico City), 223
Soconusco, 52
Sodi de Pallares, María, 91
Solache, Arturo, 211
Soldaderas, 195, 277
Soledad, 97, 117, 151, 293, 297
Soledad de Doblado, 117
Solleiro, Antonio, 129
Sonora state, 225
Sonora State Legislature, 225
Sotavento, 162

Soteapan, 11, 40, 45, 47, 49, 50–51, 52, 74, 76, 183, 300
Sotomayor, Captain, 183
Spain, 4, 16
Spaniards, 21, 36, 138, 189, 195, 206, 221, 234
Spanish, 4, 108, 221, 245, 259
Spanish Conquest, 43
Spanish interests, 17
Standard Oil Co., 110
State sovereignty, 71, 249–51, 258, 310, 312
  CAM removed to federal level, 205
  Dehesa's and Reyes's position on, 84–85
  delahuertista rebellion and, 238
  Quertaro Convention and, 216
  in Porfiriato, 79
  oil and, 244
  Plan of Agua Prieta and, 225–30
  Raúl Ruiz and, 211
  violated in Veracruz by federal government, 172, 249
State sovereignists, 216, 246
Steamships
  Antonio López, 207
  City of Tampico, 196
  Ipiranga, 123
  Monterrey, 177
  M.V. *Corsica*, 7
  Princess Cecilia, 149
Stevens, Donald Fithian, 27
Sub-soil rights, 46, 182, 186, 196, 199, 216–17, 245, 248, 251
Sub-soil rights, state, 196
Sulvarán, Genaro, 212
Supreme Court, 160, 206, 245
Survey Law, 29

*T*abasco state, 2, 233, 259, 311
Taft, William Howard, 166
Tamalín, 192
Tamaulipas state, 2, 177, 186, 223, 233, 311
Tamesí River, 2
Tamiahua, 181, 192
Tamiahua lagoon, 109
Tampico, 159, 166, 185, 188, 289, 291, 300, 301, 302, 304, 309, 312
Tantima, 192

Tantoyuca, 142, 150, 181, 182, 186, 191, 199, 265, 300
Tantoyuca canton, 98, 109
Tapia, José, 281
Tapia, Rafael, 104, 131, 162, 281, 282, 283, 284, 286, 287, 288, 289, 290, 291, 293, 296, 298, 299
  arrested and executed, 176
  attacks Orozquistas, 150
  begins rebel activity, 95–96, 98–102
  calms populace of Orizaba, 119
  Cándido Aguilar suspected, 141
  ideological position, 122, 124, 148
  named Rurales commander, 129
  posted to Tlaxcala, 165
  sent to Huatusco, 143–44
  suspected of disloyalty, 152–53
  tactics, 105–7
Tatlauqui, 101
Teatro Principal, 166
Tehuacán (Pueb.), 154
Tehuantepec Railroad, 45, 149
Tejeda, Adalberto, 178, 218, 228–35, 237–41, 246–48 250, 256, 258, 312, 313, 314
Tello, Facundo, 170
Temapache, 162, 186, 199
Teocelo, 112, 116, 154, 183, 192, 286, 287
Tepeyahualco, 123
Tequila, 155
Texas, 48
Texistepec, 53
Texmalaca, 154
Textile industry, 2, 5, 22, 242
Teziutlán (Pueb.), 110, 168, 192–93, 200, 286
Tezonapa, 183
Third Pedagogical Congress, 206
Tiburcio, Simón, 152, 186
Tienda de raya, 66–67, 69
Tierra Blanca, 107, 118, 150, 151, 155, 166, 173, 199, 214, 224
Tierra caliente, 6
Tinterillos, 16
Tlacolula, 121
Tlacotalpan, 8, 10, 75, 117, 211
Tlacotepec, 116
Tlacotepec de Mejía, 235, 309, 308
Tlacualpicán, 107
Tlalixcoyan, 101, 103, 209, 214
Tlaxcala state, 10, 66–67, 80, 144, 166, 176, 266

Tobacco industry, 4, 43
Tonalá River, 2
Torreón (Coah.), 191
Torres, Alejandro, 149
Totonac-Huasteca Indians, 11, 26, 32–34,
    39–42, 109, 265, 268
Tovar, Colonel, 86
Tram Company, 213
Treaty of Ciudad Juárez, 120, 129
Treaty of Teoloyucan, 195
Trejo y Lerdo de Tejada, Carlos, 135, 290
Trinidad Herrera, Gonzalo, 190
Trinidad Herrera, José, 190
Tron, Enrique, 65
Tula, 155
Tuxpán, 3, 109–10, 142, 158–59, 162, 166,
    181–82, 186–87, 199, 205, 208, 218,
    225, 293, 294, 296
    provisional state capital, 192
Tuxpán canton, 23, 32, 152, 182
Tuxtepec, 2, 99
Tuxtepecanos Puros, 81–82, 84
Tuxtepec (Oax.), 215

Ugarte, Gerzayn, 197
Ulloa, Luis, 30–31
Unión Mexicana de Obreros, 273
Unión de Obreros Ferrocarrilleros del
    Puerto, 242
Union of Conductors and Motorists, 201
Unions, 205
United States, 177, 182, 302, 303, 308,
    310, 311, 314
    anti-Carranza backers in, 206
    backs down under Aguilar's threat, 187
    cloth imports from, 66
    consul in Veracruz, 164, 199
    diplomacy with Mexico, 248
    enters World War I, 210
    hostility to Mexico, 250
    ignores Félix Díaz, 224
    industrial development, 83
    invasion of Mexico (1914), 190
    oil companies and, 245–46
    perceived interest in Isthmus of
        Tehuantepec, 45
    resistance to invasion in Veracruz, 191
    supports Carranza movement, 209, 220
    supports Obregón, 239
    Tehuantepec expedition, 1871, 43

    ultimatum from Admiral Fletcher, 187
    withdrawal from Veracruz, 197
Upper class, 83, 254
Urrutia, Francisco, 152, 294
Urueta, Jesús, 197, 201, 306
U.S citizens, 137, 150, 155, 159, 166, 234
    owners of Mexican property, 174
U.S. Foreign Relations Committee
    Investigation of Mexican Affairs, 200

Valdés, General, 159, 297
Valdéz, General, 169
Valentín Gómez Farías Club, 47
Valle Nacional (Oax.), 18, 173, 263
Vanderwood, Paul, 276
Vanilla, 32, 34, 36–37
Varela railway, 128
Vargas Barranco, Benito, 140
Vásquez, Cristóbal, 54
Vázquez Gómez, Emilio, 130, 132,
    134–35, 138–39, 141, 145–46, 148,
    290
Vázquez Gómez, Francisco, 88, 91, 94–95,
    116, 134–35, 139, 141, 146, 280, 281,
    288, 290
Vázquez, Mario, 145–46, 148, 152, 294
Vazquistas, 132, 139, 142, 146, 152, 157
Vega, Alejandro, 185
Vega, Celso, 185
Vega, General, 153, 159, 294
Vela, Eulalio, 98, 283
Velasco, José Refugio, 169,175, 177, 298,
    300
Veracruzans, 12, 172, 174, 180, 204, 255
    reelection, 8
    Madero's manipulation upsets, 153
    regionalism, 211
Veracruz canton, 170, 178, 211
Veracruz city (port), 265, 267, 268, 281,
    292, 293, 303, 306, 307
    anti-Porfirians, 94
    anti-reelectionist clubs, 88
    attacked by Garrido Huerta, 111–12
    capital of Mexico, 197
    Congress of the Labour
        Confederation of the Mexican
        Region, 133
    delahuertista rebellion in, 238
    First Preliminary National Workers
        Congress, 213

garrison declares for Félix Díaz, 158
garrison fortified, 178
gateway to Mexico, 2, 157
inflation, 213
liberalism, 158
Madero greeted enthusiastically, 90–91
popularity of Félix Díaz, 160
population, 212
Renters' League (union), 213, 219
renters' strike, 233
strikes, 201, 212, 213, 233
Third Pedagogical Congress, 206
Veracruz Civil Guard, 237, 241
Veracruz Communist Party, 234
Veracruz Liberal Club, 179
Veracruz-Pacific Railway, 103
Veracruz state, x, xi, 253–56, 258, 259,
    260, 265, 266, 272, 273, 281, 282,
    285, 286, 287, 288, 289, 290, 291,
    292, 293, 294, 295, 296, 297, 298,
    299, 300, 301, 302, 303, 305, 306,
    307, 309, 310, 311, 312, 313, 314
Acayucan uprising, 43
agrarian revolt in, 174
agraristas, 239–40
agricultural potential, 3
agriculture, 4, 25
anti-Constitutionalist rebel activity,
    203, 209
anti-Madero uprisings, 139–40
bandits in, 189
civil war, 197
climate, 3–4
Constitutionalist campaign in, 181–92
counter-revolution, 153–55, 161
discontent with Madero's policies,
    130, 136–38
economic development, 22–24
economic potential, 5
enmity with central government, 184
fascism in, 238
Felicistas, 198, 207–12, 214–24
Félix Díaz revolt, 156
foreign clergy expelled from, 195–96
Gaviristas, 141–46, 149, 157
geographical potential, 6
geography, 6, 259
Indian rebellions, 40
industrial output, 25
importance to Mexican economy, 25
industrial potential, 5

Jara (governor) ousted, 249
land distribution, 200–201, 204, 231
landlord backlash, 231
land question, 25–26
labour, 213
manufacturing, 6
military situation, 163
mineral deposits, 4, 25
Mutual Savings Society, 61
nineteenth century, 1
nineteenth century rebellions, 47
oil industry, 245
opposition to Constitutionalists, 204
Orozquistas in, 145–46, 149–50, 152,
    157
PLM clubs in, 47–48
political turmoil in, 127, 208
population, 4, 24–25, 30, 35, 38
Porfiran coup d'état, 9
Porfirian movement, 8
Porfirian system, 14–22
radicalization of, 230
rebel activity, 98–113
Renters' Union, 213
riparian structure, 3
repression by Constitutionalists, 206
"Republican Club," 7
rural and indigenous revolts, 25
soil conditions, 4
Spaniards expelled, 206
strikes, 72, 146, 213, 233
textile industry, 6, 57–58
Tuxtepec Revolution, 10
U.S. invasion (second) expected, 210
Vazquista, 141–46, 152, 157
Veracruz Civil Guard, 237, 241
Veracruz Peasant League, 235, 240–41
Villa abandons state, 199
violations of state sovereignty, 73, 172,
    225, 227–28, 238, 249–50
wealth, 5
"White Guards," 232, 247
Zapatistas, 141–42, 148, 183, 203–4,
    214, 219, 226
Veracruz State Legislature, 8, 14–15, 17,
    19–20, 38, 45, 64, 124, 127, 129–33,
    140, 153–54, 164, 172, 181, 185, 193,
    217–18, 235, 238, 249, 267, 300, 313
Veracruz Tram Company, 201
Vicente Guerrero Club, 47
Viceroyalty of New Spain, 259

Vidal, Juan, 36
Villa, Pancho, 197–202, 207–8, 210, 215,
   226, 303, 304, 311
Villar, Lauro, 141, 291
Villarauz, Crescencio L.., 146
Villareal, José María, 48, 70
Villegas, Colonel, 148, 292, 293
Villistas, 198–99, 202–3, 208, 214
Vista Hermosa Sugar Mercantile
   Company, 174
Viveros, Juan, 7
Voigt, Robert, 75
"Volcano Volunteers," 198
"Volunteers of Córdoba," 102

Wall Street crisis of 1907, 59
Warships
   Bravo (gunboat), 50, 162
   El Morelos (gunboat), 76
   Guerrero (gunboat), 225
   H.M.S. Melpomene (destroyer), 149,
     173, 293
   Libertad (frigate) , 10
   U.S.S. Nebraska (destroyer), 187
   Veracruz (gunboat), 188
   Yucatan (gunboat), 50
   Zaragoza (gunboat), 188
Washington, D.C., 188, 209, 246, 298
Wells, Allen, 15
White Guards, 232
   employment of foreigners as, 247
Wilson, Henry Lane, 169
Wilson, Woodrow, 190–91, 209, 220, 308,
   310
Womack, John, 118, 154, 286, 289
Women
   in Santanón's guerilla group, 75
   Yaquis, 75
Wood, Andrew, 258
Workers, 84, 121, 176, 180, 226, 256
   271, 273, 274, 275, 276, 281, 298,
   299, 310, 314
   demand payment in gold, 212–13
   demands, 70
   enganchados, 173
   expectations of Plan of San Luis
     Potosí, 124

gains, 242
ideological motivation of, 56
industrial, x, 61
join Armenta movement, 203
join PLM rebels, 74
lectured on political situation, 132,
   201
massacre of, 56, 72, 183
Mexican Revolution and, 232
militants, 143
Obregón and, 231, 238
petroleum, 244
plantation, 155
radicalization of, 233
railway, 120, 242–44
rural, xi, 258
socialist convention supports
   Obregón, 223
sugar, 174
support Aguilar, 196
textile, 56–71, 205, 254, 256
tobacco, 43
urban, xi, 258
Worker-soldiers, 202
Workers' Party, 241
Working class, 43, 223, 247, 248, 257–58
   armed by Tejeda, 250
   consciousness of, 84
   Dehesa's popularity among, 88, 92
   Mexican Revolution and, 232
   oppposed to capitalist development,
     55
   radicalized by events at Río Blanco,
     229
   resistance, xi
   supported by state government,
     218–19, 230
World War I, 220, 245

Xalapa, 25, 110, 113, 262, 264, 269, 286,
   287, 288, 289, 290, 291, 292, 293,
   294, 295, 296, 297, 298, 299, 300,
   301, 302, 303, 314
Aguilar attacks, 192
bloody Maderista rivalry in, 125–27
captured by Aguilar, 195–96
Felicista support, 180

Inter-Oceanic Railway, 11, 102
land distribution, 231
Maderistas enter, 121, 124
Mexico City corridor, 4
Porfirian coup d'état, 9
reinforced, 97, 140
state capital returned to, 202
strikes, 72
surrounded by Maderistas, 111–12,
    115, 117
textile factory, 5, 57
tobacco factory, 59
volunteer battalion, 146–47
Xico, 111, 116, 146
Xonotipam, 183
Xoxocotla, 155, 294

'Yankee' invasion plans, 18
Yaqui Indians, 75, 225, 312
Yecautla, 208
Yturbide, Mr., 206
Yucatan state, 6, 21, 107, 177, 227, 233,
    260, 262

Zacatecas state, 141
Zamora, Manuel, 103, 112, 117, 142, 286
Zapata, Emiliano, 141, 209, 215, 286, 299,
    303, 304, 305, 310, 311
    declares form Madero, 107
    killed, 221
    names Armenta governor of Veracruz,
        203
    rejects demand to surrender arms, 134
Zapatismo, 148
Zapatistas, 142, 149, 162–63, 165, 183,
    197–98, 202–4, 208, 210, 214, 219,
    226, 230
Zongólica canton, 7, 260, 291, 294, 296,
    297, 299, 300, 302, 303
    Aguilar, Higinio, in, 155–56, 161–62
    Constitutionalists capture, 195
    Felicistas in, 170, 198
    jefe político of, 18
    Martínez, Panuncio, in, 151
    rebel activity in, 141, 147, 182–83
    rubber plantation, 23
    Ruiz, Raúl G., attacks, 183
    uprisings of hill people, 168
Zontecomatlán, 120, 168, 286